Impact
of Leadership

Contributors

Bruce J. Avolio
Bernard M. Bass
William T. Bergman
Patrick J. Bettin
Rex J. Blake
Lee G. Bolman
Daniel Booth
Cheryl D. Bruff
W. Warner Burke
David P. Campbell
Kenneth E. Clark
Miriam B. Clark
Benjamin C. G. Cotton
Ian Cunningham
Gordon J. Curphy
Larry G. Daniel, Jr.
Laura A. Davenport
Terrence E. Deal
Ronald J. Deluga
Richard P. DeShon
Peter W. Dorfman
Mark R. Edwards
Fred E. Fiedler
Patricia K. Fullagar
Frederick W. Gibson
Mary Ann Glynn
George B. Graen
Jack R. Greene
Keith M. Halperin
Peter K. Hammerschmidt
Diane E. Hartley
Joy Fisher Hazucha
Jane M. Howell
Jon P. Howell
Charles Huff
Peggy S. Hunt
Mansour Javidan
Andrew C. Jennings
E. B. Knauft
Bas A. S. Koene
Rick Lepsinger

Ariel S. Levi
David Lohmann
Toni Lucia
Jennifer L. Macaulay
Larry E. Mainstone
Steven E. Markham
Phyllis P. Marson
J. Patrick Murphy
Susan E. Murphy
William D. Murry
Diana B. Osborn
T. Noel Osborn
Larry A. Pace
Johannes M. Pennings
Larry W. Penwell
Kent D. Peterson
Earl H. Potter III
Louis N. Quast, Jr.
Donna Riechmann
Michael A. Rosebush
William E. Rosenbach
Paul E. Roush
Marshall Sashkin
Hein Schreuder
K. Dow Scott
John F. Settich
Frank Shipper
Joan Slepian
Juliann Spoth
Daniel J. Svyantek
Richard S. Tallarigo
Uday Tate
Walter W. Tornow
Mary L. Tucker
Mary Uhl-Bien
Ann M. Van Eron
Charlotte Jacobsen Weddle
Willie L. Williams
Clark L. Wilson
Jane Wilson
Nina Wrolstad
Gary Yukl

Impact
of Leadership

**Edited by Kenneth E. Clark,
Miriam B. Clark, and David P. Campbell**

Center for Creative Leadership
Greensboro, North Carolina

©Copyright 1992 by
CENTER FOR CREATIVE LEADERSHIP
One Leadership Place
Post Office Box 26300
Greensboro, North Carolina 27438–6300

ISBN 0–912879–95–5
CIP 92–081214

Judy Rock Allen, Managing Editor

CONTENTS

Foreword

The two years of unimaginable change in the world's political and economic systems which preceded the publication of this book have been of historic dimension in every sense. Exploding technology—particularly in data processing and distribution—was perhaps the major catalyst, although fundamental human needs for self-fulfillment and for creative latitude were also crucial in these continuing societal transformations.

As nations, organizations, and families respond to the unrelenting stimuli of our era, calls for "leadership" intensify. These calls stimulate a review of pat investigations of leadership phenomena and rekindle our efforts to refine concepts, clarify definitions, and perhaps most importantly, put ideas about leadership and leaders into context.

The Center for Creative Leadership intends to continue to play a significant role in both investigating the nature and subject matter of leadership, and in facilitating an understanding of linkage between theory and practice. The ultimate questions are not about leadership characteristics or behaviors, or even about the essential integrating concepts that would place leadership in context. Most fundamental is the question of "Leadership for what purpose . . . for what impact?" It is not the optimum process—however critical that may be—but the optimum impact that counts.

This book reveals once again the profound insights and comprehensive overview which Kenneth and Miriam Clark and David Campbell bring to bear. Derived from the papers and discussions at the Center's 1991 conference in Colorado Springs on the impact of leadership, this book complements *Measures of Leadership* which recorded the presentations and observations of the 1988 sessions in San Antonio. Both volumes contain previously unpublished research papers by internationally recognized scientists, and these collections alone represent a formidable contemporary contribution to the study of leaders and leadership. The thoughtful, sometimes provocative, well-documented papers are—in the cases of both books—made richer and more useful by their being a compilation; and by Campbell's and the Clarks' introductions, explanations, and analyses.

Leadership as a subject remains exciting, challenging, somewhat elusive, and, in all aspects of our world, relevant and important. The Center for Creative Leadership remains committed to the support of quality research and education which this timely book represents.

Walter F. Ulmer, Jr.
President and Chief Executive Officer
Center for Creative Leadership

Preface

The October 1988 conference on leadership research examined measures of leadership and their usefulness in the world of affairs—the world in which leaders must be found and efforts organized to accomplish the work of society. The report of that conference was published in 1990 in *Measures of Leadership* (K. E. Clark & M. B. Clark, Eds., Leadership Library of America).

The July 1991 conference on leadership research centered its attention on the impact of leadership. A call for papers produced over 80 responses, with details about proposed offerings ranging from a half page to many pages. From these proposals, 42 papers were selected for publication in this volume. One or more of the authors of each paper attended a conference in July 1991 in Colorado Springs, Colorado, sponsored by the Center for Creative Leadership. While discussions at that conference affected the final form of the papers, they probably had a much greater effect on the way in which the conference attendees will view the field and their future contributions to it.

The conferences were planned to help fill an obvious void in the literature on leadership. The deficiency is not in quantity, but in the lack of focus. There are only a few general theories of leadership, and even the best are not sufficiently comprehensive. Reports are written for many audiences, studies are built on various assumptions using many methods, and reviews are written for professional colleagues, not for users. Studies appear in many forms and usually stand by themselves. As a result, insufficient guidance is given those who most need to apply the best findings.

Impact is defined broadly to relate both to the outcomes of good leadership and to the ways in which leadership produces those effects. Many studies report data on important impacts: In some organizations they examine unit performance or worker satisfaction and in others explore school reputation, effectiveness of work teams, or presidential turnover.

A glance at the Table of Contents reveals the variety of topics covered in these reports. The reader may select the order for study or may read them in the nearly random sequence in which they are presented.

Chapter 1 introduces the studies of the impact of leadership, a center-stage topic in many parts of the world today. The ramifications of the issue and the growing need for a well-prepared set of leaders and followers in a world beset with turmoil are discussed. We recommend reading this chapter first.

Chapter 2 invites the reader to join in discussion of the best ways to learn about leaders and leadership. Written in the form of a mock debate or panel discussion, it highlights the thoughts of a number of participants at the Colorado Springs conference about studying the complexities of organizations and how leaders and followers function within them. In later reports in this volume, differences of viewpoints become clearer, and the study of pure leadership may appear to be contaminated by such factors as power, authority, perceptions, stereotypes, customs and traditions, and leader and follower expectations.

The conference chairman was David P. Campbell, Smith Richardson Senior Fellow at the Center for Creative Leadership. As the author of chapter 3, he reports his most recent work with the Campbell Work Orientation Surveys (CWO) and the uses of the CWO to study

the researchers assembled for the conference. His portrayal of leaders and of those who study them may be unique in the annals of leadership study.

Chapter 4 is different from all the papers that precede and follow it, for it summarizes a major applications program within the nonprofit sector. This chapter is placed early in the volume to alert all readers that many of the papers herein deal with things other than making a profit or gaining a competitive advantage. The enormous variety of community, cultural, and services organizations can find much to apply in the studies reported in this summary.

Each of the chapters that follows has its own introduction and its own review of relevant prior work. Each stands alone, in the sense that its conclusions are supported by the evidence presented in the paper itself. Each has its own list of references to related work. This assembly of chapters may be used by scholars who need to acquaint themselves with the most recent work in a given area, as well as by those who need to use the findings.

We, the editors, have found these papers intriguing in their design and content and their authors a most interesting assembly of dedicated persons. We are grateful to them for their willingness to aid in the process of editing aimed toward a common form of reporting and acknowledge their greater knowledge in each of their individual specialties. We trust that the reader will find their work equally engaging.

Our thanks to Walter F. Ulmer, Jr., whose trust in us made this project possible, and to our two able aides, Judith R. Allen, the managing editor for this volume, and Ellen Hamman, who entered it all into the computer and made sure it came out again.

K. E. C.
M. B. C.
D. P. C.

Introduction

**Kenneth E. Clark and
Miriam B. Clark**

Some organizations prosper more than others. Some teams perform better than others. Some persons in a group contribute more than others. Societies, organizations, groups, teams, and individual persons differ. These differences can bring benefits or problems; when they are associated with group performance, they are examined carefully. Success is applauded, but concern mounts when progress falters and failure looms. This is when leaders are blamed and "heads roll." Baseball teams change managers. Churches change ministers. Corporations change chief executive officers. Universities change presidents. Democracies vote out the old leadership.

Why do leaders receive so much of the praise and blame for a group's performance? Should they? Do leaders make that much of a difference in an organization? If so, at what levels? What is the role of followers or supervisors? Are they as important as leaders? Are not group members equally critical in setting the performance level of a team?

Focusing on Leaders and Leadership

Over the past 15 years, articles on leadership have increased at twice the rate of articles in general, and new books abound on leaders and on aspects of leadership. Research studies pertaining to leadership are also proliferating, although not as abundantly as books and articles about leaders. Most of the persons involved in leadership research identify with such academic disciplines as psychology, political science, sociology, and economics. These disciplines study the way individuals, groups, and societies deal with problems and allocate resources in order to attain their goals. Research support comes from corporations, government agencies, military services, large and small public foundations, and individuals. All seek to assure that the next generation will be more fully supplied with leaders better prepared to assume greater responsibilities. Generally, the supporting organizations have already found a direct use for applications of prior research and are searching for even better results.

The Critical Role of Leaders

In a "joiners" society like the United States, every year 1 out of 10 adults is asked to take on some sort of leadership responsibility. Committees must be chaired. Clubs must have presidents. Candidates must be found for political office. A new supervisor for a work team must be located. A new plant manager, a new president, a new chairman of the board must be selected. Action groups, cultural organizations, churches, welfare associations, service organizations, and community groups regularly seek new leaders. Any intelligent college student or any concerned citizen who thinks leadership does not fit into his or her prospects for the future had better notice the way the world works and begin preparing for a future which is sure to be affected by leaders and the influence they exert.

When a new leader is selected, the selecting group too often thinks its work is done. Training sessions are often minimal or nonexistent. The new leader assumes that the job is obvious and that having been selected means that others noted the presence of appropriate qualities. Few are advised to change behaviors in order to lead properly. No one says, "You have a lot to learn." Instead they say, "Congratulations!" A few might add, "Good luck!"

The number of prominent leaders who encounter disaster seems to be incredibly high. General disappointment with leaders is common in all sectors of society. Perhaps we expect too much. Moreover, it is possible that we select and prepare our leaders poorly. Maybe we ask too much of them. But we cannot ask for less than the best from leaders—especially in government and business—to whom we entrust such great power and authority.

Widely publicized data show that over 60% of immediate superiors are the major cause of stress in the workplace. Workers who see the reports agree, and many have a sad tale they are eager to tell. Bosses who see the data do not disagree; they just do not see themselves as the bad guys or as awesome persons who cause stress. Only those superiors who have subjected themselves to anonymous evaluation by their subordinates have any right to feel comfortable about this widespread problem. In fact, many of them already may have heard the bad news about themselves and even may be working on the problem.

Most leaders start out with many flaws which they need to discover and correct. Otherwise, as leaders, they become part of the problem. Appointed because they were well liked and seen as fair and approachable, they make mistakes, lose their popularity, and select all sorts of defensive facades. Yet many of these "failures" could have been turned into brilliant successes. They failed because they did not or could not get the help, support, and education required for them to improve.

Definitions

This book deals with *leadership*, *leaders*, and the *impact* of leadership. *Managers* and *management* will also be discussed. Although we have already used these words, the following definitions are provided to clarify how these terms will be used and to avoid misunderstanding.

"*Leadership* is an activity—an influence process—in which an individual gains the trust and commitment of others and without recourse to formal position or authority moves the group to the accomplishment of one or more tasks" (W. F. Ulmer, personal communication, November 14, 1991). The processes of leadership in organizations involve leaders, followers, members, and subordinates or constituents as they interact, create visions, become inspired, find meaning in their work and lives, and gain in trust and respect. Leadership is critical in organizations of all sizes and types, whether public, private, or independent.

Leaders are people, humans with all their strengths, weaknesses, and special traits. They are people who are persuaded to accept extra responsibilities in the workplace or in the community, persons who seek out a position of advantage to promote progress toward valued goals, individuals who take charge in order to help a group achieve important objectives, people elected or appointed to a position who want to make a difference, and people who simply have a compulsion to get things moving. Great leaders are those who inspire their followers to believe, to expend more effort, and to accomplish great things that otherwise would not get done. No one merits the title of leader whose group or organization has accomplished little: "By their fruits ye shall know them" (Matthew 7.20).

Managers are persons who hold positions in a formal organization and are charged with supervising the accomplishment of given tasks. Usually they operate with the power and authority of position, with responsibility for the effective accomplishment of certain tasks with the resources provided. *Management* and *leadership* often overlap in function, but rarely in process. The exercise of leadership accomplishes goals more effectively than the usual management methods of trading rewards for performance.

The *impact* of leadership refers not only to the effects of good or bad leadership, but also to the processes of leadership that affect followers. The study of impact includes the ways in which leaders and followers interact and thus influence the functioning of an organization. Each study in this book should advance understanding of at least one aspect of leadership as it relates to improved organizational performance.

Impact

Why emphasize impact? There are two reasons. First, those who attend to results, productivity, or efficiency must be concerned with issues of leadership and its impact. The success or failure of any enterprise depends in large part on the way leaders and followers commit themselves wholeheartedly to attaining their goals.

Second, the study of impact reveals secrets about the process of leadership, telling us which leader behaviors produce which follower responses and what conditions moderate or accent these influences.

The findings of leadership studies are hard to ignore. They identify practices that need change and those that are producing the desired results. They also highlight deficiencies in our selection and training of those who are elevated to leadership positions. Curiously, though, the findings are often ignored. The important literature in leadership is neither read nor heeded by most of the people described as movers and shakers in our society. Frequently, people with power and resources consider leadership study a "soft" domain that can be neglected. In business, those seeking large profits or attempting to escape large losses as they merge, divest, plan buyouts, or engage in downsizing or plant closings overlook such variables as worker motivation and satisfaction, subordinate attitudes about superiors, and processes that enhance unit performance. In government, political leaders concern themselves more with actions that help keep them in office than in responding to the needs and the voices of all constituents.

Searching for the Effects of Good Leadership

Many factors influence the success or failure of an organization. Ideology may prevent progress, a crop failure may bring down a regime, and war and pestilence beget unpredictable consequences. Demand for a product or need for a service may be high at one time and low at another; competition increases and decreases. The quality of the workforce, the loyalty of customers, and the effectiveness of promotional efforts all affect sales and profits. The mood of people and how they perceive the world benefits organized religion in one generation and leisure-time industries in another. Outdoor activities may consume one community while cultural events appeal in another.

In addition, one organization may prosper by virtue of a charismatic leader, whereas another may prosper in spite of a dull one. Some teams need a great coach, while some generate their own fire and zeal; occasionally the team is applauded when little is known about the role of the leader. Persons in leadership positions often take credit for achievements they may have impeded. Studies of the ways in which groups work and accomplish their ends and the ways in which their leaders help and hinder this process must take account of the various effects not controllable by those in charge. Simple studies of leadership do not explain much. As studies progress, they necessarily become more complex. We must also separate the effects of good leadership from those of good management. Well-organized managers are essential, but the need for them differs from the need for effective leaders. Managing and leading are different entities. A leader's well-articulated vision truly induces extra effort in a workforce and engenders higher commitment; intellectual stimulation provided by the leader gives purpose to effort and the quality of relationships improves. These factors affect the health of the organization. What we have described as the impact of leadership on outcomes is the domain encompassed by the research in this book.

What We Already Know about Leadership

Some writers perpetuate the myth of leadership as mystical and elusive. Even persons studying the field of leadership sometimes speak of how little is known and how difficult it is to gather knowledge. The lament goes, "After all, all of the great leaders are dead or inaccessible—how can I study them?"

In truth, leaders exist in abundance all over the world. Well-planned studies are in progress; methods of study have been developed; many acts of leadership have been documented in detail. Analytical methods have been greatly refined. Among the most discerning observers of leadership events are the followers; there are plenty of them, and they are usually willing to talk, for they suffer (or benefit) most. Their descriptions of good and poor leader behavior are worth collecting and analyzing. Organizations have a great stake in such studies.

What propositions about leadership are now generally accepted? Do we really know more than we knew before? Some common threads provide the basis for a better weaving of theory about leadership. Not all persons will agree with every one of the following propositions, but we will claim them as those to which we subscribe.

1. The Ohio State Studies (Stogdill & Coons, 1957) of leadership begun in the late 1940s have been confirmed repeatedly. These studies identified two general dimensions of leadership: *Consideration* and *Initiating Structure*. *Consideration* refers to those activities that provide support, encouragement, and attention to the persons who do the work. *Initiating Structure* refers to those activities that clarify the tasks to be accomplished, the quality required, the steps in the process, and other task-related specifics.

2. These two leadership dimensions— *Consideration* and *Initiating Structure*—have been found worldwide. In the many studies by Misumi (1985) in Japan, slight variations were found in the two dimensions which he called *Performance* and *Maintenance*. His studies found them as closely related to overall performance in Japanese companies as had been found by other studies conducted in U.S. companies. These two major dimensions of leader-

ship behavior have been identified in many cultures.

3. Some people can lead well without much training; others perform badly without training. Leadership performance varies widely in the population. While personality characteristics and style relate to performance, there is no single pattern of leader qualities and no single pattern of leadership style.

4. Leadership potential can be measured. Cognitive variables, in addition to personality and other noncognitive measures, are important to help predict which persons will be successful in positions of leadership. Unfortunately, the measurement of leadership potential remains in an unsettled state, even after 45 years of work. No single measure or group of measures has emerged as the best way to measure potential. No measures can be used across cultural lines without some modifications either in form or in the interpretation of results.

5. Self-ratings of leadership performance have much lower correlations with performance than estimates by others. Subordinates give more consistent and more valid estimates of leadership performance than do superiors, but both are more valid than self-ratings. These findings indicate that many leaders think they are doing much better than they are, suggesting that subordinates are better judges of performance.

6. Descriptions of leader behaviors are better predictors than measures of leader traits. Descriptions of leader behaviors by others relate highly to (a) measured unit performance, (b) subordinate estimates of how hard they work, and (c) subordinate expressed satisfaction with the organization and its purposes.

7. Charismatic and transformational leadership, concepts that have been around for a while, have acquired operational definitions in terms of measurable effects on followers. These qualities are exhibited at all organizational levels. The transformational leader motivates followers, earns their respect and trust, and leads them to better performance and expenditure of more effort. Charisma relates more to the personality of the leader and produces more of an emotional response. Wide individual differences exist in exhibiting charismatic and transformational leadership.

8. Leader behaviors are trainable, and the effects of training have been proven to persist. Trained leaders outperform untrained leaders.

9. The outcome measures used to test leader performance in the workplace have attracted the attention of the executive suite, for they relate directly to needs for improving quality and productivity. When the setting is an educational institution, measures of student learning, retention rates, and school reputation are affected.

10. Intelligence becomes a more critical variable as the leader's responsibilities expand in scope or in time dimensions. The cognitive demands are better measured by devices aimed specifically at the job requirements.

11. Stress degrades the use of intelligence in leadership performance. Some organizations have taught leaders to use their intelligence under stress.

12. Experience and organizational policies are often substitutes for intelligence in decision making under stress. Relying on experience often leads to regressive acts under stress.

13. The prevalence of stress produced by the immediate superior must be noted. Boss stress is almost universal. Most persons in managerial or leadership positions behave in too authoritarian a manner for the circumstances

and, for many of these bosses, changes in behavior will not happen without some intervention. Perhaps they carry too much stress from their relations with superiors, but the culture has also instilled in them expectancies and stereotypes about boss behavior. Job stress may be hard to reduce; boss stress can be reduced with appropriate management attention to the problem.

14. Experience is a good teacher for leaders, if they have learned to solicit and accept feedback from others about their behavior in critical incidents. People in authority often resist learning from their mistakes, so the question remains: how to sort out those who will not learn from those who will.

15. Quality of leadership cannot be ignored at any level of an organization. Quality of leadership has been shown to have strong effects on (a) profitability of cost centers, (b) performance of work units, (c) quality of work output, (d) reduction of stress in the workplace, (e) worker satisfaction and morale, (f) reduced absenteeism, and (g) reduced accidents. Good research studies support the view that good management and leadership make at least a 24% difference in productivity. No wonder CEOs are paying attention to leadership issues.

16. Many excellent studies of leadership have been done abroad. Strong cultural differences have been documented that influence the effects of leader behavior. The propositions already listed have been supported as much by studies done outside as those done within the U.S.

Clearly, those who utilize the results of research on leadership need to learn more about the studies that have been conducted worldwide. It is essential to know how the principles of human behavior identified in U.S. research are moderated by differences in cultures, values, and lev-els of economic development. Worldwide research findings suggest that work forces outside the U.S. respond well to the sort of leadership we rate highly in America. These studies deserve to be identified and examined carefully, for they may strengthen our convictions about what behavior is appropriate as power and authority are assigned. We may find ways to capitalize on the unique characteristics of the U.S. workforce and adapt our practices of leadership so as to deal more effectively with the expected increased diversity in that workforce.

Much remains to be done. Some methods for identifying good leadership behaviors exist, but too often we use devices for identifying leadership that were developed for another purpose or were based on too narrow a population. Each time we use a measuring instrument in a new organization or a different culture, we need to reexamine each component to make sure it is appropriate. We have not yet coordinated successfully all our efforts and findings. For example, although the work of Geert Hofstede (1980) on the differences among cultures has been known for more than 10 years, today's most widely used measures do not incorporate his dimensions of national differences as moderator variables in their measures of leadership.

Another example is illustrated by the only recently developed methods used to study charismatic and transformational leadership. Findings show that leaders who behave in certain ways generate a great influence on their followers, and useful things happen. How did they do it? We can only identify charismatic and transformational leadership by asking those who are under its influence. What leader behaviors led to these perceptions by followers? We do not know. We know when the effects occur, but not what produced them. We can run training programs and see the effects increase, but we cannot assure that all trainees will become charismatic or transformational. When a great leader emerges, there is tremendous excitement and increased effort. How are such leaders produced? Can we identify them early?

This relative lack of understanding is balanced by burgeoning theories of how leadership works. Some of these general theories are formulations based on social psychology; some come from studies in economics and sociology; some are the results of close study of the work environment and personal relations among persons in different roles; some use general learning theory as the base on which programs are built. Few students of leadership and management are fully satisfied with the current state of integrated theories about the processes involved. This leaves us with much to accomplish.

The rest of the world is in the same early stage of leadership research as the United States. The propositions listed earlier are not well enough known or practiced universally, and they are often disbelieved. Even (especially?) in the U.S., many persons in authority think these findings undermine the base on which they work and therefore fight against their implementation. Generalized methods are not yet available to apply these principles to persons of a certain personality in a given country, in a given culture, or in a given organization. Maps of leadership behavior continue to require customized design. Statements of principles of leadership need formulation in the language of the culture and modification in terms of modes of conduct consonant with the culture. Therefore, *individualized* consideration, for example, may be wrong for the Japanese, for whom the welfare of the work *group* is the accepted mode.

Behaviors of leaders are susceptible to assessment. Moreover, these behaviors are also subject to modification through all avenues of education and training and through experience in the role of leader. The research community and the training centers must take the lead in providing better tools for assessment and better guides to training.

Embedded in all of the points we have made thus far are three issues of high salience:

1. Any organization, group, or society, in order to reap the benefits of improved leadership and followership, must evidence integrity. Leaders must be honest. Leaders must earn trust and inspire loyalty. They must exhibit respect for their followers and must work for their interests. Organizational policies must be in accord with leaders' pronouncements and behaviors.

2. Values of individuals and their organizations must be well articulated and adhered to universally. Organizational efforts to make values more explicit are healthy and beneficial.

3. Major efforts are required in every society and every organization to instill those behaviors that are most effective and to battle stereotypes to the contrary.

This third point is triggered by a recent research report (see the article by Larry A. Penwell in this volume) using the Meier New-Truck Exercise with students in a business school class. In this game a supervisor and his team of truck drivers must decide who should get a new truck just made available. Each participant plays the role of truck driver, and each participant also plays the role of boss. In this report, when the student acted as boss, the student's preferred style was authoritarian. When the same student played the role of truck driver, the student preferred group participation as the best mode for decision making. The imputed requirements of the role clearly determined the behavior of the incumbent: "If you are the boss, you act like a boss is supposed to act in our society," and "If you are a subject in an experiment, you do what the experimenter tells you to do."

How Leadership Is Studied

Learning new things can occur in many ways, and each researcher develops a particular preference. There are also preferred disciplinary methods which change from one domain to another. To find oil, a geologist does a computer analysis of sonic reflections collected in a specific way. To learn why the dinosaurs died, paleontologists, biologists, and geologists collaborate, using the methods in which each was trained. Students trained in an academic discipline tend to use whatever methods they have mastered. This tendency in scientific study will be noted in later chapters in the reports which demonstrate useful ways to identify the impact of a particular practice. If, at first reading, a report appears arcane and technical, read on! Reports are edited carefully to assure that conclusions are properly stated. Wary readers are cautioned to keep an eye out for limitations to the generalization of findings.

In this book, 84 of the world's most active students of leaders and leadership have presented 42 studies to expand insight into the many questions about the impact of leadership. Central to their inquiries are some very practical questions: What is it that leaders and their followers, managers and their subordinates, visionaries and those who share their vision, or presidents and their supporters do that leads to greater commitment, extra effort, increased loyalty, greater satisfaction, and increased performance? Is there a distinctive role for the leader, the follower, and the group as a whole in producing the admirable effects of leadership found in many organizations? What behaviors can be copied by others to make them more effective leaders or followers?

Behavioral scientists, and psychologists in particular, rely heavily on measures such as (a) potential for performance, (b) behaviors toward others, (c) attitude, (d) performance on the job, (e) preferred styles of operating, and (f) personality characteristics. Myriads of persons in different organizational levels have been measured by these devices. Such measures must meet high technical standards if they are to be interpreted correctly, and each study must present evidence on the quality of the measures used.

Impact of Leadership contains the ideas of many people. Each report aims not merely to present an idea, but also to describe the implementation of that idea in a given setting and the results. The test of the idea is a critical part of its presentation. Without such tests, every idea is idiosyncratic. We can always persuade ourselves that our own idea is good, and our own way is best. When an idea is put into play, some honest tests must be run to make sure it works. Even when an idea is lifted from pages in which tests with favorable outcomes are reported, it is wise to test it again in every new setting.

Research—The Test of an Idea

The testing of an idea about leadership to see whether it "works" is more like testing a new rocket launcher than testing a light bulb. Merely screwing it into a socket to see if it lights is not enough. Conditions must be specified, extraneous variables must be controlled, and priorities must be set to decide what tests to run. Even so, most studies of leadership are pretty straightforward: An idea—usually called a hypothesis or a proposition—is translated into action followed by carefully designed observation and collection of data to determine whether the idea worked. The researcher has the responsibility to provide the reader with as much context as possible, to aid in decisions about application of the findings. The reader then must decide if the given trial fits the circumstance that needs better leadership.

A well-respected approach to leadership study is that of Clark L. Wilson and his associates. Two of their studies are reported in this volume. Their method usually involves entering an organization and identifying key groups of managers whose performance seems to need improvement. The team develops and conducts a training program for the group with components aimed at producing desired changes in behavior. The performance of these managers' work units is then examined over a period of time to determine the effects of this intervention. Wilson and his group found increases in productivity ranging from an average of 8% to 30%. Clearly, the training paid off far beyond its cost. Wilson's central principle is that many highly effective managerial and leadership behaviors must be learned, and special teaching and learning sessions are often needed.

Past studies of leadership provide substantial guidance to practice by reporting tested procedures which had the desired effects. Principles with definite payoffs are known. It is not always easy to identify the paths through which leadership influences workers to increase performance, change attitudes, or expend more effort. Some current studies may seem minimally important or even irrelevant, especially when the bottom line is the primary issue, but none is trivial. All are directed at some part of the complex processes of leadership; finding where the part fits requires patience and time due to the difficulty of building a coherent framework from the many ideas of students of leadership.

You will find differences in perspective among authors about methods and results. Some reports are particularly "skeptic-friendly." The skepticism you will note is worth emulating. Tremendous changes are occurring worldwide. The shifts in power, the escalation of aspirations, the demise of some of the world's despots, the moves towards fairness and egalitarianism, the opening of world trade with its effects on national competitiveness, and the driving forces of new technologies all promise continuing change which may persist for generations. The need for leadership that can accommodate to such massive changes has never been more compelling. The United States has led the world in finding solutions to many problems; we have no choice but to join with the rest of the world in helping develop leaders to fulfill the needs of all society.

References

Hofstede, G. (1980). *Culture's consequences*. Beverly Hills: Sage.

Misumi, J. (1985). *The behavioral science of leadership: An interdisciplinary Japanese research program*. Ann Arbor: University of Michigan.

Stogdill, R. M., & Coons, A. (Eds.). (1957). *Leadership behavior, its description and measurement*. Columbus: Ohio State University, Bureau of Business Research.

Kenneth E. Clark is Smith Richardson Senior Scientist and former President and Board Chairman of the Center for Creative Leadership, Greensboro, NC. He earned his PhD at Ohio State University. He was Chair of the Department of Psychology at the University of Minnesota and Dean of the College of Arts and Science at the University of Colorado and at the University of Rochester.

He was president of the American Board in Professional Psychology and the American Psychological Foundation, appointed to the National Medal of Science Committee, Chairman of the Association for the Advancement of Psychology and the American Conference of Academic Deans. He authored *America's Psychologists* and *The Vocational Interests of Nonprofessional Men*, co-authored *The Graduate Student as Teacher*, *Psychology*, and *Measures of Leadership*, and edited for 10 years the *Journal of Applied Psychology*.

He was consultant to the White House, the Office of Science and Technology, the Central Intelligence Agency, the National Science Foundation, the National Institutes of Health, the Veteran's Administration, the Army, and the Navy. He was awarded Ohio State University's Centennial Achievement Award, the American Personnel and Guidance Association's award for research excellence, and the E. K. Strong, Jr., Gold Medal for contribution to interest measurement. He received the Gold Medal Award of the American Psychological Foundation in 1986 for a lifetime of exceptional contributions to professional psychology.

He is a founding fellow of the American Psychological Society, a fellow of the American Association for the Advancement of Science and the American Psychological Association, and an honorary life fellow of the Canadian Psychological Association.

Miriam B. Clark served as Associate Dean in the College of Arts and Science at the University of Rochester, retiring in 1980. Her primary responsibilities included undergraduate curriculum, academic advising, and career planning. She has been a member or the President of the board of numerous Rochester, NY, community agencies or civic groups. She is currently a member of the Board of Directors of the Naples Philharmonic Center for the Arts. In collaboration with others, her publications include: *The Graduate Student as Teacher*, *Leadership Education: A Source Book* (in three editions: 1985, 1987, 1990); and *Measures of Leadership*.

Direct inquiries to Kenneth or Miriam Clark, Apt. 702, 4551 Gulfshore Blvd., N., Naples, FL 33940, 813/263–8967.

Panel Discussion on Quantitative Versus Qualitative Research Methods

Walter W. Tornow

Is qualitative research of any value if it does not lead to quantification? Does quantifiable research make a difference — has it improved our understanding of leadership? Is leadership research valuable in its own right — can it be justified if it cannot be applied? Can there really be an objective science of leadership independent of the subjectivity that researchers bring when observing and interpreting data?

These are some of the epistemological questions sparked by a "challenge" letter from Henry Mintzberg (personal communication to David Campbell, January 15, 1991). David Campbell had sent out a Call for Proposals for the 1991 research conference sponsored by the Center for Creative Leadership (CCL). That call listed as acceptance criteria that studies should be focused on "The Impact of Leadership," with both *Impact* and *Leadership* broadly defined, and that studies must be data based with no conceptual papers, anecdotes, or testimonials unless accompanied by quantifiable data.

This second acceptance criterion proved controversial! In his letter to Campbell, Henry Mintzberg's challenge revolved around concerns with restricting scientific inquiry to quantification. These concerns are eloquently expressed by the following excerpts from his letter:

The hope that more science, or better science, will make up for all the past failings of science—in a domain like leadership, at least—is an illusion, in my opinion. I had lots of data in my original study, but the key to it all was observing activity and inducing concepts.

I believe in measurement, when things are measurable (like, say, products shipped or people employed), but I don't believe "data" should ever be confused with quantifiable data, nor do I believe that anecdote and impression can ever be removed from effective research.

Quantification is not bad, appropriately applied, and some papers are bound to be good. But if it doesn't . . . think about the religion we call science itself, and not just the inadequacies of our prayers to it.

A panel discussion was convened at the conference in response to a mock debate resolution: "Resolved, Henry Mintzberg was right. Quantitative leadership research is usually trivial, often presented in insufferable jargon, and will do little to change the world." The panel members included, in order of appearance:

1. Walter Tornow, Center for Creative Leadership

2. Mansour Javidan, University of Calgary

3. Fred Fiedler, University of Washington

4. Gary Yukl, State University of New York-Albany

5. Mark Edwards, Arizona State University

6. Dede Osborn, Tecnología Administrativa Moderna

7. Sean Gadman, Digital Equipment Corporation

Because Henry Mintzberg was unable to attend the conference, Mansour Javidan started the panel discussion, stating what he believed to be the basis and rationale of the argument. Mansour's remarks provide a strategic perspective on this topic by focusing on the link between research and the generation of knowledge. His presentation helps us understand the complexity of this link in terms of the journalistic questions *what*, *why*, and *how* and helps explain the divergent views toward research in the social sciences. Mansour ended his presentation with a plea for cooperation and communication between what he called the "two camps" of quantitative and qualitative methodologies.

Fred Fiedler's remarks focused on the issue of generalizability of research. He said the potential for generalizing is low when research uses only a case-study approach. However, case studies can be a good source for hypotheses when complemented by quantifiable, data-based research. The issue is not whether we should use qualitative methods, but rather whether they can stand alone if we want to develop a science.

Gary Yukl pointed out that each type of research methodology—quantitative and qualitative—has its own strengths and weaknesses. The limitations of each type of methodology make it desirable to use multiple methods in research on leadership. The two approaches need to be seen as complementary, not contradictory. A more balanced use of the varied tools available will allow us to make better progress in "unraveling the mysteries of leadership."

Mark Edwards introduced some humor to the "quantitative versus qualitative debate" by using the honeybee as an analogy, harking back to the previous day's luncheon speaker on "Theory Bee." Mark argued that without good measures, there cannot be "survival and afterlife" of leadership research, no matter how good it is. That is, there cannot be generalization, dissemination, continuity, and building of knowledge in our study of leadership unless we can operationalize and measure the constructs and quantify our observations.

Dede Osborn, as the Director of Tecnología Administrativa Moderna's (TEAM) leadership development program and an Associate of CCL, approached the panel discussion from her perspective as a trainer, rather than a researcher, with an applications orientation. Dede argued that it is not so much a question of quantitative or qualitative research, but what the implications are for the practitioner. In other words, research needs to lead to knowledge; importantly, that knowledge then needs to be translated into a non-jargon language so practitioners can apply it in useful ways.

Sean Gadman ended the panel discussion by questioning the ontological and epistemological assumptions by which science is built. "Old" assumptions, according to Sean, lead us to believe that there are "objective truths"; it is only a matter of applying the right measurement to discover these truths. In contrast, Sean argued that "new" assumptions about science recognize the inevitable confounding between the observer and the object of observation, that "truth is relative" and influenced by the unique perspective of the observer. In Sean's words, "knowing is doing, and doing is knowing."

When looking at the presentations as a whole, three major themes emerge from the panel discussion:

1. Rather than quantitative *versus* qualitative, both methodologies are useful for developing an understanding of leadership. The challenge for researchers is to capitalize on their respective strengths to complement each other and to avoid each others' weaknesses.

2. The nature and interpretation of inquiry in social science research may be influenced by the personal, social, and political "lenses" of the inquirer. What is assumed by some as "objective reality," discoverable only by good measurement, is seen by others as an evolving and complex set of constructs resulting from the subjective reality of the observer.

3. Research findings, whether obtained through quantitative or qualitative means, have little value unless they are usable. This means that the results need to be translated to the world of the practitioner, ultimately in ways that can enhance the quality and practice of leadership. Toward that end, we need to avoid statistical and other methodological jargon which may obstruct the dissemination of research-based knowledge.

Following are the presentations of the six panelists in response to the mock debate resolution on quantitative versus qualitative research methods.

Mansour Javidan
University of Calgary

Rather than arguing for one or the other, I will try to provide a "strategic" perspective and overview of the issues regarding qualitative and quantitative methodologies. My thesis is that differences between the two "camps" go beyond simple issues of methodology, and much can be gained by better understanding of both. Furthermore, there is much synergy to be achieved if the two sides are prepared to learn and incorporate their divergent views, rather than rejecting the other perspective. The following graphic summary presents the basis for my comments.

It is widely accepted that the basic reason for conducting research is to create and disseminate knowledge. This premise leads us to three ontological and epistemological questions: What? Why? How? The answers to these questions help us understand the boundaries between the two alternative approaches to research.

The first question is knowledge about *what*. What is it that we want to know? The simple answer to this question is: truth and reality! We conduct research to increase our knowledge and understanding of reality. But this leads us to another

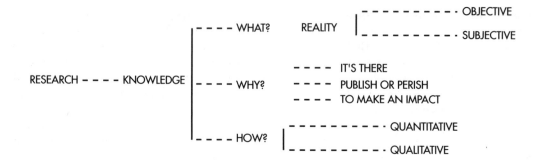

much more complex issue. Natural sciences traditionally assume the existence of an objective reality. It is independent of the researcher and can be identified, measured, and examined through verifiable, empirical evidence. Social sciences have traditionally borrowed the above basic assumption from natural sciences. Most social scientists have presumed that it is mandatory to represent the reality in an objective manner. Like their natural scientist brethren, they have pursued the scientific quest for the objective truth about humans and the human world.

While still a predominant paradigm, this view of reality has recently been challenged. Several modern philosophers, mostly from Europe, have argued that in social sciences there is no objective reality. What the scientist identifies is not the independent, external world but the scientist's perception of that world. In short, our knowledge of the world is simply a socially constructed knowledge. It is not independent of the researcher; it is part of the researcher and is based on the researcher's cognition, psyche, and background.

The second question is *why*. Why do we want to know, and what is the purpose of knowing? One answer to this question is: because it's there! We want to know because we want to describe our world and to better understand the reality around us.

An alternative response is the P.O.P. syndrome: Publish or Perish! Academic institutions need to evaluate the performance of their members. It is widely believed that the output of academics should be generation and dissemination of knowledge. But this is easier said than measured. The ideal situation is, of course, to measure the impact of the academics' work, and that is not easy. The second best alternative, therefore, is to measure the academics' research and publication productivity. The assumption here is that if a manuscript is accepted for publication, it has passed the test and, therefore, will have impact. This approach to performance evaluation has led academics and researchers on a path of increasing their number of publications rather than paying attention to their impact. As a result, there are those who argue that the literature is filled with published works which are nothing but great exercises in mindless number crunching.

Finally, a third answer is: to make an impact! Qualitative social research is based on the premise that to make an impact, one has to understand the phenomena. Since social phenomena are dynamic in nature, they can only be studied via process methodologies whereby the researcher comes into contact with the subject under study. She or he then develops an in-depth knowledge of the process through which the phenomenon comes into being. Most quantitative methdologies are at a disadvantage on this point. Due to their static and cross-sectional nature, they are void of process.

The final question is: *How* do we know when we know? At what point are we convinced that we have discovered the truth? Quantitative research is based on the premise that since there is an objective reality out there, there has to be an independent point of reference to reach the conclusion that we know. The concept of statistical significance is applied for this purpose. When our results are statistically significant, we know!

In contrast, qualitative research is premised on the notion that reality is subjective. Therefore, the researcher is in the position to decide when she or he knows. The researcher does not need external objective verification. That conclusion is reached intuitively. An interesting example will help clarify this point. The pioneering work on the nature of management by the French engineer Henri Fayol (1949) suggested that managers need to plan, motivate, direct, and control. This simple classification was adopted by most scholars and accepted as truth in spite of lack of empirical evidence. Mintzberg (1975) was the first in North America—although not in Europe—to investigate managers in action. His findings were reported in a *Harvard Business Review* article called "The Manager's Job: Folklore and Fact." He criticized the academic community for their blind following of Fayol's fictions and then presented the "facts" based on his own empirical evidence—in-depth interviews with and observation of five executives.

Mintzberg's ideas have had a major impact on the literature on managerial work. Every textbook in management has some form of reference to his work. Despite such popularity, his ideas have not had much empirical support. Several authors have tried to verify his findings with large-scale statistical samples but have had limited success, at best (see Lau, Newman, & Broadling, 1980; McCall & Segrist, 1980; Snyder & Wheelen, 1981).

In conclusion, I tried to provide a brief overview of the issues that have resulted in a divergence of views towards research in social sciences. It would be unfortunate if debate on this subject degenerates into dysfunctional competition, instead of communication and cooperation. In this regard, two points need attention. First, quantitative and qualitative methodologies are suitable for different types of research questions. Second, much can be gained if the proponents of each methodology learn from each other. Our pursuit of knowledge will proceed at a faster pace if each side of the debate takes advantage of the other side's strengths, rather than focusing on its weaknesses.

References

Fayol, H. (1949). *General and industrial management.* London: Pitman.

Lau, A. W., Newman, A. R., & Broadling, L. A. (1980). The nature of managerial work in the public sector. *Public Management Forum, 19,* 513–521.

McCall, M. W., & Segrist, C. A. (1980). *In pursuit of the manager's job: Building on Mintzberg.* Greensboro, NC: Center for Creative Leadership.

Mintzberg, H. (1975). The manager's job: Folklore and fact. *Harvard Business Review, 53*(4), 49–61.

Snyder, N. H., & Wheelen, T. L. (1981). Managerial roles: Mintzberg and the management process theorists. *Proceedings of the Annual Meeting of the Academy of Management,* 249–253.

Fred E. Fiedler
University of Washington

The issue of this debate, as I understand it, is to respond to Henry Mintzberg's letter of January 15, 1991, which suggests that we give up quantitative research in favor of "plenty of concepts and anecdotes, a few testimonials, and all kinds of data, much of the best of it not quantitative . . . the lack of impact of leadership research . . . is the overwhelming conclusion to come out of eighty years of exactly the kind of [quantitative] research you call for." If we are to take these assertions seriously for the sake of this discussion, the main issue is the relative merit of qualitative versus quantitative research. I will address just a few relevant issues.

The first question is whether qualitative and quantitative research are real alternative courses of action. According to Asher (1984) in *The Encyclopedia of Psychology*, qualitative research seeks to "conceptualize new dimensions of behavior, thought, feelings, and aspects of the inner and exterior environments that elicit them. . . . It is almost inevitably a forerunner to all the other methods since it is often here that the new variables are discovered that are more fully developed in the quantitative, descriptive method; and later more rigorously studied in the experimental methods" (pp. 228–229).

Two points are clear. First, the value of qualitative research depends largely, if not entirely, on the sensitivity and insights of the particular observer. In the ordinary course of events, the qualitative data, based on observations, interviews, documents, and so forth, are the stuff of which hypotheses for rigorous research are made. It is, therefore, not a question of using either qualitative or quantitative research. Few good researchers would launch a study without observations, interviews, and perusal of relevant documents which are the raw data of qualitative research.

Second, if we believe that we must be able to replicate and possibly disconfirm scientific observations, "plenty of anecdotes, a few testimonials, and plenty of data, most of them not quantitative," are not likely to do this job. Few researchers have rivaled Freud, Barnard, or von Clausewitz in insight, and their anecdotes and testimonials make good reading. But their hypotheses were supported or disconfirmed by quantitative research rather than more anecdotes and testimonials or observations. Consider the continuing controversies surrounding the work of Freud and the psychoanalysts or the diametrically opposed interpretations we find in historical writings.

A case study, no matter how well done or how elaborately and insightfully described, still represents only one case. How far can we generalize from one case — or from five cases? Moreover, the companies, managers, or leaders who let themselves be studied intensively tend to be a different breed from those who value a low profile or are reclusive. I am reminded of the irreverent saying that "you can lie with statistics, but one good example does a better job."

Unless we are willing to stop with story telling and anecdotes, good qualitative research attempts to generalize beyond the data. This means that we are forced to develop categories, and this means quantification. As Kerlinger (1986) pointed out, "The term, 'quantitative variables' has sometimes been applied to categorical variables, especially to dichotomies, probably in contrast to 'quantitative variables' (or continuous variables). Such usage reflects the distorted notion of what variables are. They are always quantifiable or they are not variables. If x can take on only two values, 0 and 1, these are still values and the variable varies" (p. 36).

Qualitative research certainly has its place, as does the development of new concepts and theoretical formulations. The writings by Barnard, Fayol, Machiavelli, Drucker, Peters and others have had a great deal of impact on management thinking, but none of them has been either confirmed or disconfirmed by anecdotes and testimonials. The question is not whether we should use qualitative methods, but rather, whether they can stand alone.

Finally, have we really learned nothing new from our quantitative research during the past 80 years, or are we only told that nothing has been done that properly celebrates the particular writer's wit and wisdom? The cry that the whole field (with the exception of one's own work) is sterile and trivial is heard not only in the leadership literature but in just about every other field. It goes along with the frequently voiced assertion by those who have finally managed to publish their master's thesis that there has been no progress until their own study of 23 college freshmen broke into print.

Whether there has been progress depends on whether one has read the literature for more than 6 or 12 months. Have we really learned nothing about leadership from quantitative studies over the last 80 years? And will we really not learn much in the next 80 years unless we forego quantitative research in favor of qualitative methods?

For the moment, let us call on more objective observers. Writers of business school texts, although not infallible, have to judge the impact of leadership research on the basis of how much good it will do the prospective manager. Kerr (1984) surveyed 30 management texts published between 1981 and 1983 in order to count the number of texts which described various theories in reasonable detail. These theories presumably have the most impact on the field as well as contributing to business school students' future careers.

Kerr lists the number of texts (shown in parentheses) in which the various theories were described. These were the Contingency Model (30), Path-Goal Theory (29), the Ohio State measures (28), the trait theories (28), Vroom-Yetton model (19), Tannenbaum-Schmidt model (19), the University of Michigan studies (18), the Managerial Grid (13), and Substitutes for Leadership (12). No other theory had as many as five serious mentions. Where are the theories derived from plenty of concepts and anecdotes, a few testimonials, and plenty of nonquantitative data? Granted that this list is 8 years old, which theory, based on qualitative data, would recent texts describe with equal frequencies?

There can be no question that such writers as Douglas McGregor, Peter Drucker, or Tom Peters have had a great deal of impact on management thinking. But here we are talking about research, and the question is, how much of their thinking has contributed to the scientific body of knowledge? If impact is measured by name familiarity or familiarity with certain concepts, then we are not talking about research but about intuitive, insightful, and sometimes accurate observations.

That the names of these authors are much better known than most of those on Kerr's list is relevant only if we assume that name recognition is critical. The fact that more people know about, and have been influenced by, Ann Landers than Carl Rogers or Albert Bandura does not mean that she has had more impact on psychological theory.

Finally, I would like to comment on the statement that we have learned nothing from quantitative studies in the last 80 years. The answer is, of course, in the eyes of the beholder. In a chapter for the *International Review of Industrial and Organizational Psychology* (Fiedler & House, 1988), Bob House and I drew up a partial list of what we think we have learned over the past 50 years. Here, for what it may be worth, is a shortened version of this list:

1. The field has identified two major categories of leader behavior, one concerned with interpersonal relations (e.g., consideration, social-emotional behavior) and the other with task-accomplishment (e.g., structuring, task-orientation).

2. There is no one ideal leader personality. However, effective leaders tend to have a high need to influence others and to achieve, and they tend to be bright, competent, and socially adept rather than stupid, incompetent, and social disasters.

3. Leader-follower relations affect the performance, satisfaction, motivation, self-esteem, and well-being of followers. Therefore, the study of leadership is of substantial social, as well as organizational, significance.

4. Different situations require different leader behaviors, in part to compensate

for deficiencies in the followers' environment and abilities. There are no behaviors exclusively manifested by leaders.

5. The motivations attributed by leaders to group members in judging their behavior and performance determine in large part how leaders behave toward them.

6. Leader experience correlates with performance when the leader feels under stress; intelligence tends to correlate with performance only when stress is low.

7. Charismatic or transformational leadership is the result of such clearly identifiable behaviors as articulating transcendent goals, demonstrating strong self-confidence and confidence in others, setting a personal example for followers, showing high expectations for followers' performance, and communicating one's faith in one's goals.

8. There is considerable evidence supporting several leadership theories. Among the more prominent are McClelland's (1961) need-achievement theory, Fiedler's (1964) Contingency model, House's (1971) Path Goal Theory, Vroom and Yetton's (1973) Theory of Leader Decision Making, Graen & Cashman's (1975) Vertical Dyad Linkage Theory, charismatic and transformational theories of leadership (House, 1977; Bass, 1985), and Misumi's (1985) PM theory.

9. Several leadership training methods have been successfully validated (Burke & Day, 1986). These include behavior modeling (Sorcher & Goldstein, 1972), Leader Match training (Fiedler & Chemers, 1984), motivation training (McClelland, 1965; Miner, 1978), and Goal Setting (Latham & Saari, 1979; Locke, 1968).

Whether these accomplishments are trivial depends on one's point of view. They don't seem trivial to me, and the next 50 years will, undoubtedly, document equal if not greater progress.

References

Asher, W. (1984). Research methodology. In R. J. Corsini (Ed.), *Encyclopedia of Psychology* (Vol. 3, pp. 228–229). New York: Wiley.

Bass, B. M. (1985). Leadership—good, better, best. *Organizational Dynamics, 13*, 28–40.

Burke, M. J., & Day, R. R. (1986). A cumulative study of training. *Journal of Applied Psychology, 71*(2), 232–265.

Fiedler, F. E. (1964). A contingency model of leadership effectiveness. In L. Berkowitz (Ed.), *Advances in Experimental Social Psychology* (Vol. 1, pp. 149–190). New York: Academic Press.

Fiedler, F. E., & Chemers, M. M. (1984). *Improving leadership effectiveness: The leader match concept* (2nd ed.). New York: Wiley.

Fiedler, F. E., & House, R. J. (1988). Leadership theory and research: A report of progress. In C. I. Cooper & I. Robertson (Eds.), *International review of industrial and organizational psychology* (pp. 73–92). New York: Wiley.

Graen, G., & Cashman, J. F. (1975). A role-making model of leadership in formal organizations: A developmental approach. In J. G. Hunt & L. L. Larson (Eds.), *Leadership frontiers* (pp. 143–165). Kent, OH: Kent State University Press.

House, R. J. (1971). A path goal theory of leadership effectiveness. *Administrative Science Quarterly, 16*, 321–338.

House, R. J. (1977). A 1976 theory of charismatic leadership. In J. G. Hunt & L. L. Larson (Eds.), *Leadership: The cutting edge* (pp. 189–207). Carbondale: Southern Illinois University Press.

Kerlinger, F. N. (1986). *Foundations of behavioral research*. Orlando, FL: Holt.

Kerr, S. (1984). Leadership and participation. In A. Brief (Ed.), *Research on productivity*. New York: Praeger.

Latham, G. P., & Saari, L. M. (1979). Importance of supportive relationships in goal setting. *Journal of Applied Psychology, 64,* 151–156.

Locke, E. A. (1968). Toward a theory of task motivation and incentives. *Organizational Behavior and Human Performance, 3,* 157–190.

McClelland, D. C. (1961). *The achieving society.* Princeton, NJ: Van Nostrand.

McClelland, D. C. (1965). Achievement motivation can be developed. *Harvard Business Review, 43*(6), 6–24.

Miner, J. B. (1978). 20 years of research on role-motivation theory of managerial effectiveness. *Personnel Psychology, 31,* 739–760.

Misumi, J. (1985). *The behavioral science of leadership. An interdisciplinary Japanese research program.* Ann Arbor: University of Michigan Press.

Sorcher, M., & Goldstein, A. P. (1972). A behavior modeling approach in training. *Personnel Administration, 35*(2), 35–41.

Vroom, V. H., & Yetton, P. W. (1973). *Leadership and decision-making.* Pittsburgh: University of Pittsburgh Press.

Gary Yukl
State University of New York—Albany

A major controversy about research methodology in leadership is the relative merits of quantitative and descriptive-qualitative research. In the past half century, leadership research has been dominated by quantitative methods, especially questionnaires, and we have made only limited use of qualitative-descriptive methods. Each type of research methodology has its strengths and weaknesses.

In much of the quantitative research on leadership behavior, respondents are given the difficult task of retrospectively rating how often or how much a leader exhibited some behavior over a period of several months or years. There is growing evidence that leader behavior descrip-tions obtained with questionnaires may be biased by attributions, stereotypes, and implicit assumptions about the nature of leadership. However, the extent of the problem remains to be determined, because most research on biases in questionnaires consists of laboratory studies in which subjects had little or no opportunity to observe leaders directly. Research presented at the CCL conference two years ago indicates that some tests and questionnaires may provide a moderately accurate measure of leadership skills and specific, observable leadership behaviors (Clark & Clark, 1990).

Critics of questionnaire-correlational research advocate greater use of descriptive methods such as observation, interviews, and intensive case studies. The proponents of qualitative-descriptive methods believe that these methods are more suitable for studying the complex, dynamic processes involved in leadership. However, the qualitative-descriptive methods also have limitations. Standards for the application and evaluation of qualitative methods are not as explicit as those for traditional quantitative methods, and interpretation of findings is sometimes very subjective. Just as in quantitative research, the data collection methods used in qualitative research are susceptible to biases and distortions. Information obtained from diaries, critical incidents, and interviews may be biased by selective memory for aspects of behavior consistent with the respondent's stereotypes and implicit theories about effective leadership. Direct observation is susceptible to selective attention and biased interpretation of events by the observer due to stereotypes and implicit theories. Attribution errors may occur if an observer or interviewer has information about the performance of the leader's unit. Observation of leaders is often done in a very superficial way, with a small number of random observation periods and little effort to understand the context and the prior history of events. Most observation studies of leadership do not use supplementary methods, such as interviews with key figures, to discover the meaning of the events being observed.

The limitations of each type of methodology make it desirable to use multiple methods in research on leadership. The two approaches are complementary, not incompatible. Both types of research should be used in more systematic and effective ways. Research with questionnaires and skill inventories can be improved by using interviews to gather supplementary information about the way respondents interpret the questions. I have found in my own research that respondents sometimes interpret questionnaire items in a very different way than I do, and their answers do not make much sense unless I understand their interpretation of the questions. Qualitative research can be improved by quantifying key findings so they can be verified and evaluated with statistical tests. Use of a coding system to indicate the frequency of various behaviors or event sequences makes it easier to determine if the same pattern occurs in other contexts or other organizations. However, use of coding to quantify behavior and event sequences does not imply that the richness and meaning inherent in the qualitative descriptions need be lost or ignored. In some observation studies, the observer merely checks off predetermined categories to classify events, rather than writing narrative descriptions to be coded at a later time. This highly structured observation loses much valuable information and may focus attention away from the most interesting aspects of the observed events.

It is important to select methods appropriate to the type of knowledge sought, rather than merely using whatever methods seem most convenient. The purpose of the research should dictate the methodology and choice of samples, not the other way around. Leadership researchers are not limited to questionnaire studies and descriptive case studies based on interviews and observation. Controlled experiments in laboratory and field settings are appropriate for some types of leadership research and should be utilized more often. Simulations, such as the Center for Creative Leadership's Looking Glass, can be used with interviews, observations, tests, and questionnaires to study complex leadership processes. Field experiments can be conducted over a fairly long time interval with a combination of descriptive methods (e.g., interviews, observation, and diaries) and with the repeated application of questionnaires. We need to make a more balanced use of the varied research tools available to us in order to make better progress in unraveling the mysteries of leadership.

Reference

Clark, K. E., & Clark, M. B. (Eds.). (1990). *Measures of leadership*. West Orange, NJ: Leadership Library of America.

Mark R. Edwards
Arizona State University

Background Analogy: Honeybees need strong measures to map their territory in search of pollen. They then communicate their findings with a precise dance that maps their specific flowers to other workers.

The impact of leadership research may be assisted with an analogy to the ubiquitous honeybee. Without strong measures, this bee finds:

1. No search pattern—no systematic plan to search out pollen.

2. No navigation—no way to tell where it's been.

3. No dance—no way to dance a map of the pollen location to others.

4. No survival—it's flying blind, and it's just a matter of time before it crashes and burns.

5. No afterlife—no one remembers its dance.

Fred Fiedler's leadership research, for example, will last for decades because he used empirical measures to determine where specific styles of leadership work best. Every one of his graduate students, over 100 people, know Fred's "dance." He shared his methods and findings in a manner that is universal: measurement. His students can pick up his dance and sustain the line of research that represents Fred's lifelong quest.

Quantitative measures leave clear tracks in the sand. Measures separate truths from legends. Failing another way to understand the difference between a good story and truth, science uses measurement. These measures create an "afterlife" for our leadership research that others can follow.

Use quantitative measures for leadership so others can build on your research. Measures allow others to see real differences in research so they do not have to follow your work based on just faith. Use good measures so others will understand how you have separated fads, facts, and fiction. Power your research with measures so those who follow you will see and understand the beauty of your dance.

Please dance.

Dede Osborn
Tecnología Administrativa Moderna

I have been selected to represent a training practitioner's orientation in this discussion of quantitative versus qualitative research. Although Noel Osborn and I are here presenting our own quantitative research in TEAM, as associates of the Center for Creative Leadership working with Latin America we are also actively involved in the training of managers in San Antonio, Mexico, and in South America.

I say, yes, we need the hard, data-oriented research. Most of the managers we work with are very practical, data-focused people; they want quantitative kinds of information. The more statistics, numbers, and facts that we have for our participants, the better they like it. (You might be surprised to know that a Colombian manager would be very interested in the break-out of U.S. naval plebes on the Myers-Briggs types, or that Mexican executives might be curious as to the FIRO norms on a Japanese managerial sample, or that the women in the San Antonio Leadership Development Program need to know that women are significantly more self-deprecating on the Management Skills Profile than are men.)

However, findings from quantitative research need to be "translated" and applied to become useful to the practitioner. For example, we incorporate data-based knowledge into our leadership training to help people who want to understand themselves and their world in order to be more effective and impactful.

Now, I must say that from a psychological point of view, it is really amazing to me to see grown, mature people who have been in a semicomatose state in some of these presentations open their eyes, come to attention, and lean forward with quickened breath just hearing terms like "coefficient alphas," or "Eigen values," or "varimax rotations"! I'm glad someone here speaks your language! But sometimes I think the language gets in the way of understanding. I feel like I'm running around from session to session with a big colander, collecting all these quantitative facts and information, hoping something understandable and usable will fall out that I can take back with me next week.

On the other hand, yes, qualitative research and theory are useful to us as well! If transformational leadership theory was never rigorously researched, it would still be a useful concept to us (especially when discussing the development of leadership theory over time). We can know, in many ways and by many modes, whether the data are derived quantitatively or qualitatively. From our perspective, it is all interesting and all potentially useful.

There is an old African proverb that says, "Never test the depth of the water with both feet." Even though the world needs both quantitative and qualitative dimensions of research, we need to stick with the approach that we do best. If you are a "numbers cruncher," keep "rotating your varimaxes and validating your Eigens," and do it with joy and gusto! The world needs you.

If you're a theoretical "dabbling dilettante" (as Clark Wilson recently called them), keep dabbling just as hard and as best you can, with curiosity and excitement. Those who are out there trying to make a difference need everything you can produce.

If I have one suggestion to make, it is to all parties—quantitative and qualitative types. Make the fruits of your labor more accessible to all of us. It isn't enough for just your colleagues to understand. Your potential impact is much greater than that. Your learnings become our tools.

Sean Gadman
Digital Equipment
Corporation

Paradigms, whether old or new, carry with them certain assumptions about the nature of the world and how it might be viewed. First, there are assumptions of an ontological nature which question whether the world is external to the individual or a product of the individual's consciousness. Second, there are questions of an epistemological nature which determine how an individual understands the world and communicates this as knowledge to others.

These "old" assumptions are coming under increasing pressure as the world becomes more globally interconnected, with biological, social, psychological, and environmental phenomena being inextricably linked. To describe this world appropriately, we need a perspective not offered by these old assumptions. We need a new vision of reality, a fundamental change in our thoughts, perceptions, and values. According to Bateson (1972), such a vision is one which:

1. Does not separate the knower from what was known—is nondualist.

2. Avoids making processes into things.

3. Has a deep reverence for all forms of life.

From this "new" perspective, truth would be relative; knowledge would develop into a coherent system through a philosophy of speculation. This contrasts with the somewhat rational approach of assuming that it is possible to describe in clear terms the nature of problems and the path leading to their solution.

For research, such a perspective implies that the task of confronting all possible experience lies beyond the powers of any one person. Progress must be slow in the search for elements which are both simple and universal, without the expectation of immediately grasping their full significance. Instead, a picture would be created, first in outline only, then become more detailed wherever possible.

It is ironic that the scientific community which, through Newton, brought notoriety to empiricism has also invented the very instruments which allow us to see beyond it. Microprocessors and electronic communication systems are rapidly altering the way in which we live, work, and communicate. They are also enabling a greater understanding of how our mental and physical domains are related and how our perceptions and thoughts relate to our worlds.

Many believe that this new understanding has yet to crystalize and, until it does, confusion and anxiety will remain as we attempt to deal with a world that can no longer be understood in terms of traditional Newtonian concepts. I prefer to think of the search for a new paradigm as a process of "uncrystallization" where ambiguity, confusion, and anxiety are the primary initiators of new learning, awareness, and action.

In conclusion, new paradigms offer an alternative way of thinking about the world. They seek to create a new vision of reality and foster fundamental changes in our thoughts, perceptions, and values. They are an attempt to respond to Bateson's (1972) challenge to learn to think in a new way which is nondualist, in that it does not separate the knower from what is known, which avoids making processes into things, and which has a deep reverence for all forms of life.

Reference

Bateson, G. (1972). Pathologies of epistemology. In W. P. Lebra (Ed.), *Transcultural research in mental health* (pp. 383–390). Honolulu: University of Hawaii Press.

Walter W. Tornow is Vice President, Research and Publication, at the Center for Creative Leadership. His experience in industry includes responsibility for survey research and strategic applications of human resource research programs in a cross-section of U.S. companies while at Business Advisors, Inc. At Control Data Corporation, he was responsible for Human Resource Research and Human Resource Planning functions. As a visiting professor, he has taught courses in graduate business schools. He has published widely on the topics of human resources, executive management, service quality, job evaluation, and performance management. He received his PhD in Industrial-Organizational Psychology from the University of Minnesota.

Direct inquiries about this article to Walter W. Tornow, Vice President, Research and Publication, Center for Creative Leadership, P. O. Box 26300, Greensboro, NC 27438–6300, 919/288–7210.

CHAPTER 3

The Leadership Characteristics of Leadership Researchers

David P. Campbell

This chapter is slightly different from the remaining chapters in this book in that its topic is essentially the other authors. As part of the conference that produced this book, each researcher (or at least 42 of them) completed the Campbell Leadership Index (CLI), a structured adjective checklist covering leadership characteristics, and then had three to five observers of their choice also fill it in on them. This technique, known as "self-plus-observers," provides a standardized profile of leadership characteristics whereby the individuals' self-descriptive profile can be compared with a parallel profile based on the description of the individual by knowledgeable observers.

Campbell Leadership Index, CLI, Campbell Work Orientations, and CWO are trademarks owned by David P. Campbell, PhD.

The Leadership Theory

The leadership theory underlying the Leadership Index can be thought of in three phases: first, a *definition of leadership* which emphasizes productivity within organizational settings; second, a listing of the *necessary tasks* for leadership to occur; and third, a listing of the *personal characteristics* necessary to accomplish those tasks.

A Definition of Leadership

Before a measuring instrument for leadership characteristics can be developed, a working definition of leadership must be established. For these purposes, the following definition has been used for guidance: *Leadership is actions which focus resources to create desirable opportunities.*

The *actions* of leadership include a wide range of behaviors such as planning, organizing, managing, deciding, speaking, writing, producing, cajoling, motivating, creating, economizing, inspiring, disciplining, politicking, persuading, compromising, confronting, and perhaps even litigating—that is, any behavior that leads to a higher probability of a desirable organizational outcome.

The *resources* to be focused include not only the usual list of people, money, time, space, and materials, but also nebulous assets such as public opinion, legislative power, unique talents, opportunistic accidents (for instance, disasters that can be turned to some useful end), geographic advantages, and personal contacts.

The resulting *desirable opportunities* include the normally recognized fruits of leadership such as higher profits, better educational systems, and an expanded national security, as well as other less obvious but still noble outcomes such as an improved environment, a healthier population, a reduction in international tensions, an increase in knowledge, or specific or general increase in truth, beauty, and happiness. The adjective *desirable* is used here to insure that this definition of leadership does not include tyranny. Hitler and Stalin may have influenced millions of people but, by this definition, their actions did not constitute leadership. (A further discussion of this definition as well as the leadership tasks and personal leadership characteristics which are listed next, can be found in Campbell, 1991a. A lengthier discussion can be found in Campbell, 1991b.)

The Necessary Tasks of Leadership

For leadership to occur, the next step is to specify the necessary tasks that must be achieved. The position taken here is that there are seven such tasks, each of which can be succinctly represented by a word or phrase: vision, management, empowerment, politics, feedback, entrepreneurship, and personal style.

Vision. The task of vision is to clarify the overall goals of the organization. "Organization" is taken to mean whatever collective activities the "leader" is responsible for or can influence. If the person is at the top of a formal organization, the situation is obvious. However, others who have responsibilities for departments or project teams, or who are working in other diverse settings such as church

choirs, neighborhood clean-up committees, or professional organizations, must also accept the leadership responsibility of clarifying the group's goals. In highly structured, highly disciplined organizations, the vision usually flows from the top, from the leader. In more consensual settings, the leader usually must be the catalyst for the vision to arise from below.

Management. The task of management is, first, to focus resources on the organization's goals and, second, to monitor and manage the use of these resources. Every organization has resources available, but they are never sufficient to do everything that everyone wants to do. Consequently, allocation systems have to be established. Further, because resources do not manage themselves, and because all subordinates are not necessarily thrifty and responsible, monitoring and follow-up systems must be devised.

Empowerment. The task of empowerment is to select, develop, and share power with subordinates committed to the organization's goals. In the complex world of organizations, decision making and responsibility must be dispersed, both to accomplish current tasks and to prepare those who will be responsible for future leadership.

Politics. The task of politics is to forge coalitions, both formal and informal. The dynamics of politics are ever present, both within and without, and political forces can be a constant threat or a continuing source of support. A leader must recognize these dynamics and spend time and energy developing supportive networks.

Feedback. The task of feedback is to listen carefully to relevant sources and then to react appropriately. Because they are at the center of streams of information, leaders know more about their organization than does anyone else. The feedback task is to sift through the deluge of information, decide what needs attention, route the necessary ideas or instructions to the proper recipient for action, and then follow up to see that something is done.

Entrepreneurship. The task of entrepreneurship is to find future opportunities and then create desirable change to take advantage of these opportunities. Every organization has a certain amount of momentum pushing it in the direction it is heading. This momentum is essential for continuity and is inevitable because all organizations are ruled by their immediate histories. Yet, due to unpredictable forces both internal and external, this momentum must often be guided in new directions. The task of redirecting people and resources is the entrepreneurial task of the leader.

Personal style. The "task" of personal style is to set an overall organizational tone of competence, integrity, and optimism. The leader is the most visible individual in the organization and, consequently, influences the spirit of everyone else. If the leader is competent, optimistic, and trustworthy, a positive spirit will usually pervade the organization. If, in contrast, the leader is incompetent, mean-spirited, or unethical, a less productive atmosphere will likely prevail.

These, then, are the seven tasks of leadership. Because these tasks collectively are both physically and psychologically demanding, the leader also has the additional "task" of being energetic and resilient, a conclusion that has some relevance in the measurement of leadership characteristics, which is the next topic.

Personal Characteristics of Leaders

Working from the preceding formulation, a long list of descriptive adjectives was developed to reflect the personal char-

acteristics necessary to carry out the tasks of leadership. One hundred of these adjectives were gathered together into a survey termed the Campbell Leadership Index (CLI); analytical scoring scales were constructed, normed, and organized into a profile report form. (More details on these steps and extensive statistical information on the scoring scales and profile can be found in Campbell, 1991a, along with standardization data on over 30 samples of "leaders" from various settings.)

The scoring scales. Using statistical clustering techniques, 22 scoring scales were developed and organized into 5 major leadership "Orientations," again on the basis of statistical clustering. These Orientations, the scoring scales within each of them, and examples of adjectives used to construct each scale are listed in Table 1. Each scoring scale and each Orientation, along with an Overall Index based on 96 of the CLI adjectives, has been standardized in T-Score format, which means that the population average is about 50, with a standard deviation of 10. Thus scores above 55 can be considered "high," scores below 45 can be considered "low." The population distribution is bell-shaped, and about two-thirds of the population falls between the scores of 40 and 60, so these scores can be considered "very low" and "very high," respectively.

Surprisingly, and perhaps regrettably at least for theoretical simplicity, the clusters of descriptive adjectives did not fall out in parallel with the seven listed tasks. That is, the adjectives did not statistically cluster into groups such as "Vision," "Management," "Empowerment," and so forth. Rather, the adjectives clustered into scales such as "Dynamic," "Experienced," "Friendly," and "Optimistic." Basically, this means that when people describe leaders they do not use the "tasks" approach; rather, they focus more on what psychologists usually refer to as "traits." Thus, although the seven tasks provided a useful framework for developing this measuring system, there is not a one-to-

TABLE 1   Campbell Leadership Index (CLI): Explanatory Notes

Orientations / Scales	Typical Adjectives	Psychological Interpretation
LEADERSHIP		
Ambitious	Competitive, forceful	Determined to make progress, likes to compete.
Daring	Adventuresome, risk-taking	Risk oriented, willing to try new experiences.
Dynamic	Enthusiastic, a leader	Takes charge, inspires others, seen as a leader.
Enterprising	Impressive, resourceful	Works well with the complexities of change.
Experienced	Savvy, well-connected	Has a good background, well-informed.
Farsighted	Insightful, forward-looking	Looks ahead, plans, a visionary.
Original	Creative, imaginative	Sees the world differently, has many new ideas.
Persuasive	Convincing, fluent	Articulate and persuasive in influencing others.
ENERGY	Active, healthy	Physically fit, energetic.
AFFABILITY		
Affectionate	Emotional	Acts close, warm, and nurturing.
Considerate	Cooperative, helpful	Thoughtful, willing to work with others.
Empowering	Encouraging, supportive	Motivates and helps others to achieve.
Entertaining	Extroverted, humorous	Clever and amusing; enjoys people.
Friendly	Cheerful, likeable	Pleasant to be around, smiles easily.
DEPENDABILITY		
Credible	Candid, trustworthy	Open and honest; inspires trust.
Organized	Orderly, methodical	Sets up systems and follows through.
Productive	Dependable, effective	Uses time and resources well.
Thrifty	Frugal, not extravagant	Uses and manages money wisely.
RESILIENCE		
Calm	Easy-going, serene	Has an unhurried, unruffled manner.
Flexible	Adaptable, not stubborn	Easily adjusts to changes.
Optimistic	Resilient, well-adjusted	Positive; handles challenges well.
Trusting	Trusting, not cynical	Trusts and believes in others.

one correspondence between these leadership "tasks" and commonly described leadership "traits." Until we better understand how traits lead to the performance of tasks, we will have to accept this discontinuity in this formulation. However, the measuring scales, which are reliable and standardized, can provide a wealth of information on both individual leaders and designated groups of leaders, as shown in the following section.

The samples. Two samples of leadership professionals were surveyed with the CLI, and their profiles are reported here. The first sample included 42 *Leadership Researchers* (with 171 observers, an average of 4.1 each), mostly academics with advanced degrees who participated in the conference that resulted in this book and who filled in the Leadership Index on themselves. (Each person had a minimum of three observers, else he or she was not included in this analysis.) Because an invitation to the conference was restricted to those who had completed research projects and submitted abstracts to a screening committee, each person at the conference was experienced and competent in some academic, scientific research area.

The second sample included 38 *Leadership Educators* (with 169 observers, for a 4.4 observer average) who attended a leadership education conference in the summer of 1990 at the Jepson School of Leadership Studies at the University of Richmond. This conference focused on teaching leadership in various higher education settings, and the typical attendee was a college or university staff member who had some administrative responsibility for student leadership programs. Often they were individuals who had, through imagination and persistence, created the student leadership program in their institution. Informally, the Leadership Educators seemed somewhat less "academic" and somewhat more action-oriented than did the Leadership Researchers.

The profile scores. The CLI graphic profile for the Leadership Researchers is presented in Figure 1 and for the Leadership Educators in Figure 2. These profiles are arranged so that each Orientation and its subscales are grouped together, with the Orientation scale, which is a collection of all of the adjectives in the subscales on that Orientation, listed first. (As there is only one scale in the Energy Orientation, no subscales are listed.) As can be seen, both groups scored above average on every scale, at least in the eyes of their observers; within each sample, one Self score fell slightly below average: for the Educators, it was the Calm scale; for the Researchers, it was the Organized scale. Though interesting because they were the lowest scores, neither of these scale scores is particularly noteworthy because they are both in the midrange.

The Overall Index, reported in Figures 1 and 2 for both samples for both Self and Observers, indicates that on average, the Educators saw themselves as somewhat better leaders than did the Researchers (59 versus 52); that tendency was reflected, though more muted, in the Observer scores (58 versus 56). The main reason for the muting is that the Researchers' Observers rated them more highly than they rated themselves. The Researchers were more modest than the Educators who were, however, more accurate.

(Considerable experience with standard scores has indicated that mean differences of three points or more, e.g., one-third standard deviation, are the smallest differences that are worth noting. Differences of five points or more, e.g., one-half standard deviation, are definitely important as differences of this magnitude will be observable in the performance of groups. Larger differences are obviously even more important.)

These overall profiles suggest that both groups were composed, on average, of people who were seen as effective leaders by their observers. Considering that both groups were populated by people with impressive career records and a history of accomplishments, these data seem quite reasonable.

The most noteworthy difference between the profiles of the two samples was the degree of average discrepancy between Self and Observers; this comparison can be made by noting the length of line separating the average Self and average Observer score on each profile. The differences in average discrepancies, which showed up mostly in the Leadership and Affability Orientations, suggest that, on average, the Educators have a more accurate, and slightly more favorable, picture of how they are viewed by others than do the Researchers.

Although the complete CLI profile, with its 22 scales and 5 Orientations, is informative, it has too much information for easy comparisons between group profiles. For that reason, Figure 3 reports only the five Orientations and the Overall Index for both samples, with both Self

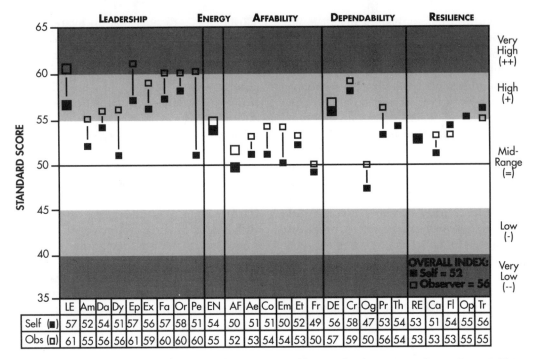

Figure 1   CWO Campbell Leadership Index group profile: Leadership Researchers (■ = Self Average, N = 42; □ = Observer Average, N = 171).

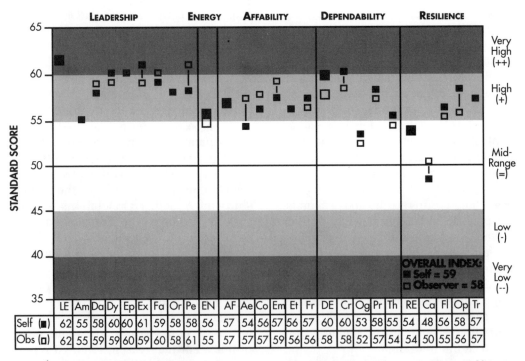

Figure 2   CWO Campbell Leadership Index group profile: Leadership Educators (■ = Self Average, N = 38; □ = Observer Average, N = 169).

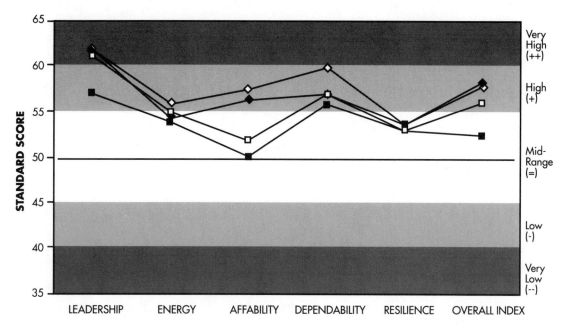

Figure 3 CWO Campbell Leadership Index: Leadership Educators (Self = ♦, Observer = ◇) vs. Leadership Researchers (Self = ■, Observer = □).

and Observer scores for each. This graphic presentation makes more evident the two main differences between these two samples: First, the Researchers underevaluated their characteristics in the Leadership Orientation (as shown in their subscale scores in Figure 1, resulting mainly from their underestimating how dynamic and persuasive they were as seen by others); second, the Researchers saw themselves, and were seen by their Observers, as somewhat less affable than the Educators, so much so that in a pragmatic sense, if one wanted to advise these Researchers on how to be perceived as better leaders, they might well be encouraged to focus on their interpersonal relationships. Their other leadership characteristics were, as a group, quite satisfactorily high.

Two validity studies. Two more sets of CLI profiles are presented in Figures 4 and 5 to demonstrate the validity of the CLI scales. These profiles document CLI scale differences between people demon-

strating different levels of leadership effectiveness. Again, only the Orientation scores and Overall Index are reported because the overall differences are easier to see.

The profiles in Figure 4 came from a marketing corporation study where "savvy insiders" in the Human Resources Department identified two samples of managers with differently perceived leadership performances. The first sample included 11 middle managers with good track records and good reputations; they were deemed "Executive Potential," worthy of possible future promotions to the executive level. The second sample included 16 middle managers who were seen as "Plateaued," which meant that although they were making valuable contributions in their current positions, they had little chance of further advancement.

Both groups of managers were asked "to participate in an experimental leadership assessment research project" by completing the CLI. Each of them selected their own observers, none of whom were

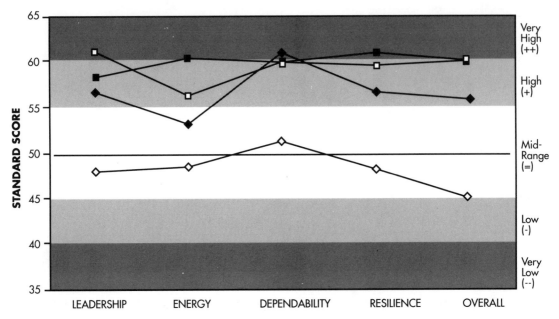

Figure 4 CWO Campbell Leadership Index Marketing Managers: Executive Potential (■ = Self, N = 11; □ = Observers, N = 50) vs. Plateaued (♦ = Self, N = 16; ◇ = Observers, N = 75).

the "savvy insiders" who made the external judgment of Executive Potential or Plateaued.

The Self and Observer profiles for the two marketing manager samples are presented in Figure 4. As can be seen, the two profiles for the Executive Potential sample are in substantial agreement, and both profiles are high. These effectively functioning managers were seen as good leaders by their observers, and they also rated themselves highly. In contrast, although the Plateaued sample also rated themselves high, though not quite as high as the Executive Potential Self scores, their observers rated them substantially lower. The results, which are somewhat painful, indicate that the managers in the Plateaued sample had an unrealistic view of their own performance. Such discrepancies are what make performance appraisal interviews so difficult. These results indicate that the CLI scales are working as they should; they appropriately reflect external judgements of people in leadership positions.

The second set of Self and Observer profiles, presented in Figure 5, are for two samples of cadets at a military academy. Both samples were seniors, within a year of commissioning. One sample included "typical" cadets who completed the CLI as a project in a psychology class in which they were enrolled; they were essentially a random sample from the entire body of cadets. The second sample included cadet commanders who had been selected by the academy administration to serve in important cadet posts during their senior year; they were, in the eyes of the institution, their most outstanding members.

Although the pattern of cadet scores was somewhat different from the scores of the corporate samples just described, the pattern indicated again that the CLI is working well in its assessment function. The outstanding cadets of the second sample were rated highly by their observers, though they modestly rated themselves slightly lower; the typical cadets of the first sample were rated mostly mid-range by themselves but somewhat lower

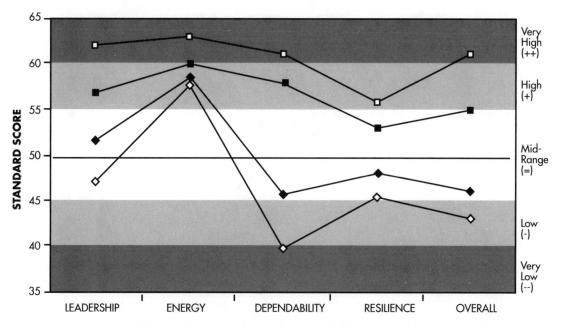

Figure 5 CWO Campbell Leadership Index Officer Candidates: Excellent (■ = Self, N = 46; □ = Observers, N = 213) vs. Average (◆ = Self, N = 111; ◇ = Observers, N = 473).

by their observers. Again, the Observer ratings appear to be a more accurate reflection of reality than the Self ratings. Note that the Energy Orientation scores were elevated on all profiles, obviously reflecting the intense physical fitness emphasis of the academy.

Individual profiles. Although the scale averages are the important statistics for understanding any differences between designated samples, these averages do conceal the widely varying differences between individuals within the samples. To illustrate this point more vividly, three individual profiles are presented in Figures 6, 7, and 8. These three profiles were selected to represent three common patterns of profiles scores. The first, reported in Figure 6, is a profile showing substantial congruence between the Self and Observer scores; the Overall Index scores were 69 and 71, respectively. The second, reported in Figure 7, is a profile showing an amazing gap in Self versus Observer perceptions with the Observer scores much higher; the Overall

Index scores were 36 and 73, respectively, almost a four standard deviation gap. The third profile, reported in Figure 8, is a profile showing the Self versus Observer gap in the opposite direction, with the Self scores being much higher; the Overall Index scores were 66 and 48, respectively.

More extensive research on other samples has indicated that over a wide range of people, these three profiles patterns are each representative of about one-third of people surveyed. That is, about one-third of those surveyed show congruence with their observers, about one-third rate themselves more modestly than do their observers, and about one-third rate themselves more favorably than do their observers.

The practical implication of these widely differing individual profiles is obvious: Any advice given or decisions made on the basis of these profiles needs to be at the individual, not group, level which is, of course, the recommended way that the Leadership Index should be used. Differences between people are too

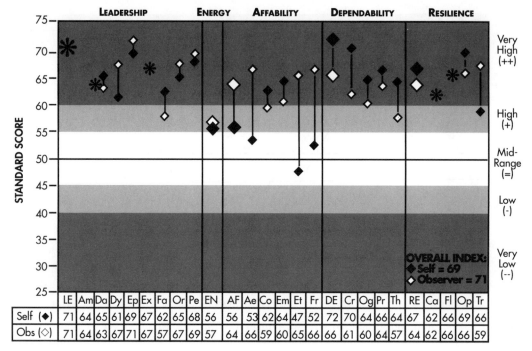

Figure 6 CWO Campbell Leadership Index individual profile (♦ = Self; ◇ = Observer Average; * = Self and Observer Values are Equal): Number of Observers: 5.

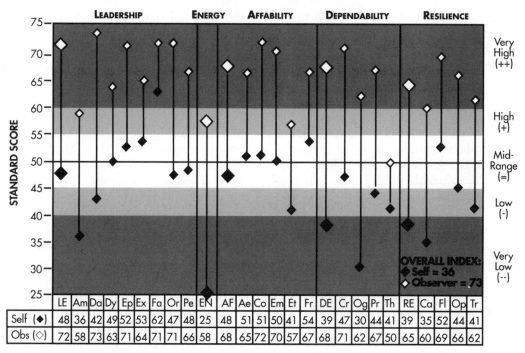

Figure 7 CWO Campbell Leadership Index individual profile (♦ = Self; ◇ = Observer Average; * = Self and Observer Values are Equal): Number of Observers: 4.

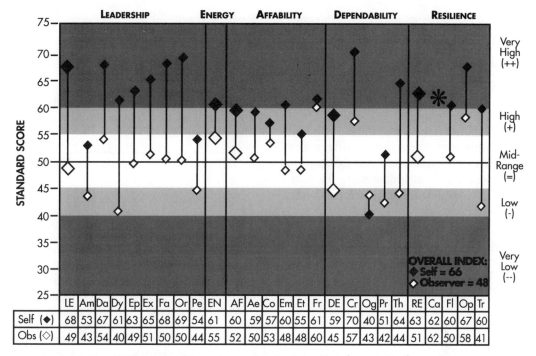

Figure 8 CWO Campbell Leadership Index individual profile (♦ = Self; ◇ = Observer Average; * = Self and Observer Values are Equal): Number of Observers: 5.

	LE	Am	Da	Dy	Ep	Ex	Fa	Or	Pe	EN	AF	Ae	Co	Em	Et	Fr	DE	Cr	Og	Pr	Th	RE	Ca	Fl	Op	Tr
Self (♦)	68	53	67	61	63	65	68	69	54	61	60	59	57	60	55	61	59	70	40	51	64	63	62	60	67	60
Obs (◇)	49	43	54	40	49	51	50	50	44	55	52	50	53	48	48	60	45	57	43	42	44	51	62	50	58	41

great to justify group suggestions. (To support this individualistic use, a comprehensive workbook is handed out to each individual who completes the Leadership Index.)

This does not mean that the group profiles cannot serve useful, educational functions. Because I was both the moderator for the entire conference that resulted in this book and the presenter who returned these individual results to the participating researchers (which was done in a group setting but in a way to protect individual privacy), I was able to make some interpretive and advisory comments to the entire group. Projecting the profile comparisons between the Educators and Researchers on the screen, which showed that the Educators were seen as substantially more affable than the Researchers and, even more notable, that the Researchers saw themselves as even less affable than did their observers, I suggested that, to improve their leadership effectiveness, they "lighten up" and recognize that friendliness is possible, desirable, and trainable. This "Improvement of Affability" topic became a minor theme of the conference, so much so that at the final dinner, the level of boisterous camaraderie was so high that I closed the conference by telling them they had improved to the point that "you are now indistinguishable from life insurance agents."

The conference final evaluation ratings for Value and Enjoyment were 4.5 and 4.7, respectively, on a 5-point scale, and the encouraged affability probably contributed to those high ratings.

Summary

This has been a report of scores on the Campbell Leadership Index for two samples of professionals involved in the field of leadership. One sample included 42 attendees of the Center for Creative Leadership's 1991 Conference on the

Impact of Leadership, which was the conference that produced the papers in this book; the sample mainly included academic writers and researchers. The other sample included 38 attendees at the Leadership Education Conference sponsored by the Jepson School of Leadership Studies at the University of Richmond in 1990; this sample mainly included college and university educators and administrators who had primary responsibility for conducting student leadership programs on their campuses.

The Campbell Leadership Index is a list of descriptive adjectives focused on leadership characteristics. It is designed to be filled in by the Self and three to five Observers selected by the Self. Scoring scales have been normed and standardized, permitting comparisons between Self and Observers, between individuals on both Self and Observer ratings, and between groups of individuals.

Comparisons between Leadership Researchers and Leadership Educators showed that both groups were above average on most of these measures of leadership traits. The most notable differences between the groups were, first, a greater congruence, on average, between the Self and Observers scores within the Educators sample as contrasted with the Researchers sample, indicating that the former had a more accurate perception of how they were viewed by others, and second, a somewhat lower score of the Researchers than of the Educators in the Affability area, as seen by both themselves and their observers.

Overall, the results were quite positive for both groups.

References

Campbell, D. P. (1991a). *Manual for the Campbell Leadership Index*. Minneapolis, MN: National Computer Systems.

Campbell, D. P. (1991b). The challenge of assessing leadership characteristics. *Issues & Observations, 11*(2), 1–8.

David P. Campbell, PhD, is Smith Richardson Senior Fellow at the Center for Creative Leadership in Greensboro, NC. He teaches and researches in creativity and leadership programs in the United States and abroad and is the author of Campbell Work Orientations (CWO), a new series of psychological surveys designed to analyze leadership effectiveness, career interests and skills, and working satisfaction. He has published widely in the professional journals and has authored *Inklings; If You Don't Know Where You're Going, You'll Probably End Up Somewhere Else; Take the Road to Creativity and Get Off Your Dead End;* and *If I'm In Charge Here, Why Is Everybody Laughing?* He coauthored the widely used Strong Interest Inventory. He was a Distinguished Visiting Professor in the Department of Behavioral Sciences and Leadership at the U.S. Air Force Academy in Colorado Springs and has recently completed a widely acclaimed study of brigadier generals. His honors include the E. K. Strong, Jr. Gold Medal for excellence in psychological testing research. He received his PhD in Psychology from the University of Minnesota.

Direct all inquiries about this article to David Campbell, Center for Creative Leadership, 850 Leader Way, P. O. Box 1559, Colorado Springs, CO 80901, 719/633–6348.

CHAPTER 4

Translating Research Results into Action

A Case Study from the Nonprofit Sector

E. B. Knauft

Experiences gained from INDEPENDENT SECTOR's Profiles of Excellence project are analyzed. The project studied the process of translating research findings on organizational performance of nonprofits into applications useful to nonprofit managers and volunteer board members. Research data from eight studies are classified from "soft" to "hard," and problems of generalizing from narrative and quantitative data are examined. Challenges encountered in translating research on leadership into action steps are described with examples. The concluding section suggests how researchers can more effectively respond to needs of practitioners.

INDEPENDENT SECTOR's Profiles of Excellence project was undertaken to identify and describe factors which characterize effective nonprofit organizations, to provide information useful to nonprofit managers and board members, and to analyze the translation of research findings into useful practice. The final product of the project was the book *Profiles of Excellence: Achieving Success in the Nonprofit Sector* (Knauft, Berger, & Gray, 1991).

The Research Data

The data on nonprofit effectiveness were derived from four projects carried out by INDEPENDENT SECTOR and from four studies recently completed by other organizations or researchers. Table 1, which describes the eight sources and lists them in approximate rank order, represents the relative precision of data from "soft" to "hard": anecdotal, subjective, and narrative information at one end of the continuum to a carefully designed and controlled experimental study at the other. The ranking represents a subjective judgment and does not imply that any study is necessarily "better" than another.

Table 1 illustrates the variety of data used to reach generalizations about organizational excellence and develop action steps for achieving improvement.

Since the focus of the entire effort was to identify characteristics of organizational excellence, the majority of the studies involved either comparisons of more effective with less effective organizations or in-depth study of groups identified as relatively most effective compared to their peers.

For example, the 10 case studies (Item 2 in Table 1) represent organizations carefully selected from a much larger sample of nonprofits. Community foundations and local associations of foundation and corporate donors in 15 cities across the country were each asked to nominate several voluntary organizations in their community that had achieved outstanding records of success over a period of time. From a list of 65 nominees, 10 organizations of various types, size, geographical location, and ethnic or racial make-up were selected for the in-depth case studies.

The Criterion Problem: Can Organizational Excellence Be Measured?

A literature survey of organizational performance indicated a lack of consensus among researchers as to what constitutes excellence or effectiveness. Comments by two scholars who surveyed the field serve to illustrate the problem. The first studied 25 separate variables as possible criteria of organizational effectiveness and concluded that it is "an extremely untidy construct" (Campbell, Bownas, Peterson, & Dunnette, 1974, p. 27). The second concluded that the literature on this topic is "the most ambiguous in the field of management" (Dalton, Todor, Spendolini, Fielding, & Porter, 1980, p. 51).

The measurement dilemma is especially acute in the nonprofit voluntary field where there is tremendous organizational diversity in size, type, and purpose. The nearly 3 million nonprofits in the United States range from tiny local groups staffed largely or wholly by volunteers, to large multipurpose national organizations with budgets in the tens of millions of dollars. The nonprofit sector includes neighborhood health clinics, shelters for the homeless, scout troops, groups advocating for a better environment, zoos, art museums, symphony orchestras, and national organizations such as the United Way and the American Red Cross. Should effectiveness be measured by the current state of an organization, by its ability to survive over time, or by its responsiveness to different issues and challenges at various stages in its growth curve? Even if one concentrates on the organization's current status, there is a choice of such measures as financial condition, number of clients served, client satisfaction, ability to raise funds, size and growth of membership, extent to which program objectives are achieved, quality of staff and board, and the nature and extent of volunteer involvement. And what about the spirit and "heart" of the organization and how it is perceived in the community?

All the studies involved in this project relied on composite or macro judgments of organizational effectiveness by individuals familiar with the performance of a number of nonprofits of the same type or in the same geographic area. In several of the studies, a list of criteria of organizational performance was also provided to the appraisers; in some instances, the organization was considered excellent only when two or three appraisers were in agreement as to the rating. The global criterion, which lacks the apparent precision of a composite of quantitative measures, has the advantages of face validity and of being understood and generally accepted by practitioners seeking to take advantage of the research findings.

TABLE 1 Summary of Data Sources

Title	Description	Procedure and Output
1. INDEPENDENT SECTOR Focus Group	One-day Focus Group of 20 heads of nonprofits and consultants, to discuss factors constituting organizational effectiveness	Report of conclusions of Focus Group, speaking from their experience
2. Narrative Case Studies of Organizations (Knauft, Berger, & Gray, 1991)	In-depth profiles of 10 nonprofits of varying size and type identified by community foundations as excellent examples	Analytical/reportorial/anecdotal description of 10 organizations by one researcher
3. Literature Survey: The Effectiveness of Nonprofit Organizations	Literature search & theoretical paper on organizational effectiveness	Over 200 references examined and synthesized; emphasis on definition and measurement of organizational effectiveness
4. Beatrice Foundation Awards of Excellence (Beatrice Foundation, 1989)	Analyses of nonprofits that received Beatrice Awards of Excellence	Analysis of narrative and financial data of 22 Beatrice finalist organizations selected from among 193 Chicago nonprofits
5. Self-Perceptions of Effectiveness: A Survey of Nonprofit Voluntary Organizations (INDEPENDENT SECTOR, 1990)	Questionnaire survey of 1) national sample of CEOs & board chairpersons, and 2) CEOs of "leadership" sample representing local affiliates designated by their national executives as "excellent"	Wide range of results from 900 respondents, including characteristics of organizations and items differentiating 1) CEOs & Chairs of organizations self-rated as well above average, and 2) leadership sample from National Assembly Study (see item (6) below)
6. A Study in Excellence: Management in the Nonprofit Human Services (National Assembly, 1989)	Interview & questionnaire study to determine 1) how an "excellent" manager carries out the job, and 2) personal qualities that distinguish the excellent manager from others	270 "excellent" managers of local or state affiliates of national human service organizations were compared to other managers
7. The Personal Equation: A Critical Look at Executive Competency in Associations (Foundation of American Society of Assn. Execs., 1989)	Questionnaire study to identify behaviors & skills that distinguish between more successful and less successful association executives; development of instrument for personal assessment and self-assessment	120 "very successful" executives from trade and professional associations were identified; completed questionnaire to identify key competencies
8. "Effective Managers of Nonprofit Organizations" (Herman & Heimovics, 1987)	A "critical incident" procedure to identify behaviors which differentiated "effective" CEOs from others	Interview study of 50 CEOs of nonprofits in one city (24 nominated as "effective" vs. comparison group of 26)

Generalizing from the Research Data

The Problem of Selective Reporting

A primary challenge in analyzing and interpreting data from a collection of studies is that of "selective reporting"— how does one select from diverse sources those findings that deserve emphasis and provide a basis for generalizations? What relative weight should be given anecdotal, ethnographic, and statistical information collected under varying conditions? Where data are amenable to statistical tests of significance; should only results at the .01 or .05 level be considered when interpreting the findings of practitioners? The bias of this project was to strive for a final product as simple and straightforward as possible, with emphasis on the applicability of the findings. *Profiles of Excellence* is intended primarily for an audience of nonprofit practitioners; the goal of practicality was balanced with that of scientific precision.

The first step was to review all information in the eight studies and data sources to identify common themes that best described the excellent organization, that distinguished top organizations from all others. This process resulted in the identification of what we termed the four Hallmarks of Excellence of nonprofit organizations (see Table 2).

The raw data, with the exception of one study of trade association executives, were derived from 501(c)(3) charitable organizations and were largely exclusive of religious groups, hospitals, colleges, and universities. Table 3 presents demographic information from one of the studies to illustrate major characteristics of organizations included.

The Special Challenges of the Subject of Leadership

One of the four Hallmarks of Excellence was "The presence of an individual who truly leads the organization and creates a culture that enables and motivates the organization to fulfill its mission."

Examples of evidence supporting this hallmark included:

1. Strong agreement by the participants in the focus group of experienced nonprofit executives and consultants that the presence of an individual described as a "leader" was an essential characteristic of outstanding organizations.

2. The focus group concluded that the best leaders:

   • Have clear goals and a vision to look beyond the day's crisis, the quarterly report, the immediate horizon;

   • Exhibit a willingness to stand up and be shot at;

   • Have the courage to make extremely tough decisions;

   • Understand their constituents' motivations and identify intimately with their needs and concerns;

   • Exhibit a special presence that enables them to motivate and inspire their constituents, staff, and volunteers beyond the authority conferred by a title.

3. Sixty nonprofit executives of organizations that had been identified as outstanding in the National Assembly study (1989) (Item 6 in Table 1) identified these characteristics of leadership:

   • Unqualified commitment to the mission of the organization;

TABLE 2   The Four Hallmarks of Excellence

1. A clearly articulated sense of mission that serves as the focal point of commitment for board and staff and is the guidepost by which the organization judges its success and makes adjustments in course over time.

2. The presence of an individual who truly leads the organization and creates a culture that enables and motivates the organization to fulfill its mission.

3. The presence of an involved and committed volunteer board that relates dynamically with the chief staff officer and provides a bridge to the larger community.

4. An ongoing capacity to attract sufficient financial and human resources.

Note. From Knauft, Berger, & Gray, 1991.

- An entrepreneurial attitude coupled with an action or risk-taking orientation;

- A vision for the organization.

4. The chief executives of the 10 organizations selected for case studies had these characteristics in common:

- Strong commitment to the organization's mission;

- A high energy level and ability to work long hours;

- Ability to inspire and motivate their staffs;

- Tended to measure success in terms of the achievements of the organization rather than through personal recognition and publicity;

- Worked very hard at being good listeners and at networking, but varied in the extent to which they were highly articulate in verbal and written communications.

In spite of such information about leadership characteristics, the data provided few clues about how a manager might analyze and improve his/her leadership skills. In developing the "how-to-do-it" section of the book, three recent works were relied on to identify types of behavior that might be amenable to self-improvement. The books by Bennis (1989), Gardner (1990), and O'Connell (1984, 1985), which are based primarily on the authors' wide experience in the field and their first-hand knowledge of various kinds of leaders, place relatively little emphasis on research results from controlled studies. Gardner reviewed much of the current psychological research and talked with scholars; Bennis conducted in-depth interviews with persons he identified as national leaders. But both authors apparently concluded that their analysis of narrative information from many sources was most relevant for their intended audience.

In the chapter, "Developing Leadership Skills," six characteristics of leadership that emerged from all three of the above sources are identified, followed by a series of Questions for Self-Analysis for each characteristic of leadership. The following excerpt from *Profiles of Excellence* (Knauft et al., 1991) illustrates this approach by identifying six characteristics, followed by an example of the self-analysis questions developed for the first characteristic, "A Guiding Vision."

We draw our portrait of the effective leader from the conclusions of the focus group of experienced consultants and nonprofit executives convened for this project, and from the writings of John Gardner, Warren Bennis, and Brian O'Connell. From these, six fundamental characteristics of quality leadership emerge.

1. Presence of a guiding vision characterized by long-term thinking.

2. Ability to convey the vision to others, to motivate and excite them.

3. Strong self-understanding, integrity, candor, and maturity.

4. Strength of convictions and toughness to stand by them.

5. Willingness to take risks, to be daring, and to learn from mistakes.

6. Ability to master the organization and its context, rather than surrendering to it.

A Guiding Vision

The effective leader takes a long-term view of his or her organization, looking beyond the latest crisis or the quarterly report. The leader has a clear idea where the organization should go and what it should be several years in the future. Vision is what distinguishes the top-notch leader from the ordinary manager. Or, as Bennis puts it: "The manager has his eye always on the bottom line; the leader has his eye on the horizon."

Questions for Self-Analysis

- What is your long-range vision for your organization? Are you fully satisfied with it?

- How does this vision differ from what was present before you assumed your current position?

- What process did you follow in developing this vision?

- If you became the staff head of another nonprofit organization, how would you go about developing a vision for it?

- To what extent would you modify your vision as a result of pressures from board and staff? How do you

TABLE 3 Key Characteristics of 856 Nonprofit Organizations Responding to Survey of Chief Executive Officers and Board Chairs

I. **Distribution of Organizations by Revenues**

Annual Revenues	% of Organizations
Under $100,000	38.5
100,000–249,999	20.1
250,000–499,999	12.5
500,000–999,999	10.3
1,000,000–2,499,000	9.0
2,500,000 and above	9.6

II. **Distribution by Geographical Focus of Activities**

Focus	% of Organizations
Local	74
National	18
Statewide	8

III. **Distribution by Location of Organizational Headquarters**

Region in USA	% of Organizations
East	30
South	26
Midwest	24
West	20

IV. **Distribution by Purpose of Organizations**

Organizational Purpose or Type	% of Organizations
Human Services	31
Health	17
Education	15
Arts, Culture, Humanities	12
Advocacy or Public Benefit	11
Other	7
Religion	3
Environment	2
International	2

Note. From INDEPENDENT SECTOR, 1990.

draw the line between compromising with the views of others and maintaining your own beliefs about the organization's needs?

- What has your presence and your vision added to this organization?
- Have you challenged the status quo? (pp. 128–130)

Suggestions for the Researcher

How can the researcher effectively respond to the needs of the practitioner in the design, conduct, and reporting of a study? Research activities typically reflect the interests of the scholar, involve collection of data from sources that are readily available, and apply technology familiar to the researcher. The nonprofit field generally has not reached the point where professionals are employed or retained to conduct research specifically for the sponsoring organization—such as the research chemist in a pharmaceutical firm or the opinion researcher employed by an advertising agency. The scholarly researcher, in contrast, is free to choose the extent to which the study is practitioner oriented. Unfortunately, much current research on nonprofit organizations seems to have limited applications for practitioners. Exceptions are found in the well-designed research of Herman and Heimovics (1987) on the relationship between the chief staff officer and the volunteer board and studies of corporate philanthropy by Galaskiewicz (1985).

Scholars interested in conducting research of greatest value to practitioners should consider these possibilities:

1. Get input from key persons in nonprofit organizations about problems and challenges they face which may be amenable to research and are likely to produce findings with wider application.

2. Obtain practitioner participation when the study is designed and when data are analyzed and interpreted.

3. Ask practitioners to review a draft of the report to determine what it means to them. Consider the appropriateness of two versions of the report: one for a scholarly publication and one for practitioners.

Issues in the Collection and Use of Data

The three methodological issues involved in the processes described in this paper are (a) the extent to which one can or should rely upon data collected under varying degrees of scientific precision (ranging from a focus group generating narrative data to a well-designed experimental study), (b) how one analyzes and interprets such research data to arrive at generalizations about organizational effectiveness, and (c) how one translates the generalizations into self-improvement suggestions for an individual or organization.

With regard to the first issue, the project proceeded on the premise that organizational effectiveness is a concept best studied by methods that capture and reflect its complex and dynamic character. That is, the methods should fit the problem to be studied, rather than the other way around. Abraham Maslow (1970, 1987) has commented on "means centered" versus "problem centered" approaches to psychological research. Means centering is the tendency for research to be driven by available instruments, techniques, and methodology without adequate consideration for the complexity of the subject matter and the broader goals of the research. Maslow's (1987) arguments are essentially these:

1. Undue emphasis on elegance of experimental design and precision of data collection tends to minimize the

significance of the problem being studied and stifles creativity.

2. Means centering tends to overvalue quantification as an end in itself.

3. Means centering creates a hierarchy of sciences in which physics is considered to be more "scientific" than biology, biology than psychology, and psychology than sociology.

This line of reasoning supports the judgment that, for example, the essence of leadership behavior and the dynamics of a leader's impact on an organization are not captured completely by quantitative data collected under controlled conditions. Narrative data from experienced, perceptive observers in a broad sampling of real life situations may often be more relevant.

In the current context, there is a lack of controlled longitudinal studies of nonprofit organizations. As an alternative, the project conducted 10 case studies which, although documented at a point in time, did include historical data covering a number of years on each organization.

With respect to the second issue, that of making generalizations from available data, the project relied on studies that attempted to identify a cause and effect relationship between excellence and antecedent or existing organizational factors. Also relied on was replication: The four Hallmarks of Excellence and their accompanying characteristics were each supported by data from three or more studies from different organizations using various methods of data collection.

The third issue is the most challenging of all. It involves translating key findings into prescriptive actions to enable organizations and individuals to become more effective. As discussed in the examples concerning leadership, the research produced examples of effective leader behavior but did not indicate how that behavior was induced. It was necessary to (a) rely largely on anecdotal descriptions from researchers who observed and interviewed many "leaders," and then (b) use that information to generate questions for self-analysis to assist the reader in examining his/her behavior. This is clearly the weakest link in the process of moving from research data through generalizations to practical applications. And, unfortunately, the process is weakest of all in the leadership area; the application steps are much clearer for the other three Hallmarks of Excellence. There is ample evidence from many sources to support action steps for effectively developing, communicating, and carrying out the organization's mission, for assisting the volunteer board in defining and carrying out its responsibilities, and for prescribing how financial and volunteer resources can best be mobilized.

What Was Learned from the Profiles of Excellence Project?

The experience of identifying and interpreting research findings for nonprofit staffs and board members suggests several generalizations for those facing a similar challenge:

1. A "practitioner orientation" to the project was achieved through involvement of an advisory committee of persons with wide experience in nonprofit management and governance. This involvement included participation in the design of studies, interpretation of the significance of the findings, and reaction to drafts of the final report.

2. The use of narrative and anecdotal data was not a drawback to arriving at generalizations because there was an abundance of data collected by many observers working independently in different settings. The recurrence of certain findings provided a basis for generalizations.

3. Lack of quantitative criteria of organizational excellence was not the drawback that had been anticipated. Greater precision could have been achieved if more of the studies had attempted to increase the reliability of the ratings of excellence by relying on agreement among several raters or employing alternation ranking or similar techniques. However, of greater importance to practitioners was the face validity of the criterion data representing judgments by persons familiar with the performance of a number of similar organizations.

4. In-depth case studies of 10 organizations identified as outstanding by their local community foundations indicated that every organization, when examined in detail, (a) was not necessarily excellent in every respect, and (b) was not likely to be considered excellent at every stage of its history. With regard to the first point, each of the organizations provided clear examples of at least several hallmarks of excellence. The lack of a high level of excellence in one or two areas did not detract from the general success of the organization and emphasized the point that nonprofits which face no significant challenges are rare indeed, if they exist at all!

On the second point, each of the 10 organizations had survived for a number of years, had overcome problems they had encountered, and were currently outstanding in comparison with their peers. It is not surprising that organizations are not forever excellent. The same variation over time applies to the for-profit world which has the advantage of widely-accepted quantitative performance criteria. For example, over the past 20 years, more than half of the 30 companies comprising the Dow Jones Industrial Average have been dropped and new companies added.

Conclusion

Our experience indicates it is possible to design, conduct, and interpret research studies that produce findings useful to the practitioner. Reliance on a wide data base from a number of sources resulted in generalizations about excellence that could be translated into action steps for nonprofit managers and key volunteers.

Acknowledgments

The research from which this paper has been derived was supported by grants from Primerica Foundation, Beatrice Foundation, Exxon Corporation, William and Flora Hewlett Foundation, and AT&T Foundation.

References

Beatrice Foundation. (1989). *Awards for excellence—1989 observations*. Chicago: Author.

Bennis, W. (1989). *On becoming a leader*. Reading, MA: Addison-Wesley.

Campbell, J., Bownas, D., Peterson, N., & Dunnette, M. (1974). *The measurement of organizational effectiveness*. San Diego: Navy Personnel Research and Development Center. NTIS No. Ad-786–462.

Dalton, D. R., Todor, W. D., Spendolini, M. J., Fielding, G. J., & Porter, L. W. (1980). Organizational structure and performance: A critical review. *Academy of Management Review, 5,* 49–64.

Foundation of the American Society of Association Executives. (1989). *The personal equation: A critical look at executive competency in associations*. Washington, DC: ASAE Publications.

Galaskiewicz, J. (1985). *Social organization of an urban grants economy: A study of business philanthropy and nonprofit organizations*. Orlando, FL: Academic Press.

Gardner, J. W. (1990). *On leadership*. New York: Free Press.

Herman, R. D., & Heimovics, R. D. (1987). Effective managers of nonprofit organizations. *1987 Spring Research Forum Working Papers*. Washington, DC: INDEPENDENT SECTOR.

INDEPENDENT SECTOR. (1990). *Self-perceptions of effectiveness: A survey of nonprofit voluntary organizations*. Washington, DC: Author.

Knauft, E. B., Berger, R. A., & Gray, S. T. (1991). *Profiles of excellence: Achieving success in the nonprofit sector*. San Francisco: Jossey-Bass.

Maslow, A. H. (1970). *Motivation and personality* (2nd ed.). New York: Harper & Row.

Maslow, A. H. (1987). *Motivation and personality* (3rd ed.). Revised by Frager, R., Fadiman, J., McReynolds, C., & Cox, R. New York: Harper & Row.

National Assembly of National Voluntary Health and Social Welfare Organizations. (1989). *A study in excellence: Management in the nonprofit human services*. Washington, DC: Author.

O'Connell, B. (1984). *The search for excellence: Lessons for philanthropy*. Speech to Annual Meeting of the New York Regional Association of Grantmakers.

O'Connell, B. (1985). *The board member's book: Making a difference in voluntary organizations*. New York: The Foundation Center.

E. B. (Burt) Knauft is Executive Vice President and Chief Operating Officer of INDEPENDENT SECTOR, a national coalition of voluntary organizations, foundations, and corporations. He has conducted research and published in the fields of nonprofit management and leadership and corporate philanthropy. He earned his PhD from the University of Iowa.

Direct inquiries about this article to E. B. Knauft, Executive Vice President, INDEPENDENT SECTOR, 1828 L Street, N.W., Ste. 1200, Washington, DC 20036, 202/223–8100.

CHAPTER 5

Managers on Leaders
Developing a Profile of Effective Leadership in Top Management

Mansour Javidan

This paper reports the findings of a survey of over 500 managers in middle, upper-middle, and senior management ranks who assessed their own immediate superiors. A comparison of those senior executives who were perceived to be highly effective and those who were rated as highly ineffective shows major differences in behaviour and personal attributes. Effective executives are reported to be dedicated and tenacious visionaries who succeed in mobilizing their subordinates. They act as concerned coaches who are always in touch with their employees, support and encourage self-reliance, recognize accomplishment, and are effective representives of their units to the outside world.

American executives have been criticized for a multitude of reasons, most of which relate to their inability to evidence leadership and to make their organizations more competitive. There is no shortage of advice. An army of authors have written on what top managers are supposed to do and how they should do it (e.g., Bennis & Nanus, 1985; Conger, 1989; Kotter, 1988). While there is merit in what most authors have to say, much that is prescribed is based on limited and impressionistic data collected through either case studies or general observations. We need a more rigorous scrutiny of these ideas. We need to verify the intuitive recipes prescribed and offer empirically supported suggestions useful to senior managers.

To accomplish this, we report here the results of a large-scale study of effectiveness in top management. Presented are the findings of a survey of over 500 managers in middle and higher ranks who evaluated their own superiors in top management. Profiles are compared of those senior executives who were perceived as highly effective with those who were perceived as highly ineffective; managerial implications are discussed.

Mintzberg's (1975) study of the nature of senior executives' work was a pioneering attempt to understand the role of top managers. He studied a small group of senior executives and concluded that they perform 10 roles which he categorized into 3 groups of interpersonal, informational, and decision making.

While Mintzberg's work has had substantial impact on the literature, attempts to replicate and confirm his findings have been inconclusive. Lau, Newman, and Broedling (1980) attempted to confirm his findings but failed to do so. McCall and Segrist (1980) suggested that the roles had too much overlap to be considered separate. Similar concerns were raised by Snyder and Wheelen (1981) who showed that Mintzberg's roles are too broadly defined and are not confirmed by statistical evidence.

Another perspective on managers' work is generally labelled as leadership research. It attempts to identify the determinants of success in top management by identifying the behavioral and personal characteristics of well-known and highly regarded executives. The empirical base of this stream of work is in either personal observations (Blanchard & Johnson, 1982; Katz, 1975; Leavitt, 1986; Wrapp, 1975) or a limited number of case studies (Conger, 1989; Kotter, 1982; Levinson & Rosenthal, 1984; Tichy & Devanna, 1986). These authors agree that successful executives are visionaries. They have strong views on what their organization should be and the values which should guide their organization's actions (Bennis & Nanus, 1985). These values are anchored in their own strong personal beliefs (Bass, 1985). By constantly preaching and living these values, they provide a sense of purpose to their subordinates (Javidan, 1991).

Successful executives manage to turn their vision into reality by drawing their subordinates to· their dreams (Kotter, 1988). They are effective communicators and storytellers (Blanchard & Johnson, 1982). They create a positive atmosphere where individuals feel self-confident and empowered to do their best to contribute to their dreams (Conger, 1989). Successful

executives are also shown to have special personal characteristics such as self-confidence (Levinson & Rosenthal, 1984), willingness to act against status quo (Tichy & Devanna, 1986), competence (Carroll & Gillen, 1987), and realism (Conger, 1989).

The main deficiency of this literature is the issue of validity and generalizability. The recipes by various authors are only a series of propositions which have to be tested and validated. While they may be intuitively appealing, they lack rigorous empirical scrutiny.

Several authors have attempted to address this problem. Luthans (1988) conducted an observational study of 248 managers and showed that success (defined by the pace of promotion) is different from effectiveness (defined as a composite of quantity and quality of performance of the manager's unit along with subordinate satisfaction). He further showed that successful managers tend to engage in a set of activities different from those attributed to effective managers. Effective managers spent more time on conflict management, staffing, training, and employee motivation; successful managers spent more time on socializing, politicking, and interacting with outsiders.

Quinn (1988) conducted another study with 295 part-time MBA and MPM students who described the best manager they knew in terms of eight roles: mentor, innovator, broker, producer, director, coordinator, monitor, and facilitator. Quinn's cluster analysis of responses showed that there is no one universal profile for effective managers. He did show, however, that "master managers" performed better than average on all the roles.

Another series of large-scale studies conducted by Bass and his colleagues (Bass, 1985; Hater & Bass, 1988; Seltzer & Bass, 1990) investigated the concept of transformational and transactional leadership. In a variety of settings, they showed transformational leaders as charismatic individuals who instill pride and transmit a sense of mission and purpose, stimulate their subordinates intellectually, and act as mentors. Transactional leaders, on the other hand, tend to emphasize contingent rewards and management by exception.

Although the findings of Luthans (1988), Quinn (1988), and Bass (1985) have provided useful, empirically rigorous insights into managerial activities, they also have a few shortcomings. Quinn's work is based on the best managers described by people who knew them best. It is not clear in what capacity and under what circumstances they knew the manager, nor is the nature of their interaction obvious. Luthans' observational study examined the observed behaviour of managers in the study and, therefore, does not shed light on the reasons for behaviour (Carroll and Gillen, 1987). For example, the study showed that effective managers spent more time planning than did successful managers but does not explain the reasons for this. One possible explanation is that successful managers are better at planning than effective managers and thus do not need to spend as much time on planning-related activities.

Bass and his colleagues focused on a narrow aspect of managers' jobs. They examined only the specific ways in which managers motivate and inspire their subordinates. While their research has been quite useful in shedding light on this important issue, it does not provide a broad view of what the job entails for senior managers.

This study will provide insights into what senior executives should do. These ideas are based on the findings of a large-scale study where the profiles of highly effective and highly ineffective senior managers are contrasted. The implications of these findings are discussed.

Managerial Effectiveness Defined

The dependent variable in this study — senior management effectiveness — is defined in terms of effectiveness as perceived by the executives' subordinates. This approach is based on the premises of the role theory (Katz & Kahn, 1978) which stipulates that each person occupying a position in an organization has to contend with the demands and expectations of a variety of individuals and groups interacting with that position. These expectations may relate to desired behaviour or they may deal with acceptable values, attitudes, and personal styles. The role theory further postulates that the focal individual's success in his position depends on his ability to satisfy these demands (Tsui, 1984). A key group in any senior executive's role set is the subordinates who are themselves in middle and upper-middle management. In a survey of 6,000 managers, Posner and Schmidt (1984) showed that executive managers rated their subordinates as their second most important stakeholder group after their customers.

Given their importance in the senior managers' role set, it is critical to understand the subordinates' views on the determinants of effective performance in top management. Subordinates have direct contact with senior executives on a regular basis and are usually responsible for implementing their ideas. Therefore, they are able to provide insights into top management performance. Furthermore, the respondents themselves are in middle, upper-middle, and even senior management positions with years of experience in dealing with managerial issues.

In line with the previous work on managerial effectiveness (i.e., Luthans, 1988; Quinn, 1988; Tsui, 1984), the construct of perceived effectiveness was operationalized in terms of seven Likert-type scales which are presented in Table 1. Each measure has a 7-point scale where 7 means "strong agreement with the statement" while 1 indicates "strong disagreement." Items refer mostly to the superior's impact on his subordinates and identify the extent to which top managers are perceived as natural leaders, stars, ideal managers,

TABLE 1 Measures of Perceived Top Management Effectiveness

No.	Item	Strongly Disagree						Strongly Agree
1.	I feel fortunate to work for my superior.	1	2	3	4	5	6	7
2.	My superior is a natural leader.	1	2	3	4	5	6	7
3.	My superior is widely recognized as a star.	1	2	3	4	5	6	7
4.	My superior is highly regarded by his subordinates.	1	2	3	4	5	6	7
5.	My superior is known by his subordinates as an ideal manager.	1	2	3	4	5	6	7
6.	My superior is known by his superiors as an ideal manager.	1	2	3	4	5	6	7
7.	My superior is my role model.	1	2	3	4	5	6	7

and role models. While these measures are all subjective, they have been shown to be positively correlated with advancement rates and performance appraisal ratings (Tsui, 1984).

In a recent review of the literature on top management effectiveness, Javidan (1991) identified six managerial roles. These are *visionary*, *symbolizer*, *mobilizer*, *auditor*, *ambassador*, and *innovator*.

As *visionaries*, top managers bring a sense of order to their subordinates by developing and communicating a picture of where the organization is headed. While it does involve some degree of wishful thinking, that picture is not just a dream. The vision has two critical features: First, it is based on a set of strong personal values and beliefs; without such an anchor, the executive's commitment and credibility is in doubt. Second, it is based on a realistic assessment of the organization's capabilities, strengths, and shortcomings. As *symbolizers*, top managers need to practice their espoused values and make personal sacrifices to accomplish them.

As *mobilizers*, executives develop and maintain a pool of skilled managers and subordinates who feel a sense of ownership, self-confidence, and purpose. They ensure that their subordinates have the required resources and are recognized for good performance.

As *auditors*, managers are in touch with their subordinates and aware of their performance level through formal and informal means. They also provide timely and useful feedback and encourage self-monitoring.

As *ambassadors*, executives view their role in terms of its interface with the rest of the organization and recognize that their effective performance depends on their ability to satisfy the various needs and demands of their constituents. Furthermore, they understand that their success is also dependent on their ability to represent their unit to other members of their network.

Finally, as *innovators*, top managers take risks and challenge the status quo. They also encourage their subordinates to be independent thinkers not necessarily bound by the organization's past history and tradition but willing to undertake new initiatives.

Based on the preceding literature review, a preliminary questionnaire of 140 items was designed. After pretests and modifications, the revised questionnaire was distributed to 1,881 middle and upper-middle managers in two very large organizations, each of whom was asked to assess his/her immediate superior on the six managerial roles.

A total of 1,133 questionnaires were returned for a response rate of 60%. A factor analysis of the results identified five factors; the specific items in each factor are presented in Tables 2 and 3. The first factor confirmed the Mobilizer role and consisted of five subfactors: (a) Subordinate development and recognition, (b) Coaching, (c) Concern for employees, (d) Support for self-reliance, and (e) Openness.

The second factor, which confirmed the Ambassador role, consisted of items that indicate the executive's ability to develop a global view of his responsibilities and his role in representing his unit to the rest of the organization.

The Symbolizer role emerged not as one factor but instead was confirmed as two separate factors, namely Tenacity and Dedication. The former referred to the manager's self-confidence, energy level, and ambition. The latter related to his willingness to pursue his vision in spite of the odds and regardless of any potential risks to his status, power, and promotion possibilities.

The fifth factor confirmed the Auditor role, which related to the executive's emphasis on obtaining results through comprehensive analysis, high-performance expectations, and regular progress reports.

For this study, the factors generated in the factor analysis were used as the independent variables. They were empirically based components of top management work as perceived by subordinates, used to contrast effective and ineffective executives.

Data Collection

The data were collected in 1990 in a telecommunication company, a corporation of over 10 thousand employees. Upon approval of the CEO, the Vice President for Human Resources provided a list of managers and executives who would receive the questionnaire. Each manager who received the questionnaire was asked to assess his/her immediate superior. A cover letter from the CEO accompanied the research instrument. Participants were asked to return the completed questionnaire in an enclosed self-addressed envelope directly to the researcher. A total of 715 questionnaires were distributed via internal mail; 554 completed responses were received (77% response rate). Table 4 presents the characteristics of the respondents.

Results

The principal components factor analysis of the dependent variable items produced one factor with eigenvalue of 5.17. The item loadings ranged from 0.61 to 0.92. Cronbach's Alpha was 0.94. These results confirmed our premise that the scales used were all related to the construct of perceived effectiveness. Reliability coefficients, means, standard deviations, and correlations for dependent and independent variables are presented in Table 5 and Table 6.

An examination of Table 5 shows that perceived effectiveness correlates significantly with all five factors and is strongly correlated with the Mobilizer and Ambassador roles. The table also shows that the five roles in the profile are all significantly correlated, which confirms that they are all different aspects of one construct—the perceived profile of top management.

To understand more fully the variables that distinguish effective from ineffective

TABLE 2 Factor Analysis of the Items in the Senior Executive Profile

Factor	Loading	Description
1. MOBILIZER (Eigenvalue 57.77)		—SEE TABLE 3 FOR DETAILS—
2. AMBASSADOR (Eigenvalue 5.63)	0.72	Understands interdependencies between his unit and the rest of the organization.
	0.72	Understands interdependencies between the organization and the outside world.
	0.70	Knows the organization's products/services.
	0.69	Understands the interdependence between the unit and the outside world.
	0.64	Knows the organization's history.
	0.60	Is technically competent.
	0.60	Is aware of the internal political realities of the organization.
	0.59	Is well aware of what happens in the rest of the organization.
	0.56	Has a firm grasp of how his unit fits in the organization.
	0.56	Frequently meets with people from other parts of the organization in task-related occasions.
	0.50	Knows his/her strengths.
	0.49	Has influence over his subordinates.
3. TENACITY (Eigenvalue 3.46)	0.76	Likes to shake things up.
	0.69	Is ambitious.
	0.62	Wants to make a difference.
	0.58	Has high energy level.
	0.58	Is determined.
	0.46	Is self-confident.
4. AUDITOR (Eigenvalue 2.71)	0.65	Expects the subordinates to follow rules and procedures.
	0.55	Believes any new initiative should be completely analyzed.
	0.52	Expects regular progress reports.
	0.52	When approached with a proposal, says let's do all the necessary analysis.
	0.48	Has high performance expectations.
	0.47	Is persistent in what he wants done.
	0.42	Meets with subordinates in formal task-related occasions.
5. DEDICATION (Eigenvalue 1.87)		Would do anything to accomplish his vision even if it involved:
	0.64	a risk of loss of power
	0.64	a risk of loss of status
	0.63	a risk for his promotion

TABLE 3   Factor Analysis of the Mobilizer Role

Dimension	Loading	Description
1. SUBORDINATE DEVELOPMENT & RECOGNITION (Eigenvalue 31.68)	0.61	Is always on the lookout to identify high performers.
	0.49	Provides high performers with opportunities to grow.
	0.48	Publicly recognizes good performance.
	0.47	Spreads enthusiasm.
	0.44	Is a cheerleader for subordinates.
	0.44	Helps employees feel appreciated.
	0.41	Publicly recognizes successful new initiatives.
2. CONCERN FOR SUBORDINATES (Eigenvalue 1.75)	0.63	Tolerates subordinates' mistakes.
	0.57	Creates a relaxing atmosphere.
	0.56	Is sensitive.
	0.49	Shows concern in dealing with subordinates.
	0.48	Is a good listener.
	0.41	Goes to bat for subordinates.
	0.39	Practices what he preaches.
	0.38	Helps create a positive atmosphere.
	0.33	Is sincere in his praise.
	− 0.75	When subordinate fails, he blames him.
	− 0.75	When subordinate fails, he protects himself.
3. SUPPORT FOR SELF-RELIANCE (Eigenvalue 1.25)	0.79	Sometimes, temporarily relaxes rules.
	0.61	Is willing to take new initiatives even if they may fail.
	0.43	Encourages independent thinking.
	0.42	Encourages self-monitoring.
4. OPENNESS (Eigenvalue 1.22)	0.87	Socializes with subordinates.
	0.43	Helps make work fun.
	0.41	Shares information with subordinates.
5. COACHING (Eigenvalue 1.00)	0.55	If doesn't like subordinate's performance, explains his concern.
	0.50	Communicates his expectations to subordinates.
	0.50	Helps subordinates understand issues.
	0.48	Is accessible.
	0.45	Manages by example.
	0.43	Provides constructive feedback.
	0.41	Keeps track of subordinates' concerns.
	0.39	Prefers face-to-face contact.
	0.39	Makes sure everyone knows where the unit is going.

executives, the "effectiveness" score of managers in the top 20% and in the bottom 20% were selected as highly effective and highly ineffective executives, respectively. We then conducted T-Tests to compare the average scores of the two groups on the five factors described earlier. The results, presented in Table 7, show that the effective group has significantly higher ratings on all five factors.

On the Mobilizer role, the effective executives' ratings were significantly and

TABLE 4 Participants in the Survey

1. **Response**

   - No. of Questionnaires sent — 715
   - No. of Questionnaires returned — 554
   - Rate of return — 77%

2. **Individual Characteristics**

   a. Length of service with organization:

   - less than 1 year — 4%
   - 1–5 years — 10%
   - 5–10 years — 11%
   - 10–15 years — 15%
   - 15–20 years — 12%
   - over 20 years — 47%

   b. Length of service with supervisor:

   - less than 1 year — 45%
   - 1–3 years — 39%
   - 3–5 years — 13%
   - over 5 years — 3%

   c. Age of respondents:

   - under 30 years — 0%
   - 30–34 years — 11%
   - 35–39 years — 17%
   - 40–49 years — 48%
   - 50–59 years — 22%
   - 60 years and over — 2%

   d. Sex

   - male — 88%
   - female — 12%

substantially higher than those of the ineffective group. Furthermore, a comparison of the subroles in this factor showed higher ratings for effective executives on all subroles. Of interest is the top group's average range between 5.29 and 6.00, a very positive range, while the ineffective group's range between 2.66 and 3.58 is a decidedly negative range. Perceptions of the top group included their emphasis on subordinate development and their ability to be open, to encourage independent thinking, and to show sincere concern for their employees. Effective executives are believed to be significantly better ambassadors when representing their units to their external stakeholders, more tenacious, and more dedicated. Finally, they are closer to their subordinates and more aware of their concerns.

TABLE 5 Reliability Coefficients, Means, Standard Deviations, and Correlations

Variable	Items	α	Mean	SD	1	2	3	4	5
1. Effectiveness	7	0.94	4.27	1.34	—	—	—	—	—
2. Mobilizer	34	—	4.62	1.04	0.83	—	—	—	—
3. Ambassador	12	0.93	5.31	0.95	0.70	0.71	—	—	—
4. Tenacity	6	0.84	5.53	1.03	0.58	0.53	0.57	—	—
5. Auditor	8	0.76	5.14	0.87	0.43	0.45	0.59	0.55	—
6. Dedication	3	0.95	3.71	1.59	0.60	0.59	0.45	0.37	0.23

Note. Sample size = 480. All correlation coefficients are significant at .001 level.

TABLE 6 Reliability Coefficients, Means, Standard Deviations, and Correlations for the Mobilizer Role

Variable	Items	α	Mean	SD	1	2	3	4
1. Coaching	9	0.89	4.70	1.19	—	—	—	—
2. Concern for Employees	11	0.95	4.57	0.88	0.80	—	—	—
3. Support for Self-Reliance	4	0.80	5.01	1.12	0.70	0.72	—	—
4. Openness	3	0.78	4.24	1.34	0.69	0.69	0.65	—
5. Subordinate Development & Recognition	7	0.97	4.61	1.29	0.84	0.79	0.73	0.75

Note. Sample size = 487. All correlation coefficients are significant at .001 level.

Tables 5, 6, and 7 reveal that the most important variable in distinguishing the two groups is the Mobilizer role and its subroles. The ineffective group receives very low ratings for its performance of this role.

Discussion and Conclusion

This research was triggered by an important question: What distinguishes effective and ineffective senior execu-

TABLE 7 A Comparison of the Profile of Highly Effective and
Ineffective Executives

Variable	Group Mean		T-Test	Group Size	
	Effective	Ineffective		Effective	Ineffective
1. MOBILIZER	5.65	3.15	26.38	113	89
A. Coaching	5.84	3.19	23.81	118	92
B. Concern for subordinates	5.33	3.42	23.29	116	89
C. Openness	5.28	2.66	17.58	119	92
D. Support for self-reliance	6.00	3.58	18.91	120	92
E. Subordinate Development	5.84	2.85	24.43	120	92
2. AMBASSADOR	6.16	4.16	18.68	118	89
3. TENACITY	6.33	4.56	13.67	120	91
4. AUDITOR	5.72	4.66	8.49	113	88
5. DEDICATION	4.93	2.09	15.78	117	93

Note. All T-Values are significant at $p < .001$.

tives? Although there is no shortage of answers to this question, most prescriptions, with few notable exceptions, are not based on rigorous statistical evidence. We approached this question from an important but generally ignored perspective. Effectiveness was defined in terms of the executive's impact on his/her subordinates, the extent to which he/she was regarded as a role model, a star, and an ideal manager.

Our findings point to what, in the minds of managers in middle and higher levels, distinguishes those executives who succeed in going beyond extrinsic rewards in motivating their subordinates from those who have no deep personal impact and thus have to rely on external rewards to mobilize their manpower. A comparison of the effective and ineffective executives showed that managers attach great importance to the executives'

ability to mobilize their human resources. The ineffective executives received particularly low ratings for their failure to perform in this role.

As supported by our findings, effective top managers need to demonstrate what Bass (1985) referred to as transformational leadership. The following are a few suggestions:

1. Make sure subordinates understand what is expected of them. Provide a sense of direction by communicating a vision of what the organization stands for and where it is headed. Explain the role of subordinates in accomplishing the organization's goals and, through open discussion, help clarify the issues.

2. Help subordinates develop a sense of self-worth and self-confidence through training, development, en-

couragement, mentoring, and public recognition.

3. Provide intellectual stimulation to subordinates by encouraging independence and self-reliance.

Executives who succeed in implementing these ideas leave a deep imprint on subordinates and command their respect and moral commitment. Those who lack such bonding are mere transactional leaders (Bass, 1985) whose only lever for directing their subordinates is reward for performance.

Our findings also show that executives are expected to be more than just transformational leaders. The second variable which distinguished effective executives is their ability to perform as ambassadors for their units. These executives need a global view of their function and a recognition of its fit in the overall organization. They need a profound knowledge of the organization's history and its internal politics. Such an understanding helps them appreciate the balance and distribution of power in their company, enabling them to better represent their unit's views and interests.

The third distinguishing feature is the executives' ability to perform the auditor role by establishing high performance standards and persistently demanding results. Due to their ability to raise their subordinates' level of confidence, these executives succeed in elevating their subordinates' own expectations and willingness to perform over and beyond acceptable levels of performance. They are also in touch with and aware of the issues and obstacles to be resolved.

Two key personal characteristics are also attributed to effective executives: tenacity and dedication. They are perceived as tenacious individuals; they are obsessed with their dreams and pursue them with great determination and energy. Ineffective executives received their lowest rating for their perceived lack of dedication. They are not credible to their subor-

dinates because they are not perceived to be committed to their espoused values and vision: Their pronouncements and enunciations lack any real impact and fail to mobilize their employees.

In summary, one needs a profile consisting of a particular set of behaviours and personal attributes to be regarded as an effective senior executive. All components of such a profile, including the attributes, can be trained and nurtured. The research reported here sets the stage for future work on this important topic. We need to learn more about perceived effectiveness. The role theory (Katz & Kahn, 1978) provides fertile ground to conceptualize this construct but has not been used in relation to top managers. The essence of this theory is that to understand managerial behaviour, we need to understand the network of relationships and the expectations of those with whom top managers interact.

This premise leads to several noteworthy questions: What are the expectations of the constituents of senior managers? What criteria are used by constituents to assess the executives' performance? How are these demands communicated to top managers? How do top managers reconcile different and conflicting expectations? How does the organization's reward system value the different expectations? Finally, are the answers to these questions the same across such varied contexts as different industries, organizations of different sizes, and different national cultures? To answer these questions, research is needed to develop and extend the notion of perceived effectiveness.

References

Bass, B. M. (1985). *Leadership and performance beyond expectations.* New York: Free Press.

Bennis, W. G., & Nanus, G. (1985). *Leaders.* New York: Harper & Row.

Blanchard, K., & Johnson, S. (1982). *The one minute manager*. New York: Morrow.

Carroll, S. J., & Gillen, D. J. (1987). Are the classical management functions useful in describing management work? *Academy of Management Review, 12*(1), 38–51.

Conger, J. A. (1989). Leadership: The art of empowering others. *Academy of Management Executive, 11*(1), 17–24.

Hater, J. J., & Bass, B. M. (1988). Superiors' evaluations and subordinates' perceptions of transformational leadership. *Journal of Applied Psychology, 73*(4), 695–702.

Javidan, M. (1991). Leading high commitment organizations. *Long Range Planning, 24*(2), 28–36.

Katz, D., & Kahn, R. L. (1978). *The social psychology of organizations*. New York: Wiley.

Katz, R. L. (1975). Skills of an effective administrator. *Harvard Business Review on Management* (pp. 19–39). New York: Harper & Row.

Kotter, J. P. (1982). *The general managers*. New York: Free Press.

Kotter, J. P. (1988). *The leadership factor*. New York: Free Press.

Lau, A. W., Newman, A. R., & Broedling, L. A. (1980). The nature of managerial work in the public sector. *Public Management Forum, 19*, 513–521.

Leavitt, H. J. (1986). *Corporate pathfinders*. Homewood, IL: Dow-Jones-Irwin.

Levinson, L., & Rosenthal, S. (1984). *CEO: Corporate leadership in action*. New York: Basic Books.

Luthans, F. (1988). Successful vs. effective managers. *Academy of Management Executive, 11*(2), 127–132.

McCall, M. W., & Segrist, C. A. (1980). *In pursuit of the manager's job: Building on Mintzberg*. Greensboro, NC: Center for Creative Leadership.

Mintzberg, H. (1975). The manager's job: Folklore and fact. *Harvard Business Review, 53*(4), 49–61.

Posner, B. Z., & Schmidt, W. H. (1984). Values and the American manager: An update. *California Management Review, 26*(3), 202–216.

Quinn, R. E. (1988). *Beyond rational management*. San Francisco: Jossey-Bass.

Seltzer, J., & Bass, B. M. (1990). Transformational leadership: Beyond initiation and consideration. *Journal of Management, 16*(4), 693–703.

Snyder, H. H., & Wheelen, T. L. (1981). Managerial roles: Mintzberg and the management process theorists. In K. H. Chung (Ed.), *Proceedings of the Meeting of the Academy of Management* (pp. 249–253). San Diego, CA.

Tichy, N. M., & Devanna, M. A. (1986). *The transformational leader*. New York: Wiley.

Tsui, A. S. (1984). A role-set analysis of managerial reputation. *Organizational Behaviour and Human Performance, 34*, 64–96.

Wrapp, H. E. (1975). Good managers don't make policy decisions. In *Harvard Business Review on Management* (pp. 5–19). New York: Harper & Row.

Mansour Javidan is Professor and Chairman in the Policy and Environment Area of the Faculty of Management at the University of Calgary in Canada. His research interests are in strategic planning and executive leadership. He received a PhD in Strategic Management from the University of Minnesota.

Direct inquiries about this article to Mansour Javidan, Professor, Faculty of Management, The University of Calgary, 2500 University Drive, N.W., Calgary, Alberta, Canada T2N 1N4, 403/220-8244.

The Impact of Leadership on Corporate Success

A Comparative Analysis of the American and Japanese Experience

David Lohmann

The impact of leadership on corporate success is examined through attitudinal and descriptive data gathered from 358 executives in the multinational setting of Honolulu, Hawaii. While there is consensus on the importance of leadership, its degree of impact is influenced by organizational factors, the work situation, culture, and individual characteristics such as age and level of responsibility. Support is lent to the views that leadership and corporate success are related, that leadership has both strategic and interpersonal components, and that there are few substitutes for the unique contributions of leaders to corporate success. A synthesis is suggested, which distinguishes between the immediate and the latent impact of leaders, to explain why American executives value leadership so much more highly than do Japanese executives.

Is leadership an important factor in the success of the firm? When asked by Keidanren, the Japanese trade association, to explain the remarkable success of Japanese industry, none of the CEOs polled mentioned leadership as a significant factor. Humility aside, this is an unusual omission (Coates, 1988).

This research sought to determine if differences exist in the relative importance of leadership as a factor in corporate success between American and Japanese firms. Leadership seems to be a more important success factor in the American setting than in the Japanese setting because the need for leadership is greater in the American firm. American workers are individualistic and the need for dynamic corporate change is great, whereas in Japan, workers are culturally expected to be supportive of corporate objectives and the external environment is more controllable. It is also possible that substitutes for leadership are utilized in the Japanese firm to a far greater extent than in the American firm. These substitutes could include, after Athos, strategy, structure, systems and procedures, superordinate goals, the inherent skills of the firm, and the competence of the staff (Waterman et al., 1980).

Leadership Ambiguities and Definitions

Leadership is many things. Unfortunately, its ambiguity confounds research into determining whether or not leadership really matters. A consistent theme in the leadership literature, however, is that leadership is a process involving certain logically ordered functions. Called by a variety of titles, each seems distinct from the others. The first involves strategic processes, sensing opportunities and outcomes, and formulating a vision. The second is a process of articulating a vision and establishing a climate of trust within the organization. The third is empowering others (Bass & Avolio, 1989; Bennis, 1989; Conger, 1989, 1991; Manz, 1986; Manz & Sims, 1989; Senge, 1990). These three functions of leadership appear to be complementary and logical components of an integrated process of leadership. In this study, leadership is defined as an individual-centered process whose requirement derives from the need for an organization to take coordinated collective action in response to external change. It involves three functions: strategic leadership, transformational leadership, and superleadership. Strategic leadership is the creative process of anticipating the needs of customers, finding new competitive advantages, and exploiting new strategies. Transformational leadership is the establishment of standards and values and the creation of the means to guide collective efforts toward corporate goals. Superleadership is the coalescence for collective action and the release of individual motivation through empowerment to achieve shared goals.

Is Leadership Important?

"Effective leadership is one of the most powerful competitive advantages an organization can possess today" (Conger, 1989).

Leading management theorists argue that leadership is desperately needed to face worldwide competition. Among these are Zaleznik, Kotter, and Drucker ("Take me," 1990). Tichy and Devanna (1986) note that "Corporate leadership is America's scarcest natural resource" (p. 14). Others contend that leadership is the decisive factor that can turn around corporate America and allow it to regain its competitive edge (Hitt, Hoskisson, & Harrison, 1991). Zaleznik (1989) attributes the decline in American competitiveness to American leadership's failure to respond to external dynamic forces. The relationship between corporate performance and individual leadership, however, while intuitively well-founded, lacks empirical support. Previous studies have been inconclusive. Lieberson and O'Connor (1972) report that while leader differences do account for performance variations within firms, their influence is generally insufficient to outweigh the structural differences among firms. Another study found a relation between corporate performance and leader succession when using capital acquisition as a proxy for top management decision making (Weiner & Mahoney, 1981). Other studies either have not supported a linkage between leadership and corporate success (Smith, Carson, & Alexander, 1984) or contend that subjects interviewed had a bias toward viewing leadership as a likely causal factor for success (Meindl & Ehrlich, 1987). In the Japanese literature on corporate success, leadership is seldom mentioned (Coates, 1988; Wokutch, 1990). The Japanese government attributes Japanese business success to 21 factors. None of them even remotely encompasses leadership (Coates, 1988). There are those who hold negative views of the impact of leadership. Some are derisive, describing the emphasis on leadership as trendy (Kiechel, 1989). Machan (1989) notes that a strong leader is required during periods of crisis but during stable periods may, with his self-possessed and autocratic style, do more harm than good. According to Weiner and Mahoney (1981), leaders are needed only in times of organization growth, development, or crisis; since most organizations require only maintenance, the leader is therefore not important. Others are alarmed by the pervasiveness of bad leadership. Hogan, Raskin, and Fazzini (1990) estimate that 60 to 75% of American managers have significant deficiencies that will ultimately lead to failure.

Are There Substitutes for Leadership?

"There is no substitute for leadership" (Drucker, 1988, p. f3).

"Substitutes for [leadership] can be developed" (Lawler, 1988, p. 11).

Are there other forces that can perform the functions normally associated with leadership? Waterman, Peters, and Phillips (1980) believe that organizational effectiveness depends upon the relationship among structure, strategy, systems, style, skills, staff, and superordinate goals. Some of these have potential for providing the influence that the hierarchical leader brings to the work place. There is support for the contention that substitutes for hierarchical leadership exist (Kerr & Jermier, 1978). The influence of leadership may emanate from worker capabilities, task characteristics, and organization characteristics. Less leadership may be needed when workers are well qualified, when the tasks are certain and have intrinsic feedback, reward, and satisfaction, when organizational rules are clear, when there are adequate resources, and when work groups are cohesive (Pitner, 1988; Szilagyi & Wallace, 1990). Other research has lent support to the relationships between work factors and leader influence. These factors include staff (Kelley, 1988), policy and structure (Waterman et al., 1980), and work design and self-leadership (Lawler, 1988). In addition, the employment of the seven Ss (strategy, systems, style—what leaders do—staff, skills, superordinate goals, and structure) appears to be different between Japanese and American leaders. While Japanese and American leaders both use the hard "Ss," strategy, structure, and systems, the Japanese also capitalize on using the soft "Ss," skill, staff, and superordinate goals (Pascale & Athos, 1981). This suggests that the differences in the importance of leadership between American and Japanese firms may be attributable to different uses of these substitutes.

Japanese Leadership Is Different

"In America," says Noritake Kobayashi, Dean of the Business School at Keio University, "the boss is the boss, and he gives orders. Here, that can be very dangerous" (Miller, 1991, p. 60). The primary functions of a Japanese leader are to facilitate group performance, to avoid friction, and to develop a strong sense of group identity and solidarity. His primary skill is interpersonal, he plays a nonvisible role, and his main focus is to create a proper atmosphere for the group to achieve its objective. He is not a strong individual directing and inspiring others to achieve goals set by himself (Yoshino, 1968). The focus is on the group, not the leader. The leader, trained to treasure his employees, is a servant of the group and treats them as equals (Hasegawa, 1986).

In a leadership survey of American and Japanese executives, Bass and Burger (1979) found that Japanese executives were more prone to use persuasion, to exhibit more concern for subordinates, and to be more participative than their American counterparts. Misumi's (1985) analysis of 15 Japanese studies involving

5,200 nonsupervisory personnel showed that effective Japanese leaders are those who are performance (job task) oriented while counterbalancing the pressures associated with performance-oriented leadership with group maintenance (people) activities. Some writers recommend that American executives adopt these people-oriented styles. In Theory Z, Ouchi (1981) suggests that American leaders reorient from technology to people. Wriston (1990) recommends that American executives need to become more reliant on the talents of workers. Others say, with criticism implied, that emphasis on teamwork and participation has weakened the concept of personal leadership and that the fascination with Japanese management practices has led to the replacement of the charismatic with the consensus-seeking leader (Conger, 1989).

While there are "one-man shachos," founder-run companies which operate with a highly visible leader (e.g., Soichiro Honda, Sony's Akio Morita, Kyocera's Kazuo Inamori), these are the exceptions. It is often difficult, if not impossible, to judge the quality and competence of a Japanese organization by the caliber of its formal leaders (Yoshino, 1968). The strengths of the Japanese company lie elsewhere. If a Japanese leader is important to the success of his company, it appears to be in ways which are so subtle that it is questionable whether he can be described with any conventional definition of a leader. When self-leadership is taken to its logical conclusion and the workers are totally empowered, self-motivated, and in tune with the group and corporation objectives, one reaches the most apt definition of a Japanese leader: a facilitator of a productive process in which he does not participate. A summary of the characteristics of the Japanese and the American executive is in Table 1.

The Japanese work force being led has distinctive characteristics. Loyalty to one's employer takes precedence over other duties (Wokutch, 1990). Informal group leaders have standards supportive of the organization (Hasegawa, 1986; Yoshino, 1968). The Japanese worker is predisposed to internalize his motivation by his education. According to a 1990 study of Japanese elementary education conducted by Sato, the training provided quickly shifts responsibility for discipline, organization, and the student's actions from the teacher to the student. In contrast, in the American school system, responsibility for organization, control, and discipline rest and remain exclusively with the teacher ("A Fresh Look," 1991).

According to a study by Maciariello, Burke, and Tilley (1989), the American work force has undergone a pronounced cultural shift since World War II. There has been a reduction in loyalty, an increase in mobility, a decline in pride in workmanship and concern for quality, and a focus on short-term rewards. There has also been a breakdown in manager-worker communication, and a weakening of the link between corporate strategy formulation and operational implementation. Other works have pointed to similar differences between American worker goals (leisure and material goods) and those of the Japanese worker (work satisfaction and a sense of duty) (Bass & Burger, 1979). The Japanese worker has a level of dedication and commitment to his company's welfare and growth that in the United States is reserved for more noble causes. His long-term security and success rests with the company's growth and profitability. The Japanese company is a community of motivated people, cohesive groups working toward a common goal (Hasegawa, 1986). When Japanese companies venture abroad they may or may not attempt to bring the community environment that prevails at home. Sixty thousand Japanese companies have offices in the United States. They are staffed with some 50,000 Japanese-born managers. Almost one half of the top officials in Japanese-owned subsidiaries abroad are

TABLE 1   Differences between Japanese and American Executives

Characteristic	Japanese Executive	American Executive
Managerial View	Organic	Systems
Principal Duty	Facilitator	Decision Maker
Work Focus	Social Leader	Professional
Strength from	Group	Individual
Emphasis	Human Relations	Organization Relations
Priority	Company	Family or Self
Communications	Vague	Explicit
Work Relations	Getting Along	Aggressiveness
	Versatility	Talent
Promotion by	Seniority	Merit and Tenacity
Decision Making	Consensual	Swift, Top Down
	"Family at Work"	"General on a Horse"
Confrontation	Avoid at all costs	Inevitable
Time Orientation	Past, Present & Future	Present

Note. After Okuma (1990) and Fukuda (1988).

transferred from the home office (Mroczkowski & Linowes, 1990). Overseas Japanese firms adopt one of two management styles when they go overseas. In the first style, no attempt is made to either adapt to the local ways or to integrate local executives into decision making. Japanese executives perceive that they can work well among themselves and assume that foreigners cannot be included in the same working relationships. In the second style, the local and Japanese management systems are integrated, and a new culture of corporate values is adopted. The decision of which style to choose depends upon how crucial the local executive's skills are to the success of the venture (Fukuda, 1988; Maruyama, 1988).

Method

On average, Japanese businesses invest $2 billion per year in Hawaii, the third largest investment volume in the United States after New York and California. Japanese business interests in Hawaii take many forms, including purchases of existing companies, new businesses, subsidiaries of Japan-based companies, equity partnerships and joint ventures with U.S. firms, and major positions in U.S. development projects (Lohmann, 1991). As a result of this extensive Japanese business presence in Hawaii, there are many Japanese business executives in residence, numbers of American executives working for Japanese firms, and a business community well informed and experienced on the matter of comparative American and Japanese leadership styles.

Hawaii business leaders who represented a cross section of senior executives working in Japanese and American firms with business interests in Hawaii were surveyed. A profile of the 358 respondents and their companies is shown in Figures 1 to 9.

The survey instrument asked respondents to assess the demands placed on their company and the factors giving them an international competitive advantage. Forced rankings were used to assess the relative importance of the types of leadership, the activities of the leader,

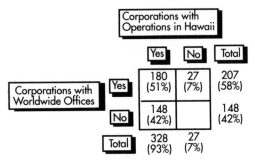

Figure 1 International interests of firms.

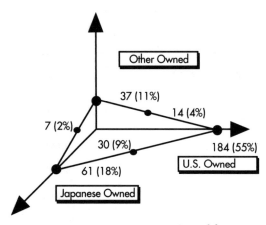

Figure 3 Firm ownership (number of firms).

and six potential substitutes for leadership to corporate success. According to Bass and Avolio (1989), forced rankings are less subject to lenient ratings and snap judgment when evaluating leadership factors and elicit a more controlled, disciplined form of information processing and evaluation. Subjects were asked to judge the relative importance of leadership to their organization's competitive success. Internal organizational stresses were gauged by asking for the respondents' assessment of the internal strengths of their companies and the capability of the staff to perform the work assigned, and through a question which ascertained whether or not the organization was undergoing major change. The success of the firm was also ascertained in a similar fashion. Measurements of perceived decision-making authority and span of discretion were also collected. Chi-square (χ^2) cross tabulations were performed on the nominal data. The measure of association used to quantify the strength and

nature of the relationships was the normalized coefficient of contingency (C). Friedman's two-way ANOVA was used to analyze the ordinal data. Correlation was used with the interval and ratio data. The Kendall coefficient of concordance was used to measure the extent of agreement across respondents.

Results and Discussion

Strategic, transformational, and super-leadership were differentiated by the respondents. The respective importance rankings (1.70, 2.26, 2.04) were significantly different (χ^2 (2, N = 352) = 56.52, p < .001). The importance and the relationship expressed in terms of negative correlation coefficients are shown in Figure 11. Leader activities were also differentiated. The average rank orders (see Table 2) are significantly different (χ^2 (7, N = 349) = 1220, p < .001). The seven "Ss" factors were rank ordered by the respondents according to their importance to the success of the organization. The results, whose rank order differences are significant (χ^2 (6, N = 350) = 337, p < .001) are shown in Table 3. The Japanese executive population subset had the same rank order (χ^2 (6, n = 49) = 43, p < .001). The relationships among these factors is shown in Table 8. As shown in Table 4,

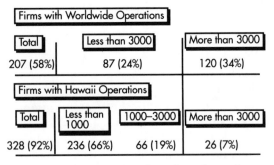

Figure 2 Firm size (number of employees).

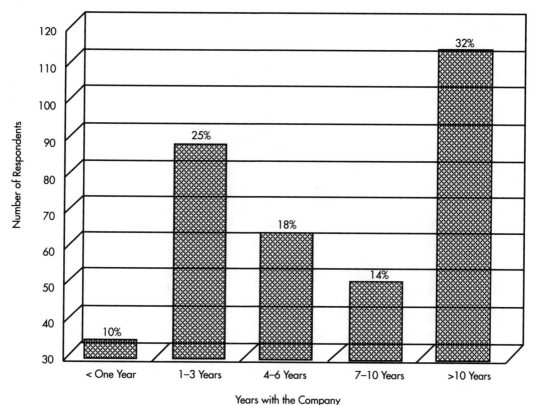

Figure 4 Length of employment.

the respondents were in agreement concerning the relative importance of the leader activities but the relative importance of the types of leadership and the seven "Ss" showed considerable diversity of view.

The Impact of Leadership on Corporate Success

Do the organization's leaders play an important role in the success of the organization? Seventy-four percent of the Hawaii executives responding believe so. Thirteen percent believe that individual leaders are the single most important reason for the competitive success of the organization, and an additional 36% believe leaders are a major force in the organization's success. Less than 2% believe that leaders are not a very impor-

tant factor at all. However, when asked to identify those factors among 12 that were important in giving a country an international competitive edge, executive leadership ranked only 6th. This finding is contrary to the widely held belief that executive leadership is a critical variable in achieving international competitive advantage. The other factors with the number of votes received for each are shown in Figure 10. In a forced choice against the other seven "Ss," the personal impact of the leader was ranked next to last as a factor important to the success of the firm (see Table 2).

Three analyses were performed to better understand these differing results. Differences in the respondent population were examined to identify those factors which may cause respondents to judge the impact of leadership differently. The

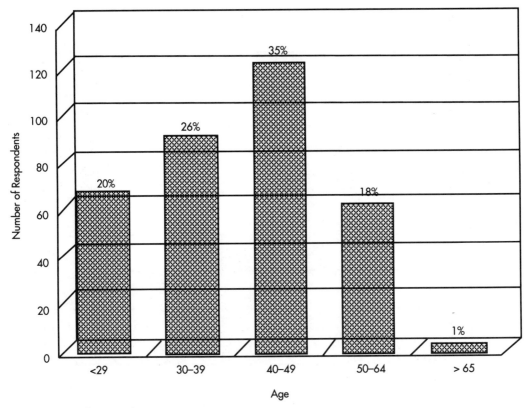

Figure 5   Age of respondents.

different types of leadership (Strategic, Transformational, and Superleadership) were examined to determine if respondents had different perceptions of the concept of leadership. The various activities of leaders were examined to see if some of their activities had greater impact than others.

The Influence of the Characteristics of the Population

The importance of leadership was related to organizational characteristics, which included the nature of the work, ownership nationality, type of industry, and the firm's financial strength. Significant individual characteristics affecting the importance of leadership were organization level, length of service, age, and citizenship. Respondents in challenging work environments considered leader-

ship to be more important than those from firms with routine work environments (χ^2 (2, N = 351) = 10.00, p < .01, C = .17). A greater percentage of executives from wholly owned U.S. firms thought leadership was an important factor (79%) than did those from firms with no U.S. ownership interest (60%) (χ^2 (2, N = 330) = 13.99, p < .001, C = .22). These firms are owned primarily by ethnic Chinese who are citizens of Singapore, Hong Kong, and Taiwan. Australian, Canadian, and Indonesian companies also have major holdings in Hawaii. Firms with no Japanese or American ownership had the lowest percentage of respondents who believe leaders were important (50%). Mixed ownership firms had the highest percentage of respondents believing that leadership had high impact (86% in partly U.S. owned, 80% in partly other owned). These results indicate that leadership may be particularly well suited to meet the additional

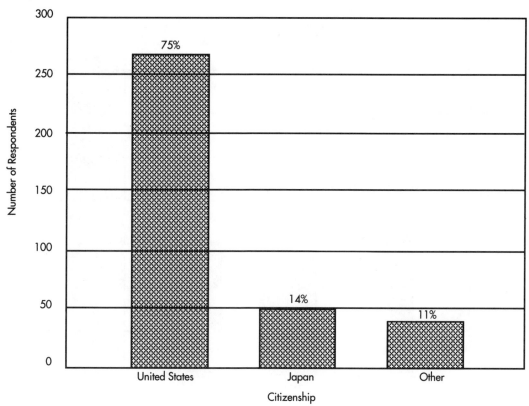

Figure 6   Respondent citizenship.

challenges placed on firms with mixed ownership. Employees of international firms of less than 3,000 employees believe that the personal influence of the leader has a greater impact on the firm's success than those in larger multinational corporations (χ^2 (6, N = 204) = 21.35, p < .001). One leadership factor was significantly different between companies that were in a strong financial position and those that were not: Financially strong companies tended to give less importance to the need for the leader to make all the decisions than did the respondents from companies in weak financial positions (χ^2 (7, N = 349) = 18.67, p < .01).

Individual characteristics also held important differentiations. A greater percentage of chairmen of the board and chief executive officers and those reporting directly to them believed that leadership had a major impact on the success of the firm than those in lower positions (see

Table 5). There was also a significant difference on this measure by citizenship. The percentages of Americans, Japanese, and others who responded that leaders were important to the success of the organization were 82%, 62%, and 47% respectively (χ^2 (2, N = 352) = 22.76, p < .001, C = .27). This finding supports the hypothesis that culture influences how importantly leadership is perceived.

The Types of Leadership

Three types of leadership were described to the respondents. These were strategic leadership (determining the strategic direction of the organization in response to external forces), transformational leadership (changing the organization, redirecting the staff, and motivating subordinates), and superleadership (growing, developing, and empowering subordinates to lead themselves). Respondents

---

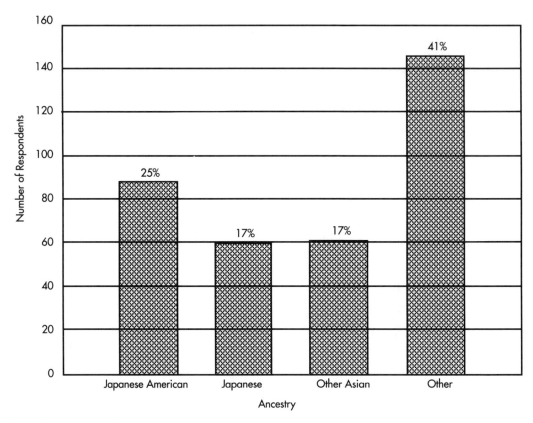

Figure 7 Respondent ancestry.

force ranked these three. The results are shown in Figure 11. Japanese respondents, both by citizenship and ancestry, gave higher priority to strategic leadership than did others, but the rank order of the three was the same (χ^2 (4, N = 329) = 9.18, p < .05).

While strategic leadership was accorded top priority by virtually every population subset, more experienced executives gave it top billing with far less frequency than did more junior executives. Only 50% of the executives with 10 or more years of experience gave the top spot to strategic leadership, whereas 67% of those with less than 3 years in the firm believed that it was the most important of the three to the success of the firm.

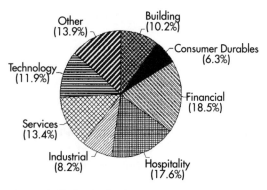

Figure 8 Industry by type.

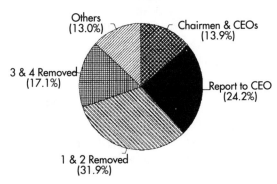

Figure 9 Organizational level of respondents.

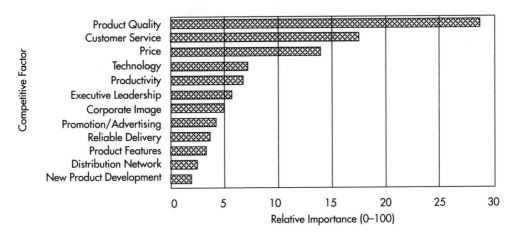

Figure 10   Competitive advantage factors.

TABLE 2   Rank Ordered Importance of Leader Activities to the Success
of the Firm

Rank	Mean Rank	Activity
1.	2.4	Conveys Vision of the Company's Future
2.	2.8	Frequently Communicates with Employees
3.	3.4	Promotes Training and Development
4.	4.0	Links Compensation to Performance
5.	4.5	Emphasizes Ethics
6.	5.2	Rewards Loyalty and Tenure
7.	6.8	Makes All Decisions
8.	6.9	Uses Consultants

TABLE 3   Rank Ordered Importance
of the Seven "Ss"

Rank	Mean Rank	Factor
1.	2.8	Strategy
2.	3.1	Skills
3.	3.2	Staff
4.	3.9	Systems
5.	4.4	Super-ordinate Goals
6.	4.5	Style
7.	5.4	Structure

The importance of the two other types of leadership also depended upon situational and individual characteristics. Respondents from 100% Japanese-owned firms held transformational leadership to be important while those from mixed ownership firms did not (χ^2 (4, N = 329) = 9.18, p < .05). A Japanese firm in Hawaii may feel the need to transform the organization to a different external culture.

Superleadership, the empowerment of subordinates, was more highly valued by certain subsets of the respondent population. Japanese citizens gave it more first place votes than did any other group, followed by the Americans. Other citizens

TABLE 4 Concordance Within Respondent Rankings

Factors Rated	Kendall Coefficient of Concordance	
	Sample Population	Japanese Subset
Leadership Type	.08	a
Leader Activities	.50	.33
Seven "Ss"	.16	.16
N	349	45

Note. A value of 0 indicates no agreement, a value of 1 indicates complete agreement
among all respondents.

[a]not significant.

(mainly from Singapore, Hong Kong, and Taiwan) significantly undervalued the empowerment of subordinates (χ^2 (4, N = 350) = 13.45, p<.05, C = .14). Other groups which gave the empowerment of others a significantly higher percentage of importance were respondents in U.S., Japanese, or jointly-owned U.S.-Japanese firms, regardless of citizenship (χ^2 (4, N = 329) = 11.60, p<.05, C = .13), and those reporting high levels of professional standards among their company's work force (χ^2 (2, N = 351) = 6.3, p<.05, C = .13).

These findings support the contention that the nature of leadership and the impact of leadership is perceived differently by executives of different cultures and experience levels and is affected by the work situations in which these executives find themselves.

Leader Activities

Eight leader activities were described in the 1990 Korn/Ferry International Study of CEOs. These were used in modified form; their rank order is shown in Table 2. Individual and organizational factors influenced the relative importance respondents gave to these leader activities. The significant ones, together with

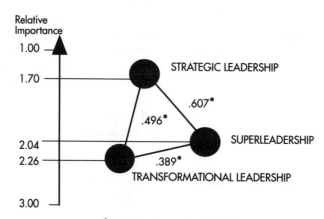

Figure 11   Types of leadership.

TABLE 5 Importance of Leadership by Organizational Level

Organization Level	Percent Affirmative Responses
Chairmen and CEOs	88%
Reporting to the CEO	84%
One & Two Levels Removed	69%
Three & Four Levels Removed	74%
All Lower Levels	56%

Note. $\chi^2(4, N = 336) = 15.66, p < .01.$

pertinent statistics, are shown in Tables 6 and 7. Table 6 is the result of the cross tab analysis, Table 7 of the correlation with the numerical variables which had interval and ratio characteristics.

Respondents in financially strong companies, and those in the financial and industrial sectors, believed that conveying a vision is a more important leader function than did those in financially weak companies and those in real estate and construction. Americans gave more importance to ethics as a leader function than did other nationalities. In companies with 100% American ownership, linking compensation to performance held more weight than in mixed or non-U.S. owned companies. The relative importance of the ethical dimension of leadership seemed to be situationally dependent. Respondents from companies with high professional standards, strong informal group values, or excellent worker initiative rated ethics as above average in importance. The first and last associations of these institutional factors were stronger for Americans than for other nationalities. Age was also a relevant characteristic. Those under 40 gave less value to the importance of ethics than those 40 years of age and older. When worker initiative was rated not very good or only good, respondents believed that the leader should promote growth, train-

ing, and development of his staff as a priority activity. In addition, female respondents valued the activity more highly; 18% of them gave it the first rank compared to 5.0% of the men. (This was the only statistically significant difference between the responses of the female subset (N = 87) and the male subset (N = 268) in the study.) The distinctive groups which believed that rewarding loyalty and longevity was an important leader activity included those with inexperienced work forces and weak informal group values (perhaps due to high turnover). Senior executives gave high priority to rewarding loyalty, while middle managers give it less emphasis. Lower level workers did not believe it was important. Young workers wanted leaders to emphasize rewarding loyalty and longevity; middle age executives thought it was less important. Those over 50 did not believe it was important at all. Not surprisingly, those of Japanese ancestry or citizenship accorded very high priority to this long-standing characteristic of the Japanese work place.

The leader activity of seeking outside consultation was rated high in importance by Japanese citizens and low by Americans. Established companies with strong financial positions and experienced work forces rated outside consultation low. American companies with high perceived professional standards and Japanese companies with high informal group values saw less need for the leader to seek outside advice.

There were significant differences among the respondents when judging the need for the leader to make all decisions. Those who perceived that their company had below-average professional standards believed that it was necessary for the leader to make all the decisions. Americans did not believe that it was important for the leader to make all the decisions, particularly if the respondent came from a company with perceived high professional standards. Respondents of Japanese citizenship or ancestry, however,

TABLE 6 Factors Influencing the Impact of Leader Activities
on Corporate Performance

Leader Activity and Factor	Category	χ^2(d.f.,N), p
Conveys Vision of Company's Future		
Financial strength	O	13.67 (7,315),.05
Type of industry	O	72.86 (42,345),.01
Citizenship	I	26.24 (14,347),.05
Links Compensation to Performance		
Ownership nationality	O	30.66 (14,327),.05
Emphasizes Ethics		
High performance standards	O	17.38 (7,348),.01
Strong group values	O	22.78 (7,348).001
Excellent worker initiative[a]	O	14.62 (7,231),.01
Ownership nationality	O	34.99 (14,347),.001
Age	I	29.20 (14,345),.001
Ancestry	I	54.75 (21,346),.001
Promotes Training and Development		
Below average worker initiative	O	16.96 (7,348),.01
Gender	I	14.15 (7,347),.05
Ownership nationality	I	14.14 (7,347),.05
Rewards Loyalty and Tenure		
Low worker experience levels	O	18.43 (7,348),.01
Strong informal group values	O	18.03 (7,348),.01
Seniority	I	44.08 (28,331),.05
Age	I	39.04 (14,345),.001
Japanese citizenship	I	47.10 (14,347),.001
Japanese ancestry	I	34.35 (21,346),.05
Uses Outside Consultants		
Financial strength	O	20.20 (7,315),.01
Experienced work force	O	17.72 (7,348),.01
High professional standards[a]	O	18.12 (7,261),.01
Citizenship	I	44.84 (14,347),.001
Makes All Decisions		
High professional standards	O	14.22 (7,348),.05
Citizenship	I	60.32 (14,347),.001
Ancestry	I	73.77 (21,346),.001

Note. O = organizational subgroup; I = individual characteristic subgroup.

[a]American subset only.

TABLE 7   Correlation Matrix of Leader Activities

	1.	2.	3.	4.	5.	7.	8.
Intracorrelations							
1. Vision	—						
2. Comp = Perf	.[a]	—					
3. Ethics	.	−.19**	—				
4. Comm.	−.23**	−.17*	.	—			
5. Trng. & Dev.	−.20*	−.21**	.	.	—		
6. Loyalty	−.29**	.	.	.	−.14*		
7. Consultants	.	.	−.24**	.	.	—	
8. Decisions	.	−.15*	−.33**	−.30**	−.21**	.	—
Intercorrelations							
US Ownership	.	.	−.22**	.	.	.16**	
JA Ownership	.	.	.16*	.	.	.	−.17*
Org Level	.	.	.16*	.14*	.	−.15*	−.18**
Authority	.	−.14*	.	.	.	.	.15*

Note. Strategic/Decision Making Cluster composed of factors 1, 2, 7 & 8; Interpersonal Cluster composed of factors 3, 4 & 5.

[a]not significant.

*p < .01.   **p < .001.

believed it is very important for the leader to make all the decisions. Twenty-five percent of all Japanese respondents gave this activity the first or second priority compared to only 4% for American citizen respondents.

The correlation matrix, displayed in Table 7, appears to contain two clusters of leader activity: those that are essentially strategic and decision oriented, and those which involve interpersonal dimensions. Only one of the activities, rewards loyalty and tenure, does not fall into either cluster. Those in the strategic and decision-making cluster are conveying a vision, linking compensation to performance, seeking outside consultation, and making all the decisions. The interpersonal cluster includes emphasizing ethics, communication, and promoting training and development. All of the statistically significant correlations, which are all negative, are with leader activities in the opposite cluster.

The intercorrelation matrix in Table 7 indicates that ethics was considered more important in firms with a greater percentage of ownership. The opposite is true for the level of Japanese ownership. Also, the greater the Japanese ownership, the more highly valued is use of outside consultant and autonomous leader decision making.

The higher the individual was in the organization, the greater he or she valued ethics and communications as leader activities. The greater the decision-making latitude given the respondent, the greater he or she wished leaders to link compensation to performance and to not make autonomous decisions.

TABLE 8   Correlation Matrix of the Seven "Ss"

	1.	2.	3.	4.	5.	6.
Intracorrelations						
1. Strategy (H)	—					
2. Systems (H)	.	—				
3. Style (S)	− .25**	− .28**	—			
4. Staff (S)	− .26**	.	.	—		
5. Skills (S)	− .25**	− .24**	.	.	—	
6. Supergoals (S)	− .17*	− .28**	.	− .18**	− .21**	—
7. Structure (H)	− .20**	.	− .25**	− .20**	.	− .17*
Types of Leadership						
Strategic Leadership	.40**	.	.	− .14*	.	− .17*
Transformational Leadership	.	.	.	.	.	
Super-Leadership	− .30**	.	.	.19**	.	.15
Activities of Leaders						
Vision	.20**	.	.	.		.15*
Comp = Perf	.16*	.	.	.	.	− .15*
Ethics	− .14	.	.	.14*	.	.16*
Comm.	.		.	.14*	.	.
Trng. & Dev.	− .17*	.	.	.	.	
Decisions	.	.13 +	.	.	.	

Note. (H) = hard "Ss"; (S) = soft "Ss."

*p < .01.   **p < .001.   +p < .05.

The Seven "Ss" as Leader Substitutes

Respondents rank ordered the seven "Ss" factors (Waterman et al., 1980) against the standard, "which are most important to the success of your organization?" The rank orders are shown in Table 3. The correlations are shown in Table 8. These factors were also correlated with the interval and ratio descriptive information collected. The more senior an executive, the higher he or she rated style—the personal influence of the leader (r = .1718, p < .01). The rating accorded staff development was correlated with the percentage of Japanese ownership. The greater the Japanese ownership, the less the factor skills (the unique capabilities of the firm) were valued (r = .1688, p < .01). The greater percentage of the decisions made by one's superior, that is, the less autonomy one had, the higher the leader activity of developing the staff was ranked (r = .1362, p < .01).

The seven "Ss" were categorized as hard or soft using the Waterman definitions (1980). It appears that hard (H) and soft (S) factors cluster. Ten of the 13 significant negative correlations are against factors in the opposite cluster. It appears that these paired factors are distinctively different and can be eliminated as substitutes for one another. Similarly, it appears that the two clusters are so substantively different that members of one cannot be considered substitutes for members in the other. Within the hard cluster, strategy

LOHMANN

and structure are negatively correlated. Structure, therefore, is probably not a substitute for the leader activity of strategy. Within the soft cluster, superordinate goals are negatively correlated with both staff development and staff skills, indicating that the leader task of conveying vision cannot be replaced by either staff development or differentiating the company through the collection of unique skills. An examination of the activities of leaders shows that they too cluster into strategic decision-making (SD) activities and interpersonal (IP) activities. With one exception, all strategic activities are positively correlated with hard "Ss" and all interpersonal activities correlate positively with soft "Ss." The opposite regarding negative correlations is also true (see Table 8). It is interesting to note that the rank orders of the importance of the "Ss" to corporate success alternate: 1. Hard, 2. Soft, 3. Hard, 4. Soft, 5. Soft, 6. Soft, 7. Hard. This may indicate that the respondents believe that leadership contributes in both strategic and interpersonal ways to the success of the firm. Eliminating those in the opposite cluster and those within the cluster which have negative correlation yielded a matrix of possible leader substitutes. These are shown in Table 9. Style is what leaders do, their personal influence, and their presence. There appear to be, at most, only three means to substitute for this individual influence. These are to develop the staff, to establish a distinctive set of skills and culture in the firm, and to establish commonly held superordinate goals. A similar analysis of leader activities is shown in Table 10. There are only 9 possible substitutions from the 28 possible combinations.

Summary

Leadership has a significant impact on the success of the firm. However, the impact of leadership is perceived differently by executives of different cultures and experience levels and is significantly affected by work situations.

There appear to be two distinctive clusters of leader activities. These are strategic activities and interpersonal activities. Substitution across these clusters does not appear possible; within clusters, substitution opportunities appear very limited.

As noted by Hollander and Offerman (1990), organization level is important in the interpretation of leadership. There are differences among front-line supervisors and more senior leaders. Fukuda (1988) reports on research by Harai and Zeira in 1974 which was confirmed by Whitehall and Takezawa in 1978, that Japanese workers had similar values regardless of whether they were working for Japanese or non-Japanese firms, or whether they were working in Japan or overseas. These findings are supported here. Badaracco and Ellsworth (1989) advocate constancy of vision, purpose, and personal beliefs as a required ingredient for successful leadership. This view is supported by this study. The leader requirement to create and maintain an ethical climate was a consistent theme found among the American responses and the analyses. It is the thread that is common to all types, perceptions, and definitions of leadership.

Conclusions and Implications

The executives surveyed in this study believed that leadership was important to the success of the organization. Leaders have impact. Leadership importance, however, varied across culture; for example, American business executives thought it more important to corporate success than did Japanese executives. It varied by industry; it was credited with greater importance in high skill industries. Its importance was also influenced by the health of the work force in the respondent's company; higher ratings for

TABLE 9 Possible Substitutions among the Seven "Ss"

	Strategy	Systems	Style	Staff	Skills	Supergoals
Strategy	—					
Systems	P	—				
Style	O	O	—			
Staff	O	O	P	—		
Skills	O	O	P	P	—	
Supergoals	O	O	P	X	X	—
Structure	X	P	O	O	O	O

Note. P = possible substitute; X = negatively correlated; O = opposite cluster.

leadership as a corporate success factor were associated with strong, healthy companies with a motivated and experienced work force. Individual characteristics such as age, seniority, and level of responsibility also affected the perception of the importance of leadership. Upper echelon executives thought it more important than did their subordinates.

Contrary to the findings of this study, other researchers have concluded that leadership is not important to corporate success (Thomas, 1988). Bensimon, Neumann, and Birnbaum (1989) cite four studies which support the view that leaders are no more than figureheads whose symbolic acts signal to sponsors and supporters that everything is going well. According to these studies, leader activities have little effect over the tangible outcomes of the organization. Do leaders have impact, as this study concludes, or are they no more than window dressing, as suggested by others? These two views can be reconciled by considering two points. Firstly, according to the executives surveyed, leaders perform certain specific, nonsubstitutable functions which are necessary for the success of the enterprise but not sufficient in themselves to assure success. Leaders are one of many necessary ingredients for success. They cannot do it alone. Secondly, the impact that leaders have on an organization may

TABLE 10 Possible Substitutions among Leader Activities

		VI	CP	ET	CO	TD	LT	OC
Vision	(VI)	—						
Comp = Perf	(CP)	P	—					
Ethics	(ET)	O	O	—				
Comm.	(CO)	O	O	P	—			
T & D	(TD)	O	O	P	P	—		
Loyalty	(LT)	X	—	—	—	X	—	
Consultants	(OC)	P	P	O	O	O	—	—
Decisions	(MD)	P	P	O	O	O	—	P

Note. P = possible substitute; X = opposite cluster; O = negatively correlated.

not be obvious at the time of their actions. Leaders increase the capability of the organization. That capability may be turned into tangible results at a later time.

Leaders need strong, healthy organizations to accomplish great things. This research showed that leaders are considered important to the success of the firm only when there was both a challenging task to be done and there was the capability within the organization to accomplish it. When the staff was judged to be weak and inadequate, leaders were not considered important. The best leader cannot accomplish something with nothing. Also, just as leaders cannot do it alone, they cannot do everything. This study showed that leaders perform two principle tasks: A leader gives meaning and direction to an organization, and he obtains the commitment of the work force to that meaning and direction. These are his two contributions to corporate success. Everything else the individual executive does is more properly defined as management.

To have a positive impact on the organization, the leader must perform these two functions effectively. The meaning and direction that he or she gives to the organization must be significant to the followers. The significance is judged, in part, by the leader's commitment. If the leader makes visible sacrifices for the goal, the goal becomes credible. According to Fuller (1936), military men who command from protected positions and, by analogy, executives who are obscenely overpaid, violate this principle of sacrifice. Personal involvement and commitment are required to convince followers of the worthiness of the goal. Perhaps this is the reason that sacrifice and courage are words commonly associated with the concept of leadership. The worthiness of the goal is also judged by its consistency with the follower's value structure, which may differ from one culture to another. As shown by this study and by others, Americans valued

ethically-based systems whereas Japanese respondents placed higher value on pragmatically-based criteria. The leader must also have the tools necessary to perform his functions. A personal ability to communicate meaning and direction, and the base of power to influence others, are required for success.

Leaders are visibly more important to the organization's success during periods of crisis than during quiet times. The consequences of excellent leadership, or failed leadership, are immediate and significant. In a crisis, leaders are accorded greater discretion and freedom to set new direction, and followers are more willing to commit themselves to a trusted leader during times of confusion, uncertainty, and shared threat from outside the organization. Crises demand leadership. It is not surprising, therefore, that in this study the American executives, who are short-term and solution oriented, would think that visible leadership is more important than would the Japanese executives, who are long-term and crisis-avoidance oriented. However, leadership can have long-term impact on the organization as well. Leader actions during quiet times can impact on the organization's ability to respond during a future crisis.

Leaders are responsible for managing the capability and competent human energy of an organization to accomplish important tasks. According to Ohmann (1983), people want an opportunity to take part freely in a cooperative effort that has a moral purpose. This willingness to commit to an organization's goal is the human energy with which leaders work. In a crisis, there is no time to build these assets. They are then prudently expended by the good leader to achieve a common goal. In quiet times, however, the good leader's purpose is to build the capability of the organization and to store up competent human energy. By so doing, he or she enhances the organization's capacity for performance. It seems that American leaders are more comfortable in the role of capability users, while Japanese leaders are more likely to be capability builders. The human energy that is managed by the leader can be stored in staff capabilities, an agreed-upon organization mission of noble purpose, a distinctive philosophy and ethos, effective systems and procedures, a well-conceived strategy, and in the loyalty and commitment of the followers. The storage of human energy is the work of the effective leader that will have the greatest impact on the success of the organization. Bad leaders, in contrast, expend human energy without meaningful purpose, allow the human energy of the organization to erode, and fail to maintain a climate of trust, ethical standards, and the confidence of the followers.

Leadership is management of the heart. Obtaining and utilizing the enthusiastic commitment and human energy of others to accomplish a noble goal is a responsibility of the highest order and is the essence of leadership.

References

A Fresh Look at Japanese Education. (1991, January). *Stanford Observer*, pp. 9–12.

Badaracco, J. L., Jr., & Ellsworth, R. R. (1989). *Leadership and the quest for integrity*. Boston: Harvard Business School.

Bass, B. M., & Avolio, B. J. (1989). Potential biases in leadership measures: How prototypes, leniency, and general satisfaction relate to ratings and rankings of transformational and transactional leadership constructs. *Educational and Psychological Measurement*, 49, 505–526.

Bass, M., & Burger, P. C. (1979). *Assessment of managers: An international comparison*. New York: Free Press.

Bennis, W. (1989). *On becoming a leader*. New York: Addison-Wesley.

Bensimon, E. M., Neumann, A., & Birnbaum, R. (1989). *Making sense of administrative leadership: The 'L' word in higher education*. Washington, DC: George Washington University.

Coates, N. (1988). Determinants of Japan's business success: Some Japanese executives' views. *The Academy of Management Executive, 2*(1), 69–72.

Conger, J. A. (1989). *The charismatic leader*. San Francisco: Jossey-Bass.

Conger, J. A. (1991). Inspiring others: The language of leadership. *Academy of Management Executive, 5*(1), 31–45.

Drucker, P. (1988, January 6). Leadership: More doing than dash. *Wall Street Journal*, p. f3.

Fukuda, J. K. (1988). *Japanese style management transferred: The experience of East Asia*. New York: Routledge.

Fuller, J. F. C. (1936). *Generalship: Its diseases and their cure*. Harrisburg, PA: Military Service Publishing Co.

Hasegawa, K. (1986). *Japanese-style management: An insider's analysis*. Tokyo: Kodansha International.

Hitt, M. A., Hoskisson, R. E., & Harrison, J. S. (1991). Strategic competitiveness in the 1990s: Challenges and opportunities for U.S. executives. *The Executive, 5*(2), 7–22.

Hogan, R., Raskin, R., & Fazzini D. (1990). How charisma cloaks incompetence. *Personnel Journal, 69*(5), 73–76.

Hollander, E. P., & Offerman, L. R. (1990). Power and leadership in organizations. *American Psychologist*, 45, 179–189.

Kelley, R. E. (1988, November-December). In praise of followers. *Harvard Business Review*, pp. 142–148.

Kerr, S., & Jermier, J. M. (1978). Substitutes for leadership: Their meaning and measurement. *Organizational Behavior and Human Performance*, 22, 375–403.

Kiechel, W. (1989, October 23). A hard look at executive vision. *Fortune*, pp. 207–209.

Korn/Ferry International & Columbia University Graduate School of Business (1990). *Reinventing the CEO*. New York.

Lawler, E. E., III (1988, Summer). Substitutes for hierarchy. *Organizational Dynamics*, pp. 4–15.

Lieberson, S., & O'Conner, N. (1972). Leadership and performance: A study of large corporations. *American Sociological Review*, 37, 117–130.

Lohmann, D. P. (1991). A balance sheet on Japanese investment in Hawaii. *Proceedings of the Fourth Annual Meeting of the Association of Japanese Business Studies.*

Machan, D. (1989, January 23). The Charisma Merchants. *Forbes*, pp. 100–101.

Manz, C. (1986). Self-leadership: Toward an expanded theory of self-influence processes in organizations. *Academy of Management Review, 11*(3), 585–600.

Manz, C. C., & Sims, H. P., Jr. (1989). *Superleadership: Leading others to lead themselves.* New York: Prentice-Hall.

Maciariello, J., Burke, J. W., & Tilley, D. (1989). Improving American competitiveness: A management systems perspective. *The Academy of Management Executive, 3*(4), 294–303.

Maruyama, M. (1988). The inverse practice principle in multicultural management. *The Academy of Management Executive, 2*(1), 67–68.

Meindl, J. R., & Ehrlich, B. (1987). The romance of leadership and the evaluation of organizational performance. *Academy of Management Journal, 30*, 91–109.

Miller, K. (1991, April 1). How Japan vaccinates its CEOs. *Business Week, 1*, p. 60.

Mroczkowski, T., & Linowes, R. (1990). American professionals inside Japanese firms: A study of Japanese financial services in the U.S. *Proceedings of the Third Annual Conference of the Association of Japanese Business Studies.*

Ohmann, O. A. (1983). Skyhooks. In E. G. C. Collins (Ed.), *Executive success: Making it in management* (pp. 186–201). New York: John Wiley.

Okuma, D. in Pepper, J. (1990, March 26). Japanese bosses get in the way of executive go-getters. *Detroit News*, pp. A5-A7.

Ouchi, W. (1981). *Theory Z: How American business can meet the Japanese challenge.* Reading, MA: Addison-Wesley.

Pascale, R. T., & Athos, A. G. (1981). *The art of Japanese management: Applications for American executives.* New York: Simon & Schuster.

Pitner, N. J. (1988). Leadership substitutes: Their factorial validity in educational organizations. *Educational and Psychological Measurement, 48*, 307–315.

Senge, P. M. (1990). The leader's new coach: Building learning organizations. *Sloan Management Review, 31*(1), 7–23.

Smith, J. E., Carson, K. P., & Alexander, R. A. (1984). Leadership: It can make a difference. *Academy of Management Journal, 27*, 765–776.

Szilagyi, A. D., Jr., & Wallace, M. J., Jr. (1990). *Organizational Behavior & Performance* (5th ed.). New York: Scott Foresman.

Take me to your leader. (1990, June 2). *The Economist*, p. 73.

Thomas, A. B. (1988). Does leadership make a difference to organizational performance. *Administrative Science Quarterly, 33*, 388–400.

Tichy, N. M., & Devanna, M. A. (1986). The transformational leader. *Training and Development Journal, 40*(7), 14–26.

Waterman, R. H., Peters, T. J., & Phillips, J. R. (1980, June). Structure is not organization. *Business Horizons*, pp. 14–26.

Weiner, N., & Mahoney, T. (1981). A model of corporate performance as a function of environmental, organizational, and leadership influences. *Academy of Management Journal, 3*, 453–470.

Wokutch, R. E. (1990). Corporate social responsibility Japanese style. *Academy of Management Executive, 4*(2), 56–74.

Wriston, W. (1990). The state of American management. *Harvard Business Review, 1*, 78–83.

Yoshino, M. Y. (1968). *Japan's management system: Tradition and innovation.* Cambridge, MA: MIT Press.

Zaleznik, A. (1989). *The managerial mystique: Restoring leadership in business.* New York: Harper & Row.

David Lohmann is Professor of Management and Executive Assistant to the President at Hawaii Pacific University. His research interests include assessing the impact of leadership, management, and motivation on the international competitiveness of American firms as developing simulation models of international competition.

Direct inquiries about this article to David Lohmann, Professor of Management, Hawaii Pacific University, 1164 Bishop Street, Honolulu, HI 96813, 808/544–0200.

CHAPTER 7

Shidō
Effective Leadership in Japan

Patrick J. Bettin,
Peggy S. Hunt,
Jennifer L. Macaulay,
and Susan E. Murphy

Although there may be unique cultural differences associated with specific leadership behaviors, there is significant commonality associated with effective leadership that transcends cultural boundaries. This study examined the applicability of several leadership theories in a large Japanese service organization. Additionally, the impact of individual, work group, and environmental factors on organizational performance and worker satisfaction were investigated. The data support the Performance-Maintenance Theory of Leadership. Also, transformational leaders received better performance ratings by both their supervisors and their subordinates than did transactional leaders, and their groups performed well and were satisfied. While few of the individual, group, and environmental variables were significantly related to performance or satisfaction, they often were related to the leadership factors and had an indirect effect on performance.

"Leadership is one of the most observed yet least understood phenomena on earth" (p. 2).

James MacGregor Burns
Leadership

Without question, leadership is emphasized by organizations as a critical process to enhance the performance and effectiveness of individuals, teams, and organizations. The Japanese have a word for this process of guiding individuals, teams, and organizations: Shidō. Even W. Edwards Deming's (1986) philosophy of transformation highlights the requirement for leadership as a supplement to the traditional management competencies practiced for the last 40 years. As organizations strive to create and sustain competitive advantages in an increasingly complex global economy, they must emphasize the value-added contributions of leaders. A widely shared view is that effective leadership taps into the potential of individuals and enables groups to function synergistically.

Given the continuing emphasis on international business activities, there is increased worldwide need to address leadership activities and processes in other nations and cultures. This research focused on identifying some of the unique factors and processes that influence organizational effectiveness within a large Japanese organization. Additionally, it provided an opportunity to investigate potential cross-cultural differences in variables known to predict leadership performance in the United States. Cross-cultural research on managerial style and leadership has found mixed evidence for the validity of predominantly American models of leadership (cf. Ronen, 1986). Explanations for lack of support focus on aspects of a country's culture that might determine whether a leadership model is predictive of leadership performance (Farmer & Richman, 1965; Harbison & Myers, 1959). For example, Farmer and Richman's model of comparative management proposes that attitudes toward achievement, risk-taking preferences, and needs are important cultural values affecting managerial style. The present study investigated the validity of two leadership models, the Transformational Leadership model (Bass, 1985; House, 1977) and Misumi and Peterson's (1985) Performance Maintenance Model of Leadership, for predicting leadership performance in Japan. In addition, such individual, group, and environmental factors as interpersonal style, self-esteem, stress, and group atmosphere were investigated.

Using a modification of McGrath's (1964) model of group interaction (see Figure 1), this research attempted to identify some of the individual, work group, and environmental factors that, when coupled with the leadership processes, influence individual performance and satisfaction.

Performance-Maintenance Model

The Performance-Maintenance (PM) Theory of Leadership evolved from a systematic, interdisciplinary research program conducted in Japan during the last 30 years (Misumi & Peterson, 1985). The PM Theory of Leadership focuses on lead-

ership behaviors similar to those defined in the original Ohio State studies on situational leadership. The concepts of "Performance" (P) behaviors and "Maintenance" (M) behaviors were derived from ideas about basic functions of leadership. Performance-oriented behaviors focus on forming and achieving group goals, such as fast work speed, good quality, high accuracy, high quantity, and observation of rules and procedures. Although these behaviors are related to the structuring behaviors defined in the Ohio State studies, they are unique in that they look at the processes being used by the leader as well as the results that are attained. The maintenance-oriented leadership function refers to the activities and processes the leader uses to maintain the cohesion and integration of the work group. These behaviors focus on preserving group social stability by demonstrating a concern for subordinate feelings, providing comfort, reducing stress, and displaying appreciation. These behaviors are closely related to the concept of consideration.

Empirical tests of the Performance-Maintenance leadership theory have led to the conclusion that the most effective lower- and middle-level leaders in Japan exhibit a consistent combination of high performance-oriented behaviors and high maintenance-oriented behaviors. In essence, there is empirical support for the notion that the most effective leaders create a general leadership philosophy that consistently emphasizes the need to focus on the use of appropriate processes to achieve task accomplishment and, simultaneously, address the needs to maintain effective interpersonal relationships within the work group (Misumi & Peterson, 1985).

Transformational Leadership

Originally coined by J. M. Burns (1978), the term "transformational leadership" refers to a class of theories that describe effective leaders as those able to in-

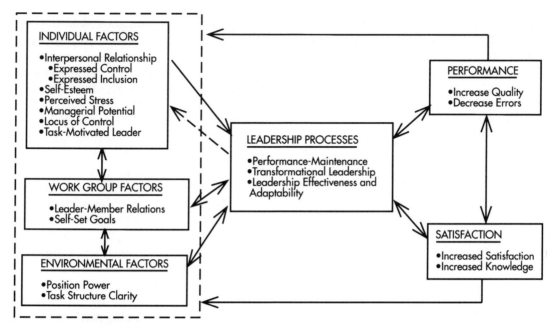

Figure 1 Adaptation of McGrath's model (1964).

spire their followers to perform at higher levels than they would under normal circumstances. Burns referred to the concept of transforming followers into leaders, thereby creating a sense of shared responsibility within the work group. Bass (1985) emphasized the need for leaders to arouse and satisfy higher level needs while engaging the full person of the follower. In essence, transformational leaders influence others through emotional appeals and increasing followers' devotion to duty. Often, theories of this type are also referred to as theories of charismatic leadership (Conger & Kanungo, 1988; House, Spangler, & Woycke, 1991).

Transformational leaders influence their followers to transcend their own self-interests for the good of the group (Bass, 1985; Burns, 1978). The ability of these leaders to communicate goals and values to the group increases the motivation and commitment to the group. Transformational leaders provide high standards of performance and the inspiration to meet such goals.

Transformational leaders are assumed to have high confidence and a conviction

of the righteousness or correctness of their cause. They are thought to affect the emotions of their subordinates by expressing high performance expectations and high confidence in their followers' abilities to perform the task (House, 1977). Through these high expectations, transformational leaders are hypothesized to have higher performing groups. In addition to higher task performance, transformational leaders are hypothesized to generate higher levels of group cohesion and consensus within the group, as well as to deepen the commitment by followers to the goals of the leader (Conger & Kanungo, 1987).

Individual, Work Group, and Environmental Factors

A number of individual, work group, and environmental factors potentially affect the usage and effectiveness of leadership processes, as well as the performance and satisfaction of work-group members. The Fundamental Interpersonal Relationship Orientation-Behavior (FIRO-B) questionnaire measures three fundamental dimensions of interpersonal relationships (Ryan, 1977): (a) *Inclusion* assesses the degree to which a person associates with others; (b) *Control* measures the extent to which a person assumes responsibility, makes decisions, or dominates other people; and (c) *Affection* reflects the degree to which a person becomes emotionally involved with others. Research on interpersonal relations orientations in Japan shows that the Japanese score higher than Americans on masculinity, uncertainty avoidance, and power distance (Hofstede, 1980). Even without any specific hypotheses regarding the FIRO-B scale, its use allows a comparison of scores in Japan with U.S. managerial norms and an examination of how differences in scores affect leadership behavior of the Japanese sample of managers.

Another individual difference variable of interest is self-esteem. Although most research finds no direct relationship between self-esteem and job performance, research has shown that people high in self-esteem are more likely to emerge as group leaders (Andrews, 1984), and a high level of leader self-esteem can transfer to the subordinate (Bennis & Nanus, 1985). Furthermore, Bass (1985) hypothesized that charismatic leaders have higher self-esteem and higher performing and more satisfied work groups. Self-esteem is expected to relate both to transformational measures of leadership and performance-maintenance measures in the present study. Leaders with higher self-esteem will be seen as more transformational, having higher performance (P) and higher maintenance (M) scores than leaders with lower self-esteem.

Intragroup relations is another factor likely to contribute to the overall leadership model. Leaders need supportive group members in order to create a synergistic atmosphere in which excellent performance can be achieved. Clearly, leaders with groups in revolt are not likely to perform well (Fiedler & Garcia, 1987). Therefore, group relations should have a direct effect on performance as well as an indirect effect on leadership processes. Stronger group relations should be found for leaders who score high on the transformational leadership scale and high on both the P and M scales as opposed to leaders who score low on these scales.

Stress is an important environmental factor that influences the performance of leaders (cf. Bass, 1990). Stress may affect the leader's behavior, the behavior of other individuals within the work group, and the working relationships among group members. Consequently, it is reasonable to expect that stress will influence performance and satisfaction (Fiedler & Garcia, 1987). This is predicted to be an important variable in the overall leadership model. Leaders who perceive more stress in their lives will have lower scores on the transformational leadership scale and the P and M scales; stress will interfere with their effectiveness as leaders.

Method

Overview

This study was conducted for a major Japanese utility and its relevant contractor and subcontractor companies. The primary purpose of this research effort was to understand the reasons for more effective or less effective leadership and to create a focused leadership development program that would be integrated into their 20-year long training curriculum for maintenance supervisors. Several instruments and questionnaires were used in this study. However, only those pertaining to transformational leadership, the Performance-Maintenance Leadership Theory, and selected individual, work group, and environmental factors are described here.

Subjects

The subjects consisted of 566 male maintenance employees from six distinct supervisory positions (Hancho, Sagyo Cho, Tanto Sha, Tokatsu Sekininsha, Sagyo Sekininsha, and Sagyo Group Leaders), working at three nuclear power stations in Japan.

Procedure

Initial data were collected through critical incident interviews (Flanagan, 1954). These interviews were conducted to identify general criteria linked to effective and ineffective supervisory behavior. Seven interviews were conducted at each of the three nuclear power stations included in this study. Three researchers, each accompanied by an interpreter, conducted the 2-hour interviews. As a result of the interviews, 38 distinct critical incidents involving effective leadership were identified. The information obtained in the interviews was then content analyzed by two individuals who did not participate in the data collection. The inter-rater reliability was .81. An additional 30 critical incidents involving ineffective leadership were also identified. The content analysis by two independent assessors resulted in an inter-rater reliability of .70. A random sample of 15% of the critical incidents was withheld and categorized at the end. No new job behaviors or categories emerged from this holdout sample.

Subsequent analysis reduced the listing of 161 effective leadership behaviors to 32 categories which were grouped into 8 dimensions by affinity diagramming. The 30 critical incidents involving ineffective leadership resulted in a listing of 116 behaviors broken into 33 categories. These categories were also grouped into 9 different dimensions through affinity diagramming (see Table 1).

Questionnaires and Instruments

Performance evaluation. Using the content analysis of the critical incident interviews, a 32-item performance evaluation scale was developed that focused on supervisory behaviors shown to be important within that company and its culture. The scale was factor analyzed, and one main performance factor was found. Specifically, the concepts of technical competence, interpersonal consideration, and appropriate planning and decision making were addressed in this performance evaluation scale. Each subject indicated the frequency with which his supervisor or his subordinate leader exhibited this behavior. For example, items included "Restrains overeager workers from acting haphazardly until specific assignments can be made" and "Gives exact step-by-step instructions about how to solve a problem."

Leadership processes. The 22-item Performance-Maintenance Leadership Questionnaire (Misumi & Peterson, 1985) was administered to all subjects. Each leader's behavior was rated by one, two, or three team members. The two subscales, P and M, were scored separately and compared to the group means. After the group means were computed, each leader was classified by his scores on both of the scales. A leader with scores above the mean on both the Performance scale and the Maintenance scale was classified as a "PM" leader. A leader with scores above the mean on the Performance scale only was a "P" leader; likewise, a leader with a score above the mean on the Maintenance scale only was an "M" leader. A leader who was at or below the mean on both scales was a "pm" leader. These classifications are used to predict overall performance. According to this theory, a "PM" leader is the most desirable type of leader and a "pm" is the least desirable.

A shortened version of the Multifactor Leadership Questionnaire (MLQ ; Bass,

TABLE 1   Categories Derived from Critical Incident Interviews

Effective Leadership Behaviors

Category	Frequency[a]
Involvement of Others	42

Meets/discusses/consults with group members
Solicits subordinate input
Informs superior of problems
Informs/communicates with superior
Communicates effectively (2-way communication)

Assignment of Responsibilities and Instructions	29

Assigns specific responsibilities
Provides specific instructions
Clarifies issues
Gives safety instructions/checks equipment
Emphasizes quality (TQC) during meetings
Holds technically-oriented meetings to resolve problems

Technical Competence	24

Studies technical issues/content/processes
Seeks expertise
Possesses/demonstrates technical expertise
Pays attention to detail

Physical Involvement	21

Physically present at the work site
Participates in work/demonstrates correct behavior

Interpersonal Consideration	16

Knowledgeable about the people in the group
Uses meetings to calm people down
Is thoughtful/considerate
Calms workers down
Good interpersonal skills (is not pushy)

Work Assessment and Feedback	15

Assesses work
Provides feedback on job performance

Planning and Decision-Making	14

Allocates time/adjusts schedule
Devises plans to complete work
Improves procedures
Develops alternative plans (when necessary)
Makes appropriate decisions
Analyzes problems

Composure	4

Is not overcome by emotions in emergencies
Is not confused

[a]Frequency = the number of times a behavior occurred.

Ineffective Leadership Behaviors

Category	Frequency[a]
Assignment of Responsibilities and Instructions	22

Gives vague/incorrect/unclear instructions
Assigns work inappropriately (beyond capability of workers)
Does not give written instructions

Physical Involvement	21

Stays at desk (gives instructions from office)
Does not supervise
Is not at the work site during stressful period
Does not help subordinates/other work group
Is not available to give advice/supervise (is not present)

Involvement of Others	18

Does not listen to subordinates
Does not solicit ideas/suggestions from below
Does not listen to ideas of others (outside the company)
Does not meet with subordinates
Does not give explanation/rationale for orders (instructions)
Does not give feedback

Abrasive Communications	15

Gets angry/irritated (yells)
Criticizes/blames/scolds
Never compliments
Leader is "pushy" (uses abrasive language)
Fails to communicate effectively

Planning and Decision-Making	14

Fails to plan/coordinate properly
Is unable to make decisions
Fails to act promptly

Work Assessment and Feedback	10

Does not inspect machinery
Does not check work

Incorrect Procedures	10

Does not use correct procedures/equipment/tools
Rushes the job/performs superficial work
Skips steps to keep on time
Does not follow rules
Does not provide appropriate rest
Ignores supervisor's orders/instructions

Technical Competence	4

Lacks technical knowledge/expertise

Inflexible	2

Does not ask for expertise/directions
Does not consider alternatives

[a]Frequency = the number of times a behavior occurred.

1985) was administered. This 20-item questionnaire measured charisma, contingent reward, individual consideration, extra effort, satisfaction, and performance. Each supervisor was rated by up to three subordinates.

Individual, work group, and environmental factors.

Stress was assessed using Cohen's Perceived Stress scale, a 14-item scale that asks leaders to indicate the frequency with which certain stressful events have occurred during the last month (Cohen et al., 1983). *Interpersonal relations* was assessed using the FIRO-B, a 54-item questionnaire where leaders indicate their own preferences and behavior in interpersonal situations. *Self-esteem* was measured with the Rosenberg (1965) Self-Esteem measure, a 10-item scale on which leaders indicate their agreement with statements about their self-attitudes. *Leader-Member relations* scale, an 8-item scale, was used to assess group members' agreement with statements about the cohesiveness and atmosphere of the group in which they work. Each supervisor had up to three subordinates rate the group.

The questionnaires and instruments were translated into Japanese and back-translated into English prior to being administered. The back-translated instruments were compared to the original English version; some minor modifications were made. The Japanese versions were piloted with 21 leaders from a variety of supervisory positions at two of the power stations. All instruments were retained after the pilot study.

Results

Leadership Models

Performance-Maintenance results.
Each subject in this study had (a) a Performance-Maintenance score completed by his subordinate(s), (b) a Perfor-

mance Evaluation completed by his subordinate(s), and (c) a Performance Evaluation completed by his supervisor. Subjects were grouped into one of four categories (TYPE) based upon their scores on the "P" and "M" scales. As stated, subjects above average on both the "P" and "M" scales were "PM" leaders; subjects scoring above average on the "M" scale only were "M" leaders; subjects scoring above average only on the "P" scale were "P" leaders; and subjects not scoring above average on either scale were classified as "pm" leaders.

Analyses of variance were conducted to determine the relationship between leader type (based upon the Performance-Maintenance Scale) and leader effectiveness. The Performance Evaluations were used as the dependent outcome measures; the four leadership types "PM," "P," "M," and "pm" were used as the independent or predictor variables.

The analysis of variance of subordinates' rating of leader performance by TYPE provided statistically significant results that supported the hypothesis: [F (3, 376) = 42.76. $p < .001$]. Post hoc tests were performed to determine the significant differences. The "PM" leaders were rated as significantly better performers than the three other types of leaders. Additionally, as hypothesized, the "M" leaders and the "P" leaders were rated as significantly more effective leaders than the "pm" leaders. Nearly as predicted, the highest effectiveness ratings were associated with "PM" leaders, followed by "P" leaders, then "M" leaders, and lastly by "pm" leaders. Figure 2 presents these results in graphic form.

The analysis of variance of the superiors' rating of leader performance by TYPE also found statistically significant results that supported the hypothesis: [F (3, 291) = 2.61, $p < .05$]. In this case, the "PM" leaders were rated as significantly better performers than the "pm" leaders. However, the highest ratings were given to "P" leaders, followed by "PM" leaders, then

BETTIN, HUNT, MACAULAY, AND MURPHY

"M" leaders, with the lowest ratings given to "pm" leaders.

Transformational Leadership results.

Each subject in this study had (a) a Multifactor Leadership Questionnaire completed by his subordinate(s), (b) a Performance Evaluation completed by his subordinate(s), and (c) a Performance Evaluation completed by his supervisor. The resulting sample consisted of 406 supervisors.

The MLQ includes measures of leader behavior (individual consideration, charisma, contingent reward) and outcome measures. Bass (1985) originally portrayed only two outcome measures in the MLQ—satisfaction and performance. Factor analysis of this data set revealed three distinct outcome measures: Group performance, Leader Performance, and Satisfaction. The other two outcome measures used in this study are the subordinate and superior performance ratings.

Correlations were calculated between each of the leadership factors and the five outcome measures (see Table 2). As the model predicts, the two transformational factors are more highly correlated with the outcome factors than is the transactional factor; all three factors, however, are clearly related to the outcomes. Also, Supervisory Ratings and Group Performance are not predicted well by the factors, while the other three outcomes are predicted quite well by the factors.

Bass (1985) hypothesized that extra effort mediates the relationship between the three leadership factors and performance. He argued that transformational characteristics motivates followers to give extra effort, which in turn leads to higher performance. According to this model, charisma, individual consideration, and contingent reward should be correlated with extra effort, which should, in turn, be correlated with performance. In fact, this was the case. Results indicate that extra effort is highly related to each of the leadership factors of charisma, individual consideration, and contingent reward (r = .68, .74, and .64, respectively; $p <$ .001). Results also indicate that extra effort is significantly correlated with each outcome measure, with the exception of supervisory ratings. These results support Bass's hypothesis that extra effort mediates the leadership factor-performance relationship. It also provides support for his hypothesis that both transformational and transactional behaviors are necessary for outstanding performance.

Performance-Maintenance and Transformational Leadership.

There were high intercorrelations between the P and M scales and each of the subscales of the transformational leadership scale. The correlations ranged from r = .48 between Maintenance (M) and Contingent Reward to r = .71 for Performance (P) and Individual Consideration, with a median correlation of r = .53.

Individual, Group, and Environmental Factors

While none of the individual, group, and environmental variables was significantly related to performance or satisfaction (except self-esteem and subordinate ratings of leader performance), they often were related to each other or to the leadership factors; they thus had an indirect effect on performance. Following is a report by variable of these significant relationships.

Fundamental Interpersonal Relationship Orientation-Behavior (FIRO-B).

In comparing the FIRO-B scores of this group of Japanese managers to normative data collected from U.S. managers, several differences were discovered (see Table 3). The most striking findings are that, compared to the U.S. managers, the Japanese managers appear to desire much more control and direction from others and to desire much less inclusion and affection. These differences may indicate a cultural difference or may be

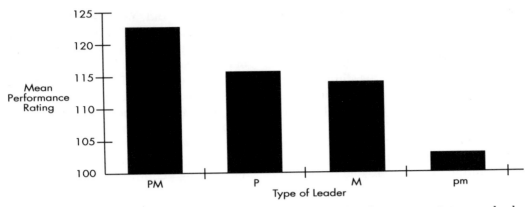

Figure 2   Means of performance ratings by subordinate by type of performance-maintenance leader.

specific to the Japanese organization sampled. None of these measures was related to any measures of leadership processes. However, expressed inclusion, control, and affection correlated r = .25, r = .25, and r = .21, respectively, with self-esteem. They were unrelated to perceived stress or leader-member relations.

Self-esteem.   Self-esteem of the leader was related to several other variables studied. It was found that leaders with higher reported self-esteem reported lower perceived stress (r = -.39, p < .001). It may be that more confident leaders view situations as challenging, whereas less confident leaders view these same situations as stressful. Also, a significant correlation was found between self-esteem and group relations (r = .15, p < .003). Leaders with more confidence seemed better able to create and sustain positive interpersonal relationships within their work groups than less con-

TABLE 2   Correlations between Transformational and Transactional Leadership Factors and the Five Outcome Measures

Leadership Type/Factor	Overall Measures				
	Group Performance	Leader Performance	Satisfaction	Supervisor Ratings	Subordinate Ratings
Transformational					
Charisma	.23*	.52*	.59*	.17*	.57*
Individual Consideration	.29*	.55*	.61*	.10	.57*
Transactional					
Contingent–Reward	.23*	.42*	.39*	.00	.46*
Extra Effort	.37*	.60*	.59*	.11	.57*

*p < .001.

BETTIN, HUNT, MACAULAY, AND MURPHY

TABLE 3 FIRO-B Scores: A Comparison of Results between Managers in the United States and Japan

	Japanese Overall n = 540		
	Inclusion	**Control**	**Affection**
expressed	3.1 sd = 1.5	3.8 sd = 2.2	3.3 sd = 1.9
wanted	1.9 sd = 2.1	4.7 sd = 1.8	3.4 sd = 2.3

	U.S. Managers n = 1800		
	Inclusion	**Control**	**Affection**
expressed	4.1 sd = 2.0	4.7 sd = 2.7	3.5 sd = 2.3
wanted	3.4 sd = 3.3	3.0 sd = 1.9	5.0 sd = 2.4

Note. Differences greater than 0.2 scale points between Japanese and U.S. managers are statistically significant ($p < .05$).

fident leaders. Lastly, leaders with high self-esteem were more likely to have followers who reported that their leader inspired them to put forth extra effort as measured by the MLQ ($r = .19, p < .001$); leaders with high self-esteem were rated higher on performance by their subordinates on the performance measure developed from the critical incident interviews ($r = .15, p < .005$). This supports Bass' hypothesis that self-esteem is important in the transformational leadership processes.

Group relations. As mentioned, self-esteem and group relations were found to be positively related. Group relations and perceived stress of the leader are significantly related ($r = -.27, p < .003$). This result indicates that leaders who perceive less stress in their lives have better interpersonal relationships within their work groups. Leaders under less stress may be more effective leaders. On the other hand, group relations may be a form of social support that helps alleviate or buffer the leader from stress.

Perceived stress. As previously mentioned, stress was negatively correlated with both self-esteem and group relations. It was not related to rated performance or satisfaction.

Overall model. Of the individual factors, FIRO-B was related to self-esteem but not to other factors in the model. Self-esteem was positively related to LMR and

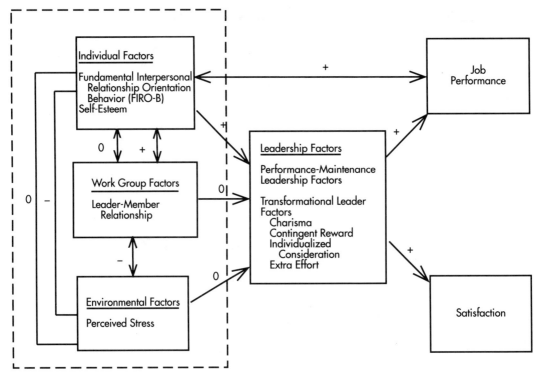

Figure 3 Effective leadership model.

extra effort and was negatively related to perceived stress. Self-esteem was also related to performance as rated by subordinates. LMR was negatively related to stress and had no relationship to any of the leadership scales in the two leadership models. Stress was also unrelated to the leadership factors. Performance-Maintenance measures were highly related to both superior and subordinate ratings of performance. Transformational leadership was related to a number of measures of performance. Figure 3 depicts the relationship of the variables in the model.

Discussion

This study has demonstrated that, although there may be unique cultural differences associated with specific leadership behaviors, there is significant commonality associated with effective leadership that transcends cultural boundaries. It appears that the most effective leaders have developed an overarching philosophy of transformational leadership, while emphasizing the importance of task performance and attending to the general group atmosphere and the interpersonal relationships between team members.

This research effort investigated the impact of input variables and process activities on leadership effectiveness and subordinate satisfaction. The input variables, individual characteristics, work group factors, and environmental/organizational considerations were shown to have a limited impact on the leadership processes used and on the overall outcome measures (performance and satisfaction). The process activities, on the other hand, accounted for the significant overall variance in this study. In essence, the way in which leaders behave, the priorities they establish for themselves and the work group, and the activities and relationships they engage in with other team members are the most important factors in determining leadership effectiveness.

In general, this study found few cross-cultural differences with respect to leadership effectiveness. The Performance-Maintenance model of leadership effectiveness developed in Japan was supported by these data. The Transformational Leadership theory, which has been tested almost exclusively in Western cultures, was also supported by data from this sample of Japanese managers. To a lesser extent, the effects of stress, self-esteem, and group relations were found to be contributing factors to leadership behavior which, in turn, predicted performance and satisfaction.

These results enabled the creation of a basic model of effective leadership for the Japanese company. The model was then used as the foundation for a training program designed to enhance safety, efficiency, and effectiveness through leadership development. This is a significant example of improving processes as a means to enhance organizational performance. This research supported the company philosophy that performance can be improved by preparing leaders to perform more effectively.

This research supports the belief that there are important minimum levels of input that influence the leadership process. Investigation should persist into the various individual, work group, and environmental factors that may shape a leader's relationship with team members. In the near term, the emphasis should continue to be on the leadership processes and activities.

References

Andrews, P. (1984). Performance, self-esteem, and perceptions of leadership emergence: A comparative study of men and women. *Western Journal of Speech Communication, 48*, 1–13.

Bass, B. (1985). *Leadership and performance beyond expectations*. New York: Free Press.

Bass, B. (1990). *Bass and Stogdill's Handbook of Leadership* (3rd ed.). New York: Free Press.

Bennis, W. G., & Nanus, B. (1985). *Leaders: The strategies for taking charge*. New York: Harper & Row.

Burns, J. M. (1978). *Leadership*. New York: Harper & Row.

Cohen, S., Kamarck, T., & Mermelstein, R. (1983). A global measure of perceived stress. *Journal of Health and Social Behavior, 24*, 385–396.

Conger, J. A., & Kanungo, R. N. (1987). Toward a behavioral theory of charismatic leadership in organizational settings. *Academy of Management Review, 12*, 637–647.

Conger, J. A., & Kanungo, R. N. (1988). Behavioral dimensions of charismatic leadership. In J. A. Conger & R. N. Kanungo (Eds.), *Charismatic leadership: The elusive factor in organization effectiveness*. San Francisco: Jossey-Bass.

Deming, W. E. (1986). *Out of the crisis*. Cambridge: Massachusetts Institute of Technology, Center for Advanced Engineering Study.

Farmer, R., & Richman, B. (1965). *Comparative management and economic progress*. Homewood, IL: Irwin.

Fiedler, F., & Garcia, J. (1987). *New approaches to effective leadership*. New York: Wiley.

Flanagan, J. C. (1954). The critical incident technique. *Psychological Bulletin, 51*(4), 327–358.

Harbison, F., & Myers, C. (1959). *Management in the industrial world: An international study*. New York: McGraw-Hill.

Hofstede, G. (1980). *Culture's consequences: International differences in work-related values*. Beverly Hills, CA: Sage.

House, R. J. (1977). A 1976 theory of charismatic leadership. In J. G. Hunt & L. L. Larson (Eds.), *Leadership: The cutting edge*. Carbondale, IL.: Southern Illinois University Press.

House, R. J., Spangler, W. D., & Woycke, J. (1991). Personality and charisma in the U.S. presidency: A psychological theory of leader effectiveness. *Administrative Science Quarterly, 36*, 364–396.

McGrath, J. (1964). *Groups: Interaction and performance*. Englewood Cliffs, NJ: Prentice-Hall.

Misumi, J., & Peterson, M. F. (1985). The performance-maintenance (PM) theory of leadership: Review of Japanese research program. *Administrative Science Quarterly, 30*, 198–223.

Ronen, S. (1986). *Comparative and multinational management*. New York: Wiley.

Rosenberg, M. (1965). *Society and the adolescent self-image*. Princeton, NJ: Princeton University Press.

Ryan, L. (1977). *Clinical interpretation of the FIRO-B*. Palo Alto, CA: Consulting Psychologists Press.

Patrick J. Bettin, PhD, is an Organizational Psychologist with Battelle Human Affairs Research Centers with expertise in leadership and management development, effective team development, small group cohesion, organizational culture, commitment, and motivation. His research interests focus on creating and sustaining organizational effectiveness by enhancing the performance and development of leaders and managers. He was formerly on the faculty of the United States Military Academy at West Point, NY.

Peggy S. Hunt received her Master's Degree in Industrial-Organizational Psychology from San Diego State University and is a Senior Research Associate with Battelle Human Affairs Research Centers. She has focused on Japanese leadership research, developed leadership training courses, and conducted organizational assessments.

Jennifer L. Macaulay is a PhD candidate in Organizational Psychology at the University of Washington, where she is associated with the Organizational Research Group. At Battelle Human Affairs Research Centers, she is involved with research on leadership and managerial effectiveness. Her research interests include leadership, small-group decision making, and gender differences in leadership.

Susan E. Murphy, PhD, is an Organizational Psychologist specializing in leadership and management research and training. Her research interests include group decision making, organizational culture, and the effects of stress in the workplace. She was associated formerly with the Organizational Research Group at the University of Washington.

Direct inquiries about this article to Patrick J. Bettin, Director, Leadership & Professional Development, Battelle Human Affairs Research Centers, P.O. Box 5395, 4000 N.E. 41st Street, Seattle, WA 98105–5428, 206/525-3130.

CHAPTER 8

The Role and Meaning of Leadership Experience

Fred E. Fiedler

This paper explicates the role and function of leadership experience in group and organizational performance. It views experience as overlearned knowledge, skills, and behavior which is incompatible with creative, logical, and analytical thinking. The paper suggests that experience for the leader provides a crash-plan or a pattern of emergency behaviors for dealing with uncertainty and stress.

Common wisdom says that experience is the best teacher. This widespread faith in the importance of experience is evidenced by organizational practices which require several years' tenure at one managerial level before being considered for promotion to the next higher level. Moreover, almost every organization's employment application form, personnel interview, and promotion board ask about previous experience or job history and use it as an important factor in hiring and promotion decisions. However, there is very little evidence to indicate that leadership experience predicts managerial performance. Correlations between various measures of experience and leadership performance have been near zero. This paper examines the seemingly conflicting evidence and proposes a model that reconciles contradictory findings.

A well-known dictionary (McKechnie, 1966) defines experience in a work setting as "anything observed or lived through, as well as time spent in a job or an organization, or the period of such activity as teaching experience" (p. 645). Other definitions emphasize breadth, diversity, quality, or relevance of previous jobs. However, everyday parlance and custom

The opinions and conclusions expressed in this paper do not necessarily reflect those of the sponsoring agency or the Department of Defense.

stress time-based definitions (e.g., "how long have you worked in that company?"). We also recognize, of course, that a 2-year job as foreman of a shipping department provides less managerial experience than heading a division of General Motors Corporation. Time-based measures are especially useful in settings such as the military services where all leaders have had very similar career tracks. These measures basically indicate the opportunity to gain job-relevant information, skills, and knowledge. Above all, they are easily available and reliable measures that permit us to begin investigating a very complex problem.

Experience as Overlearned Behavior

All definitions of experience imply the opportunity to learn and repeatedly practice behaviors that are effective in coping with recurring job-related problems. Since learning is a cognitive process, we must also understand the role of intelligence in the utilization of experience. We use here Berry's (1986) definition of intelligence as "the end-product of individual development in the cognitive psychological domain . . . but excludes motor, motivational, emotional, and social functioning" (p. 35).

This paper aims to show that (a) experience can be interpreted as overlearned knowledge, skill, or behavior to which we revert under conditions of stress; (b) actions based on experience are generally incompatible with creative and logical-analytical thinking; (c) behavior based on experience under stress tends to result in automatic, or nearly automatic, reactions, suggesting the existence of an integrated "emergency behavior pattern" if not an "emergency or stress-personality" along with a "normal" personality and behavior pattern; and (d) experience interferes with the effective utilization of the leader's intellectual abilities.

A Review of Relevant Analyses

Job and Interpersonal Stress

Our studies show that stress is of particular importance in determining how experience affects leader behavior and performance. Such notoriously stressful jobs as police work, fire fighting, the military services, emergency medical services, and the command of ships and planes typically require many years of experience, presumably to enable the leader to react effectively in emergencies and conditions of high stress.

The main value of experience may be in potentially stressful jobs. It is interesting to note that experience seems to be gained primarily in stressful situations. Thus, when we ask individuals to think of an experience from which they have learned a great deal, the incident is almost invariably remembered as stressful and unpleasant rather than as relaxed and pleasant.

Types of stress. We must differentiate between at least two types of stress: job stress and interpersonal stress. Job stress is generated by task difficulty or complexity, time pressure, or noxious and dangerous working conditions. Interpersonal stress is the consequence of threat from, conflict with, or unreasonable demands by important others in the work environment, principally by superiors and subordinates. Although moderately correlated, these two types of stress are conceptually different and have different effects on the leader.

Relatively mild job stress, usually encountered in work life, forces the individual to concentrate on the task. Therefore, more competent or intelligent leaders tend to have better performance. Very high job stress usually results in disorganization and poorer performance; under these conditions experience is helpful.

In contrast, interpersonal stress, especially when caused by the immediate superior, is emotionally very disturbing (Buck, 1963) and has major effects on the leader's ability to think creatively or to make sound decisions. It diverts the leader's intellectual focus from the task (Lazarus, 1966; Sarason, 1984; Spielberger & Katzenmeyer, 1959). As a consequence, leader intelligence cannot contribute to or correlate with performance (Fiedler & Garcia, 1987; Potter & Fiedler, 1981). Moreover, apprehension about how one will be evaluated by one's boss is quite realistic. The immediate superior has considerable fate control, and without his or her endorsement and recommendation, obtaining a promotion or transfer to a more desirable position within or outside the organization is difficult if not impossible.

When the leader is unable to concentrate on the task because of stress or high uncertainty in the situation, one important recourse is to fall back on overlearned behaviors such as past experience. Thus, when boss stress is low, leaders use their intellectual abilities but not their experience; when boss stress is high, leaders use their experience but not their intelligence. It is especially puzzling, however, that the more intelligent leaders perform less well under stressful conditions than less intelligent leaders, and that the performance of more experienced leaders tends to be poorer than that of less experienced leaders under conditions of low stress (Fiedler & Garcia, 1987; Fiedler, McGuire, & Richardson, 1989; Fiedler, Potter, & McGuire, 1992; Fiedler, Potter, Zais, & Knowlton, 1979; Frost, 1980; Potter & Fiedler, 1981).

Combat infantry leaders. Research by Borden (1980) illustrates this point. Borden conducted a study of combat infantry division officers and noncommissioned officers (NCOs), namely of 36 company commanders, 27 executive officers, 97 platoon leaders, 41 First Sergeants, and 126 platoon sergeants. Performance

evaluations were obtained from two to five superiors, using the Bons scale (Bons, 1974). Superiors were asked to rate on a 5-point scale the degree to which the subordinate's performance exceeded, met, or failed to meet performance standards on such items as "how well he carries out administrative actions," "how well he organizes his group," and "how well he handles his job when the demands are extra heavy." Stress was measured on a graphic 11-point scale which asked to what extent the relationship with the boss or the job was "very stressful" or "not stressful at all."

The subjects in each job category were divided into thirds on the job-stress and boss-stress scales, and correlations were then computed between intelligence and performance and experience as measured by Time in Service (TIS). Figure 1 shows the average standardized performance scores for relatively more intelligent and experienced leaders and less intelligent and experienced leaders who reported different levels of stress.

These consistent findings indicate that experience and intellectual abilities are not effectively utilized in the same situations and may, in fact, interfere with one another. In particular, experience appears to be detrimental to performance under low stress while intelligence is detrimental to performance under high stress, especially stress with the immediate superior.

Fire service officers. A study of fire department officers (Frost, 1980) investigated the contribution of experience under low and high stress in various working conditions. Fire fighting is physically dangerous as well as stressful. Experience should, therefore, play a major role in determining leadership performance in these jobs. A study of an urban fire department collected data on 76 lieutenants and 45 captains, each of whom headed a company of 3 to 5 fire fighters. The generally more experienced captains also had responsibility for the fire station and the re-

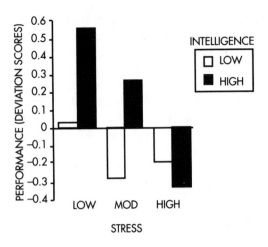

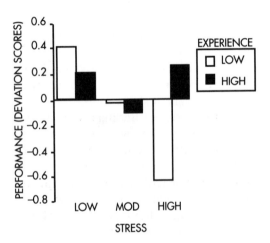

Figure 1 IQ, stress, and performance scores and experience, stress, and performance scores. (Borden [1980] data weighted across five samples).

cord keeping for all four companies which worked in that particular station.

The officers reported the degree to which the job and the relationship with their immediate superior seemed stressful. Battalion chiefs rated their subordinate officers' performance at the scene of the fire as well as in administrative tasks. Three measures of experience were obtained: time in the fire service, time in rank, and time in the unit. None of these measures predicted performance for the entire sample.

As in other studies, experience correlated positively with performance under high perceived stress but was also quite high in the negative direction under low stress. This was especially so under the presumably least stressful conditions, that is, in administrative jobs under low stress. Furthermore, 17 of the 24 correlations were negative, indicating that experience detracted from, rather than contributed to, the performance ratings of these officers. The correlations were about as high for boss stress as for job stress (see Table 1).

Stress caused by physical danger.

Fire fighting is among the most dangerous civilian jobs, with a high incidence of injuries and death. As a result, job stress is generally high. It is measured objectively in the fire service by the average number of hours per year that fire companies spend at the scene of the fire. We could ask, therefore, if this type of stress also affects the contribution of experience to fire fighting performance.

The study compared the rated mean performance of captains and lieutenants who commanded companies with relatively more and less time in fire combat. The fire captains and the lieutenants were further divided on length of time in their positions. Figure 2 shows a significant interaction, an indication that the more experienced captains were rated as performing considerably less well than were the less experienced captains of companies which faced relatively little physical danger. The performance of more and less experienced lieutenants did not differ significantly in companies which had spent little time in fire combat. However, in companies with frequent fire combat duty, the more experienced lieutenants tended to perform somewhat better than did the less experienced lieutenants (interaction significant at p.10).

The findings raised a number of ques-

TABLE 1 Correlations between Various Types of Fire Department Experience and Performance in Fire Combat and Administrative Duties Under High and Low Stress

	Boss Stress		Job Stress	
	Low	High	Low	High
Fire Combat	(22)	(23)	(25)	(20)
Time in Service	− .24	.23	− .34	.41*
Time as Officer	− .23	.25	− .40**	.68***
Time in Own Unit	− .41*	.11	− .31	.14
Administration				
Time in Service	− .31	− .19	− .41**	− .06
Time as Officer	− .40*	− .24	− .58***	.10
Time in Unit	− .66***	− .19	− .56***	− .19

*p < .10.   **p < .05.   ***p < .01.

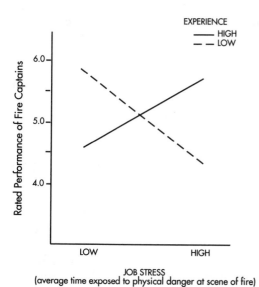

EXPERIENCE
—— HIGH
− − LOW

JOB STRESS
(average time exposed to physical danger at scene of fire)

Figure 2 Mean performance for experience and time in combat.

tions which needed to be resolved, specifically:

1. Why do leaders primarily use their experience but not their intelligence when stress is high, but their intelligence and not their experience when boss stress is low?

2. Why do we find negative correlations between leader experience and performance under low stress and between intelligence and performance under high stress?

3. How do we explain the effect of stress on intelligence and experience?

As already indicated, we cannot react automatically to a problem on the basis of old habits while simultaneously thinking creatively or weighing alternative actions and seeking novel approaches. (When we concentrate on how we hold our tennis racket, the game goes to pot.) Thus, intellectual effort seemingly interferes with overlearned behavior, nor is it easy to think of ways to improve old established work habits, as shown by Frank Gilbreth's (1911) work on improved methods of brick laying. Empirical evidence for this hypothesis comes from a recent study.

Information search study. An experiment by Locklear (1989) investigated the effect of stress on decision making by 31 relatively inexperienced officers (mean TIS = 48 months) and 27 experienced noncommissioned officers (NCOs) (mean TIS = 183 months) during a military training exercise. Officers scored substantially higher on Horn's (1968) crystallized and fluid intelligence measures than did NCOs. Since the crystallized and fluid intelligence scores were highly correlated in this study and yielded almost identical findings, the results are shown here for crystallized intelligence.

The task consisted of ranking five military training plans on the degree to which they met certain requirements. Subjects were shown a 3' x 4' "information board" (Payne, 1976) which contained all the relevant information for evaluating the training schedules (see Figure 3). Thirty-five 3" x 5" index cards contained the needed information. Each of the cards was mounted face-down on a hook and could be inspected and reinspected as often as desired. The number of items inspected by each subject was recorded. The performance score was the agreement of the subjects' ranking with that of a panel of military training experts. This task turned out to be quite difficult: Only 7 of the 58 subjects were able to get a perfect score.

Each leader performed the task under three counter-balanced conditions: (a) "base-rate," in which stress was minimized; (b) "boss stress," in which the leaders were told that their performance would be videotaped and shown to the company commander or sergeant major; and (c) "job stress" in which the leader was told that he had only half the time normally required for the task. Thus, the subjects were under time-pressure and inspected fewer information items, although the available time was, in fact, the same as for the other conditions. Table 2 shows the results.

As can be seen, leader intelligence scores correlated positively with the total number of inspected items but correlated negatively with experience (TIS) and with performance (significantly so in the job stress condition). Performance correlated negatively with intelligence but positively with experience in the job stress condition. These data can be more readily understood if we interpret the process of item inspection as indicative of intellectual effort. A person who tries hard to make use of the given information presumably is more concerned with seeking information and mulling it over than someone who just glances at a few items. Thus, the results show that the more intelligent leaders demonstrated greater intellectual effort. This supports the assumption that more intelligent leaders will rely more on their intellectual abilities than will less intelligent leaders. Why, then, did the leaders who made more intellectual effort perform less well? Although the intelligence and experience levels were confounded with officer and NCO status, essentially the same results were obtained when the data were computed separately for officers and NCOs. As mentioned, the ranking task was very complex. It required the subject to keep 35 different items of information in his head and, on the basis of these items, to rank 5 training schedules. Thus, it may have been nearly impossible to perform this task by sheer intellectual effort.

This suggests why more intelligent leaders did not perform better than those who had lower intelligence scores, and why the more experienced leaders tended to perform better. When a choice had to be made quickly, intuition and hunch served better than extensive search for information and analysis of the problem. Also, as the negative correlation between experience and intellectual effort suggests, the more experienced leaders felt that they already knew the answers and were impatient with the task of looking for informa-

Attributes of the Training Schedules							
(Categories):							
Training Schedule	1	2	3	4	5	6	7
1	[ ]	[ ]	[ ]	[ ]	[ ]	[ ]	[ ]
2	[ ]	[ ]	[ ]	[ ]	[ ]	[ ]	[ ]
3	[ ]	[ ]	[ ]	[ ]	[ ]	[ ]	[ ]
4	[ ]	[ ]	[ ]	[ ]	[ ]	[ ]	[ ]
5	[ ]	[ ]	[ ]	[ ]	[ ]	[ ]	[ ]

Figure 3   Schematic depiction of the information board.

tion they considered unnecessary. As it turned out, they were correct, especially under the presumed pressure of time imposed by the job stress condition. Boss stress did not have a major impact on relationship between intelligence and experience and performance. By way of explanation, our military consultants

TABLE 2 Correlations of Number of Item Inspections and Re-inspections (Item Inspections) with Intelligence Measures, Time in Service (TIS) and Performance (N = 58)

Correlations between Intellectual Effort and:	Intell.	TIS	Perf.
Stress Condition			
Low Stress	.40*	− .43**	− .25
Boss Stress	.39**	− .36**	− .25
Job Stress	.46**	− .37**	− .32*

Correlations between Performance and:	Intell.	TIS
Stress Condition		
Low Stress	− .15	.14
Boss Stress	− .07	− .03
Job Stress	− .38**	.29*

*p < .05.   **p < .10.

conjectured that the boss stress condition was not very realistic. (What, after all, can happen to a senior NCO or an officer if he disagrees with a panel of experts on how to rank five military training schedules?)

In general, however, the data support the interpretations that were based on earlier findings:

1. The more intelligent the leader, the more his reliance on intellectual effort.

2. The more experienced the leader, the less his inclination to put forth intellectual effort (-.26). Negative correlations between intelligence and performance also have been reported in other decision-making contexts (Langer & Imber, 1979; Wilson & Schooler, 1991).

Locklear's (1989) study also suggests an explanation for the negative correlations between performance and experience under low stress, and between intelligence and performance under high stress. The explanation is based on the old adage that "a kid with a hammer will find that everything needs pounding." That is, we assume that the more intelligent leaders will rely on intellectual effort (as already demonstrated by the correlation between intelligence scores and number of inspected items). The more experienced leaders will rely on their extensive knowledge of "how we've always done it before." They are likely to become impatient with "yet another study" or with careful reconsideration of a problem which, in their judgment, has already been resolved. They will base their decisions on their previously acquired knowledge, skills, and policies.

Since intellectual abilities usually correlate with performance under low stress, intelligence is likely to be required under these conditions. Reliance on quick reactions and on previously learned behavior and skills is bound to interfere with finding new solutions to problems. Hence, in the information search study, the correlations between number of items inspected and intelligence were positive, while correlations with experience were negative (see Table 2). Thus, the more intelligent officers made added intellectual effort while the more experienced officers made less intellectual effort.

We also expect that experience interferes with performance when intellectual solutions are appropriate, especially from leaders endlessly drilled to react on the basis of learned behavior. Correlations between leader experience and performance measures should then be negative, as was the case in the study of fire service officers. When intellectual effort is required (as in administrative work), reliance on established routines and policies, as well as automatic reactions to problems, reduces effectiveness.

The third question posed was how to explain the contribution to performance of leaders' intellectual abilities in relatively stress-free conditions while experience contributed only under conditions of stress. One explanation is that stress tends to disrupt thinking by diverting the individual's attention from the job (Sarason, 1984), thus impeding the individual's concentration on the task. Under these conditions we try to cope by falling back on behaviors that worked before on similar problems. When situational control is low or uncertainty is high, we cannot predict the outcome. Again, using previously

successful strategies is likely to be the best solution.

The strategy of relying on experience probably is not deliberate. Learning theory (e.g., Millerson, 1967) tells us that previously learned and rewarded behaviors become dominant under conditions of stress. Social facilitation theory (Zajonc, 1965) predicts that individuals perform best on simple and overlearned tasks, but poorly on new or complex tasks, when they are observed by a critical audience. In the organizational context, a threatening boss is likely to be seen as a critical observer. The boss, therefore, also is likely to become the cause for evaluation apprehension. As these theories suggest, previously learned habits, knowledge, behaviors, and policies will then become dominant under stress. In other words, the individual under stress will fall back on previous experience in dealing with his or her problems (Berkum, 1964; Zajonc, 1965).

Success in an emergency situation calls for rapid action. An already existing pattern of emergency behavior has more survival value and is more efficient for meeting a crisis or for defending oneself against a threat than is careful intellectual analysis. Reaction to threat is exemplified by the typical bureaucratic defense against stress and uncertainty, that "We've always done it this way" or "It's the rule." Since the more experienced leaders have a larger repertoire of previously successful behaviors and policies, they are more likely than inexperienced leaders to respond in a manner that fits the particular situation.

In this connection, of particular interest is the sudden shift from intellectual effort to reactions based on experience, that is, to overlearned behavior. These shifts are dramatic and imply that the individual adopts a completely different set of behaviors and attitudes under normal conditions than under conditions of stress or uncertainty. Similar sudden shifts in behavior patterns have been observed in studies based on the contingency model when there were changes in situational control or stress (e.g., Larson & Rowland, 1973; Sample & Wilson, 1965). Therefore, as stress changes, we see major changes in leader behavior as well as performance (see Fiedler, 1972; Fiedler & Garcia, 1987).

These findings suggest that an already existing integrated emergency or "crash-plan" pattern of behavior is evoked under these conditions. This same leader must behave quite differently under stress when relying on experience to guide his or her group. We may thus have two or more different behavior patterns or repertoires as part of our personality: one for normal situations, and one for conditions with which the individual cannot cope in the usual manner. While this explanation is highly speculative, it does provide one explanation for why the leader's intellectual abilities under low stress, and experience under high stress, would correlate with leadership and organizational performance.

Personality theories have not given much consideration to the possibility that we operate with a dual system of interpersonal behavior. However, it is quite commonly seen in everyday life as reflected by, for example, the remark that someone is "a completely different person at home and at the office."

It is obvious from the literature that the topic of leadership experience has received very little attention, even though "experience," in the way the term is used in organizational life, is considered of great importance in the staffing and management of organizations. Yet our understanding of the role and function of the skills, knowledge, and behaviors gained from being in an organization, or in a particular job or profession, are rudimentary at best. Our own studies, as well as those of others (e.g., Bettin & Kennedy, 1990), show that we cannot understand leadership experience without an understanding of its relationship to intelligence or apart from such situational components as stress and uncertainty.

Summary

The foregoing data and interpretations suggest that:

1. Experience and intellectual abilities appear to fall on opposite poles of a dimension which is bounded on one end by logical, analytical, and creative thinking and on the other end by relatively automatic thought and behavior patterns acquired in the course of experience. Under most conditions, we usually use either intelligence or experience, but not both.

2. Under stress, falling back on experience may well be tantamount to adopting an integrated pattern of "crash-plan" behavior, or even an "emergency personality" which is automatically evoked by stress and uncertainty, enabling the individual to deal with high uncertainty, stress, and difficult interpersonal encounters. The effective contribution of experience depends in part on the degree to which the situation requires quick response.

3. Although not discussed in this paper, the degree to which the individual will rely on experience must depend not only on how stressful the situation appears to be, but also on the leader's vulnerability to that particular type of stress.

The present model represents a highly speculative attempt to develop a framework for understanding leadership experience, a problem which, up to now, has been virtually ignored in organizational research. The role and function of experience present a fascinating problem surely worthy of further investigation.

Acknowledgment

The research reported in this paper was funded mainly by contracts MDA 903–86–

S-0300 and MDA903–89-K-0193 (Fred E. Fiedler, Principal Investigator).

References

Berkum, M. M. (1964). Performance decrement under psychological stress. *Human Factors, 6*(1), 24–26.

Berry, J. W. (1986). A cross-cultural view of intelligence. In R. J. Sternberg & D. K. Detterman (Eds.), *What is intelligence?* (pp. 35–38). Norwood, NJ: Ablex.

Bettin, P. J., & Kennedy, J. K., Jr. (1990). Leadership experience and leader performance: Some empirical support at last. *Leadership Quarterly, 1*(4), 219–228.

Bons, P. M. (1974). *The effect of changes in leadership environment on the behavior of relationship and task-motivated leaders.* Unpublished doctoral dissertation, University of Washington, Seattle.

Borden, D. F. (1980). *Leader-boss stress, personality, job satisfaction and performance: Another look at the inter-relationship of some old constructs in the modern large bureaucracy.* Unpublished doctoral dissertation, University of Washington, Seattle.

Buck, V. E. (1963). Job pressures on managers: Sources, subjects and correlates. *Dissertation Abstracts, 24,* 2164–2165.

Fiedler, F. E. (1972). Personality, motivation systems, and behavior of high and low LPC persons. *Human Relations, 25,* 391–412.

Fiedler, F. E., & Garcia, J. E. (1987). *New approaches to effective leadership: Cognitive resources and organizational performance.* New York: Wiley.

Fiedler, F. E., McGuire, M. A., & Richardson, M. (1989). The role of intelligence and experience in successful group performance. *Journal of Applied Sport Psychology, 1*(2), 132–149.

Fiedler, F. E., Potter, E. H., III, & McGuire, M. A. (1992). Stress and effective leadership decisions. In F. A. Heller (Ed.), *Decision making and leadership* (pp. 46–57). Cambridge, England: Cambridge University Press.

Fiedler, F. E., Potter, E. H., III, Zais, M. M., & Knowlton, W., Jr. (1979). Organizational stress and the use and misuse of managerial intelligence and experience. *Journal of Applied Psychology, 64*(6), 635–647.

Frost, D. E. (1980). *The mediating effects of interpersonal stress on managerial intelligence and experience utilization.* Unpublished master's thesis, University of Washington, Seattle.

Gilbreth, F. B. (1911). *Motion studies.* New York: Van Nostrand.

Horn, J. L. (1968). Organization of abilities and the development of intelligence. *Psychological Review, 75,* 242–259.

Langer, E. J., & Imber, L. G. (1979). When practice makes perfect: Debilitating effects of overlearning. *Journal of Personality and Social Psychology, 37,* 2014–2024.

Larson, L. L., & Rowland, K. M. (1973). Leadership style, stress, and behavior in task performance. *Organizational Behavior and Human Performance, 9,* 407–420.

Lazarus, R. S. (1966). *Psychological stress and the coping process.* New York: McGraw-Hill.

Locklear, J. C. (1989). *The effects of individual intelligence and organizational experience on pre-decisional information acquisition.* Unpublished master's thesis, University of Washington, Seattle.

McKechnie, J. L. (1966). *Webster's new 20th century dictionary of the English language, unabridged.* Cleveland: World Publishing.

Millerson, J. R. (1967). *Principles of behavior analysis.* New York: Macmillan.

Payne, J. W. (1976). Task complexity and contingent processing in decision making: An information search and protocol analysis. *Organizational Behavior and Human Performance, 16,* 366–387.

Potter, E. H., & Fiedler, F. E. (1981). The utilization of staff member intelligence and experience under high and low stress. *Academy of Management Journal, 24,* 361–376.

Sample, J. A., & Wilson, T. R. (1965). Leader behavior, group productivity, and ratings of least preferred co-worker. *Journal of Personality and Social Psychology, 1,* 266–270.

Sarason, I. (1984). Stress, anxiety and cognitive interference: Reactions to tests. *Journal of Personality and Social Psychology, 46,* 929–938.

Spielberger, C. D., & Katzenmeyer, W. G. (1959). Manifest anxiety, intelligence, and college grades. *Journal of Consulting Psychology, 22*, 278.

Wilson, T. D., & Schooler, J. W. (1991). Thinking too much: Introspection can reduce the quality of preferences and decisions. *Journal of Personality and Social Psychology, 60*(2), 181–192.

Zajonc, R. R. (1965). Social facilitation. *Science, 149*, 269–274.

Fred E. Fiedler is Professor of Psychology and of Management and Organization (Adj.) and Director of the Organizational Research Group at the University of Washington. He is the author of 8 books and over 200 scientific papers on leadership and managerial performance. He was Visiting Research Fellow at Templeton College, University of Oxford, holder of the Alon Chair at the Technion, Haifa, and the first psychologist to hold the S.L.A. Marshall Chair in the Army Research Institute.

His numerous awards include the Stogdill Award for Distinguished Contributions to Leadership, appointment as Distinguished Bicentennial Lecturer at the University of Georgia, and recognition by The Fourth Annual Claremont McKenna College Leadership Conference, which was entitled "The Future of Leadership Research—A Tribute to Fred Fiedler."

He has directed numerous research grants and contracts from government agencies and private foundations, consulted for federal and local government agencies and private industry, and lectured in the U.S. and abroad. He received his PhD from the University of Chicago.

Direct inquiries about this article to Fred E. Fiedler, Professor, Organizational Research Group, Department of Psychology, University of Washington, Seattle, WA 98195, 206/543-2314.

CHAPTER 9

Strategic Leadership in a Big-City Police Department
The Philadelphia Story

Willie L. Williams, Jack R. Greene, and William T. Bergman

This report examines how the Philadelphia Police Department faced a calamitous crisis and serious adverse public criticism. It describes the various methods, both quantitative and qualitative, used to improve management and leadership behaviors and to develop useful strategic group thought processes throughout the Department. The cooperative efforts required by both the Police Department and the city of Philadelphia are outlined.

Obstacles to Strategic Leadership in American Policing

Police departments in the United States have not been reputed for their capacity to develop and/or implement long-range, carefully designed plans. Too often, tactical, short-term objectives have occupied police managers, thereby precluding long-term assessment, analysis, and long-range planning.

Many police organizations do not collect or process information in a way that can inform strategic issues. Information sharing is not commonplace in most police agencies. Commenting on the state of American policing, Egon Bittner (1970) declared that police organizations were "colossal bureaucracies of systematic information denial" (p. 64).

Several observers of American policing attribute the absence of strategic emphasis on shifting internal coalitions within police bureaucracies as the cause of struggles for power (Brown, 1985) that reduce these organizations to what Gouldner (1954) referred to as "mock bureaucracies" (cf. Manning, 1977). Power sharing is not common within police organizations; instead, they are more often characterized by rigid rank and authority systems and centralized decision making.

It is clear that police managers have not been introduced to long-range planning concepts in the course of their professional development. Rather, police training has focused on short-term issues and technical mandates.

Historically, internal cultures of many police organizations, especially big-city police departments, have been clouded by political intrigue (Bent, 1974; Brown, 1981; Manning, 1977) and a focus on present crises; they have shown the results of police training which tends to reinforce this organizational myopia (Harris, 1973). Current political, social, and criminal events, coupled with a "firefighting" predisposition, have resulted in a near absence of strategic leadership in police administrative circles (Klockars, 1985, 1988). Because police managerial training has not included course content emphasizing planning, analysis, policy evaluation, and organizational change dynamics, the here-and-now has become a general and dominant theme in police management.

Burdened by an "internal-management focus" instead of an "external-institutional focus," police chiefs around the country have deferred their strategic leadership role to the mayor or to other local elected officials. The former Superintendent of the Chicago Police Department said:

> Most chiefs fail to realize that they have a very important function as a municipal policy maker. Unaware of their opportunity to be a policy initiator, they seem to feel their policy making role is subordinate to that of the mayor. (Brzeczek, 1985, p. 49)

Generally, group decisional support for strategic leadership has been absent in American policing. Decision making has tended to be rank centered and individualized, with staff work following authoritative decisions. Decisional authority in most police agencies is monopolized by those at the top. Typically, information pertaining to strategic decisions is rarely passed up the department's organizational hierarchy: Power conflict among intermediary managers has prevailed, managers have not been taught to deal with strategic concepts, and police executives have relinquished their strategic leadership roles to elected officials outside the department. The internal group processes needed to support and develop these leadership roles are insufficient.

Strategic Absence: Past and Present Implications for Policing

The implications are far reaching when strategic focus is absent. Previously, when municipal resources were expanding, police departments could—and did—hide their inefficiencies and ineffectiveness (Greene, Bynum, & Cordner, 1986). As long as resources were available, long-term perspectives appeared unnecessary, irrelevant, or both. However, beginning in the late 1970s and increasingly throughout the 1980s, municipal revenues decreased, while municipal demand burgeoned. The demand for municipal services skyrocketed, most particularly for those associated with public safety. Now, police departments, especially those in large urban areas, find themselves being pressed to improve and increase services with far fewer resources.

Additionally, consumer emphasis in the general citizenry, emerging more stridently in the last several years, has placed many public services (e.g., health care, education, police services, etc.) under greater scrutiny. In the 1990s, strategic planning has become a necessary consideration for the police.

This report examines the development and implementation of a strategic leadership initiative within the Philadelphia Police Department. It is a study of organizational change and reformulation in the nation's fifth largest police department.

Project Methodology

The impetus for change which confronted the Philadelphia Police Department since 1986 is examined. Public perceptions of the Philadelphia Police Department, in light of several major scandals confronting the organization, are described. Data were collected by a "blue-ribbon" commission formed to obtain information about departmental policy, practices, and leadership potential. Reports by internal committees, outlining necessary changes to be accomplished within the police department, were collected. These reports highlighted external demand for police organizational reform and described what was lacking in the internal dynamics concerning case flow, organizational workload, resource utilization, etc. These were the antecedents for accepting a strategic management initiative for the Philadelphia Police Department.

Information from a department-wide survey instrument was used to examine strategic needs as perceived by top-level police managers within the Philadelphia Police Department. Current assessments of "critical success factors" and organizational strengths and weaknesses were examined to establish goals, objectives, and plans needed to accomplish the aims of this strategic leadership initiative. The analysis provided insight into how organizational leaders (past, present, and future) identify organizational needs and objectives.

Research considered the linkage between strategic leadership initiatives and other organizational changes occurring within this large, complex, big-city police department and its social and political environment. Here, the focus was on understanding the forces which contributed to or detracted from strategic leadership within this organization. The final portion of the analysis examined the linkage of strategic leadership in one city agency, the police department, with leadership in other political and administrative municipal agencies and the private sector as it affected the emphasis on strategic planning for the city as a whole.

Antecedents for Strategic Leadership Change in Philadelphia

While the Philadelphia Police Department had a rich and varied past, it had played a "backstage" and less visible role in city affairs for many years. In May of 1985, a tragic and profound event shook the foundations of Philadelphia and its police department. At 5:37 p.m. on May 13, 1985, a police lieutenant leaned from the open door of a helicopter (borrowed from the Pennsylvania State Police) and dropped a satchel containing an estimated three and one-half pounds of a military explosive on the roof of a row house in West Philadelphia.

The house had been the location of a 12-hour siege with a radical "back to nature" group called MOVE, a group that had completely alienated the local neighbors, threatened violence, and actually been involved in a violent confrontation with the Philadelphia Police Department some 8 years earlier. During the first MOVE confrontation, one Philadelphia police officer had been killed.

The ensuing fire from this explosion led to the deaths of 11 people, destroyed 61 homes, and displaced hundreds of local residents. The resulting city inquiry into the incident placed the Philadelphia Police Department under more public scrutiny than it had ever experienced in the past.

This critical incident underscored the lack of a strategic emphasis in police leadership at that time. The Department was harshly criticized; it was condemned for widespread corruption and was destined to bear the scar of the MOVE tragedy for years to come.

However, these "crises of confidence" provided the opportunity to introduce major changes into the Department, into its ways of thinking, into its structure, and into its future. This opportunity paved the way for the creation of strategic emphasis within the Philadelphia Police Department—a Community Policing emphasis which stressed, among other things, a police-citizen partnership in defining and providing public safety services.

Since January 1986, the Philadelphia Police Department has addressed such issues as improving information usage, depoliticizing decision making, improving strategic training, enhancing and increasing the aggressive stance of the Department's executive strategic leadership, and providing a vehicle for group process to inform strategic planning. Virtually none of these positive processes had been present previously in the Philadelphia Police Department.

It should be noted that two police commissioners maintained continuity throughout the strategic change procedure and provided a consistent base for reaching the stated objectives. Such continuity is considered a necessary condition to effect change in an organization steeped in traditionalism and resistant to outside interventions.

Constructing a Strategic Emphasis in Philadelphia

Since 1986, the Philadelphia Police Department has designed and implemented a strategic vision for the department, its membership, and its community. A review follows of the major strategies used to accomplish change within the organization. Empirical data to underscore these changes are presented when available. Cumulatively, these efforts have resulted in two major innovations within the Philadelphia Police Department: (a) the adoption of a Departmental Strategic Plan, the first of its kind in Philadelphia, and (b) the enhancement of an organizational capability to "think" strategically.

Philadelphia Police Study Task Force. In 1986, the Philadelphia Police Department commissioned the Philadelphia Police Study Task Force, a blue-ribbon panel of police and civic experts, to assess all aspects of the police department. Primarily, this was to become a major "stock-taking" exercise to enable the police department, city officials, and the general public to understand the resources available to the department and the goods and services produced by it and to achieve public recognition and acceptance for those goods and services. For too long the Philadelphia Police Department had functioned in a political and service-delivery vacuum, one that rarely asked the question "how are we doing?" The stock-taking findings of the Task Force were illuminating.

The Task Force made 92 recommendations for massive and far-reaching change within the Philadelphia Police Department (Philadelphia Police Study Task Force, 1987). Among its major findings, the Task Force noted that:

1. Philadelphia compared favorably to other big cities in respect to overall ratios of police officers to citizens, but overspecialization in the department had stripped it of its general capacity to respond to calls for service.

2. The Police Department was under-managed and ill-equipped in comparison to standards of common practice; police facilities were dilapidated and managerial initiative was nonexistent.

3. Performance evaluation within the department was generally lacking, and while police officer entry-level salaries were comparable to other large cities, overtime police salaries, most particularly those of managers, became noncompetitive.

4. The department enjoyed some support in the community, but that support was tempered by a community belief that the police were brutal sometimes,

drank on duty, and were themselves uncivil to citizens. This perception was more strongly held in minority communities.

Another set of assessments made by the Task Force aimed to provide strategic insight to departmental management in their role of directing the department's future for years to come. Prior to publication of *Philadelphia and its Police: Toward a New Partnership* (Philadelphia Policy Study Task Force, 1987), the Police Department had neither an explicit strategic emphasis nor a clear mission and set of organizational value statements. As the Task Force Study group noted:

> We believe that the current strategy for policing Philadelphia is deeply flawed. It is flawed not only in its technical features, but also in its overall philosophy. It results in policing that is inefficient in fighting crime; is enormously expensive in terms of money and abuses of authority; and weakens and divides the community, rather than strengthening and unifying it. This, we think, is inconsistent with Philadelphia's traditions and its current interests. (p. 30)

Strategically, then, the Philadelphia Police Department was trying to break with a past era, an era that bypassed external involvement in police department matters and that divided the police from those policed.

Community policing emphasis.

Historically, and even currently, much of police work has been associated with fighting crime. As a municipal agency, the police have come to see themselves as the sole providers of crime control activities, resulting in a long-term adversarial relationship between the police and the community. After several years of research, a new and more community-oriented role for the police has emerged in twentieth century law enforcement (Greene & Mastrofski, 1988).

Community policing challenges the police to embrace a larger public safety role and to downplay the exclusive crime-fighting role of the past. This community role is socially facilitating, in that police officers look to the community for help while supporting the efforts of the community to improve informal social control. Recognition that solutions to community problems of crime and disorder cannot rest solely on police actions has resulted in many police agencies rethinking their overall missions and operating objectives.

The need for Philadelphia to improve the community focus of the Police Department produced a revised Mission Statement and Statement of Ethical Principles early in the program. By the end of 1987, the Philadelphia Police Department had begun the process of overcoming negative public response to the MOVE incident and perceptions of corruption of many of its 6,000 officers. Perhaps for the first time, the Department and the community had two documents that made the strategy of community partnership eminently important in Philadelphia. However, the move from formal prescriptions contained in these documents to an "on-the-ground" acceptance of this strategic emphasis was yet to be accomplished.

Internal and external advisory groups.

In establishing the basis for community policing and its inherent partnership implication for civic involvement, a major component is the establishment of contacts between the police organization and its wider service environment. Creating a vision for the organization and its constituents is an important aspect of strategic management and a crucial task of the chief executive (Reiss, 1985).

An outcome of the Police Task Force Study Group and its subsequent assessment of the Philadelphia Police Department was the establishment of an external Police Commissioner's Advisory Group to provide advice and counsel to the Police Commissioner about strategic purposes. This Advisory Group, composed of business, civic, and religious leaders, assisted the Department throughout 1986 and into 1987 in crafting a strategic vision; it provided a sounding board for proposed strategic changes within the police department. With the expertise of this Advisory Group, responses to proposed changes were marshalled, and subsidiary technical assistance was acquired. In its early stages (1986–87), the Commissioner's Advisory Group was concerned primarily with creating a supportive external environment.

In addition to this high-level policy group, smaller Neighborhood Advisory Councils (NACs) were created in each of Philadelphia's 23 patrol districts. The NACs made local district commanders more directly accountable to the citizens and businesses served. They provided linkage between producer and customer to: (a) improve relations between the two groups, (b) provide better "market" assessment of community wants and needs, and (c) focus local commanders on the larger questions of purpose within their immediate commands as well as within the department at large.

In 1989, each NAC prepared a "State of the Community Report" to explicate the level of service delivery and community demand for police services; each began the process of building informational flow and strategic planning from the grassroots level upward throughout the police department. These reports gave residents and businesses a stake in and an understanding of the future of police services in their immediate neighborhoods while providing grist for crafting a departmental strategic plan.

Strategic Emphasis Programs, Police Executive Research Forum, Kennedy School, and Temple University

It was important to change the internal learning curve of the managerial corps within the Philadelphia Police Depart-

ment. This was the most prolonged process due to the underdeveloped state of managerial and leadership training afforded police executives in Philadelphia prior to 1986. Some commanders had pursued training and education independently, but there had been no systematic effort by the Department to upgrade its managerial personnel in these areas.

By 1987 and throughout 1989, the leadership of the Department financed the first of several "brain-trust" developments, sending nearly 100 managerial personnel to two independent executive-level managerial training programs. The first was a program conducted under the auspices of the Police Executive Research Forum and the Kennedy School of Government at Harvard University. Groups of Philadelphia police managers and executives were sequestered for up to 3 weeks while Harvard faculty schooled them in a business, case-study approach to management. Upon their return to the Department, these police managers and executives were somewhat better prepared to address the big picture within the Department.

The initial Harvard training program had a more indirect than direct effect on the managerial culture of the Philadelphia Police Department. For many reasons, several of these "new leaders" were not strategically placed in the organization upon their return to Philadelphia. Consequently, their ability to implement what they had been taught at Harvard was somewhat diminished. Nonetheless, the Harvard program established a common identity and jargon for this newly emerging managerial class within the Department. At the time of this writing, these new leaders were ascending to positions of leadership and responsibility in the Philadelphia Police Department. Their passage through Harvard had left its stamp. Perhaps for the first time in their managerial careers, they began to see strategic issues as central to their roles.

In early 1989, another executive-level training program was germinating at

Temple University in Philadelphia. By 1990, the Public Service Management Institute was up and running, seeded with persons identified as on "the fast track." The Temple program, similar to the program designed at Harvard, had several distinguishing features. First and foremost, the Temple program was designed from the onset to produce a strategic plan by introducing group decisional processes into the Police Department. Discussion follows on widespread management group involvement in the crafting of the Department's first strategic plan, which went a long way to facilitating its internal acceptance. Furthermore, the developmental process used in Temple's Public Service Management Institute aided the Department in better grounding an internal capacity to conduct similar planning exercises in the future.

Internal feedback from command staff. To produce a strategic plan for the Philadelphia Police Department, an internal "needs assessment" was created. It was designed to involve police command personnel throughout the organization in taking stock and identifying critical success factors, key elements to future police department survival. An organizational questionnaire was sent to 195 command officers, 94 of which were completed and returned. The response rate was disappointing inasmuch as wider organizational participation was sought for this aspect of the project. Nonetheless, as anonymity was assured and subsequent general requests for additional responses were exhausted, the 48% response rate was used as the basis for analysis.

While several areas were identified for assessment in the organizational questionnaire, three areas are briefly considered: (a) organizational "critical success factors," or those things that the police department needed to do to become an excellent police agency; (b) the five most apparent organizational strengths; and (c) the five most apparent organizational weaknesses. Tables 1 through 3 provide

the rank ordering of these responses, from the most to the least mentioned items.

As can be seen in Table 1, many of the highest-ranked items for future success were expressed as traditional police needs, including preventing crime, apprehending criminals, and providing better training, equipment, and facilities. Importantly, however, several "new" ideas were also presented. For example, police commanders also identified responsiveness to the community, maintenance of high ethical standards, and increasing a "valid" partnership between the police and the community within their 120 top ranked items.

Table 2 provides some insight into how these same commanders viewed departmental strengths, presumably those things the department would build on in the future. As shown in Table 2, the Police Department was seen as a "can do" organization: Despite perceived adversity, departmental personnel would "get the job done." In fact, most of the items mentioned in Table 2 indicate that departmental commanders viewed personnel as their strongest asset.

Commanders were asked not only their impressions of departmental strengths, they were also asked about departmental weaknesses. Table 3, which presents the rank ordering of their responses to this question, shows commanders as likely to negatively evaluate internal management and "political interference with the department" as the greatest limiting factors to the Department. These commanders were more negative about the capacity of the Department's management to provide the strategic leadership needed to move the Department into the twenty-first century.

Creation of a Strategic Plan

The formal creation of the Philadelphia Police Department's Strategic Plan contributed to institutionalizing strategic planning and analysis in the Police De-

TABLE 1 Things the Department Must Do Well

Ensure all personnel are well trained.

Police department must be responsive to the community.

Prevent crime and apprehend criminals.

Implement an effective strategy against the use of illegal drugs through enforcement and public education.

Upgrade and maintain equipment and facilities, and train personnel in the use and care of equipment.

Ensure effective response time to crimes-in-progress and emergencies.

Expand our use of technology and automation.

Maintain high ethical standards.

Ensure a valid partnership between police and community.

Manage our resources more efficiently.

Reduce the fear of crime.

Ensure professional attitude, appearance, and demeanor of our personnel, through improved training, 1st line supervision and discipline.

Recruit those persons most qualified for the job.

Improve the public image of the Department.

Recruitment of personnel must be fair and effective.

Ensure that we can apprehend criminals through investigation.

Increase our ability to analyze data to improve efficient use of resources and solve community problems.

TABLE 2 Strengths of the Department

Police Department personnel are innovative, dedicated, talented, ''can do'' under adverse conditions.

Personnel endorse Community policing and desire to have community support.

Lieutenants, Captains, and Inspectors distinguish themselves as quality leaders.

There is good opportunity for management training, especially by the Career Services Division.

The Department is committed towards improving technology.

Morale is at a high level.

We enjoy good media relations and the self-image of the Department and personnel is improving.

Strengths of special units.

We are good at enforcing laws against drugs.

We have good promotional policies.

WILLIAMS, GREENE, AND BERGMAN

TABLE 3 Internal Weaknesses of the Department

There is a lack and poor condition of equipment and facilities.

There is a failure to communicate within the Department.

There are inadequate recruitment and hiring standards.

Personnel are often deployed on basis of politics or "special interest groups."

Personnel are poorly deployed for best use.

Lack of valid criteria for placing "best person" in the "right job."

The Department has insufficient personnel.

There is a lack of quality in many first-line supervisors.

Money is unavailable in the budget.

Often there is much intra-Department politics and infighting.

---

partment and to highlighting the strategic leadership role of the organization's executive corps. The ongoing project has as its central objectives: (a) the creation of a public-police partnership for the purpose of establishing a city-wide strategic vision for public safety services in Philadelphia, and (b) the implementation of a strategic leadership initiative within the Philadelphia Police Department.

The project involved three functioning groups created to address aspects of strategic analysis in the Philadelphia Police Department and to increase police and public interaction in shaping this strategic initiative. The first group, the Commissioner's Strategic Advisory Committee, an outgrowth of the Commissioner's Advisory Committee originally created in 1987, is composed of 13 representatives of the corporate, civic, and religious communities within Philadelphia. It was established in September 1990 as a governing and reference board to review and comment on strategic initiatives within the Philadelphia Police Department. These persons, identified as major civic stakeholders and representative of many cultural and ethnic interests within the City of Philadelphia, were directly involved in the creation of a Strategic Plan from the very inception of the project.

A second group, the Strategic Planning Group, is composed of 14 representatives of the Philadelphia Police Department, reflecting the major divisions of the Department. Its intensive involvement from the onset of the program has focused on creating a strategic plan overseen by the Commissioner's Strategic Advisory Committee. These internal stakeholders also reflect cultural and ethnic diversity within the Police Department.

A third group of 35 senior-level police managers, including racial minorities and females, became staff to the Advisory Committee and the Planning Group. They participated in a Public Service Management Institute intensified training and policy assessment program, conducted by Temple University from September through December of 1990, which proved to be an excellent vehicle for extending participation in the Department's first Strategic Plan.

A series of conferences, meetings, and planning sessions was held between September 1990 and March 1991 to craft a Police Department Strategic Plan approved by all concerned groups participating in this project. Their recommendations formed the basis of the Police Commissioner's 1991 Strategic Plan. The project involved:

1. The Strategic Advisory Committee met with the Police Commissioner and the Strategic Planning Group to frame the future of the Police Department within the City's development to provide a "public grounding" for subsequent efforts.

2. Using data from a department-wide survey instrument, the Advisory Committee and the Planning Group examined strategic needs as perceived by top-level police managers within the Philadelphia Police Department. They examined and explained current assessments of "critical success factors," organizational strengths and weaknesses, and the resulting goals, objectives, and strategies deemed necessary to accomplish the aims of this strategic leadership initiative.

3. As final framing of the Strategic Plan, Strategic Advisory Committee members were identified as "mentors" for subgroups of police managers staffing the project. In this way, civic contact was maintained through all levels of planning and strategic design.

Coordination of program information was maintained through a series of "overlapping committees." These committees helped assure that all members of the Commissioner's Strategic Planning Committee, the Strategic Planning Group, and the participants in the Public Service Management Institute were informed of the other's actions and advice. Face-to-face meetings between the Advisory Committee and the Planning Group occurred in 4- to 6-week intervals. Draft materials from all discussions were circulated widely to all participants, and the Police Commissioner's Executive Officer served as the primary contact and information conduit throughout the project. As a result, a constant focus on open communications and feedback was maintained.

This project was consensually based. Nearly 6 months of intensive planning, group-based discussion, community mentoring of police planning groups, as well as the circulation of numerous drafts of goals, objectives, and strategies, resulted in a Strategic Plan composed of 5 goals, 30 objectives, and 80 strategies. The refinement of goals, objectives, and strategies had at least three levels of review, each involving representatives of the advisory and planning groups. Stakeholders in the Commissioner's Strategic Advisory Committee ultimately approved the Strategic Plan and forwarded it to the Police Commissioner, a process which involved several levels of decision making. Within and across each of the strategic planning and advisory groups, decisions pertaining to departmental initiatives, priorities, and objectives were group based.

Strategic Leadership in Police Organizations: A Final Comment

This is a report of a strategic "course correction" within the Philadelphia Police Department. The reader should understand that this dramatic change took time and met with various forms of internal and external resistance. The changes in strategic emphasis within the Department have, to this point, taken nearly 5 years to accomplish, and much remains to be done. Changing the philosophy and operating processes within a large-scale public bureaucracy is not an easy task. Internal coalitions must be won over, territorial behavior must be reduced, and individuals must be prepared for their changing roles. This resulted in the need to revamp the entire organizational culture.

If such results are to be achieved, police-agency leaders confronted with such circumstances must "take the reins" of the organization in two fundamental ways. The leader must create an internal and external climate that minimally produces less resistance for change and maximally supports those change efforts. In Philadelphia, the Commissioner's Advisory Committee, the Neighborhood Advisory Committees, and the internal Strategic Planning Group proved to be invaluable in beginning the process for strategic change within the organization.

We learned in Philadelphia that many of the changes anticipated were intertwined with other changes; achieving strategic redirection required simultaneously pursuing other fundamental changes in the organization. For success to be realized in Philadelphia, it was necessary to provide better training, to implement and encourage group and nominal decision making, and to expand organizational learning systems for capturing strategically valuable information.

Finally, our experiences in Philadelphia suggest that in undertaking strategic changes, a fundamental role for the chief executive is to provide a strong linkage with other municipal, political, and administrative policy makers. We found that institutional leadership requires a strong environmental orientation, an orientation that places internal police department reform on the agenda of many organizations and individuals outside of the police department.

References

Bent, A. E. (1974). *The politics of law enforcement*. Lexington, MA: D.C. Heath.

Bittner, E. (1970). *The functions of police in modern society*. Chevy Chase, MD: National Institute of Mental Health.

Brown, L. (1985). Police-community power sharing. In W. A. Geller (Ed.), *Police leadership in America* (pp. 70–83). New York: Praeger.

Brown, M. (1981). *Working the street*. New York: Russell Sage.

Brzeczek, R. J. (1985). Chief-mayor relations: The view from the chief's chair. In W. A. Geller (Ed.), *Police leadership in America* (pp. 48–55). New York: Praeger.

Eden, C., & Radford, J. (Eds.). (1990). *Tackling strategic problems: The role of group decision support*. Newbury Park, CA: Sage.

Gouldner, A. (1954). *Patterns of industrial bureaucracy*. New York: Free Press.

Greene, J. R., Bynum, T., & Cordner, G. W. (1986). Planning and the play of power: Resource acquisition and use among criminal justice agencies. *Journal of Criminal Justice, 14,* 6.

Greene, J. R., & Mastrofski, S. (Eds.). (1988). *Community policing: Rhetoric and reality*. New York: Praeger.

Harris, R. N. (1973). *The police academy: An inside view*. New York: Wiley.

Klockars, C. (1985). Order maintenance, the quality of urban life, and police: A different line of argument. In W. A. Geller (Ed.), *Police leadership in America* (pp. 309–321). New York: Praeger.

Klockars, C. (1988). The rhetoric of community policing. In J. R. Greene & S. Mastrofski (Eds.), *Community policing: Rhetoric and reality* (pp. 239–258). New York: Praeger.

Manning, P. (1977). *Police work: The social organization of policing*. Cambridge, MA: MIT Press.

Philadelphia Police Study Task Force. (1987). *Philadelphia and its police: Toward a new partnership*. Philadelphia: Philadelphia Police Department.

Reiss, A. J., Jr. (1985). Shaping and serving the community: The role of the police chief executive. In W. A. Geller (Ed.), *Police leadership in America* (pp. 61–69). New York: Praeger.

Willie L. Williams is Police Chief of the Los Angeles Police Department, the nation's 3rd largest police department. He was formerly the Police Commissioner in Philadelphia, where he oversaw the operations of the largest, most visible arm of Philadelphia's municipal government, which employs nearly 8,500 sworn police officers and civilian personnel. He began implementation of strategic planning and community-oriented policing city-wide in Philadelphia in 1989.

Jack R. Greene, PhD, is the Director of Temple University's Center for Public Policy, a multidisciplinary institution for the design and implementation of public policy. He has conducted research and published extensively on matters pertaining to the police. His most recent book, *Community Policing: Rhetoric and Reality* (1988), examines a major institutional change occurring in law enforcement. He is a regular consultant to several police agencies and recently has been assisting the National Police College of Sweden and the Sao Paulo State Police in Brazil.

William T. Bergman, Chief Inspector and Commander of the Philadelphia Police Department's Detective Bureau, has been responsible for implementing strategic change within the police department. Currently, he is introducing victims' assistance and community-oriented policing into the department's investigative services. He received his Master's Degree from St. Joseph's University and regularly teaches for Temple University and the Federal Law Enforcement Training Center.

Direct inquiries about this article to Jack R. Greene, Director, Center for Public Policy, 10th Floor, Gladfelter Hall, Temple University, Philadelphia, PA 19122, 215/787–6696.

The Impact of Managerial Behaviors on Group Performance, Stress, and Commitment

**Frank Shipper and
Clark L. Wilson**

The impact of managerial behaviors on group performance, stress, and commitment are investigated through a longitudinal study. Industrial engineering measures are used to assess performance. The results indicate that work units with high performance, high commitment, and low tension are associated with managers with a developed set of behaviors.

The impetus for this paper comes from three sources. First, a collection of articles on stress in the work place appeared in the October 1990 issue of the *American Psychologist*. In one article, the authors tried to distinguish between avoidable and unavoidable work-related stresses (Keita & Jones, 1990). One stressor labeled as "unavoidable" is "poor management." Certainly, one would agree that probably most individuals will encounter "poor management" sometime in their career, but to label it as "unavoidable" appears unwarranted. In another article in this collection, the need for research on reducing the stress in the work place was advanced (Levi, 1990). Thus, this paper investigates the impact of management on employee stress and how improvements in managerial behaviors alleviate stress.

The second source is a series of articles which appeared in the popular press. One particularly riveting article, which appeared in *The Wall Street Journal* (Winokur, 1991), identified the immediate manager as the most stressful aspect of the job. Other articles of interest have appeared in *The New York Times* (Kagay, 1988) and *Newsweek* (Miller, 1988). Miller's article also identified the supervisor as the major source of stress in the work environment and went on to estimate that stress costs industry $18 billion per year. Such information leads one to the logical conclusion that direct interventions should be taken to alleviate the problem and not accept it as unavoidable.

The third source is two articles by Jamal (1984, 1985) and one by Shipper and Neck (1990). In the first two articles, Jamal investigated the relationship between stress and performance. Two competing models of stress and performance—Yerkes-Dodson (1908) and Meglino (1977)—hypothesize respectively that either (a) some amount of stress is required to activate behavior or (b) stresses represent challenges for improved performance. Jamal's studies, however, found a negative linear relationship between performance and stress, which contradicts both models. Findings in Shipper and Neck's study of managerial skills support the hypothesis that stress and performance are inversely related. In addition, their study suggests that improvements in managerial skills could result in improvements in performance. Jamal also found that the relationship between stress and performance is moderated by organizational commitment.

Thus, a study to investigate the relationships among management, stress, performance, and organizational commitment appeared warranted. Specifically, this study investigates (a) the relationships between management and performance, stress, and commitment; (b) the relationships between performance and commitment and stress; (c) the relationship between stress and commitment; and (d) the relationships among management, performance, and stress.

Methodology

The study was conducted in a large southwestern hospital administered by a governmental agency. The hospital is divided into approximately 15 different divisions. The size of the subunits varies from 2 to 34. All subunits of the hospital were included in the study. Due to the lack of performance data for a number of subunits, including all the administrative staff subunits, only 68 subunits were available for analysis when performance is used as a variable.

Measures and Procedures

The procedure used for collecting the longitudinal observational data of managerial behaviors was a structured questionnaire. Distributed to all employees, it asked for their observations of their superior's behavior and their levels of stress and commitment. Empirically, the use of subordinate observations could avoid the introduction of inaccuracies due to biases associated with self-observations (Tubbs, 1986). Furthermore, subordinate observations have been found previously to be more discriminatory than either self or superior observations relative to effectiveness (Wilson, O'Hare, & Shipper, 1990). Theoretically, subordinates normally have more opportunities to observe the array of managerial behaviors of interest in this study than do superiors (Bernardin, 1987). In addition, a manager's behavior may change depending on whether the observer is the superior or the subordinate.

A researcher administered the questionnaire twice to employees in their work areas at approximately a 1-year interval. The administrator was identified to the employees as being connected with a large southwestern university. The purpose of the study and questionnaire was explained to the employees, who were then given an opportunity to ask questions. They were assured that the administration was anonymous; the only identifying mark on the questionnaire was the title of the manager of the subunit.

The two-part questionnaire consisted of Wilson's Survey of Management Practices—Form J (Wilson & Wilson,

1991), to measure a set of managerial behaviors. The first part is a structured observation form of managerial behaviors, and the second part is an attitudinal questionnaire. Morrison, McCall, and DeVries (1978) rated an earlier form (Form G) to be one of the 3 best of 24 managerial behavior instruments reviewed. The instruments were reviewed on, among other criteria, linkage to theory and research as well as psychometric properties. In addition, Koser and Lussier (1987), Morrison et al., and Summers (1991) have found the instrument to contain a comprehensive inventory of managerial behaviors. The questionnaire has been examined previously for test-retest reliability, internal consistency, interrater reliability, construct validity, and criterion validity (Wilson, 1975, 1978). All scales have been reported in prior studies to exceed Nunnally's (1978) criteria for reliability in exploratory research. All scales were retested for internal consistency in this study and again found to exceed Nunnally's criteria. Since the level of analysis for this study was the subunit, the average score for all individuals who responded to the questionnaire within a subunit was used as the measure for each scale. Such aggregation is appropriate at the subunit level of analysis because it reduces random error and perceptual differences among respondents (Campion, 1988).

Due to the nature of this study, the criterion data were gathered from two sources. Additionally, the use of multiple criterion measures complies with prior suggestions that multiple measures are appropriate (Hitt, Ireland, Keats, & Vianna, 1983; Nicholas & Katz, 1985). Nicholas and Katz advocate the use of "hard criteria" such as worker behavior, productivity, or profitability as well as "soft criteria" such as attitudinal and perceptual measures. Hitt et al. found that subunit effectiveness was best represented by multiple criteria reflective of multiple constituents. Thus, the use of measures of subunit productivity, stress, and commitment integrates the multiple constituents

perspective with the hard versus soft criterion position.

Productivity was measured using standard industrial engineering procedures. The figure used in this study was for the year preceding each administration of the questionnaire. A full year's figure was felt to be more representative of the managers' skills, since one skill of interest was planning. Although the data were gathered at both the first and second administrations, the number of managers traced in the same positions was too low for meaningful interpretation.

Commitment and tension were measured by 6-item and 5-item Likert scales in the second part of Wilson's questionnaire. Cronbach's alpha for these scales in this hospital was .90 and .79, respectively. These alphas compared favorably with those previously reported (Wilson, 1978). As with all other measures, the average score for all individuals within a subunit who completed the scales was used as the measure for subunit commitment and tension.

Analysis

The analysis was performed in four ways. The first analysis was an examination of the zero-order Pearson correlations among performance, tension, and commitment to examine for agreement with prior research.

The second analysis was a set of zero-order Pearson correlations between each of the behavioral scales and performance, tension, or commitment. This analysis was undertaken to find the degree of association between each of the managerial behaviors and either the performance, tension, or commitment of the work unit.

The third analysis was a set of dynamic zero-order Pearson correlations which measures the degree of association among changes in the managerial behaviors and changes in either tension or commitment. This analysis was undertaken to examine the degree of association between changes in each of the managerial behaviors and tension and commitment.

The fourth analysis was a two-step procedure. The first step was an oblique cluster analysis of the managerial behavior scales. This analysis was undertaken to find if managers with distinct patterns of behavior could be identified. Oblique cluster analysis was used due to its ability to replace a larger set of variables with a smaller set of cluster components with little loss of information. In addition, oblique cluster analysis has a commonly accepted criterion, eigenvalue greater than one, for determining the appropriate number of clusters (SAS User's Guide: Statistics, 1982). Once the individual clusters were identified, they were tested to determine the association of different patterns of managerial behaviors with differences in subunit performance, commitment, and tension using Duncan's multiple range test.

Results

In the first set of zero-order Pearson correlations, a negative relationship was found between performance and tension, a positive relationship between performance and commitment, and a negative relationship between commitment and tension (see Table 1). The directions of these correlations were as one would expect from Jamal's (1984, 1985) and Shipper and Neck's (1990) research. The magnitude of the first correlation was similar to that reported by Jamal. The magnitudes of the second and third correlations, however, were considerably stronger. The relationship between performance and tension was examined for curvilinearity. No support was found for such a relationship.

The results from the static, zero-order Pearson correlations between each managerial behavior and either performance, tension, or commitment show that rela-

TABLE 1 Static Correlations among Performance, Tension, and Commitment

	Performance	Tension
Tension	r = − .17 p = .094 n = 61	
Commitment	r = .29 p = .012 n = 61	r = − .65 p = .000 n = 84

tionships do exist between the behaviors and either performance, tension, or commitment (see Table 2). With the exception of goal pressure, all behaviors were positively and significantly associated with performance. Goal pressure, the degree of coercion a manager uses with an employee to obtain performance, was neither positively nor negatively significantly associated with performance. In contrast, all the behaviors except for goal pressure were negatively associated with tension. Goal pressure was positively and significantly associated with tension. Relative to commitment, the pattern of signs reverted to the same pattern as for performance. Goal pressure, however, was significantly and negatively related to commitment. These results parallel prior findings which compared the use of managerial behaviors by managers of high- and low-performing subunits (Shipper, 1991).

The dynamic correlations between changes in each managerial behavior and changes in either tension or commitment over a 1-year period are shown in Table 3. The pattern of the direction of the relationships followed exactly the pattern found in the static correlations. The relationships between change in tension and change in either time emphasis, control of details, or delegation/permissiveness were, however, nonsignificant. Similarly, the relationship between a change in goal

TABLE 2 Static Correlations between Managerial Behaviors and
Performance, Tension, and Commitment

Scales	Performance n = 61	Tension n = 85	Commitment n = 84
Making goals clear and important	r = .36 p = .002	− .59 .000	.58 .000
Upward communication and participation	.28 .02	− .54 .000	.53 .000
Orderly work planning	.38 .001	− .55 .000	.50 .000
Expertise	.38 .001	− .64 .000	.56 .000
Facilitating work of others	.32 .007	− .59 .000	.56 .000
Providing feedback	.39 .001	− .59 .000	.59 .000
Time emphasis	.46 .000	− .31 .002	.44 .000
Control of details	.33 .004	− .24 .01	.36 .000
Goal pressure	.06 N/S	.49 .000	− .22 .02
Delegation/ Permissiveness	.22 .05	− .48 .000	.45 .000
Recognition for good performance	.36 .002	− .58 .000	.61 .000

pressure and a change in commitment was nonsignificant.

The oblique cluster analysis yielded a two-equation, four-cluster solution using eigenvalue greater than one as the criterion for determining the number of clusters. The equations are reported in Table 4. The two equations for assigning managers to clusters were examined to figure out the underlying dimensions. The first equation appeared to represent instrumental behaviors because the scales for goal setting, communication, planning, expertise, facilitation, feedback, delegation, and recognition loaded on it. Instrumental managerial behaviors are those employed by a manager which facilitate the accomplishment of objectives with the least expense of human or other capital resources. The second equation appeared to represent controlling skills because time emphasis, control of details, and goal pressure loaded on it.

Correlations between the cluster scores and performance, tension, and commitment were analyzed. The correlations be-

TABLE 3 Dynamic Correlations between Managerial Behaviors and Performance, Tension, and Commitment

Scales	Tension n = 46	Commitment n = 46
Making goals clear and important	r = .36 p = .008	.41 .003
Upward communication and participation	− .26 .044	.27 .036
Orderly work planning	− .42 .002	.34 .010
Expertise	− .44 .001	.45 .001
Facilitating work of others	− .42 .002	.43 .001
Providing feedback	− .38 .005	.40 .003
Time emphasis	− .17 N/S	.45 .001
Control of details	− .19 N/S	.37 .005
Goal pressure	.33 .012	− .18 N/S
Delegation/Permissiveness	− .18 N/S	.28 .03
Recognition for good performance	− .39 .005	.36 .007

tween the cluster equations and performance, tension, and commitment are reported in Table 5. The scores for both cluster equations correlated positively with performance and commitment. In contrast, the scores for both equations correlated negatively with tension.

The standardized cluster equations were then used to assign managers to clusters (see Figure 1) and to test if managers with different behavioral patterns have significantly different unit performance, tension, and/or commitment (see Table 6). The differences between clusters were tested using Duncan's multiple range test with a significance level of .05. The results show that the only managers whose unit performance was significantly different were those who exhibited high use of both instrumental and controlling behaviors. In addition, with one exception, managers who exhibited high instrumental behaviors had significantly higher commitment and significantly lower tension in their units than managers who exhibited a low competency on these behav-

TABLE 4 Standardized Coefficients of Oblique Cluster Analysis

Equations:	1	2
1. Goal Setting	.140	.000
2. Upward Communication	.139	.000
3. Orderly Planning	.136	.000
4. Expertise	.137	.000
5. Facilitation	.140	.000
6. Providing Feedback	.140	.000
7. Time Emphasis	.000	.489
8. Control of Details	.000	.515
9. Goal Pressure	.000	.247
10. Delegation	.118	.000
11. Recognition	.139	.000

iors. No significant difference was found for the difference in commitment levels of the units with managers high on instrumental behaviors and low on controlling behaviors versus those managers who exhibited high controlling behaviors and low instrumental behaviors. One possible explanation for the later finding is that the sample sizes for these two groups were small, 11 and 12 respectively.

TABLE 5 Pearson, Zero-Order Correlations between Performance, Tension, and Commitment, and Cluster Scores

Equations:		1	2
1. Performance	r	.38	.45
	n	61	61
	p	.001	.000
2. Tension	r	− .62	− .16
	n	85	85
	p	.000	.075
3. Commitment	r	.60	.35
	n	84	84
	p	.000	.001

Discussion

The results of the first analysis support Jamal's (1984, 1985) work on a negative, linear relationship between performance and stress. The only differences between this study and Jamal's work on the relationships between performance, stress, and commitment is one of magnitude and not direction. These differences could easily occur due to differences in populations, measures, and analysis. This analysis was done at the subunit level of analysis whereas Jamal's analysis was performed at the individual level of analysis. Taken together, the results from both studies suggest that stress is a detriment to both performance and organizational commitment.

The second set of static correlations indicates that managerial behaviors, except for goal pressure, may be important determinants of performance, tension, and commitment. Wilson et al. (1990) theorized that the response of the subordinates, both behavioral and attitudinal, to managerial behaviors is more a function of the pattern of behaviors than of any one managerial behavior. In a comparative study, goal pressure was not significantly different for managers of high- versus low-performing subunits, whereas all the other behaviors were significantly different (Shipper, 1991).

The dynamic correlations indicate that an improvement in managerial behaviors is likely to be significantly associated with both a decrease in tension and an increase in commitment, with a few exceptions. The few exceptions appear to be more a function of sample size than whether the relationships exist.

The results from the scores of the cluster equation loaded with instrumental behaviors are supportive of earlier findings. The correlations with the scores from the equation loaded with controlling behaviors might appear at first glance to contradict the earlier results. Interviews with groups of employees, however, explained

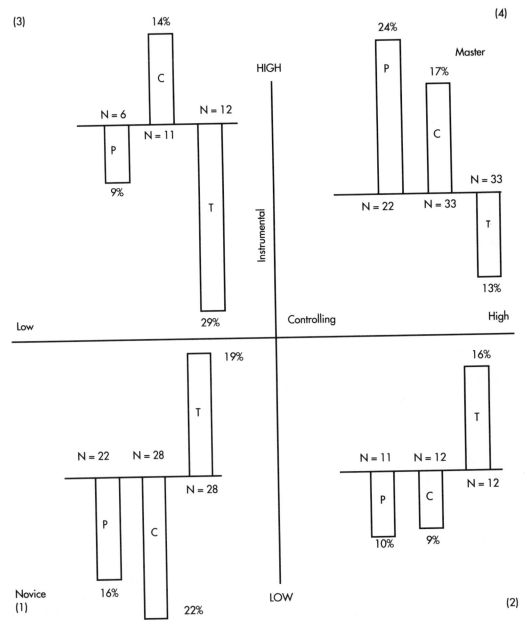

Figure 1 Managerial behaviors matrix—Performance (P), Commitment (C), and Tension (T).

these results. First, the use of goal pressure had the lowest coefficient of the three behaviors. Second, employees approved the selective use of goal pressure on non-productive members of their work units, especially when they had known all along what was expected of them. The employees went on to say that emphasizing when the work was to be done was appreciated.

To them, the best surprise was no surprise. Even a manager who was aware of the performance-related details was seen as beneficial. As one employee said, "No one skates," meaning that if an employee was doing a superficial job, the manager would inform the employee. The underlying issue to many of their comments was that the selective use of control on those

TABLE 6   Results from Duncan's Multiple Range Tests

Quadrants	1	2	3	4
1. Performance	− 16%	− 10%	− 9%	24%
2. Tension	19%	16%	− 29%	− 13%
3. Commitment	− 22%	− 9%	14%	17%

Note. Means with a common solid line are significantly different (p ≤ .05) from means with a common dotted line.

not performing was not only accepted, but appreciated, by the performers in the group. They saw such use of control as only fair. Thus, the appropriate use of control improved commitment, lessened tension, and improved performance.

The results from the managers with similar behavioral patterns suggest that only those managers with a balance of skills can have units with high performance, low tension, and high commitment. In other words, to have such a work unit, a manager must master both the controlling and the instrumental behaviors.

This study is also in agreement with Hogan's estimate that between 60% and 75% of current managers are incompetent (Winokur, 1991). In this study, 61% of the managers did not exhibit the appropriate managerial behaviors which would classify them in the mastery quadrant in Figure 1. Collectively, these findings have implications relative to the competitiveness of both the organization and the economy. Assuming that (a) Hogan's low estimate that 60% of the managers in the domestic economy are incompetent, (b) the average competent manager outproduces the incompetent by 24%, and (c) the domestic corporate gross national product for 1990 was $3,086.4 billion (Bureau of Economic Analysis, 1991), the cost of incompetent managers to the domestic corporate economy in 1990 was $676 billion.

Limitations of the Study

One limitation of this study is its inability to show that a change in managerial behavior is associated with a change in performance. Due to organizational turbulence, this study was unable to track a sufficient number of managers in work units with hard performance data for the 2-year period. The attrition rate of managers occupying the same position during the period of this study was 46%.

A second limitation of this study is that the analysis did not test directly for the interplay among the variables. Jamal (1985) demonstrated that organizational commitment may be a moderator between performance and stress. In future research, additional conceptual formulation and statistical testing of possible interactions among the variables will need to be done.

A third limitation of this study is that only relationships and degree of association were investigated. None of the analyses demonstrated a causal relationship.

Additional work and analyses need to be performed to establish the causal relationships among managerial skills, stress, and commitment. Only when this work is done can some of the criticisms of managerial studies by Davis and Luthans (1979) and Morrison et al. (1978) be laid to rest.

A fourth limitation is the generalizability of this study. As mentioned previously, this study was conducted in one hospital over a 2-year period. The period coincided with an interval of budget cuts that might have placed a premium on the need for superior management skills. Whether the same degree of skill of all behaviors would be needed for success in another organization is unknown. Subsequent studies in three other organizations in two other industries have found similar results.

Conclusions

This study clearly demonstrates that managerial behaviors relate to performance as well as to the commitment and tension felt by employees, as shown in Figure 1. Along with other studies cited, this study indicates that managers with an undeveloped set of managerial behaviors are very costly. In addition, this study suggests that improvements in managerial behaviors will be associated with increased employee commitment and performance and decreased tension. This study also suggests that organizations and employees can have it all — improved performance, improved commitment, and decreased tension. The key to such changes is an improved set of managerial behaviors. This study also supports Wilson and Shipper's (1990) contentions that (a) managerial behaviors are interactive in determining organizational success and (b) a balance of managerial behaviors is needed to optimize the success of a work unit.

Additional work is needed to test directly for cause and effect relationships between managerial behaviors and performance, commitment, and tension. In addition, work needs to be done on how the different behaviors interact to lead to the success of the work unit and to determine if and how managers can best improve their behaviors. Finally, additional work needs to be done to understand when and how control can be exercised effectively.

References

Bernardin, H. J. (1987). Can subordinate appraisals enhance managerial productivity? *Sloan Management Review, 30,* 63–73.

Bureau of Economic Analysis (1991, February). *Survey of current business.* Washington, DC: U.S. Government Printing Office.

Campion, H. J. (1988). Interdisciplinary approaches to job design: A constructive replication with extensions. *Journal of Applied Psychology, 73,* 467–481.

Davis, T. R. V., & Luthans, F. (1979). Leadership reexamined: A behavioral approach. *Academy of Management Review, 4,* 237–248.

Hitt, M. A., Ireland, R. D., Keats, B. W., & Vianna, A. (1983). Measuring subunit performance. *Decision Science, 14*(1), 87–102.

Jamal, M. (1984). Job stress and job performance controversy: An empirical examination. *Organizational Behavior and Human Performance, 33,* 1–21.

Jamal, M. (1985). Relationship of job stress to job performance: A study of managers and blue-collar workers. *Human Relations, 38,* 409–424.

Kagay, M. R. (1988, June 14). Workers want their employers to listen to them, survey shows. *The New York Times,* p. A25.

Keita, G. P., & Jones, J. M. (1990). Reducing adverse reaction to stress in the workplace: Psychology's expanding role. *American Psychologist, 45,* 1137–1141.

Koser, K., & Lussier, R. R. (1987). *A summary of the research related to middle management.* Long Beach, CA: Veterans Administration Medical Center.

Levi, L. (1990). Occupational stress: Spice of life or kiss of death? *American Psychologist*, 45, 1142–1145.

Meglino, B. M. (1977). Stress and performance: Are they always incompatible? *Supervisory Management*, 22(3), 2–12.

Miller, A. (1988, April 25). Stress on the job: It's hurting morale and the bottom line. How can workers and bosses cope? *Newsweek*, pp. 40–45.

Morrison, A. M., McCall, M. W., Jr., & DeVries, D. L. (1978). *Feedback to managers: A comprehensive review of twenty-four instruments*. Greensboro, NC: Center for Creative Leadership.

Nicholas, J. M., & Katz, M. (1985). Research methods and reporting practices in organizational development: A review and some guidelines. *Academy of Management Review*, 10, 737–749.

Nunnally, J. C. (1978). *Psychometric theory* (2nd ed.). New York: McGraw-Hill.

SAS User's Guide Statistics (1982). Cary, NC: SAS Institute.

Shipper, F. (1991). Mastery and frequency of managerial behaviors relative to subunit effectiveness. *Human Relations*, 44, 371–388.

Shipper, F., & Neck, C. P. (1990). Subordinates' observations: Feedback for management development. *Human Resource Development Quarterly*, 1, 371–385.

Summers, L. (1991). [Review of *Measures of leadership*]. *Personnel Psychology*, 44, 152–157.

Tubbs, M. E. (1986). Goal setting: A meta-analytical examination of the empirical evidence. *Journal of Applied Psychology*, 71(3), 474–483.

Wilson, C. L. (1975). Multi-level management surveys: Feasibility studies and initial applications. In *JSAS: Catalog of selected documents in psychology* (Vol. 5, Ms. No. 1137). Washington, DC: American Psychological Association.

Wilson, C. L. (1978). The Wilson multi-level management surveys: Refinement and replication of the scales. In *JSAS: Catalog of Selected Documents in Psychology* (Vol. 8, Ms. No.

1707). Washington, DC: American Psychological Association.

Wilson, C. L., O'Hare, D., & Shipper, F. (1990). Task cycle theory: The processes of influence. In K. E. Clark & M. B. Clark (Eds.), *Measures of leadership* (pp. 185–204). West Orange, NJ: Leadership Library of America.

Wilson, C. L., & Shipper, F. M. (1990). *Task cycle management: A competency-based course for operating managers*. New Canaan, CT: Clark Wilson Publishing.

Wilson, C. L., & Wilson, J. L. (1991). *Teams and leaders: A manual for the Clark Wilson Publishing Company training and developing programs* (rev. ed.). Silver Spring, MD: Clark Wilson Publishing.

Winokur, L. A. (1991, January 10). Well, they say there are lies, damn lies, statistics, and bosses. *The Wall Street Journal*, p. B1.

Yerkes, R., & Dodson, J. D. (1908). The relationship of stimulus to rapidity of habit formation. *Journal of Comparative Neurological Psychology*, 18, 459–482.

Frank Shipper is Professor of Management in the Franklin P. Perdue School of Business at Salisbury State University, with prior experience in biomechanical and structural engineering. His current research and consulting interests are leadership and social issues in management. He has authored numerous works, including *Task Cycle Management: A Competency-Based Course for Operating Managers* (Clark Wilson Publishing Company, 1990) and *Avoiding and Surviving Lawsuits: The Executive Guide to Strategic Legal Planning* (Jossey-Bass, 1989).

Clark L. Wilson is President of Clark Wilson Publishing Company, New Canaan, CT. He is the author of numerous articles on assessment of managerial, leadership, and organization skills. He received his PhD from the University of Southern California.

Direct inquiries about this article to Frank Shipper, Concord Lane, Route 5, Box 693, Salisbury, MD 21801–6837, 410/543-6315.

Assessing Transformational Leadership and Its Impact

Marshall Sashkin,
William E. Rosenbach,
Terrence E. Deal, and
Kent D. Peterson

This paper has two major themes: the assessment of leadership, using quantitative approaches, and the assessment of leadership *impact*, using both qualitative and quantitative methods. Leadership assessment is based on Sashkin's Leader Behavior Questionnaire (LBQ). The first section reports the latest research results on the development of the LBQ, including normative data for various samples and some international comparisons. LBQ norms will also be compared with norms on the Leader Description Questionnaire (LDQ), a version of Bass' Multifactor Leadership Questionnaire, using equivalent populations. The second section focuses on the issue of impact; quantitative data are provided to demonstrate the relationship between leadership (assessed using the LBQ) and culture building in schools and school districts. In addition to culture, some of these studies include data on student performance outcomes as related to both culture and leadership. Finally, interim results are reported on an in-process long-term leadership training program for executives in fire departments, the same population used to compare LBQ with LDQ norms (U.S. and Australia).

This paper has two themes: the assessment of *leadership*, using quantitative approaches, and the assessment of leadership *impact*, using both qualitative and quantitative methods. Leadership assessment is based on Sashkin's Leader Behavior Questionnaire (LBQ) and on the Leader Description Questionnaire (LDQ), a version of Bass' Multifactor Leadership Questionnaire (MLQ). The first major section of the paper reviews briefly the latest research results on the development of the LBQ, including normative data for various samples. The primary focus, however, is on a more basic issue: Is there really evidence that "transformational" leadership theories represent a coherent new paradigm for understanding leadership? We examine this issue by comparing large-sample results, using the LBQ and LDQ on similar populations, to see if the conceptual commonalities of the two instruments are paralleled by empirically similar results.

The second part of the paper focuses on the issue of impact; quantitative data are provided to demonstrate the relationship between leadership (assessed using the LBQ) and culture building in schools and school districts. In addition to culture, some of these studies include data on student performance outcomes as related to both culture and leadership. Finally, results are reported on an in-process long term leadership training program for executives in fire departments, one of the populations used to compare LBQ with LDQ norms.

The Assessment of Leadership

This section reports an effort to establish a degree of validity for the construct of transformational leadership. We first review briefly the development of our principal measure, the Leader Behavior Questionnaire (Sashkin, 1990; Sashkin & Fulmer, 1985). Our focus, however, is not on the LBQ per se but on determining if we could uncover some evidence to support the concepts that undergird the so-called new paradigm of "transformational" or "visionary" leadership.

We explore this issue by examining two relatively large data sets which consist of leadership questionnaire data for private industry business leaders, all of whom are at the executive level. One group of over 600 leaders completed the LDQ, while almost 400 filled out the LBQ. Overall, the two populations are very similar. We wanted, then, to see whether or not these two widely used transformational leadership assessment tools produce similar empirical normative results for scales and sets of scales that should logically yield similar results.

The Leader Behavior Questionnaire (The Visionary Leader) was developed in the early 1980s in an effort to quantitatively assess the new construct of "transformational leadership." The first LBQ in 1984 had just five scales, based on the work of Bennis (1984). A sixth scale was added to examine the relationship between transformational behaviors and charismatic affect (Sashkin & Fulmer, 1985). In its first formal publication, another four scales were added based on the Michigan Four-Factor theory of leadership (Bowers & Seashore, 1966). The aim was for the LBQ to assess both "traditional" and transformational (visionary) leadership. In 1988, the LBQ was revised to incorporate two entirely new sets of scales. The scales that had measured traditional managerial behavior using the Michigan Four-Factor concept were dropped (along with the charismatic affect scale). Five new scales took their place. The first three measured personal characteristics believed to relate to visionary leadership: self-efficacy (Bandura, 1977), need for power (McClelland & Burnham, 1976), and time-span of vision (Jaques, 1986). The last two were constructed in an attempt to assess the leader's impact on the organization's culture, using concepts similar to those developed by Parsons (1960) and elaborated by Schein (1985). The aim was for the LBQ to provide a more complete assessment of transformational leadership by including measures of behavior, of personal characteristics, and of the effects of the leader's actions on the organizational culture.

The initial development of the new scales, reported by Sashkin and Burke (1990) at the 1988 Center for Creative Leadership conference in San Antonio, included data from five samples with over 500 cases. Since then the number of samples has more than tripled: The total number of cases is over 2,000. The latest psychometric research results are reported in Appendix A; new normative LBQ data are shown in Appendix B.

The Construct of Transformational Leadership

Our purpose in this paper is not to report in detail on the continuing work using the LBQ. Rather, we hoped to explore and, if possible, validate the construct of transformational or visionary leadership. The concept originated in the work of James McGregor Burns (1978) and has been elaborated by many, especially Bennis (1990; Bennis & Nanus, 1985) and Bass (1985). We will not try to describe the content of this concept in detail; the reader is referred to the works just cited or to various chapters in Clark and Clark (1990), including those by Sashkin and Burke, Yammarino and Bass, and Posner and Kouzes.

The preponderance of research activity and opinion does *not* seem to be consistent with the concept of transformational leadership as a new paradigm for understanding leadership in organizations. As evidenced by the reports published in Clark and Clark (1990), the most current and comprehensive resource concerning the study of leadership, researchers seem to continue to focus on relatively traditional concepts and measures, often using extant scales on existing instruments to assess leadership. Indeed, some, such as Hollander and Offerman (1990), explicitly reject the notion of a new paradigm and continue to assert that the classic transactional model (expressed as social exchange) is able to encompass all leadership theory and research. Obviously, we disagree.

In Clark and Clark (1990), Sashkin and Burke (1990) noted that the Kouzes and Posner (1987) Leadership Practices Inventory (LPI) consists of five scales that fit remarkably well with the five LBQ behavior scales (which were based largely on the work of Bennis, as reported in Bennis and Nanus, 1985). The five LBQ behavior scales and the five LPI scales were developed independently, using very different methodology. Despite this, the similarity of outcomes suggests that transformational or visionary leaders engage in a set of common and measurable behaviors. While this provides at least an inkling of construct validity support for the concept of transformational leadership (as described by Sashkin and Fulmer, 1985, and various authors already cited), it is a weak argument. The present report attempts to strengthen the argument using quantitative analyses.

Examining the Construct: A Quantitative Test

Over the past four years, we have obtained several substantial sets of data using a version of Bass' MLQ. This version, the Leader Description Questionnaire (LDQ), was originally developed with the permission of Bass for use with students at the Air Force Academy (Clover & Rosenbach, 1986). It has undergone considerable reliability and internal validity testing, including repeated factor analysis. The results are consistent with work by Bass and his colleagues on the MLQ; some are reported in Rosenbach and Mueller (1989).

During the same time period, Rosenbach and his colleagues began to use Sashkin's LBQ with the same populations. While they did not generally collect both LBQ and LDQ data from the same *individuals*, they developed substantial data sets for the same *populations*, using the LBQ and the LDQ. Our approach here has been to exploit these data.

Our aim was to determine if these different instruments would yield similar assessment results for the same populations, in terms of a set of specific dimensions for which there are logical reasons to expect similarities. If so, then the basic construct of transformational leadership on which both instruments are based is supported. Our method is simply to compare scale or dimension distributions, all of which use 5-point Likert scales, using t-tests.

Predicted Relationships and Results

The LDQ has four primary transformational leadership dimensions: charisma, inspiration, individualized consideration, and intellectual stimulation. Each of these dimensions might logically relate to one or more of the LBQ scales. We developed three specific predictions about relationships between LDQ and LBQ scores, focused on what we felt should be the most clear and strong connections. Note that results showing no significant difference between the two means will support the prediction, while finding such a difference means that the two measures (of conceptually similar variables) are not the same, contradicting our prediction. Following are the three predictions and outcomes.

Prediction 1. Charisma would seem most likely to relate to the LBQ personal characteristics dimensions (Scales 6, 7, and 8). Thus, we examined the distribution of LDQ charisma scores and compared it with the distribution of LBQ personal characteristics scores. Our prediction was supported. While the t-test shows p < .04, the primary reason is the large sample (LDQ: N = 634, LBQ: N = 388). The actual difference is between an LDQ mean of 3.92 and an LBQ mean of 3.77, .15 points on a 5-point Likert scale (standard deviations both about 1.0). On 5-item LBQ scales, this difference would be that between a mean of 19 and a mean of 20, a practically meaningless difference even though it comes close to statistical significance due to the large sample Ns.

Prediction 2. Individualized consideration should logically relate to the LBQ behavioral measure of respect (Scale 4). The prediction was not supported. The means for individualized consideration (LDQ) and respect (LBQ) differ by about seven-tenths of a point (3.29 vs. 4.02), a difference that is highly significant (p < .001).

Prediction 3. Intellectual stimulation would seem related to the same issue as LBQ Scale 5, risk-taking, which is less about risk than about creating opportunities that others can "buy into" and "own." In our view, this should be a closely related outcome of intellectual stimulation. This third prediction was supported fully. No difference was found between scores on intellectual stimulation (LDQ) and risk taking (LBQ). The two means were 3.71 and 3.71.

Summary

Overall, two of the three specific predictions we tested proved correct. This certainly does not show that the instruments give a "true" assessment of transformational leadership. The results do, however, suggest that there is something real and constant that is "there" and that is being measured. Additional research is needed to explore the transformational leadership research paradigm. We believe, however, that this evidence, combined with evidence from various other research studies which explore the new paradigm, supports the construct of transformational leadership. The present results add quantitative weight to our view that transformational or visionary leadership is qualitatively different from the earlier "transactional" model.

The Assessment of Leadership Impact

It is our view that a major impact of leadership is on organizational culture. Schein (1985), for example, suggests that possibly the *only* important thing leaders do is create organizational cultures. It is, however, quite a problem to link leadership, in terms of individual behaviors and characteristics, to a system-level variable such as culture. The fact that organizational theorists differ on the very definition of culture does not make this task easier. Indeed, the present authors have some differences among themselves in the way they view organizational culture. Some, like Schein (1990), assert that no questionnaire can possibly assess culture. This stance seems to imply that culture cannot be measured quantitatively, a view with which we strongly disagree. We developed several instruments and approaches to both quantitative and qualitative assessment of organizational culture. Reported next are the research results we obtained using some of these measures.

Quantitative Assessment of Impact in Schools

In this section we review four studies in which leadership, culture, and, in two cases, performance outcomes were all quantitatively assessed. Leadership was in every case measured using the LBQ. Culture was assessed using a variety of questionnaire instruments. Performance outcomes, when included, were measured using the California Achievement Test.

The first study examined the relationship between school principals' leadership and student performance. Major (1988) showed that children in schools led by principals scoring high on the LBQ scored significantly higher on student outcome assessments than did students in schools in which the principals had low LBQ scores.

More recently, Sashkin and Sashkin (1990) assessed leadership and culture in each of 12 schools in a single district. The assessments were done independently; those completing culture assessment instruments were not the same persons who filled out leadership instruments, nor were data obtained at the same time. In that study, leadership was defined in a somewhat unusual manner as a *system* variable rather than an *individual* variable. Self and other LBQ scores had been obtained for principals, assistant principals, vocational education supervisors, and lead teachers in each school. These scores were averaged for each building; a single set of LBQ scores representing the condition of leadership in the school rather than the actions of a single leader, were obtained. The leadership scores were correlated with assessments of school culture, using the School Culture Assessment Questionnaire (SCAQ) and

"Frames of Reference" (Sashkin & Morris, 1987), an instrument based on Bolman and Deal's (1984) approach to organizations. The SCAQ centers on four crucial functions: adapting to change, attaining goals, working together as a team, and sharing values and beliefs. These four dimensions, derived from Parsons' (1960) structural-functional approach to organizational analysis, are also similar to the aspects of culture defined by Schein (1985). Frames of Reference assesses the extent to which organizational members use each of four possible organizational orientations defined by Bolman and Deal (1984): structural, political, human resources, and symbolic. A strong web of relationships was found among leadership variables and organizational culture measures. Some of the more substantial included a relationship between visionary leadership behavior and teamwork, between time-span of vision and adaptation, between time-span and use of symbols, between culture building (LBQ Scales 9–10) and adaptation, and between culture building and strength of shared values and beliefs. All of these relationships were statistically significant.

Endeman (1990) repeated Major's study at the school district level. In addition, she used a district-level version of the SCAQ. She found strong and significant relationships between visionary leadership and district culture. She also identified some relationships between the superintendents' leadership and student outcome measures at the building level. However, these relationships were much weaker than those found between building-level leadership and student outcomes (scores on standardized tests). Endeman's was the first report to incorporate all three measures, that is, leadership, culture, and performance outcomes.

Finally, Weese (1991) studied campus recreational programs at the Big Ten colleges, relating LBQ leadership scores of campus recreation directors to measures he developed of cultural strength and culture-building activities. Weese looked at the highest and lowest scoring directors and found that programs led by high visionary leaders had stronger cultures; in those programs there was significantly more culture-building activity, and it was especially oriented toward "customers."

Quantitative Results: Conclusions

Prior research, summarized by Sashkin and Burke (1990) and Sashkin (1991), showed that visionary (or transformational) leadership, measured using Sashkin's (1990) LBQ, is associated with positive organizational conditions and outcomes. The most recent evidence, reported here, confirms that transformational or visionary leaders obtain more positive organizational outcomes as compared with nonvisionary leaders. The recent studies also show that organizations with visionary leaders are characterized by more effective adaptation, goal attainment, and teamwork, by stronger shared values and beliefs, and by the use of symbols.

In sum, a variety of quantitative research results provides strong support for the assertion that transformational leaders have strong positive effects on their organizations. These results further suggest that the effects are obtained, at least in part, as a consequence of the organizational cultures that leaders construct. The results, however, only hint at what transformational leaders actually *do* to construct cultures or to produce desired organizational outcomes and conditions. To say that the results are caused by leaders' charisma and inspiration is to say too little. To understand *why* the results occur, we need clear concepts (theory) to drive sound measurement approaches. We believe that visionary leadership theory makes an important contribution in this regard and that the evidence presented in this paper supports that view. To under-

stand *how* the results are produced we need still more. That is, we need to understand the concrete dynamics of culture building through transformational leadership. Qualitative studies do suggest some of the specific strategies and tactics used by visionary leaders to transform organizations; it is to these findings that we now turn.

Qualitative Assessment of Impact in Schools

Organizational cultures are shaped by formal and informal leaders in a variety of ways. In a series of case studies, Deal and Peterson (1990) illustrated the ways that school principals shaped the culture, both formally and informally. They identified six major ways that these principals shaped culture:

1. Developing a sense of what the school should and could be, that is, a vision.

2. Recruiting and selecting staff whose values fit with those of the leader.

3. Resolving conflicts, disputes, and problems in ways that shape values.

4. Communicating values and beliefs in daily routines and behaviors.

5. Identifying and articulating stories that communicate shared values.

6. Nurturing the traditions, ceremonies, rituals, and symbols that communicate and reinforce the school culture the leader is constructing.

These six ways of building culture were exhibited in five schools studied by Deal and Peterson. The five cases were drawn from a variety of sources, including:

1. Original case research data obtained by Peterson on Hank Cot-

ton, principal of Cherry Creek, in Cherry Creek, Colorado.

2. A detailed case study of Frances Hedges, an inner-city principal, prepared by the Far West Regional Lab (Dwyer, Lee, Barnett, Filby, & Rowan, 1984a).

3. A second Far West Lab case study, this one of Ray Murdock, a rural school principal (Dwyer, Lee, Barnett, Filby, & Rowan, 1984b).

4. The case of Bob Mastruzzi, a New York high school principal, described by Lightfoot (1983).

5. The story of Frank Boyden, headmaster of Deerfield Academy, as reported by McPhee (1966).

These cases and descriptions provided excellent illustrative material for identifying the ways principals shape culture.

Developing a sense of what is important.
Each of the five principals had a clear notion of what the school stood for:

1. Hank Cotton focused primarily on academic performance and quality.

2. Frances Hedges, the inner-city principal, valued academic performance with a particular focus on reading skills and student self-esteem.

3. Ray Murdock, a rural elementary school principal, concentrated his attention on the importance of students' academic growth and providing an emotionally supportive environment. He sought to insure that his school was a model of rural education with a caring school climate for each child, no matter how difficult the home situation.

4. Bob Mastruzzi, a secondary school principal, emphasized diversity, attendance, and helping less fortunate members of the school as a way of communicating support and inclusion for all peoples.

5. Frank Boyden, the private school headmaster, regularly emphasized that he, the staff, and the school were there for the students and only for the students. He valued loyalty and commitment to the school and its students above all else.

While these principals had similar concerns for quality and for serving their students, each identified a unique, value-based vision for the organization. Visions need not all be based on the same values, but they must be clear and well-articulated. These five leaders each had a clear and focused sense of mission and values.

Selecting faculty.
A second important approach to shaping culture was careful recruitment and selection of faculty. Not simply a technical activity on the part of these principals, the selection of staff went deeper and focused not only on skills and abilities, but also on values. Each principal approached this task differently.

1. Hank Cotton worked hard to recruit faculty who shared the values he was trying to inculcate at Cherry Creek. He not only recruited new faculty to the school, but he helped faculty who did not fit in find positions in other schools.

2. Frances Hedges was considerably restricted in her right to hire and recruit teachers, in large part due to strict transfer policies and a high proportion of tenured faculty. But she drew on her knowledge and work in the district to attract teachers who shared her values; in 3 years she had built a substantial core of like-minded faculty.

3. Ray Murdock had the opportunity, over a period of 16 years, to hire almost every teacher at his school. He interviewed prospective staff members carefully to insure that values were consis-

tent with those of the school as a whole.

4. Because the school was new, Bob Mastruzzi was able to screen and hire all faculty for Kennedy High School. He looked for teachers who not only could perform well but who shared the school's emergent values.

5. Finally, Frank Boyden selected faculty who were loyal to Deerfield Academy and its students. He made sure that teachers were committed to the work of the school as defined by the core values of Deerfield.

It took these principals different lengths of time to get faculty who could share, express, and articulate the core values of the school. However, they all continued to seek them.

Dealing with conflict. Each of these principals was clear about what was important to the school. They stood up for those values and for the school culture they were trying to build. They faced conflicts directly and used such occasions to communicate values. These principals and the headmaster were not hesitant to deal with conflict.

1. Cotton was direct—and at times confrontational—in dealing with students and teachers whose activities or behaviors conflicted with the core purpose of the school. In the past there had been an "open campus" policy, and students had not been required to attend classes. Cotton changed this policy and the norms it created. Faculty members who resisted the changes were counseled; if they could not adapt, Cotton helped them find positions elsewhere.

2. Hedges tried to build collaboration among her faculty because of prior divisiveness. When faced with a conflict with a reading teacher she had hired, she convened a faculty retreat to resolve the issue collectively.

3. Murdock seemed to have relatively few direct conflicts, but he faced resistance in seeking resources and gaining parent support. For example, he found it difficult to confront parents who were migrant workers around issues of supporting their children's intellectual development. This took considerable energy and time. He did not hesitate to confront and resolve problems.

4. Mastruzzi's style was also more conservatory than confrontational, but he did not shy away from conflict or pressure. He worked with neighborhood residents, for example, to resolve problems they perceived concerning the behavior of students as they walked to and from the school. He dealt with community members and teachers alike over core issues that arose.

5. Boyden, unlike the other public school leaders, had considerable power over faculty members and others. He was, for example, able to communicate that a particular individual was no longer a welcome member of the school community. In such cases, individuals would either mend their ways or leave.

Each of these leaders identified a set of core values and beliefs to be communicated and enacted. They found ways of dealing with conflict and problems that not only resolved the issues but communicated those core values. They shared a willingness to deal with difficulties.

Setting a consistent and communicative example. Each of these five leaders communicated their values consistently by the examples of their behaviors and actions:

1. Hank Cotton seldom was seen without a book from which he quoted liber-

ally. He modeled self-development and academic interest.

2. Hedges' convictions were constantly identifiable in her behavior. She picked up litter, praised outstanding students, and worked extremely hard to make the school successful for her children.

3. Murdock set an example of service by supporting the school, helping individuals, repairing equipment himself, and even serving food to children in the cafeteria.

4. Mastruzzi engaged in consistent behaviors to communicate his beliefs. He regularly listened to others and showed his interest by means of frequent "tours" of the school.

5. Frank Boyden, up early every morning and working late into the evening, provided a different set of examples. Even as he passed normal retirement age, he communicated by his actions the commitment and dedication he expected of everyone in the school. Every moment of his life was focused on the school, its faculty and students. From pulling a weed on the lawn to picking up pieces of litter, he sought to make perfect every aspect of the school.

Principals' values are communicated through their daily actions and seemingly mundane routines. If consistently carried out, such daily routines can communicate strong values. All five school leaders communicated values through daily routines and concrete actions, thus reinforcing the culture of the school.

Telling stories that communicate values. One way of communicating values and purpose is by telling stories of the history and successes of teachers and students in a school:

1. Hank Cotton had a set of stories he used to communicate the values of hard work, collaboration, and success.

2. Bob Mastruzzi frequently told stories of academic and athletic success.

3. Frank Boyden often retold the story of the school hero who was a student, an athlete, a faculty member, and a war hero.

Stories about school heroes and heroines, shared experiences, and hard work become value-communicating aspects of principals' work and vision.

Ceremonies, traditions, rituals, and symbols as culture builders. One of the most commonly recognized ways of building culture is to have ceremonies, traditions, rituals, and symbols that communicate values, beliefs, and hopes. While such things as graduation ceremonies can communicate values in clear and striking ways, the daily routines and rituals engaged in by leaders can do just as well:

1. Hank Cotton made sure to be seen regularly wearing his sneakers imprinted with the school's mascot.

2. Frances Hedges did not have many formal ceremonies, but she regularly had symbolic routines such as schoolwide assemblies and poetry readings.

3. Ray Murdock created numerous ceremonies and traditions to provide a cornerstone for his school culture. He had an annual art auction, a yearly carnival, special days, and scheduled meetings with each child on his or her birthday. This helped build the close community he sought.

4. Bob Mastruzzi developed a tradition of collecting Christmas gifts for the needy to highlight the school value of helping the less fortunate.

5. Frank Boyden established important small rituals to communicate values. For example, he distributed grades

personally to each student at the end of the school year.

To varying degrees, each school leader used formal cultural statements to define, shape, and express the school's culture. It is clear that these principals understood the value of ceremonies and rituals to communicate values.

Other Examples

In looking at school principals around the country, we find that they, too, communicate values and shape their culture in the six ways we have defined. Many principals communicate a sense of what is important. We visited a principal who had to close a school: He designed and conducted a ceremony to mark its closing and incorporation into a new school. In high ceremony, he and members of the school community carried selected artifacts of the old school—bricks, books, trophies, etc.—to the new school building, thus communicating the value of continuity and history. In another school named after the famous environmentalist John Muir, the principal and staff spend a week celebrating John Muir's life, using the example of his life to communicate and reinforce the values they share.

Most principals try to select faculty for their teaching skills. In addition, culture-building principals seek faculty whose values can strongly support the core purposes of the school. In one midwestern school, the principal spent the summer identifying and selecting new faculty. He was not looking simply for technical qualifications but seeking new faculty members whose values fit with those on which his own vision of excellence was based: academic success and cultural diversity. In selection interviews, another principal tries to communicate clearly the nature of the school's culture to the job candidate. If there appears to be a match, he begins the process of socializing the potential new faculty member, inculcat-

ing values of collaboration, collegiality, and improvement.

All leaders have to face conflict in the enactment of their work. Principals who want to shape culture confront conflicts in ways that communicate and instill the values they hold. One midwestern high school principal appeared before the city council to advocate denial of a beer permit for a local gas station/grocery store located half a block from the high school. She communicated the values of the school and her commitment to blocking easy access to drugs. Another principal communicated the value of respect of others' religions by refusing to allow a Christmas tree to be set up in his school.

Leaders regularly communicate their values by the actions and routines they engage in. One high school principal in a western state spends two minutes every day in every classroom. In another school, the principal regularly sends out articles and research on new instructional ideas even if it is years before they will be used. Yet another principal spent four weeks in a training program to communicate his professional commitment to being an instructional leader.

Telling stories is a key element of culture building and one of its most enjoyable sides. But not all stories are positive. The principal of a southern school had to contend with a story—told to all incoming students and teachers—of the 34 graduates of his high school who went to prison. To overcome this negative story, the principal sought out 34 graduates successful in a wide range of careers. The "34 graduates story" is still told, but it now has a different, positive meaning.

Many principals use ceremonies, traditions, rituals, and symbols to communicate and strengthen organizational support for their values. Some principals use a formal "granting of tenure" ceremony as a means of "reconnecting" teachers with the value of serving all children. In other schools, beginning-of-the-year ceremonies are used to communicate values. In one West Virginia district, everyone joins together to share in the successes of the prior year and define common aspirations for the year to come.

Qualitative Analysis: Conclusions

The strategies we have defined, when used consistently, are major tools of school leaders. Through their skillful application, effective school cultures are built. We are beginning, through careful observational research, to understand both the nature of successful leadership and, as importantly, how it can be applied. Qualitative analyses, like that based on the work of Deal and Peterson (1990), are crucial. Such analyses help us understand, in a practical way, how leaders use the behaviors that are assessed in quantitative terms (by instruments such as the LBQ) that result in effective cultures as measured by the School Culture Assessment Questionnaire (Sashkin & Sashkin, 1990) and other instruments. The next step, of course, is to develop better methods for teaching both aspiring and current leaders how to think about and construct cultures of excellence.

Leadership Training for Impact

We believe that the transformational leadership paradigm, operationalized with quantitative assessment tools like the LDQ and LBQ and qualitative analyses such as the work of Deal and Peterson (1990), provides a sound basis for attempting to improve leadership in organizations. This sort of research is, however, only beginning.

For more than three years we have been engaged in one action-research study to see whether a leadership development program designed around the transformational construct could actually result in improvements, in terms of followers' per-

ceptions of leaders. The study involved the Melbourne (Australia) Metropolitan Fire Brigade. It was conducted as part of a formal leadership development program involving eight individuals, all of whom occupied the same executive level positions during the period of the study. The leader of the fire brigade (Chief Fire Officer) was appointed about six months prior to the beginning of the study in January 1988; he was still experiencing the positive effects of the "honeymoon." This Chief Fire Officer had a graduate degree in management. The majority of the executive fire officers were college graduates and were enrolled in or had completed graduate programs during the course of the study.

While the study was underway, the Chief Fire Officer initiated formal and informal leadership development programs, including organization-sponsored university undergraduate, graduate, and special topic courses, emergency services management courses, short courses held in Australia, Hong Kong, Europe, and the U.S., special seminars on topics such as creativity, personal growth, values, and executive leadership, and in-house seminars specifically focused on leadership effectiveness. Most notable, the Chief Fire Officer modeled his commitment to leadership development by participating in all of these programs. He emphasized education with formal and informal rewards, and this was clearly reflected in the organization's culture.

The study began with a 3-day seminar focused on leadership and team effectiveness. Prework included administration of the LDQ. Each participant asked eight fire service officers who reported directly to him to anonymously complete the LDQ and mail the form to one of the authors for scoring and analysis. The seminar included feedback on individual and group scores. Each individual prepared a personal leadership development plan which included specific strategies for improving his own effectiveness as a leader. The study concluded 30 months later with a similar seminar, including the readministration of the LDQ. Of approximately 15 participants in each seminar, 8 were the same individuals and the subjects of this analysis. Note that the data were obtained from observers, not from the trainees; in many cases the observers changed from time one to time two, and the two measurements were separated by more than two years. Therefore, there seems to be little opportunity here for contamination of time-two responses by prior exposure to the instrument.

Results

Table 1 presents the pretraining and posttraining LDQ scores. In all cases, the scores changed in the direction predicted. Results are described for each of the major categories measured:

1. Laissez-faire leadership. This is actually a measure of the absence of leadership. As expected, scores decreased significantly ($p < .05$) from T1 to T2, as leadership effectiveness improved.

2. Transactional leadership. The two LDQ scales that assess transactional leadership are contingent reward and management by exception (MBE). The scores for contingent reward, a measure of equity, remained about the same, with an equal number of individual scores going up and going down. There were no changes to the organizational reward system during the study. Although seven of the eight MBE scores went down, there was no significant change in the mean scores for the group from T1 to T2.

3. Transformational leadership. The four LDQ scales that assess transformational leadership are charisma, individualized consideration, intellectual stimulation, inspiration, and motivation beyond expectations. (The last scale has been dropped from the MLQ. Additional analyses of our data show that MBE is actually incorporated, factorially, within the inspiration dimension.) There were significant increases for charisma ($p < .01$) and individualized consideration ($p < .05$). Scores on the other two scales tended to increase, but no strong pattern was apparent nor were any significant changes found. As inspiration and motivation beyond expectation are actually a single construct, this means that on two of three transformational leadership measures we find substantial and statistically significant improvements, even with a very small sample.

4. Effectiveness. The improvements in transformational leadership, which are reflected in scores for perceived effectiveness of the leaders' units, improved significantly ($p < .05$), as did ratings of the leaders' effectiveness in representing their units to higher authority ($p < .05$). The improvement of all eight executives in representing individuals and their unit to higher authority may be a result of higher charisma scores. Despite the fact that the unit effectiveness ratings are perceptions rather than objective scores, these results add support for the promise of transformational leadership to produce improved organizational effectiveness. Although there were improvements in all three of the remaining effectiveness measures, the changes were not significant.

5. Satisfaction. Half of the subordinate managers were more satisfied with their leaders as persons at the end of the study; the changes were not significant. Seven of the eight, however, were more satisfied that the leaders now employed styles of leadership more appropriate to getting the job done right ($p < .01$). We conclude that improved transformational leadership may or may not result in individuals being more highly esteemed but will, more importantly, contribute directly to more appropriate and effective leadership behavior.

SASHKIN, ROSENBACH, DEAL, AND PETERSON

TABLE 1 Pre- and Post-Training Measures

Scale	Time 1 mean	σ	Time 2 mean	σ	Changes +	Changes −	Signif. (p <)
Laissez-Faire Leadership	2.43	.70	1.86	.51	1	7	.05
Transactional Leadership							
Contingent Reward	3.28	.25	3.33	.22	4	4	n.s.
Mgmt. by Exception	2.66	.60	2.28	.51	1	7	n.s.
Transformational Leadership							
Charisma	3.67	.71	3.93	.66	7	1	.01
Individualized Consideration	3.46	.56	3.74	.31	5	1	.05
Intellectual Stimulation	3.73	.40	3.92	.45	5	2	n.s.
Inspiration	3.05	.51	3.32	.28	4	2	n.s.
Effectiveness							
Unit	3.52	.31	3.88	.33	6	1	.05
Rep. to Higher Auth.	3.56	.59	4.00	.42	8	0	.05
Meeting Job Needs	3.33	.63	3.62	.50	5	3	n.s.
Meeting Org. Needs	3.78	.61	4.02	.56	5	3	n.s.
Meeting Personal Needs	3.13	.51	3.35	.44	6	2	n.s.
Satisfaction							
With the Person	4.11	.83	4.33	.36	4	3	n.s.
With the Leader's Style	3.83	.85	4.26	.57	7	1	.01

Summary

These results demonstrate that an organization with a transformational leadership focus that encourages, models, and rewards leadership training and development can expect higher levels of transformational leadership behavior. Such behavior does make a difference in perceived organizational effectiveness and in the satisfaction of subordinate managers. For these results to be lasting, however, the organizational culture must reflect this commitment to leadership.

Conclusion

We purposely designed this project and paper to incorporate both quantitative and qualitative research. We see the "debate" between these two research approaches as misleading at best, foolish and unworthy of serious energies at worst. But we go beyond the polite tolerance often expressed by researchers for an approach other than their own. We believe that both forms of assessment are absolutely necessary. Some suggest that qualitative research can help define the important variables and constructs and can help determine what is worth measuring, at which point it becomes appropriate to turn to quantitative measures. We see the interdependencies between qualitative and quantitative approaches as even more complex. Quantitative research also helps us understand more about the nature of leadership and culture, that is, the underlying pattern of relationships between the two. Through qualitative research, we also learn how to help leaders develop and create or change cultures. Both approaches are needed as we learn more about the nature and application of transformational leadership, including how it can be developed and used to create cultures in which both people and performance are valued.

In this report we add to the increasingly large and convincing body of research and evidence showing that transformational or visionary leadership has clear positive effects on organizational outcomes of various types. We have presented evidence that (a) supports the construct of transformational leadership; (b) directly links transformational leadership with effective organizational culture, suggesting that transformational leaders construct effective organizational cultures; and (c) demonstrates that transformational leadership can be taught, with positive changes resulting both in assessments of leadership and organizationally-relevant outcome measures. Although more work is needed, we see our efforts and those of others working in the area of transformational leadership as providing strong and convincing evidence that this new paradigm for leadership theory, research, and application is robust and will, in the near future, generate important applications for organizations struggling to compete and remain viable in a rapidly changing world.

References

Bandura, A. (1977). *Social learning theory.* Englewood Cliffs, NJ: Prentice-Hall.

Bass, B. M. (1985). *Leadership and performance beyond expectations.* New York: Free Press.

Bennis, W. (1984). The four competencies of leadership. *Training and Development Journal, 38*(8), 14–19.

Bennis, W. (1990). *On becoming a leader.* Reading, MA: Addison-Wesley.

Bennis, W., & Nanus, B. (1985). *Leaders: The strategies for taking charge.* New York: Harper & Row.

Bolman, L., & Deal, T. E. (1984). *Modern approaches to understanding and managing organizations.* San Francisco: Jossey-Bass.

Bowers, D. G., & Seashore, S. E. (1966). Predicting organizational effectiveness with a four-factor theory of leadership. *Administrative Science Quarterly, 11,* 238–263.

Burns, J. M. (1978). *Leadership.* New York: Harper & Row.

Clark, K. E., & Clark, M. B. (1990). *Measures of leadership.* West Orange, NJ: Leadership Library of America.

Clover, W. H., & Rosenbach, W. E. (1986). *Item reduction of the Multifactor Leadership Questionnaire.* Working paper, U.S. Air Force Academy, Colorado Springs, CO.

Deal, T. E., & Peterson, K. D. (1990). *The principal's role in shaping school culture.* Washington, DC: U.S. Government Printing Office.

Dwyer, D. C., Lee, G. V., Barnett, B. G., Filby, N. N., & Rowan, B. (1984a). *Frances Hedges and Orchard Park Elementary School: Instructional leadership in a stable urban setting.* San Francisco: Instructional Management Program, Far West Laboratory for Educational Research and Development.

Dwyer, D. C., Lee, G. V., Barnett, B. G., Filby, N. N., & Rowan, B. (1984b). *Ray Murdock and Jefferson Elementary School: Instructional leadership in a rural setting.* San Francisco: Instructional Management Program, Far West Laboratory for Educational Research and Development.

Endeman, J. (1990, April). *Leadership and culture: Superintendents and districts.* Paper presented at the annual meeting of the American Educational Research Association, as part of the Division A refereed symposium, "Leadership and culture: Qualitative and quantitative research approaches and results," Boston, MA.

Hollander, E. P., & Offerman, L. R. (1990). Relational features of organizational leadership and followership. In K. E. Clark & M. B. Clark (Eds.), *Measures of leadership* (pp. 83–98). West Orange, NJ: Leadership Library of America.

Jaques, E. (1986). The development of intellectual capacity. *Journal of Applied Behavioral Science, 22,* 361–383.

Kouzes, J. M., & Posner, B. Z. (1987). *The leadership challenge.* San Francisco: Jossey-Bass.

Lightfoot, S. L. (1983). *The good high school.* New York: Basic Books.

Major, K. D. (1988). *Dogmatism, visionary leadership, and effectiveness of secondary schools.* Unpublished doctoral dissertation, University of La Verne, La Verne, CA.

McClelland, D. C., & Burnham, D. H. (1976). Power is the great motivator. *Harvard Business Review,* 54(2), 100–110.

McPhee, J. (1966). *The headmaster.* New York: Farrar, Straus & Giroux.

Parsons, T. (1960). *Structure and process in modern societies.* New York: Free Press.

Posner, B. Z., & Kouzes, J. M. (1990). Leadership practices: An alternative to the psychological perspective. In K. E. Clark & M. B. Clark (Eds.), *Measures of leadership* (pp. 205–215). West Orange, NJ: Leadership Library of America.

Rosenbach, W. E., & Mueller, R. (1989). Transformational and transactional leadership of business, church, and fire service executives. In B. J. Fallon, H. P. Pfister, & J. Brebner (Eds.), *Advances in organizational psychology.* Utrecht, The Netherlands: Elsevier Science Publishers, BV (North-Holland).

Sashkin, M. (1990). *The visionary leader: Trainer guide.* King of Prussia, PA: Organization Design and Development.

Sashkin, M. (1991, February). *Strategic leadership competencies: What are they? How do they operate? What can be done to develop them?* Paper prepared for the Strategic Leadership Conference, co-sponsored by the Army War College, Army Research Institute, and Texas Tech University, Carlisle Barracks, PA.

Sashkin, M., & Burke, W. W. (1990). Understanding and assessing organizational leadership. In K. E. Clark & M. B. Clark (Eds.), *Measures of leadership* (pp. 297–325). West Orange, NJ: Leadership Library of America.

Sashkin, M., & Fulmer, R. M. (1985, July). *A new framework for leadership: Vision, charisma, and culture.* Paper presented at the Biennial International Leadership Symposium, Texas Tech University, Lubbock.

Sashkin, M., & Morris, W. C. (1987). *Experiencing management.* Reading, MA: Addison-Wesley.

Sashkin, M., & Sashkin, M. G. (1990, April). *Leadership and culture building in schools: Quantitative and qualitative understandings.* Paper presented at the annual meeting of the American Educational Research Association, as part of the Division A refereed symposium,

"Leadership and culture: Qualitative and quantitative research approaches and results," Boston, MA.

Schein, E. H. (1985). *Organizational culture and leadership.* San Francisco: Jossey-Bass.

Schein, E. H. (1990, Summer). Organization development and the study of organizational culture. *Academy of Management OD Newsletter,* pp. 3–5.

Stoner-Zemel, J. (1988). *Visionary leadership, management, and high performance work units.* Unpublished doctoral dissertation, University of Massachusetts, Amherst.

Weese, W. J. (1991). *Visionary leadership and the development and penetration of organizational culture within campus recreation programs.* Unpublished doctoral dissertation, The Ohio State University, Columbus, OH.

Marshall Sashkin is Adjunct Professor of Psychology and of Administrative Sciences at the George Washington University. His primary current assignment is in the U.S. Department of Education's Office of Educational Research and Improvement, where he develops and guides applied research aimed at improving the management and organization of schools. He is also principal partner of Marshall Sashkin & Associates, a management and organizational consulting firm. He has consulted with public and private sector organizations and conducted research on leadership, participation, and organizational change with a focus on measuring organizational excellence and changing organizational cultures through visionary leadership. He is the author or co-author of ten books and monographs and numerous research articles. He earned his PhD from the University of Michigan.

William E. Rosenbach is the Evans Professor of Eisenhower Leadership Studies and Professor of Management at Gettysburg College. Dr. Rosenbach teaches courses in organizational behavior and leadership, followership, and teamwork. He is the co-author of the third edition of *Contemporary Issues In Leadership* and the second edition of *Military Leadership*.

Terrence E. (Terry) Deal is Professor of Education and Human Development at Peabody College of Vanderbilt University and serves as Co-Director of The National Center for Educational Leadership (NCEL) and as Senior Research Associate at the Center for Advanced Study of Educational Leadership (CASEL). He has consulted with numerous organizations in the United States and abroad. He has authored or co-authored several books and numerous articles concerning organizational issues such as change, culture management, reform, symbolism, theater, and theory, including *Corporate Cultures* (1982, Addison-Wesley), *Reframing Organizations: Artistry, Choice, and Leadership* (1991, Jossey-Bass), and *Modern Approaches to Understanding and Managing Organizations*, (1992, Jossey-Bass). He received his PhD in Educational Administration and Sociology from Stanford University.

Kent D. Peterson is a Professor at The University of Wisconsin-Madison. He has written extensively for both researchers and practitioners in such publications as *Educational Leadership*, *NASSP Bulletin*, *Educational Administration Quarterly*, and *Administrative Science Quarterly* and has co-authored a monograph, *The Principal's Role in Shaping School Culture* for the U.S. Department of Education. His research focuses on understanding the ways leaders think, act, and lead effective school cultures and is being applied in leadership training programs in the California School Leaders Academy, several LEAD programs, and in school leader institutes in Canada, Belgium, and Sweden.

Direct inquiries about this article to Marshall Sashkin, OERI Senior Associate, Office of Educational Research and Improvement, U.S. Department of Education, Washington, DC 20208–5644, 202/219–2120.

Psychometric analyses. In the process of data collection, further psychometric work has been done to improve the scales. The most recent printing of the LBQ (which is still referred to as the third edition) incorporates a variety of minor changes in item wording. The latest scale reliability tests show that the LBQ-Other scales have high reliabilities (as assessed by Cronbach's alpha). The lowest alpha is .52 for Scale 5 (Respect), and most are in the range of .60 to .70. The LBQ-Self data show lower internal scale reliabilities, particularly for the five behavior scales. These, however, show more than acceptable reliability when combined (Cronbach alpha = .75 for LBQ-Self scales 1–5 combined, N = 415). The power need scale (Scale 7) has a low alpha due in part to the fact that it has two separate components; the need for power per se and the extent to which that need is directed in a pro- or anti-social manner. Similarly, Scale 10 assesses the extent to which leaders inculcate four independent values within the culture of the organization; its alpha is .36 (for LBQ-Self; for Other data alpha increases to .64). Looking at the three groups of scales, 1–5, 6–8, and 9–10, we find Cronbach alphas above .80 for each group for the LBQ-Other data and from .64 (Scales 9–10) to .75 (behavior) for the Self data. Thus, grouping the scales in terms of the three aspects of the LBQ—behavior, personal characteristics, and culture-building—yields strong reliability results. As noted, the various reliability tests and results have led to still further item revision, to strengthen the inter-item correlations on each scale.

Validity research. The same large data sets used to examine reliability were factor analyzed. The LBQ-Other data (N = 578) provide support for the basic structure of the LBQ, adding construct validity. The LBQ-Self data are even more strongly supportive. This analysis (reported in detail in the latest LBQ manual; see Sashkin, 1990) gives strong support to the scale construction of the LBQ-Self, specifically Scales 1, 2, 3, 4, 6, 7, and 8. All of the personal characteristic scales appear as clear and independent factors. This is strong construct validation, as is the finding that the behavior scales all group together (except Scale 3, trust, which is a clear independent factor). In sum, factor analyses on large sets of LBQ data provide moderate to strong support for the construct validity of the instrument.

There have been several studies examining the external validity of the LBQ, since the report published in *Measures of Leadership* (Clark & Clark, 1990). Most of these center on leadership and culture, which will be discussed in the latter portion of this paper. However, Endeman (1990) also presents evidence that even at the school district level the superintendent's leadership (as assessed by the LBQ) has some impact on the performance of students. This adds support to the prior work of Major (1988), who studied principals. Similarly, Sashkin and Sashkin (1990) report that LBQ scores relate to organization members' perceptions of the quality of the work environment, supporting earlier findings by Stoner–Zemel (1988). Overall, recent external validity research using the LBQ is consistent with and supportive of earlier work. Results suggest that visionary leadership has positive effects on organizational outcomes, including performance and satisfaction.

APPENDIX B: Recent Normative Data for the Leader Behavior Questionnaire

| Sample | | N | X | | LBQ Scales | | | | | | LBQ Scales | | | | LBQ Scales | | | |
				1	2	3	4	5	VLB	6	7	8	VLC	9	10	VCB	Total
XXII	(S)	34	X	19.6	18.1	20.4	20.8	20.1	98.9	22.4	20.2	20.6	63.2	21.4	20.2	41.6	203.7
			sd	1.89	2.52	2.10	2.18	2.46	9.20	1.96	2.22	2.51	4.39	2.55	2.28	4.09	15.66
	(O)	64	X	20.5	18.4	19.9	21.3	19.4	99.4	20.8	18.5	20.2	59.5	21.1	19.7	40.8	199.7
			sd	2.39	3.05	2.86	2.36	2.89	10.11	2.85	2.69	2.94	6.03	2.71	2.06	4.18	17.54
XXIII	(S)	31	X	19.4	17.7	20.2	21.6	19.9	98.8	22.3	20.0	19.5	61.8	21.5	20.8	42.3	203.0
			sd	1.89	2.72	1.98	2.20	2.67	8.71	2.18	2.53	2.78	5.99	2.39	2.40	3.96	15.78
	(O)	62	X	19.4	17.9	19.8	20.7	18.6	96.4	20.0	18.0	19.0	57.0	20.8	19.2	40.0	193.4
			sd	2.94	3.35	2.99	3.12	4.05	13.63	2.89	2.80	3.95	8.14	3.43	2.68	5.31	25.43
XXIV	(S)	19	X	19.5	17.3	20.9	21.1	19.8	98.5	22.7	19.6	19.8	62.2	20.7	19.8	40.6	201.3
			sd	1.61	2.51	1.97	2.86	2.24	8.70	2.08	2.63	2.81	6.23	2.33	2.14	3.96	17.28
	(O)	36	X	20.0	17.9	19.9	21.7	20.2	99.6	20.9	18.4	19.9	59.2	20.6	20.1	40.8	199.6
			sd	2.48	3.59	3.36	3.19	2.79	11.53	2.59	2.85	3.31	6.32	3.02	2.38	4.78	20.66
XXV	(S)	43	X	20.7	19.5	21.2	21.8	19.8	102.9	21.7	19.6	20.0	61.2	21.9	20.9	42.8	206.9
			sd	2.05	2.46	2.06	2.08	2.17	8.05	2.62	2.53	2.98	6.44	2.01	2.17	3.48	15.93
	(O)	82	X	21.7	21.0	21.3	23.1	21.6	108.8	21.6	19.5	21.4	62.6	22.9	21.1	44.1	215.4
			sd	2.66	3.04	2.42	1.74	3.98	9.94	2.84	2.73	2.49	6.44	2.18	2.47	3.90	17.94
XXVI	(S)	200	X	21.1	20.1	21.2	22.3	20.5	105.2	22.1	19.6	20.6	62.3	22.3	20.8	43.1	210.6
			sd	1.66	2.17	1.72	1.88	2.32	6.92	2.17	2.38	2.49	5.07	1.98	2.25	3.62	13.18
XXVII	(S)	67	X	21.2	20.0	21.4	22.5	20.7	105.8	22.2	20.5	21.0	63.7	22.5	20.9	43.3	212.8
			sd	2.12	2.76	1.82	1.96	2.32	8.16	2.48	2.80	3.03	6.50	2.12	2.47	4.04	16.90
	(O)	130	X	21.9	21.1	21.7	23.0	21.6	109.4	22.0	19.7	21.0	62.6	23.1	20.9	44.0	215.9
			sd	2.20	2.63	2.00	1.86	2.42	8.38	2.32	2.64	2.95	6.50	2.11	2.61	4.08	17.07
XXVIII	(S)	81	X	20.9	20.1	20.7	21.7	20.5	104.1	21.4	20.7	20.7	62.7	21.1	20.7	41.7	208.7
			sd	2.02	2.34	2.40	1.88	2.35	7.36	2.36	2.56	2.85	6.28	2.07	2.15	3.60	14.36
XXIX	(S)	27	X	20.1	17.9	20.6	21.0	19.5	99.1	21.6	20.9	18.4	60.9	21.1	19.7	40.8	200.8
			sd	2.54	2.77	1.93	2.50	2.81	9.71	2.58	2.18	3.34	6.71	2.74	2.29	4.29	18.91
	(O)	162	X	20.3	18.3	19.4	21.0	19.0	98.1	19.6	18.3	17.6	55.6	19.7	18.8	38.5	192.2
			sd	2.54	3.26	3.33	3.12	3.32	12.55	3.11	2.83	3.71	8.25	3.70	2.66	5.76	24.56

Key to Samples
XXII: Presidents of small business firms, midwest U.S.
XXIII: Executives in small business firms, midwest U.S.
XXIV: Entrepreneurs, sole proprietors of very small businesses, midwest U.S.
XXV: School principals, suburban school districts, southeast U.S.
XXVI: School administrators, suburban school district, southeast U.S.
XXVII: Assistant principals identified as high-potential leaders, suburban district, mid-Atlantic U.S.
XXVIII: Administrators and organizational consultants, psychological health care field
XXIX: Sales managers, national high-technology service organization

© 1988, 1990 Marshall Sashkin.

SASHKIN, ROSENBACH, DEAL, AND PETERSON

The Transformational/Transactional Leadership Model

A Study of Critical Components

Ann M. Van Eron and
W. Warner Burke

Survey results of 128 senior executives and 615 subordinates from a global company confirmed that communication patterns and cognitive style differences are related differentially to belief systems of transformational and transactional leaders. These different beliefs were, in turn, related to subordinates' perceived differences in leadership practices. The study further demonstrated an association between practices and climate.

Rapidly changing environmental conditions, the need for significant organizational changes, and the remaining lack of clarity about leadership continue to make transformational leadership (Burns, 1978) a compelling paradigm to explore. Organizations experience conflicting needs to maintain the balance of operations and create new approaches (Zaleznik, 1977). Responding to these needs, individuals in leadership positions relate to their followers either as a transformational leader or as a transactional leader.

Concerned with change, the transformational leader communicates and focuses attention on a clear vision of future conditions that address the needs and values of the organization and of the leader's individual followers. The transactional leader focuses on maintaining the status quo of organizational functions by clarifying roles and tasks and managing complexity. Transactional leaders work within the existing organizational culture, norms, and beliefs and relate to followers primarily by an exchange or transaction (Burns, 1978).

Various researchers and theorists have supported the distinction between transformational and transactional leaders (Bass, 1985; Bennis & Nanus, 1985; Burke, 1986a; Kotter, 1990; Levinson & Rosenthal, 1984; Tichy & Devanna, 1986; Zaleznik, 1977). Each has distinguishing purposes, foci of attention, and characteristic activities. According to Burns (1978), transformational and transactional leadership are at opposite ends of a continuum. Kuhnert and Lewis (1987) consider transformational and transactional leaders "qualitatively different kinds of individuals who construct reality in markedly different ways, thereby viewing themselves and the people they lead in contrasting ways" (p. 649).

This study assumes that transformational and transactional leadership complement each other and are both needed for organizational success. Although individuals may display both kinds of leadership, they are disposed with varying intensities toward one form of leadership. While Kotter (1990) believes that individuals can exercise both forms of leadership, his study of senior executives indicated that over 95% reported having too few people strong at both.

Since transformational leaders respond more frequently and more effectively than transactional leaders to change in environment and needs of employees, knowledge about selecting and developing transformational leaders is becoming increasingly important in the global economy. Exploring personality differences and behaviors of transformational and transactional leaders and the relationship between these and organizational factors should prove to be useful for the development, selection, and placement of effective leaders.

Transformational/Transactional Leadership Model

This exploratory study tests empirically the key components of a proposed Transformational/Transactional Leadership model (see Figure 1). Drawing from the work of Burns (1978), Burke and Litwin (1989), and House (1988), this model is based on open systems principles. It assumes that individual differences contribute to variance in leadership disposition.

Personality factors which may distinguish between the disposition of transformational or transactional leadership include: cognitive style (Myers, 1975, 1980), need for power (Burke, 1986a; House, 1977, 1988; McClelland, 1975; McClelland & Burnham, 1976), power inhibition (Howell, 1988; McClelland, 1985), level of ego development (Kegan & Lahey, 1984; Kuhnert & Lewis, 1987; Loevinger, 1976), drive or energy level (Kotter, 1990; McClelland & Boyatzis, 1982), cognitive complexity (Kotter, 1990; Stogdill, 1974; Streufert & Streufert, 1978), mental health (Kotter, 1990), and history of leadership experiences (Bray & Howard, 1983). It is also possible that external environment and organizational culture help shape an individual's disposition to be a transformational or transactional leader.

According to the model, leadership disposition influences the exhibition of leadership practices. Other factors associated with the emergence of transformational or transactional leadership behavior include environmental conditions, organizational structure and systems, and organizational culture and climate. For example, transformational leadership is more likely to be found in times of crisis or opportunity rather than during static or stable conditions (Conger, 1989; Schein, 1985). Human resource and other organizational systems such as technology, reward, compensation, and training influence the emergence of leadership practices.

Schneider (1983) argued strongly that interaction between individual leader differences and situational factors influences leadership practices. Individual disposition is expected to be most predic-

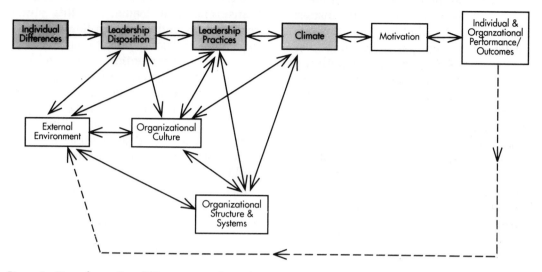

Figure 1   Transformational/Transactional Leadership model.

tive of leadership practices when conditions are unstructured or ambiguous
(House, 1988; Mischel, 1973). Similarly,
situational variables are most predictive
of an individual's behavior in less ambiguous situations.

Transactional leadership behavior,
therefore, is most likely to be congruent
with a stable environment and mechanis-
tic structure where issues of control and
power are more salient. Transformational
leadership is more likely to be effective in
a turbulent environment with an organis-
mic structure where issues of power may
be less salient. The fit between organizational context, structure, and leadership
practices is likely to influence organizational performance.

Leadership practices are expected to influence reciprocally the perceived work
climate and culture. While culture refers
to covert as well as overt rules, norms,
and values, climate is defined as the collective impressions, expectations, and
feelings regarding the local work environment (Burke & Litwin, 1989). Climate perceptions are related to organizational and
individual outcomes including performance, productivity, employee and cus-

tomer satisfaction, and evaluation of quality (Burke & Litwin, 1989; Fox, 1990).

Leadership behavior is also expected to
influence culture reciprocally (Barney,
1986; Burke & Litwin, 1989; Fox, 1990;
Schwartz & Davis, 1981). Transformational leadership has been related to cultures that support innovation and risk taking (Bass, 1985; Conger & Kanungo,
1988). Transformational leadership behavior is proposed to influence fundamental, second-order changes (Lundberg,
1986) and therefore significant cultural
changes related to the norms and values
of the organization. Transactional leadership practices, however, work to maintain
the existing order in a system and support
the current culture (Burns, 1978; Schein,
1985).

The Transformational/Transactional
Leadership model supports the view that
leadership is a function of the interaction
between the leader's individual
differences and behavior, the situation,
and subordinates with their individual
differences and behavior (Burke, 1965).

Few studies have examined the impact
of individual differences on transformational leadership (Howell & Avolio,

1989). This study is unique in that the relationship between leadership disposition—a leader's belief system or way of creating meaning—and leadership practices is examined. Furthermore, although a conceptual link has been made between leadership and climate, little empirical research addressing this connection is available (Kozlowski & Doherty, 1989).

The focus of this study, therefore, was to examine from the perspective of both leaders and their subordinates the relationship among four components of the Transformational/Transactional Leadership model: individual differences, leadership disposition, practices, and climate.

Individual Differences and Leadership Disposition

After research on personal characteristics of leaders diminished in the fifties, Stogdill (1974) indicated that many researchers had misinterpreted his earlier conclusion (Stogdill, 1948) and "overemphasized the situational and underemphasized the personal nature of leadership" (Stogdill, 1974, p. 72). Subsequently, House (1977, 1988) advocated the study of psychological characteristics of leaders. Bass (1981) proposed that some traits characterize leaders across situations. House and Baetz (1979), after reviewing the literature, concluded that traits often affect criterion variables such as measures of performance, and many traits interact with situational variables. House (1977, 1988) argued that personality traits predispose individuals to engage in certain behaviors. There has been increasing interest in the view that transformational and transactional leaders may have fundamental individual differences (Burke, 1986a). While the Transformational/Transactional Leadership model proposes an interaction between individual differences and situational variables, it was beyond the scope of this study to examine the interaction.

Although many individual differences

are likely to influence the disposition for transformational leadership, this study explored the influence of different cognitive styles and communication patterns in judgment and perception. Cognitive style characterizes the habitual processes a person uses to assimilate and evaluate information (Goldstein & Blackman, 1978; Sashkin & Fulmer, 1988). Cognitive style incorporates Stogdill's (1948) assessment that judgment (decisions reached after insight into a situation) is a distinguishing individual characteristic of leaders. Various dimensions of cognitive style can be assessed. The Myers-Briggs Type Indicator® (MBTI™) can be used as a beneficial assessment instrument since it measures the way people use their energy, perceive the outside world, and make judgments about their perceptions (Myers & McCaulley, 1985). According to Myers (1975), four continua form the basis of psychological type: (a) the preference of extraversion versus introversion (EI), (b) the preference of sensing versus intuition (SN), (c) the preference of thinking versus feeling (TF), and (d) the preference for judging versus perceiving (JP). Although individuals use all eight processes, the theory proposes that one of each pair is favored over the other. It is expected that some of the different preferences on the bipolar scales will relate to an individual's disposition for transformational or transactional leadership.

Extraversion-Introversion (EI). Leadership requires communication, sociability, and action, traits more natural for extraverts. However, conceptualizing problems clearly and thoughtfully, which comes more easily for introverts, is also required for effective leadership. While it is likely that transformational leaders tend to be extraverts, there is no reason to believe that transactional leaders tend to

Myers-Briggs Type Indicator is a registered trademark of Consulting Psychologists Press, Inc.

MBTI is a trademark of Consulting Psychologists Press, Inc.

VAN ERON AND BURKE

be introverts. Therefore, it is unlikely that preference on the EI scale will differentiate transformational and transactional leaders.

Sensing-Intuiting (SN). Since intuition is required to create and articulate a vision which motivates followers, it is hypothesized that transformational leaders will be more intuitive than transactional leaders. The open use of intuition sets transformational leaders apart from transactional leaders (Brown, 1987).

Thinking-Feeling (TF). Studies have shown that executives generally have a greater preference for thinking rather than feeling (McCaulley, 1990). Since it is likely that more of the executives in this study will prefer thinking, it is unlikely that preference on the TF scale will differentiate transformational and transactional leaders.

Judging-Perceiving (JP). Because they are more open to ambiguity and change, transformational leaders are expected to be more perceiving (P) than their transactional counterparts.

In summary, it is expected that some individual cognitive style preferences are related to disposition for transformational or transactional leadership. Individuals who use intuitive perception (N) rather than sensing (S) are more likely to have a disposition for transformational leadership. Individuals who are perceivers (P) are more likely to have a proclivity for transformational leadership. The tendencies for extraversion (E) or introversion (I) and thinking (T) or feeling (F) are not expected to distinguish leadership disposition.

Relationship between Disposition and Leadership Practices

There are two integrated aspects of leadership: (a) the belief system, or disposition of leaders, and (b) the leadership process, or practices and behaviors of leaders. This study proposed the premise that a leader's belief system or way of creating meaning is associated with behavioral practices. According to Deutsch (1982), a disposition is a "more or less consistent complex of cognitive, motivational and moral orientations to a given situation that serve to guide one's behavior and responses in that situation" (p. 15). In an interview study of transformational leaders, Lehr (1987) found "that what was most important and common to all the leaders studied was an underlying belief system which guided and directed their actions" (p. 42).

Practices are "what managers do in the normal course of events to use the human and material resources at their disposal to carry out the organization's strategy" (Burke & Litwin, 1989, p. 282). A person who has the proclivity to be a transformational leader is expected to exhibit more of the behaviors of a transformational leader, such as taking risks, providing, demonstrating, and capturing commitment for a vision.

Relationship between Leadership Practices and Climate

Climate is defined as "the collective current impressions, expectations and feelings that members of local work units have that in turn affect their relations with their boss, with one another, and with other units" (Burke & Litwin, 1989, p.16). Transformational leadership has been theoretically related to organizational climates and cultures that promote innovation and risk taking (Bass, 1985; Burke, 1986a; Conger, 1989; Kotter, 1990). Climate is expected to influence follower motivation, which is related to organizational and individual outcomes. Outcomes include performance, productivity, and employee and customer satisfaction (Burke & Litwin, 1989; Fox, 1990).

Processes that characterize the immediate organizational context, such as the nature and quality of interactions with immediate supervisors, are likely to have a major influence on subordinate climate perceptions (Kozlowski & Doherty, 1989). Studies have supported the relationship between leadership practices and climate perceptions (e.g., Litwin & Stringer, 1968). Significant and positive relationships have been found between transformational leadership and the amount of effort subordinates are willing to exert, satisfaction with the leader, ratings of job performance, and perceived effectiveness (Avolio, Waldman, & Einstein, 1988; Bass, Waldman, Avolio, & Bebb, 1987; Hater & Bass, 1988). This study proposes that differences in leadership practices of transformational and transactional leaders are likely to be reflected in climate perceptions of leaders as well as subordinates. Figure 2 provides a diagram of the propositions tested in this study.

Method

Participants

Participants in the study included 128 senior-level executives from a global Fortune 500 manufacturing firm and 615 of their subordinates. Ninety-three percent of the executives were males, which is representative of the senior executive population in the company and the industry within which this company operates. Ages ranged between 28 and 62 years, with an average age of 45. The average length of tenure was 14 years, with an average of 11 years as a manager with the company. The executives in the study represented various functional areas of responsibility. Seventy one percent of the executives and their subordinates were based in the United States, with others from various countries.

Procedure

The following procedure was used in this study:

Survey packets were sent to executives approximately 3 to 6 weeks before they were scheduled to attend an advanced management training program sponsored by the company. The Myers-Briggs Type Indicator (MBTI) (Myers & McCaulley, 1985) and the Executive Practices and Climate Questionnaire (Burke, 1986b) with demographic questions were included in the mailing. Executives were asked to forward their responses on the answer sheets provided.

Participants were told that the instruments were strictly for developmental purposes and that confidential, personal feedback would be provided. This procedure was expected to maximize the respondent's commitment to the study and to increase data validity. Participants were asked to have "Other" forms of the Executive Practices and Climate Questionnaire completed by up to six subordinates. These instruments, which contained the same content used for the executives, asked respondents to rate their leader on each item.

To emphasize confidentiality, demographic data were not collected from subordinates completing evaluations. Since the subordinates who reported directly to the participant executives were also among top management, their demographic information was not likely to be significantly different from the executives they were rating.

All questionnaires were sent directly to an independent consulting firm, which processed the data. With the help of follow-up calls, a 98% response return rate of executive and subordinate questionnaires was obtained. Burke's (1988) Leadership Report, measuring leadership disposition, was completed by participants and self-scored at the management development seminar.

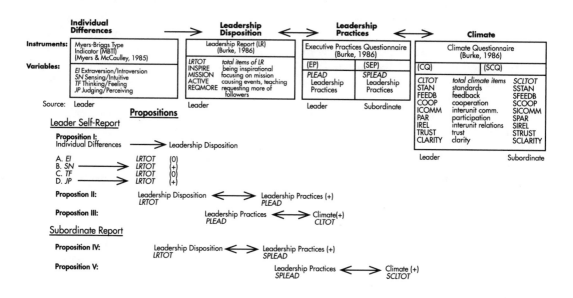

Figure 2 Tested propositions.

Instrumentation

Each executive in the study completed four instruments. Each subordinate completed an "Other" version of the Executive Practices and Climate Questionnaire. Pearson correlations were used to test the study propositions.

Individual differences. The MBTI (Myers & McCaulley, 1985) Form G, containing 126 items, was used in this study. For correlational research, the MBTI dichotomous preference scales were transformed into continuous scores. The scales were constructed so that a positive score indicated a preference for introversion, intuiting, feeling, and perceiving. A negative score identified a preference for extraversion, sensing, thinking, and judging.

Leadership belief system. The Leadership Report (LR) (Burke, 1988)

measures individual disposition for transformational or transactional leadership. The items in the Leadership Report are based on the work of Burns (1978), Bennis and Nanus (1985), and Zaleznik (1977). Respondents were given pairs of items. For each, they were asked to divide 5 points between the two alternatives, giving the higher weight to the choice more characteristic of them. In each pair, one response was indicative of transformational leadership and the other of transactional leadership, as demonstrated by the following item: "As a leader I have a primary mission of: A.---maintaining stability, B.---change." By summing the transformational scores, a continuum was formed for correlational analysis. A low score signified a more transactional belief system, and a high score signified a more transformational belief system. For more information about Burke's Leadership Report, see Sashkin and Burke (1990).

Leadership practices and climate.
The Executive Practices (EP) and Climate Questionnaire (CQ) (Burke, 1986b) consists of leadership practices and climate items on 5-point Likert-type scales. There are two versions of the Executive Practices and Climate Questionnaire, one a self-rating for leaders and the other for subordinates. Each instrument is comprised of several dimensions created by factor analysis.

The Executive Practices questionnaire measures the extent to which a statement describes a leader's behavior. After factor analysis, the Executive Practices questionnaire consisted of 35 items and 4 subscales. The 10-item Leadership Practices factor was most relevant to this study due to the hypothesis that leadership disposition is associated with those practices related to transformational leadership. Leadership Practices include providing a vision of the future that captures the commitment of people, following strong compelling goals, demonstrating commitment and persistence to achieving goals, taking risks, standing up for beliefs, encouraging others to achieve more than they think they can, showing a healthy impatience, securing through influence necessary resources, and demonstrating through behavior perception of self as a leader.

The Climate Questionnaire evaluates the last component of the Transformational/Transactional Leadership model tested in the present study. Respondents rated the extent of their agreement, from no agreement (1) to very strong agreement (5), that a statement accurately described their working conditions. Factors, similar to other climate instruments, were formed by summing item ratings. A low score on the Climate Questionnaire suggested a less favorable rating of climate perception. After factor analysis, the Climate Questionnaire consisted of 31 items, forming 8 factors.

Researchers have found that six to eight climate dimensions are generalizable across samples (James & Sells, 1981). These dimensions represent meaningful categories used by respondents to differentiate among factors in their work environment (James & Sells, 1981). The eight scales of this study are similar to those reported in other climate research (Campbell, Dunnette, Lawler, & Weick, 1970; James & Sells, 1981; Payne & Pugh, 1976). The practice and climate instruments were developed empirically using large data bases of over 4,000 executives. In the past 8 years, the instruments have been used with several thousand executives from both the business and public sectors. Climate subfactors in this study include:

1. Standards. Refers to high work unit standards and challenging goals. Members of the work unit are inspired to perform at a higher level and take pride in being members of the work unit. This factor, similar to the dependent variable used by Bass (1985), evaluates willingness to put in more effort than would be expected.

2. Feedback. Relates to recognizing people for their contribution and performance in a timely manner. It includes the leader being approachable, supporting subordinates, and regularly reviewing their performance.

3. Cooperation. Items include dealing effectively with conflicts between units, identifying problems between units to increase organizational effectiveness, responding quickly to the needs of other units, and fostering friendly, informal personal relationships between work unit members.

4. Interunit Communications. Refers to the communication of ideas, thoughts, and suggestions between work units and to the responsiveness of other units to the work unit.

5. Participation. Concerns subordinates' opportunities to influence one another's work objectives and the overall direction of the unit.

6. Interunit Relations. Corresponds to cooperative relations with other work units. When Interunit Relations are high, senior management rarely has to deal with conflicts between the work unit and other units.

7. Trust. Includes the sharing of thoughts and opinions and the support between work unit members.

8. Clarity. Items relate to operating practices and goals. When Clarity is high, work unit members are organized to plan tasks and know the tasks expected of them by others in the unit.

Results

Descriptive Statistics

Table 1 presents the descriptive statistics of the instruments used in this study. While the full range of possible scores was observed on the instruments, leaders tend to rate themselves on the higher end of the scales. The scales Interunit Relations and Trust for leaders were negatively skewed (skewness statistic is -1.39 for each), indicating that leaders tend to rate these climate factors favorably. The skewness statistic for all other scales was a normal distribution between -1 and +1, indicating that the variability of the scores on the scales was adequate for the intended correlational analyses.

The Pearson correlations related to Propositions I, II and III, leader self-report, are shown in Figure 3.

Individual Personality Differences and Leadership Disposition

Individual Differences are associated with Leadership Disposition (transformational or transactional) as measured by leader self-report. Correlations of the indices of the MBTI with the Leadership Report are presented in Figure 3.

Extraversion-Introversion and Leadership Disposition. An association was not likely between those whose preferred process is extraversion (E) or introversion (I) and their leadership disposition. The correlation between the MBTI Extraversion-Introversion (EI) scale and the total Leadership Report, presented in Figure 3, was not significant. There were significant correlations, however, between two of the four Leadership Report subscales (Mission and Requests More) and (EI), as shown in Table 2.

The correlations with these subscales suggests that transformational leaders tend to be more extraverted when they have a strong sense of mission and tend to demand more of their subordinates. There was not a significant correlation between either Inspire or Active and EI.

Sensing-Intuiting and Leadership Disposition. Those leaders whose preferred perceptive process is intuitive (N) are more likely to indicate a disposition for transformational leadership than those whose preferred process is sensing (S). As indicated in Figure 3, the correlation between the MBTI Sensing-Intuitive (SN) scale and the total Leadership Report was r = .43 (p < .001). Table 2 shows a significant positive correlation between each of the Leadership Report subscales and the Sensing-Intuitive scale (SN).

Thinking-Feeling and Leadership Disposition. There is no significant association between leaders who prefer thinking (T) or feeling (F) processes and their leadership disposition. The correlation between the MBTI Thinking-Feeling (TF) scale and the total Leadership Report presented in Figure 3 was not significant. In addition, as shown in Table 2, there were no significant correlations between the four Leadership Report subscales and TF.

TABLE 1 Descriptive Statistics for Instruments

Myers–Briggs Type Indicator N = 121

Scale	Possible Range	Observed Range	Median	Mean	SD
EI—Extraversion/Introversion	49–157 (108)	53–157 (104)	99.0	99.8	27.25
SN—Sensing/Intuitive	33–151 (118)	41–151 (110)	107.0	102.7	30.84
TF—Thinking/Feeling	35–143 (108)	39–121 (82)	71.0	74.3	19.71
JP—Judging/Perceiving	45–161 (116)	47–139 (92)	79.0	83.7	22.33

Leadership Report N = 111

Scale	# of Items	Possible Range	Observed Range	Median	Mean	SD	Cronbach Alpha
Total Leadership Report Items (LRTOT)	16	0–80 (80)	19–69 (50)	49.0	48.9	10.68	.99
Inspires Followers	8	0–40 (40)	10–34 (24)	24.0	22.7	6.62	.98
Regards Work as a Strong Sense of Mission	4	0–20 (20)	4–20 (16)	14.0	14.1	3.06	.95
Involves Being a Teacher	2	0–10 (10)	1–09 (08)	5.0	5.3	2.09	.93
Requests More of Followers	2	0–10 (10)	0–10 (10)	7.0	6.7	1.74	.93

Executive Leadership Practices Questionnaire

Scale	# of Items	Possible Range	Observed Range	Median	Mean	SD	Cronbach Alpha
Leader Ratings (PLEAD) N = 128	10	10–50 (40)	21–47 (26)	38.0	37.7	4.74	.88
Subordinate Ratings (SPLEAD) N = 615	10	10–50 (40)	10–50 (40)	36.0	35.3	6.92	.98

Climate Questionnaire—Leader Ratings N = 128

Scale	# of Items	Possible Range	Observed Range	Median	Mean	SD	Cronbach Alpha
Total Climate Items (CLTOT)	31	31–155 (124)	84–146 (62)	123.0	122.4	11.06	.94
Standards	4	4–20 (16)	10–20 (10)	16.0	15.8	2.10	.83
Feedback	6	6–30 (24)	17–30 (13)	25.0	25.0	2.65	.78
Cooperation	5	5–25 (20)	12–25 (13)	19.0	18.9	2.44	.76
Interunit Communication	2	2–10 (8)	2–10 (8)	7.0	6.7	1.40	.38
Participation	2	2–10 (8)	3–10 (7)	7.0	7.2	1.38	.45
Interunit Relations	3	3–15 (12)	5–15 (10)	14.0	13.1	2.14	.77
Trust	3	3–15 (12)	5–15 (10)	13.0	13.1	2.14	.78
Clarity	6	6–30 (24)	15–30 (15)	23.0	22.7	3.02	.84

Climate Questionnaire—Subordinate Ratings N = 615

Scale	# of Items	Possible Range	Observed Range	Median	Mean	SD	Cronbach Alpha
Total Climate Items (SCLTOT)	31	31–155 (124)	50–153 (103)	111.0	114.5	15.54	.91
Standards	4	4–20 (16)	5–20 (15)	16.0	15.6	2.86	.75
Feedback	6	6–30 (24)	6–30 (24)	23.0	22.1	4.48	.79
Cooperation	5	5–25 (20)	5–25 (17)	19.0	18.5	3.14	.76
Interunit Communication	2	2–10 (8)	2–10 (8)	6.0	6.1	1.62	.63
Participation	2	2–10 (8)	2–10 (8)	7.0	6.6	1.85	.60
Interunit Relations	3	3–15 (12)	3–15 (12)	13.0	12.4	2.43	.69
Trust	3	3–15 (12)	3–15 (12)	13.0	12.4	2.43	.60
Clarity	6	6–30 (24)	6–30 (24)	21.0	20.9	4.11	.80

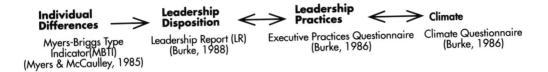

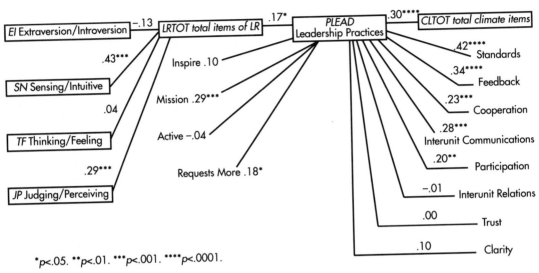

*p<.05. **p<.01. ***p<.001. ****p<.0001.

Figure 3   Pearson correlation coefficients for leader self-report.

TABLE 2   Pearson Correlation Coefficients Between the Myers–Briggs Type Indicator (MBTI) and the Leadership Report Factors   N = 111

	Inspires Followers	Regards Work as a Strong Sense of Mission	Involves Being a Teacher	Requests More of Followers
EI	− .04	− .25**	− .03	− .16*
SN	.44***	.34***	.19*	.21*
TF	.06	− .01	− .03	.02
JP	.30***	.23**	.09	.18*

Note. MBTI scales constructed so that a positive correlation indicates Leadership Report Scale was correlated with I (introversion), N (intuiting), F (feeling), and P (perceiving); a negative correlation indicates Leadership Report Scale was correlated with E (extraversion), S (sensing), T (thinking) and J (judging). Leadership Report Scale constructed so that a high score is related to transformational leadership disposition and a low score is related to transactional disposition.

*p < .05.   **p < .01.   ***p < .001.

Judging-Perceiving and Leadership Disposition.   Leaders whose preferred process is perceiving (P) are more likely to indicate a disposition for transformational leadership. As shown in Figure 3, the correlation between the MBTI Judging-Perceiving (JP) scale and the total Leadership Report was r = .29 (p < .001). As indicated in Table 2, significant correlations between three of the four Leadership

Report subscales (Inspire, Mission, and Requests More) and JP exists. There was not a significant correlation between Active and JP.

In summary, the specific propositions regarding the relationship between individual differences and leadership disposition were supported.

Leadership Disposition and Leadership Practices (Evaluated by Leader Self-Report)

Leadership Disposition has a slight association with Leadership Practices as evaluated by leader self-report. As indicated in Figure 3, the correlation between practices and disposition was r = .17 (p < .05). There were significant correlations between two of the Leadership Report factors, Mission and Requests More, and Leadership Practices.

Leadership Practices and Climate (Rated by Leader Self-Report)

A higher rating on Leadership Practices is expected to be related to higher ratings on work unit Climate dimensions. As presented in Figure 3, there was a significant positive relationship between Leadership Practices and the total Climate score of r = .30 (p < .001). Apparently, those leaders who believe they exhibit practices related to transformational leadership tend to perceive more positive work climates.

There was a significant positive correlation between Leadership Practices and the following climate factors: Standards, Feedback, Cooperation, Interunit Communications, and Participation. There were no significant correlations between practices and the dimensions of Interunit Relations, Trust, and Clarity. The negatively skewed distribution of scores for Trust and Interunit Relations accounts for the lack of correlations with these factors. According to these results, transforma-

tional leaders are more likely to communicate a vision and encourage subordinates to manage the details and thus provide less clarity.

Leadership Disposition (Evaluated by Leaders) and Leadership Practices (Evaluated by Subordinates)

Figure 4 summarizes the results of Propositions IV and V, the Pearson correlations related to subordinate reports. The Leadership Practices scale, as rated by subordinates, was correlated with the total Leadership Report instrument. Each subordinate's rating of practices was paired with his or her leader's rating of disposition. As indicated in Figure 4, the correlation between leadership disposition (the total Leadership Report) and subordinate Leadership Practices was r = .14 (p < .001). There was a significant positive correlation between three of the subscales of the Leadership Report and Leadership Practices as rated by subordinates. The size of the relationship, however, is quite small.

Leadership Practices and Climate (Rated by Subordinates)

Figure 4 shows a significant positive relationship between subordinate ratings of Leadership Practices and the total Climate score, r = .54 (p < .001). Subordinates who believe that their leaders exhibit practices of transformational leaders tend to perceive more positive work climates. There was a significant positive correlation between subordinate Leadership Practices and each of the following subordinate climate factors: Standards, Feedback, Cooperation, Interunit Communications, Participation, Interunit Relations, Trust, and Clarity.

Comparison between Leader Ratings and Subordinate Ratings

Both leader and subordinate ratings of practices were significantly related to leadership disposition and climate. Each subordinate's rating was paired with his or her leader's rating of the same dimension. There was a significant but modest association between leader and subordinate ratings of practices. Table 3 provides the correlations between leader and subordinate ratings of total Climate and the climate factors. Other research has supported the differences in practice and climate perceptions found between leaders and subordinates. However, a strong relationship existed for each group between perceptions of practices and climate.

Impact of Demographic Factors

Research findings have not shown demographic variables to be consistently associated with leadership (Bennis & Nanus, 1985; Sashkin & Fulmer, 1988; Stogdill, 1974). It is possible, however, that the hypothesized correlational results in this study could be explained by the effects of concomitant variables impacting on the hypothesized relationships. Several demographic factors that could influence the proposed relationships were taken into account through collection of demographic information from leaders. These included: years with the company, years as a manager in this company, total years as a manager, age, gender, and organizational function. Dummy variable coding was used to account for the categorical nature of functional responsibilities. To ensure confidentiality, demographic data were not collected from subordinates.

Results from this study indicated relatively little relationship between demographic factors and the scales used. Younger leaders may have a tendency toward transformational leadership disposition. The small sample of females (7%) made it difficult to evaluate the difference

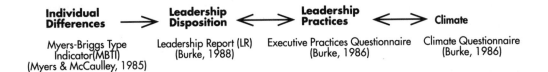

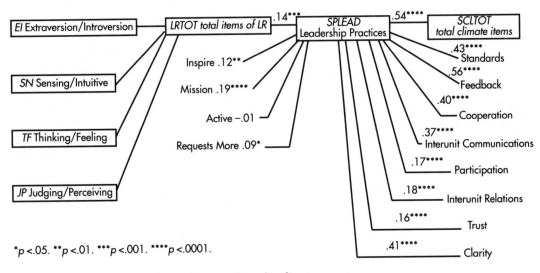

$*p <.05. **p <.01. ***p <.001. ****p <.0001.$

Figure 4 Pearson correlation coefficients for subordinate report.

TABLE 3 Pearson Correlation Coefficients Between Subordinate Ratings of Climate and Leader Ratings of Climate   N = 615

	Standards	Feedback	Cooperation	Interunit Communication	Participation
Standards	.18*				
Feedback		.12*			
Cooperation			.16*		
Interunit Communication				.16*	
Participation					.18*

	Interunit Relations	Trust	Clarity	Climate Total
Interunit Relations	.19*			
Trust		.18*		
Clarity			.17*	
Climate Total				.20*

Note. *p < .0001

---

between male and female leaders. Also, controlling for the effects of years with the company, years in management, and other demographic variables had very little impact on the relationships among key variables in this study.

Summary and Implications

The propositions tested in this study were supported by the results of the data analyses (see Van Eron, 1991, for additional details). Individual personality differences, measured by the Myers-Briggs Type Indicator (MBTI), were associated with self-ratings of leadership disposition. Those leaders whose cognitive style is intuitive are more likely to indicate a transformational belief system than those who prefer sensing. Since intuition is integral to inspiring followers and focusing attention on a vision, further re-

search is needed on using and developing intuition. The ability of perceivers to adapt and keep options open is more associated with transformational leadership than with the judging cognitive style which business organizations have primarily selected and rewarded. Rather than quickly striving for closure, transformational leaders seem to be more comfortable with ambiguity.

Leadership disposition was significantly associated with the exercise of behavioral practices related to transformational leadership, as evaluated by self-report. The low correlation portends that other situational factors—including external environment, culture, organizational structure, systems, and climate—influence leadership practices. Organizational culture and reward systems are likely to encourage some practices and discourage others. Organizational function may influence the relationship between leadership disposition and practices and is an area for further study.

Strong positive relationships were found between leader self-ratings on practices and work unit climate perceptions. Similar relationships were found for subordinate perceptions. The subordinates of leaders who have a disposition for transformational leadership rate leadership practices somewhat higher than subordinates whose bosses rate themselves as having a disposition for transactional leadership. Since subordinates did not directly evaluate disposition, the low correlation is not surprising. Again, other factors—including environment, structure, culture, climate, training, and reward systems—influence leader practices and subordinate perceptions. The study of the interaction between these factors and disposition is necessary.

There was a positive correlation between subordinates' perceptions of practices and work climate. Higher ratings on practices are related to more favorable climate ratings.

While the relationships tested in this study may be influenced by other concomitant variables, the tested demographic variables had no appreciable impact. To keep the effects of organizational culture constant, all participants in this study were from one company. Further research is needed to test whether these results generalize to other organizations.

The investigation suggests that cognitive style differences, as reflected by the MBTI, are contributing factors to leadership disposition. This study also suggests that factors other than disposition influence practices. Additional research is needed to evaluate the relationship between these factors and practices.

Since climate perceptions co-vary with leadership practices (Howell & Avolio, 1989), training and rewarding managers to use the practices of transformational leaders could have a positive effect on climate perceptions and related outcomes. In addition, identifying and evaluating leadership disposition and practices would be useful for developing effective leaders.

In summary, the present study offers support for the relationship between cognitive style, belief systems, leadership practices, and climate perceptions for transformational and transactional leaders.

References

Avolio, B. J., Waldman, D. A., & Einstein, W. O. (1988). Transformational leadership in a management game simulation: Impacting the bottom line. Group and Organizational Studies, 13, 59–80.

Barney, J. B. (1986). Organizational culture: Can it be a source of sustained competitive advantage? Academy of Management Review, 11(3), 656–665.

Bass, B. M. (1981). Stogdill's handbook of leadership: A survey of theory and research. New York: Free Press.

Bass, B. M. (1985). Leadership and performance beyond expectations. New York: Free Press.

Bass, B. M., Waldman, D. A., Avolio, B. J., & Bebb, M. (1987). Transformational leadership and the falling dominoes effect. Group and Organization Studies, 12, 73–87.

Bennis, W. G., & Nanus, B. (1985). Leaders: The strategies for taking charge. New York: Harper & Row.

Bray, D. W., & Howard, A. (1983). The AT&T longitudinal studies of managers. In K. W. Shaiel (Ed.), Longitudinal studies of adult psychological development. New York: Guilford Press.

Brown, M. D. (1987). Leadership and organization transformation: A competency model. Unpublished doctoral dissertation, The Fielding Institute, Santa Barbara, CA.

Burke, W. W. (1965). Leadership behavior as a function of the leader, the follower and the situation. Journal of Personality, 33, 60–81.

Burke, W. W. (1986a). Leadership as empowering others. In S. Srivastra & Associates (Eds.), Executive power: How executives influence people and organizations (pp. 51–75). San Francisco: Jossey-Bass.

Burke, W. W. (1986b). *Executive Practices and Climate Questionnaire.* Pelham, NY: W. Warner Burke & Associates.

Burke, W. W. (1988). *Leadership report* (rev. ed.). Pelham, NY: W. Warner Burke & Associates.

Burke, W. W., & Litwin, G. H. (1989). A causal model of organizational performance. In J. W. Pfeiffer (Ed.), *The 1989 Annual: Developing Human Resources* (pp. 277–288). San Diego: University Associates.

Burns, J. M. (1978). *Leadership.* NY: Harper & Row.

Campbell, J. P., Dunnette, M. D., Lawler, E. E., & Weick, K. E. (1970). *Managerial behavior, performance and effectiveness.* New York: McGraw-Hill.

Conger, J. A. (1989). *The charismatic leader: Behind the mystique of exceptional leadership.* San Francisco: Jossey-Bass.

Conger, J. A., & Kanungo, R. N. (1988). *Charismatic leadership: The elusive factors in organizational effectiveness.* San Francisco: Jossey-Bass.

Deutsch, M. (1982). Interdependence and psychological orientation. In V. J. Derlega & J. Grzelak (Eds.), *Cooperation and helping behavior.* New York: Academic Press.

Fox, M. (1990). *The role of individual perceptions of organization culture in predicting perceptions of work unit climate and individual and organizational performance.* Unpublished doctoral dissertation, Columbia University, New York, NY.

Goldstein, K. M., & Blackman, S. (1978). *Cognitive style: Five approaches and relevant research.* New York: Wiley-Interscience.

Hater, J. J., & Bass, B. M. (1988). Superiors' evaluations and subordinates' perceptions of transformational and transactional leadership. *Journal of Abnormal Psychology, 73,* 695–702.

House, R. J. (1977). A 1976 theory of charismatic leadership. In J. G. Hunt & L. L. Larson (Eds.), *Leadership: The cutting edge* (pp. 189–207). Carbondale, IL: Southern Illinois University Press.

House, R. J. (1988). Power and personality in complex organizations. In L. L. Cummings & B. M. Staw (Eds.), *Research in organizational behavior: An annual review of critical essays and reviews, 10,* 305–357.

House, R. J., & Baetz, M. L. (1979). Leadership: Some empirical generalizations and new research directions. *Research in Organizational Behavior, 1,* 341–423.

Howell, J. M. (1988). Two faces of charisma: Socialized and personalized leadership in organizations. In J. A. Conger & R. N. Kanungo (Eds.), *Charismatic leadership: The elusive factor in organizational effectiveness.* San Francisco: Jossey-Bass.

Howell, J. M., & Avolio, B. J. (1989, August). *Transformational versus transactional leaders: How they impact innovation, risk-taking, organizational structure and performance.* Paper presented at the Annual Meeting of the Academy of Management, Washington, D.C.

James, L. R., & Sells, S. B. (1981). Psychological climate: Theoretical perspectives and empirical research. In D. Magnusson (Ed.), *Toward a psychology of situations: An interactionist perspective* (pp. 275–295). Hillside, NJ: Erlbaum.

Kegan, R., & Lahey, L. L. (1984). Adult leadership and adult development: A constructivist view. In B. Kellerman (Ed.), *Leadership: Multidisciplinary perspectives.* Englewood Cliffs, NJ: Prentice-Hall.

Kotter, J. P. (1990). *A force for change: How leadership differs from management.* New York: Free Press.

Kozlowski, S. W. J., & Doherty, M. L. (1989). Integration of climate and leadership: Examination of a neglected issue. *Journal of Applied Psychology, 74,* 546–553.

Kuhnert, K. W., & Lewis, P. (1987). Transactional and transformational leadership: A constructive/developmental analysis. *Academy of Management Review, 12,* 648–657.

Lehr, K. A. (1987). *A descriptive study of contemporary transformational leadership.* Unpublished doctoral dissertation, The Union for Experimenting Colleges and Universities, Cincinnati, OH.

Levinson, H., & Rosenthal, S. (1984). *CEO: Corporate leadership in action.* New York: Basic Books.

Litwin, G. H., & Stringer, R. A., Jr. (1968). *Motivation and organizational climate.* Boston, MA: Harvard University Graduate School of Business Administration.

Loevinger, J. (1976). *Ego development*. San Francisco: Jossey-Bass.

Lundberg, C. (1986). The dynamic organizational contexts of executive succession: Considerations and challenges. *Human Resources Management, 25*(2), 287–303.

McCaulley, M. H. (1990). *The Myers-Briggs Type Indicator and leadership*. In K. E. Clark & M. B. Clark (Eds.), *Measures of leadership* (pp. 381–418). West Orange, NJ: Leadership Library of America.

McClelland, D. C. (1975). *Power: The inner experience*. New York: Irvington Publishers.

McClelland, D. C. (1985). *Human motivation*. Glenview, IL: Scott, Foresman.

McClelland, D. C., & Boyatzis, R. E. (1982). Leadership motive pattern and long-term success in management. *Journal of Applied Psychology, 67*, 737–743.

McClelland, D. C., & Burnham, D. H. (1976). Power is the great motivator. *Harvard Business Review, 54*(2), 100–110.

Mischel, W. (1973). Toward a cognitive social learning reconceptualization of personality. *Psychological Review, 80*, 252–283.

Myers, I. B. (1975). *Manual: The Myers-Briggs Type Indicator*. Palo Alto, CA: Consulting Psychologists Press.

Myers, I. B., with Briggs, P. (1980). *Gifts differing*. Palo Alto, CA: Consulting Psychologists Press.

Myers, I. B., & McCaulley, M. H. (1985). *A guide to the development and use of the Myers-Briggs Type Indicator*. Palo Alto, CA: Consulting Psychologists Press.

Payne, R. L., & Pugh D. S. (1976). Organizational structure and climate. In M. D. Dunnette (Ed.), *Handbook of industrial and organizational psychology* (pp. 1125–1173). Chicago: Rand McNally.

Sashkin, M., & Burke, W. W. (1990). Understanding and assessing organizational leadership. In K. E. Clark & M. B. Clark (Eds.), *Measures of leadership* (pp. 297–325). West Orange, NJ: Leadership Library of America.

Sashkin, M., & Fulmer, R. M. (1988). Toward an organizational leadership theory. In J. G. Hunt, B. R. Baliga, H. P. Dachler, & C. A. Schriesheim (Eds.), *Emerging leadership vistas* (pp. 51–65). Lexington, MA: Lexington Books.

Schein, E. H. (1985). *Organizational culture and leadership*. San Francisco: Jossey-Bass.

Schneider, B. (1983). Work climates: An interactionist perspective. In N. W. Feimer & E. S. Geller (Eds.), *Environmental psychology directions and perspectives* (pp. 106–128). New York: Praeger.

Schwartz, H., & Davis, S. M. (1981). Matching corporate culture and business strategy. *Organizational Dynamics, 10*(2), 30–48.

Stogdill, R. M. (1948). Personal factors associated with leadership: A survey of the literature. *Journal of Psychology, 25*, 35–71.

Stogdill, R. M. (1974). *Handbook of leadership*. New York: Free Press.

Streufert S., & Streufert, S. J. (1978). *Behavior in the complex environment*. New York: Halsted.

Tichy, N. M., & Devanna, M. (1986). *The transformational leader*. New York: Wiley.

Van Eron, A. M. (1991). *Key components of the transformational/ transactional leadership model: The relationship between individual differences, leadership disposition, behavior and climate*. Unpublished doctoral dissertation, Columbia University, New York, NY.

Zaleznik, A. (1977). Managers and leaders: Are they different? *Harvard Business Review, 55*(5), 67–78.

Ann M. Van Eron is the principal of Potentials, an organization development and management consulting firm based in New York and Wisconsin. She is a member of the Academy of Management and the American Psychological Association. She earned her PhD from Columbia University.

W. Warner Burke is Professor of Psychology and Education and Director of the graduate program in Organizational Psychology at Teachers College, Columbia University, as well as President of W. Warner Burke Associates, Inc. Formerly with NTL and the OD Network, he was the Editor of the *Academy of Management Executive* and has been on the board of governors of both the Academy of Management and the American Society for

Training and Development. He has received the Public Service Medal from the National Aeronautics and Space Administration and the Distinguished Contribution to Human Resource Development Award from ASTD. He has published over 60 works on organization development, training, and social and organizational psychology. He received his PhD from the University of Texas.

Direct inquiries about this article to Ann M. Van Eron, Principal, Potentials, 1511 Briarcliff Drive, Appleton, Wisconsin 54915, 414/832–9788 or 212/399–0708.

CHAPTER 13

Transformational Leadership's Impact on Higher Education Satisfaction, Effectiveness, and Extra Effort

Mary L. Tucker, Bernard M. Bass, and Larry G. Daniel, Jr.

Leaders in higher education have been widely criticized for failure to apply the literature on leadership and management to maintain and advance their institutions in today's increasingly complex internal and external environments. Using the Multifactor Leadership Questionnaire (MLQ), based on Bass' transformational leadership paradigm, this research investigated the perceived organizational leadership profile of a southern urban university. Transformational leadership was the predominant style in this university, affirming that transformational leadership subsumed transactional leadership qualities in this higher education sample. Leaders intent on maximizing satisfaction of and obtaining extra effort from followers would benefit from transformational leadership behaviors.

Unquestionably, universities are among the worst managed institutions in the country. . . One reason, incredibly enough, is that universities—which have studied everything from government to Persian mirrors and the number '7'—have never deeply studied their own administration. (Bennis, 1976, pp. 25–26)

Whether or not Bennis' statement about university management is true, there are those who believe that higher education leadership phenomena are insufficiently researched. Immegart (1988) notes that between 1980 and 1985, the *Educational Administration Quarterly* published only one university-level leadership article. In fact, so few higher education leadership studies have been published that the topic was omitted in the 1982 *Encyclopedia of Educational Research*.

Researchers agree that strong and versatile university leadership is critical during times of great flux (Bensimon, 1987; Bolman & Deal, 1984). Ironically, however, as universities experience accelerating rates of change, with unpredictable futures that prohibit long-term goal formation, and increasing dependence on rules, regulations, and external environments, it is difficult to find leaders who survive. Kerr (1975) predicted that between the years 1980 to 2000, 10 thousand presidents will have served American universities with an average tenure of 2 1/2 years.

Bennis and Nanus (1985) suggested that organizations are being underled and overmanaged, a concern echoed by Terrey (1986) in regard to universities. Terrey observed that there is a craving for leadership in higher education and bemoaned "the absence of leadership and vision, the tendency to select survivalism over risk, [and] the control by managers rather than leaders" (p. 6).

Educational leadership research in this direction has been encouraged (Bass & Avolio, 1990; Sergiovanni, 1984) but still remains behind research in other fields. Immegart (1988) feels "there are only a few minor differences between education and other areas, and it is also quite apparent that studies in education tend to mirror other work and to lag behind the empirical, conceptual, and methodological advances realized elsewhere" (p. 267).

Purpose

The specific focus of this research was to investigate the perceived organizational leadership of a southern urban university using the Multifactor Leadership Questionnaire (MLQ), which is based on the transformational leadership paradigm developed by Bass (1985). The independent variables for this research were transactional leadership, transformational leadership, and laissez-faire leadership. Outcome variables included satisfaction, effectiveness, and extra effort. All six variables were measured by the MLQ. The present study evaluated possible augmentation effects of transformational leadership. Specifically, this research intended to determine whether transformational leadership accounts for more of the variance in (a) followers' perceived satisfaction with their leader, (b) followers' perception of leader effectiveness, and (c) followers' perception of their extra effort beyond that accounted for by transactional leadership alone.

Sample and Procedures of Data Collection

A comprehensive urban university in the southern United States served as the institution for study. Sampling for the study was obtained from members of the university's dominant coalition: chancellor, administration, deans, department chairs, and selected faculty. Responses of individual participants were used to prepare university-level leadership profiles. Each respondent described his or her immediate supervisor: Faculty respondents described their department chairperson, chairpersons described their dean, and so on. The chancellor was the only participant asked to use a self-rater form.

Copies of the MLQ (Form 5) were hand delivered to 200 administrators and faculty. The university organizational chart and campus directory were used to identify a purposive sampling (Kerlinger, 1986) of representative participants. The MLQs were coded to identify departments, colleges, divisions, and administration, while maintaining individual anonymity.

Usable responses were obtained from 106 (53%) of the subjects. Of the 106 usable responses, 31 respondents held the position of chancellor, vice chancellor, associate vice chancellor, dean, or director; the remaining 75 were department chairs and faculty. On the average, most leaders were described by three respondents; in some instances, one or two respondents provided an individual leadership profile.

University Profile

The university being researched (XSU) opened its doors in 1958. In 1987 to 1988, XSU's enrollment ranked second in the state with 16,109 students and graduated 1,201 bachelor, 428 masters, and 25 doctoral students.

XSU had 29.4 Full Time Equivalent (FTE) students per full-time faculty, organized in six colleges: Business Administration, Education, Engineering, Liberal Arts, Sciences, and Urban and Public Affairs. The current chancellor was appointed in 1987, and University documents refer to his "visions" for the university. Under the chancellor's leadership, the strategic mission for the university was revised, and five major goals of the institution and university-wide objectives were established. For accomplishment of these goals, the administration revised the organizational structure of XSU to include vice chancellors for Academic and Student Affairs, Business Affairs, Graduate Studies and Research, and University Relations.

Instrumentation

The Multifactor Leadership Questionnaire (MLQ) was developed by Bass (1985) and refined by Bass and Avolio (1990) in an effort to expand "the dimensions of leadership measured by previous leadership surveys and to provide a concise computerized feedback form that could be used for individual, team, and organizational development" (p. 1). The MLQ measures seven factors of leadership grouped within three dimensions of leadership: transactional, transformational, and laissez-faire (or nonleadership).

The transactional leadership dimension consists in the factors of Contingent Reward (CR) and Management-by-Exception (MBE). Use of contingent reward signifies an exchange. Rewards are recommended or provided by the leader if followers have met agreed-upon objectives. Needs of followers are identified and associated with leader expectations and with rewards if objectives are reached. Management-By-Exception is less active, occurring when the leader avoids intervening as long as performance goals are met. Outcomes from effective transactional leadership are the expected effort and expected performance of followers.

The transformational dimension consists in the factors of Charisma (CH), Inspirational Motivation (IM), Intellectual Stimulation (IS), and Individualized Consideration (IC). Charisma is found in the interaction between the leader's attributes and the values, needs, beliefs, and perceptions of followers. Inspirational Motivation is exhibited in understanding what is important, voicing shared goals, and engaging the followers for successful attainment of organizational objectives. Intellectual Stimulation engages followers to think creatively, fostering problem solving and reasoning. Individualized Consideration is shown when the leader (a) delegates projects to followers to foster learning experiences and (b) mentors followers, treating followers individually. Outcomes derived from effective transformational leadership are higher levels of satisfaction, effectiveness, and extra effort than those realized with transactional leadership alone. Bass and Avolio (1990) point out that this "newer paradigm adds transformational leadership to previous transactional leadership models" (p. 16), not to replace transactional leadership but to augment it with transformational factors to reach the goals of the organization, group, leaders, and followers.

The seventh factor, Laissez-Faire (LF), is indicative of nonleadership. This type of "avoiding" leadership generally is without transactions or agreements between leaders and followers. Laissez-Faire leadership results in negative outcomes of satisfaction, effectiveness, and extra effort.

Research Analyses

Intercorrelations of MLQ-derived factors and outcome variables for the 106 respondents are illustrated in Table 1. All variables were statistically significant and were intercorrelated with all other variables at an alpha level of .05 except for Management-By-Exception, which only covaried with Contingent Reward and Laissez-Faire at a statistically significant level.

Illustrated in Table 2 are the Pearson correlation coefficients for each predictor variable with each of the outcome variables and the other predictor variables, as well as the variable means and standard deviations. Of the three predictors, transformational leadership had the highest correlations with university satisfaction (r = .73), university leaders' effectiveness (r = .87), and university extra effort for their leaders (r = .86). Transactional leadership had the next highest correlations with the outcome variables (r = .49 to .59). Transactional leadership was also highly correlated with transformational leadership (r = .59). In turn, Laissez-Faire leadership, as expected, was inversely correlated with transformational leadership (r = -.41) and also had negative correlations with the outcome variables (r = -.29 to -.41).

Canonical Correlation Analysis

The MLQ-derived function subscale scores for transformational, transactional, and laissez-faire leadership were designated as the independent, or predictor, variables; MLQ-derived function subscale scores for Satisfaction, Effectiveness, and Extra Effort were designated as the criterion, or dependent, variables. All six of these variables were entered into a canonical correlation analysis using the SSPSx MANOVA procedure.

Since both the predictor and criterion sets used in the present study contained three variables, the analysis yielded three canonical functions. The standardized function and structure coefficients for all three possible uncorrelated canonical functions are presented in Table 3.

The first canonical function yielded an Rc of .93 (R_c^2 = .87). Leadership variables thus predicted approximately 87% of the variance in the outcome variables on the first canonical function, which accounted for 98% of the total canonical analysis variance. Only Function I had an eigenvalue greater than 1 (6.698), and Wilks' lambda showed the F approximation to be statistically significant at $p < .001$. Transformational leadership explained most of the variance of the first canonical function with a structure coefficient of 1.00. Satisfaction, Effectiveness, and Extra Effort were highly correlated with Function I, as illustrated by structure coefficients ranging from .79 to .93.

Transactional leadership had the largest structure coefficient (.78) on the second canonical function. Satisfaction correlated moderately with Function II (.62) but only correlated minimally with Extra Effort (.10) and minutely (.03) with Effectiveness. Although Function II explained only 10% of total variance and had an eigenvalue less than 1 (.116), it did have a Wilks' lambda showing the F approximation to be statistically significant at $p < .05$.

Laissez-Faire had a structure coefficient of .89 on the third canonical function. However, Function III only contained .01% of the total variance explained, and the likelihood ratio associated with lambda for the third function (p = .319) was not statistically significant. This function explains virtually no correlation to Satisfaction and only small amounts of correlation to Effectiveness and Extra Effort.

Commonality Analysis

The canonical correlation analysis was followed up with a multivariate commonality analysis (Thompson, 1985) of Function I. Based on the commonality analy-

TABLE 1 Intercorrelations of MLQ-Derived Factors and Outcome
Variables for University Data

| | **Pearson Product-Moment Correlations** | | | | | | | | | |
	CH	**IM**	**IS**	**IC**	**CR**	**MBE**	**LF**	**EE**	**EFF**	**SAT**
CH	----									
IM	.87	----								
IS	.84	.85	----							
IC	.89	.88	.86	----						
CR	.77	.73	.66	.82	----					
MBE	− .07*	− .15*	− .11*	− .06*	.13	----				
LF	− .36	− .41	− .38	− .40	− .26	.51	----			
EE	.81	.80	.86	.80	.65	− .08*	− .34	----		
EFF	.86	.81	.78	.84	.69	− .12*	− .41	.73	----	
SAT	.74	.65	.67	.70	.66	.10*	− .29	.66	.72	----

Note. n = 106.

Note. CH = Charisma; IM = Inspirational Motivation; IS = Intellectual Stimulation;
IC = Individualized Consideration; CR = Contingent Reward; MBE = Management-
By-Exception; LF = Laissez-Faire; EE = Extra Effort; EFF = Effectiveness;
SAT = Satisfaction.

*Not statistically significant at alpha = .05.

TABLE 2 Intercorrelations of MLQ-Derived Predictor Variables and
Outcome Variables for Entire University Data with Means and
Standard Deviations

| | **Pearson Product-Moment Correlations** | | | | | | **Means and Standard Deviations** | |
	TF	**TA**	**LF**	**EE**	**EFF**	**SAT**	**M**	**SD**
TF	---	.59	− .41	.86	.87	.73	2.47	.889
TA	.59	---	.04*	.49	.50	.59	2.07	.556
LF	− .41	.04*	---	− .34	− .41	− .29	1.54	.611
EE	.86	.49	− .34	---	.74	.66	2.15	1.207
EFF	.87	.50	− .41	.74	---	.72	2.58	.953
SAT	.73	.59	−.29	.66	.72	---	2.47	1.427

Note. n = 106.

Note. TF = Transformational Leadership; TA = Transactional Leadership; LF = Laissez-
Faire Leadership; EE = Extra Effort; EFF = Effectiveness; SAT = Satisfaction.

*Not statistically significant at alpha = .05.

TABLE 3 Canonical Standardized Function and Structure Coefficients and Variance Explained

	Function I		Function II		Function III	
	Func.	Struc.	Func.	Struc.	Func.	Struc.
TF	.98	**1.00**	.91	.00	.61	.02
TA	.01	.59	1.33	**.78**	.19	.21
LF	.03	.43	.29	.13	1.15	**.89**
R_c^2		.870		.104		.010
EE	.49	**.93**	.61	.10	1.32	.37
EFF	.50	**.93**	.65	.03	1.43	.36
SAT	.10	**.79**	1.49	**.62**	.15	.01

Note. Structure coefficients > .6 are presented in bold.

Note. TF = Transformational Leadership; TA = Transactional Leadership; LF = Laissez-Faire Leadership; EE = Extra Effort; EFF = Effectiveness; SAT = Satisfaction.

sis, transformational leadership had the most unique share of the variance (38.8%) explained in the canonical correlation analysis, with transformational and transactional leadership variables having the most shared variance (32.2%). Little of the variance (.005%) individually was explained uniquely by transactional leadership. Laissez-Faire leadership also shared 17.6% of additional variance with transformational leadership. (See Tucker, 1990, for an in-depth review of research analyses for this study.)

Profile of XSU Leadership Style

The overall XSU leadership profile, presented as means in Table 2, suggests that transformational leadership is perceived as the predominant leadership style used by leaders at XSU (M = 2.47, SD = .9). Although there is a perception of the presence of transactional leadership (M = 2.07, SD = .6), the standardized effect size for the difference between transformational and transactional leadership is 53% [[2.47 − 2.07] / [(.9 + .6) / 2]]. A laissez-faire leadership (M = 1.54, SD

= .6) style is less frequently ascribed to this university's leaders.

Table 2 suggests that participants throughout this university are fairly satisfied (M = 2.47, SD = 1.4) with their leaders as a whole and perceive them to be effective (M = 2.58, SD = .9). In addition, extra effort (M = 2.45, SD = 1.2) is perceived to be expended for these leaders by followers. Satisfaction ratings were the most variable (SD = 1.43).

Summary and Conclusions

The university MLQ-derived profile suggests an overall transformational leadership style, although individual leaders' profiles spanned from laissez-faire leadership styles to transformational leadership styles. Transactional leadership, particularly Contingent Reward, was associated with satisfaction, effectiveness, and extra effort. However, such transactional leadership, augmented by transformational leadership, generated perceived increases of satisfaction, effectiveness, and extra effort. Although laissez-faire leadership had a negative correlation with the outcome variables for this university, some individual laissez-faire and management-by-exception items were considered in a positive vein by the respondents. This may reflect the unique functions of higher education organizations as compared to organizations of other types.

Replication of this research is called for to substantiate these findings. However, three implications can be drawn from this data analysis. First, although intuitively different from leaders in business, industry, and the military, leaders in higher education are perceived by followers as possessing qualities attributable to the newer transformational leadership paradigm. Second, higher education leaders who scored in the transformational domain are perceived by their followers as more effective than other leaders. Followers of these transformational leaders are more satisfied with their leaders. In addition, followers of these transformational leaders in higher education are more willing to expend extra effort for their leaders than are followers of predominately transactional or laissez-faire leaders. Third, educational leaders wishing to increase their impact of perceived satisfaction, effectiveness, and extra effort may enlist the behaviors of transformational leadership to enhance their job relationships with subordinates and peers.

Training using this paradigm and the MLQ would provide higher education leaders with a working knowledge of the benefits of augmenting transactional leadership with transformational leadership. It would also demonstrate how various components of leadership style can be harnessed to intensify leadership effectiveness, follower satisfaction, and extra effort expended by followers.

References

Bass, B. M. (1985). *Leadership and performance beyond expectations*. New York: Free Press.

Bass, B. M., & Avolio, B. J. (1990). *Transformational leadership development: Manual for the Multifactor Leadership Questionnaire*. Palo Alto, CA: Consulting Psychologists Press.

Bennis, W. (1976). *The unconscious conspiracy: Why leaders can't lead*. New York: AMACOM.

Bennis, W., & Nanus, B. (1985). *Leaders: The strategies for taking charge*. New York: Harper & Row.

Bensimon, E. M. (1987, November). *The meaning of "Good presidential leadership": A frame analysis*. Paper presented at the meeting of the Association for the Study of Higher Education, Baltimore, MD.

Bolman, L. G., & Deal, T. E. (1984). *Modern approaches to understanding and managing organizations*. San Francisco: Jossey-Bass.

Immegart, G. L. (1988). Leadership and leader behavior. In N. J. Boyan (Ed.), *Handbook of research on educational administration: A project of the AERA* (pp. 259–277). New York: Longman.

Kerlinger, F. N. (1986). *Foundations of behavioral research* (3rd ed.). Fort Worth, TX: Holt, Rinehart & Winston.

Kerr, C. (1975). The trustee faces steady state. *AGB Reports, 17*, 2–15.

Sergiovanni, T. J. (1984). Leadership and excellence in schooling. *Educational Leadership, 41*, 6–13.

Terrey, J. N. (1986, April). *Leadership can create excellence*. Paper presented at the National Convention of the American Association of Community and Junior Colleges, Orlando, FL.

Thompson, B. (1985, April). *Heuristics for teaching multivariate general linear model techniques*. Paper presented at the meeting of the American Educational Research Association, Chicago, IL.

Tucker, M. L. (1991). Higher education leadership: Transformational leadership as a predictor of satisfaction, effectiveness, and extra effort. *Dissertation Abstracts International, 52*, 773A. (University Microfilms No. 91–21, 558)

Mary L. Tucker, PhD, is Assistant Professor in the College of Business at Nicholls State University. She has published and presented academic and professional articles on leadership, communication, and statistical methods.

Bernard M. Bass, PhD, is Distinguished Professor of Management at State University of New York-Binghamton and Director of the Center for Leadership Studies. He has authored 13 books and published over 250 articles and papers. He is co-author of the Multifactor Leadership Questionnaire and has conducted leadership workshops in over 40 countries and in numerous Fortune 500 companies.

Larry G. Daniel, Jr., PhD, is Assistant Professor of Educational Leadership and Research at the University of Southern Mississippi. He has published and presented in the research areas of teacher education and evaluation, higher education, ethics, and statistical methods.

Direct inquiries about this article to Mary L. Tucker, Assistant Professor, Office Information Systems, Nicholls State University, P.O. Box 2042, Thibodaux, LA 70310–2042, 504/448–4922.

An Empirical Investigation of the Effects of Transformational and Transactional Leadership on Organizational Climate, Attrition, and Performance

Gordon J. Curphy

This study extends the construct validity of Bass' (1985) theory of transformational and transactional leadership by examining how these variables relate to indices of organizational climate, attrition, and performance. Neither transformational nor transactional leadership were found to be related to organizational turnover. Organizational performance indices which required independent effort among subordinates were also unrelated to either leadership dimension. However, both types of leadership were significantly related to organizational climate and performance indices which required interdependent effort among subordinates. The possibility of training individuals to be transformational leaders is discussed.

From the 1920s through the 1970s, charismatic leaders and movements were studied primarily by historians, sociologists, and political scientists. Psychologists did not show much interest in studying charisma until the appearance of an article by House (1977). House posited that many aspects of charismatic leadership were empirically testable. A number of researchers have since examined the traits and behaviors of leaders, the characteristics of followers, and the situational variables necessary for charisma to be attributed to certain leaders. Although a number of different charismatic leadership theories have been offered (Bass, 1985; Boal & Bryson, 1987; Conger & Kanungo, 1988; Graham, 1987; Howell, 1988; Kets de Vries, 1988; Kuhnert & Lewis, 1987; Roberts & Bradley, 1988; Sashkin, 1988; Tichy & Devanna, 1986; Willner, 1984), none is as comprehensive or as thoroughly researched as Bass' (1985) theory of transformational and transactional leadership.

Bass (1985) maintains that transforma-

The opinions expressed in this paper are the author's; they do not necessarily reflect those of the United States Air Force nor the United States Air Force Academy.

tional and transactional behaviors comprise two conceptually independent dimensions of leadership. Transformational leadership consists of those behaviors which are typically associated with charismatic leaders, such as having a vision of the future and causing subordinates to rethink the way in which they see the world. These behaviors are believed to result in heightened emotions, which in turn inspire followers to exert extra effort toward goal accomplishment. On the other hand, transactional leadership primarily consists of the administration of rewards and punishments contingent upon subordinates' performance.

Bass (1985) operationally defined transactional leadership as the composite score from the Contingent Reward and Management by Exception scales on the Multifactor Leadership Questionnaire (MLQ). The Contingent Reward scale measures behaviors that emphasize the rewards to be gained or exchanged for subordinates' performance. These behaviors can be effective, particularly when leaders have a high level of authority and subordinates' performance is due to skill or effort (Yukl, 1981). However, due to time pressures and a general disbelief in the efficacy of contingent reward behaviors, many managers are content to intervene only when problems occur (Avolio & Bass, 1988). Managers who firmly believe in the status quo and do not take proactive organizational roles are likely to manifest a variety of Management by Exception behaviors.

On the other hand, transformational leaders constantly interact with subordinates in order to cause organizational change. Bass (1985) originally conceptualized transformational leadership as having three major subcomponents, which were charisma, individualized consideration, and intellectual stimulation. Charisma is the most important subcomponent; charismatic leaders have high self-confidence, a strong need to influence others, and superior communication skills. They also articulate goals in ideological terms, engage in behaviors

that create the image of success, and have an action orientation. Transformational leaders also show individualized consideration toward subordinates; these leaders have high levels of insight into subordinates, treat them as individuals, and maintain a mentoring or developmental attitude rather than fostering blind obedience in followers. Moreover, transformational leaders intellectually stimulate their followers by getting them to question the status quo and think about problems in new ways. Bass operationally defined transformational leadership as the composite score of the charisma, individualized consideration, and intellectual stimulation scales of the MLQ.

Bass and his associates investigated (a) the covariance structure of the transformational and transactional leadership scales; (b) the relationship between the two leadership dimensions and subordinates' satisfaction, leaders' performance, and unit performance; (c) whether transformational leadership accounts for criterion variance over and above transactional leadership (i.e., the augmentation hypothesis); and (d) whether followers of transformational leaders model their leader's behaviors (i.e., the cascade hypothesis).

Curphy (1991) reviewed the studies which shed light on these four research areas and found that covariance structure analyses showed only mixed support for the independence of transformational and transactional leadership; the contingent reward scale often loaded on the same factor as the three transformational scales, and the intercorrelations between these four scales often exceeded r = .7. Thus, although Bass and his associates claimed transformational and transactional leadership were conceptually independent, empirically they were not.

Subordinates' ratings of transformational leadership were usually found to correlate above r = .5 with subordinates' ratings of satisfaction and of leader effectiveness. These correlations were often higher than those noted for transactional leadership. However, substantially smaller correlation coefficients were found when single source bias was eliminated or if promotion rates or unit performance indices were used as the criterion. Moreover, transformational leadership accounted for variance in subordinates' satisfaction ratings over and above transactional leadership only when hierarchical regression analysis (Cohen & Cohen, 1975) was used and both the predictor and criterion variables came from the same questionnaire. Studies utilizing stepwise regression analyses techniques or unit performance indices found much less support for the augmentation hypothesis. Finally, some evidence was found to support the cascade hypothesis; however, transactional leadership behaviors were more likely to be modeled by subordinates.

Method

The study described in this paper further explores the construct validity of Bass' (1985) theory. The data reported herein were collected four times (i.e., once per semester) over a 2-year period and were collected from a large number of individuals (N = 11,668). Furthermore, individuals were randomly assigned to one of 40 identical organizations, and multiple indices of unit performance were utilized.

Setting

Data were collected at the United States Air Force Academy (USAFA). Its mission is "to provide instruction and experience to each cadet so that he/she graduates with the knowledge and character essential to leadership and the motivation to become a career officer in the United States Air Force (Schmeling, 1974, p. 185). Thus, USAFA is one of the few undergraduate institutions in the United States whose primary charter is to gradu-

ate future leaders. One of the ways in which the Academy accomplishes its mission is by having cadets experience a number of leadership opportunities prior to graduation. These opportunities are found primarily in the 40 cadet squadrons, which are self-contained organizations with identical hierarchical structures. Cadets are randomly assigned to one of the squadrons and experience a different aspect of leadership each year. Freshmen perform a follower role, sophomores spend a majority of their time being trained to become first-line supervisors, juniors are the first-line supervisors, and senior cadets fulfill a middle-level management role in the squadron.

The top-level management role in each squadron is played by the Air Officer Commanding, or AOC. The AOC is a commissioned military officer with 10 to 13 years of active duty experience. As the commander, an AOC is responsible for guiding, advising, counseling, representing, rewarding, and disciplining all 110 cadets in his squadron. This study examines how cadets' ratings of their AOC are related to squadron climate, attrition, and performance.

Measures

The Squadron Assessment Questionnaire (SAQ). The SAQ was developed to assess cadets' perceptions of their AOC, their squadron, and Academy-wide issues. This study utilized 36 SAQ items which measured cadets' perceptions about squadron climate, reward and punishment policies, resignation from the Academy, and the degree of transformational and transactional leadership exhibited by their AOCs. Six-point Likert and 5-point magnitude estimation scales were used by cadets when rating the items. The 16 transformational and transactional items were adapted from the MLQ.

Squadron attrition. The number of cadets who resigned from the Academy in

TABLE 1 Pattern Matrix for a Five Factor Solution for SAQ Items

	Factor Loadings				
Items	**One**	**Two**	**Three**	**Four**	**Five**
My AOC is a symbol of success and accomplishment.	.89				
I am ready to trust my AOC to overcome any obstacle.	.89				
I'm proud to be associated with my AOC.	.88				
I have complete faith in my AOC.	.86				
My AOC arouses in me the effort to work harder.	.84				
My AOC gets us to use reasoning and evidence.	.82				
My AOC is a good officer role model.	.78				
My AOC gives me reasons to change the way I think.	.77				
We can count on our AOC to express his/her appreciation when we do a good job.	.76				
If we work hard for our AOC, he/she gets us things.	.76				
My AOC places special emphasis on careful problem solving.	.74				
My AOC makes sure I think through my problems.	.74				
My AOC finds out what I want and helps me achieve it.	.73				
My AOC gives recognition when we perform at the standard or higher.	.72				
My AOC gives special attention for good work.	.66				
My AOC gives attention to neglected squadron members.	.63				
A friendly atmosphere prevails in this squadron.		− .80			
I'm proud to be part of this squadron.		− .76			
I'm glad to be in this squadron.		− .75			
Our squadron sticks together to do a job.		− .72			
I feel good about being in this squadron.		− .70			
Cadets in this squadron trust each other.		− .64			
Different classes cooperate in this squadron.		− .60			
There is hostility between classes in this squadron.		.56			
I'm satisfied with the relationship between classes in this squadron.		− .56			
Cliques divide and split my squadron.		.37			
This semester I've been motivated to do more.			.81		
I have a higher motivation to succeed this semester.			.74		
I have done more than I expected this semester.			.68		
I frequently think about leaving the Academy.				.74	
I often get discouraged about being a cadet.				.74	
There is not enough recognition or reward in the squadron.					− .69
Punishments exceed rewards in the squadron.					− .64
There are sufficient rewards for good work in the squadron.					.64
Discipline is handled fairly in the squadron.					.41
Cadets know why they get hits in my squadron.					.32

Note. Factor loadings < .3 were omitted; N = 11,668.

each cadet squadron from August 15, 1985 through January 15, 1986 and January 16, 1986 through June 16, 1986 was used to define the first two attrition data sets. The same information was collected in the 1986–1987 academic year and made up the last two attrition data sets.

Squadron performance. The five performance indicators available for anal-

Scales and Items

Transformational Leadership

Charisma

I'm proud to be associated with my AOC.
I have complete faith in my AOC.
My AOC is a symbol of success and accomplishment.
I am ready to trust my AOC to overcome any obstacle.
My AOC arouses in me the effort to work harder.
My AOC is a good officer role model.

Individualized Consideration

My AOC gives attention to neglected squadron members.
My AOC finds out what I want and helps me to achieve it.
We can count on our AOC to express his/her appreciation when we do a good job.

Intellectual Stimulation

My AOC gives me reasons to change the way I think.
My AOC places special emphasis on careful problem solving.
My AOC gets us to use reasoning and evidence.

Transactional Leadership

If we work hard for our AOC, he/she gets us things.
My AOC gives special recognition for good work.
My AOC gives recognition when we perform at the standard or higher.

Note. Almost all of these items were rated on a 1 through 5 scale which ranged from not at all to frequently. The exception was the item "My AOC is a good officer role model." This item was rated on a 6-point Likert scale.

ysis include the squadrons' intramural, Professional Competency Exam (PCE), academic, and overall (called the squadron-of-the-semester) rank orderings, as well as the standards evaluation (stan eval) rating performance at the end of each semester. Squadrons were rank ordered from 1 to 40 on the first three performance indicators depending on the number of intramural victories, overall knowledge of the Academy and the Air Force (i.e., mean PCE performance), and overall academic performance respectively. Each squadron also went through a rigorous 2-day inspection of personnel and operational procedures, which resulted in a 5-point stan eval rating ranging from outstanding (1) to unsatisfactory (5). Finally, the squadron-of-the-semester results encompass these four indicators as well as a number of other indices of squadron performance. These rankings ranged from 1 to 10, as only the first 10 squadrons, second 10 squadrons, and so forth competed against each other for this award.

Samples

The subjects used in this study were freshman, sophomore, junior, and senior cadets at USAFA from August 1985 until April 1987. Because the cadet squadron is the unit of analysis and the performance and attrition data were calculated at the squadron level, sampling is only a con-

TABLE 3 Descriptive Statistics for the April 1987 SAQ Scales

Scales	Mean	Standard Deviation
Transformational Leadership	3.20	.67
Charisma	3.26	.79
Individualized Consideration	3.07	.58
Intellectual Stimulation	3.20	.57
Transactional Leadership	3.28	.58
Climate	4.08	.41
Extra Effort	3.57	.26
Intent to Resign	3.23	.24
Reward and Punishment	3.72	.48

Note. Cronbach (1951) alphas for eight of the nine scales exceeded .8; the Intent to Resign scale had internal consistency reliability indices averaging .72. Similar descriptive statistics and reliability results were found for the November 1985, April 1986, and November 1986 data sets.

Note. The Intent to Resign scale was reverse scored. Higher scores indicate that cadets are thinking less about leaving USAFA.

cern for the SAQ ratings. The SAQ data were collected over four different administrations, in November 1985, April 1986, November 1986, and April 1987. The SAQ was administered to the entire cadet population (N = 4,400) each semester, and the number of usable returns ranged from 2,300 to 3,500 (average return rate of 63%). Thus, 60–90 cadets per squadron per semester provided ratings concerning their AOC, squadron climate, and squadron reward and punishment policies.

Analyses and Results

The first step in the analyses consisted of creating scales for the 36 SAQ items. The pattern matrix found in Table 1 corresponds to the Leadership, Climate, Intent to Resign, and Reward and Punishment scales created using factor analytic techniques. Because the 16 transformational and transactional items loaded on a single factor, the Transformational and Transactional Leadership scales found in Table 2 were created using rational scale construction techniques. Descriptive statis-

tics for the nine scales can be found in Table 3.

Both Transformational and Transactional Leadership scores were significantly correlated with the Climate, Extra Effort, and Reward and Punishment indices across the four data sets (see Table 4). In addition, fall semester leadership scale scores often correlated significantly with spring semester Climate, Extra Effort, and Reward and Punishment indices. Additional analyses indicated that these correlation coefficients remained unchanged after controlling for single source bias.

Both Transformational and Transactional leadership were generally unrelated to organizational turnover. However, the fall 1986 leadership scales ratings were positively related to spring 1987 turnover rates (see Table 5).

Table 6 reveals that squadron performance indices which required independent effort, such as the PCE and academic rankings, were for the most part unrelated to AOCs' Transformational or Transactional Leadership ratings. On the other hand, indices which required interdependent effort, such as stan eval, intramurals,

TABLE 4 Zero-Order Correlations of Transformational and Transactional Leadership with Other SAQ Scales

	Semester					
Scales	Nov 1985	Apr 1986	Nov 1986	Apr 1987	1985[a]– 1986	1986[b]– 1987
Climate						
Transformational	.38	.51	.41	.43	.29	.29
Transactional	.45	.61	.50	.43	.34	.30
Extra Effort						
Transformational	.53	.39	.39	.50	.48	.26
Transactional	.60	.50	.47	.47	.52	.28
Intent to Resign						
Transformational	−.19	−.43	.15	.25	−.17	.24
Transactional	−.18	−.42	.13	.30	−.14	.31
Reward and Punishment						
Transformational	.67	.68	.63	.73	.56	.60
Transactional	.70	.80	.73	.77	.61	.64

Note. r's > .31 are significant at the .05 level. r's > .40 are significant at the .01 level. r's > .50 are significant at the .001 level.

[a]These are the correlations between the November 1985 Leadership scales and the April 1986 Climate, etc., scales.

[b]These are the correlations between the November 1986 Leadership scales and the April 1987 Climate, etc., scales.

and squadron-of-the-semester standings were often significantly correlated with Transformational and Transactional Leadership ratings. (The negative correlations indicate that higher Transformational and Transactional Leadership ratings were associated with squadrons which were either ranked higher—e.g., 1st or 2nd as opposed to 39th or 40th—or rated as outstanding on these performance indicators.) Furthermore, AOCs' fall leadership ratings were often more highly correlated with spring rather than fall performance standings.

Discussion

This study examined different aspects of Bass' (1985) theory of transformational and transactional leadership. Both types of leadership had moderate to strong relationships with squadron Climate, Extra Effort, and Reward and Punishment ratings. Both leadership dimensions were generally unrelated to cadets' Intent to Resign ratings or objective indices of organizational turnover. Therefore, cadets giving their AOCs higher leadership ratings reported being more motivated and

TABLE 5 Descriptive Statistics and Zero-Order Correlations of Squadron Attrition with Transformational and Transactional Leadership Ratings

	Semester					
	Nov 1985	Apr 1986	Nov 1986	Apr 1987	1985[a]– 1986	1986[b]– 1987
Descriptive Statistics for Attrition						
Mean	3.5	5.0	3.3	5.0	—	—
Std. Dev.	2.3	2.2	1.9	2.1	—	—
Zero-Order Correlations						
Transform.	.07	.19	– .27	.20	.22	.41
Transact.	.08	.24	– .20	.28	.22	.43

Note. r's > .31 are significant at the .05 level. r's > .40 are significant at the .01 level. r's > .50 are significant at the .001 level.

[a]These are the correlations between the November 1985 leadership ratings and the spring 1986 attrition rates. [b]These are the correlations between the November 1986 leadership ratings and the spring 1986 attrition rates.

having a more cohesive squadron than did cadets giving their AOCs lower leadership ratings.

Perhaps the most interesting finding of this study has to do with the impact of transformational and transactional leadership on organizational performance. Neither leadership dimension was found to have much impact on performance indices which reflect the independent efforts of subordinates. However, AOCs' Transformational and Transactional Leadership ratings had a positive impact on organizational performance indices which required interdependent effort. This was particularly true when AOCs' fall scores on Transformational and Transactional Leadership were correlated with spring performance indices requiring interdependent effort (i.e., stan eval, intramural, and squadron-of-the-semester standings).

These leadership-performance findings have several implications. As described by Campbell (1977, 1988), it may be somewhat naive to assume that a leader's behaviors will have an equal impact on all organizational performance indices. The recommendation from this study is that leadership will only affect those performance indices which require interdependent effort; indices which require independent effort will be relatively insensitive to a leader's behaviors. Moreover, it may take time for the leader behaviors to have an effect. Table 6 revealed that fall leadership-spring performance correlations were often higher than the fall leadership-fall performance correlations. Studies concurrently collecting leadership and performance data may underestimate the long-term impact of leadership on organizational performance.

Although these findings are promising, much more work needs to be done to

TABLE 6 Zero-Order Correlations of Transformational and Transactional Leadership with Squadron Performance Measures

Measures	Nov 1985	Apr 1986	Nov 1986	Apr 1987	1985[a]– 1986	1986[b]– 1987
PCE4[c]						
Transformational	−.16	.10	.04	.00	−.28	−.08
Transactional	−.17	.08	−.05	.06	−.32	−.06
PCE3[d]						
Transformational	—	.17	—	.19	.21	.12
Transactional	—	.20	—	.17	.20	.13
PCE1[e]						
Transformational	—	−.10	—	−.17	.08	−.10
Transactional	—	−.06	—	−.23	.03	−.04
Academics						
Transformational	−.05	−.27	.21	.23	−.27	.21
Transactional	−.10	−.32	.18	.22	−.27	.24
Intramurals						
Transformational	−.28	−.35	−.21	.00	−.51	−.15
Transactional	−.30	−.33	−.20	.02	−.50	−.12
Stan Eval						
Transformational	−.03	−.43	.03	−.32	−.36	−.23
Transactional	−.07	−.40	.04	−.29	−.36	−.24
Squadron of the Semester						
Transformational	−.27	−.35	−.18	−.32	−.35	−.31
Transactional	−.29	−.34	−.22	−.30	−.36	−.30

Note. r's > .31 are significant at the .05 level. r's > .40 are significant at the .01 level. r's > .50 are significant at the .001 level. Negative correlations indicate that AOCs with higher leadership ratings had better squadron performance.

[a]These are the correlations between the November 1985 leadership ratings and standings on the April 1986 performance measures. [b]These are the correlations between the November 1986 leadership ratings and standings on the April 1987 performance measures. [c]PCE4 = Professional Competency Exam for freshmen. [d]PCE3 = Professional Competency Exam for sophomores; these tests were given only in the spring. [e]PCE1 = Professional Competency Exam for seniors; these tests were given only in the spring.

select those individuals with the potential to be transformational leaders, identify the behaviors comprising charismatic leadership, and determine how to train these charismatic behaviors. Until these last three issues are resolved, the idea that we can now train people to be transformational leaders seems fairly unrealistic.

In conclusion, it seems clear that both transformational and transactional leadership had immediate effects on organizational climate. Regarding organizational performance, both types of leadership had particularly strong effects when (a) the leadership ratings were collected six months prior to the performance data, and (b) the performance measure required interdependent effort among subordinates.

Acknowledgments

This paper is a condensed version of my doctoral dissertation. It was written under the guidance of my advisor, John Campbell.

I would like to thank Dianne Nilsen, Paul Grunzke, Dave Porter, Tom McCloy, and Rich Hughes for their help in preparing this manuscript.

References

Avolio, B. J., & Bass, B. M. (1988). *Test manual for the Multifactor Leadership Questionnaire.* Unpublished manuscript, State University of New York, Center for Leadership Studies, School of Management, Binghamton.

Bass, B. M. (1985). *Leadership and performance beyond expectations.* New York: Free Press.

Boal, K. M., & Bryson, J. M. (1987). Charismatic leadership: A phenomenological and structural approach. In J. G. Hunt, B. R. Baliga, H. P. Dachler, & C. A. Schriesheim (Eds.), *Emerging leadership vistas* (pp. 11–28). Lexington, MA: D. C. Heath & Company.

Campbell, J. P. (1977). The cutting edge of leadership: An overview. In J. G. Hunt & L. L. Larson (Eds.), *Leadership: The cutting edge* (pp. 221–234). Carbondale, IL: Southern Illinois University Press.

Campbell, J. P. (1988). Training design for performance improvement. In J. P. Campbell, R. J. Campbell, & Associates (Eds.), *Productivity in organizations: New perspectives from industrial/organizational psychology* (pp. 177–215). San Francisco: Jossey-Bass.

Cohen, J., & Cohen, P. (1975). *Applied multiple regression/correlation analysis for the behavioral sciences.* Hillsdale, NJ: Erlbaum.

Conger, J. A., & Kanungo, R. N. (1988). Behavioral dimensions of charismatic leadership. In J. A. Conger & R. N. Kanungo (Eds.), *Charismatic leadership: The elusive factor in organizational effectiveness* (pp. 78–97). San Francisco: Jossey-Bass.

Cronbach, L. J. (1951). Coefficient alpha and the internal structure of tests. *Psychometrika, 16,* 297–334.

Curphy, G. J. (1991). *An empirical evaluation of Bass' (1985) theory of transformational and transactional leadership.* Unpublished doctoral dissertation, University of Minnesota, Minneapolis.

Graham, J. W. (1987). Transformational leadership: Fostering follower autonomy, not automatic followership. In J. G. Hunt, B. R. Baliga, H. P. Dachler, & C. A. Schriesheim (Eds.), *Emerging leadership vistas* (pp. 73–79). Lexington, MA: D. C. Heath.

House, R. J. (1977). A 1976 theory of charismatic leadership. In J. G. Hunt & L. L. Larson (Eds.), *Leadership: The cutting edge* (pp. 189–207). Carbondale, IL: Southern Illinois University Press.

Howell, J. M. (1988). Two faces of charisma: Socialized and personalized leadership in organizations. In J. A. Conger & R. N. Kanungo (Eds.), *Charismatic leadership: The elusive factor in organizational effectiveness* (pp. 213–236). San Francisco: Jossey-Bass.

Kets de Vries, M. F. (1988). Origins of charisma: Ties that bind the leader and the led. In J. A. Conger & R. N. Kanungo (Eds.), *Charismatic leadership: The elusive factor in organizational effectiveness* (pp. 237–252). San Francisco: Jossey-Bass.

Kuhnert, K. W., & Lewis, P. (1987). Transactional and transformational leadership: A constructive/developmental analysis. *Academy of Management Review, 12,* 648–657.

Roberts, N. C., & Bradley, R. T. (1988). Limits of charisma. In J. A. Conger & R. N. Kanungo (Eds.), *Charismatic leadership: The elusive factor in organizational effectiveness* (pp. 253–275). San Francisco: Jossey-Bass.

Sashkin, M. (1988). The visionary leader. In J. A. Conger & R. N. Kanungo (Eds.), *Charismatic leadership: The elusive factor in organizational effectiveness* (pp. 122–160). San Francisco: Jossey-Bass.

Schmeling, C. E. (Ed.). (1974). *Contrails: The Air Force cadet handbook* (Vol. 20). Colorado Springs: United States Air Force Academy.

Tichy, N. M., & Devanna, M. A. (1986). *The transformational leader*. New York: Wiley.

Willner, A. R. (1984). *The Spellbinders*. Ann Arbor, MI: Bookcrafters.

Yukl, G. A. (1981). *Leadership in organizations*. Englewood Cliffs, NJ: Prentice-Hall.

Gordon J. Curphy is a Tenure Associate Professor in the Department of Behavioral Sciences and Leadership at the United States Air Force Academy. He is actively conducting research in leadership selection and training, whistleblowing, integrity testing, and the evaluation of a new undergraduate physics curriculum.

Direct inquiries about this article to Gordon J. Curphy, Tenure Associate Professor, Department of Behavioral Sciences, USAF Academy, CO 80840–5701, 719/472–3860.

CHAPTER 15

An Examination of Leader Behaviors, Organizational Climate, and Subordinate Reactions

**Richard S. Tallarigo and
Michael A. Rosebush**

The Leadership Development Questionnaire (LDQ) is used at the U.S. Air Force Academy to provide feedback to cadet supervisors from subordinates on aspects of leadership behavior, organizational climate, and perceptual/attitudinal reactions. Relations of leader behaviors, organizational climate, and hierarchical position to subordinates' reactions are examined. It is concluded that leader behaviors, while significantly accounting for satisfaction with supervision, had minor impact on reactions to the organization. Organizational climate, although significantly accounting for reactions to the organization, had little impact on satisfaction with supervision. Hierarchical position had only weak effects.

Throughout four years at the United States Air Force Academy (USAFA), cadets are exposed to a wide variety of academic, military, and athletic programs designed to develop the leadership skills and commitment required of professional military officers. One aspect of the leadership training received by all cadets is provided by the organizational structure of the cadet wing. Through this structure, all cadets exercise leadership and followership roles in various capacities. Over the past several years, the USAFA Department of Behavioral Sciences and Leadership has developed survey programs tailored to the cadet wing structure. These surveys have been designed to provide cadets the opportunity to assess the leadership behaviors of their immediate cadet supervisors and the climate within their respective cadet organizational units (i.e., squadrons). Factor analyses of responses to hundreds of items from thousands of cadets over several years have resulted in the Leadership Development Questionnaire (LDQ) (Tallarigo & Rosebush, 1991).

The LDQ is a hypothetical model of leadership consisting of leader behaviors (individualized consideration, task orientation, and leadership demeanor), organi-

TABLE 1 Internal Consistency Reliability Estimates of LDQ Scales

LDQ Scale	No. Items	Alpha
1. Supervisor Individualized Consideration	7	.93
2. Supervisor Task Orientation	5	.90
3. Supervisor Leadership Demeanor	3	.87
4. Squadron Goals/Responsibilities	4	.75
5. Squadron Class Relations	4	.81
6. Squadron Equity	4	.63
7. Squadron Communication	3	.80
8. Satisfaction with Supervision	3	.92
9. Personal Growth	2	.79
10. Satisfaction with Squadron	3	.86
11. Perceived Squadron Productivity	2	.87
	Total: 40	Median: .86

zational climate (equity, communication, goals, and cadet class relations), and subordinate reactions of satisfaction with supervision, satisfaction with the organization, personal growth, and perceived organizational productivity. The purpose of the present study was to examine a few preliminary questions regarding the appropriateness of the LDQ model. Specifically, are the effects of leader behaviors and climate contingent on supervisory levels? What are the relative impacts of leader behavior and of climate in accounting for subordinate reactions to supervision and to the organization? By way of introduction, a description of the LDQ and some of its psychometric properties is appropriate.

Psychometric Properties of the LDQ

One of the practical realities that has shaped the LDQ is user acceptance, particularly of the length of the survey instrument. Previous instruments were lengthy (over 100 items), and there was marked resistance to their administration. By con-

trast, the LDQ consists of 11 scales and 40 core items (excluding demographics). Table 1 presents the scales, the number of items, and the coefficient alpha (Cronbach, 1951) estimate of internal consistency reliability associated with each. Conceptually, the LDQ consists of three types of items (and scales): (a) leader behaviors rated on 10-point scales of observed frequency (Scales 1 through 3), (b) organizational processes rated on 10-point scales of observed frequency (Scales 4 through 7), and (c) perceptual and attitudinal reactions to leader behaviors and the organization rated on 10-point adjectival scales (Scales 8 through 11). This structure was the result of factor analytic research spanning several years and based on responses from over 10,000 cadets.

Table 2 presents the results of a canonical correlation analysis of scales 1 through 7 with scales 8 through 11. This test, based on data obtained in the fall of 1990 from 3,759 cadets, addressed the construct validity of the observation scales (Scales 1 through 7) and the reaction scales (Scales 8 through 11). If the conceptual framework outlined above is correct, the canonical solution (similar to factor analysis) should demonstrate distinct factors of leadership and organizational climate across the observation and reaction scales. This appeared to be the result. The overall test was highly significant (p < .0001), and the overall test effect (Wilks lambda = .17) can be interpreted as an R-squared of .83 between the two sets of scales (Tatsuoka, 1988). More importantly, the solution suggested that two major dimensions, or canonical roots, accounted for most of the variance in the data. (The third and fourth dimensions accounted for less than 1% of the total variance.) Root I represented scales 1, 2, 3, and 8. These scales measure Supervisor Individualized Consideration, Supervisor Task Orientation, Supervisor Leadership Demeanor, and Satisfaction with Supervision. Root II represented scales 4, 5, 6, 7, 10, and 11. That is, Root II represented the organizational climate observation scales (Squadron Goals and Responsibilities, Squadron Class Relations, Squadron Equity, and Squadron Communication) and subordinate reactions to the organization (Satisfaction with Squadron and Perceived Squadron Productivity). Note that scale 9, Personal Growth, did not clearly load on either canonical root and was crossloaded on both. The canonical correlation analysis suggested that the LDQ consists of two independent construct domains, leader behaviors (and subordinate reactions to them) and organizational processes (and subordinate reactions to them).

To assess criterion-related validity, criteria for organizational and leader effectiveness were obtained. The organizational units of interest in the LDQ are the 40 squadrons comprising the cadet wing. At the end of the academic year, squadrons are assigned scores based on military, athletic, and academic effectiveness cumulated over the year. The winner of this competition is named the Outstanding Squadron of the Year. Multivariate analysis of variance was used to test for differences on LDQ scales between the higher and lower squadrons (based upon a median split). Table 3 shows the mean

TABLE 2   Canonical Correlation Analysis of LDQ Observation Scales with LDQ Subordinate Reaction Scales

Canonical Root: Canonical Correlation:	I .81	II .70
LDQ Observation Scales:		
1. Supervisor Individualized Consideration	.89	– .31
2. Supervisor Task Orientation	.84	– .21
3. Supervisor Leadership Demeanor	.84	– .23
4. Squadron Goals and Responsibilities	.51	.69
5. Squadron Class Relations	.52	.59
6. Squadron Equity	.55	.56
7. Squadron Communication	.56	.70
LDQ Reaction Scales:		
8. Satisfaction with Supervision	.97	– .25
9. Personal Growth	.62	.41
10. Satisfaction with Squadron	.59	.75
11. Perceived Squadron Productivity	.55	.75

Note. Table entries are correlations between scales and respective canonical variates.

scores and t-tests on the LDQ scales obtained from this analysis. The scales that were significantly related to squadron end-of-year performance were those that measured organizational processes and subordinate reactions to them. The leader behavior scales, however, showed no significant relationships with squadron performance.

The validity of leader behavior and squadron ratings was also investigated in a user acceptance study of the LDQ and the associated feedback processes (Rosebush & Tallarigo, 1991). Each Air Officer Commanding (AOC), that is, the commissioned officer in charge of supervising all cadets in a squadron, was asked to rate the validity of the LDQ in identifying high- and low-performing cadet supervisors. Fifty percent said the LDQ correctly identified all true low-scoring cadets; 69%

TABLE 3 Differences between LDQ Ratings of Cadets in Higher and
Lower Performing Squadrons

LDQ Scale		Higher Performing	Lower Performing	*t*
Supervisor Individualized Consideration[a]	M	3.40	3.41	.22 n.s.
	SD	.96	.93	
	N	1492	1212	
Supervisor Task Orientation[a]	M	3.58	3.58	.05 n.s.
	SD	.89	.87	
	N	1492	1212	
Supervisor Leadership Demeanor[a]	M	3.77	3.81	1.09 n.s.
	SD	.87	.88	
	N	1512	1223	
Squadron Goals and Responsibilities	M	5.76	5.44	5.26**
	SD	1.71	1.72	
	N	1897	1496	
Squadron Class Relations	M	4.98	4.83	2.32*
	SD	1.80	1.85	
	N	1897	1496	
Squadron Equity	M	5.27	4.98	4.28**
	SD	1.90	1.96	
	N	1897	1496	
Squadron Communication	M	5.23	4.86	5.48**
	SD	1.86	1.93	
	N	1897	1496	
Satisfaction with Supervision	M	7.00	6.92	1.11 n.s.
	SD	2.08	2.02	
	N	1492	2704	
Personal Growth	M	5.40	5.05	4.57**
	SD	2.20	2.29	
	N	1897	1496	
Satisfaction with Squadron	M	5.32	4.76	7.79**
	SD	2.09	2.11	
	N	1897	1496	
Perceived Squadron Productivity	M	5.69	5.13	7.49**
	SD	2.11	2.20	
	N	1897	1496	

Note. Data are based on spring 1990 administration of the LDQ and
Outstanding Squadron results.

[a]Based on 5-point scale, 5 being most positive; all other scales based
on 10-point scale, 10 being most positive.

*$p < .05$.   **$p < .001$.

said most or all true high-scoring cadets were identified. Regarding the squadron organizational measures, 89% of the AOCs reported that the LDQ accurately assessed their squadron's performance.

In terms of measurement properties, the LDQ appears to be a useful instrument for measuring leader behaviors, organizational climate, and perceptual/attitudinal reactions to them. However, additional validation, particularly of the leader behavior scales, would be appropriate.

Hierarchical Level of the Leader as a Situational Factor

A major theme in the extensive leadership research literature has been the situational factors impacting both leader behavior and their consequences (Yukl, 1989). No model of leadership impact can be complete without consideration of such factors.

In the present research, the hierarchical level of the immediate supervisor was examined as a potential situational factor. The highest level included 46 supervisors: the cadet wing commander and a vice wing commander, 4 group commanders, and 40 squadron commanders. Each squadron commander supervised 3 flight commanders (totalling 120 middle-level supervisors). Each flight commander supervised 3 element leaders (totalling 360 first-line supervisors). To test for the effects of these three hierarchical levels, two analyses were conducted. The first was a multivariate analysis of variance which tested the effects of level on leader behaviors of Individualized Consideration, Task Orientation, and Leadership Demeanor. The second examined the effects of level on the functional relationships between leader behaviors and outcome scales.

Effects of Level on Leader Behaviors

Each respondent in the sample was classified on the basis of the immediate supervisor rated (i.e., one of the three supervisory levels previously mentioned). A one-way multivariate analysis of variance was performed on the three leader behavior scales by position. The overall test was significant (Wilks lambda = .97), with a sample size of 2,777. The effect size, however, was rather small, with only about 3% of variance in leader behavior explained by level. Univariate F-tests with post hoc Scheffe contrasts indicated that the level effect was significant for Individualized Consideration with $F (2, 2774) = 8.73, p < .001$. The contrast was significant between top-level commanders ($M = 6.89$) and lowest-level supervisors ($M = 6.42$). For the Task Orientation scale, the F statistic was also significant ($F (2, 2774) = 14.57, p < .0001$). Again, the only significant Scheffe contrast was between the top supervisors ($M = 7.65$) and the lowest ($M = 7.12$). The F statistic for the Leadership Demeanor scale was not significant.

Overall, the effects of the hierarchical level of the leader in the cadet wing did not demonstrate strong effects on observed leader behavior. With increasing level, however, a trend toward higher scores on observed Individualized Consideration and Task Orientation was evident.

Are Subordinate Reactions Contingent on Leader Level?

To address this question, the regression of the outcome scales on leader behaviors was tested for consistency across the three supervisory levels. That is, did leader behaviors exhibited by element leaders produce satisfaction with supervision in the same manner as did the behaviors of other supervisors? Two series of hierarchical regression analyses were performed to test the significance of the increment in explained variance provided by the interaction of supervisory position with each of the leader behavior scales. The dependent variables were Satisfaction with Immediate Supervision and Personal Growth. The analyses, based upon responses from 2,753 cadets, provided no meaningful support to a contingency explanation for leader behavior based upon supervisory position. The largest increment in explained variance due to the position interaction term was .009.

Leader behaviors accounting for Satisfaction with Supervision and Personal Growth were not meaningfully different across the three leader hierarchical levels. Consequently, the following tests were based upon combined data from the cadet wing sample.

Relative Impacts of Leadership Behavior and Climate on Subordinate Reactions

By virtue of its design, the Leadership Development Questionnaire incorporates behavioral observations of leadership and organizational climate within a single instrument. This provides the opportunity to assess the joint and the unique effects of these factors on the LDQ outcomes measured at the level of the individual respondent. An advantage of this type of analysis is in the modeling of leader behaviors, organizational climate, and subordinate reactions to supervision and the organization.

Table 4 provides an analysis of the unique contributions to the four LDQ outcome scales (Scales 8 through 11) provided by the leader behavior scales, partialing out the effects of the climate scales, and by the climate scales, partialing out the effects of the leader behavior scales. Due to the large sample, all R-squared increments were statistically significant.

Consequently, interpretations of these results were made on the basis of the relative sizes of the effects. Computations were performed following the procedures outlined by Pedhazur (1982).

The leader behavior and climate scales appeared to exert independent and specific effects, depending upon the outcome measure being considered. For example, in predicting Satisfaction with Supervision, the R-squared increment provided by climate was .008, whereas the increment provided by leader behavior was .501. While this suggests the "common-sense" notion that leader behavior is very important for predicting satisfaction with supervision, it also implies that perceptions of the organization may have little to do with how one appraises one's supervisor.

Similarly, the climate scales explained 38% and 40% of the variance in Perceived Squadron Productivity and Satisfaction with the Squadron, respectively. However, leader behavior explained extremely small percentages of variance in those outcomes (see Table 4).

Personal Growth was predicted more strongly by the climate scales (18%) than by the leader behavior scales (4%). Overall, Personal Growth related less strongly to leader behavior and climate than any of the other outcome scales. As a follow-up to these findings, a series of step-wise multiple regression analyses were performed which indicated, from the 30 leader behavior and climate observation items, those most predictive of the outcome scales. Table 5 lists the items most predictive of each LDQ outcome scale. As can be seen in the table, each dependent variable (with the exception of Personal Growth) was best predicted by a cluster of either leadership or climate items. For example, of the 12 items most predictive of Perceived Squadron Productivity, all were from climate items except for 2, which also contributed the least explained variance. Of the 16 items that predicted the Personal Growth scale, only 6 were from the leader behavior scales. Re-

TABLE 4 Incremental Validity of Leader Behavior (LB) and Organization Climate (OC) Scales in Predicting LDQ Reaction Scales

Dependent Variable	Predictor Set					N
	LB[a]	OC[a]	LB + OC	RSQinc–LB[b]	RSQinc–OC[c]	
Satisfaction with Supervision	.634	.141	.642	.501	.008	3768
Personal Growth	.155	.295	.335	.040	.180	3766
Satisfaction with Squadron	.097	.501	.503	.002	.406	3771
Perceived Squadron Productivity	.082	.464	.467	.002	.385	3767

[a]R-squared for predicting dependent variable from predictor scales.
[b]Squared multiple semi-partial correlation of the leader behavior scales (scales 1–3) with each dependent variable. Denoted as $R^2y(123.4567) = R^2y.1234567 - R^2y.4567$.
[c]Squared multiple semi-partial correlation of the organizational climate scales (scales 4–7) with each dependent variable. Denoted as $R^2y(4567.123) = R^2y.1234567 - R^2y.123$.

gression statistics for the preceding analyses are available from the first author.

Summary and Theoretical Considerations

This study explored a tentative model of leadership for the cadet wing at the United States Air Force Academy. A number of conclusions are suggested by the research thus far. These concern the taxonomy of leadership behaviors and organizational climate, the role of contingency factors, and possible causal directions in the model.

Taxonomies of leader behavior have grown substantially in size since the Ohio State and Michigan studies of decades past (Yukl, 1989). The taxonomies emerging from the present research, however, included a three-factor structure of leader behavior and a four-factor structure of organizational climate. The leader behavior scales appeared to represent the traditional components of task orientation, relationship orientation, and a third factor (Leadership Demeanor) that may be suggestive of participative or charisma behaviors. Further research on the construct and criterion-related validity of these scales is needed. The climate model represents traditional processes, such as equity and communication, but also cadet-relevant issues such as squadron goal setting and class relationships.

The role of contingency factors in leadership research with the LDQ is also in a very early stage of exploration. Situational moderators such as work group size, nature of the work, or leader/subordinate tenure are not likely to be operative in the highly standardized cadet organizational structure. The analyses reported here suggested a minimal effect due to hierarchical level. That is, a small effect was found for increased Task Orientation and Individualized Consideration at higher levels. The small effect may be at

TABLE 5   Items Best Predicting Subordinate Reactions

Predicted Scale: Satisfaction with Supervision

Acts in a very encouraging manner to me. (Individualized Consideration)
Seems to have a solid plan to accomplish tasks. (Task Orientation)
Tells me that he/she is willing to help me. (Individualized Consideration)
Appears friendly and approachable. (Leadership Demeanor)
Holds effective meetings. (Task Orientation)
I am kept up-to-date on important events and situations. (Squadron Communication)
Leads by providing an example of what is required. (Task Orientation)

Predicted Scale: Personal Growth

Information is shared upward so decisions are based on the best available know-how.
   (Squadron Communication)
Lets me know that he/she believes in my performance capabilities. (Individualized
   Consideration)
The tasks I am given to do by other cadets are important. (Squadron Class Relations)
I am kept up-to-date on important events and situations. (Squadron Communication)
I am rewarded based on my performance. (Squadron Equity)
Maintains a positive outlook. (Leadership Demeanor)
If I make an unintentional mistake, I receive verbal correction or retraining—not punishment.
   (Squadron Equity)
I can see when and where we are making progress toward our squadron's goals.
   (Squadron Goals & Responsibilities)

Predicted Scale: Satisfaction with Squadron

Information is shared upward so decisions are based on the best available know-how.
   (Squadron Communication)
I can see when and where we are making progress toward our squadron's goals.
   (Squadron Goals & Responsibilities)
I see cadets from different classes cooperating to help those not in their class.
   (Squadron Class Relations)
If I make an unintentional mistake, I receive verbal correction or retraining—not punishment.
   (Squadron Equity)
New ideas are welcomed and encouraged. (Squadron Communication)
I receive the same level of consequences as any other cadet under the same circumstances.
   (Squadron Equity)

Predicted Scale: Perceived Squadron Productivity

Information is shared upward so decisions are based on the best available know-how.
   (Squadron Communication)
I can see when and where we are making progress toward our squadron's goals.
   (Squadron Goals & Responsibilities)
I see cadets taking their squadron responsibilities seriously. (Squadron Goals & Responsibilities)
I am rewarded based on my performance. (Squadron Equity)
New ideas are welcomed and encouraged. (Squadron Communication)

least partially explained by the scales included (and excluded) in the analysis. Because of its brevity, the LDQ does not include other potential factors of leader behavior, many of which, if included in the model, could exhibit effects due to hierarchical position. For example, Jago and Vroom (1977), among others, found that increases in hierarchical level are associated with increased use of participative supervisory style and decreased autocratic styles. The leader behavior scales of the LDQ do not measure participative versus autocratic leadership styles and consequently could not indicate such relationships. The slight tendency for top-level supervisors to exhibit higher levels of Task Orientation and Consideration may be related to differences in the task characteristics, peer relations, or position power associated with those positions (Badin, 1974). Future research may need to examine these and other factors, to determine how the cadet supervisory levels may differ in situational variables. The role theory approach of Tsui (1984) may also provide an interesting basis for analysis of expected differences in behaviors of the cadet positions.

Finally, causal assumptions underlie all leadership impact research. Causal assumptions can be acknowledged explicitly; less preferably, they may remain implicit. Indeed, the very notion of "the impact of leadership" implies a causal order. For example, arguments have been made on both sides of the leadership-causes-performance debate (Lieberson & O'Connor, 1972; Thomas, 1988). There is also evidence on both sides of the leadership-causes-climate debate (Joyce, Slocum, & Abelson, 1977; Litwin & Stringer, 1968). The issues surrounding causal ordering of leadership and organizational processes are complex (see Kozlowski & Doherty, 1989, for a review). The complexity of modeling causal pathways increases when, in addition to leadership and climate, the outcomes of satisfaction and organizational performance

are included (Barrow, 1976; LaFollette & Sims, 1975; Pritchard & Karasick, 1973).

While not testing a causal model, the present data suggest that leader behaviors were not strongly related to organizational outcomes such as perceived productivity, measured performance, or satisfaction with the organization. Causal model testing programs such as LISREL (Joreskog & Sorbom, 1989) will be necessary to study causal relationships among leader behaviors, climate, reaction factors, and organizational performance. If leader behaviors do not exert direct effects on organizational outcomes, then alternative models must be considered. One alternative, that leader behaviors impact organizational outcomes indirectly through organizational climate processes, would be consistent with the findings reported in this study: Leader behaviors had negligible direct impact on organizational outcomes when climate processes were taken into consideration. An alternative model, also consistent with present findings, is that climate processes impact satisfaction with supervision indirectly through direct influence on leader behaviors. The determination of the more appropriate model to the present data is an objective for additional research.

Conclusions

How does leader behavior impact subordinate reactions? Conclusions from the present study suggest that leader behaviors may have a direct and strong impact on satisfaction with supervision. With regard to organizational outcomes, the impact of leader behaviors may be very small or mediated by other factors such as organizational climate. Finally, for the behaviors measured in this study, the influence of leadership was not contingent upon the leaders's level of responsibility in the larger organization.

References

Badin, I. (1974). Some moderator influences on relationships between consideration, initiating structure, and organizational criteria. *Journal of Applied Psychology, 59*, 380–382.

Barrow, J. (1976). Worker performance and task complexity as causal determinants of leader behavior style and flexibility. *Journal of Applied Psychology, 61*, 433–440.

Cronbach, L. (1951). Coefficient alpha and the internal structure of tests. *Psychometrika, 16*, 297–334.

Jago, A., & Vroom, V. (1977). Hierarchical level and leadership style. *Organizational Behavior and Human Performance, 18*, 131–145.

Joreskog, K., & Sorbom, D. (1989). *LISREL VII: User's reference guide*. Mooresville, IN: Scientific Software.

Joyce, W., Slocum, J., & Abelson, M. (1977). A causal analysis of psychological climate and leader behavior relationships. *Journal of Business Research, 5*, 261–273.

Kozlowski, S., & Doherty, M. (1989). Integration of climate and leadership: Examination of a neglected issue. *Journal of Applied Psychology, 74*, 546–553.

LaFollette, W., & Sims, H. (1975). Is satisfaction redundant with organizational climate? *Organizational Behavior and Human Performance, 13*, 257–278.

Lieberson, S., & O'Connor, J. (1972). Leadership and organizational performance: A study of large corporations. *American Sociological Review, 37*, 117–130.

Litwin, G., & Stringer, R. (1968). *Motivation and organizational climate*. Boston: Harvard University Press.

Pedhazur, E. (1982). *Multiple regression in behavioral research* (2nd ed.). New York: Holt, Rinehart, & Winston.

Pritchard, R., & Karasick, B. (1973). The effects of organizational climate on managerial job performance and job satisfaction. *Organizational Behavior and Human Performance, 9*, 126–146.

Rosebush, M., & Tallarigo, R. (1991). *Assessment of the usefulness of subordinate survey feedback to supervisors*. Paper presented at the Third Annual Convention of the American Psychological Society, Washington, DC.

Tallarigo, R., & Rosebush, M. (1991). *Psychometric characteristics of the United States Air Force Academy Leadership Development Questionnaire*. Paper presented at the Third Annual Convention of the American Psychological Society, Washington, DC.

Tatsuoka, M. (1988). *Multivariate analysis* (2nd ed.). New York: Macmillan.

Thomas, A. (1988). Does leadership make a difference to organizational performance? *Administrative Science Quarterly, 33*, 388–400.

Tsui, A. (1984). A role set analysis of managerial reputation. *Organizational Behavior and Human Performance, 34*, 64–96.

Yukl, G. (1989). *Leadership in Organizations* (2nd ed.). Englewood Cliffs, NJ: Prentice-Hall.

Richard S. Tallarigo is a Captain in the United States Air Force. His specialties include job design, survey feedback, and performance appraisal. He received a PhD in Industrial-Organizational Psychology from Bowling Green State University.

Michael A. Rosebush is the Director for Curriculum and Faculty Development at the U.S. Air Force Academy and a Lieutenant Colonel in the Air Force. He is the author of "Implementing the Academy Training Philosophy," a manual governing supervisory behaviors at several of the officer commissioning programs in America. He received a PhD in Counseling Psychology from the University of North Carolina.

Direct inquiries about this article to Richard Tallarigo, Research Directorate, Defense Equal Opportunity Management Institute, Patrick Air Force Base, FL 32925-6685, 407/494-2675.

CHAPTER 16

The Relationship between Leaders' Management Skills and Their Groups' Effectiveness

Louis N. Quast, Jr., and Joy Fisher Hazucha

This paper investigates the relationship between subordinates' perceptions of their leader's management skills and of their group's effectiveness. The instruments used were the Management Skills Profile and the Team Success Profile. Group effectiveness was more strongly related to the leader's Initiating Structure and Consideration skills and less strongly related to the leader's Technical Knowledge. Most of the leaders' skills were related to some aspect of organizational effectiveness. Results suggest that a leader's management skills, especially empowerment and clarity of objectives, are important to organizational effectiveness and that management selection and development can be effective strategies for increasing organizational effectiveness.

Do leaders' skills have an impact on their groups' effectiveness? The wide use of human resource initiatives such as succession planning and management development implies that executives assume a link between management skills and organizational effectiveness. However, the bulk of leadership research has focused only on leaders, assuming that "more effective" leaders make for more successful organizations. Empirical documentation of a relationship between the leader's skills and group effectiveness has not received the same attention. In this paper we will briefly review the evidence from several approaches and then describe this study and the questions it addresses.

A few studies have investigated the relationship between leadership and global organizational outcomes such as approval ratings, financial performance (e.g., sales or profits), or sports team win-loss records. Weiner and Mahoney (1981) concluded that leadership accounts for more variance in organizational performance than do environmental or organizational factors. Thomas (1988) reanalyzed studies by Lieberson and O'Connor (1972) and a replication by Weiner (1978), together with a new set of data correlating leader behavior and organizational outcomes.

Thomas concluded that leaders have a substantial impact on variations in organizational performance that is not accounted for by contextual factors. Few studies have been conducted in business settings because it is difficult to find enough organizations with comparable measures of organizational effectiveness to make the study feasible.

Typically the studies which include both leader and group measures have used global measures on one side or the other. Global measures of individual performance include previous team win-loss records for sports coaches (Brown, 1982; Pfeffer & Davis-Blake, 1986) and salary progression for ministers (Smith, Carson, & Alexander, 1984). Corresponding measures of group performance include sports team win-loss records and church membership growth. These studies and others are part of the ongoing debate about whether or not leaders really impact the group (cf. Fiedler, 1972, 1986; Lieberson & O'Connor, 1972; Thomas, 1988).

Some theorists hold that the effectiveness of a particular leadership behavior varies depending on the situation; several of them maintain that effective leaders shape their behaviors to fit the nature of the given situation. Ralph Stogdill (1974), author of the *Handbook of Leadership*, observed that "the most effective leaders appear to exhibit a degree of versatility and flexibility that enables them to adapt their behavior to the changing and contradictory demands made on them" (p. 7).

Contingency theories include Fiedler's (1964) theory of leadership, Hersey and Blanchard's (1988) Situational Leadership model, Yukl's (1971, 1989) multiple linkage theory, House's (1971) path-goal theory of leadership, and Vroom and Yetton's (1973) leadership and decision-making model. These theories differ in both their theoretical frameworks and their specifications for leader action. Common to all is the assertion that behaviors effective in one situation may be less effective in another situation but that the right behaviors, under the right conditions, yield better results. Also common to all are mixed results from studies attempting to empirically document their effectiveness (e.g., Ashour, 1973a, 1973b; Graen, Alvares, Orris, & Marletta, 1970; Gumpert & Hambleton, 1979; Hambleton & Gumpert, 1982; Michaelsen, 1973; Peters, Hartkey, & Pullman, 1985; Podsakoff, Todor, Grover, & Huber, 1984; Schriesheim & Kerr, 1977; Thomas, 1988). House and Baetz (1979) integrated contingency and "one best way to lead" models when they concluded that, while situational moderators of effectiveness exist, some traits are required across leadership situations.

In this study, we consider multidimensional measures of both leadership and organizational effectiveness. While overall effectiveness is important as a "bottom-line" measure, Dunnette (1963) called for using multiple measures to gain a better understanding of the domains of interest.

We simultaneously investigate managerial skills and group characteristics in this study. We expect that the manager's skills are related to group effectiveness, but we also expect that other influences not included in this study (e.g., group composition and economic factors) will have an effect. Models of the dimensionality of leadership typically include task and person components. However, the dimensionality of group effectiveness is much less clear, partly because it is more difficult to obtain large numbers of groups to study at one time. The results of this study should shed light on the dimensions of group effectiveness and on the relationships between manager and group dimensions.

The specific questions addressed by this study include:

1. Which management skills, displayed by leaders in organizations, are associated with indices of organizational effectiveness? Which are least associated with organizational effectiveness?

2. Which group effectiveness dimen-

sions are most related to the leader's management skills? Which are least related?

The results have implications for the development of both leaders and organizations.

Methodology

Sample

The sample consists of 104 managers from one organization who attended a leadership program some time between 1987 and 1990. Of these participants, 70 were business-unit general managers; the remaining 34 were functional managers from within various business units. The businesses which the general managers directed varied in size but were similar in function. Each unit had been a distribution company acquired by an old-line manufacturing firm over the last 25 years. In the mid-1980s, the manufacturing firm itself was acquired by a large international corporation. The firm allowed these general managers to operate their businesses fairly independently and to retain their original local identity.

Each session of the development program included 18 people, approximately 6 from each of three divisions. One objective was to provide the managers with an empirical foundation for personal development planning, using a number of feedback instruments. As prework, participants first asked their coworkers to complete two questionnaires, one designed to measure management skills and the other to tap organizational practices.

All but one of the managers in the study were white and male. Their ages ranged from 29 to 60 years, with a median of 43. The majority (71%) classified their organizational level as "executive," 25% chose "middle management," and the remaining 4% described themselves as "first-line management." Consistent with

their organizational level, their experience in management was quite long: 44% had been in management more than 10 years, and only 10% had less than 3 years of management experience. Tenure in their current position was evenly distributed across the whole range of options from "less than 1 year" (24%) to "more than 10 years" (11%).

The Management Skills Profile

The first questionnaire, the Management Skills Profile (MSP) (Sevy, Olson, McGuire, Fraser, & Paajanen, 1985), contains 122 items which tap 19 dimensions including skills, characteristics, and results orientation. Each item describes an effective management behavior; respondents are asked to indicate on a Likert scale "to what extent" the manager performs the behavior, from 1 "not at all" to 5 "to a very great extent." Typically, one boss, three peers, three subordinates, and the developing manager (self) complete the MSP. Internal consistency reliabilities (alphas) for the dimensions range from .70 (Conflict Management) to .91 (Human Relations). For this study, the average subordinate ratings were of the most interest for two reasons. First, subordinates were usually at the same geographic location as the manager being rated and therefore saw them more frequently than did peers or superiors, who tended to be geographically dispersed. In fact, when leaders were asked about the geographic location and frequency of contact between them and "most of the people you manage," 85% reported working in the same building as their subordinates, and 90% saw them at least once per week. Second, the Team Success Profile was also completed by subordinates. Sevy et al. (1985) reported interrater reliabilities for groups of three subordinates which ranged from .49 (Conflict Management) to .78 (Personal Organization). These internal consistency and interrater reliability coefficients are shown in Table 1.

TABLE 1 MSP Subordinate Ratings: Internal Consistency and
Interrater Reliabilities

	Alpha	Intraclass Correlation	# of Items
Consideration			
Listening	.82	.63	5
Human Relations	.91	.67	8
Conflict Management	.70	.49	6
Motivating Others	.89	.61	6
Personal Adaptability	.80	.56	7
Initiating Structure			
Planning	.87	.69	7
Organizing	.81	.68	8
Personal Organization & Time Mgt.	.81	.78	8
Informing	.85	.62	6
Leadership Style & Influence	.85	.62	7
Delegating & Controlling	.77	.65	7
Coaching & Developing	.89	.63	10
Technical Skills			
Written Communications	.74	.64	4
Financial & Quantitative Skills	.83	.73	5
Occupational & Technical Knowledge	.82	.58	6
Other Skills			
Oral Communications	.87	.57	6
Problem Analysis & Decision Making	.77	.54	8
Personal Motivation	.81	.65	5
Results Oriented	.90	.70	6

Note. Based on Sevy et al., (1985); 8,500 raters, 1,089 ratees.

Data were used for every manager who had at least three questionnaires completed by subordinates, bringing the sample size down to 84. In addition to the 19 subordinate dimension ratings, 4 broader clusters were used. These clusters were formed based on factor analysis results and were named Consideration, Initiating Structure, Technical Skills, and Other Skills. These first two cluster names were selected because of the striking similarity between these results and those of the Bureau of Business research at Ohio State University (Stogdill & Coons, 1957). The dimensions included in each grouping, and their definitions, are shown in Table 2.

The Team Success Profile

The second questionnaire, the Team Success Profile (TSP), includes 118 items which measure several dimensions of organizational effectiveness. The Likert scale for this questionnaire ranges from 1 "strongly disagree" to 5 "strongly agree." Typically this questionnaire is completed by up to 20 direct and indirect subordinates of the manager who represent a wide (and in many cases complete) sample of employees in the business unit.

The Team Success Profile was developed by Personnel Decisions, Inc. in 1987 as an organizational development tool. To

TABLE 2 Management Skills Profile Dimensions and Definitions

Consideration

Listening Demonstrating attention to, and conveying understanding of, the comments or questions of others.

Human Relations Developing and maintaining smooth, cooperative working relationships with peers, subordinates, and superiors; showing awareness of, and consideration for, the opinions and feelings of others.

Conflict Management Bringing conflict or dissent into the open and using it productively to enhance the quality of decisions; arriving at constructive solutions while maintaining positive working relationships.

Motivating Others Creating an environment in which subordinates and others are rewarded for accomplishment of group and individual goals.

Personal Adaptability Responding appropriately and competently to the demands of work challenges when confronted with changes, ambiguity, and adversity, or other pressures.

Initiating Structure

Planning Setting goals and developing strategies and schedules for meeting those goals; anticipating obstacles and defining alternative strategies.

Organizing Scheduling and coordinating work of others; setting priorities, establishing efficient work procedures to meet objectives.

Personal Organization & Time Management Allocating one's own time efficiently; arranging information systematically and processing paperwork and other information effectively without getting bogged down in detail.

Informing Letting people know of decisions, changes, and other relevant information on a timely basis.

Leadership Style & Influence Taking charge and initiating actions, directing the activities of individuals and groups toward the accomplishment of meaningful goals and commanding the attention and respect of others.

Delegating & Controlling Clearly assigning responsibilities and tasks to others and establishing effective controls, ensuring that employees have the necessary resources and authority, and monitoring progress and exercising control.

Coaching & Developing Evaluating employees, providing performance feedback, and facilitating professional growth.

Technical Skills

Written Communications Writing clearly and effectively; using appropriate style, grammar and tone, in informal and formal business communications.

Financial & Quantitative Drawing accurate conclusions from financial and numerical material and applying financial principles and numerical techniques to management problems.

Occupational & Technical Knowledge Applying the knowledge and skills needed to do the job, including technical competence in one's own field and familiarity with policies and practices of the organization and the industry.

Other Skills

Oral Communications Speaking effectively one-to-one and in groups; making effective presentations.

Problem Analysis & Decision Making Identifying problems; recognizing symptoms, causes, and alternative solutions, making timely, sound decisions even under conditions of risk and uncertainty.

Personal Motivation Displaying a high energy level, working long and hard to get things done, and seeking increased responsibility on the job.

Results Orientation Producing high quality work, managing productively, getting results.

use Rousseau's (1990) distinctions, it taps patterns of behavior and behavioral norms but not values, fundamental assumptions, or artifacts. Because the unit of analysis is the group, a database takes longer to build and no technical report exists. Thus, we began with an investigation of the instrument's psychometric properties.

The first step was a factor analysis of the items. The second step was to regroup the items based on the factor analysis and compute the internal consistency of the resulting scales. The third step was to factor analyze the scales and group them into clusters. This approach was chosen as an alternative to using scale scores because factor analysis revealed considerable shared variance, indicating overlap among most of the dimensions. However, scale scores, rather than factor scores, were used to maintain interpretability. The scale titles (grouped into clusters) and definitions are shown in Table 3. The number of items and alphas for each dimension are shown in Table 4. An analysis of variance on the scale scores was computed to compare the variance within the groups in this study to the variance between groups. These results are also displayed in Table 4. All of the Fs were highly significant, indicating more variance between groups than within groups. The corresponding interrater reliabilities range from .49 (Clarify Jobs and Roles) to .78 (Facilities), with a median of .66. This signifies that group members' responses were more similar to the responses of others in their group than to the responses of people in other groups, an indication of interrater reliability. These analyses showed that the instrument was sufficiently reliable to yield meaningful results.

Intercorrelations

We then intercorrelated the MSP and TSP dimensions. The complete correlation matrix is shown in Table 5. Table 6 shows the median correlations for the 20

cells formed by crossing the 4 MSP clusters with the 5 TSP clusters. Table 7 shows median and maximum rs for each MSP dimension; Table 8 shows the same statistics for each TSP dimension.

Results

Many of the 418 correlations between the MSP and the TSP (shown in Table 5) were quite high; 129 exceeded r = .33 (p < .001). The range of correlations was from -.10 to .52, with most in the .2 to .3 range. These were lower than the within-instrument correlations, which ranged from .6 to .7 for the TSP and .5 to .7 for the MSP. At this high threshold of significance, we would expect only 0.4 (418 x .001) of the correlations to be significant by chance alone. This indicates that subordinates see a relationship between the leader's management skills and group effectiveness.

A closer examination of Table 6 reveals several areas where the correlations were especially high. The clusters with the highest median correlation were MSP Initiating Structure with TSP Clarity of Purpose (median r = .38, p < .001), MSP Consideration with TSP Empowerment (median r = .34, p < .001), and MSP Initiating Structure with TSP Empowerment (median r = .34, p < .001). Performing the statistical correction for attenuation of correlation due to interrater unreliability in both instruments yielded corrected correlations of r = .56, .50, and .57, respectively. These findings indicate that leaders with stronger Initiating Structure skills have groups with greater Clarity of Purpose, and leaders with stronger Consideration and Initiating Structure skills are associated with groups reporting higher levels of Empowerment.

Conversely, the median correlations with MSP Technical Skills and TSP External Inhibitors were quite low (r = .07 to .21). The lowest median correlation (r = .07) occurred at the intersection of these

TABLE 3 Team Success Profile: Dimensions and Definitions

Teamwork	Teamwork within and among group members.
Flexibility	The group is willing to take risks, seeks ways to improve, and capitalizes on opportunities.
Enjoy Coworkers	People in the group enjoy working with each other.
Contribute Equally	People all do their fair share of the work.
Support Each Other	People treat each other well.
Work with Other Groups	The group works well with other groups in the organization.
Execute Plans	The group works effectively to achieve objectives—"like a well-oiled machine."
Share Responsibility	The group members take responsibility for getting things done.
Empowerment	Empowerment of group members by management.
Participation & Openness	Group members have input and give and receive feedback.
Allow Latitude	Group members are allowed leeway in decisions and actions.
Deal with Differences	The group handles conflict in healthy ways, allows opinions to be aired, and treats people fairly.
Share Power & Information	Power and information are shared fairly in the group.
Reward Merit	Good performance is encouraged and rewarded.
Clarity of Purpose	Group members understand objectives and plans.
Direct & Plan	The group has clear direction, makes and uses plans.
Work toward Goals	The group plans and works to achieve goals.
Clarify Jobs & Roles	Group members understand what is expected of them.
Establish Budgets	The group has, and uses, budgets.
Monitor Expenditures	The group keeps a close watch on expenses.
External Inhibitors	External factors which inhibit group effectiveness.
Absence of Obstacles	The group does not face a lot of obstacles which seem beyond their control.
Resources to do Job	The group has the resources it needs.
Facilities	The group has adequate space and equipment.
Human Resource Management	The group effectively staffs and trains.
Staff Effectively	The group does a good job of recruiting and hiring.
Train & Develop	The group encourages and rewards development.

two clusters. These results suggest that the strength of the leader's technical skills is only slightly related to group effectiveness and that External Inhibitors were not strongly related to the leader's skills. Correlations with the Teamwork TSP cluster were moderate.

These patterns indicate that the leader's

	N of Items	Alpha	F Ratio	Interrater Reliability
Teamwork				
Flexibility	7	.86	3.41	.71
Enjoy Coworkers	3	.77	2.96	.66
Contribute Equally	4	.70	2.94	.66
Support Each Other	9	.86	3.58	.72
Work with Other Groups	3	.66	2.05	.51
Execute Plans	10	.85	3.21	.69
Share Responsibility	5	.67	2.54	.61
Empowerment				
Participation & Openness	9	.88	3.80	.74
Allow Latitude	2	.61	2.68	.63
Deal with Differences	7	.86	3.50	.71
Share Power & Information	9	.85	2.98	.66
Reward Merit	4	.80	3.93	.75
Clarity of Purpose				
Direct & Plan	9	.89	3.71	.73
Work toward Goals	4	.70	4.87	.79
Clarify Jobs & Roles	3	.71	1.97	.49
Establish Budgets	5	.75	2.41	.58
Monitor Expenditures	3	.67	2.12	.53
External Inhibitors				
Absence of Obstacles	3	.60	3.09	.68
Resources to do Job	4	.51	2.92	.66
Facilities	4	.75	4.53	.78
Human Resource Management				
Staff Effectively	5	.66	2.83	.65
Train & Develop	4	.71	2.59	.61

Note. df (92,1351); all p < .0001.

skills are most strongly related to the group's Clarity of Objectives and Empowerment and are moderately related to Teamwork. Finally, External Inhibitors are only slightly related to the leader's management skills. Tests for significant differences among these medians showed that .38 is significantly greater than .18, .34 is greater than .14, and .30 is greater than .07.

TABLE 5 Correlation Matrix of Subordinate Ratings
of MSP with TSP

Team Success Profile \ Management Skills Profile	Consideration	Listening	Human Relations	Conflict Management	Motivating Others	Personal Adaptability	Initiating Structure	Planning	Organizing	Personal Organization/Time Mgmt.	Informing	Leadership Style & Influence	Delegating & Controlling	Coaching & Developing	Technical Skills	Written Communications	Financial & Quantitative	Occupational/Technical Knowledge	Other Skills	Oral Communications	Problem Analysis/Decision Making	Personal Motivation	Results Orientation
Teamwork																							
Flexibility		18	16	34	30	30		35	40	28	25	41	42	36		31	18	30		32	36	21	35
Enjoy Coworkers		25	22	32	28	28		23	29	24	29	32	34	26		21	06	19		21	24	16	27
Contribute Equally		19	15	26	27	25		26	29	23	22	29	34	29		13	15	17		13	24	20	28
Support Each Other		32	30	33	34	36		30	36	26	27	35	33	29		26	07	20		25	32	17	30
Work with Other Groups		14	16	21	22	24		23	30	23	22	28	28	23		15	04	16		13	23	20	28
Execute Plans		35	31	38	40	41		42	45	37	37	46	50	39		30	13	31		32	42	25	43
Share Responsibility		25	26	27	28	30		28	35	22	23	32	30	25		24	07	20		22	31	17	32
Empowerment																							
Participation & Openness		45	40	41	49	45		42	47	33	36	47	44	47		22	10	25		30	41	22	42
Allow Latitude		34	31	24	32	28		24	19	16	16	29	21	16		28	18	17		33	28	08	17
Deal with Differences		46	43	39	43	45		35	40	26	31	42	36	37		20	10	27		29	40	19	38
Share Power & Information		34	30	33	36	39		34	38	28	28	37	36	34		22	15	26		24	37	21	34
Reward Merit		27	24	27	33	29		32	32	26	26	35	38	31		27	17	25		25	33	21	32
Clarity of Purpose																							
Direct & Plan		31	29	40	37	41		43	47	40	37	49	47	39		34	19	32		34	46	29	49
Work toward Goals		27	25	40	35	39		43	45	37	41	46	48	43		24	20	31		24	42	32	46
Clarify Jobs & Roles		33	35	43	44	43		43	48	38	31	52	46	40		30	16	40		30	45	39	53
Establish Budgets		27	23	25	26	26		33	27	27	28	29	31	26		10	06	16		09	24	18	32
Monitor Expenditures		15	17	16	19	19		19	22	12	24	26	19	15		09	05	27		08	22	22	29
External Inhibitors																							
Absence of Obstacles		17	14	13	21	17		18	20	16	12	25	26	17		14	13	07		20	18	03	23
Resources to do Job		16	13	19	24	22		23	23	17	19	34	27	18		21	07	17		25	22	15	26
Facilities		09	14	10	09	10		07	05	-01	12	08	02	05		02	-10	-01		-04	02	-01	06
Human Resource Mgmt.																							
Staff Effectively		20	17	27	26	25		25	30	19	22	32	31	22		19	08	23		23	30	17	26
Train & Develop		36	35	40	39	37		36	39	26	37	43	39	40		31	01	30		36	40	19	36

Note. Bold/italicized numbers indicate p < .001. Decimal points omitted. n = 84.

TABLE 6 Median Correlations between MSP and TSP Clusters

Management Skills Profile	Consideration	Initiating Structure	Technical Skills	Other Skills
Team Success Profile				
Teamwork	28	29	18	26
Empowerment	34*	34*	21	30
Clarity of Purpose	28	38*	20	31
External Inhibitors	14	17	07	17
HR Management	31	31	21	28

Note. Decimal points omitted. n = 84.

Note. Significant differences between correlations: .38 > .18; .34 > .14; .30 > .07.

*p < .001.

Table 7 shows the median and maximum correlations of the TSP with each MSP dimension. The two highest median correlations, Leadership Style and Influence and Delegating and Controlling, were statistically significant (r = .34, p < .001, corrected r = .52). This indicates that the leader's skills in taking charge, directing others' activities, and commanding respect, and their skills in clearly assigning tasks and following up on these tasks, were associated with a number of group effectiveness variables.

All but one of the maximum correlations attained significance at p < .001 (r = .33). The exception was Financial and Quantitative Skills, where the correlation (r = .20) fell short of the critical value of .33. This suggests that the leader's Financial and Quantitative Skills had little impact on group effectiveness. The three strongest correlations exceeded .50. In descending order, they were MSP Results Orientation with TSP Clarify Jobs and Roles (r = .53, corrected r = .90), MSP Leadership Style and Influence with TSP Clarify Jobs and Roles (r = .52, corrected r = .94), and MSP Delegating and Controlling with TSP Execute Plans (r = .50, corrected r = .75). The two latter MSP dimensions were also those with the highest median correlations.

Table 8 shows the median and maximum correlations of each TSP dimension with the MSP. Several of the median correlations were significant at p < .001 (r = .33). These included Execute Plans (r = .38, corrected r = .59), Participation and Openness (r = .34, corrected r = .59), Deal with Differences (r = .37, corrected r = .54), Share Power and Information (r = .34, corrected r = .50), Direct and Plan (r = .39, corrected r = .55), Work toward Goals (r = .39, corrected r = .58), Clarify Jobs and Roles (r = .40, corrected r = .74), and Train and Develop (r = .37, corrected r = .60). These results indicate that these are the organizational dimensions most strongly related to the leader's management skills.

Of the maximum correlations, all but four exceeded the critical value (r = .33, p < .001). These exceptions were Work with Other Groups, Monitor Expenditures, Absence of Obstacles, and Facilities. This indicates that the leader's management skills were quite strongly related to most of the organizational effectiveness dimensions. However, intergroup cooperation, the monitoring of expenditures, obstacles beyond the group's control, and the adequacy of space and equipment were not under the leader's direct influence.

TABLE 7 Management Skills Profile: Median and Maximum Correlations
with TSP Scales

MSP Dimension	Median r	Maximum r: scale (r)
Consideration		
Listening	27	Deal with Differences (46)
Human Relations	24	Deal with Differences (43)
Conflict Management	27	Clarify Jobs & Roles (43)
Motivating Others	30	Participation & Openness (49)
Personal Adaptability	29	Participation & Openness/ Deal with Differences (45)
Initiating Structure		
Planning	30	Direct & Plan/Clarify Jobs & Roles (43)
Organizing	32	Clarify Jobs & Roles (48)
Personal Organization & Time Mgmt.	26	Direct & Plan (40)
Informing	26	Work toward Goals (41)
Leadership Style & Influence	34*	Clarify Jobs & Roles (52)
Delegating & Controlling	34*	Execute Plans (50)
Coaching & Developing	29	Participation & Openness (47)
Technical Skills		
Written Communications	22	Direct & Plan (34)
Financial & Quantitative	10	Work toward Goals (20)
Occupational & Technical Knowledge	24	Clarify Jobs & Roles (40)
Other Skills		
Oral Communications	25	Train & Develop (36)
Problem Analysis & Decision Making	31	Direct & Plan (46)
Personal Motivation	20	Clarify Jobs & Roles (39)
Results Orientation	32	Clarify Jobs & Roles (53)

Note. Decimal points omitted. n = 84. *p < .001.

Discussion

This study reveals substantial relationships between the leader's demonstrated management skills and the observed effectiveness of the group. With the exception of Financial and Quantitative Skills, all of the management skills measured in this study correlated significantly (r = .33, p < .001) with at least one measure of organizational performance; many were related to more than one. Our design did not allow us to prove direction of causality; additional research is required to do so.

The most highly correlated management skills fell into two skill clusters: Initiating Structure and Consideration. The implication of these findings is direct: both selecting for and developing these skills in individuals targeted for leadership roles are likely to improve organizational effectiveness. In contrast to Initiating Structure and Consideration, leaders' Technical Skills had much weaker rela-

TABLE 8 Team Success Profile: Median and Maximum Correlations
with MSP Scales

TSP Dimension	Median r	Maximum r: scale (r)
Teamwork		
Flexibility	31	Delegating & Controlling (42)
Enjoy Coworkers	26	Delegating & Controlling (34)
Contribute Equally	24	Delegating & Controlling (34)
Support Each Other	30	Organizing/Personal Adaptability (36)
Work with Other Groups	22	Organizing (29)
Execute Plans	38*	Delegating & Controlling (50)
Share Responsibility	27	Organizing (35)
Empowerment		
Participation & Openness	42*	Motivating Others (49)
Allow Latitude	24	Listening (34)
Deal with Differences	37*	Listening (46)
Share Power & Information	34*	Personal Adaptability (39)
Reward Merit	27	Delegating & Controlling (38)
Clarity of Purpose		
Direct & Plan	39*	Leadership Style & Influence/ Results Orientation (49)
Work toward Goals	39*	Delegating & Controlling (48)
Clarify Jobs & Roles	40*	Results Orientation (53)
Establish Budgets	26	Planning (33)
Monitor Expenditures	19	Results Orientation (29)
External Inhibitors		
Absence of Obstacles	17	Delegating & Controlling (26)
Resources to do Job	21	Leadership Style & Influence (34)
Facilities	05	Human Relations (14)
Human Resource Management		
Staff Effectively	23	Leadership Style & Influence (32)
Train & Develop	37*	Leadership Style & Influence (43)

Note. Decimal points omitted. n = 84. *p < .001.

tionships with organizational effectiveness. This skill area (especially Financial and Quantitative Skills) should not be the primary focus of attention in either selecting or developing leaders.

While virtually all management skills were related to organizational effectiveness, not all dimensions of organizational effectiveness were related to management skills. Thus, some aspects of organizational behavior, namely External Inhibitors, appear to be beyond the direct reach of individual leaders. These may be more strongly affected by corporate policies and the availability of capital funds which may depend on the economy and the business cycle. The moderate relationship between the manager's skills and Group Teamwork indicates other factors of influence which may include the personalities and cooperativeness of the group members.

In conclusion, these findings strongly support the assertion that leaders' skills do have specific, quantifiable impact on organizational effectiveness. Moreover, the results point to specific areas in which leaders have greatest, and least, impact. Careful selection and development of managers are important for enhancing group members' clarity and empowerment but are insufficient for substantially increasing teamwork. Teamwork may be more likely to respond to large-scale organizational development interventions or team-building. It is naive to presume that a leader would account for all the variance in organizational performance; based on this research, it would be equally unproductive to ignore the influence of leadership.

Future research should investigate the direction of causality and the nature of other influences on group effectiveness. The causality questions are: Does the leader influence the group? Does the group influence the leader? Do the leader and group influence each other? Does a third factor influence both? These could be examined by conducting succession studies similar to those conducted with sports teams (Gamson & Scotch, 1964; Pfeffer & Davis-Blake, 1986). This would require managerial and group data collection both before and after leadership transitions. A comparison of how much and in what direction the groups and leaders changed after the transition would show how much each influenced the other. Other influences on group effectiveness may include the characteristics of the group members (e.g., skills, personality, and satisfaction) and broader organizational influences beyond the leader's direct control (e.g., compensation, performance appraisal systems, and organizational structure). Isolating the influences of each set of factors would require multilevel data across several groups and organizations. In addition, collecting business performance criteria, such as productivity or profitability, would help to elucidate the relationship between organizational effectiveness and these "bottom-line" criteria.

Acknowledgments

We wish to thank Sally Neverman for her assistance with the literature review, Chris Carraher and Scott Birkeland for their help with the data and the analyses, and Douglas Yost for his assistance with the manuscript.

References

Ashour, A. S. (1973a). The contingency model of leadership effectiveness: An evaluation. *Organizational Behavior and Human Performance, 9,* 336–356.

Ashour, A. S. (1973b). Further discussion of Fiedler's contingency model of leadership effectiveness. *Organizational Behavior and Human Performance, 9,* 369–376.

Brown, M. C. (1982). Administrative succession and organizational performance: The succession effect. *Administrative Science Quarterly, 27,* 1–16.

Dunnette, M. D. (1963). A note on the criterion. *Journal of Applied Psychology, 47,* 251–254.

Fiedler, F. E. (1964). A contingency model of leadership effectiveness. In N. L. Berkowitz (Ed.), *Advances in experimental social psychology* (Vol. 1, pp. 149–190). New York: Academic Press.

Fiedler, F. E. (1972). The effects of leadership training and experience: A contingency model interpretation. *Administrative Science Quarterly, 17*(4), 453–470.

Fiedler, F. E. (1986). The contribution of cognitive resources and leader behavior to organizational performance. *Journal of Applied Social Psychology, 16*(6), 532–548.

Gamson, W. A., & Scotch, N. R. (1964). Scapegoating in baseball. *American Journal of Sociology, 70*, 69–76.

Graen, G., Alvares, K., Orris, J. P., & Marletta, J. A. (1970). Contingency model of leadership effectiveness: Antecedent and evidential results. *Psychological Bulletin, 74*(4), 285–296.

Gumpert, R. A., & Hambleton, R. K. (1979). Situational leadership: How Xerox managers fine-tuned managerial styles to employee maturity and task needs. *Management Review, 68*(12), 8–12.

Hambleton, R. K., & Gumpert, R. A. (1982). The validity of Hersey and Blanchard's theory of leader effectiveness. *Group and Organization Studies, 7*(2), 225–242.

Hersey, P., & Blanchard, K. H. (1988). *Management of organizational behavior* (5th ed.). Englewood Cliffs, NJ: Prentice-Hall.

House, R. J. (1971). A path-goal theory of leader effectiveness. *Administrative Science Quarterly, 16*, 321–339.

House, R. J., & Baetz, J. L. (1979). Leadership: Some empirical generalizations and new research directions. In B. Staw & L. Cummings (Eds.), *Research in Organizational Behavior* (Vol. 1). Greenwich, CT: JAI Press.

Lieberson, S., & O'Connor, J. F. (1972). Leadership and organizational performance: A study of large corporations. *American Sociological Review, 37*, 117–130.

Michaelsen, L. K. (1973). Leader orientation, leader behavior, group effectiveness, and situational favorability: An empirical extension of the contingency model. *Organizational Behavior and Human Performance, 9*, 226–245.

Peters, L. H., Hartkey, D. D., & Pullman, J. T., (1985). Fiedler's contingency theory of leadership: An application of the meta-analysis procedures of Schmidt and Hunter. *Psychological Bulletin, 97*, 274–285.

Pfeffer, J., & Davis-Blake, A. (1986). Administrative succession and organizational performance: How administrator experience mediates the succession effect. *Academy of Management Journal, 29*(1), 72–83.

Podsakoff, P. M., Todor, W. D., Grover, R. A., & Huber, V. L. (1984). Situational moderators of leader reward and punishment behaviors: Fact or fiction? *Organizational Behavior and Human Performance, 34*, 21–63.

Rousseau, D. M. (1990). Assessing organizational culture: The case for multiple methods. In B. Schneider (Ed.), *Organizational climate and culture*. San Francisco: Jossey-Bass.

Schriesheim, C. A., & Kerr, S. (1977). Theories and measures of leadership: A critical appraisal of current and future directions. In J. G. Hunt & L. L. Larson (Eds.), *Leadership: The cutting edge*. Carbondale: Southern Illinois University Press.

Sevy, B. A., Olson, R. D., McGuire, D. P., Fraser, M. E., & Paajanen, G. (1985). *Management Skills Profile research report and technical manual*. Minneapolis, MN: Personnel Decisions.

Smith, J. E., Carson, K. P., & Alexander, R. A. (1984). Leadership: It can make a difference. *Academy of Management Journal, 27*(4), 765–776.

Stogdill, R. M. (1974). Historical trends in leadership theory and research. *Journal of Contemporary Business, 3*(4), 1–17.

Stogdill, R. M., & Coons, A. (1957). *Leader behavior: Its description and measurement* (Research Monograph No. 88). Columbus: Ohio State University, Bureau of Business Research.

Thomas, A. B. (1988). Does leadership make a difference to organizational performance? *Administrative Science Quarterly, 33*, 3.

Vroom, V. H., & Yetton, P. W. (1973). *Leadership and decision making*. Pittsburgh, PA: University of Pittsburgh Press.

Weiner, N. (1978). Situational and leadership influences on organization performance. *Proceedings of the Academy of Management*, 230–234.

Weiner, N., & Mahoney, T. A. (1981). A model of corporate performance as a function of environmental, organizational, and leadership influences. *Academy of Management Journal, 24*, 453–470.

Yukl, G. A. (1971). Toward a behavioral theory of leadership. *Organizational Behavior and Human Performance, 6*, 414–440.

Yukl, G. A. (1989). *Leadership in organizations*. Englewood Cliffs, NJ: Prentice-Hall.

Louis N. Quast, Jr., is a Senior Consultant in the Training and Development Division at Personnel Decisions, Inc., where he creates and delivers leadership development workshops. His previous experience was in marketing management and training with two Fortune 100 corporations. He is a PhD candidate in Business and Marketing Education from the University of Minnesota.

Joy Fisher Hazucha is Director of Research at Personnel Decisions, Inc. Her research interests include management and executive effectiveness, career development, management development, and multirater feedback. She holds a PhD in Industrial-Organizational Psychology from the University of Minnesota.

Direct inquiries about this article to Joy Fisher Hazucha, Personnel Decisions, Inc., 2000 Plaza VII Tower, 45 South Seventh Street, Minneapolis, MN 55402–1608, 612/339–0927.

Leadership, Organizational Culture, and Organizational Outcomes

Bas A. S. Koene, Johannes M. Pennings, and Hein Schreuder

This study presents a first analysis of data from an empirical study into leadership and organizational culture in a sample of 50 stores of one of the larger European food retailers. The paper examines the relationships of leadership and organizational culture with the dependent variables of employee motivation, satisfaction, and a measure for financial performance. The results show that initiation, consideration, and charismatic leadership are strongly related with these dependent variables. Furthermore, while organizational culture moderates the effects of initiation and consideration, no such interaction was detected for charismatic leadership.

In this study, the effects of leadership on organizational culture and the joint effects of leadership and organizational culture on motivation, satisfaction, and performance are examined. Leadership is differentiated with respect to both Ohio State constructs (Fleishman, 1953) of Consideration and Initiating Structure, as well as Charismatic Leadership (Bass, 1985). Culture is similarly viewed as a multifaceted attribute and is operationalized using the organizational culture construct of Hofstede and colleagues (Hofstede, Neuijen, Ohayv, & Sanders, 1990). Hypotheses on leadership, culture, and their outcomes are investigated in a sample of 50 stores of one of the larger European food retailers.

Background

A large number of studies have examined possible relationships between leadership and performance as well as between organizational culture and performance. Strong arguments are made in the literature for expecting a significant relationship between leadership and organizational culture, both from the cultural perspective (Peters & Waterman, 1982; Schein, 1985) and the leadership perspective (Bass, 1985; Smith & Peterson, 1990). This study attempts to bring together organizational culture and leadership and investigate their influences on organizational effectiveness. In examining the outcomes of leadership and culture, two psychological indicators, employee motivation and job satisfaction, and one financial indicator, shrinkage, are considered. Shrinkage is a measure of a store's level of controllable costs.

First, we look at the relationship between leadership and organizational culture. Pairs of leadership dimensions, such as task orientation and relations orientation (Bass, 1990), performance and maintenance (Misumi & Peterson, 1987), consideration and initiating structure (Philipsen, 1965, 1970; Syroit, 1979), and transformational and transactional leadership (Bass, 1985), all convey the assumption that leaders differ in how they relate to their subordinates. This leads to questions like: What aspects of culture are influenced by leadership? What kinds of leadership are most influential in promoting certain kinds of culture?

Second, there is the question of the mediating influence of organizational culture on the effectiveness of leadership. Under what cultural conditions is leadership most effective? What kinds of leadership are most suitable to motivate and satisfy employees in certain cultures? But also, are there cultural conditions that prohibit certain leadership styles, that is, conditions under which those styles have a negative impact on organizational outcomes?

At this moment, it is generally accepted that an organization's structure influences the effectiveness of different leadership styles. House and Mitchell's (1983) path-goal theory, for example, indicates that the influence of consideration and initiating structure is contingent upon the structure of the job. When job structure is high, consideration often serves as a mitigating factor in aligning—and even motivating—employees. Initiation, on the other hand, only has an effect when job structure is low and the supervisor alleviates the ambiguity and stress that might be associated with a job that is ill-specified, whose objectives are poorly articulated, and where the technology is fuzzy. Kerr and Jermier (1978) also investigated this relationship between structure and leadership. They came up with a list of "substitutes for leadership," these substitutes really being structural factors which moderate the impact of leadership. Organization design, technology, and task structure specify behavior and performance and render certain styles of leadership superfluous; they "substitute" for the structuring and controlling effects of leaders. The recently revived interest in the charisma of leaders, however, presents an interesting challenge to leadership being substitutable. Charismatic leaders do not rely on organizational vehicles of control, incentives, and structure (e.g., job description, MBO, performance appraisal, persuasion, and other "transactional" leadership mechanisms). Rather, they lead on the basis of their personality attributes and interpersonal dispositions. They are capable of rallying their followers behind their views, strategy, and mission. Therefore, culture might moderate leadership effects, but the interactions vary by leadership attributes. Consideration (co) and initiating structure (is) are measured with questions like "He lets his subordinates know what is expected of them (is)," "He gives advance notice of changes (co)," "He schedules the work to be done (is)," and "He makes sure that his part in the group is understood by the group members (is)." Charismatic leadership is measured with questions like "I have complete confidence in him," "He serves as a role model for me," and "He makes me aware of what we try to accomplish in this store."

A complicating factor, when looking at organizational culture, is whether culture should be treated as a situational variable. The controlling or structuring effects of culture, attributed by the previously noted studies to organization design and task structure, need to be examined. Organizational culture, defined as a set of shared meanings or as a group-specific set of practices, is different from the more behaviorally oriented concept of organizational design. Culture underpins social behavior and confers legitimacy and regularity, but it is more difficult to operationalize and to observe. As shared meanings or practices, culture provides employees with the cognitive premises of behavior (Eyoang, 1985). Being dispositional, motivation and satisfaction should be more closely tied to organizational culture than to technology or structure. By the same token we expect a less direct link with the outcomes of actual behavior. Similarly, charismatic leadership can be presumed to have a comparatively strong impact on psychological outcomes such as motivation and satisfaction. A charismatic leader contributes to the nature and strength of culture (Burns, 1978), thereby influencing subordinates' cognitive foundations of behavior. Charismatic leadership might be less germane to financial outcomes which are influenced only indirectly *through* its influence on subordinate's work attitudes.

Method

The study was conducted in a large retail firm in the Netherlands to determine whether and how leadership and organizational culture could predict variations of store performance. The firm had been observing large differences in store performance; senior firm executives speculated that managerial attitudes and store culture might constitute an unexplored reason for these "mysterious" performance differences. The investigators were approached to determine whether managerial attitudes and store culture were causative factors.

After an initial round of intensive exploratory interviews with store middle managers throughout the country, the possible relationships between leadership, organizational culture, and organizational performance were investigated more systematically. In the exploratory interviews, the middle managers were questioned

about their experiences in different stores, about differences in the day-to-day operations of stores, and about their perceptions of cultural differences between stores. After that, questionnaires were used to chart employee opinions; structured interviews were conducted to get to know the store manager and to draw a rough picture of store-specific circumstances. Company head-office information was searched to compare the stores on various performance criteria (e.g., gross sales, profit, employee turnover) and store classification indicators (store size, type, main objectives, etc.).

A sample was selected of 25 pairs of company-owned stores that matched on size and geographical location but differed on store performance as measured by shrinkage. Shrinkage was selected by company executives as the best measure of a store manager's control over store operations. It featured a store's "unaccounted-for stock differences" and its controllable costs as a percentage of the store's gross sales. Shrinkage can be interpreted as a measure of sloppiness of a store's employees in performing their day to day work. A high score on shrinkage is bad, a low score is good.

A questionnaire was sent to all employees who worked more than 12 hours a week in the stores in the sample; the store managers were interviewed for two hours. The questionnaire (amongst other scales) included: (a) an abbreviated 18-item version of Hofstede's (Hofstede et al., 1990) organizational culture questionnaire measuring six dimensions of culture, (b) a scale measuring work satisfaction (Vogelaar, 1990), and (c) a scale measuring motivation. The scales were chosen and, where necessary, adapted on the basis of results from the exploratory interviews with store middle managers. Leadership style was investigated using a Belgian Dutch-language instrument measuring consideration and initiating structure (Syroit, 1979), adapted for use in our specific (Dutch) setting. A new translation of Bass's (Bass, 1988; Bass & Avolio, 1990) leader charisma scale was employed. Bass's research shows charismatic leadership to be the most important of three factors (charisma, individualized consideration, and intellectual stimulation) which together describe transformational leadership.

This study focuses on the results of the employee questionnaire, emphasizing the relationship between leadership, organizational culture, employee motivation, and satisfaction. Shrinkage was included in the analysis as a first, rough measure of financial performance. For expository reasons, in addition to conceptual and psychometric considerations, the analysis of organizational culture was limited to two of the six dimensions of organizational culture identified by Hofstede (Hofstede et al., 1990): job versus employee orientation (P2) and closed versus open cultures (P4). Job-orientation is measured with questions like: "Where I work the organization is only interested in the work people do" and "Where I work there is little concern for personal problems of employees." Closedness is measured with questions like: "Where I work only very special people fit in the organization" and "Where I work new employees need more than a year to feel at home." Conceptually we chose the dimensions most closely related to the salient dimensions of leadership (see Table 4 for our expectations on the relationships between leadership and culture). Psychometric considerations pertained to the internal consistency and face validity of the abbreviated scales.

The questionnaires were sent to a sample of employees in each store. The percentage returned varied from store to store. The total number of questionnaires mailed was 2,290, yielding a response rate of 53% (n = 1229). The internal consistency of the leadership scales and the scales measuring motivation and satisfaction was satisfactory. In a first analysis, the (short) organizational culture scales did not do so well. This might be due to the use of a measurement instrument developed for comparisons between organizations in a comparison of units within one

TABLE 1 Alpha-Scores for Scales

	Standardized alphas	# items
Individual level (n = 1229):		
Charismatic leadership	.96	13
Initiating structure	.78	9
Consideration	.90	7
Motivation	.77	6
Satisfaction	.88	7
Store level (n = 50):		
Job orientation (P2)	.60	3
Open vs. closed (P4)	.72	3

organization or to setting-specific adaptations made in the questions. Table 1 shows the Cronbach alphas for the scales used in this study. The organizational culture scales were calculated on the level of the 50 units to avoid getting caught in the "reverse ecological fallacy": trying to interpret organizational culture, a concept defined at the level of social systems, with individual-level data (Hofstede, 1980; Hofstede, Bond, & Luk, 1991).

In studying the results, it is important to note the pecularities of data on the ecological level. Few cases are needed because the store scores, based on the mean of a (large) number of employee scores, tend to be very stable. Also, because ecological correlations tend to be stronger than individual correlations, high percentages of explained variance can be expected (Hofstede et al., 1990).

Results

Table 2 presents the means and standard deviations of the variables of interest for the 50 stores. A one-way analysis of variance revealed strong differences in leadership and culture among the 50 stores. The high F-ratios are testimony to the assumption that each store would have a distinct and unique culture, while the leadership style that prevailed in these stores was likewise different. These results permit us to aggregate individual data in order to generate store-level indicators of culture and leadership.

Significant relationships between leadership, organizational culture, and organizational outcome variables were found. Table 3, which provides an overview of the correlations between variables on the store level, indicates that most of the correlations are highly significant. Correlation coefficients with a p-value higher than .05 are presented as not significant (ns). Only the correlation between initiating structure and job orientation (P2) (r = -.35) was very different from what was expected. Charismatic leadership showed the strongest relation with the outcome variables (r = .72, .49, and -.29), initiating structure the weakest (r = .49, .31, ns). Consideration showed the strongest relation with both dimensions of culture, and initiating structure, again, the weakest (r = -.56, -.45, and r = -.35, ns, respectively). Overall, leadership seemed to be more strongly associated with a job orientation (r = -.52, -.35, -.56) than with closedness (r = -.39, ns, -.45).

Shrinkage showed only reasonably significant correlations with charismatic leadership (r = -.29) and the open-closed culture dimension (r = .33).

To investigate the mediating influence of organizational culture on the effectiveness of leadership, a partition was imposed at the median which classified stores as low and high on job orientation (see Table 4) and on closedness of the group (see Table 5). The results indicate a clear influence of culture on the correlation of leadership with motivation, satisfaction, and shrinkage: Initiating structure shows a strong correlation with the outcome variables in cultures that are closed or show a job orientation.

Consideration, on the other hand, showed the strongest correlations in cultures that are open or employee oriented. The effects of charismatic leadership

appeared to be least moderated by these cultural differences. Correlations with outcome factors under differing cultural conditions were virtually the same.

Discussion

To investigate the relationships between leadership and organizational culture, we decided to measure three dimensions of leadership using the following scales:

1. The consideration scale, because it provides a measure of employees' perception of their manager's *dedication to team-building*, respect for others, and being considerate of other people's feelings. It shows how much the leader values "acting as a loyal group member."

2. The initiating structure scale describing the *quality of guidance and control* people feel in *what* they do, because it identifies how well a leader is able to communicate and structure the workload. It shows the subordinates' perception of the manager's ability to control the unit's work. It also indicates their perception of the importance to the manager to have everything done one best way—his/her best way.

3. The charismatic leadership scale, because it adds to the analysis by addressing specifically the aspects in leadership that pertain to *raising individual employee's self-confidence and responsibility*, making them aware of the importance of their work to the company as a whole.

On the basis of these definitions of the three dimensions of leadership, strong relationships were expected between these leadership attributes and culture. We expected that (a) consideration mainly added to an employee orientation (p2) and to openness (p4), (b) initiating structure mainly added to a job orientation, and

TABLE 2 Mean, Standard Deviation, F-ratio on Store Level (n = 50)

Variable	Mean	Std Dev	F-ratio	pr > F
charismatic leadership (cl)	3.24	.44	5.07	.0001
initiating structure (is)	3.47	.27	3.77	.0001
consideration (co)	3.46	.44	7.26	.0001
motivation (mot)	3.64	.25	1.96	.0001
satisfaction (sat)	3.76	.19	1.32	.0648
shrinkage (shr)	3.42	.55	ns	ns
Organizational culture				
job orientation (p2)	33.85	21.81	2.10	.0001
org culture closed (p4)	8.66	23.15	2.19	.0001

(c) charismatic leadership mainly added to an employee orientation (p2). The results show that for the two dimensions of organizational culture included in this study, the correlations were mostly as expected.

Probably the most striking difference between expectations and actual results is the slightly negative correlation between initiating structure and job orientation (p2). It suggests that a stronger emphasis on structuring work is related to a greater concern for people instead of to a concern for the work to be done. This negative correlation might be explained by the clarifying influence of initiating structure on individual tasks, obligations, and rights. Overall, the correlation with organizational culture seems weaker for initiating structure than for the other leadership factors. This was unexpected. We expected that charismatic leadership and consideration would show stronger correlations with motivation and satisfaction, but there was no reason to expect differences in the

TABLE 3 Pearson Product Moment Correlations on Store Level

	cl	is	co	mot	sat	shr	p2	p4
cl	1	.78***	.86***	.72***	.49***	−.29*	−.52***	−.39**
is		1	.53***	.49***	.31*	ns	−.35**	ns
co			1	.68***	.39**	ns	−.56***	−.45***
mot				1	.84***	ns	−.67***	−.62***
sat					1	ns	−.49***	−.50***
shr						1	ns	.33*
Organizational culture								
p2							1	.62***
p4								1

Note. cl = charismatic leadership; is = initiating structure;
co = consideration; mot = motivation; sat = satisfaction;
shr = shrinkage; p2 = job orientation; p4 = culture closed.

*significant at .05 level.   **significant at .01 level.   ***significant at .001 level.

TABLE 4 Analysis of Effect of Leadership on Motivation, Satisfaction, and Performance (Shrinkage), as Moderated by Culture on Store Level

	Low On Job Orientation			**High On Job Orientation**		
	mot	sat	shr	mot	sat	shr
cl	.72[a] .001[b]	.41 .04	− .30 .15	.66 .001	.43 .02	− .28 .17
is	.21 .3	− .01 .96	− .03 .87	.70 .001	.54 .001	− .22 .27
co	.72 .001	.31 .14	− .04 .84	.56 .001	.28 .17	− .30 .14

[a]Indicates correlation.　[b]Indicates p-value.

strength of relationships of the leadership factors with organizational culture.

When looking at the influence of organizational culture on the effectiveness of leadership, the most significant result seems to be the relative insensitivity of charismatic leadership (as perceived by subordinates) to cultural differences. The data show clearly a mediating influence of organizational culture on the effectiveness of consideration and initiating structure. In contrast, charismatic leadership appears to have strong effects regardless of the cultural context. Both openness and employee orientation seem to increase the effectiveness of consideration. Initiating structure, on the other hand, seems more effective in a closed culture or in a culture with a preoccupation with the job. In short, while the impact of consideration and initiating structure on motivation and satisfaction seems to be contingent on the organizational culture, the charismatic style appears strong regardless of the different cultural surroundings in which a leader operates.

Although qualitative differences between the mediating influence of the different dimensions of culture were expected, this seemed not to be the case for job orientation and closedness. This might be due to the conceptual relationship

TABLE 5 Analysis of Effect of Leadership on Motivation, Satisfaction, and Performance (Shrinkage), as Moderated by Culture on Store Level

	Open Culture			**Closed Culture**		
	mot	sat	shr	mot	sat	shr
cl	.67[a] .001[b]	.35 .09	− .02 .93	.72 .001	.50 .01	− .31 .13
is	.28 .18	.001 1	.01 .95	.68 .001	.57 .001	− .19 .36
co	.72 .001	.32 .12	.28 .18	.58 .001	.27 .18	− .31 .12

[a]Indicates correlation.　[b]Indicates p-value.

between the two factors, underlined by the strong correlation between them.

The weak and often insignificant direct relation of shrinkage with the leadership factors is somewhat disappointing. However, the interaction effect of organizational culture and consideration on shrinkage seems quite high: In an open culture, the correlation between consideration and shrinkage is .28; in a closed culture, this correlation is -.31.

The influence of culture on consideration and initiating structure seems to fit nicely in the row of contingency factors which influence the outcomes of leadership. However, the absence of situational contingency for charismatic leadership seems to point to a conceptual difference with the other two dimensions of leadership. Charismatic leadership is a recently rediscovered concept which revives attention to the personal characteristics of a leader, focusing on how deeply a leader can influence his subordinates' behavior and way of thinking. It might be that this charismatic approach influences employee satisfaction and motivation in a more direct way because it is defined as a personal attribute of the leader, rather than as a statement on the relational position of a leader in the whole of the organization. This means a charismatic leader can motivate and satisfy subordinates regardless of the organizational culture.

Overall, the relationships with shrinkage were weak; this is possibly attributable to the influence of external, store-specific factors on the shrinkage level. Examples of such factors include store size, the socio-economic or demographic make-up of the area being served, and the quality of the local labor pool. Company executives pointed to shrinkage as the best measure of a store manager's control over store operations due, in part, to the garbage-can function of shrinkage, buffering for several store-specific factors for which the store manager is responsible. Because shrinkage is not exclusively influenced by leadership and culture, but instead represents a buffer for a multitude of other factors, correla-tions might be weaker than for other financial performance variables.

Conclusion

Overall, the leadership factors—initiating structure, charismatic leadership, and consideration—showed significant relationships with the outcome variables, as well as with the studied dimensions of organizational culture. Most importantly, however, the data showed organizational culture to have a mediating influence on the effectiveness of consideration and initiating structure but not on the effectiveness of charismatic leadership. The other two leadership dimensions seemed to have situationally dependent effects, whereas charismatic leadership reflected more of the influence of the leader.

Acknowledgments

This publication was made possible by grants from the 'Stichting Wetenschappe-lijk Onderwijs Limburg' (SWOL) and the Netherlands Organization for Scientific Research (NWO).

We would like to thank Geert Hofstede for helpful comments on the final drafts of this paper.

References

Bass, B. M. (1985). *Leadership and performance beyond expectations*. New York: Free Press.

Bass, B. M. (1988). Evolving perspectives on charismatic leadership. In J. A. Conger, R. N. Kanungo, & Associates (Eds.), *Charismatic leadership, the elusive factor in organizational effectiveness*. San Francisco: Jossey-Bass.

Bass, B. M. (1990). *Bass & Stogdill's handbook of leadership*. New York: Free Press.

KOENE, PENNINGS, AND SCHREUDER

Bass, B. M., & Avolio, B. J. (1990). *Multifactor leadership questionnaire (MLQ)*. Palo Alto: Consulting Psychologists Press.

Burns, J. M. (1978). *Leadership*. New York: Harper & Row.

Eyoang, C. (1985). Culture as cognition. In L. Pondy, P. Frost, G. Morgan, & T. Dandridge (Eds.), *Organizational symbolism*. Greenwich, CT: JAI Press.

Fleishman, F. E. (1953). The description of supervisory behavior. *Journal of Applied Psychology, 37,* 1–6.

Hofstede, G. (1980). *Culture's consequences: International differences in work-related values*. Beverly Hills: Sage.

Hofstede, G., Bond, M. H., & Luk, C. (1991). *Individual perceptions of organizational culture*. Unpublished manuscript.

Hofstede, G., Neuijen, B., Ohayv, D. D., & Sanders G. (1990). Measuring organizational cultures: A qualitative and quantitative study across twenty cases. *Administrative Science Quarterly, 35,* 286–316.

House, R. J., & Mitchell, T. R. (1983). Path-goal theory of leadership. In J. M. Pennings (Ed.), *Decision making, an organizational behavior approach*. New York: Markus Wiener.

Kerr, S., & Jermier, J. M. (1978). Substitutes for leadership: Their meaning and measurement. *Organizational Behavior and Human Performance, 22,* 375–403.

Misumi, J., & Peterson, M. F. (1987). In B. M. Bass & P. J. D. Drenth (Eds.), *Advances in organizational psychology*. Beverly Hills: Sage.

Peters, T. J., & Waterman, R. H. (1982). *In search of excellence*. New York: Harper & Row.

Philipsen, H. (1965). Het meten van leiderschap. *Mens en onderneming, 19,* 153–171.

Philipsen, H. (1970). Het meten van leiderschap nader beschouwd. *Mens en onderneming, 24,* 128–135.

Schein, E. H. (1985). *Organizational culture and leadership: A dynamic view*. San Francisco: Jossey-Bass.

Smith, P. B., & Peterson, M. F. (1990). *Leadership, organizations, and culture*. London: Sage.

Syroit, J. (1979). Mens-en taakgerichtheid: Constructie en validering van een verkorte leiderschapsschaal. *Gedrag, tijdschrift voor Psychologie, 3,* 176–192.

Vogelaar, A. (1990). *Arbeidssatisfactie: Een consequentie van behoeftenstructuur en kenmerken van werk en werksituatie*. Unpublished doctoral dissertation, University of Leiden, The Netherlands.

Bas A. S. Koene is a doctoral student at the University of Limburg, Maastricht, The Netherlands. His research interests focus on managerial effectiveness and the influence of organizational culture on financial performance of organizations. He received his MBA from the University of Limburg.

Johannes M. Pennings is Professor at the Wharton School of the University of Pennsylvania and is on the faculty of the University of Limburg, Maastricht, The Netherlands. Previously he taught at Carnegie Mellon University and Columbia University. His research interests include organizational innovation, compensation, and contingency theory.

Hein Schreuder is Director of Planning and Development of DSM Polymers and Hydrocarbons and an affiliated Professor of Business Economics at the University of Limburg, Maastricht, The Netherlands. He has been a fellow of the European Institute for Advanced Studies in Management, Brussels, Belgium, for 10 years. His research focuses on corporate and business strategy and economic theories of organization.

Direct inquiries about this article to Bas A. S. Koene, Faculty of Economics and Business Administration, University of Limburg, P.O. Box 616, NL-6200 MD Maastricht, Netherlands, (043) 883638, 883812.

The Impact of Leadership Behavior and Leader-Follower Personality Match on Satisfaction and Unit Performance

**Bruce J. Avolio and
Jane M. Howell**

This study examined the degree to which leader behavior predicted follower satisfaction and business unit performance, considering the match between selective characteristics of the leader's and follower's personality. Survey measures of personality and leadership behavior were administered to 76 senior managers and their direct reports (N = 237). One year later, business unit performance data were gathered from company records. Results revealed that the personality of both the leader and follower, as well as the level of congruence between their personalities, moderated followers' satisfaction with the leader and the performance of the leader's business unit. Implications for research on leader-follower personality congruence are considered.

Over the last five years, a number of studies have demonstrated the importance of differentiating transactional from transformational styles of leadership. The purpose of the current study is to examine the degree to which leader behavior predicts follower satisfaction and work unit performance, based on the match between selected characteristics of the leader's and follower's personality. Previous authors, including Evans (1974), have suggested that the personality characteristics of the leader and his or her followers may moderate the relationship between the leadership exhibited and the performance levels achieved. It is expected that certain characteristics of the leader and his or her followers will moderate unit performance and follower satisfaction with the leader.

The typical study in literature which examines the linkage between leadership and personality traits has focused on how one or more personality traits of the leader contribute to the prediction of leadership outcomes. Minimal attention has been paid to the characteristics of followers and how they may affect or moderate the leadership influence process. To understand fully the leadership influence process, more attention needs to be directed towards establishing follower-centered approaches to leadership research (Hollander & Offermann, 1990). The lack of attention to follower characteristics in the development of leadership theory and research is curious in light of Stogdill's (1963) observation concerning the Leadership Behavior Description Questionnaire (LBDQ). Stogdill commented that "the significance of consideration and structure is to be explained, not in terms of leadership, but in terms of followership" (p. 141).

The importance of personality traits to the study of leadership was recently revived in the literature (Kenny & Zaccaro, 1983; Lord, DeVader, & Alliger, 1986; Schneider, 1985). Lord and his associates (1986) reanalyzed previous research on leadership and personality traits in an extensive meta-analysis, reporting that "personality traits are associated with leadership perceptions to a higher degree and more consistently than popular literature indicates" (p.407). Supporting earlier arguments in this literature, Lord et al. concluded that the examination of personality traits with respect to leadership perceptions, effectiveness, and performance may have been dropped prematurely by leadership researchers.

Perceptions of leadership style have been shown to vary as a function of their followers' dispositional characteristics. For example, Misumi and Seki (1971) reported that followers high on need for achievement tended to be more aware of the leader's task orientation than those rated low on need for achievement. Pryer and Distefano (1971) showed that subordinates who believed they had little control over events affecting their lives (external locus of control) rated their leaders as being less considerate than those subordinates who felt they controlled events (internal locus of control). Evans (1974) reported that internally-oriented followers evaluated their leaders as more considerate and more task oriented than did externally-oriented followers.

Durand and Nord (1976) argued that a leader's influence with followers is likely to be affected by the personality characteristics of the follower as well as by the leader's personality. They found that the locus of control scores of the leader and his or her followers independently contributed to predicting the amount of initiation of structure attributed by followers to the leader. For instance, externally-oriented subordinates rated their leaders *higher* on initiation of structure and *lower* on consideration.

Leader-Follower Compatibility

Graen and Cashman (1975) proposed that level of compatibility between group member characteristics and the leader can affect the nature of the exchange between the leader and followers, as well as the performance and satisfaction levels of the work group. Fujii (1977) provided support for Graen and Cashman's position, reporting that follower performance and satisfaction were positively related to greater interpersonal compatibility between the leader and his or her respective followers. Similarly, Weed, Mitchell, and Moffitt (1976) reported that leaders who initiated more structure with dogmatic subordinates were more likely to achieve higher levels of performance, whereas leaders who displayed more consideration yielded greater performance with subordinates who scored low on dogmatism.

Several studies have examined the effect of leader-follower value compatibility (a construct considered central to individual personalities) on a variety of individual outcome measures. For example, Weiss (1978) reported that value congruence between superiors and subordinates was associated with subordinates' evaluations of the leader's level of success and competence. Conversely, Senger (1970) found that managers rated higher those followers who had values similar to the manager. Meglino, Ravlin, and Adkins (1989) reported that value congruence between subordinates and supervisors resulted in higher levels of follower satisfaction and greater organizational commitment; however, in contrast to earlier research, leader-follower congruence was unrelated to performance.

Personality Factors Linked with Transactional and Transformational Leadership

Bass (1985) postulated several key personality characteristics associated with transformational and transactional leadership. According to Bass, transformational leadership calls for personalities that are more likely to be proactive than reactive in their thinking; more creative, novel, and innovative in their ideas; more radical or reforming than reactionary or conservative in ideology; more risk prone; and less inhibited in their ideational search for solutions. In contrast, on average, transactional leaders remain more reactive and less involved, particularly if they practice management-by-exception rather than a contingent reward style of leadership. Such leaders focus on what can work, keep time constraints in mind, and do what seems to be most efficient and free of risk.

Prior research has supported a positive impact of transformational and transactional contingent reward leadership on the performance and satisfaction of followers, at both individual and group levels (see Bass & Avolio, 1990, for a review of this literature). For example, Avolio, Waldman, and Einstein (1988) reported that leaders rated by immediate followers as transformational and transactional more successfully motivated their teams to achieve higher levels of productivity and profits than leaders who frequently practiced management-by-exception. Waldman, Bass, and Yammarino (1990) provided further support for the "augmentation effect" of transformational leadership noted by Bass (1985). Transformational leadership accounted for a significant amount of unique variance—beyond the variance accounted for by transactional leadership—when used to predict supervisory ratings, thus augmenting transactional leadership as a performance predictor. Howell and Avolio (1991) confirmed the augmentation effect reported by Waldman et al. (1990) by predicting unit performance over a one-year time span.

Locus of control is a key personality characteristic that has been associated repeatedly with ratings of leadership and performance (Bass, 1990; Runyon, 1973). Locus of control was examined in the current study because it has already been shown to be predictive of leadership performance (Miller & Toulouse, 1986). However, previous research had not examined locus of control with respect to leader-follower compatibility. The current study, therefore, extends earlier research by examining the locus of control of both leader and follower, considering the level of compatibility and how it moderates the relationship between ratings of transactional and transformational leadership behavior and work unit performance and satisfaction.

Additional personality measures were collected from all leaders and their respective followers using Jackson's Personality Inventory (Jackson, 1976). These measures included risk-taking and innovation. Since there is little empirical research linking these two measures to transformational leadership, testing of a specific hypothesis is not proposed. However, moderating effects are expected to generalize to these additional measures of personality.

Method

Sample

Participants included 76 senior executives and their immediate subordinates (N = 237) in a large Canadian financial institution. Executives ranged in age from 29 to 64, with the average age being 47 years. The executives and their subordinates represented all divisions of the company including investments, finance, market development, sales, administration, and customer service.

Measures

Locus of control. Rotter's (1966) locus of control scale was used in the current study. Rotter's 23-item scale measures whether people believe events are contingent on their own behavior (internal control) or on external forces (external control). Scores were reversed so that higher scores represented an internal locus of control. Internal consistency of this scale as estimated by Cronbach's alpha was .68.

Risk-taking and innovation. Items for risk-taking and innovation came from Jackson's Personality Inventory (Jackson, 1976). The risk-taking scale assesses an individual's willingness to "go out on a limb" when he or she really wants something. High risk-takers are willing to engage in activities that have a low probability of success but a potentially high payoff. The innovation scale reflects willingness to work in areas that are at the forefront of knowledge, venturing into areas where there are minimal guidelines to follow. The Cronbach alpha values and a sample item for each scale are as follows: risk-taking—"If the possible reward was very high, I would not hesitate putting my money into a new business that might fail" (α = .76); and innovation—"I often try to invent new uses for everyday objects" (α = .77).

Leadership. Three transformational and one transactional leadership factors were measured using Bass and Avolio's (1990) Multifactor Leadership Questionnaire (MLQ-Form 10). Subordinates were asked to judge how frequently they observed their respective manager engaged in different leadership behaviors included in the survey. Each behavior was rated on a 5-point frequency scale ranging from 0 = not at all, through 4 = frequently, if not always. Prior research by Bass, Cascio, and O'Connor (1974) has shown that these scale anchors bear a magnitude-estimated based ratio to each other of 4:3:2:1:0.

The four leadership scales were comprised of 30 behavioral items. Subordinate ratings for each manager were added to obtain an overall score on each scale. The four scales included: Charisma, Individualized Consideration, Intellectual Stimulation, and Contingent Reward Leadership. A sample item and internal consistency reliabilities for each scale follow.

1. Charisma (α = .92): "Uses symbols and images to get his/her ideas across."

2. Individualized Consideration (α = .90): "Observes what I do so that he/she can offer me suggestions for improvement."

3. Intellectual Stimulation (α = .89): "Provides reasons to change my way of thinking about problems."

4. Contingent Reward (α = .81): "Points out what I will receive if I do what needs to be done."

Since the three transformational leadership scales were highly intercorrelated (r = .85), they were combined and averaged to form a single standardized weighted index (α = .89), using a procedure recommended by Hotelling (1933) for weighting each independent lower-order factor.

Satisfaction. Two items were used to assess the subordinates' satisfaction with the leader (α = .92).

Consolidated business unit performance. Consolidated business unit performance data were generated from company records for each of the 76 senior executives. The unit performance scores for each executive were based on a detailed management-by-objective system. Specifically, each manager worked with his or her boss to establish the financial goals for the unit during the upcoming year. The goals were set based on the unit's prior performance, expectations regarding external demand for the unit's product(s), and the financial goals for the overall organization. Unit performance scores represent the percentage of goals met by the manager's unit over a 12-month period.

The index representing the percentage of goals achieved by each manager provides an excellent opportunity to assess performance beyond (or below) expectations. Bass (1985) suggested that transformational rather than transactional leadership will stimulate performance levels beyond what is expected or standard levels. The method used here for calculating unit performance can directly test Bass's prediction. Further, the performance data were collected for each leader's business unit *one year* following the collection of all survey data.

Procedure

Executives and their immediate subordinates completed each of the respective personality measures on themselves. After a 2-week delay to prevent contamination of responses, another survey was sent to all subordinates of each participating executive. In this second mailing, subordinates were asked to describe the leadership behavior of their boss and their level of satisfaction. Surveys were returned directly to the authors via self-addressed stamped envelopes. All respondents completed the surveys anonymously and were assured by letters from the authors and from the company's CEO that their responses would remain confidential. The response rate was 92% for executives and 89% for subordinates.

Data Analysis

Hierarchical regression analysis was used to examine the moderating effects of leader-follower personality match or congruence on the links between ratings of leadership, satisfaction, and performance. Cohen and Cohen (1975) recommend hierarchical regression analysis to test the significance of moderator variables. The leadership variables were entered first, followed by leader-follower personality, personality congruence (measured as D^2), and an interaction term representing leadership x personality match. In this analysis, the interaction term represents the moderator variable. D^2 is the absolute difference between the leader and each follower's personality score computed for locus of control, risk-taking, and innovation (see Nunnally, 1978).

Results and Discussion

Means, standard deviations, and correlations between leadership, leader-follower personality and personality congruence, satisfaction, and unit performance are reported in Table 1. Supporting previous research, transformational leadership was significantly and positively correlated with contingent reward leadership, follower satisfaction, and unit performance. Contingent reward leadership was significantly correlated with risk-taking and follower satisfaction, but not with unit performance. Confirming earlier research, leaders and followers who rated higher on internal locus of control produced higher unit performance over a one-year period. Rated satisfaction with the leader was also positively correlated with unit performance.

Congruence item 5 in Table 1 (which refers to the personality match between leader and follower for locus of control calculated as D^2) was significantly and positively correlated with unit performance. The remaining congruence scores calculated for risk-taking and innovation were not significantly correlated with either rated satisfaction or unit performance. Similarly, scale scores for risk-

TABLE 1 Descriptive Statistics and Intercorrelations among Predictors, Moderators, Satisfaction, and Unit Performance

	M	SD	1.	2.	3.	4.	5.	6.	7.	8.	9.	10.	11.	12.	13.
Leadership[a]															
1. Transformational	2.38	.42	—												
2. Contingent Reward	1.86	.50	.62*	—											
Locus of Control[b]															
3. Leader	7.52	2.52	.17	-.06	—										
4. Follower	7.51	3.16	.22	-.19	.17	—									
5. Congruence	12.76	18.55	-.01	-.01	.21	.10	—								
Innovation[c]															
6. Leader	1.67	.21	.00	.01	.05	-.07	-.04	—							
7. Follower	1.70	.21	.01	.09	-.23	-.23	-.05	.06	—						
8. Congruence	.09	.10	.19	.14	.33*	.23	-.24	-.27*	-.16	—					
Risk-Taking[c]															
9. Leader	1.68	.20	.17	.28*	-.08	-.08	-.20	.20	.25	-.15	—				
10. Follower	1.63	.29	-.04	.07	-.23	-.05	-.04	-.04	.34*	.00	.07	—			
11. Congruence	.11	.15	-.16	-.05	.21	-.17	.10	.07	-.04	-.13	.11	-.50*	—		
Dependent Variables															
12. Satisfaction	2.85	.65	.78*	.46*	.18	.18	.11	-.05	-.16	.15	-.06	-.02	-.12	—	
13. Performance	93.73	50.99	.26*	.06	.50*	.42*	.31*	-.21	-.05	.20	-.25	.01	.07	.28*	—

[a]The possible range of scores for the leadership and satisfaction measures was 0 to 4.
[b]The possible range of scores for Rotter's Locus of Control scale was 0 to 23.
[c]The possible range of scores for innovation and risk-taking measures was 1 to 2.

* p < .05. ** p < .01

AVOLIO AND HOWELL

TABLE 2 Hierarchical Regression Predicting Overall Satisfaction and
Unit Performance

Predictors	Satisfaction		Unit Performance	
	R^2	$\triangle R^2$	R^2	$\triangle R^2$
Transformational Leadership[a]	.64	—	.08	—
Locus of Control (Leader/Follower)	.65	.01	.47	.39
Personality Congruence	.66	.01	.50	.03
Leadership–Personality Congruence	.66	.00	.51	.01
Risk–Taking (Leader/Follower)	.66	.02	.25	.17
Personality Congruence	.66	.00	.26	.01
Leadership–Personality Congruence	.66	.00	.27	.01
Innovation (Leader/Follower)	.66	.02	.19	.11
Personality Congruence	.66	.00	.19	.00
Leadership–Personality Congruence	.67	.01	.24	.05
Contingent Reward[b]	.17	—	.04	—
Locus of Control (Leader/Follower)	.32	.15	.49	.45
Personality Congruence	.32	.00	.52	.03
Leadership–Personality Congruence	.36	.04	.54	.02
Risk–Taking (Leader/Follower)	.20	.03	.17	.13
Personality Congruence	.21	.01	.17	.00
Leadership–Personality Congruence	.40	.19	.25	.08
Innovation (Leader/Follower)	.22	.05	.13	.09
Personality Congruence	.22	.00	.16	.03
Leadership–Personality Congruence	.36	.14	.32	.16

[a]Represents the weighted average of the three transformational leadership factors
entered on the first step in the regression analysis. Since the R^2 values for transformational leadership are identical for each subsequent analysis, these values were
not repeated in this table for subsequent analyses using risk-taking and innovation.

[b]Contingent Reward was entered on the first step of the analysis. Since the R^2 values
for contingent reward are identical in each subsequent analysis, these values were
not repeated in this table for subsequent analyses using risk-taking and innovation.

taking and innovation (for both leader and followers) were not correlated with satisfaction or unit performance. As a group, the three personality scores for each leader and their respective followers were generally uncorrelated.

Six separate hierarchical regression analyses were calculated to examine the contribution of both the leader's and followers' personality to the prediction of satisfaction and unit performance (see Table 2). In addition, the moderating effects of leader-follower personality congruence on the relationship between leader behavior and follower satisfaction and business unit performance were examined in these hierarchical regression analyses. Leadership (transactional or transformational) was entered on the first step, followed by the personality scores for each leader and their respective followers, the personality congruence score (D^2), and finally the interaction term (i.e., leadership x personality congruence). Again, the interaction term was used to test the moderating effects of personality congruence on the linkage between leadership, satisfaction, and performance.

In three of the six regression analyses, all involving contingent reward leadership, the interaction term added unique variance to the prediction of follower satisfaction. For both transactional and transformational leadership, each of the respective interaction terms added unique variance to the prediction of unit performance. Locus of control scores for both leader and follower moderated the impact of ratings of leadership on unit performance. The same pattern emerged for each of the two remaining personality scales for both transformational and transactional leadership.

One possible reason for the lack of unique variance being added by the interaction term in analyses involving transformational leadership and satisfaction is the relatively high correlation ($r = .78$) between these two scales as compared to the correlation between contingent reward leadership and satisfaction ($r = .46$). Transformational leadership accounts for such a large share of the variance in ratings of satisfaction that it may be difficult to find a significant moderating effect due to the interaction term.

All three personality measures added a substantial amount of unique variance to the prediction of both criterion variables augmenting both transactional and transformational leadership. Regarding unit performance, the use of the term prediction refers to the one-year interval over which performance data were collected. Again, satisfaction ratings were collected concurrently with leadership ratings, thus potentially resulting in an inflated relationship (Avolio, Bass, & Yammarino, 1991).

The current results indicate that the personality of both leader and follower, as well as the level of congruence (or lack thereof) between a leader's and follower's personality, may moderate the satisfaction of the follower with the leader as well as the performance of the leader's work unit. The examination of two conceptually distinct leadership constructs demonstrated the importance of considering leader and follower dispositions in the prediction of standard outcome measures commonly used in prior leadership research.

The current findings support Fujii (1977) and Graen and Cashman (1975) who proposed that compatibility between leader and group member characteristics can impact performance and satisfaction levels within the leader's unit. It now seems appropriate to extend the current study by evaluating a broader range of personality measures, in addition to other variables, to determine the degree to which level of compatibility between the leader and follower affects measures of satisfaction and performance. These additional variables might include similarity in experiences, personal values, and/or attitudes.

In addition to predicting satisfaction and performance, other criterion measures more directly relevant to the level of leader-follower compatibility could be incorporated in future research. These might include level of conflict within the unit, turnover rates, number of innovations produced, and organizational commitment.

Another avenue for future research is the evaluation of the variance in personality characteristics within work units and the effect of changes in group composition on the leader's ability to influence followers (Dansereau, Alutto, & Yammarino, 1984). For example, a relatively homogeneous group of followers who are moderate risk-takers may be willing to support the leader's innovative initiatives. However, a new member who is highly resistant to change and innovation may enter the work group and significantly affect the leader's ability to influence the group's level of innovation.

Level of leader-follower compatibility is particularly relevant to the construct of transformational leadership since such leaders work assiduously to align followers around their mission and vision. A moderate degree of incompatibility between leader and follower may be needed to question the leader's vision in order to avoid "blind obedience" by followers. Yet, too little compatibility, which may lead to mistrust and apprehension, may result in a lack of alignment and the leader's inability to rally followers behind his or her vision. Since research on transformational leadership is in the very early stages of development, many of these questions must await further investigation.

Some Practical Implications and Conclusions

This preliminary investigation reconfirmed the importance of personality variables in the study of leadership. Specifically, both the leader's and followers' personality were shown to be important in the prediction of satisfaction and performance.

The trend in many organizations towards team-based management necessitates closer scrutiny of the characteristics of the leader as well as the members of the teams. For example, with short-term projects where the strategy for project completion is clear and interdependence among team members is required, team members need to work cooperatively with each other. In this situation, a relatively homogenous group, with respect to individual backgrounds, personality, and/or attitudes, may be optimal for project completion. In contrast, a team which develops unique solutions to a particular problem, which require minimal cooperation to implement, may necessitate a team composition which is highly diverse. Minimally, the nature of the project, coupled with team member characteristics, may affect the impact that a leader can have on the team's performance. Consequently, these factors need to be considered to optimize team performance.

In many instances it is difficult, if not impossible, to consider the level of congruence among team members and the leader with respect to personalities, attitudes, and values. Yet, there are also instances where temporary project teams, formed to tackle a particular problem, are disbanded when the problem is resolved. These represent ideal settings in which to consider the composition of the team with respect to the nature of the problem. In departmental settings with less discretion over group composition, leader sensitization to differences in personalities, values, or attitudes among departmental members may force the leader to consider those differences in his or her attempt to build a more cohesive unit.

In sum, future research is required. It must include a broader range of individual difference and criterion measures to differentiate further the impact of transactional and transformational leadership on various outcome measures. Also, to the extent possible, it is important to collect such measures from independent sources, to avoid single source bias that can result when measures such as leadership and satisfaction are collected from a single rater.

References

Avolio, B. J., Bass, B. M., & Yammarino, F. (1991). Identifying common methods variance with data collected from a single source: An unresolved sticky issue. *Journal of Management, 17,* 571–587.

Avolio, B. J., Waldman, D. A., & Einstein, W. O. (1988). Transformational leadership in a management game simulation: Impacting the bottom line. *Group and Organization Studies, 13,* 59–80.

Bass, B. M. (1985). *Leadership and performance beyond expectations.* New York: Free Press.

Bass, B. M. (1990). *Bass and Stogdill's handbook of leadership.* New York: Free Press.

Bass, B. M., & Avolio, B. J. (1990). *The multifactor leadership manual.* Palo Alto, CA: Consulting Psychologists Press.

Bass, B. M., Cascio, W. F., & O'Connor, E. J. (1974). Magnitude estimations of expressions of frequency and amount. *Journal of Applied Psychology, 59*, 313–320.

Cohen, J., & Cohen, J. (1975). *Applied multiple regression/correlational analysis for the behavioral sciences.* Hillsdale, NJ: Lawrence Erlbaum Associates.

Dansereau, F., Alutto, J. A., & Yammarino, F. J. (1984). *Theory testing in organizational behavior: The varient approach.* Englewood Cliffs, NJ: Prentice-Hall.

Durand, D. E., & Nord, W. R. (1976). Perceived leader behavior as a function of personality characteristics of supervisors and subordinates. *Academy of Management Journal, 19*, 427–438.

Evans, M. G. (1974). Extensions of a path goal theory of motivation. *Journal of Applied Psychology, 59*, 172–178.

Fujii, D. S. (1977). A dyadic interactive approach to the study of leader behaviors. *Dissertation Abstracts International, 37*, 5415–5416.

Graen, G., & Cashman, J. F. (1975). A role-making model of leadership in formal organizations: A developmental approach. In J. G. Hunt & L. L. Larson (Eds.), *Leadership frontiers* (pp. 143–165). Carbondale, IL: Southern Illinois University Press.

Hollander, E. P., & Offermann, L. R. (1990). Power and leadership in organizations. *American Psychologist, 45*, 179–189.

Hotelling, H. (1933). Analysis of a complex of statistical variables into principal components. *Journal of Educational Psychology, 24*, 417–441, 498–520.

Howell, J. M., & Avolio, B. J. (1991). *Predicting consolidated unit performance: Leadership ratings, locus of control and support for innovation.* Paper presented at the Meeting of the Academy of Management, Miami, FL.

Jackson, D. N. (1976). *Jackson personality inventory.* Goshen, NY: Research Psychologists Press.

Kenny, D. A., & Zaccaro, S. J. (1983). An estimate of variance due to traits in leadership. *Journal of Applied Psychology, 68*, 678–685.

Lord, R. G., DeVader, C. L., & Alliger, G. M. (1986). A meta-analysis of the relation between personality traits and leadership perceptions: An application of validity generalization procedures. *Journal of Applied Psychology, 71*, 402–410.

Meglino, B. M., Ravlin, E. C., & Adkins, C. L. (1989). A work-values approach to corporate culture: A field test of the value congruence process and its relationship to individual outcomes. *Journal of Applied Psychology, 74*, 424–432.

Miller, D., & Toulouse, J. M. (1986). Strategy, structure, CEO personality and performance in small firms. *American Journal of Small Business, 15*, 47–62.

Misumi, J., & Seki, F. (1971). Effects of achievement motivation on the effectiveness of leadership patterns. *Administrative Science Quarterly, 16*, 51–59.

Nunnally, J. C. (1978). *Psychometric theory* (2nd ed.). New York: McGraw-Hill.

Pryer, M. W., & Distefano, M. K. (1971). Perceptions of leadership, job satisfaction and internal-external locus of control across three nursing levels. *Nursing Research, 2*, 534–537.

Rotter, J. B. (1966). Generalized expectancies for internal versus external locus of control of reinforcement. *Psychological Monographs: General and Applied, 80*(Whole No. 609).

Runyon, K. E. (1973). Some interactions between personality variables and management styles. *Journal of Applied Psychology, 57*, 288–294.

Schneider, B. (1985). Organizational behavior. *Annual Review of Psychology, 36*, 573–611.

Senger, J. (1970). The religious manager. *Academy of Management Journal, 13*, 179–186.

Stogdill, R. M. (1963). *Manual for the leader behavior description questionnaire — Form XII.* Columbus, OH: Bureau of Business Research.

Waldman, D. A., Bass, B. M., & Yammarino, F. J. (1990). Adding to contingent reward behavior: The augmenting effect of charismatic leadership. *Group and Organization Studies, 15*, 381–394.

Weed, S. E., Mitchell, T. R., & Moffitt, W. (1976). Leadership style, subordinate personality and task type as predictors of performance and satisfaction with supervision. *Journal of Applied Psychology, 61*, 58–66.

Weiss, H. M. (1978). Social learning of work values in organizations. *Journal of Applied Psychology, 63,* 711–718.

Bruce J. Avolio, PhD, is Director of Graduate Programs in the School of Management at the State University of New York-Binghamton and Associate Professor in Organizational Behavior. A leading expert on the study of transformational leadership, he has published numerous articles and conducted training and organizational development programs worldwide.

Jane M. Howell, PhD, is Assistant Professor of Organizational Behavior at the University of Western Ontario. She has published numerous articles on transformational leadership, organizational champions, and technological innovation. She conducts leadership, organizational change, and management skill development programs in Canada and abroad.

Direct inquiries about this article to Bruce J. Avolio, Associate Professor, Center for Leadership Studies, State University of New York at Binghamton, P.O. Box 6000, Binghamton, NY 13901–6000, 607/777–4181.

The Relationship of Leader-Member Exchanges with Laissez-Faire, Transactional, and Transformational Leadership in Naval Environments

Ronald J. Deluga

The augmenting and dyadic nature of transformational leader-subordinate relationships was studied. High-quality leader-member exchanges may merge with transformational leadership in a mutually stimulating fashion, generating organizationally advantageous outcomes. The findings suggested that charisma and individual consideration are the transformational leadership factors most closely associated with high-quality exchanges.

Understanding the impact of leadership requires recognizing the social exchange nature of leader-subordinate relationships (Hollander, 1978). That is, leaders and subordinates engage in giving and receiving to obtain personal rewards and achieve organizational objectives. Laissez-faire, transactional, transformational, and leader-member exchange are four approaches which address the participation of leaders and subordinates in social reciprocity.

Laissez-Faire Leadership

Laissez-faire or passive leadership is characterized by a highly permissive, "hands off" approach wherein the leadership role and duties are relinquished. Laissez-faire leaders have minimal confidence in their ability to supervise and exhibit low initiation and participation with subordinates (Bass, 1990). They avoid influencing subordinates (Bradford & Lippitt, 1945), do not set lucid objectives, and generally leave too much responsibility to disorganized subordinates (Bass, 1990). As a consequence, laissez-faire leaders frequently generate detached, unproductive, and dissatisfied followers. Relative to transactional and transformational leadership, laissez-faire leadership has been uniformly viewed as the least effective supervisory approach (Bass, 1990).

Transactional Leadership

Transactional leadership focuses on the social exchange nature of the leader-subordinate relationships (e.g., Hollander, 1979). In a quid pro quo process, transactional leaders implicitly and explicitly contract with subordinates to barter services rendered in return for rewards (Bass, 1985; Burns, 1978). The typical leader is transactional as he or she appeals to subordinate lower level needs and decides their goals (Zaleznik, 1983).

For Bass (1985, 1990), transactional leadership is associated with two factors. First, contingent reward characterizes the familiar work-for-pay arrangement where subordinates are rewarded for their effort, support, and doing what needs to be done. Second, management-by-exception describes how the transactional leader only exerts corrective action in response to subordinates who deviate from expectations or fail to meet goals. Transactional leaders promote subordinate self-interest, routine performance, and general organizational mediocrity (Bass, 1985).

Transformational Leadership

Referred to as the augmentation effect, transformational leadership incorporates and moves beyond transactional leadership. The transformational leader catalyzes conventional social exchanges between leaders and subordinates. Subordinates are stimulated to surpass initial performance goals and self-interests by generating commitment to designated outcomes. Subordinates place considerable confidence and trust in the transformational leader (Bass, 1985, 1990; Burns, 1978; Yukl, 1989).

Transformational leadership appears in varying degrees at all organizational levels and has been observed in diverse settings, including the military (Bass, 1985, 1990). Moreover, the advantageous nature of transformational leadership has been corroborated by numerous organizational studies (e.g., Deluga, 1988; Hater & Bass, 1988) and is viewed as a function of each subordinate's unique relationship with the leader, apart from other subordinates (Yammarino & Bass, 1990a). Transformational leaders cultivate high-level devotion, loyalty, and performance by exhibiting charisma and inspiring subordinates, as well as through intellectually stimulating and treating subordinates as individuals (Bass, 1985, 1990).

Charisma characterizes the influence of the transformational leader on subordinates by appealing to their emotions and encouraging identification with the leader. Charisma is considered the most important, but not entirely sufficient, condition for the emergence of transformational leadership.

Next, transformational leaders inspire subordinates by sharing a compelling vision of what can be accomplished. Energized and confident subordinates are motivated to make a strong effort toward reaching the desired objectives.

In addition, intellectual stimulation fosters creative thinking among subordinates. Subordinates are encouraged to develop new cognitive patterns targeted toward conceptualizing and solving complex problems. Finally, individual consideration describes the transformational leader's mentoring orientation and the treatment of subordinates as special contributors to the work group's mission. Subordinates are assigned developmental tasks and are provided with coaching and teaching support.

Leader-Member Exchanges

Leader-member exchange theory proposes a role-making approach to leadership. That is, nearly all leaders develop different social exchange relationships with different subordinates. These dyadic relationships range from higher quality to lower quality exchanges (e.g., Graen & Cashman, 1975). High-quality exchanges are characterized by mutual influence (Yukl, 1989), loyalty, support (Liden & Graen, 1980), and a sense of a common fate (Dansereau, Graen, & Haga, 1975). High-quality exchange subordinates receive a large proportion of formal and informal benefits while, in return, leaders obtain dedicated and committed subordinates (Dansereau et al., 1975; Yukl, 1989).

Conversely, lower quality exchanges feature a relatively low level of mutual support and upward influence. Leaders acquire routine subordinate commitment and performance while out-group subordinates receive ordinary benefits (Graen & Cashman, 1975; Yukl, 1989).

Further, the strength of leader-member exchange relationships can predict organizationally significant outcomes (Graen & Scandura, 1987). For instance, improved leader-member exchanges have been linked with elevated productivity (Graen, Novak, & Sommerkamp, 1982; Scandura & Graen, 1984) and enhanced subordinate career progress (Graen, Wakabayashi, Graen, & Graen, 1990) and have played a moderating role in influencing managerial decisions (Scandura, Graen, & Novak, 1986). Finally, high-quality exchanges have been associated with superior effectiveness, satisfaction with the superior, and upward influence effectiveness (Deluga & Perry, 1991).

Present Study

In summary, laissez-faire, transactional, and transformational leadership have been examined extensively. Laissez-faire and transformational leadership have consistently emerged as, respectively, the least and most effective supervisory approaches (Bass, 1985; Deluga, 1990; Yammarino & Bass, 1990a). However, the relationship of

leader-member exchange theory with these three approaches needs empirical investigation. An understanding of these relationships will help illuminate the mutual impact of subordinates and leaders. For example, could the organizational benefits of high-quality exchanges be more closely associated with transformational than with either laissez-faire or transactional leadership? Accordingly, the purpose of this investigation was to examine the relationship of leader-member exchanges with laissez-faire, transactional, and transformational leadership.

Recall that transformational leadership promotes subordinate commitment to the organization's mission (Bass, 1985), while high-quality exchanges are similarly comprised of subordinates dedicated to achieving task goals (Liden & Graen, 1980). In addition, both transformational leadership and leader-member exchanges appear to operate at the individual subordinate-leader or dyadic level. Thus, it seems possible that these two leadership processes may combine in an organizationally productive manner. It was therefore predicted that high-quality exchanges (as reported by subordinates) combined with, respectively, subordinate extra effort, perceived leader effectiveness, satisfaction with the leader, and perceived upward influence effectiveness will be most closely associated with transformational, then transactional, leadership and least closely associated with laissez-faire leadership.

Method

Sample and Procedure

A U.S. Navy facility located on the East Coast was the setting for the study. Subjects were 145 advanced male U.S. Navy officers (average age = 32 years) who were completing a 26-week professional development program. During classroom training and at approximately 1-week intervals, officers confidentially completed three self-report instruments describing their relationship with their most recent immediate superior. Approximately 95% of the officers had worked with their superior (all males) for two years or less.

Data were collected at multiple points in time to diminish the threat of single-source bias. That is, because ratings of the constructs were generated by the same subordinates, effect sizes may be overestimated due to the subordinates' inclination to maintain uniformity in their responses (Podsakoff & Organ, 1986). However, a temporal delay between data collection points for several constructs from identical sources may reduce the possibility of inflated relationships (Avolio, Yammarino, & Bass, 1991).

Instruments

To assess perceptions of laissez-faire, transactional, and transformational leadership, the officers completed the Multifactor Officer Questionnaire-Form R (MOQ-R) (Bass, Yammarino, & Kowalewski, 1987). The instrument has been used in previous military leadership studies (e.g., Deluga, 1991; Yammarino & Bass, 1990a, 1990b) and employs a 5-point Likert-type format with sample response choices ranging from "frequently, if not always" (4) to "not at all" (0).

First, laissez-faire leadership is measured by six MOQ-R items which describe how the leader avoids making decisions and permits near total freedom for subordinates to perform as they wish. A sample item was "however I do my job is OK with him/her."

Next, the MOQ-R employs 14 items to measure transactional leadership. Three items assess General Contingent Reward described as the pervasive use of rewards by the leader, while an additional three items measure Individual Contingent Re-

ward, characterized as rewards targeted toward each subordinate's priorities. Similarly, four items assess Active Management-by-Exception, characterized by how the leader vigorously searches for subordinate deviations from expectations. Finally, four items measure Passive Management-by-Exception which describe the leader's reactive approach to substandard subordinate performance.

Additionally, the MOQ-R uses four sets of six items which assess charisma, inspiration, individual consideration, and intellectual stimulation as the factors linked with transformational leadership. Finally, the MOQ-R assessed officer perceptions regarding their most recent immediate superior's effectiveness (four items), satisfaction with their superior officer (two items), and self-reports of their own extra effort (four items).

Approximately one week later, the officers completed a second instrument also referencing their most recent immediate superior: Form M of the Profiles of Organizational Influence Strategies (POIS-M) (Kipnis & Schmidt, 1982). The POIS-M, although not directly related to the study's hypothesis, was included in order to conduct a subsequent single-source bias analysis.

The 27-item instrument uses a 5-point Likert-type response format ranging from "Almost always" (5) to "Never" (1). The POIS-M measured how frequently the officers employed six strategies to influence their superior. The strategies include friendliness, assertiveness, bargaining, coalition, higher authority, and reason. As an additional outcome variable, that is, perceived upward influence effectiveness, the officers also completed an item reporting their effectiveness in influencing their most recent immediate superior using the aforementioned strategies.

Finally, about one week after finishing the POIS-M, the officers completed the Leader-Member Exchange Scale-17 (LMX-17) (Graen & Scandura, 1985). The 17-item instrument employs a 5-point Likert-type format similar to the POIS-M. The LMX-17 reveals the extent to which officers reported high-quality exchanges (high scores) or low-quality exchanges (low scores) with their most recent immediate superior. A sample question was, "How would you characterize your working relationship with your most recent immediate superior?"

The descriptive statistics for the key instruments used in the study appear in Table 1. Results with scales having alpha coefficients below the recommended level of .70 (Nunnally, 1978) should be interpreted with caution.

Results

First, the four transactional and four transformational factors were combined to form single measures of transactional and transformational leadership, respectively. Second, because the data were collected from the same subordinates, a procedure implemented by Kozlowski and Doherty (1989) was adopted to address single-source bias as an alternative explanation for the findings. That is, if single-source bias was artificially inflating the relationship among the four leadership approaches and outcome variables, it would be anticipated that the approaches and variables would also emerge strongly associated with the POIS-M. However, the average correlation between the POIS-M and the focal instruments was limited: $r = .01$ (range, $r = .07$ to $-.09$). Consequently, due to these findings, the temporal nature of the data collection, and the strength of the observed relationships, it was concluded that the potential impact of single-source bias on the findings was minimal. The data analysis then proceeded as follows.

Hierarchical regression analysis was used to test the prediction that subordinates reporting high-quality exchanges combined with the outcome variables (e.g., subordinate extra effort) would be most closely associated with transformational, then transactional, leadership and least closely associated with laissez-faire leadership. Hierarchical regression reveals the increase in outcome variable (e.g., subordinate extra effort) variance accounted for by the addition of an independent variable (e.g., transactional leadership) exceeding that accounted for by previously entered independent variables (Cohen & Cohen, 1975). By concurrently adding the independent variables to the regression equation, the procedure also decreases multicollinearity among independent variables (Seltzer & Bass, 1990).

Accordingly, a series of regression models were constructed. In model one, laissez-faire leadership served as a regressor variable while subordinate extra effort, combined with leader member exchange, operated as a response variable. Model two was identical to model one except for the addition of transactional leadership as the last entered regressor variable. Thus, the increase in variance accounted for by the addition of transactional leadership was determined by subtracting the variance accounted for by model one (R^2_1) from the variance accounted for by model two (R^2_2).

Model three was identical to model two except for the addition of transformational leadership as the last entered regressor variable. The additional variance accounted for by transformational leadership was calculated by $R^2_3 - R^2_2$. A similar hierarchical procedure was conducted for leader-member exchange combined with, respectively, perceived leader effectiveness, satisfaction with the leader, and perceived upward-influencing effectiveness as response variables.

Next, a second series of hierarchical regression analyses were conducted whereby laissez-faire, transformational, and transactional leadership were, respectively, sequentially entered into the regression equation. The purpose was to determine the extent to which transactional leadership could explain a significant amount of variance in the outcome

TABLE 1   Descriptive Statistics for Key Study Variables

	N	M	SD	alpha coefficient	2	3	4	5	6	7	8	9	10	11	12	13	14	15	16
1. Laissez-faire leadership	144	1.37	0.69	.66	-37	-23	-43	-43	26	-59	-60	-45	-57	-57	-43	-16	-53	-50	03
2. Transactional leadership	143	8.37	2.43	.76		80	85	50	39	77	67	76	73	67	69	17	63	67	30
3. General contingent reward	144	1.36	0.89	.68			72	18	08	61	53	60	61	52	56	02	46	53	18
4. Individual contingent reward	145	2.08	1.17	.95				20	11	82	70	85	77	71	72	08	69	73	29
5. Active management-by-exception	144	2.48	0.85	.74					-03	31	35	17	29	23	22	18	26	18	01
6. Passive management-by-exception	145	2.45	0.77	.54						14	05	23	10	15	21	19	11	16	26
7. Transformational leadership	139	9.02	3.7	.97							90	91	95	95	84	16	85	88	23
8. Intellectual stimulation	144	2.37	0.92	.91								75	83	80	73	12	75	74	13
9. Individual consideration	142	2.27	0.91	.87									84	81	82	16	75	81	34
10. Inspiration	143	2.13	0.88	.86										86	75	15	79	79	24
11. Charisma	145	2.18	1.29	.96											79	12	85	89	15
12. Leader-member exchange	138	71.07	15.23	.92												24	74	77	43
13. Subordinate extra effort	143	3.36	0.57	.72													17	03	19
14. Perceived leader effectiveness	145	2.79	0.93	.89														82	19
15. Satisfaction with leader	145	2.50	1.41	.95															23
16. Perceived upward influence effectiveness	141	2.87	0.92 [a]																

Note. Ns differ due to missing values. Decimal points were omitted from intercorrelations.
[a]Equals a single item measure.

variables beyond that accounted for by laissez-faire and transformational leadership.

The results for the first series of hierarchical regression analyses (i.e., transformational leadership as the last entered regressor variable) are shown in Table 2. In model one, the laissez-faire beta weights were significantly and negatively associated with the response variables. Laissez-faire leadership explained from 3% to 27% of the response variable variance.

In model two, in every instance, transactional leadership contributed a level of variance accounted for in the response variables significantly exceeding that associated with laissez-faire leadership (range from 22% to 36%). The transactional beta weights were significantly and positively associated with the response variables.

Finally, in model three, also in every case, transformational leadership contributed a level of variance accounted for in the response variables significantly beyond that associated with both laissez-faire and transactional leadership (range from 8% to 26%). In contrast to those of laissez-faire and transactional leadership, the transformational leadership beta weights were significantly and positively associated with the response variables.

By comparison, there were no significant increases in variance accounted for beyond laissez-faire and transformational leadership when transactional leadership was the last entered regressor variable (i.e., second regression series). That is, transactional leadership did not explain a significant amount of variance beyond the 32% to 85% already accounted for by transformational leadership. In short, transformational leadership augmented transactional leadership, but not the reverse.

To further explore the relationship between transformational leadership and leader-member exchanges, a follow-up multiple regression analysis was conducted. Here, the response variable was leader-member exchange, while the four transformational leadership factors served as regressors. The intent was to reveal those factors most closely linked with leader-member exchanges. Table 3 shows that individual consideration ($beta = .48$, $p < .0001$) and charisma ($beta = .31$, $p < .01$) appeared as significantly associated with leader-member exchanges.

Discussion

These data support the prediction that transformational leadership produces desirable organizational outcomes surpassing those of laissez-faire and transactional leadership. In this respect, the findings sustain the augmentation effect of transformational leadership reported in previous studies (e.g., Seltzer & Bass, 1990). That is, transformational leadership is not simply the flip side of transactional leadership but incorporates and adds a highly significant incremental effect to the social-exchange nature of transactional leadership. As a consequence, desirable organizational consequences are likely to emerge.

At the same time, this investigation supports prior work which suggests that, relative to transactional leadership, the heightened outcomes associated with transformational leadership result from the individualized, dyadic relationship between a given subordinate and the leader. The essence of the relationship with a transformational leader is perceived as unique by each subordinate, independent of other subordinate-leader interactions (Yammarino & Bass, 1990a).

Also, this study contributes to the research literature by supporting the notion that the advantages of transformational leadership may fuse with high-quality leader-member exchanges in a mutually stimulating fashion. Transformational leaders may foster the formation of high-quality relationships and a sense

TABLE 2 Hierarchical Multiple Regression Analysis Evaluating the Relationship of Laissez-Faire, Transactional, and Transformational Leadership with Leader-Member Exchanges, Subordinate Extra Effort, Upward Influence, Satisfaction with the Leader, and Leader Effectiveness

Response variables	df	F	Adjusted R^2	Leadership approaches (regressors)		
				Laissez-Faire beta	Transactional beta	Transformational beta
LMX–17 combined with subordinate extra effort						
Model 1	1,133	24.52**	.15	−.40**		
Model 2	2,130	40.88**	.38	−.19*	.53**	
difference[a]	1,142	57.50**	.23			
Model 3	3,125	41.86**	.49	−.01	.14	.58**
difference[b]	1,141	27.50**	.11			
LMX–17 combined with perceived leader effectiveness						
Model 1	1,135	51.63**	.27	−.53**		
Model 2	2,132	92.52**	.58	−.29**	.61**	
difference[a]	1,142	103.33**	.31			
Model 3	3,126	220.63**	.84	.02	.03	.91**
difference[b]	1,141	260.00**	.26			
LMX–17 combined with satisfaction with the leader						
Model 1	1,135	47.11**	.25	−.51**		
Model 2	2,132	103.77**	.61	−.25**	.65**	
difference[a]	1,142	120.00**	.36			
Model 3	3,126	234.66**	.85	.04	.10	.87**
difference[b]	1,141	240.00**	.24			
LMX–17 combined with perceived upward influence effectiveness						
Model 1	1,131	5.25*	.03	−.20*		
Model 2	2,128	23.08**	.25	.00	.52**	
difference[a]	1,142	44.00	.22			
Model 3	3,123	21.47**	.33	.16	.21	.48**
difference[b]	1,141	16.00**	.08			

Note 1. $N = 145$. LMX–17 = leader-member exchange.

Note 2. A second series of analyses with transactional leadership as the last entered regressor variable did not explain any significant amount of variance beyond that already accounted for by laissez-faire and transformational leadership.

[a]Indicates $R^2{}_2 - R^2{}_1$.   [b]Indicates $R^2{}_3 - R^2{}_2$.

$* p < .05$. $** p < .0001$.

TABLE 3 Results of Leader-Member Exchange Regression Analysis
with Transformational Leadership Factors as Regressors

Response variable	F	Adjusted R^2	Transformational leadership factor betas			
			Intellectual stimulation	Inspiration	Individual consideration	Charisma
Leader-member exchange	86.38**	.72	.11	.01	.48**	.31*

$*p < .01$ $**p < .001.$

of a common fate with individual subordinates while, in a social-exchange process, these subordinates strengthen and encourage the leader. Through the leader's charismatic and magnetic demeanor, inspired subordinates may gravitate toward those characteristics chiefly associated with high-quality exchanges (e.g., subordinate extra effort).

Moreover, charisma and individual consideration could be the key factors by which transformational leadership merges with high quality leader-member exchanges. Support for this idea is provided in two ways. First, the data reveal that charisma and individual consideration were the factors most closely associated with high-quality exchanges. Second, previous research has suggested that charisma primarily operates at the dyadic level, rather than at a group-leader level (Seltzer & Bass, 1990). Parallel to the leader-member exchange process, individual subordinates and leaders— perceived as charismatic—form varying relationships as a function of their own unique interactions.

Also, individual consideration operates at the dyadic level by definition; that is, the leader serves as a mentor and provides personal attention when necessary. Accordingly, the dyadic nature of leader-member exchanges corresponds with the transformational charisma and individual consideration processes functioning at the subordinate-leader level. As a consequence, high-quality exchange subordinates may, for example, exert extra effort beyond those levels associated with laissez-faire and transactional leadership.

In total, the findings support the augmenting effect of transformational leadership. Further, the transformational leader and empowered high-quality exchange subordinates may impact each other as they jointly work to accomplish individual and organizational goals. The dyadic nature of individual consideration and charisma could be the key factors producing these outcomes.

Future studies might explore the relationship of transformational leadership and leader-member exchanges in a variety of organizations. By examining longitudinal data from superiors and subordinates, the evolution of transformational and leader-member exchanges could subsequently be traced. In turn, an understanding of these dynamics would promote the development of leadership training programs, guide individual career progress, and facilitate organizationally advantageous outcomes.

References

Avolio, B. J., Yammarino, F. J., & Bass, B. M. (1991). Identifying common methods variance with data collected from a single source: An unresolved sticky issue. *Journal of Management, 17*, 571–588.

Bass, B. M. (1985). *Leadership and performance beyond expectations.* New York: Free Press.

Bass, B. M. (1990). *Bass & Stogdill's handbook of leadership* (3rd ed.). New York: Free Press.

Bass, B. M., Yammarino, F. J., & Kowalewski, S. M. (1987). *Multifactor officer questionnaire (Form R).* Binghamton: State University of New York, University Center.

Bradford, L. P., & Lippitt, R. (1945). Building a democratic work group. *Personnel, 22*(3), 142–148.

Burns, J. M. (1978). *Leadership.* New York: Harper.

Cohen, J., & Cohen, P. (1975). *Applied multiple regression/correlation analysis for the behavioral sciences.* Hillsdale, NJ: Erlbaum.

Dansereau, F., Graen, G. B., & Haga, W. J. (1975). A vertical dyad linkage approach to leadership within formal organizations — a longitudinal investigation of the role-making process. *Organizational Behavior and Human Performance, 13*, 46–78.

Deluga, R. J. (1988). Relationship of transformational and transactional leadership with employee influencing strategies. *Group & Organization Studies, 13*, 456–467.

Deluga, R. J. (1990). The effects of transformational, transactional, and laissez-faire leadership characteristics on subordinate influencing behavior. *Basic and Applied Social Psychology, 11*, 191–203.

Deluga, R. J. (1991). The relationship of leader and subordinate influencing activity in naval environments. *Military Psychology, 3*, 25–39.

Deluga, R. J., & Perry, J. T. (1991). The relationship of subordinate upward influencing behavior, satisfaction, and perceived superior effectiveness with leader-member exchanges. *Journal of Occupational Psychology, 64*, 239–252.

Graen, G. B., & Cashman, J. (1975). A role-making model of leadership in formal organizations: A developmental approach. In J. G. Hunt & L. L. Larson (Eds.), *Leadership frontiers* (pp. 143–165). Kent, OH: Kent State University Press.

Graen, G. B., Novak, M., & Sommerkamp, P. (1982). The effects of leader-member exchange and job design on productivity and satisfaction: Testing a dual attachment model. *Organizational Behavior and Human Performance, 30*, 109–131.

Graen, G. B., & Scandura, T. A. (1985). *Leader-member exchange scale-17.* Cincinnati, OH: University of Cincinnati.

Graen, G. B., & Scandura, T. A. (1987). Toward a psychology of dyadic organizing. In L. L. Cummings & B. M. Staw (Eds.), *Research in organizational behavior* (Vol. 9, pp. 175–208). Greenwich, CT: JAI Press.

Graen, G. B., Wakabayashi, M., Graen, M. R., & Graen, M. G. (1990). International generalizability of American hypotheses about Japanese management progress: A strong inference investigation. *Leadership Quarterly, 1*, 1–23.

Hater, J. J., & Bass, B. M. (1988). Superiors' evaluations and subordinates' perceptions of transformational and transactional leadership. *Journal of Applied Psychology, 73*, 695–702.

Hollander, E. P. (1978). *Leadership dynamics: A practical guide to effective relationships.* New York: Free Press.

Hollander, E. P. (1979). Leadership and social exchange processes. In K. Gergen, M. S. Greenberg, & R. H. Willis (Eds.), *Social exchange: Advances in theory and research* (pp. 103–118). New York: Winston-Wiley.

Kipnis, D., & Schmidt, S. M. (1982). *Profiles of organizational influence strategies (Form M).* San Diego, CA: University Associates.

Kozlowski, S. W. J., & Doherty, M. L. (1989). Integration of climate and leadership: Examination of a neglected issue. *Journal of Applied Psychology, 74*, 546–553.

Liden, R., & Graen, G. B. (1980). Generalizability of the vertical dyad linkage model of leadership. *Academy of Management Journal, 23*, 451–465.

Nunnally, J. C. (1978). *Psychometric theory.* New York: McGraw-Hill.

Podsakoff, P. M., & Organ, D. W. (1986). Self-reports in organizational research: Problems and prospects. *Journal of Management, 12*, 531–544.

Scandura, T. A., & Graen, G. B. (1984). Moderating effects of initial leader-member exchange status on the effects of a leadership intervention. *Journal of Applied Psychology, 69,* 428–436.

Scandura, T. A., Graen, G. B., & Novak, M. (1986). When managers decide not to decide autocratically: An investigation of leader-member exchange and decision influence. *Journal of Applied Psychology, 71,* 579–584.

Seltzer, J., & Bass, B. M. (1990). Transformational leadership: Beyond initiation and consideration. *Journal of Management, 16,* 693–703.

Yammarino, F. J., & Bass, B. M. (1990a). Transformational leadership and multiple levels of analysis. *Human Relations, 43,* 975–995.

Yammarino, F. J., & Bass, B. M. (1990b). Long-term forecasting of transformational leadership and its effects among naval officers: Some preliminary findings. In K. E. Clark & M. B. Clark (Eds.), *Measures of leadership* (pp. 151–169). West Orange, NJ: Leadership Library of America.

Yukl, G. (1989). *Leadership in organizations* (2nd ed.). Englewood Cliffs, NJ: Prentice-Hall.

Zaleznik, A. (1983). The leadership gap. *Washington Quarterly, 6*(1), 32–39.

Ronald J. Deluga is an Associate Professor of Psychology at Bryant College. The Coordinator of the Learning for Leadership Program, his research interests include leader-follower influencing activity and impression management.

Direct inquiries about this article to Ronald J. Deluga, Associate Professor of Psychology, Bryant College, 1150 Douglas Pike, Smithfield, RI 02917–1284, 401/232–6279.

CHAPTER 20

The Impact of Who Leaders Are and What They Do

Ian Cunningham

This paper focuses on strategic leadership. It summarizes research on chief executives and others over a 5-year period, research which has aimed to use the analysis of language patterns as one way of understanding leaders. It also raises issues around abstract concepts such as "centering" and "grounding" as they apply to leaders. Some final points are made about learning to lead.

This paper is dedicated to Gregory Bateson, another Brit who enjoyed so much being in the USA that he was prepared to offer perspectives from another culture (sometimes critical perspectives, but always from a basis of caring and support). The paper is unashamedly personally and culturally biased—but then, like Hofstede (1980), I am not sure if those who claim objectivist universalism and culture-free truths are not deluding themselves and, worse, others. Leadership par excellence is a classic concept subject to postmodern relativism. I am not, though, as extreme a deconstructionist as my Derridaean colleagues across the English Channel. Leadership is a concept worthy of global concern, in part because of the internationalizing of business. We must therefore grapple with generalized statements, models, and hypotheses. However, not only is the "doing" of leadership culturally bound, but the thinking and researching about it as well. Hence we ought to be humble about our invented theories. I hope this paper will be read in this vein, despite my apparent dogmatism in places.

The focus of this paper is on strategic leadership. In this respect, I have been interested mainly in researching CEOs and others at the top of organizations. I can accept Hambrick's (1989) characterization of strategic leaders as those who are: (a) concerning themselves with external and internal spheres; (b) dealing with ambiguity, complexity, and information over-load; (c) addressing multifunctional tasks; and (d) covering the whole of an organization and essentially managing through others.

The research upon which this paper is based has been conducted since 1985 and has included studies in the UK and USA. Early research based around interviews and company case studies has been published elsewhere (Cunningham, 1988), and a specific study on chief executives' learning has also been published (Cunningham, 1986, 1991). This paper builds on these earlier works and refers to them, although not in great detail.

This paper begins with comments about my approach to research before an examination of some implications of studying the language of leaders. I will then look at concrete examples of language patterns prior to discussion of more abstract concepts about leadership.

Approach to Research

Elsewhere I have elaborated a stance on research methods (Cunningham, 1984, 1989). I have worked with the supporters of New Paradigm Research (Reason, 1989; Reason & Rowan, 1981) while not always agreeing with the specifics of this position. This has led me away from questionnaires and "content-based interviews," as exemplified by Bennis (1989). As one of Bennis's interviewees states, "The things people always talk about in any interview about leadership aren't the things that are the most difficult or the most interesting about leadership" (Bennis, 1989, p. 145). Bateson (1973) suggests that as someone becomes more able at what they do (for example, a great artist), they become less able to describe what makes them successful. The great artist becomes increasingly unconscious of the fundamentals and may only be able to articulate surface issues or idiosyncratic features of performance of little use to others.

In my own studies, I have not discarded the content of what leaders say, but I have focused mainly on process and pattern dimensions. By "patterns" I mean, among other things, regularities in the behavior of leaders—aspects that recur or repeat.

As leadership in organizations cannot be conducted without language, studying the language patterns of leaders provides a unique insight into their thoughts and actions. An analysis of language might bring one closer to unconscious patterns in leaders which may provide new clues to their impact on organizations. Bateson (1973) and those he has influenced (especially the Neuro-Linguistic Programming proponents) argue that what we raise into consciousness at any one time is a tiny outcropping of who we are. Even under intensive interviewing, probably most of the facets of ourselves that are contributory to our work and our lives remain unconscious and therefore hidden, both to others and to ourselves. My interest has been to tap into unconscious processes on the basis that even if such analysis is flawed, it may be infinitely more useful to access such factors than to focus on conscious surface issues.

Linguistic Analysis

While the socio-linguists and discourse analysts have taken their analyses into the "real world" (rather than working on the idealized language of mainstream linguistics), they still seem to address issues of little direct use. My interest is in helping leaders, or those desiring to be leaders, through tentative, prescriptive offerings. By "tentative prescriptive" I mean such statements as "If you want to get that result, try this." "Try this" means "I do not have a truth to offer," and the prescriptive/injunctive language gives a basis for scientific experiment. The comparator is with, say, the biologist who says "If you want to see X, look down this microscope at this slide"; or the chemist who says, "If you want to make that compound, do this" (Spencer-Brown, 1969). Science is dependent upon injunctive language and progresses often when injunctions do not work. The so-called social sciences are often impoverished by their refusal to move beyond description and analysis.

Hence, in leadership research, I am most interested in theoretical generalizations which are formulated so that they can be used, tried out and, if found wanting, modified or rejected. I am not a full-blown Popperian in demanding falsifiability, but testability in action is important to me. The "me" I am referring to is a researcher, a consultant, a trainer, and a leader. In all these roles I have found limited value (in terms of usability) in what I term "middle ground theories." Such theories are middle ground on a continuum from abstract to concrete: They are neither highly abstract generalizations nor specifically and concretely linked to observable action. Examples of middle ground theoretical notions include: transformational versus transactional, task versus relationships, lists of qualities of leaders (such as "trust," "integrity," "curiosity").

These latter concepts are, to me, unclearly unclear. That is, when leaders or aspiring leaders read these kinds of words in order to learn, the lack of clarity of the words is not necessarily apparent, except in their failures to improve from trying to follow these dictums. A word like "curiosity" or "integrity" is a description of something and is itself an outcropping of something. For example, X —— [curiosity] —— Y; X is the basis of curiosity — the reason why a person might be curious — and Y is the observable activity. But if we think that labels such as curiosity actually refer to real things, we are in danger, as Bateson (1973) warns, of eating the menu card instead of the meal.

In Figure 1, I have outlined "The U Procedure" for removing ourselves from middle ground, unclearly unclear concepts into the abstract, clearly unclear, being-

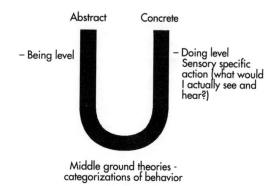

Figure 1   The U procedure.

level on the one side, and the concrete, clearly clear, doing-level on the other. Integration across the top of the "U" can be accomplished through invoking the concept of "patterns." We can postulate that there are patterns of being and of doing which are linked.

One route into patterns is through language patterns. Leaders have patterns of language use; these could be seen as verbalizations (doing) which emanate from deeper underlying patterns (being). Figure 2 suggests a model for this process. In this model, the influence of Bateson (1973) and Whorf (1956) is on the link of thought and language (without implying a narrowly deterministic cause-effect relationship).

In the following section, I shall move into the concrete linguistic arena, before later returning to the abstract (being) domain.

Language Patterns Analysis (LPA)

In this section, I will indicate the use of what I term *language pattern analysis* (LPA). I have used the LPA method on interview data, on letters and memos, on speeches made by leaders, on informal conversations, and on formal board meetings. The source matters little if the analysis has actual language as produced by the person. The objective is to identify pat-

Figure 2   Language patterns.

terns: that is, the language modes must repeat and must be a regular feature of the leader's language use. "One off" statements are not sufficient.

A typical repeating pattern identified, through LPA, in successful leaders is the "I. . . we. . ." or "I. . . us. . ." pattern. This is used typically in the same sentence or in succeeding sentences. Four examples follow:

1. *I* was very puzzled about what to do, but *we* did change (from a speech by David Johnson, General Manager, UK Health Authority).

2. *I* learned two lessons. One was that *we* were too small in financial terms to withstand the long haul required in the Soviet Union. The second was that *our* expertise in Europe offered the most profitable way forward (Creenagh Lodge, Chairman of Craton Lodge and Knight).

3. *I* hate to get into litigation. It put *us* off contested takeovers for years (Swraj Paul, Chairman, Caparo Group).

4. *I* believe *we*'re responsible to them (from an interview with Robert Dockson, Bennis, 1989, p.140).

The interesting aspect of examples 2 and 3 is that they come from a British newspaper (*The Independent on Sunday*) in a weekly series called "My Biggest Mistake," in which business leaders own up to their biggest mistake. At one level, it confirms a standard view that good leaders (a) do make mistakes, and (b) own up to them and learn from them. Interest-

ingly, Sophie Mirman, the founder of the failed Sock Shop chain, used a language pattern common with unsuccessful leaders. She typically used a "they" pattern. The reasons for her failure were ascribed to "them"—the bankers and the drug pushers in railroad stations. Similarly, Asil Nadir, Chairman of the bankrupt Polly Peck empire, when interviewed about the group's disaster blamed financiers and others. His language again was a "they" language.

One hypothesis about the "I. . . we. . ." pattern is that it is a connective one. It connects the person (I) to the collective (we, us). Often the "I" is followed by a verb defining a state, "I feel. . .," or "I believe. . .," whereas the "we/us" is followed by an active verb, "I. . . we do. . .," or "I. . . we make. . ." This often links a being level (I am) to the doing level (we do).

This is the opposite of a language pattern common amongst the British upper class who use "one" instead of "I" or "we," as in "one does" instead of "I do" or "we do." A more general pattern is the use of "you" instead of "I." This move from the first person (singular or plural) to the second or third person seems highly significant.

Linking back to the issue of ownership of failure or problems, I found in my evaluation of a successful development program for chief executives that they said repeatedly that a key to learning was personal ownership of problems. A typical comment was "When I started the program I thought the problems were out there. They were with other people or with my need to learn about, say, marketing. Gradually I came to realize that the problem was me. I had to change if we were to become more successful." The language pattern here is congruent with the content. There is heavy use of "I" in the language process; in the content, the CEO is referring to ownership of problems. The sequence ends with an "I. . . we. . ." connection which links the CEO to the organization.

There are other patterns which are associated with successful leaders, but some CEOs, while overall seeming to perform well, have weak spots which create problems for others. An example was a president of a company in which I conducted an intensive study over a period of 5 years. The president used a lot of "I. . . we. . ." patterning as well as other patterns I had observed in other CEOs. These included the use of: (a) rich metaphors that created new meanings for people; (b) time patterns specifically linking present issues to future needs (with appropriately sequenced tense changes in verbs); (c) noun to verb switches (technically denominalizing) including, for example, a memo in which the president said, "I want sales to sell, marketing to market, engineering to engineer"; (d) linking "is" to "should" (switching verb modality) in order to move from data to action; and (e) using mainly visual predicates with appropriate links to kinaesthetic predicates such as, for example, where he explored how he felt (kinaesthetic) about what he saw (visual) for the future. This area of analysis was stimulated by Bandler and Grinder's (1976) work in developing Neuro-Linguistic Programming.

Despite these strengths, the president had also developed a strong pattern over time of hiding and disowning his personal authority in certain situations. He used patterns such as "X is expected to. . ." rather than "I expect X to. . .," a passivising pattern in which he deletes reference to his role as the authority figure. He also used, in memos, "The president. . ." instead of "I. . ."

Parallel research undertaken with my colleagues at Roffey Park on organization culture in the same company made it clear that the CEO's congruent connective style was deemed successful and valuable by his "followers." The company, set up by the CEO over 30 years ago, also had a long history of financial success and growth and was regarded as an industry leader. However, while we found a strong Achievement element in the culture (using Harrison's, 1987, typology), we found that the Power dimension which was also strong was a source of confusion and difficulty and directly linked to the way the CEO used authority, as demonstrated by his language pattern.

Centering and Grounding

I have made reference to the link between language and congruence and connectedness. Earlier, I indicated the value in going to both the concrete and the abstract from middle ground theory. Language provides a concrete arena of analysis, and it needs linking to the abstract domains at the top of the U (see Figure 1).

The concepts of "centering" and "grounding" provide one such link. Centeredness is a concept originally derived from Eastern thought. My own influences have been Ki Aikido and Taoism (and its links to Tai Ji). These approaches have a quality of integrating physical, emotional, spiritual, and cognitive domains. Centeredness can be thought of as harmonizing and focusing energy, as bringing together and balancing polar opposites such as yin and yang (in Chinese philosophy), hard and soft, inner and outer, reactive and proactive, control and freedom, rigidity and flexibility, and so on.

Much of the leadership literature has recognized the apparent paradox of leaders displaying opposite traits (e.g., Cunningham, 1988). Such paradoxes are only so because of the trap of Aristotelian logic. The concept of centeredness can be used to explain the balance of opposites. Centered leaders show a congruent integration of theory and practice. They meet the challenge of Argyris and Schon (1974) to bring together espoused theory and theory-in-use.

However, centeredness is not sufficient. Groundedness is about rooting ourselves in something. The CEO of the company previously discussed was grounded in a number of ways:

1. Physical. He is not a pushover. He looks solid and impressive as he walks around the organization.

2. Spiritual. He is a devout Christian who lives his Christian values at work.

3. Profession. He is rooted in his engineering background, and refers to it in his work. He still thinks of himself as an engineer.

4. Location. He has lived in the same house for 30 years (and remained married to the same wife).

Centeredness can be a showy, fizzy energy if it is not grounded in something—values, ideals, a vision. But grounding on its own can be inertial. A speculative observation is that European leaders are often more grounded than centered; they have a sense of history, of place, of permanence. But they may operate in disconnected ways and not "walk the talk." The USA may often have the opposite situation—centered leaders who are able to operate effectively but who become trapped in short-termism and quick fixes.

My use of groundedness and centeredness is in part linked to linguistic analysis, but only in part. The physical domain plays an important part. Through observation of physical characteristics, I have been able to predict aspects of the impact of a leader. Simple acts like standing, sitting, and walking reveal a great deal about a person and can be used for analysis.

Further discussion of this dimension is outside the scope of this paper. In some respects it is outside the scope of any paper: the language on a page can only describe. The physical dimension is experienced physically.

Conclusion—Learning

Evidence of leadership development (Cunningham, 1991) is that leaders can develop their impact on their organizations. The evidence suggests that middle ground theory learning is of limited value, for it may merely accentuate the gap between espoused theory and theory-in-use, as demonstrated by Argyris and Schon (1974). Approaches which challenge leaders to look at themselves and to analyze, amongst other things, their language use, seem to work. This concrete, microlevel activity appears to have the most payoff when explicitly linked to assisting leaders to address underlying factors (such as centering and grounding). For instance, when leaders raise the issue of the qualities needed to be effective, it is possible to assist them by pushing them in both directions (concrete and abstract). So where a quality such as "charisma" is invoked, one can (a) challenge the leader about specific charismatic behaviors they have observed and use the language generated as a further basis for challenge, and (b) ask what lies behind charisma—what would enable a leader to be charismatic? Such questioning can lead to an examination of concepts such as centering and grounding as explanatory factors.

My conclusion, then, is that leaders can learn to increase their positive impact on organizations. However, such changes occur not through taught courses and didactic pedagogy, but through open exploration and challenge.

References

Argyris, C., & Schon, D. (1974). *Theory in practice.* San Francisco: Jossey-Bass.

Bandler, R., & Grinder, J. (1976). *The structure of magic* (Vols. I–II). Palo Alto, CA: Science & Behavior Books.

Bateson, G. (1973). *Steps to an ecology of mind.* London: Paladin.

Bennis, W. G. (1989). *On becoming a leader.* Reading, MA: Addison-Wesley.

Cunningham, I. (1984). *Teaching styles in learner centred management development programmes.* Unpublished doctoral dissertation, Lancaster University, England.

Cunningham, I. (1986). *Action learning for chief executives.* Berkhamsted, England: Ashridge Management College.

Cunningham, I. (1988). The leading question—leadership development re-visited. *International Management Development, 2,* 13–16.

Cunningham, I. (1989). Interactive holistic research. In P. Reason (Ed.), *Human inquiry in practice* (pp. 163–181). London: Sage.

Cunningham, I. (1991). Evaluation of action learning. In M. Pedler (Ed.), *Action learning in practice* (2nd ed., pp. 319–340). Farnborough, Hants: Gower Press.

Hambrick, C. D. (1989). Putting top managers back in the strategy picture. *Strategic Management Journal, 10,* 5–15.

Harrison, R. (1987). *Organization culture and quality of service.* London: Association for Management Education and Development.

Hofstede, G. (1980). *Culture's consequences.* London: Sage.

Reason, P. (Ed.). (1989). *Human inquiry in practice.* London: Sage.

Reason, P., & Rowan, J. (1981). *Human inquiry.* New York: Wiley.

Spencer-Brown, G. (1969). *Laws of form.* New York: Dutton.

Whorf, B. L. (1956). In J. B. Carroll (Ed.), *Language thought and reality.* Cambridge, MA: MIT Press.

Ian Cunningham, PhD, is the Chief Executive of the Roffey Park Management College, England. He has been Chairman and Managing Director of the management consultancy Meta-communications Ltd., a Senior Research Fellow at Ashridge Management College, Head of the Personal Development Division at the Anglian Regional Management Centre, a management trainer, a chemistry lecturer and researcher, and a visiting professor in the U.S. and India. He has published 90 works on leadership, management, learning, and development.

Direct inquiries about this article to Ian Cunningham, Chief Executive, Roffey Park Management College, Forest Road, Horsham, West Sussex RH12 4TD, U.K., 44 293 851644.

CHAPTER 21

High-Involvement, High-Performance Teams in Higher Education
The Impact of Leadership

Donna Riechmann

This paper reports findings of an ongoing study of high-involvement, high-performance teams in higher education. It focuses on five administrative teams in academia, representing a range of purpose and task. Seven characteristics of effectiveness are reported for teams, highlighting the impact of the team leader on team effectiveness.

Organizational innovation and change, coupled with the increased emphasis on productivity and quality of work life, have produced a number of new approaches to the design and implementation of work in the United States. Current initiatives signal a change from the control model of management, typified by the Taylor and Fayol models of the early 1990s, to a commitment organizational model (Walton, 1980).

Underlying these initiatives is a growing realization of the requirement for new models of management that emphasize participation and collaboration. The trend toward participation produces fundamental changes in the ways organizations are designed and managed. Leaders are more often developing participative environments that emphasize high involvement of individuals and teams in work processes (Bennis & Nanus, 1985; Burns, 1978; Peters & Waterman, 1982). As Lawler (1986) said, "Participative management is an idea whose time has come" (p.1).

Some groups in higher education settings are adopting team structures to respond more effectively to an increasingly difficult environment. Every team in this study is experiencing fiscal constraints, if not fiscal crisis. The need exists to improve productivity and/or quality with the same or decreased level of funding. Like most institutions of higher education, the teams in this study are grappling with fundamental questions about strategic direction, governance, resource allocation, and recruiting and staffing.

The purpose of this research was to examine high-involvement, high-performance teams in higher education settings. Specifically, the study examined the characteristics of high-involvement, high-performance teams, characteristics of team leaders, and team leader behaviors that contribute to the development and maintenance of high-performing teams.

A "high-involvement team" was defined as a unit with authority to modify the design of the unit itself which manages members' and the unit's performance and carries out the unit's work (Hackman, 1987). A "high-performance team" was defined initially as one which has a clear, elevating goal, a results-driven structure, competent members, unified commitment, a collaborative climate, standards of excellence, and principled leadership (Larson & LaFasto, 1989). "Team leader" was the formally designated manager or administrator of the unit.

Most studies on participation and individual or team self-management have focused on production environments (Goodman, Devadas, & Hughson, 1988; Manz & Sims, 1984; McMahon, 1976). Little research exists about autonomous work teams in other settings (Hackman, 1987). Nonmanufacturing organizations are increasingly adopting self-managed teams, but few studies are complete at this point (Cohen & Ledford, 1990; Hackman, 1990).

High-involvement, high-performance (HIHP) teams are rare in academia, and an extensive literature review revealed no research on teams in that setting. Most of the literature on leadership and participation in higher education addressed either the role of leaders or the need for assuming more participative practices, none of which are directly team based (Alfred, 1985; Powers & Powers, 1983; Walker, 1979). Thus, this study charts new ground in the arena of academia.

Method

Using the recommendations of 22 experts, 18 potential HIHP teams were identified. Of these, 11 teams participated in the selection process. Selection of the sample was criterion based. A minimum of four external evaluators familiar with each team's performance completed an 18-item Team Performance (TP) checklist which asked them to rate the current performance of the team. The six teams which rated highest on the TP checklist were asked to participate in the qualitative portion of the research.

The sample for this study consisted of five teams, including team leaders and all team members. Team size ranged from a minimum of 3 to a maximum of 10 people. Teams were from throughout the United States and included four universities and one community college. All five teams were administrative in nature, although most team leaders and team members had teaching responsibilities. Three of the leaders were female and two were male. Team leader titles were Provost, Vice President and Academic Dean, Dean, Associate Dean, and Department Head.

The researcher reviewed written documents for each team and then conducted in-depth 1- to 2-hour individual interviews at the organization's site. Five team leaders and 33 team members participated in the audiotaped interviews. Questions for the semi-structured interviews appear in Appendix A.

Data Analysis

The taped interviews were transcribed and then coded for preliminary categories and themes. Subsequently, manual and computer coding schemes were used to conduct content analysis of the data to define themes and patterns. (See Appendix B for coding examples.) Differences between teams, discrepancies, and alternative interpretations were noted. Three of the study's team leaders and four academic researchers reviewed preliminary results of the analysis.

The focus for the analysis centered on characteristics and behaviors of team members and team leaders. To confirm or contradict the findings on nonacademic team leadership (see Appendix C), emergent patterns were compared to team and leadership dimensions found in the literature. Additional dimensions that emerged in the interview process were also noted.

Results and Discussion

A description follows of the characteristics that emerged as evidence of superior, sustained performance in teams.

Structure and Results Orientation

All teams made a *conscious* decision to become a team and worked hard at achieving "teamness," enabling them to use the structure to work together to achieve common ends. Structures varied from matrix to hierarchical, but effective teams were structured in ways that team members perceived as conducive to achieving results. Structure was seen as cohesive, not divisive.

One team reorganized and established a matrix that combined academic and administrative decision-making authority in the team. Other teams were traditional hierarchies but felt free to circumvent re-porting relationships and policies to be more effective. The more rigid the structure, the more team members complained about bureaucracy and barriers to performance. For example, one team had organizational subunits within the team, and several members complained about "fiefdoms" that interfered with getting the job done.

Teams were results oriented and evidenced clarity about goals, programs, and standards for achievement. People often intermingled descriptions of mission, purpose, values, and vision, but they always described those elements as components of a results orientation with an *institutional* focus. Often there was an "overarching goal" for the team that provided focus and generated excitement.

A strong sense of commitment to the team and the team's goals existed. For example, one leader said, "Whatever the mission statement is, we intend to be a first-rate learning institution that has an environment not only well-designed in terms of the educational and instructional components, but also an environment where the student is respected and loved." Every person on that team repeated that theme.

Participation and Collaboration

Participation and involvement were evident in the teams and in their subunits. Members felt a sense of belonging to the team and easily were able to cooperate and share expertise. Each person's opinion was valued and sought. Spontaneous discussions occurred in offices, reception areas, hallways, and bathrooms.

Decision making was described as consensual, democratic, or participative. Common phrases were: "We discuss and thrash it out," "We argue wonderfully well," and "The majority must agree and the minority has to accept, or we keep on talking." Any issue could be raised and debated, with input accepted from all interested parties. Members felt equal responsibility for resolving problems and implementing decisions. Once consensus was reached, team members backed decisions almost without exception because it was for the well-being of the institution to do so.

Faculty and staff were routinely and frequently involved in decisions, and iterative loops existed to resolve issues. One team member said, "The power is in the group, and the power from the group is in the faculty and staff." People sometimes groused about the time it took to reach the best decision and the "messiness" of the process, but most indicated a willingness to involve as many people as often as possible.

Authority was rather well-defined. Each person was expected to manage his or her own area of responsibility for the good of the institution. Many members talked about an absence of power struggles and a lack of ego in their colleagues. They reported willingness to work cooperatively and trusted other team members not to further their unit at the expense of another.

Individuation and Synthesis

There were two components to this dimension. One was integration of diversity within the team. Without exception, the teams considered diversity a special attribute. For some, this meant integration in terms of race, religion, gender, and age. For others, it meant strength of diversity in experience, background, education, and personal attributes. Whatever the definition of diversity, members perceived the differences as a contribution to team synthesis.

A second component was the concept of uniqueness and union, or differentiation of self versus integration of self with others' goals and ideas (Csikszentmihalyi, 1990). A key to successful teams was accommodating the needs of both the individual and the team. In superior teams, individuals contributed their unique abilities and special talents: "They're all so lovable in their eccentricities."

At the same time, a synthesis of group goals, decisions, and actions transcended the individual agenda. Many team members described satisfaction in belonging to a team that joined them in a common quest. They were motivated to achieve results in a collective fashion: "We used to be competitive, but now we're a part of something bigger. We're one hell of a team!"

Competence and Performance

Members were able to use and develop their skills and abilities to the fullest extent. Leader and team members drew on each others' strengths and made full use of each person's competencies. Many comments referred to members' experience, knowledge, successes, and the power of mobilizing the collective ability. People held each other in high regard, to the point of using a reverential tone when talking about the strengths of fellow team members.

People worked well together, not only because of individual competencies but also because they knew each other. To illustrate: "We almost know what the other person is going to say before he says it. We understand each person and his role and responsibility." This did not occur through happenstance. There seemed to be a connection between time spent together and team effectiveness, between efforts at team development and team effectiveness.

Teams were asked about formal and informal evaluation processes. Teams rarely set aside time to evaluate themselves formally. Most often, this happened once a year in a retreat. However, there was a great deal of routine, informal, spontaneous discussion about goals and progress. The group frequently fine-tuned team decisions.

In the best teams, there was an emphasis on positive evaluation of performance.

Shortfalls were seen as a team issue regardless of the source, and members tended to "self-correct" based on colleagues' comments. Performance appraisal systems were designed to be developmental, not punitive.

Communication Processes

Interpersonal and team interactions were open and effective. Typically, there was a lot of communication between team members and between team members and their work units—what one person called "ad hocing." Teams met frequently, and debate and conflict were valued and resolved. Members demonstrated excellent skills in interpersonal and group processes.

Considerable effort was expended to disseminate information in an open and honest fashion. The result was to make decisions and "move the institution" quickly with a lot of "buy in" from faculty and staff. The emphasis on open communication ensured the greatest amount of involvement and commitment of team and faculty. Communication was characterized by quality and frequency.

Emotional Climate

Teams had a certain emotional tone. People frequently described their feelings about the team and its purpose. Common words were trust, chemistry, pride, and enthusiasm. Good teams had high morale, energy, and camaraderie, and they valued honesty, sincerity, and integrity. Members talked at length about respecting each other as persons and as professionals. People *liked* each other, and they had fun. ("We take work seriously, but not much else.") In the best teams, there was a strong sense of equality: "I can't say any one person has any position of preeminence."

These were optimistic groups. People tended to emphasize the good rather than the bad, and the successes helped them persevere through the crises and difficulties. Members recognized adversity as ever present, but they actively demonstrated a positive viewpoint. They bolstered staff spirits through modeling optimism, celebrating successes, and creating symbols of achievement. For example, one team held a July 1st "New Year's Party" to celebrate the beginning of their fiscal year.

Leadership

A major purpose of this study was to examine team leadership. Leadership was demonstrated in many ways by individual members, teams, and designated leaders. Considerable evidence exists that each person fully exercised leadership over his or her unit and was viewed by peers as a leader both personally and professionally.

Additionally, many examples suggested that the team exhibited leadership as a group. Leadership was fluid, dynamic, and freely shared. Everyone, including the team leader, deferred to the individual who had expertise or represented a particular programmatic area and allowed that person to assume leadership within the team at that point in time. Yet the expectation was that the *team* would make decisions, take actions, and support its individual leaders.

An important aspect of this study was the designated team leader and his or her leadership ability. The initial assumptions and avenues of inquiry were based on the literature on leadership in nonacademic teams (Harris, 1989; Larson & LaFasto, 1989; Lawler, 1986; Manz & Sims, 1989; McCann & Margerison, 1989). A summary appears in Appendix C.

Initial results of this study suggest that the attributes each leader brought to the team have a significant impact on team and organizational performance. Every theme described in the section on team characteristics can be applied to superior team leaders, although special characteristics and behaviors also existed. Again, not every leader demonstrated every characteristic and behavior to the same degree. Each characteristic and behavior can be viewed as a continuum, with each leader at a different point on the continuum.

HIHP team members described their leaders as people who demonstrated intellectual and conceptual leadership. Phrases included "a conceptual thinker," "an idea person," and "someone who can see the big picture." Leaders brought education and experience to their positions and were seen as having considerable knowledge of academia, administration, and their institution. They were variously portrayed as intelligent, honest, fair, optimistic, and caring. They seemed to have a strong sense of self and of personal values.

As with characteristics, leaders of HIHP teams demonstrated behaviors in varying degrees. However, all team leaders demonstrated all of the following behaviors to some degree. All leaders of HIHP teams were able to:

1. *Provide a vision and communicate it.* This concept appears frequently in the literature on leaders in every type of setting, including academia (Boyer, 1988; Dempsey, 1988–89). The outstanding leader in the present study developed the vision, sometimes collaboratively, and was primarily responsible for disseminating the vision to the organization. The leader set challenging goals for the organization, created a commonality of purpose and effort, and developed the group as a team. There was a clarity of purpose that engaged members in the overarching goal of their team.

Illustrative behaviors of this concept include: using a 1-day team retreat to forge a vision statement, starting every faculty meeting with a statement of mission and purpose, and questioning what is best for the institution every time a decision needs to be made.

2. *Create a favorable climate.* Leaders played a strong role in creating a favorable environment. Members described the climate as one characterized by openness, equality, sharing, fairness, trust, and mutual respect. They "did not pull any punches" because people were not constrained by hierarchy. They had access to the leader, and they spent a great deal of time with the leader and other unit members.

Leaders trusted their people's work and their opinions. By supporting others and soliciting their input, a sense of trust was created. Leaders operationalized respect by recognizing work quality, skills and talents, and expertise. Generally, the atmosphere was positive, marked by humor and fun. The leader set a norm for celebrating successes and creating symbols of achievement.

Illustrative behaviors included: acknowledging, in faculty meetings, the achievements of team members; giving each team member complete responsibility for their unit; ensuring that every opinion was expressed and discussed, even when the team leader disagreed; and handing out balloons and buttons to students and alumni.

3. *Foster collaborative practices.* The best leaders believed in participatory management, disseminated information freely and openly, involved others in decision making, and treated problems as common issues to be resolved. Extraordinary amounts of time were devoted to these activities. Expertise was the benchmark for authority, and deference to position was discouraged. Even though the approach was collaborative in terms of authority and decision making, the leader clearly accepted final responsibility for the result.

Illustrative behaviors included: use of formal questionnaires to obtain feedback from faculty, periodic retreats for team development, spontaneous agenda-setting in team meetings with input from all, and knowing everyone on the faculty by name.

4. *Enable others.* The superior leader enabled members by requiring and facilitating team decision making and ensuring that members had authority to implement actions. The team leader empowered each member by supporting members' decisions and actions in their arena of authority. Despite the difficulty, the leader developed reward systems that recognized individual *and* team contributions. He or she encouraged each person to develop personally and professionally.

Illustrative behaviors included: accepting team decisions with which the leader did not agree, delegating complete responsibility for a program area, supporting members' disparate management styles, and assigning developmental activities such as committee chairmanships.

5. *Model excellence.* The excellent leader was described as someone who set high standards, met those standards, and expected others to do the same. Yet the leader treated people fairly and compassionately, with an expressed concern for the individual good. At the same time, he or she championed the organization and expended considerable energy to meet its goals. "Hard worker" was a phrase frequently heard.

These were people of experience, talent, integrity, honesty, and humor. They were aware that their actions set the leadership tone and they were determined to "practice what they preach." For example, four of the five leaders taught classes in order to model their commitment to education and to students.

Illustrative behaviors included: disseminating countless articles to staff on leadership and related topics, spending four days and three nights with little sleep to avert a budget crisis, meeting three times with the parents of a student on pro-

bation, and mediating a conflict between two staff members.

For these teams and team leaders, no "one best way" emerged as the means to excellent team performance. The teams appeared to be in varying stages of development, with some at higher levels of involvement and performance. Each team and each leader had their own strengths and weaknesses, their own "personality." Yet commonalities did emerge.

In summary, these findings suggest that HIHP teams and team leaders share certain identifiable characteristics and behaviors. These findings suggest implications for leadership development in academic settings. The characteristics and behaviors of the teams in this study provide a framework for discussions about teamwork, developing teams, and improving team involvement and performance. For the increasing numbers of academic leaders who urge the use of teams and teamwork in higher education, these findings suggest possibilities for informed action for academic groups.

Implications exist for further research. More studies of academic teams are needed. We need to know when teams are appropriate in academia and how they compare to teams in other settings. Also, some HIHP teams are more effective than others. Although this study offers tentative explanations for the variation in teams, the question needs further exploration. Future research would add to the body of knowledge on team leadership and HIHP teams.

References

Alfred, R. (1985). Organizing for renewal through participative governance. *New Directions for Higher Education, 13*(1), 57–63.

Bennis, W., & Nanus, B. (1985). *Leaders: Strategies for taking charge.* New York: Harper & Row.

Boyer, E. L. (1988). Leadership: A clear and vital mission. *The College Board Review, 150,* 6–9.

Burns, J. M. (1978). *Leadership*. New York: Harper & Row.

Cohen, S. G., & Ledford, G. E. (1990, August). The effectiveness of self-managing teams in service and support functions: A field experiment. Paper presented in the symposium "*Creating Conditions for Team Effectiveness in White Collar Settings*" at the annual meeting of the Academy of Management, San Francisco.

Csikszentmihalyi, M. (1990). *Flow: The psychology of optimal experience*. New York: Harper Perennial.

Dempsey, J. R. (1988–89, Winter). A president's perspective on leadership. *The College Board Review, 150*, 16–19, 34.

Goodman, P. S., Devadas, R., & Hughson, T. L. (1988). Groups and productivity: Analyzing the effectiveness of self-managing teams. In J.P. Campbell, R.J. Campbell, & Associates (Eds.), *Productivity in organizations* (pp. 295–325). San Francisco: Jossey-Bass.

Hackman, J. R. (1987). The design of work teams. In J. W. Lorsch (Ed.), *Handbook of organizational behavior* (pp. 315–342). Englewood Cliffs, NJ: Prentice-Hall.

Hackman, J. R. (Ed.). (1990). *Groups that work (and those that don't)*. San Francisco: Jossey-Bass.

Harris, P. R. (1989). *High performance leadership: Strategies for maximum career productivity*. Glenview, IL: Scott Foresman.

Larson, C. E., & LaFasto, F. M. (1989). *Teamwork: What must go right/what can go wrong*. Newbury Park, CA: Sage Publications.

Lawler, E. E. (1986). *High-involvement management*. San Francisco: Jossey-Bass.

Manz, C. C., & Sims, H. P. (1984). Searching for the "unleader": Organizational member views on leading self-managed groups. *Human Relations, 37*(5), 409–423.

Manz, C. C., & Sims, H. P. (1989). *Super-Leadership: Leading others to lead themselves*. New York: Prentice-Hall.

McCann, D. J., & Margerison, C. (1989). Managing high performance teams. *Training and Development Journal, 43*(11), 53–60.

McMahon, T. (1976). Participative and power-equalized organizational systems. *Human Relations, 29*, 203–214.

Peters, T. J., & Waterman, R. H. (1982). *In search of excellence*. New York: Warner.

Powers, D. R., & Powers, M. F. (1983). *Making participatory management work*. San Francisco: Jossey-Bass.

Walker, D. E. (1979). *The effective administrator*. San Francisco: Jossey-Bass.

Walton, R. E. (1980). Establishing and maintaining high commitment work systems. In J. R. Kimberly & R. H. Miles (Eds.), *The organizational life cycle*. San Francisco: Jossey-Bass.

Donna Riechmann is the owner of DRC Associates in Greensboro, NC, which specializes in building high-performance teams and implementing continuous improvement projects. She received her PhD from the University of North Carolina, Chapel Hill.

Direct inquiries about this article to Donna Riechmann, DRC Associates, P.O. Box 10061, Greensboro, NC 27404, 919/288-7187.

Interview Questions

1a. Define the structure of your team.

1b. What are the major tasks (or purposes) of the team?

1c. What is your position and what are your major job responsibilities?

2a. How would you define the value and/or vision of your team?

2b. What is the team's mission? How does the team determine its mission/goals?

3. Who decides what work the team is to do?

4a. Who manages the team's performance?

4b. Who manages the team members' performance?

4c. Is there a difference in the way that performance is managed when things go well and when things go badly?

5. What are the major strengths of your team?

6. How is leadership exercised in the team? (Is leadership shared or is leadership assumed by the team leader?)

7. Describe a recent incident in which your team leader helped the team to function more effectively. (Behavioral)

8. What could your team leader do to help your team function more effectively?

9a. What is special about your team?

9b. What is special about your team leader?

10. Anything else?

Appendix B

Examples of Coding

Manual Core Code	Manual Category	Computer Category	Transcription Data
Strategies	Mission	Mission/ Values/ Vision	"The College has a planning process where we talk about collegiate mission a lot but with our team that would . . . those sorts of over-arching value issues tend to emerge out of day-to-day decisions rather than precede them."
Consequences	Values		

Manual Core Code	Manual Category	Computer Category	
Interactions	Communication	Communication	"We talk about it. If the three of us think something's wrong, it's probably wrong. If the three of us think something went right, it probably went right. Whereas, if all thought exactly the same way, you're not as certain. It's, it's the difference between a tripod and a pole."
Diversity	Picture		

Manual Core Code	Manual Category	Computer Category	
Performance	Formal Evaluation	Performance	"We meet with them to discuss their distribution of effort and essentially write a contract. And we use that as the basis for reviewing their performance during the year."
Tactics/ Activities			

Summary of the Literature on Team Leadership

Lawler (1986)

(1) build trust and openness
(2) provide a vision and communicate it
(3) move decisions to the proper location
(4) empower others

Harris (1989)

(1) provide more communication and information
(2) create more autonomy and participation
(3) promote an entrepreneurial spirit
(4) enhance the quality of work life
(5) generate innovative high performance norms
(6) use informal synergistic relations (to create cooperation and trust)
(7) advance technology transfer and venturing and research and development

McCann & Margerison (1989)

(1) listen before deciding
(2) keep team members up-to-date on a regular basis
(3) be available and responsive to people's problems
(4) develop balanced teams
(5) allocate work to people based on their capabilities
(6) encourage respect and understanding among team members
(7) delegate work that is not essential for them to do
(8) set a high-quality example for the team
(9) coordinate and represent team members
(10) involve team members in solving key problems

Manz & Sims (1989)

(1) model—practice behavioral and cognitive self-leadership in a vivid and recognizable manner
(2) guide participation—question, suggest, reinforce others to encourage self-administered rewards
(3) gradually develop others—reinforce task behaviors first and later reinforce target behavior, independence, and self-goals

Larson & LaFasto (1989)

(1) establish a vision
(2) create change
(3) unleash talent
(4) establish expectations for the team leader and team members
(5) establish a supportive decision-making climate

CHAPTER 22

Reframing Leadership
The Effects of Leaders' Images of Leadership

**Lee G. Bolman and
Terrence E. Deal**

This paper explores the implications of four different images that managers often use as implicit theories of leadership: structural, human resource, political, and symbolic. The structural image is associated with effectiveness as a manager but not as a leader. The symbolic image is the best predictor of leadership effectiveness but is unrelated to effectiveness as a manager. Human resource and political images are moderately associated with effectiveness as both manager and leader. Men and women in comparable jobs are more alike than different in their images of leadership.

The concept of frames has many synonyms in the social science literature — maps, images, schemata, frames of reference, perspectives, orientations, lenses, and mindscapes (Boulding, 1956; Goffman, 1974; Markus & Zajonc, 1985). The different labels share an assumption that individuals see the world in different ways since they are embedded in different paradigms or world views. Because the world of human experience is ambiguous, frames of reference shape how situations are defined and determine what actions are taken.

Several years ago, we distilled theories of organizations into four traditions, which we labeled frames (Bolman & Deal, 1984, 1991). We believed that these four distinct images existed not only in textbooks but in the ways that leaders think and act in response to everyday issues and problems.

The first of those perspectives, the *structural* frame, derives its outlook particularly from the discipline of sociology. The frame emphasizes goals and efficiency. It posits that effective organizations define clear goals, differentiate people into specific roles, and coordinate diverse activities through policies, rules, and formal chain of command. Structural leaders value analysis and data, keep their eye on the bottom line, set clear directions, hold people accountable for results, and try to solve organizational problems with new policies and rules—or through restructuring.

The *human resource* frame borrows its assumptions from the fields of psychology and organizational behavior. It focuses attention on human needs and assumes that organizations that meet basic needs will work better than those that do not. Human resource leaders value relationships and feelings and seek to lead through facilitation and empowerment. They tend to define problems in individual or interpersonal terms and look for ways to adjust the organization to fit people—or to adjust the people to fit the organization through, for example, training and workshops.

The *political* frame emphasizes individual and group interests that often displace organizational goals. Borrowing ideas from political science, the frame assumes continuing competition among different interests for scarce resources. Conflict is seen as a normal byproduct of collective action. Political leaders are advocates and negotiators who value realism and pragmatism. They spend much of their time networking, creating coalitions, building a power base, and negotiating compromises.

The *symbolic* frame synthesizes concepts and imagery from a number of disciplines but most notably from anthropology. It sees a chaotic world in which meaning and predictability are social creations and facts are interpretative rather than objective. Organizations develop symbols and cultures that unobtrusively shape human behavior and provide a shared sense of mission and identity. Symbolic leaders instill a sense of enthusiasm and commitment through charisma and drama. They pay diligent attention to myth, ritual, ceremony, stories, and other symbolic forms. The origination of problems is seen to be in an organization's history, existing cultural patterns, or its visions of the future.

Our experience has convinced us that the frames are more than academic constructs. They are often visible in leaders' thoughts and actions. Leaders carry images that correspond to one or more of the four lenses; they use those images to interpret what is going on, to decide what to do, and to interpret the results of their action.

The Idea of Leadership

Leadership is offered as a solution for most of the problems of organizations everywhere. Schools will work, we are told, if principals provide strong instructional leadership. Around the world, middle managers say that their organizations would thrive if senior management provided strategy, vision, and "real leadership." Though the call for leadership is universal, the term is surrounded by misunderstanding and myth.

One myth views the leader as hero: the towering individual who can single-handedly clean up a whole town (Murphy, 1989). Such images of leadership, although vivid and comforting, are counterproductive when they induce leaders to believe they should do it all themselves because everyone around them has less of the right stuff. A second myth equates leadership with position, suggesting that leadership is whatever administrators do. Yet it is common knowledge that many managers could not "lead a squad of seven-year-olds to the ice cream counter" (Gardner, 1990, p. 2).

A third myth views leadership largely as a one-way process: leaders act, and followers react; leaders are powerful, and followers are dependent. Such a view blinds us to the reality that leadership fundamentally involves a relationship between leaders and their constituents (Bolman & Deal, 1991; Gardner, 1990). Leadership is better understood as a process of mutual influence that produces collective action in the service of shared or compatible purposes and values, usually in the context of uncertainty and conflict (Bolman & Deal, 1991). Such a view is emerging in recent contributions to leadership theory (Bennis

& Nanus, 1985; Burns, 1978; Gardner, 1990; Kotter, 1990; Kouzes & Posner, 1988). The new view clearly differentiates leadership from management while recognizing that modern organizations require both the manager's objectivity and the leader's flashes of vision (Bolman & Deal, 1991; Kotter, 1990).

Leadership is not a magic cure nor a solution to everything that ails organizations, but it does play a key role in efforts to effect significant organizational change and improvement in teaching, curriculum, and the relationship between schools and their communities. Leadership is critical for its central role in shaping missions, articulating values, setting directions, and building motivation. Leadership helps organizations move forward when faced with uncertainty about what to do, disagreements about how to do it, and doubts that it can be done.

We have undertaken a series of empirical investigations into how leaders use frames: how many they use, which ones, and with what results. Our methods include a combination of qualitative and quantitative methods, because each has different advantages in studying leaders' world views. Qualitative methods are particularly effective in getting at the subtleties of how leaders think and how they frame their experience. Quantitative methods are particularly useful in examining the relationship between the frames of leaders and their constituents in different settings and in examining the impact of different frames.

Qualitative Investigations

Our qualitative work focuses on the frames implicit in narratives provided by administrators about their experience. We used those narratives to answer two questions: (a) How many frames do leaders use? and (b) which frames do they use?

We developed a set of indicators to use in coding those narratives, summarized in Table 1. The coding system is not very fine-grained: We simply made a global judgment about the presence or absence of each frame, using the criteria previously listed.

Table 2 shows data from different samples of educational administrators in terms of the number of frames they use. The first population is a sample of 32 college presidents reported by Bensimon (1989, in press). Bensimon asked each president, "How would you describe yourself as a leader?" and coded the interview transcripts for use in each of the four frames. Bensimon also asked senior administrators on campus to describe the president as a leader. Colleagues typically saw less versatility than the presidents saw in themselves. The presidents' self-descriptions contained an average of 2.2 frames, while the average colleague reported only 1.7.

The second population is a sample of 75 senior administrators in higher education who participated in Harvard's Institute for Educational Management. Members of that group were highly diverse with respect to geography and institutional type. Most held positions at the level of Dean, Vice President, or President. The third population is a sample of 15 central-office administrators from school districts in a midwestern state. Each administrator in the second and third samples was asked to write a "case," an account of a challenging leadership incident in which he or she had been involved. The cases were typically one or two pages long (typed, double-spaced), though some were as short as a paragraph and others went on for several pages. Each case was scored for the presence or absence of each of the frames.

The results in all three samples show that leaders rarely use more than two frames, and almost no one uses four frames. In every sample, the percentage of leaders who appeared to use more than two frames was less than 25%, and the number who relied on all four frames was 1% or less.

TABLE 1   Criteria for Coding Frame Responses

Frame	Frame-related Issues	Frame-related Actions
Structural	Coordination and control; clarity or lack of clarity about goals, roles or expectations; references to planning, budgeting, and evaluation; discussion of analysis or its absence (e.g., feasibility studies, institutional analysis); issues around policies and procedures	Reorganizing, implementing, or clarifying policies and procedures; developing new information, budgeting or control systems, adding new structural units, planning processes
Human Resource	Discussions of individuals' feelings, needs, preferences, or abilities (e.g., problems of individual performance or staff quality); references to the importance of participation, listening, open communications, involvement in decision-making, morale; discussion of interpersonal relationships; emphasis on collaboration, win-win and a sense of family or community	Processes of participation and involvement (task forces, open meetings, etc.), training, recruiting new staff, workshops and retreats, empowerment, organization development, and quality-of-work life programs
Political	Focus on conflict or tension among different constituencies, interest groups, or organizations; competing interests and agendas; disputes over allocation of scarce resources; games of power and self-interest	Bargaining, negotiation, advocacy, building alliances, and networking with other key players
Symbolic	Discussions of institutional identity, culture, or symbols; discussions of the image that will be projected to different audiences; discussion of the symbolic importance of existing practices, rituals, or artifacts (e.g., symbolic attachment to an old building on campus); emphasis on influencing how different audiences will interpret or frame an activity or decision	Creating or revitalizing ceremonies and rituals, working to develop or restate the institution's vision, working on influencing organizational culture, using self as a symbol

Which Frames Do Leaders Use?

Table 3 reports which frames were employed by the leaders in the same three samples. In their self-descriptions, Bensimon's (1989, in press) presidents most often described themselves as using the symbolic frame, though they were least often described that way by their colleagues. Bensimon also conducted an analysis comparing single-frame to multi-frame presidents. Single-frame presidents were mostly seen as structural or political and never seen as using the human resource frame. More than half of those presidents described themselves as symbolic, but their colleagues almost never agreed. Multi-frame presidents were most likely to use the human resource frame but usually used the political and symbolic frames as

TABLE 2 How Many Frames Do Leaders Use?

How Many Frames?	College Presidents (Bensimon, 1989) (N = 32)	Higher Education Administrators (N = 75)	School Administrators (N = 15)
One	42%	33%	40%
Two	35%	55%	55%
Three	22%	11%	5%
Four	1%	1%	—

well. They were least likely to use the structural frame. Strikingly, the single-frame presidents were mostly seen as managers; the multi-frame presidents were seen as leaders.

Even in the colleagues' reports, though, the symbolic frame was more common for the presidents than for the other two samples. This may reflect the symbolic importance of the presidency on most college campuses, but methodological differences might account for some of the difference. Bensimon's (1989, in press) presidents were asked to describe themselves as leaders, whereas administrators in the other samples described a set of events in which they tried to exercise leadership. Moreover, Bensimon's study was conducted independently of our work, and she used her own coding scheme to analyze her data.

We recognize several caveats about these data. Except for Bensimon's study, the data came from convenience samples (participants in executive programs) of educational administrators. The sample of verbal data from each participant was relatively brief, and the coding system can be refined further. But the data are still encouraging. They suggest that free-form verbal accounts can be coded into the four frames and can help us learn about leaders' orientations to leadership.

Quantitative Investigations

Our quantitative investigations employ a survey instrument, "Leadership Orientations," derived from the four organization frames. It contains 32 items with 5-point response scales. The instrument is de-

TABLE 3 Which Frames Do Leaders Use?

Which Frames?	College Presidents (Bensimon, 1989, in press) (N = 32)		Higher Education Administrators (N = 75)	School Administrators (N = 15)
	Self	Colleague		
Structural	53%	49%	53%	50%
Human Resource	53%	39%	55%	40%
Political	47%	45%	59%	70%
Symbolic	66%	36%	11%	5%

signed to measure eight separate dimensions of leadership, two for each frame. Following are the eight dimensions:

1. Human Resource Dimensions
   a. Supportive—concerned about the feelings of others; supportive and responsive.
   b. Participative—fosters participation and involvement; listens and is open to new ideas.

2. Structural Dimensions
   a. Analytic—thinks clearly and logically; approaches problems with facts and attends to detail.
   b. Organized—develops clear goals and policies; holds people accountable for results.

3. Political Dimensions
   a. Powerful—persuasive, high level of ability to mobilize people and resources; effective at building alliances and support.
   b. Adroit—politically sensitive and skillful; a skillful negotiator in the face of conflict and opposition.

4. Symbolic Dimensions
   a. Inspirational—inspires others to loyalty and enthusiasm; communicates a strong sense of vision.
   b. Charismatic—imaginative, emphasizes culture and values; is highly charismatic.

The instrument has two parallel forms: one for individuals to rate themselves and another in which their colleagues (superiors, peers, subordinates, etc.) can rate them.

We collected data from respondents in schools, higher education, government, and the private sector. We used the data to address a number of significant questions about leadership; in this paper, we present evidence on three of those questions:

1. How well do the frames capture administrators' thinking?

2. How well do the frames predict administrators' effectiveness?

3. How does gender relate to leadership orientations?

Do the Frames Capture How Administrators Think?

We conducted a number of factor analyses of responses to our leadership instruments, including analyses of both administrators' self-ratings and ratings by others. Factors associated with the four frames consistently emerge from the data. The factor structures are somewhat different for colleague and self-ratings, but in both cases all four frames emerge clearly. Table 4 shows an analysis using data from about 680 senior administrators in higher education. Using a conventional procedure (principal components analysis followed by varimax rotation of all factors with an eigenvalue > 1.0), the analysis produced four factors, each of which represents one of the frames. We found similar results in other populations. The factors are usually very clean. A bleed of items across frames arises from overlap of the symbolic frame with the human resource or political frames. However, the political and human resource frames show little overlap with each other, and none of the frames overlaps with the structural frame.

Do the Frames Predict Effectiveness?

We used regression analysis to explore the link between the frames and effectiveness. Dependent variables were obtained by asking colleagues to rate a manager's overall effectiveness as a manager and overall effectiveness as a leader. We did not define the meaning of the terms manager or leader because we wanted to learn about the implicit meanings managers give to the two concepts. The independent variables were the four organizational frames. The results, shown in tables 5, 6, and 7, are provocative. First, using the four frames we are able to predict a minimum of 66% of the variance in perceived manage-

TABLE 4   Leadership Orientations Factor Analyses

Factor 1: Human Resource
(Percent of variance explained = 21%)

Shows high sensitivity and concern for others' needs	.85
Shows high support and concern for others	.84
Is consistently helpful and responsive to others	.83
Builds trust through open, collaborative relationships	.77
Listens well and is unusually receptive to others' input	.71
Gives personal recognition for work well done	.64
Generates loyalty and enthusiasm	.63

Factor 2: Structural
(Percent of variance explained = 17%)

Strongly emphasizes careful planning and clear timelines	.79
Has extraordinary attention to detail	.75
Develops and implements clear, logical policies	.75
Approaches problems with facts and logic	.73
Uses logical analysis and careful thinking to solve problems	.72
Sets specific, measurable goals and holds people accountable	.69
Strongly believes in clear structure and a chain of command	.67
Thinks very clearly and logically	.65

Factor 3: Political
(Percent of variance explained = 17%)

Is politically very sensitive and skillful	.78
Gets support from people with influence and power	.73
Is a very skillful and shrewd negotiator	.74
Is unusually persuasive and influential	.68
Succeeds in the face of conflict and opposition	.63
Anticipates and deals adroitly with organizational conflict	.59

Factor 4: Symbolic
(Percent of variance explained = 13%)

Uses celebrations and symbols to shape values, build morale	.68
Sees beyond current realities to create new opportunities	.63
Communicates strong and challenging sense of mission	.63
Is highly imaginative and creative	.60
Inspires others to do their best	.54

Note. Principal components analysis with Varimax rotation of all factors with
    eigenvalue > 1.0.

N = 681 higher education raters.

rial effectiveness and 74% in leadership effectiveness. Even more interesting, the array of independent variables associated with effectiveness as a manager is almost the reverse of those associated with effectiveness as a leader. For two of the three samples, the structural frame is the best predictor of managerial effectiveness but

TABLE 5 Regression Analyses: School Administrators

Dependent variable: Effectiveness as a Manager (R-square = .66)

Frame	Standard coefficient	T for H_0: Parameter = 0	Probability
Structural	.30	3.411	.001
Human Resource	.29	3.208	.01
Political	.27	2.366	.05
Symbolic	.02	0.185	N.S.

Dependent variable: Effectiveness as a Leader (R-square = .75)

Frame	Standard coefficient	T for H_0: Parameter = 0	Probability
Structural	.10	1.452	N.S.
Human Resource	.17	2.197	.05
Political	.36	3.591	.001
Symbolic	.28	2.670	.01

Note. Ratings of 24 school administrators (superintendents and other central office) by 147 colleagues.

is, for all three, the worst predictor of effectiveness as a leader (nonsignificant for two, a significant negative predictor for the third). For the symbolic frame, the pattern is reversed: It is consistently the worst predictor of effectiveness as a manager but is the best predictor of effectiveness as a leader in two of the three samples, and second best in the third.

These analyses also show that the human resource and the political frames are positively related to effectiveness as both manager and leader in every sample. What is more stunning is that, across sectors, the political frame is usually a better predictor of both managerial and leadership effectiveness than is the human resource frame. This runs counter to the widespread feeling that politics is a negative feature to be avoided as much as possible in organizations. This pessimistic view of politics is embodied in one widely used management-style instrument in which an effective profile for managers includes a *low* score on politics. Our data suggest the opposite: People adept in understanding and using the political frame are perceived by their colleagues, superiors, and subordinates as better managers *and* leaders. Our international corporate sample (see Table 7) suggests that this is true across sectors and cultures.

The patterns in regression coefficients for the three samples are sufficiently different to suggest that the contribution of the frames to effectiveness is influenced by contextual factors. As one example, it seems initially surprising that the corporate sample is the only one in which the structural frame does not contribute to effectiveness as a manager. But the pattern of scores across the three sectors (see Fig-

TABLE 6   Regression Analyses: Higher Education Administrators

Dependent variable: Effectiveness as a Manager (R-square = .67)

Frame	Standard coefficient	T for H_0: Parameter = 0	Probability
Structural	.45	8.92	.001
Human Resource	.20	3.34	.001
Political	.38	4.94	.001
Symbolic	− .01	− 0.23	N.S.
Gender	.01	0.33	N.S.

Dependent variable: Effectiveness as a Leader (R-square = .74)

Frame	Standard coefficient	T for H_0: Parameter = 0	Probability
Structural	.10	2.23	.05
Human Resource	.14	2.68	.01
Political	.35	5.12	.001
Symbolic	.41	5.64	.001
Gender	.03	0.71	N.S.

Note. Ratings of 187 higher education administrators by 1,342 colleagues.

ure 1) suggests that the apparent anomaly may result from a ceiling effect. Corporate managers, on average, had high scores on the structural frame and relatively low scores on everything else. If everyone in a group is high on a particular frame, there may be a truncated range (too little variance). Alternatively, there may be a cutoff point beyond which more is no longer better. A similar result can be seen for the higher education administrators, who were particularly high on the human resource frame. The frame had lower predictive coefficients for them than for the other two groups. Conversely, the corporate managers were notably weak on the symbolic frame, while the relationship between the symbolic frame and leadership effectiveness was stronger in that group than in either of the others. In a group where everyone is weak, it may be that any movement above the floor has a big impact on an individual's perceived effectiveness as a leader.

Gender and the Frames

Because there are still too few women in administrative roles, only one of our samples—higher education administrators—contains enough women to analyze gender as a variable. About 40% of this group of senior and midlevel administrators was female; they came from public and private colleges and universities all over the United States. In this sample, gender shows virtually no relationship to any of the other variables (see Table 8). Stereotypically, we might expect that women would rate themselves higher on the human resource frame (warm, supportive, participative) and lower on the political frame (powerful, shrewd, aggressive). But the data give no support to those stereo-

TABLE 7   Regression Analyses: Corporate Middle Managers

Dependent variable: Effectiveness as a Manager (R-square = .77)

Frame	Standard coefficient	T for H_0: Parameter = 0	Probability
Structural	.17	1.61	N.S.
Human Resource	.30	1.78	.01
Political	.40	3.84	.01
Symbolic	.12	0.69	N.S.

Dependent variable: Effectiveness as a Leader (R-square = .87)

Frame	Standard coefficient	T for H_0: Parameter = 0	Probability
Structural	− .28	− 2.31	.05
Human Resource	.31	2.63	.01
Political	.36	2.38	.05
Symbolic	.73	5.17	.001

Note. Ratings of 90 corporate managers from Asia, Europe, Latin America, and the U.S.
by 500 colleagues.

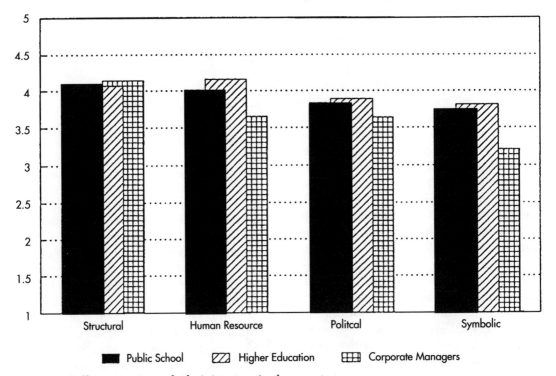

Figure 1   Colleague ratings of administrators in three sectors.

TABLE 8 Correlation of Gender with Frames and Effectiveness for Self and Colleague Ratings

Frame	Self-Ratings	Ratings by Colleagues
Structural	.02	− .03
Human Resource	.03	− .12
Political	.00	− .13
Symbolic	.04	− .15
Managerial Effectiveness	(not asked)	− .07
Leadership Effectiveness	(not asked)	− .10

Note. Gender: 0 = Female; 1 = Male. N = 187 (76 female, 111 male).

types. Women do not consistently rate themselves higher or lower on the any of the frames. In this sample, there is a slight tendency for colleagues to rate men slightly lower on every frame except structure, but the correlations are very small. Moreover, there were no statistically reliable differences between men and women in their ratings by colleagues on effectiveness as both manager and leader. (If anything, men were rated slightly *lower* on both effectiveness measures, but none of the relationships is statistically significant.)

This was a sample of *successful* men and women who held positions ranging from department chair to college president. We do not know if the results would generalize to a less selective population, but they certainly raise questions about many conventional views of differences between men and women as administrators.

Where We Are: A Summary

We have shown that the frames can be measured using both qualitative and quantitative methods. The qualitative work suggests that most administrators in both schools and higher education use only one or two of the frames. With the possible exception of college presidents, administrators use the symbolic frame much less than the other three frames. For college presidents, comparison of self-perceptions with colleague ratings suggests that presidents think they use the symbolic frame much more than they actually do. Both the qualitative and quantitative results suggest that the ability to use multiple frames is important to effectiveness in senior administrative positions.

Factor analysis of survey instruments shows that responses cluster around the conceptual categories as anticipated. Results from three different populations show that, implicitly, administrators distinguish between good managers and good leaders. The frame instrument is able to predict effectiveness as both manager and leader, but the pattern is different for the two variables. Leadership effectiveness is particularly associated with high scores on the symbolic dimensions but is largely unrelated to the structural frame. For managerial effectiveness, the results are almost reversed: The symbolic frame is never a significant predictor but is always a significant predictor for the structural frame.

The other two frames—human resource and political—are both significant positive predictors of success as both leader and manager, but the political frame is consistently the more powerful of the two. Across sectors, professional programs for administrators rarely give much attention to symbolic and political skills, yet our results show they are crucial components for effective leadership.

Acknowledgment

This research was supported in part by a grant from the Office of Educational Research and Improvement of the U.S. Department of Education to the National Center for Educational Leadership.

References

Bennis, W., & Nanus, B. (1985). *Leaders: Strategies for taking charge*. New York: Harper.

Bensimon, E. M. (1989). The meaning of "good presidential leadership": A frame analysis. *The Review of Higher Education, 12*, 107–123.

Bensimon, E. M. (in press). Viewing the presidency: Perceptual congruence between presidents and leaders on their campuses. *The Leadership Quarterly*.

Bolman, L. G., & Deal, T. E. (1984). *Modern approaches to understanding and managing organizations*. San Francisco: Jossey-Bass.

Bolman, L. G., & Deal, T. E. (1991). *Reframing organizations: Artistry, choice and leadership*. San Francisco: Jossey-Bass.

Boulding, K. (1956). *The image*. Binghamton, NY: Vail-Ballou.

Burns, J. M. (1978). *Leadership*. New York: Harper.

Gardner, J. W. (1990). *On leadership*. New York: Free Press.

Goffman, E. (1974). *Frame analysis: An essay on the organization of experience*. Cambridge, MA: Harvard University Press.

Kotter, J. (1990). *A force for change*. New York: Free Press.

Kouzes, J. M., & Posner, B. Z. (1988). *The leadership challenge: How to get extraordinary things done in organizations*. San Francisco: Jossey-Bass.

Markus, H., & Zajonc, R. (1985). The cognitive perspective in social psychology. In B. Hall and G. Lindzey (Eds.), *The handbook of social psychology* (pp. 137–230). New York: Random House/Knopf.

Murphy, J. T. (1989). The unheroic side of leadership: Notes from the swamp. *Phi Delta Kappan, 69*, 654–659.

Lee G. Bolman is Lecturer on Education and Director of the National Center for Educational Leadership at the Harvard Graduate School of Education. A specialist in leadership and organizational behavior, his publications include *Reframing Organizations: Artistry, Choice and Leadership* (written with Terrence E. Deal). He received his PhD in Organizational Behavior from Yale University.

Terrence E. Deal is Professor of Education at Peabody College of Vanderbilt University and Co-Director of the National Center for Educational Leadership. He is the author of six books, including the best-seller *Corporate Cultures* (with A. A. Kennedy, 1983). He received his PhD from Stanford University.

Direct inquiries about this article to Lee G. Bolman, Director, National Center for Educational Leadership, Harvard Graduate School of Education, 6 Appian Way, Cambridge, MA 02138, 617/496–4808.

The Impact of Executive Ideology on Structural Change

Juliann Spoth

This case study traces the impact of an executive's ideology on a divisional change in a strategic business unit structure. The research demonstrates that the executive's organizational ideology is the best explanation for the structure chosen. Furthermore, it shows that the executive used the selection process and falling financial performance to promote his ideology and the structural change.

Questions regarding the impact of executive ideology on structural change remain largely unanswered. Structural change in organizations is most often attributed to other factors: external environment, size, technology, performance, and strategy (Chandler, 1962; Ford & Slocum, 1977; Inkson, Pugh, & Hickson, 1970). Only recently has organizational ideology been directly linked to structural change (Brunsson, 1982; Pettigrew, 1986; Starbuck, 1982; Weiss & Miller, 1987), and research on the subject is sparse. The research that does exist focuses on corporate-level ideology and does not link executive ideology to structural change (Bartunek, 1984; Child & Smith, 1987; Meyer, 1982; Starbuck, 1982).

This research addresses some of the unanswered questions. It offers a methodology to accurately identify executive ideology, demonstrates that executive ideology can drive structural change, and identifies how ideology may be used to change structure. Following are the conceptual and operational definitions of the two main variables in this study, organizational ideology and structure. Operational definitions for environment, strategy, size, technology, and performance are outlined in another section and in Table 4.

Ideology

The conceptual definition of ideology is based on Wilson's (1973) definition of ideology in social movements. Ideology in an organizational setting is a constellation of beliefs and values about the organizational world and how it operates and contains statements about preferences for organizational arrangements that imply compatible actions. It is both a cognitive map and a set of accompanying values in which expectations, standards, and imperatives are proclaimed. Operationally, organizational ideology is the set of constructs that defines the person's beliefs and values about organizations as measured by the Repertory Grid (Kelly, 1955) technique.

Structure

For the purposes of this study, organizational structure is the "sum total of the ways in which the organization divides itself and its labor into distinct tasks and how it achieves coordination among them" (Mintzberg, 1979, p. 2).

Operationally, divisional structure is: (a) structuring or structure as defined by Galbraith & Nathanson (1979) and organizational charts, and (b) perceptions of structural complexity, decision making (centrality), amount of administrators and staff (administrative intensity), number of rules, policies, and procedures (formalization), and appropriateness of division structure. Complexity, centrality, and formalization are structural dimensions most frequently reported in the literature (Fredrickson, 1986). Administrative intensity, while reported less frequently, is included because the pilot data indicated that changes in numbers of staff and management were core to restructuring efforts.

Methods

Research Strategy

This paper reports the research results of two questions: First, what is the content of the decision maker's organizational ideology?, and second, did the decision

maker's ideology impact the structural change? These research questions were answered through an in-depth case study, which triangulated methods at four levels of analysis, of one Fortune 500 company (ABC).

Five research strategies were used to answer these questions. These strategies and their corresponding units of analysis and data sources are outlined in Table 1.

Sample

The sample included seven key organizational leaders who had participated in the structural change from a traditional bureaucracy to strategic business units (SBU). These men were identified as key informants through pilot interviews. They included the Group Vice President (FB), who initiated the structural change within a year after being hired; the divisional Presidents before (WM), during (CA), and after (AA) the divisional change; four SBU managers; and the Human Resource manager. Their length of time in ABC ranged from 4 to 35 years.

Data and Analysis

Information was obtained for the years 1975 to 1989, nine years before and five years after the 1984 structural change.

Repertory Grid. George Kelly's (1955) Repertory (REP) Grid technique was used to identify the content of the executives' ideology. Elicitation triads were used with 11 organizations as the Grid elements. Nineteen ideology elements were elicited for FB and then distilled through thematic analysis into eight elements.

The three divisional Presidents' (i.e., WM, CA, and AA) rated Grids were compared to FB's to obtain the degree of overlap between ideology elements. This analysis creates a sequence of sociometric diagrams from a matrix of similarity measures between pairs of individual grids (Shaw & Gaines, 1988).

TABLE 1   Research Design

Research Question	Strategy	Level of Analysis	Data Source
1. What was the content of the decision maker's (FB's) ideology?	Describe FB's ideology.	Individual	Repertory Grid Interviews Archival Records
2. Did the decision maker's ideology impact structural change?	Compare the division's structure before and after 1984 to see if it changed.	Division	Questionnaire Interviews Archival Records
	Compare FB's ideology against the characteristics inherent in SBU's vs. other possible structural forms to see if it best fits the SBU form.	Division	Literature Review
	Compare contingency and performance characteristics before and after the 1984 structural change to see if they can be eliminated as explanations for the structural change.	Division Group Corporate	Questionnaire Annual Reports Archival Records Interviews
	Compare FB's ideology with the ideology of the division presidents he selected to see the degree to which FB's ideology is shared.	Individual	Repertory Grid

While the REP Grid has not been specifically used to measure ideology, it has been used to measure closely related phenomena such as values (Fransella & Bannister, 1967) and organizational references frames (Dunn & Ginsberg, 1986). The REP test is the method of choice for studying ideology, as it can elicit latent cognitive and value content in the individual's own language.

The questionnaire. A 9-item questionnaire measured the seven experts' perceptions of the division's structure and factors believed to affect structural change: general environment, strategy, size, technology, and performance. Each question was rated on a 7-point scale for the post-1984 structural era of the MED Division and the structural era of the ATD Division immediately preceding it from 1980–1983. Respondents' answers were not included in the analysis if they indicated a low level of confidence in their response for that era. Each 7-point scale was trichotomized into low (1, 2, or 3), medium (4), and high (5, 6, or 7) categories, and mean values were calculated. In some cases, measures of central tendency were misleading due to the range of responses. Therefore, the trichotomized responses were used to draw conclusions.

Interviews and archival data. Three critical incidents were solicited for one decision made during each of the Division's structural periods. Another critical incident was solicited for the Division's change to the SBU.

Several types of internal and external archival data were collected. Data from annual reports were used to determine structural change, size, and the presence of FB's ideology in certain documents, as well as to calculate division, group, and corporate profit margins.

The Executive's Ideology

FB's organizational ideology is described in order to answer the first research question: What was the content of the decision maker's ideology? FB was credited by the division's executives as the most influential decision maker shaping the change to SBU's. This was also supported by documentary evidence. If organizational ideology did have an impact on the structural change, then FB's ideology was the dominant ideology shaping that change.

The thematic analysis of FB's 19 ideology elements elicited by the REP test resulted in 5 ideology themes (see Table 2). Since some themes contained more than

TABLE 2   FB's Ideology

---

1. Contingency thinking
2. Contingency theories of organizing and change:
   - Organizational/environment interface
   - Change
   - Organization of resources
3. Management theory:
   - Management philosophy
   - Management characteristics
4. Simplified, localized control
5. A healthy organization/business

---

one element, there was a total of eight themes.

An abbreviated description of each element follows:

1. Contingency Thinking values thinking that reflects a thorough understanding of the situation and the tradeoffs involved. Final decisions should be based on the fit between all factors considered.

2. Contingency Theories promote actions or decisions that vary depending on certain criteria. First, the organization/environment interface describes the importance of identifying the nature of product lines and markets and the match between them when making decisions about structure. The second theory on change states that an organization always looks for ways to improve. However, the rate of change varies and is incremental in the face of success and radical if the organization is failing. Third, the theory of organization of resources states that all resources are located in the business unless these resources are expensive or scarce.

3. Management Theory includes FB's general philosophy of management which contains five items (e.g., "organizational structure should address critical motivational forces" and "man-

agement development is a priority to insure managers for succession"). A second area, Management Characteristics, includes seven necessary traits (e.g., contingency-based thinking, realistic, and committed).

4. Simplified and Localized Control states that (a) control should be decentralized, (b) organizations should be structured to support this, and (c) managers should be held accountable for their actions. Corporate interference with business and management autonomy should be minimal.

5. A Healthy Organization, as described by FB, has good profit and growth rate, soundness (e.g., stable, robust, good condition), and quality people with good skills and capacity.

FB's Ideology and the Structural Changes

Four research strategies (outlined in Table 1) were pursued to answer the second research question: Did the decision maker's ideology impact the structural change? These strategies demonstrated that (a) the divisional structure did change, (b) FB's ideology best matched the characteristics of the SBU, and (c) other possible contingency and performance factors did not mandate the change to the SBU structure. The fourth strategy confirmed that one way FB crafted the change was through executive selection.

Strategy One: Were Perceptions of the Structural Change Myth or Fact?

When the ATD Division became the MED Division in 1984, the common perception was that there had been a dramatic change. Questionnaire results, or-

ganizational charts, and annual report and interview data were used to construct a comparison of the structural elements in ATD and MED. The results showed that MED differed dramatically from ATD in all structural dimensions reviewed: grouping, product lines, centralization, formalization, complexity, and administrative intensity (Spoth, 1990).

Strategy Two: Does FB's Ideology Best Match the Characteristics Inherent in SBU's as Compared to Other Structural Options?

The first part of the strategy was the comparison to the SBU concept. There are five SBU characteristics reported in the literature (Bettis & Hall, 1983; Coate, 1983; Govindarajan, 1988; Hall, 1978; Haspeslagh, 1982). Table 3 aligns these five SBU characteristics with FB's corresponding ideology elements.

In each case there is a match between the SBU characteristic and at least one of FB's elements. Of the elements represented, organizational/environment interface and organization of resources are particularly relevant. Contingency thinking, conditional change, the management philosophy, and some management characteristics were not represented. The focus on SBU structure, rather than management or process, may partially explain these missing elements.

The second part of this strategy was to determine whether structures other than the SBU structure were more compatible with FB's ideology. This was accomplished by matching alternative divisional structures against FB's ideology. A literature search revealed no one source for divisional-level structures. Galbraith and Nathanson's (1979) topology of structures was adapted by eliminating the holding company structure, which was applicable only to the corporate level, and by adding a matrix structure (Davis & Lawrence, 1977). This topology was used

TABLE 3 Comparison of SBU Characteristics and FB's Ideology

SBU Characteristics	FB's Elements
1. Independence	Organization/environment interface and Organization of resources
2. Product/market segment defines the business unit	Organizational/environment interface
3. Resources allocated in SBU	Organization of resources
4. Business manager has authority and responsibility for strategy and business decisions	Management Characteristics (controls destiny) and Simplified and Localized Control
5. Strategy and decisions use models focused on long-term welfare	Healthy organization and Management Characteristics (realistic, rational, perpetuates business)

because it compares structures according to the influence of product line(s), which is one of FB's elements. It also compares structural types by degree of centralization, function or product orientation, control of strategic decisions, and allocation of resources.

The final topology included the following structures: simple, functional, divisionalized, and matrix. Each structure was eliminated based on mismatches with the nature of the products, FB's ideology, and the existing structural problems that FB was correcting.

The simple structure was eliminated because the complexity of MED's products and technology surpasses its capability. This structure also conflicted with FB's ideological elements of localized control and allocation of resources.

The functional structure was also too simplistic for MED's products, and the degree of centralization and control over resource allocation conflicted with FB's ideology. In fact, FB's first structural change

was to eradicate the group's functional structure by reallocating group staff to the divisions.

The matrix structure was the least aligned with FB's desired structure. MED's products neither required complex coordination nor information processing. The dual manager system interfered with individual managerial autonomy and responsibility and conflicted with FB's element of simplified, localized control. The allocation of resources across product groups also conflicted with FB's value of allocating resources to specific units.

The divisional type was the one structure most aligned with the nature of the Division's products and FB's ideological elements of simplified localized control, allocation of resources, and management style. ABC had, in fact, divisionalized MED before the 1984 change. However, this fell far short of the ideal described in this topology. FB's changes, on the other hand, went far beyond this ideal description. The SBU structure pushed profit

TABLE 4 Environment, Strategy, Size, Technology, and Performance:
Definitions and Data Source

	Operational Definitions	**Data Source**
Environment	Perceptions of the division's environmental attributes: • Certainty • Simplicity • Stability	Expert Questionnaire
Strategy	1. Perceptions of divisional diversification and growth 2. Statements about strategy 3. Implicit signalling of strategy through statements about market orientation, acquisitions, mergers, etc.	Expert Questionnaire Annual Reports Archival Records Interviews
Size	Magnitude of the labor force for the division, group, and corporation	Annual Reports
Technology	Perceptions of the division's technology: automation/simplicity, and control/coordination	Expert Questionnaire Annual Reports
Performance	Profit margin • Corporation = $\dfrac{Net\ Income}{Sales}$ • Division & Group = $\dfrac{Operating\ Income}{Sales}$	Annual Reports Annual Divisional Reports

center concepts into even smaller business units. Comparing all structural options, the business unit concept remains the most compatible with FB's ideology.

Strategy Three: Can Other Factors Be Eliminated as Explanations for the Structural Change?

Table 4 lists the operational definitions and data sources used to explore the impact of other variables commonly believed to be the cause of structural change: environment, technology, size, strategy, and performance. (See Spoth, 1990, for definitions and literature support for these variables.) Each variable was measured for the ATD era of 1980–1983, the structural era immediately preceding the structural change, and during the MED era of 1984–1989. All variables were measured at the divisional level. In addition, strategy, size, and performance were measured at the corporate and group levels; changes at these levels could impact the division even if the division variable was stable. The intent was to determine if any variable in the preceding era was sufficiently different from the MED era and, if so, would the difference require a change to the particular structural dimensions found in SBU's (Chandler, 1962; Ford & Slocum, 1977; Gerwin, 1981; Ouchi & Harris, 1974).

A summary of the findings for each variable is presented in Table 5. (See Spoth, 1990, for a detailed description of the questionnaire results and other data used to support the conclusions for each level and category.)

The only variable that could have an impact on the structural change was performance. Profit margins were falling at every level, and corporate and group margins hit their lowest point in 1983. The interview data clarifies the impact of this situation on the structural change. Interviews indicate that FB was brought in by the Chairman to make the group more profitable rather than to change the structure per se. Thus, low profits facilitated corporate acceptance of the SBU change proposed by FB as a partial solution.

Within the group, the medical businesses had shown greater profitability than the other businesses. Thus, the need to protect the more profitable medical businesses shaped the structural change by identifying the products worthy of focus. It did not, however, dictate how these businesses should be organized once they were grouped together. Hence, poor financial performance created the urgency, opportunity, and support for FB to make his structural change but did not dictate the nature of the change.

Strategy Four: Did FB's Ideology Affect Selections for the Divisional Presidency?

The speculation that FB's ideology influenced his selection of presidents for MED assumed a good match between FB's organizational ideology and the ideology of those he chose for Divisional Presidents. These presidents included WM, whom FB reassigned and replaced with CA, who implemented the structural change; upon his retirement two years later, CA was replaced by AA. Table 6 indicates the percent of FB's ideology elements that encompass each of these men's elements. The majority of AA's and CA's elements correspond to FB's; of the two, AA has a greater correspondence than CA. In comparison, fewer of WM's elements correspond to FB's. A possible explanation for the greater similarity in AA's elements is that AA had more consistent and intensive contact with FB. CA and WM, however, also had consistent, intensive contact with FB for several years. If the degree of contact with FB was the underlying explanation, then correspondence with both CA and WM should be higher.

These results are supported through AA's, CA's, and WM's descriptions of why FB selected or reassigned them and then interacted with them, as well as through FB's description of the same processes. Hence, the quantitative results merely confirm what the participants themselves acknowledged. In each case, perceived ideological compatibilities fueled FB's decisions about the person best suited for MED's Presidency.

Conclusions and Implications for Practice

FB's ideology is the best explanation for the change to the structure of the SBU. FB's ideology matches the characteristics of the SBU structure better than other structural options. Furthermore, there were no changes in technology, strategy, performance, or size that would have mandated this type of structural change. While these variables did not mandate the change, corporate, group, and divisional financial performance facilitated the change, as did FB's selection of the division's presidents.

Although these results are clearly documented in this case study, further verification is needed before generalizations can be made. However, one major implication open to speculation is that executives *can* impact structural change, and

TABLE 5 Impact of Environment, Strategy, Size, Technology, and
Performance on MED's Structural Change

	Environment	Strategy	Size	Technology	Performance
Division	no	no	no	no	yes
Group	NA	no	no	NA	yes
Corporation	NA	no	no	NA	yes

Note. NA indicates "not applicable."

their ideology is an important factor in determining the nature of the change. This study indicates that despite the complexities of the modern organization, it is still possible for an executive to be the source of major structural change. Although this may seem obvious, structural change is most often reported as being determined by contextual factors (Chandler, 1962; Ford & Slocum, 1977; Inkson, Pugh, & Hickson, 1970).

While this study supports executive choice, it also suggests that neither the issue of contextual determinism nor executive choice is as clear as typically presented. The choice models that state that executives' decisions affect structural change largely ignore the role of the executive's ideology in these decisions (Bob-

bitt & Ford, 1980). They also hold that executive choice is constrained by context (Khandwalla, 1976). This study suggests that the executive's own ideology also constrains choice, for it limits the options the executive is willing to consider. Context may also facilitate, not merely constrain, executives' decisions. It can provide an opportunity, as did ABC's financial performance, for executives to implement their preferred structure. Thus, as Hrebiniak and Joyce (1985) suggest, executive choice and contextual determinism may be independent variables that interact in varying ways. If so, then there is need for better and more detailed theories of how and why changes in structure occur in organizations.

Other applications from this study arise from the link between an executive's organizational ideology and the popular notion of vision. Organizational ideology is the basis for vision. Vision is the outcome of an executive's or a dominant coalition's core beliefs and values about the way an organization should be. Thus, the beginning step in articulating a vision is eliciting an executive's or a collective's organizational ideology. This study indicates that ideology can be identified in the person's or group's own language, and the REP Grid test appears to be an accurate way to do so.

Promoting a vision also requires more than constructing a statement or enacting it in ceremonies (Meyer & Rowan, 1977),

TABLE 6 Percent of FB's Ideology Elements
Shared by Other MED Presidents

President	% of Shared Ideology
AA	95.0
CA	66.7
WM	38.5

Note. Shared ideology is the percent of an individual's elements each of which had greater than 80 matches when individually compared against one of FB's elements (Shaw & Gaines, 1988).

as popularly prescribed. An ideology and corresponding vision should be managed (Starbuck, Greve, & Hedberg, 1988) in concrete, everyday forms. This study suggests that it is critical for executives to promote ideologies by translating them into concrete structural and managerial activities as a way of managing the invisible through the visible. Aligned changes in organizational form or activities anchor the vision and allow others to concretely experience the new ideology. When structure is changed and the ideology/vision is embedded within it, the structure itself can help convert skeptics to the new ideology and vision.

This happened in ABC when the managers in the old structure were promoted to general managers of the SBUs. Although initially they thought FB's ideas sounded good, they questioned whether the ideas could work in ABC and vacillated in their support. Once they experienced their new autonomy and influence under the SBU structure, they became advocates for the changes and worked to make the businesses successful to ensure survival of this vision. Thus, there is a reciprocal determinism between executive ideology and structure; executive ideology can shape structural change and, in turn, structure can shape the ideology of others.

Besides structural change, another concrete way an executive can promote a desired ideology/vision is the intentional selection and placement of personnel who share the ideology, as did the two divisional presidents. These people act as ideological carriers. They promote and act out the ideology in their daily organizational life. The more aligned the ideology of the executive and manager, the more independent the manager can be and still be in concert with the desires of the executive. When strategically placed and given positional power, these people can be potent forces in the organization for further ideological and visionary change.

There is no longer a question about whether an executive's ideology can impact structural change. There are, however, still unanswered questions about how an executive's ideology affects structural change. Undoubtedly there are other factors and dynamics than those uncovered in this research which affect this process. Additional case studies are needed to provide the thick descriptions (Geertz, 1973) necessary to understand these dynamics.

References

Bartunek, J. (1984). Changing interpretive schemes and organizational restructuring: The example of a religious order. *Administrative Science Quarterly, 29,* 355–372.

Bettis, R., & Hall, W. (1983). The business portfolio approach—where it falls down in practice. *Long-Range Planning, 16,* 95–104.

Bobbitt, H., & Ford, J. (1980). Decision-maker choice as a determinant of organizational structure. *Academy of Management, 5,* 13–23.

Brunsson, N. (1982). The irrationality of action and action rationality: Decisions, ideologies and organizational actions. *Journal of Management Studies, 19,* 29–43.

Chandler, A. (1962). *Strategy and structure.* Cambridge, MA: M.I.T. Press.

Child, J., & Smith, C. (1987). The context and process of organizational transformation—Cadbury limited in its sector. *Journal of Management Studies, 24,* 565–593.

Coate, M. (1983). Pitfalls in portfolio planning. *Long Range Planning, 16,* 47–56.

Davis, S., & Lawrence, P. (1977). *Matrix.* Reading, MA: Addison–Wesley.

Dunn, W., & Ginsberg, A. (1986). A sociocognitive network approach to organizational analysis. *Human Relations, 40,* 955–976.

Ford, J., & Slocum, J. (1977). Size, technology, environment and the structure of organizations. *Academy of Management Review, 2,* 561–575.

Fransella, F., & Bannister, D. (1967). A validation of repertory grid technique as a measure of political construing. *Acta Psychologica, 26,* 97–106.

Fredrickson, J. (1986). The strategic decision process and organizational structure. *Academy of Management Review, 11*, 280–297.

Galbraith, J., & Nathanson, D. (1979). The role of organizational structure and process in strategy implementation. In D. Schnedel & C. Hofer (Eds.), *Strategic management* (pp. 249–283). Boston: Little, Brown.

Geertz, C. (1973). *The interpretation of cultures.* New York: Basic Books.

Gerwin, D. (1981). Relationships between structure and technology. In P. C. Nystrom & W. H. Starbuck (Eds.), *Handbook of organizational design* (Vol. 2, pp. 3–38). New York: Oxford.

Govindarajan, V. (1988). A contingency approach to strategy implementation at the business-unit level: Integrating administrative mechanisms with strategy. *Academy of Management Journal, 31*, 842–853.

Hall, W. (1978, February). SBUs: Hot, new topic in the management of diversification. *Business Horizons,* 17–25.

Haspeslagh, P. (1982). Portfolio planning: Its uses and limits. *Harvard Business Review, 60,* 58–73.

Hrebiniak, L., & Joyce, W. (1985). Organizational adaptation: Strategic choice and environmental determinism. *Administrative Science Quarterly, 30*, 336–349.

Inkson, J., Pugh, D., & Hickson, D. (1970). Organization and context: An abbreviated replication. *Administration Science Quarterly, 15*, 318–329.

Kelly, G. (1955). *The psychology of personal constructs* (Vols. 1–2). New York: W. W. Norton.

Khandwalla, P. (1976). Some top management styles, their context and performance. *Organization and Administrative Science, 7*, 21–51.

Meyer, A. (1982). How ideologies supplant formal structures and shape responses to environments. *Journal of Management Studies, 19,* 45–61.

Meyer, J., & Rowan, B. (1977). Institutionalized organizations: Formal structure as myth and ceremony. *American Journal of Sociology, 83*, 340–363.

Mintzberg, H. (1979). *The structuring of organizations.* Englewood Cliffs, NJ: Prentice Hall.

Ouchi, W., & Harris, R. (1974). Structure, technology and environment. In G. Strass, R. Miles, C. Snow, & A. Tannenbaum (Eds.), *Organizational behavior* (pp. 107–140). Madison, WI: Industrial Research Association.

Pettigrew, A. (1986). Some limits of executive power in creating strategic change. In S. Srivastva (Ed.), *The functioning of executive power* (pp. 132–154). San Francisco: Jossey-Bass.

Shaw, M., & Gaines, B. (1988). *A methodology or recognizing consensus, correspondence, conflict and contrast in a knowledge acquisition system.* Paper presented at the Workshop on Knowledge Acquisition for Knowledge-Based Systems, Banff, Canada.

Spoth, J. (1990). *Spirit and substance: The impact of organizational ideology on structural change.* Unpublished doctoral dissertation, Case Western Reserve University, Cleveland, OH.

Starbuck, W. (1982). Congealing oil: Inventing ideologies to justify acting ideologies out. *Journal of Management Studies, 19*, 3–27.

Starbuck, W., Greve, A., & Hedberg, B. (1988). Responding to crisis. In J. Quinn, H. Mintzberg, & R. James (Eds.), *The strategy process* (pp. 13–20). Englewood Cliffs, NJ: Prentice Hall.

Weiss, R. M., & Miller, L. E. (1987). The concept of ideology in organizational analysis: The sociology of knowledge or the social psychology of beliefs? *Academy of Management Review, 12*, 104–116.

Wilson, J. (1973). *Introduction to social movements.* New York: Basic Books.

Juliann Spoth is an independent consultant in organizational development and has held faculty positions and taught graduate students. She received her PhD in Organizational Behavior from Case Western Reserve University.

Direct inquiries about this article to Juliann Spoth, Spoth and Associates, 4441 Lamar Court, Richmond Heights, OH 44146, 216/531-6910.

Leaders and Organizational Outcomes in Established Industries

An Analysis of Lee Iacocca and the American Automobile Industry

**Daniel J. Svyantek and
Richard P. DeShon**

An analysis of Lee Iacocca and the American automobile industry's performance was conducted to assess the executive leader's impact on performance. The analysis showed that Iacocca's influence on sales and profit was less than expected. A discussion describes the relationship between industry inertia and leadership in mature organizations.

There is a controversy in organizational behavior research over the effect of top-management decisions and actions on organizational performance in mature, established companies. The answers to this question have rarely been consistent with folk wisdom that leaders have a significant impact on the performance of their companies (Barney & Ouchi, 1986). The purpose of this study was to assess the impact of CEO leadership on objective organizational performance indices for mature, established organizations. A longitudinal analysis was conducted to examine the effects of one leader hypothesized to be the exemplar of a charismatic visionary leader, Lee Iacocca (Chung, Lubatkin, Rogers, & Owers, 1987; Nadler & Tushman, 1990). The performance of the American automobile industry as a whole was investigated to differentiate performance outcomes attributable to Iacocca's leadership from those attributable to extraorganizational events.

One view of leadership holds that, for established companies, the effect of a leader on organizational performance is much smaller than commonly believed. Chung et al. (1987) have shown that long-term performance is more a function of that organization's performance trend prior to succession of a new CEO than it is to the new CEO. There was an interaction effect between executive origin and prior performance on short-term stock prices. High-performing organizations that hired outsiders as CEOs had the greatest increase in short-term stock prices (8.5%). Low-performing organizations that hired outsiders as CEOs had the lowest increase in short-term stock prices (-19%). The authors conclude that leadership does not affect the life of an organization and its performance. Perceived leadership by investors, however, was seen as the possible explanatory factor accounting for the difference in the short-term profits of organizations. The current performance of the organization to which a CEO is succeeding, therefore, will influence the characteristics attributed to that leader. In addition, Meindl and Erlich (1987) argued that individuals (e.g., internal or external stakeholders) have a bias towards seeing the leader as a causal factor when accounting for organizational performance under ambiguous conditions.

This view of the value of leadership in organizational performance has been questioned. Day and Lord (1988) interpreted the results of executive succession studies using economic aspects of organizational performance as criteria. Executive leadership is seen as explaining 20% to 45% of the variance in organizational outcomes in their studies. Barrick, Day, Lord, and Alexander (1991) used utility analysis concepts to assess the financial impact of executive leadership on organizational performance as estimated by financial analysts. A mean utility point estimate for the value of executive leadership of $26 million was found. In addition, the mean of the financial analysts' subjective estimates of the percent by which leadership impacted performance (15.1%) was found to be nearly identical to the average effect size found in executive succession studies. This study, however, is a study of perceptions and does not utilize objective criteria of organizational performance.

The question of the impact of leadership on organizational performance has clearly not been resolved. Further research is necessary to determine when and what leadership activities influence organizational performance and the conditions under which these activities may have maximum effect.

Chung et al. (1987) suggested that leadership does play an important part in organizational renewal efforts. It may be that this influence derives from the effects of perceived leadership on internal stakeholders. The succession of CEOs perceived as good leaders may be as important to organizational members as it is to investors. The careful symbolic manipulation of organizational renewal efforts may be more important than the actual changes being made. Chung et al. (1987) proposed that only exceptional leaders, when faced with a company turnaround, may counteract the "momentum effect" of an organization's prior performance. Lee Iacocca was one CEO cited as a possible exceptional leader by these authors. O'Toole (1985) argued that the success of Lee Iacocca at Chrysler is not a lesson in leadership but a lesson in followership. Iacocca's success is hypothesized to be the result of marketing to internal and external stakeholders instead of improved managerial performance on behavioral criteria such as improved strategy or decision making.

Method

The method used to conduct this analysis was a quasi-experimental longitudinal design. Romanelli and Tushman (1986) advocate the use of quasi-experimental designs in comparative longitudinal organizational research as a method for comparing the decisions and behaviors of managers. This method allows (a) the comparison of the persistence in a pattern of organizational activity over time as environmental conditions change in one organization, (b) the comparison of the persistence in patterns of organizational activity as a function of organizational origin across environmental changes, and (c) the comparison of patterns of organizational activity across organizations within the same environmental conditions.

Quasi-experimental designs support internally valid inferences if it can be shown that threats to internal validity are controllable (cf. Campbell & Stanley, 1966; Cook & Campbell, 1979; Komaki, 1986). Organizations must be classified according to their similarities so that the effects of history may be controlled; significant environmental changes must be identified as points of comparison of changes in organizational activity patterns (Romanelli & Tushman, 1986). Cook and Campbell stated that threats to internal validity are minimized by studying systems which are subject to similar environmental changes and have common histories.

The American automobile industry is ideally suited to the analysis of potential leader impact on objective organizational performance criteria. The American automobile industry is commonly held to have similar origins and history (relative to foreign automobile industries). The *Forbes* (1967–1986) *Annual Reports on American Industry*, for example, have emphasized the common fate in a changing environment of the American automobile industry for the past 20 years.

This study combined the logic of the quasi-experimental longitudinal design advocated by Romanelli and Tushman (1986) with that of Komaki's (1986) organizational reversal (or ABA) design to assess the effects of Iacocca's leadership (an "intervention" in the terminology of ABA designs). Lee Iacocca was a leader in both Ford and Chrysler during the period of the study. The hiring of Lee Iacocca as president of Ford in 1970 and as CEO of Chrysler in 1979 were treated as treatment interventions in a multiple-baseline ABA design.

If Iacocca is an effective leader, it is hypothesized (in terms of objective performance of a company) that (a) organizational performance for the company promoting or hiring him will improve after he is hired, and (b) there should be a drop in the performance of companies from which he leaves.

The data used to assess these trends were gathered from *Business Week's* (1971–1988) *Quarterly Reports on American Industry*. Data were collected on the performance of Chrysler, Ford, and General Motors, organizations which represent the primary American automakers from 1971 through 1988. The assessment of executive performance is best done using organizational-level variables such as organizational growth, profit, or stock prices (Day & Lord, 1988). Therefore, the dependent variables used in this study were quarterly sales, quarterly earnings-per-share, quarterly profits, and quarterly return-on-equity. All dependent variables using the dollar as their metric were corrected for inflation.

Analysis

Although the preferred method of analyzing longitudinal economic data is through time-series analysis, there were too few data points for this method (Cook & Campbell, 1979). Instead, moderated regression in adjunct with a careful focus on correlated error was used. Before a potential regression model is considered adequate for interpretation, residual plots and Durbin-Watson (1971) statistics must indicate no serious autocorrelation. In addition to identifying autocorrelation, this method also assesses model fit (Myers, 1988).

The data were divided into two sections: Iacocca at Ford (before 1979) and

Iacocca at Chrysler (after 1979). The years 1979 and 1980 were not used in the analysis to allow for any variation in corporate performance due to the political maneuvering between Iacocca and Henry Ford II during Iacocca's last year at Ford (cf. Halberstam, 1986) and to allow a 1-year lag after Iacocca became CEO at Chrysler, compensating for the short-term influences on stock prices due to perceptions of stakeholders upon CEO succession (cf. Chung et al., 1987) and giving Iacocca time to institute his own plans. The eight years within each section (before and after Iacocca's move) each had four quarters of data which were coded as organizational tenure. This led to 32 data points before Iacocca's move and 32 data points after his move. The premove and postmove data were effects coded to create one variable called PRE-POST. By focusing on the change in organizational performance across time, both before and after Iacocca's move, it was possible to assess changes in the slope of the dependent variables as a function of Iacocca's leadership and test the hypotheses.

Results

Initial inspection of residual plots indicated substantial violation of the homogeneity of variance assumption. A significance test for violation of this assumption (White, 1980) demonstrated that, in fact, there was heterogeneity of variance in all dependent variables across time. The logarithmic transformation recommended by Draper and Smith (1981) was used to remedy this situation. After the log transformation, White's test indicated that the homogeneity of variance assumption was met in all the models involving sales and profit. Earnings-per-share and return-on-equity, on the other hand, were not helped by the log transformation. Inspection of the raw data yielded a surprising result. The data for return-on-equity and earnings-per-share were discontinuous

over time. Neither time-series nor regression analysis is appropriate when data are explosively nonlinear, as in this case. Tong's (1983) piecewise linear regression technique is recommended for this type of data. Hence, the remainder of the analysis focused on changes in sales and profit over time.

In order to test the hypotheses, moderated multiple regression was performed. The variables used in the model were organizational TENURE (32 levels), the effects coded PRE-POST variable (2 levels), and a dummy coded COMPANY variable (3 levels). The test of the hypotheses focused on the significance of the three-way interaction term for these three variables. Specifically, the slopes in organizational performance, across time, were tested to see if they were different across the companies as a function of Iacocca's presence. When this model was tested, the Durbin-Watson (1971) statistics, residual plots, and White's (1980) variance test indicated lack of model fit. A conceptually and statistically equivalent alternative to this procedure is to drop the company variable from the analysis and focus on the two-way interaction between organizational TENURE and the effects coded PRE-POST variable (Armitage, 1971; Kleinbaum & Kupper, 1978) for each company separately. To test whether this interaction is different across companies, the regression weights for the two-way interaction are compared against each other using simultaneous bonferroni confidence intervals (Myers, 1988). The model used in all of the analyses took the following form: $Y = b_0 + b_1$ PRE-POST $+ b_2$ TENURE $+ b_3$ PRE-POST $\times$ TENURE.

Sales

The PRE-POST variable and the TENURE variable were both significant in all analyses for the sales data, which means that average sales were different after 1979 than before 1979 for all companies.

TABLE 1 Analysis of the Sales of the American Automobile Industry

Company	R²	Beta	Prob	Bonferroni Confidence Interval
Ford	.982	0.0059	0.0003	0.00949 – 0.00222
Chrysler	.966	– 0.00348	0.0670	0.00092 – (– 0.00788)
GM	.974	0.0077	0.0001	0.01222 – 0.00338

Sales increased monotonically over time within each time period. The remainder of the analyses focused on the interaction term, which directly tests the hypotheses. Table 1 provides the overall model R^2, regression weights for the interaction term, the significance level of the weights, and the bonferroni confidence intervals for each company. The interaction term for Ford was significant, indicating that sales slowed after 1979. The critical test, though, was whether Ford's sales decreased at a higher rate than GM's sales. Table 1 illustrates the overlap of the bonferroni confidence intervals on the regression weights for Ford and GM, demonstrating that the decrease in Ford's sales was not significantly different than the decrease in sales at GM. In other words, Ford's decrease in sales resulted from a market trend rather than from the lack of Iacocca's leadership.

The regression results further indicated that the interaction term for Chrysler failed to reach significance. Chrysler's sales increased at the same rate before and after Iacocca became CEO. The confidence interval around the regression weight for the interaction term did not overlap with either of the confidence intervals for Ford or GM. Chrysler's slopes have a different rate of change than Ford or GM. This difference, however, is a more negative slope (see the confidence interval).

Sales data are plotted for Ford, GM and Chrysler in Figures 1, 2 and 3. These figures demonstrate the remarkably similar rates of increases in sales after 1979 of the American automobile industry.

Profit

The profit data, when compared across companies, present a similar picture of the actual results of Iacocca's leadership. Here, an identical pattern emerged across the three companies. The PRE-POST variable was marginally significant across all companies and the TENURE variable was not. Again, the focus was on the interaction term. Table 2 provides the overall model R^2, regression weights, for the interaction term, the significance level of the weights, and the bonferroni confidence intervals for each company. The data in the table clearly demonstrate that the rate of change in all three companies followed the same pattern across time. The regression weights for each company were nonsignificant, and the bonferroni confidence intervals overlapped. In other words, Iacocca's change in company affiliation in no way influenced the change in profits across time for either Ford or Chrysler.

Summary

The magnitude of the predicted variance in both the sales and profit data is impressive. Given the strength of the model in predicting these variables, it would be difficult to argue that Iacocca's apparent lack of influence on organizationally important variables was artifactual. Analyses overwhelmingly suggest that Iacocca's move from Ford to Chrysler

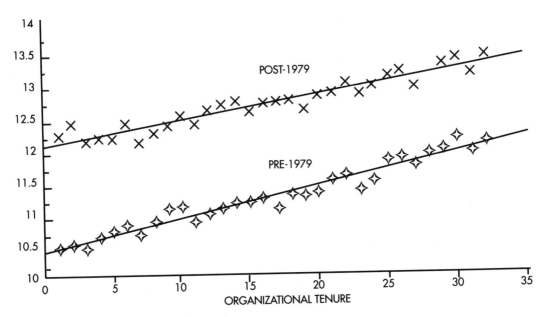

SALES

Figure 1 Log-transformed sales for Ford.

neither adversely affected Ford's performance nor did it improve Chrysler's performance relative to the other auto makers. The data analyzed in this study did not support the contention that Lee Iacocca is an exceptional leader, at least in terms of sales and profit-dependent variables. Rather, the performance data supported the contention of general trends in the American automobile industry.

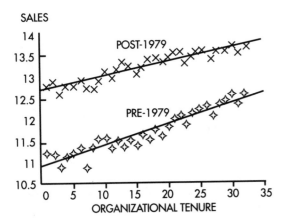

SALES

Figure 2 Log-transformed sales for GM.

Discussion

This study showed that those executives commonly held to be excellent may not impact objective performance measures for their organizations in an established industry. Iacocca, an executive accepted as being an exceptional leader in both popular and academic literature, was shown to have little or no positive effect on sales and profit during the 8-year period in which he was lionized as the prototypical executive of the future. From an objective performance perspective, Iacocca has not turned Chrysler around as would be expected if, as hypothesized, he was truly the exceptional leader.[1]

The results of this quasi-experimental, longitudinal design show that executive leadership does not always positively influence organizational-level performance measures such as sales and profit. An exceptional leader is one who should be able to increase performance across situations *and* in situations where others cannot. There is little support for this from

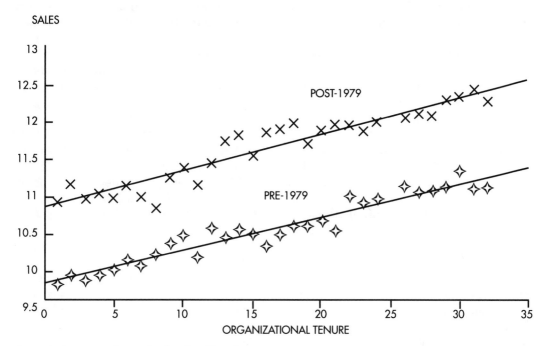

Figure 3 Log-transformed sales for Chrysler.

TABLE 2 Analysis of the Profits of the American Automobile Industry

Company	R²	Beta	Prob	Bonferroni Confidence Interval
Ford	.718	− 0.01389	0.1749	0.00996 − (− 0.03776)
Chrysler	.412	− 0.02622	0.2871	0.03133 − (− 0.08377)
GM	.441	− 0.00647	0.5662	0.01997 − (− 0.03291)

the analysis of Iacocca's effects on Ford and Chrysler. A more appropriate interpretation is that American carmakers followed the same general pattern of sales and profits during the past 20 years. The "momentum effect" (Chung et al., 1987) was not overcome by Iacocca. Chrysler was on a 10-year downward slide when Iacocca became CEO. Any changes in this slide were related to general changes in the industry. For research and practical purposes, it is necessary to understand why this occurred.

The Role of Industry Inertia in Organizational Performance

One explanation for the results of this study may be found in the literature on the relationship between organizational culture and corporate performance in mature organizations. Barney (1986) proposed that organizational culture is seldom a source of sustained financial value to a company. To provide a sustained competitive advantage, the culture of an organization must (a) allow the firm to do things which add value to the firm's output, (b) be rare (in relation to the cultures found in competitor firms), and (c) be imperfectly imitable by other firms in the same industry.

Davis (1984) stated that organizational cultures reflect a company's orientations toward the management of internal human resources and ability to compete against external competitors. Svyantek and Hendrick (1987) hypothesized that these two orientations are reflected in complementary but separate cultural systems *and* that changes in orientations towards competition are the easiest to make. Gordon (1991) suggested that the formation of these two orientations is dependent largely on industry-wide assumptions about customers, competitors, and society. Therefore, organizations in the same industry will use similar procedures to implement similar strategies derived from these assumptions. CEOs will be constrained by the cultures in which they develop and reside (cf. Tushman & Romanelli, 1985). Therefore, outside succession of CEOs *within an industry* is no guarantee of new ideas, because the cultures of the two companies (here Ford and Chrysler) will share similar assumptions.

It has been hypothesized that the lack of innovation in most mature, established companies is due to the need to allocate resources to compete with rivals in the same industry and to avoid losses due to experimentation (Svyantek & Hendrick, 1987). Leaders within an industry are constrained by this need to avoid losing against competitors (Svyantek & Hendrick) and, in order to survive, will imitate others in the industry (Gordon, 1991). The result is that CEOs in established industries do not take risks which offer the chance of exceptional return. A pattern of incremental changes imitated by competitors becomes common within an industry. But, as with organizational culture, such advances must be imperfectly imitable in order to offer sustained competitive advantage. Any advances by one company (e.g., the minivan at Chrysler or the use of airbags) are easily imitated by other companies in the industry. An industry, therefore, develops similar patterns of performance on objective measures of performance due to the similar strategies used by CEOs across companies in the industry.

The external environment must be considered as well. Both managerial skill and luck must be accounted for in explanation of firm performance (Barney & Ouchi, 1986). Luck may be better defined as the constellation of internal and external contextual factors in which the leader finds him- or herself. These factors also help determine the range of leadership behavior possible within a situation *and* the range of possible effects of these behaviors. Therefore, no matter how charismatic or visionary the leader, objective performance of a firm is clearly not solely dependent on that leader.

Subjective Criteria of Successful Leaders

The external strategies chosen by Iacocca for Chrysler were based on marketing and advertising (O'Toole, 1985) and easily imitated changes in product lines (e.g., the minivan and airbags). The critical decisions which were made in salvaging Chrysler were not made by Iacocca. The policies were developed by Iacocca's predecessor or mandated as part of the governmental loan program to Chrysler. Iacocca, however, did an excellent job of marketing these policies to internal and external stakeholders of Chrysler. O'Toole (1985) proposed that Iacocca's success was more a function of followership than leadership; people wanted to believe Iacocca was a great leader, and he was. This strategy, while allowing Chrysler to remain afloat and making Iacocca a popular hero in the United States, has not translated into increases in objective measures of performance.

As previously noted, organizational

culture reflects assumptions about how to compete against external rivals and how to manage the internal human resources of a company. Thus, it may be that successful leaders are those who create new assumptions about managing human resources for a company. Their performance would be reflected in subjective measures instead of objective performance criteria.

Therefore, it is possible that somehow Iacocca has galvanized the workforce of Chrysler. This is unlikely, however. Studies of Iacocca and Chrysler's revival (e.g., Reich & Donahue, 1985) do not touch on this aspect. Iacocca has not changed the basic assumptions about how human resources are to be used. In 1985 and 1986, Roger Smith (CEO of GM at the time) created controversy when he paid himself large bonuses while requesting austerity measures from the rank and file (Byrne, 1991a). In 1990, Iacocca increased his total compensation 25% while Chrysler's earnings dropped 79%, and he asked for cost-saving sacrifices from workers (Byrne, 1991b). Iacocca's assumptions about how to manage the human resources of a company seem consistent with that of the American automobile industry.[2]

Conclusions

The resolution of the question of when leadership affects organizational performance and when it does not will require, at a minimum, more in-depth analyses of (a) the specific strategies and behaviors exhibited by a leader, (b) the organization in which the leader resides, (c) the industry in which a leader resides, and (d) events in the environments of the organization and the industry. The use of such a research strategy has shown that leaders commonly accepted as exceptional may not have great impact on objective, organizational performance measures. The nature of subjective perceptions of leadership was touched on as well. It was shown that internal and external perceptions of a leader may not always match. Understanding must be advanced of how these perceptions of leadership are formed. Do we attribute leadership to an individual (such as Iacocca) because he or she makes charismatic commercials? Is the effect of a leader based on form or substantive behavioral differences from other managers? Is leadership a phenomenon of the leader or of the followers? These are issues which must be answered to understand the construct of leadership and its relationship to organizational performance.

Acknowledgments

This research was supported by research grants from the University of Akron Faculty Research Fund and the Ohio Board of Regents Research Challenge Program.

References

Armitage, P. (1971). *Statistical methods in medical research*. Oxford: Blackwell Scientific Publications.

Barney, J. B. (1986). Organizational culture: Can it be a source of sustained competitive advantage? *Academy of Management Review*, 11, 657–665.

Barney, J. B., & Ouchi, W. G. (1986). Evolutionary theory: Questioning managerial impact on firm performance. In J. B. Barney & W. G. Ouchi (Eds.), *Organizational economics* (pp. 299–319). San Francisco: Jossey-Bass.

Barrick, M. B., Day, D. V., Lord, R. G., & Alexander, R. A. (1991). Assessing the utility of executive leadership. *Leadership Quarterly, 2*, 9–22.

Business Week (1971–1988, February, May, August, November). Quarterly reports on American industry.

Byrne, J. A. (1991a, April 15). Salaries at the top finally stop defying gravity. *Business Week*, p. 30.

Byrne, J. A. (1991b, May 6). The flap over executive pay. *Business Week*, pp. 90–96.

Chung, K. H., Lubatkin, M., Rogers, R. C., & Owers, J. E. (1987). Do insiders make better CEOs than outsiders? *Academy of Management Executive, 1*, 325–329.

Campbell, D. T., & Stanley, J. C. (1966). *Experimental and quasi-experimental designs for research*. Chicago: Rand-McNally.

Cook, T. D., & Campbell, D. T. (1979). *Quasi-experimentation: Design and analysis issues for field settings*. Boston: Houghton-Mifflin.

Davis, S. M. (1984). *Managing corporate culture*. Cambridge, MA: Ballinger.

Day, D. V., & Lord, R. G. (1988). Executive leadership and organizational performance: Suggestions for a new theory and methodology. *Journal of Management, 14*, 111–122.

Draper, N. R., & Smith, H. (1981). *Applied regression analysis*. New York: Wiley.

Dumaine, B. (1988, January 4). Donald Peterson: A humble hero drives Ford to the top. *Fortune*, pp. 23–24.

Durbin, J., & Watson, G. S. (1971). Testing for serial correlation in least-squares regression III. *Biometrika, 58*, 1–19.

Fisher, A. B. (1985, December 23). Ford is back on track. *Fortune, 114*, pp. 18–22.

Forbes, (1967–1986, January). Annual report on American industry.

Gordon, G. G. (1991). Industry determinants of culture. *Academy of Management Review, 16*, 396–415.

Halberstam, D. (1986). *The reckoning*. New York: William Morrow.

Kleinbaum, D., & Kupper, L. (1978). *Applied regression analysis and other multivariate methods*. North Scitate, MA: Duxbury.

Komaki, J. L. (1986). Applied behavior analysis and organizational behavior: Reciprocal influence of two fields. In B. M. Staw & L. L. Cummings (Eds.), *Research in organizational behavior* (Vol. 8, pp. 297–334). San Francisco: Jossey-Bass.

Meindl, J. R., & Erlich, S. B. (1987). The romance of leadership and the evaluation of organizational performance. *Academy of Management Journal, 30*, 91–109.

Myers, R. (1988). *Classical and modern regression with applications*. Boston: PWS-Kent.

Nadler, D. A ., & Tushman, M. L. (1990). Beyond the charismatic leader: Leadership and organizational change. *California Management Review, 32*, 77–97.

O'Toole, P. (1985). *Corporate messiah*. New York: New American Library.

Reich, R. B., & Donahue, J. D. (1985). *New Deals: The Chrysler revival and the American system*. New York: Penguin.

Romanelli, E., & Tushman, M. L. (1986). Inertia, environments, and strategic choice: A quasi-experimental design for comparative longitudinal research. *Management Science, 32*, 608–621.

Shook, R. L. (1990). *Turnaround: The new Ford Motor Company*. New York: Prentice-Hall.

Svyantek, D. J., & Hendrick, H. L. (1987). The nature of change: An extension of new developments in evolutionary theory to the study of organizational systems. *Proceedings of the Association of Human Resource Management and Organizational Behavior, I*, 243–247.

Tong, H. (1983). *Threshold models in nonlinear time series analysis*. New York: Springer-Verlag.

White, H. (1980). A heteroscedasticity-consistent covariance matrix estimator and a direct test for heteroscedasticity. *Econometrics, 48*, 817–838.

Yates, B. W. (1983). *The decline and fall of the American automobile industry*. New York: Empire.

Endnotes

1. Ironically, the best performing American carmaker during this period was Ford, the company which Iacocca left to join Chrysler. More ironically, when Iacocca became CEO at Chrysler, he made it a policy to hire as executives individuals he knew from Ford (O'Toole, 1985). He did this both to add to Chrysler's performance and subtract from Ford's performance. Therefore, the executive leadership who have not turned Chrysler around are old Ford people, while the executive leadership who have turned Ford around are individuals who might not be in those positions if Iacocca had remained at Ford. Ford now enjoys a reputation for excellent management and the development of new, innova-

tive automobiles (Yates, 1983). In 1987, for example, Ford was the only American carmaker to increase its market value and market share (Fisher, 1985). Although Ford suffered a short-term loss in the early 1980s after the departure of Iacocca during the general downturn felt by American carmakers from 1980 through 1982, Ford has since been recognized as the comeback story of the 1980s and the world's most profitable car company (Dumaine, 1988).

2. One aspect of the strategy implemented at Ford, however, emphasized the change from a highly autocratic organizational culture to a more participative one (Dumaine, 1988). This change was in the assumption about how to manage human resources (Shook, 1990) and was combined with a commitment to quality and innovative car designs. Ford has been the best performing American automobile company during the 1980s and early 1990s.

Daniel J. Svyantek is Assistant Professor of Industrial-Organizational Psychology at the University of Akron. His research interests include the effects of environments, industry type, organizational culture, and leaders on organizational performance. He has developed new evaluation methods for organizational change efforts and is working on a new method of productivity measurement for use with large-scale organizational change interventions. He received his PhD in Industrial-Organizational Psychology from the University of Houston.

Richard P. DeShon is a PhD candidate in Industrial-Organizational Psychology at the University of Akron. His primary research interests are quantitative assessments of organizational performance, cognitive issues in strategy and decision making, and the development of methods for predicting the likelihood of organizational intervention success.

Direct inquiries about this article to Daniel J. Svyantek, Assistant Professor, Department of Psychology, University of Akron, Akron, OH 44325–4301, 216/972–6705.

CHAPTER 25

Leaders and Transitions
The Role of Leadership in Corporate Name Change

**Mary Ann Glynn and
Joan Slepian**

With organizational name change becoming an increasingly common event, it is interesting to assess the role and impact of leadership in organizations undergoing a renaming. This study contrasts leadership events in 30 firms undergoing a name change against a matched sample of 31 firms not undergoing a name change in the computer and financial services industries. Increased leadership changes and more dramatic leadership changes, such as external successions, were associated with organizational name change. The results indicate that leaders play vital strategic and symbolic roles in affecting organizational change.

When we changed the name, we realized that this wasn't just a matter of taking down one sign and putting up another. What we were doing was changing the institution and its culture. (J. R. McDougal, Chair and CEO, Apple Bank for Savings, 1987, p. 13)

The decision to change a company's name is not trivial: "The selection of a name can be one of the most significant decisions in the creation of the corporate image" (Marquis, 1970, p. 77). Long-familiar corporate names such as United States Steel, International Harvester, and the American Can Company have recently been changed to USX, Navistar, and Primerica, respectively. Proclaimed as "the last word in name recognition," one trucking company renamed itself "G.O.D.," an acronym of its earlier name, Guaranteed Overnight Delivery (Brokaw, 1988). Over the last decade, over 10% of the Fortune 500 companies have changed their legal names (McQuade, 1984). The phenomenon is not limited to Fortune 500 firms; in the 6-year period from 1982–87, nearly 2,000 firms—some large, some small—changed their names. The majority of these firms (78%) attributed the name change to major strategic issues such as mergers, acquisitions, and changes in the organization's business, products, markets, services, and/or geographic locations (Glynn & Slepian, 1990).

Corporate name change seems to signal a profound organizational transformation. For example, when General Radio Company made extensive system-wide changes in 1973 by adopting a marketing-oriented strategy, cutting its product line, and redesigning the organizational structure, it also changed its name to GenRad in order to "more formally symbolize these changes and the sharp move away from the 'old' General Radio" (Tushman, Newman, & Romanelli, 1986, p. 706). These organizational changes were accompanied by leadership changes. GenRad's new President, Bill Thurston, initiated many important changes in the firm. Furthermore, to implement these changes, Thurston "went outside for a set of executives" (Tushman et al., 1986, p. 706) and ushered new officers into the executive suite.

The case of General Radio suggests that changes in organizational names, and the strategic reorientation that a name change implies, are associated with dramatic changes in leadership. Leadership change seems to be a necessary and vital part of any organizational change. Romanelli and Tushman (1988) argue that "leaders have their most profound and important influence on organizational outcomes where pressures for change emerge" (p. 141). During periods of organizational reorientation (Lant & Milliken, 1991; Virany, Tushman, & Romanelli, 1985) and following mergers and acquisitions (Drucker, 1981; Walsh, 1988), executive turnover rates are typically higher. Top management turnover is often a form of organizational adaptation to change (Pfeffer & Moore, 1980; Salancik, Staw, & Pondy, 1980). New leaders can import necessary new knowledge, skills, energy, and strategic perspective into the organization. A change in top management can symbolize the new organizational direction represented by the new corporate name. Executive turnover often facilitates organizational change because new leaders have less psychological investment in the organization's past strategic stance (Milliken & Lant, 1991) and may encourage the organization to "unlearn" past routines that would hamper an organizational transformation (Nystrom & Starbuck, 1984).

In an organization undergoing a name change, the leadership function is both strategic and symbolic. Bolman and Deal (1991) propose that effective leaders typically employ multiple views or frames in the way they think and act in the organization. For an organization undergoing a name change, effective leaders probably use at least two of the frames proposed by Bolman and Deal: the "structural" frame, which involves strategic goal setting and planning, and the "symbolic" frame, which involves creating and managing the institution's identity and symbols. The symbolic role of leadership in managing change is "to provide explanations, rationalizations, and legitimation for the activities undertaken in the organization" (Pfeffer, 1981, p. 4). By articulating their vision of the new organization, leaders drive corporate transformations (Tichy & Devanna, 1986). Leaders should be involved in building commitment to the new corporate identity. John Diefenbach, President of Landor Associates, cogently summarizes the relationship: "Behind a name change always lies the passion of one person, usually the chief executive" (McQuade, 1984, p. 250).

One purpose of this research is to establish the association of leadership change with organizational name change, as suggested in the literature. The rate of leadership change is expected to be higher in organizations undergoing a name change than in comparable organizations not undergoing a name change.

A second purpose of this research is to investigate the nature of executive succession associated with a name change. A corporate name change suggests that a fundamental organizational reorientation may be taking place. During organizational reorientations, executive turnover is more severe in nature: External succession is more frequent than internal promotion (Virany et al., 1985). A persistent theme resonates in the management succession literature: "Organizational outsiders are more likely to make changes as they take charge than insiders" (Gabarro, 1988, p. 248). Because organizational renaming generally involves major organizational changes, organizations undergoing a name change may tend to bring in more leaders from outside the organization (external succession) than to promote leaders from within (internal succession). Executives who enter an organization undergoing a name change are expected to be organizational outsiders. This study examined the relationship of external succession to organizational name change. More change and more discontinuous change in the top management team is believed to characterize firms undergoing a name change.

Research Methods

Data Sources

Companies that changed their names in 1986 and 1987 were identified using annual volumes of *Predicasts F & S Index of Corporate Change* (1986, 1987), which contains lists of organizations that amended their corporate charter to change their legal names. *Predicasts Company Thesaurus* (1986, 1987) was used to obtain 5-digit SIC Industry Codes for these firms in order to classify them by industry. Fifteen firms in the computer industry and 16 firms in financial services were randomly selected. These two industries were chosen for the study because an examination of leadership events in two very different environmental contexts would enhance the generalizability of results.

This group of 31 firms (labelled "Name Change" or "NC" firms) was matched with a corresponding group of 31 firms (14 computer firms and 16 financial services firms) that did not change their name in the period 1984–1989 (labelled "non-Name Change" or "non-NC" firms). Bogus name change dates were randomly assigned to firms in the non-NC group in the same proportion as their appearance in the NC group. This was done to control for potential effects of the year of the name change in assessing differences in leadership changes between the NC and non-NC firms. For the total sample of 62 firms, information was obtained on the number of executives per company, mean executive tenure, and the arrival and exit of members of the executive constellation (Chair, CEO, and President) for each company for each year for the period 1984–1989 (N = 374 company years). Executive background information, including his/her organizational position/title, tenure, and type of succession (internal vs. external) was collected for each executive (N = 130 executives) from the following sources: Datext, Dun & Bradstreet's Reference Guide to Corporate Management, Who's Who in Banking (1971 edition), Corporate 10K's and annual reports, and various industry and trade journals.

Variables

Name change firms. NC firms were identified by *Predicasts F&S Index* (1986, 1987). The period of the name change, or the time firms were considered to be undergoing a name change, was defined as the 5-year interval surrounding and including the date of the name change. For firms that changed their name in 1986, the period under study is 1984–1988; for firms that changed their name in 1987, the period under study is 1985–1989.

Leadership change. Leadership change refers to a change in occupancy of any one of the three positions in the executive constellation (Chair, CEO, President) during the name change period.

Succession type. An external succession event is defined as one in which an executive was brought into the organization from the outside; an internal succession event is one in which an executive was promoted from within the organization (Gabarro, 1988).

Creating a Matched Sample of NC and Non-NC Firms

The non-NC group of firms was matched to the NC group of firms by industry segment (firm's 5-digit SIC code), size (sales in 1986), and performance (Earnings Per Share (EPS) in 1986). It was important to control for these organizational characteristics because executive turnover has been related to firm size (Grusky, 1964) and performance (Allen, Panion, & Lotz, 1979; Lubatkin, Chung, Rogers, & Owers, 1989).

For the 5-year interval surrounding the name change event, there were no significant differences in organizational size $(t(80.7) = 0.94)$ or performance $(t(104.9) = 0.85)$ between the NC and non-NC groups of firms.

Description of Leadership Changes

Since all firms in the sample did not use the same titles for executives and did not have all three executive positions (Chair, CEO, and President) occupied for each year of the study, the number of individuals in the executive constellation varied across firms. However, there was not a significant difference in the mean number of executives between the NC firms $(M = 2.67)$ and the non-NC firms $(M = 2.33; t(49) = 1.10)$.

A leadership change was coded if there was a change in any member of the executive constellation. Table 1 reports the frequency of leadership changes by types of executive position. Of the organizations that changed their leadership, approximately 75% changed the President, 50% changed the Chair, and 37% changed the CEO. Nearly half the organizations (46.8%) made changes in two or more of these positions simultaneously. There was not a significant difference in the distributions of these changes across executive positions between the NC and the non-NC firms (Chi-Square (3) = 0.35).

Industry Effects

Exploratory analyses were conducted to determine if there were industry effects on the relevant leadership variables. It was important to do this because differences in an industry's environmental uncertainty and munificence have the potential to affect leadership change in organizations (Virany et al., 1985). Environmental uncertainty, which describes the extent to which future states of the environment can be anticipated or accurately predicted (Pfeffer & Salancik, 1978), was assessed using Tushman and Anderson's (1986) measure of Forecast Error (FE); higher FE values indicate greater environmental uncertainty. Mean FE was significantly higher for the computer industry $(M = 105.11)$ than for the financial services industry $(M = 4.59; t(44) = 28.52, p < .0001)$. Environmental munificence, which describes the extent to which an environment can support future growth (Tushman & Anderson, 1986), was measured by assessing mean sales growth for the firms by industry over time. For the period under study (1984–1989), mean sales for firms in the financial services group $(M = \$370.73 \text{ mil})$ were significantly greater than for those in the computer group $(M = \$95.82 \text{ mil}; t(96.3) = 2.39, p < .05)$. Thus, firms in the two industries operated in very different environmental contexts in 1986–1987: The computer industry was characterized by relatively higher environmental uncertainty and lower munificence than financial services.

Differences by industry were examined

TABLE 1 Leadership Changes by Executive Position

Position	Number of Executives (N = 130)	% All Firms (N = 62)	% Non-NC Firms (N = 31)	% NC Firms (N = 31)
Chair	31	50.0	50.0	50.0
CEO	23	37.1	40.6	33.3
President	47	75.8	78.1	73.3
Combinations:	29	46.8	53.1	40.0
Chair/CEO	3	4.8	6.2	3.3
Chair/Pres	7	11.3	15.6	6.7
CEO/Pres	9	14.5	15.6	13.3
Chair/CEO/Pres	10	16.1	15.6	16.7

in the number of executives per organization (M [computers] = 2.29; M [financial services] = 2.62); mean executive tenure (M [computers] = 6.72; M [financial services] = 8.03); and in the frequency of leadership changes (67% for computers; 68% for financial services), internal succession (56% for computers; 60% for financial services), and external succession (44% for computers; 40% for financial services). There were no statistically significant differences by industry (all t's < 0.50).

Given the lack of industry effects on relevant leadership variables, industry explanations for any observed differences in leadership changes can be eliminated. Consequently, firm data across industries were combined to conduct the analyses.

Results

In the 5-year interval surrounding the name change, 82% of the name change firms experienced leadership changes, while only 57% of the non-name change firms experienced leadership changes; this difference is statistically significant (Z = 2.10, p < .05). Changing an organi-

zation's name involves changing its leadership as well.

An exploratory analysis was conducted on a subsample of 18 firms which changed both their name and their leadership to determine if executive changes occurred before, during, or after the year of the name change. Leadership changes occurred in the same year as the name change for 44% of the firms. However, leadership change also occurred in the period prior to the name change in 17% of the firms and in the period following the name change in 28% of the firms. In 11% of the organizations, leadership changes occurred both before and after the name change. This evidence suggests that leadership change most often occurs (72% of the time) during or shortly following a name change. However, a goodness-of-fit test (following Siegel, 1956, pp. 42–47) did not reveal a significant difference in the frequency of leadership changes by temporal period (Chi-Square (3) = 4.67). While it was not possible to establish a clear causal link between name changes and leadership changes, the findings suggest that leadership changes and name changes are fairly contemporaneous outcomes of a broader, underlying process of strategic organizational change.

Types of succession events (internal vs. external) for executives in the NC and

TABLE 2 Executive Succession by NC and Non-NC Firms

	External Succession	Internal Succession
Number of executives assuming leadership positions in:		
Non-Name Change Firms	12 (52.2%)	11 (47.8%)
Name Change Firms	23 (92.0%)	2 (8.0%)

non-NC firms are reported in Table 2. In NC firms, external successors assumed leadership positions more often (92%) than did internal successors (8%); in non-NC firms, internal successors (47.8%) assumed leadership positions with nearly the same frequency as external successors (52.2%). The pattern of succession types by types of firms shown in Table 2 is significant (Chi-Square (1) = 9.62, p < .01).

Implications

This study indicates that firms undergoing a name change changed their leadership more frequently and more radically than firms not undergoing a name change. The results offer clear evidence of the link between organizational leadership and symbolic change. The corporate name is a visible and potent organizational symbol; as part of the organizational language, it represents a form of symbolic action (Pfeffer, 1981). While the results do not suggest that the visionary leader always directs the renaming process, it was obvious that leaders were involved in managing important changes in organizational symbolism and identity.

Schein (1985) suggests that executives insure organizational survival and integration primarily by their impact on the organizational culture. While performance effects associated with a name change were not assessed, there is existing evidence that symbolic changes do affect organizational outcomes. Empirical research has demonstrated that name changes are associated with improved organizational performance (Argenti, Hansen, & Neslin, 1988; Horsky & Swyngeduow, 1987). This study further suggests that these outcomes may be influenced by new leadership.

In addition, the association between leadership change and name change is consonant with evolutionary theories of the firm. During major upheavals or reorientations, firms tend to replace key executives with outsiders; it is rare that an organization undergoes dramatic changes, including a name change, with existing leadership at the helm (Tushman et al., 1986). One explanation for this relationship between leadership and organizational change lies in the role of managerial interpretations. Lant and Milliken (1991) found that strategic reorientations were significantly affected by managers' awareness of environmental changes and their attributions of organizational success and failure. This suggests that the interpretation and explanation of an organizational name change by leaders to key internal and external constituencies is an important component of organizational renaming and reorienting.

Conclusions

It is apparent that an organizational name change demands both substantive and symbolic managerial leadership. Two corporate executives describe the management challenge that attended the transition from International Harvester to Navistar: "What seemed initially to be a relatively simple project of changing a name quickly became the challenge of developing a new identity for a 150-year-old corporation with worldwide recognition" (Decyk & McDonald, 1987).

These findings indicate that name change involves an important and active role for an organization's leadership. The results reinforce the work of other researchers (Bolman & Deal, 1991; Drucker, 1981; Pfeffer, 1981; Virany et al., 1985) who emphasize the real and symbolic value of leadership change in managing corporate identity and strategically redirecting an organization. Changing the name means changing the institution; one way in which the institution changes is by its leadership. Managing the newly christened enterprise represents a real challenge for the organizational leadership but, in the long run, should also revitalize the organization and its members. The findings of this study highlight the importance of this managerial challenge.

Acknowledgments

The authors wish to thank Bob Gann, Frances Milliken, and Victor Vroom for their assistance, encouragement, and support.

References

Allen, M., Panion, S., & Lotz, R. (1979). Managerial succession and organizational performance: A recalcitrant problem revisited. *Administrative Science Quarterly, 24*, 167–180.

Argenti, P., Hansen, R., & Neslin, S. (1988). The name game: How corporate name changes affect stock price. *Tuck Today, 17*, 20–27.

Bolman, L. G., & Deal, T. E. (1991). *Reframing organizations: Artistry, choice and leadership*. San Francisco: Jossey-Bass.

Brokaw, L. (April, 1988). The miracle of the name. *INC.*, p. 14.

Decyk, R. J., & McDonald, J. D. (1987). The campaign as case study: Navistar. In M. Simpson (Ed.), *Corporate identity: Name, image and perception* (pp. 17–18). New York: The Conference Board, Inc.

Drucker, P. (1981, October 15). The five rules of successful acquisition. *The Wall Street Journal*, p. 28.

Gabarro, J. J. (1988). Executive leadership and succession: The process of taking charge. In D.C. Hambrick (Ed.), *The Executive Effect* (pp. 237–268). Greenwich, CT: JAI Press.

Glynn, M. A., & Slepian, J. (1990). *An organization by any other name: An examination of institutionalization and adaptation over time*. Paper presented at the annual meeting of the Academy of Management, San Francisco.

Grusky, O. (1964). Reply to scapegoating in baseball. *American Journal of Sociology, 70*, 72–76.

Horsky, D., & Swyngeduow, P. (1987). Does it pay to change your company's name? A stock market perspective. *Marketing Science, 6(4)*, 320–335.

Lant, T. K., & Milliken, F. J. (1991). *An empirical exploration of the determinants of strategic persistence and reorientation* (Working Paper No. Mgt:91.1). New York: New York University.

Lubatkin, M., Chung, K., Rogers, R., & Owers, J. (1989). Stockholder reactions to CEO changes in large corporations. *Academy of Management Journal, 32(1)*, 47–68.

Marquis, H. H. (1970). *The changing corporate image*. New York: American Management Association.

McDougal, J. R. (1987). The underlying strategic decisions. In M. Simpson (Ed.), *Corporate identity: Name, image and perception* (pp. 12–13). New York: The Conference Board, Inc.

McQuade, W. (1984, April 30). Cosmetic surgery for the company name. *Fortune*, 249–250.

Milliken, F. J., & Lant, T. K. (1991). The effect of an organization's recent performance history on strategic persistence and change: The role of managerial interpretations. In J. Dutton, A. Huff, & P. Shrivastava (Eds.), *Advances in Strategic Management* (Vol. 7, pp. 125–152). Greenwich, CT: JAI Press.

Nystrom, P. C., & Starbuck, W. H. (1984). To avoid organizational crises: Unlearn. *Organizational Dynamics*, 12(4), 53–65.

Pfeffer, J. (1981). Management as symbolic action: The creation and maintenance of organizational paradigms. In L.L. Cummings & B.M. Staw (Eds.), *Research in organizational behavior* (Vol. 3, pp. 1–52). Greenwich, CT: JAI Press.

Pfeffer, J., & Moore, W. L. (1980). Average tenure of academic department heads: The effects of paradigm, size, and departmental philosophy. *Administrative Science Quarterly*, 25, 387–406.

Pfeffer, J., & Salancik, G. (1978). *The external control of organizations*. New York: Harper & Row.

Predicasts F & S Index of Corporate Change (Vols. 22–23). (1986, 1987). Cleveland: Predicasts.

Predicasts Company Thesaurus (Vols. 7–8). (1986, 1987). Cleveland: Predicasts.

Romanelli, E., & Tushman, M. L. (1988). Executive leadership and organizational outcomes: An evolutionary perspective. In D.C. Hambrick (Ed.), *The Executive Effect* (pp. 129–146). Greenwich, CT: JAI Press.

Salancik, G. R., Staw, B. M., & Pondy, L. R. (1980). Administrative turnover as a response to unmanaged organizational interdependence. *Academy of Management Journal*, 23, 422–437.

Schein, E. H. (1985). *Organizational culture and leadership*. San Francisco: Jossey-Bass.

Siegel, S. (1956). *Nonparametric statistics for the behavioral sciences*. New York: McGraw-Hill.

Tichy, N., & Devanna, M. (1986). *The transformational leader*. New York: Wiley.

Tushman, M. L., & Anderson, P. (1986). Technological discontinuities and organizational environments. *Administrative Science Quarterly*, 31, 439–465.

Tushman, M. L., Newman, W. H., & Romanelli, E. (1986). Convergence and upheaval: Managing the unsteady pace of organizational evolution. In M. L. Tushman & W. L. Moore (Eds.), *Readings in the management of innovation* (pp. 705–717). Cambridge, MA: Ballinger.

Virany, B., Tushman, M., & Romanelli, E. (1985). A longitudinal study of the determinants and effects of executive succession. In R. Robinson & J. Pearce (Eds.), *Proceedings of the Academy of Management* (pp. 186–190). Madison, WI: Omnipress.

Walsh, J. (1988). Top management turnover following mergers and acquisitions. *Strategic Management Journal*, 9, 173–183.

Mary Ann Glynn is an Assistant Professor of Organizational Behavior in the School of Organization and Management at Yale University. Her research interests focus on cognitive processes in organizational contexts. She has authored several journal articles and her book, *Contemporary Management: An Integrative Approach*, co-authored with Paul Berney and Gary Brewer, will be published in 1993. She earned her PhD at Columbia University.

Joan Slepian is a PhD candidate in Organizational Behavior in the School of Organization and Management at Yale University. Her research interests include organizational learning, group dynamics, and belief structures.

Direct inquiries about this article to Mary Ann Glynn, Assistant Professor, School of Organization and Management, Yale University, Box 1A, New Haven, CT 06520, 203/432-6008.

Novice Leaders, Novel Behaviors, and Strong Culture
Promoting Leadership Change beyond the Classroom

Rex J. Blake and
Earl H. Potter III

Effective leadership is generally assumed to be essential to the success of organizations, but it is not the only factor which determines the performance of an organization's members. Furthermore, an organization's "success" is likely to depend on a number of other variables — employee commitment, loyalty, satisfaction, and attrition — in addition to performance. Expensive training efforts aimed at reshaping the leadership style of an organization may or may not have a substantial impact on any of these variables. This paper presents a case study of an effort to change the leadership culture of an organization which recognized that its existing leadership behaviors were detrimental to the achievement of its objectives. The cornerstone of the intervention was a week-long leadership training program based on behavioral modeling principles. Change did not come easily and was evident only after system interventions were made to support the transfer of behaviors learned in the classroom. Survey-based data provided evidence of behavior change and suggested that the impact of particular behaviors varied across a set of subjective and objective outcome criteria.

People are concerned about the quality of leadership in their organizations for a number of reasons. Flagging American competitiveness may be the most notable reason, but changes in the environment within which leaders must lead are more significant. Flatter organizations, technological advances, and self-managed teams demand that leaders and followers find new ways of working together. With all that has been written about leadership, it is not hard to say what we want — the problem is getting it. What do you do when you recognize that the culture of your organization supports a style of leadership that works against your best interests? Can you change the day-to-day behavior of leaders? And, if you are successful in changing leaders' behavior, what will be the impact of the new behaviors in your organization? Is a change in their followers' performance the only or even the most important index of success?

In this paper, we examine one effort to shape leadership behavior within the context of a strong organizational culture which had long supported a different style of leadership. This is as much a paper about cultural change as it is about leadership. And, while we will not address directly the political aspects of change, it should be obvious that someone saw the changes in the external and internal environments of the organization, recognized a need to steer the culture in a new direction, and secured the support of the people "at the top" of the organization for the introduction of something new and different. Thus, vision, as always, was the step that opened the way to change.

The Organization and Its Leadership Culture

As our model, we chose an organization which stereotypically is not easy to change—a military academy. As a class of institutions, the academies exist for the purpose of shaping leaders. The peculiar cultures of academies and the military are more conservative and their overall style of leadership is more directive, but the recognition of a need to change places them in the company of other organizations that are trying to increase employee involvement and commitment. Growing awareness that leadership development is one of the tasks of undergraduate education has meant that academies now have much more in common with colleges and universities than they once did. The military academies' traditions are embodied in a culture that is more than 200 years old. In this regard they resemble other organizations whose strong traditions shape the character of their leadership. So, rather than seeing this example as unique, we see it as a "tough case" and believe that success here should bode well for any who hope to change the leadership culture in their organizations.

Each summer, a group of young women and men enter the U.S. Coast Guard Academy. Most have graduated from high school less than a month before. For the next 7 weeks, they participate in a program intended to assimilate them into the Coast Guard. The experience has features common to most indoctrination pro-

grams. Activities focus on the acquisition and practice of important aspects of Coast Guard culture—customs, courtesies, language, norms, and values. Identification with the group is promoted; rewards accrue to individuals primarily as a result of their contribution to the group's success in various sports and military competitions. Physical activity and fitness are emphasized.

At the military academies, however, the indoctrination program for the new students or "cadets" is intended to help fulfill an additional objective. The new cadets provide the opportunity for more senior cadets to practice leadership skills. In other military accession programs—at enlisted basic training programs ("boot camp") and officer candidate schools— training is conducted by experienced, hand-picked, and well-trained commissioned and noncommissioned officers, carefully selected on the basis of *demonstrated* leadership ability. At the academies, indoctrination is conducted by cadets in their junior year, limited in experience and only 2 years senior to first-year students or "fourth class" cadets. For these more senior or upper class cadets, the process of indoctrinating new cadets is intended to help them *develop* leadership skills. It is a leadership practicum; for most, it constitutes their first leadership role in a military context.

The degree to which this leadership experience contributes to the development of effective military leaders at the nation's service academies is questionable (Campbell, 1987). Some have argued that the practice of assigning young, inexperienced leaders to conduct an "initiation" of members new to the organization may actually promote behaviors antithetical to the development of effective leadership and supervisory skills. In the mid-1980s, the U.S. Coast Guard Academy was confronted with survey data suggesting that, while its graduates were adequately prepared to assume their duties in a variety of technical areas (e.g., navigation, engineering, etc.), they had difficulty performing supervisory functions. This feedback prompted a look at the cadets' behaviors in leadership roles at the academy. During the summer training program, we found behaviors that would have met few people's definition of "leadership." The upper class cadets were verbally abusive, subjected their followers to individual humiliation and public embarrassment, and relied almost exclusively on punishment (especially physical punishment) as a means of influencing behavior.

A number of factors appeared to contribute to the prevalence of these behaviors. The first was the supervising cadets' own definition of the nature of the summer training event. Asked about their role, the upper class cadets did not talk about leadership. Instead, they focused solely on the entering cadets and defined the summer as an "initiation" or "rite of passage" for the newest cadets. Their objective was to make it difficult for the initiates, to test their motivation and resolve, to "weed out" those who were different, unqualified for membership in the organization, unsure of themselves, and who did not belong. They expended little effort on providing clear and complete directions for task accomplishment or on thoroughly teaching their subordinates the requisite skills for successful task accomplishment. The upper class cadets made poor performance virtually inevitable, characteristically attributed the poor performance to a "bad attitude" on the part of the performer, and punished the performer accordingly. The degree to which the subordinate continued to expend effort in the pursuit of impossible task accomplishment was deemed evidence of his/her motivation to become an officer. Overall, the upper class cadets' behaviors clearly seemed intended to diminish rather than promote their followers' performance and satisfaction.

Second, the staff and faculty of the academy, perhaps inadvertently, lent support to the cadets' perception of the summer program's objective. Despite enacting prohibitions against physical abuse and the most serious examples of hazing during the early 1970s, the academy staff nevertheless maintained a laissez-faire policy toward the supervision and direction of the upper class cadets during the summer program. The upper class cadets were supervised only by former cadets who had graduated less than two months before; more senior staff members paid little attention to the events taking place in the barracks unless something truly deviant occurred. The upper class cadets were tacitly given a role as experts in charge of the training of the new cadets; little emphasis was placed on their own role as leadership trainees. This tacit support reflected a significant ambivalence about the appropriateness of the cadets' leadership style. There were faculty members who argued that abuse and harassment were essential to indoctrinate the newest members of the organization. It was specifically argued that upper class cadets who were harsh and created an adversarial relationship with the trainees would engender increased group cohesiveness and inspire teamwork. Additionally, harsh treatment was said to actually make the training experience more rewarding; it tested trainees' limits and showed them what they were capable of achieving. Individuals would graduate from the training program with a greater sense of accomplishment and self-knowledge. Thus, while the academy had undertaken some earlier efforts to change the upper class cadets' leadership behaviors, the efforts were limited and largely unsuccessful; the organization's "will" to change was not clear.

Third, Bandura (1971, 1973, 1977) has presented substantial evidence of the role played by behavioral modeling processes in the acquisition of behavior. Two years after their initiation, the "initiates" become the "initiators." As available research suggests, they generally imitate the behavior of those who initiated them, that is, the credible, successful, expert cadets they encountered when they first entered the organization. Combined with the influence of similar models provided by television and movies and the absence of alternative models of leadership in this context, role modeling increased the chances that the prevalent leadership behaviors would remain relatively consistent from one year to the next.

Finally, cadets have much in common with other novice supervisors who rely on punishment to shape the behavior of their subordinates. After reviewing the literature, Podsakoff (1982) tentatively identified a number of factors affecting supervisors' use of rewards and punishments. First, consistent with what might have been expected, supervisors tended to punish low performers and reward high performers. By definition, entering cadets are low performers in the eyes of their supervisors. Second, Podsakoff found the following:

> Supervisors who have less experience and self-confidence, or who feel that their behavior is more externally controlled, tend to rely more on the use of punishment. Third, leaders with a greater span of control tend to spend less time with problem workers and to use punishment more than do leaders with narrower spans of control. Fourth, leaders punish more for poor performance when it is perceived to result from a lack of motivation rather than a lack of ability or task difficulty, or when it is perceived to be dispositionally as opposed to situationally produced. (p. 76)

This amounts to a fairly succinct description of the cadets and their situation.

In summary, the leadership behaviors of the first-line supervisors at this military academy were enmeshed in a strong culture which ensured their maintenance. Previous efforts to influence leadership styles and substitute alternative behaviors were limited and regularly unsuccessful. The matrix of belief and habit led to a repeating cycle of abusive supervisory behavior. Similarly enmeshed in the culture, the academy's senior management was not persuaded of the need for change until faced with external evidence of the ineffectiveness of the current training program. Given these circumstances, it seemed unlikely that merely participating in this culture would cause/allow the cadets to spontaneously discover and begin to practice new leadership behaviors on their own. Therefore, when senior management did determine to change, we first took steps to overhaul the leadership education and training program—to supplement the cadets' experiences with a more structured and formal introduction to basic leadership principles and skills.

A Leadership Training Program—Initial Efforts

With ample opportunity to observe the cadets in supervisory roles, it was relatively simple to identify problematic behaviors. Most problems occurred in the context of direct interpersonal relations with the fourth-class cadets and included behaviors intended to both direct and provide consequences for performance. With that circumscribed catalogue of concerns, we chose an operant conceptualization of the leadership/supervisory role as the foundation for a training program.

Operant models of leadership are focused on a subset of the larger domain of leadership tasks and functions. Their focus is limited to supervisory behavior—the leaders' interpersonal efforts to influence the behavior of followers toward the accomplishment of work-related goals (Komaki, 1986; Scott, 1977; Sims, 1977). Three categories of behavior generally form the basis of operant taxonomies of supervisory activities. According to Komaki, Zlotnick, and Jensen (1986), these include "performance antecedents (providing instructions about performance), performance monitors (collecting performance information), and performance consequences (indicating knowledge of performance)" (p. 260). Regarding prescriptions based on operant models of supervisory behavior, Komaki et al. state:

> Although operant conditioning theory per se does not contain an explicit model of an

ideal manager, it was inferred that an effective manager would make appropriate behaviors clear, accurately and fairly appraise performance, and regularly provide consequences contingent on performance. An ineffective manager, on the other hand, would probably leave tasks ambiguously defined, appraise performance sporadically, if at all, and provide infrequent or non-contingent consequences for performance. (p. 260)

Based primarily on operant models of leadership, a number of authors have extrapolated more extensive guidelines for supervisors' application of "positive discipline" or "positive motivation" (Arvey & Ivancevich, 1980; Haimann & Hilgert, 1977; Preston & Zimmerer, 1978; Schoen & Durand, 1979; White, 1975; Yukl, 1989). These prescriptions formed the basis of a week-long, 40-hour curriculum emphasizing a variety of specific supervisory skills organized into an operant chronology. The program was inaugurated in the summer of 1987. A textbook for the course was based on one written 2 years earlier for a leadership program at the U.S. Air Force Academy (Rosebush, 1985).

Instruction focused first on performance antecedents, emphasizing the need for clear communications, clear articulation of priorities, full explanation of tasks, and the modeling of correct task performance for complex psychomotor tasks. In response to performance, the curriculum emphasized the need for accurate diagnosis or analysis of performance (especially poor performance) before attributing causes of performance to internal (ability, motivation) or external (luck, degree of task difficulty, adequacy of training provided) causes and administering consequences. Instructors discussed with cadet supervisors the range of consequences available, their potential impact on performance and satisfaction, and the decision to reinforce or punish to encourage behavior change. The curriculum introduced, for example, the notion of positively reinforcing successive approx-

imations of desired performance. Instructors also encouraged increased support of the cadets' subordinates and increased individual, routine contact with subordinates under circumstances other than the administration of punishment.

The actual process of instruction relied heavily on behavioral modeling. During the week, instructors described and modeled the components in a classroom setting. The students then practiced basic skills in role playing exercises, viewed their performance on videotape, and received individual feedback from peers and instructors.

Following the classroom introduction, the students were directed to apply the model during their training of the new cadets. Our informal observations during the remainder of that summer, however, suggested that the cadets failed to do so; their behaviors seemed indistinguishable from those we had seen the year before. They were negative, abusive, and continued to intentionally create no-win situations for their followers. Follow-up interviews with the cadets (as well as discussions that had occurred during the training) indicated that the persistence of these behaviors may have had less to do with skill deficits than with a resilient conceptualization of their role as directors of an initiation. Furthermore, and most significantly, we discovered that the recent graduates assigned as intermediate supervisors had willfully refused to reinforce the behaviors taught in the leadership program.

Completing the Program

The following year, in addition to the emphasis on skill building, greater attention was paid to reframing the organization's goals for the summer program and the upper class cadets' role in accomplishing those goals. Briefly, they were told explicitly that their role was that of *student* leaders. The purpose of the summer training program was to give them an opportunity to practice these leadership skills; they could expect to be observed, to receive feedback, and to be evaluated and graded on their performance. As concrete demonstration of the organization's commitment to these objectives, the cadets' performance evaluation forms were rewritten to incorporate a set of behaviorally anchored rating scales exactly matching the supervisory dimensions they had practiced in class. Instead of recent graduates, faculty members, each with some 8 to 15 years of experience in the Coast Guard, were assigned to oversee the summer training program. Each faculty member met daily with six student leaders to continue the process of guiding, monitoring, and reinforcing effective leadership behavior.

Now more than a simple classroom training exercise, the effort to establish this leadership program became an effort to reshape the organization's culture. It began with the recognition by senior management that the existing culture did not support effective leadership. It eventually required that the organization's goals be clearly articulated and that the contribution that each member was expected to make to the accomplishment of those goals be described in detail. It relied on a team of change leaders and coaches who taught new behaviors and reinforced their development. Finally, it depended on the realignment of reward structures to support and maintain new leadership styles.

Assessing the Impact of the Program

Contemporary leadership theories are generally consistent concerning the effects we could expect if the cadet leaders' behaviors changed in the desired direction. Path-goal (House, 1971; House & Mitchell, 1974), social exchange (Hollander, 1978), and operant (Scott, 1977; Sims, 1977) models of leadership all suggest that fair, equitable rewards and punishments, valued by the subordinate and delivered contingent on performance, are more likely to produce desirable subordinate behaviors and positive attitudes.

Available research contrasting contingent and noncontingent reward and punishment behaviors by supervisors has produced data consistent with these notions (e.g., Arvey, Davis, & Nelson, 1984; Podsakoff, Todor, & Skov, 1982) and has raised questions as well. While not perfectly analogous to the harassment that goes on at the academy, noncontingent punishment seems to represent a similar phenomenon in civilian organizations. Podsakoff, Todor, and Skov (1982) defined noncontingent punishment as "the degree to which a supervisor uses punitive events independent of the performance levels of his/her subordinates" (p. 811). Their data indicated a negative relationship between the supervisor's noncontingent punitive behavior and subordinates' satisfaction with work and with the supervisor. Arvey, Davis, and Nelson (1984) also investigated supervisors' use of discipline and employed a number of similar constructs, distinguishing between supervisors who were "quite 'mature' and consistent in their application of discipline" and others who used discipline "in rather arbitrary, inappropriate, and inconsistent ways" (p. 453). Arvey et al. found the perceived punitive behaviors of the supervisors to be related to satisfaction with the supervisor: "To the extent that supervisors are abusive and childish in their application of discipline, are inconsistent in their application of discipline, are apt to use informal punishers, and are not supportive of their employees, employees express dissatisfaction with them" (p. 456). However, neither punitive nor reward behaviors of supervisors demonstrated a significant relationship to overall job satisfaction, leading Arvey et al. to suggest the possibility of other variables in the job context as more important determinants of job satisfaction.

These findings highlight the risk of assuming that a relationship exists between particular leadership behavior and a particular organizational outcome or that, once found, such a relationship would automatically generalize from one organization's context to another. Therefore, anticipating the specific impacts of changed leadership behavior at the academy is problematic. It is conceivable that military indoctrination represents a very different set of organizational conditions and that there is something about either the environment, the individuals involved, or both, that is different in important ways from the civilian organizations studied by Arvey et al. (1984). For example, noncontingent punishment presumably constitutes an exceptional and infrequent behavior in civilian organizations; at the Coast Guard Academy in 1987, it occupied center stage, a de rigueur technique for the socialization of young men and women. Much of the impact of such behavior should depend on what the behavior means to subordinates; it may not be the case that military initiates would interpret the behavior in the same way as civilian employees. Furthermore, there are likely to be other important differences — in the values and interests of the subordinates, the availability of other rewards in the work environment, the nature of the work itself, the quality of relationships within the work group, and so on — that would have effects on individuals' performance and satisfaction independent of leaders' behaviors. At the academy, satisfaction, commitment, retention, and performance could have a variety of more powerful determinants than the leadership behaviors of upper class cadets. We depended on this outcomes analysis both to validate our observations that leadership behavior had changed and to determine the impact of those changes on entering cadets. The result was by no means clear from an a priori application of the research literature.

Method

Subjects

Entering classes range in size from 250 to 320 students. Students are selected by the Coast Guard Academy on a competitive basis, weighing prior academic performance, standardized achievement test scores, and extent of participation in sports, student government, and other extracurricular activities. Unlike the other military academies, congressional nominations are not required. Virtually all cadets are from 18 to 20 years of age. Twenty percent of the cadets are women.

The samples consist of 220 cadets who completed the indoctrination program during the summer of 1987 and 280 cadets who entered in the summer of 1990. The academy's admissions policies remained consistent throughout this period. From 1980 through 1986, attrition during the 8-week period of swab summer ranged from 10 to 16% of the entering class (mean = 12.5%). During the summer of 1987, 14.5% of the cadets resigned before the end of the summer; in 1990, the attrition rate was 6.9%.

Survey

Each sample group completed a survey 8 to 10 weeks after the end of the swab summer training program, during the fall academic term. Some members of each class were not surveyed due to their participation in intercollegiate sports events or scheduling conflicts with other academic or military obligations. There seemed to be no systematic pattern to these absences that would have biased the results. Cadets in both groups were told that the survey's purpose was to collect data for research and curriculum development. The cadets in the 1987 sample completed the survey anonymously; no effort was made to match survey forms with particular individuals. In 1990, however, we asked the cadets to include their identification number on the back of the form and assured them that their responses would be kept confidential.

The survey was prepared in the summer of 1987. The item content was based largely on a survey developed at the U.S. Air Force Academy to assess various components of their Positive Motivation curriculum (Rosebush, 1985), with items added to address areas of interest peculiar to the Coast Guard Academy. When completed, the various components of the questionnaire were as follows:

1. Behavior of upper class leaders. This section included 25 items eliciting the fourth-class cadets' perceptions of the frequency with which the upper class cadets exhibited certain behaviors (e.g., "My platoon cadre criticized poor work," "My platoon cadre expressed appreciation when one of us did a good job," "My platoon cadre explained their actions," "My platoon cadre demanded more than we could do," etc.). Responses to these items were made on a 5-point scale (1 = never, 5 = always).

2. Evaluation of leaders' effectiveness. Unlike the descriptive items above, an additional set of five items could be characterized as primarily evaluative, asking for the respondents' reaction to the upper class cadre or an appraisal of the effectiveness of their leadership (e.g., "My platoon cadre were admired and respected by the cadets in my platoon," "My platoon cadre treated the fourth-class cadets like responsible adults," "My platoon cadre were good teachers," etc.). Responses to these items were made on a 6-point scale (1 = strongly disagree, 6 = strongly agree).

3. The cohesiveness or "climate" in the platoon. Rootman (1971) offered data suggesting that the degree of subjective interpersonal "fit" with other members of the platoon was strongly related to a cadet's decision to resign from the academy during the first year. In addition, consistent evidence of the role of social support as a buffer against the effects of stress seemed to indicate the importance of assessing this dimension as it related to the fourth-class cadets' overall appraisal of the summer experience. The items included evaluation of group cohesiveness/closeness ("It was difficult to confide in other cadets in the platoon," "Cadets in my platoon trusted one another," "No one in my platoon seemed to care much about what happened to me," "Most cadets in my platoon would go out of their way to help other members of the platoon," etc.) and group commitment ("I would not have wanted to leave my platoon"). Responses to these 10 items were made on a 6-point scale (1 = strongly disagree, 6 = strongly agree).

4. Comparison of the summer with what had been expected. Like the items describing the climate in the platoon, a series of items evaluating the cadets' prior knowledge and expectations about the summer were included in the survey based on an interest in the factors affecting summer attrition. Realistic expectations have consistently demonstrated an association with reduced rates of voluntary turnover in organizations; data collected at the U.S. Naval Academy showed a similar pattern (Ilgen & Seely, 1974). The survey contained six items addressing the accuracy of prior information about the academy ("Materials published by the admissions department provided an accurate description of swab summer," "If I really knew what to expect during swab summer, I would never have accepted my appointment," etc.) and the degree to which the academy was like or unlike their expectations in a variety of areas, including the extent of the demands for physical activity and fitness, the emphasis on military activities, and so on.

5. Overall personal appraisal and reaction to the summer. This section of the

survey consisted of 15 items eliciting the cadets' general affective reactions to the summer (e.g., "During the summer, I looked forward to each day," "During the summer, I often got discouraged about being a cadet at the academy," etc.) and their personal appraisal of the amount of personal growth and learning they attributed to the summer experience (e.g., "I learned a lot during swab summer," "I know myself a lot better now having been through swab summer," "In general, I feel proud to be a cadet at the academy," "The swab summer training program prepared me well for the academic year at the academy," etc.). Responses to these items were made on a 6-point scale (1 = strongly disagree, 6 = strongly agree).

Group Performance

Shortly after their arrival at the academy, each fourth-class cadet was assigned to 1 of 12 platoons (average size of a platoon was 20–25 students). Each platoon was intact for the entire training period, from the beginning of July to the end of August. During that time, under the direction of the upper class cadets, platoons competed for top honors in a variety of individual and group exercises — written tests of military knowledge, physical fitness tests, sports competitions, military drill and marching events. Group performance data were recorded throughout the period. The highest total score achieved on the basis of these events determined the summer "honor platoon." Scores ranged from a high of 107 total points for the first place platoon to 50 points for the platoon that finished last. The mean score was 69 points.

Individual Performance

An index of individual performance was available for the group of fourth-class cadets who completed the questionnaire in 1990. The performance rating con-

sisted of the total score obtained on a rating form filled out by the upper class cadets several times during the summer. The form consisted of a set of behaviorally anchored rating scales addressing such areas as: appearance in uniform, room condition, performance on assigned tasks, working as part of a team, and so on. The mean performance score for the group was 210 points (SD = 30.15); the highest performer received 333 points, and the lowest totaled only 103 points.

Data Analyses

The analyses reported here proceeded along three lines. First was a comparison of questionnaire data from 1987 with those collected in 1990. Second was an examination of the relationships among the survey items themselves, particularly the relationship between the cadets' perception of the frequency of particular leadership behaviors and their attendant evaluation of their leaders and of the summer program. Third was the relationship between survey items and indices of individual and group performance.

Results

Composite Scales

To facilitate further analyses, a reduced set of scales describing the leadership behavior of the upper class cadets was derived. Tentative assignment of items to scales was made on an a priori basis, consistent with the theoretical concepts underlying the leadership curriculum. Five categories were originally considered: goal setting, negative consequences, positive consequences, noncontingent punishment, and noncontingent support. The scales were refined based on an inspection of item content, item intercorrelations, and the results of a principal-components analysis of the combined 1987 and 1990 data. The means and standard deviations of the four scales that resulted are shown in Table 1, together with their constituent items. Following is a brief description of their content:

1. *Goal emphasis* contains items generally reflecting the setting and enforcement of high standards as well as responsiveness to poor performance.

2. *Positive motivation* includes items reflecting praise and positive reinforcement in response to good performance and offering encouragement as well as maintaining clear communication and a willingness on the part of the leader to explain his/her actions.

3. *Support* reflects a perception of the leaders' availability and willingness to help with problems.

4. *Harsh treatment* describes general and specific examples of inconsiderate and harsh treatment, including the imposition of excessive or impossible demands.

As noted earlier, the remainder of the survey contained items descriptive of the climate within the platoon, affective reactions to the summer program, appraisals of the leaders' effectiveness, and a few other questions of interest. The remaining items were likewise subjected to a principal components analysis. The following three additional composite scales, *group cohesiveness, personal growth,* and *negative affect,* were compiled based on the analysis:

5. *Group cohesiveness* reflects the degree of helpfulness, trust, and honest communication among the members of the platoon.

6. *Negative affect* contains items reflecting themes of discouragement and disappointment with the summer program.

7. *Personal growth* describes the degree to which the respondent perceives

gains in personal growth, self-knowledge, and learning which occurred as a result of the summer program.

The means and standard deviations for these scales and their member items are reported in Table 2. Another set of items grouped together by the principal components analysis seemed too conceptually heterogeneous to allow us to summarize their content with a single composite score. These items generally reflected overall evaluation and reactions to the summer program, the platoon, and the cadet leaders. They are listed at the end of Table 2 as *miscellaneous evaluative items.*

Comparison of Results for 1987 and 1990

Table 1 presents means and standard deviations for the leadership items and the leadership composite scales for the 1987 and 1990 administrations of the survey. The means of all four of the leadership composite scales are significantly different at $p < .001$ (a .001 level of significance was chosen because of the large number of statistical tests conducted). Of the constituent items, 14 of 24 are significantly different at $p < .001$.

For the composite scales *positive motivation, harsh treatment,* and *support,* the differences between the 1987 and 1990 results are in the expected direction. Consistent with the objectives of the leadership program, the 1990 cadre group is perceived as providing more praise, encouragement, and help while at the same time being less harsh and unreasonable in its demands. On the *goal emphasis* scale, however, the difference between the year groups is also significant but in a direction that seems inconsistent with the model. The leaders of the 1990 group are perceived as less insistent on hard work and less strict in their enforcement of standards. It should be recalled from an

TABLE 1 Comparison of Group Means for Leadership Behaviors, 1987 and 1990

Scale/items	1987		1990		t
	M	SD	M	SD	
Goal emphasis (coefficient alpha = .63)	30.58	3.07	28.99	3.23	5.54*
2. Set challenging goals for the cadets in my platoon.	5.18	.90	5.09	.81	1.20
47. Insisted that fourth class cadets follow standard ways of doing things in every detail.	4.38	.73	4.24	.76	2.08
48. Saw to it that the cadets were working up to their limits.	4.33	.72	4.02	.84	4.57*
56. Encouraged low performing platoon members to greater effort.	3.98	.94	3.91	.85	.83
57. Asked for sacrifices from platoon members for the good of the entire platoon.	4.11	.87	3.70	.93	5.17*
42. Criticized poor work.	4.62	.66	4.13	.88	7.16*
52. Criticized a specific act rather than a particular individual.	3.95	.83	3.93	.82	.35
Positive motivation (coefficient alpha = .79)	24.47	4.67	26.57	4.48	5.09*
14. Praised cadets for a job well done.	4.43	1.08	4.82	.94	4.22*
40. Expressed appreciation when one of us did a good job.	3.36	.86	3.67	.91	3.87*
43. Were easy to understand.	3.40	.88	3.59	.95	2.29
46. Saw to it that a cadet was rewarded for a job well done.	3.08	1.02	3.48	.97	4.38*
51. Stressed the importance of high morale.	3.68	1.14	3.81	1.02	1.36
59. Offered encouragement when the going got tough.	3.30	1.07	3.88	.90	6.41*
58. Explained their actions.	3.23	.96	3.31	1.08	.95
Harsh treatment (coefficient alpha = .72)	19.88	3.97	17.56	3.87	6.53*
41. Ruled with an iron fist.	3.77	.79	3.31	.87	6.21*
49. Treated people under them without considering their feelings.	3.00	.94	2.59	.94	4.81*
18. Ignored the feelings of fourth class cadets.	3.19	1.28	2.70	1.23	4.24*
50. "Rode" platoon members who made a mistake.	3.52	.94	3.02	1.02	5.53*
55. Demanded more than we could do.	2.94	1.13	2.83	1.01	1.11
45. Criticized platoon members in front of others.	3.43	1.10	3.05	1.11	3.86*
Support (coefficient alpha = .82)	12.37	3.38	13.57	3.15	4.10*
53. Made it easy to talk to them.	2.68	.96	3.13	1.01	4.99*
44. Helped the fourth class with their personal problems.	3.26	1.08	3.48	1.00	2.30
60. Were available if I had a problem.	3.59	1.16	3.75	1.02	1.49
54. Went out of their way to help platoon members.	2.83	.94	3.22	.93	4.67*

*p < .001; df = 494.

TABLE 2 Comparison of Group Means for Other Survey Items, 1987 and 1990.

Scale/items	1987 M	1987 SD	1990 M	1990 SD	t
Group cohesiveness (coefficient alpha = .81)	30.31	5.98	31.46	5.57	2.21
17. Most cadets in my platoon would go out of their way to help other members of the platoon.	4.23	1.17	4.53	1.08	2.92*
15. Cadets in my platoon trusted each other.	4.61	1.06	4.88	.97	2.97*
24. No one in my platoon seemed to care much about what happened to me. (-)	2.45	1.33	2.32	1.26	1.07
16. It was difficult to talk honestly and directly to many cadets in my platoon. (-)	2.77	1.38	2.70	1.27	.60
4. A friendly atmosphere prevailed among the cadets in my platoon.	4.59	1.15	4.82	1.03	2.29
20. There were many people in my platoon who knew me well and who knew how I felt.	4.00	1.43	4.03	1.35	.19
23. It was difficult to confide in other cadets in my platoon. (-)	2.97	1.36	2.77	1.22	1.68
Negative affect (coefficient alpha = .70)	18.50	5.84	16.49	5.02	4.09*
33. Swab summer was so tough, I considered resigning almost every day.	2.38	1.58	2.07	1.27	2.36
35. If I really knew what to expect during swab summer, I would never have accepted my appointment.	2.04	1.36	1.88	1.22	1.29
19. During the summer, I often got discouraged about being a cadet at the academy.	3.88	1.63	3.28	1.43	4.30*
27. Swab summer was a discouraging experience.	2.99	1.50	2.62	1.32	2.82
34. Psychologically, swab summer left me feeling drained and ill-prepared for the academic year.	2.86	1.44	2.47	1.31	3.11*
3. During the summer, I looked forward to each day. (-)	2.63	1.38	2.80	1.37	1.35
Personal growth (coefficient alpha = .73)	24.43	4.30	24.00	4.02	1.12
28. I learned a lot during swab summer.	5.25	1.08	4.97	1.19	2.82
29. Swab summer was a time of personal growth for me.	4.96	1.16	4.87	1.17	.81
30. I know myself a lot better now having been through swab summer.	4.70	1.36	4.41	1.31	2.40
39. The swab summer training program prepared me well for the academic year at the academy.	3.98	1.44	4.24	1.24	2.13
12. In general, I feel proud to be a cadet at the academy.	5.52	.85	5.54	.76	.20
Miscellaneous evaluative items					
6. In my platoon, I felt treated like a "real" person.	2.94	1.41	3.89	1.32	7.64*
21. My platoon cadre treated the fourth-class cadets as responsible adults.	2.75	1.41	3.25	1.31	4.12*
5. My platoon cadre were admired and respected by the cadets in my platoon.	4.27	1.18	4.51	1.16	2.23
25. My platoon cadre were good teachers.	4.69	1.01	4.61	1.09	.86
8. I would not have wanted to leave my platoon.	5.18	1.12	5.20	1.14	.15
13. I felt good about being in my platoon.	5.13	1.03	5.20	.90	.77
1. In general, cadets in my platoon knew what was expected of them.	4.39	1.09	4.48	1.07	.83
7. I knew where I stood in the eyes of my platoon cadre.	4.05	1.25	4.06	1.26	.14
10. Threats and criticism outweighed rewards in my platoon.	3.71	1.46	3.25	1.45	3.45*
26. I felt I could talk to my platoon cadre about any problems.	3.49	1.62	3.89	1.44	2.86

* p < 001; df = 494.

earlier section, however, that we described the upper class cadets as intentionally setting unrealistically high standards, making failure virtually inevitable for their subordinates. More realistic setting and enforcement of standards would seem likely to produce a pattern of results like those obtained here; the upper class cadets "backed off" a bit from the unrealistic level of expectations that characterized the process in 1987 and before. Likewise, they seem to have backed off somewhat from the frequency with which they "criticized poor work" (item #42); the mean for item #42 in 1987 was 4.62 on a 5-point scale! The 1990 group of leaders seems less preoccupied with discovering and punishing *all* the mistakes made by their followers.

Table 2 contrasts 1987 and 1990 questionnaire results for the three remaining composite scales and a selection of additional items. Fewer statistically significant differences are evident. Of the composite scales, only *negative affect* is significantly different (lower) in 1990 than 1987; neither *group cohesiveness* nor *personal growth* exhibit statistically significant differences from 1987 to 1990. On individual items, the cadets in 1990 report that their leaders treated them more as "responsible adults" (item #21) and as "real" people (item #6). They also report getting discouraged less about being a cadet (item #19), greater trust and helpfulness among the members of their platoon (items #15 and 17), and a better balance of threats and criticism with rewards received from their leaders (item #10).

Aware that differences in survey administration in 1987 and 1990 may have confounded these results (recall that the 1987 survey data was reported anonymously while 1990 respondents were asked to identify themselves with their code number), we also examined survey data collected in 1988 and 1989. Like the 1990 data, the respondents reported on "postintervention" leadership behaviors and their reactions to it. As in the 1987 administration, the cadets completed the

questionnaire anonymously. While the results will not be reported here for the sake of brevity, questionnaire data from 1988 and 1989 were nevertheless quite similar to the results obtained in 1990, indicating a large number of statistically significant differences in the reported frequency of various leadership behaviors from the 1987 data. Furthermore, the pattern of differences from the 1987 survey results was consistent across all 3 years; negative behaviors were reported to have decreased in frequency while positive, supportive behaviors increased. The lack of anonymity of the group completing the questionnaire in 1990 does not appear to have influenced their responses in any important way.

Relationship among Scales/Items

Correlations among the derived composite scales are reported in Table 3. The leadership composite scales generally exhibit moderate correlations with one another, ranging from r = .63 (between *support* and *positive motivation*) to r = -.19 (between *goal emphasis* and *harsh treatment*). Given the magnitude of the intercorrelations among the leadership composites, partial correlations were also computed to gain a better idea of the independent association of specific leadership behaviors with the other outcome criteria reflected in the *group cohesiveness, negative affect,* and *personal growth* composites.

The values shown in Table 4 represent third-order partial correlations between each of the composite scales on the left and one of the leadership scales, controlling in each case for the effect of the other three leadership composite scales. The resulting matrix clarifies the pattern of relationships among the composite scales; with the effects of the other leadership scales partialled out, few statistically significant relationships remain. While *group cohesiveness* is significantly correlated with *goal emphasis*, its largest (and

TABLE 3   Correlations among Derived Composite Scales

Scales	1	2	3	4	5	6	7
1. Goal emphasis	.....	.34**	.30**	− .19**	.24**	− .14*	.40**
2. Positive motivation		.....	.63**	− .46**	.23**	− .28**	.26**
3. Support			.....	− .50**	.21**	− .17**	.23**
4. Harsh treatment				.....	− .29**	.29**	− .16**
5. Group cohesiveness					.....	− .25**	.38**
6. Negative affect						.....	− .28**
7. Personal growth							.....

*p < .05.   **p < .01.

negative) correlation is with *harsh treatment*. This suggests that, contrary to some of the "folk" notions about the military indoctrination process described earlier, the fourth-class cadets do not associate perceptions of harsh and unreasonable leadership behaviors with greater cohesiveness within the platoon. Instead, perceptions of *harsh treatment* by the leaders are associated by the fourth-class cadets with individual feelings of disappointment and discouragement during the summer (*negative affect*) and are unrelated to the amount of learning, growth, and self-knowledge they attribute to participation in the summer program (*personal growth*). Feelings of *personal growth* are associated with perceptions of leaders who set high goals and enforced standards of performance (*goal emphasis*). Somewhat surprisingly, the kind of open, noncontingent supportive behaviors that comprise the *support* composite scale are not significantly related to any of the other composites.

Table 5 presents the correlations of the composite scales with other selected items from the questionnaire. Zero-order correlations of the leadership composite scales with individual items are reported in each row of the table. The values shown in parentheses in Table 5 represent fourth-order partial correlations between the composite scale and each item, con-

trolling for the effect of the other four composite scales.

Based on the pattern of partial correlations, overall appraisal of the cadet leaders as admired and respected is associated with *positive motivation* and, to a lesser extent, with *goal emphasis*. Goal emphasis plays a somewhat larger role in the perception of the cadet leaders as "good teachers" (r = .24, p < .01). Perceptions of *support* are associated with greater reported willingness to talk with the leaders about problems (r = .42, p < .01). *Harsh treatment* demonstrates significant negative zero-order correlations with most of the other items. With the effect of the other composites partialled out, however, few statistically significant relationships remain. It does exhibit a significant negative correlation with perceptions of being treated like a "responsible adult" (r = -.20, p < .01) and is positively correlated with feelings of discouragement during the summer program (r = .14, p < .05). It does not seem to play a primary role either in the appraisal of the leaders as admired or respected (r = -.09, n.s.) or in the fourth class cadets' willingness to approach the leaders with problems (r = -.06, n.s.)

Finally, perceptions of *group cohesiveness* are more strongly associated with commitment to the platoon (r = .41, p < .01) and, negatively, with becoming dis-

TABLE 4   Partial Correlations between Leadership Composites and Other
Composite Scales

	Leadership Scales			
	Goal Emphasis	Positive Motivation	Support	Harsh Treatment
Group Cohesiveness	.18*	.05	.01	− .20*
Negative Affect	− .05	− .18*	− .09	.21*
Personal Growth	.34*	.07	.05	− .01

Note. Reported are third-order partial correlations reflecting the relationship
between each of the composite scales on the left and one of the leadership
composites, controlling for the effect of the other three leadership composites.

*p < .01.

couraged with the summer program (r = -.21, $p < .01$) than were any of the leadership composite scales.

Performance and Leadership

Efforts to identify any differences in the perception of leaders' behaviors in high- and low-performing groups yielded negative results. Based on the cumulative summer competition points, the highest and lowest scoring platoons were identified. There were no significant differences on any of the leadership composite scales. In a second analysis, the platoons were rank ordered both on summer performance and on all of the leadership composites, and correlations were computed. Again, there were no significant relationships.

The relationship between indices of individual performance and subordinates' perceptions of their leaders is presented in Table 6. High performers see their leaders as more positively reinforcing and somewhat more supportive. This may be as it should be; high performers should be rewarded more. The magnitude of these correlations is small, however, suggesting that subordinates may not observe close correspondence between leader behavior

and cadet performance. Lacking comparison data from 1987, the chief value of these data is to show that relationships conform to expectations.

Discussion

Over the course of three years, we were successful in changing the behavior of first-line supervisors in one organization. The first effort, which relied on classroom training alone, was not successful despite the commitment of top leadership. The second effort was successful in part because of a concerted effort to articulate organizational goals and roles and in part because targeted behaviors were monitored and reinforced on a regular basis by a committed team of change agents. Resistance to change in this organization was rooted in the belief that a traditional set of leadership behaviors was essential to the success and development of entering members. The results of the outcomes analysis clearly show this belief to be false. The same behaviors generally perceived to be effective in both the leadership literature and the popular press proved to be associated with positive outcomes in this organization as well.

TABLE 5 Zero-order and Partial Correlations of Composite Scales with Selected Items

Items	Composite Scales				
	Goal Emphasis	Positive Motivation	Support	Harsh Treatment	Group Cohesiveness
My platoon cadre were admired and respected by the cadets in my platoon.	.30** (.14*)	.56** (.34**)	.43** (.08)	−.34** (−.09)	.15* (−.05)
My platoon cadre were good teachers.	.38** (.24**)	.48** (.23**)	.43** (.10)	−.37** (−.14*)	.24** (.17**)
My platoon cadre treated the fourth-class cadets like responsible adults.	.09 (−.04)	.33** (.05)	.38** (.19**)	−.37** (−.20**)	.24** (.11*)
In my platoon, I felt treated like a "real" person.	.22** (.07)	.41** (.16**)	.41** (.18**)	−.37** (−.14*)	.28** (.17**)
I felt I could talk to my platoon cadre about any problems.	.26** (.07)	.51** (.17**)	.62** (.42**)	−.36** (−.06)	.16** (.00)
I would not have wanted to leave my platoon.	.26** (.17*)	.32** (.08)	.34** (.11)	−.30** (−.14*)	.48** (.41**)
I felt good about being in my platoon.	.31** (.22**)	.33** (.13*)	.28** (.03)	−.27** (−.10)	.58** (.55**)
During the summer, I often got discouraged about being a cadet. Swab summer was a discouraging experience.[a]	−.18** (−.10)	−.21** (−.11*)	−.18** (.03)	.23** (.14*)	−.26** (−.21**)
Swab summer was a time of personal growth for me.	.26** (.20**)	.20** (.03)	.22** (.11*)	−.09 (.05)	.29** (.23**)
I know myself a lot better now having been through swab summer.	.26** (.22**)	.14* (−.02)	.15* (.07)	−.04 (.04)	.26** (.19**)
I learned a lot during swab summer.	.39** (.36**)	.23** (.12*)	.13* (−.09)	−.19** (−.03)	.23** (.11*)
In general, I feel proud to be a cadet at the academy.	.25** (.21**)	.17** (.06)	.14* (.02)	−.09 (.02)	.24** (.21**)

Note. Values in parentheses are fourth-order partial correlations reflecting the relationship between each of the items on the left and one of the composite scales, controlling for the effect of the other four composite scales.

[a]These items were summed and averaged to obtain a composite score reflecting a "discouragement" theme.

*p < .05.   **p < .01.

TABLE 6 Zero-order and Partial Correlations of Individual Performance Ratings with Composite Scales

| | **Correlation with Individual Performance Rating** | |
Scale	Zero-order	Fourth-order partial[a]
Goal emphasis	.16*	.04
Positive motivation	.33**	.17**
Support	.32**	.12*
Harsh treatment	− .22**	− .04
Group cohesiveness	.12	.00

[a]Reflects the correlation of individual performance rating with each of the composite scales, controlling for the effect of the other four composites.

*p < .05.   **p < .01.

On the other hand, the impact of the changes in leader behavior was neither large nor consistent across a variety of subjective and objective outcome criteria. There was no evidence, for example, that changed leadership behavior improved subordinates' performance. This may have been due to the fact that individual cadets are already highly motivated to succeed, requirements for their success are clear, and the program is highly structured. In this case, "the system" itself may substitute for leadership. In similar fashion, the quality of peer relations within the platoon was as strongly related to feelings of personal growth, learning, and commitment to the team as was any leader behavior.

Instead of validating a simple relationship between unitary constructs of "effective leadership" and "organizational effectiveness," these data serve to remind us of the complexity of the behaviors and outcomes we try so hard to influence. These data provide reminders of the multidimensionality of leader behavior, the variety of possible outcome variables, and the significance of the context in which leadership takes place. Clearly, when we undertake efforts to change leadership behavior in a way we presume will benefit an organization, we should also routinely assess as many of these variables as possible as part of the overall evaluation of our effectiveness. It is possible to change the behavior of leaders, but the peculiar culture of every organization will either limit or enhance the impact of new behaviors on those who follow. What we hope to achieve may not be exactly what we get.

What of the academy? Attrition of the fourth-class cadets during the summer of 1990 was dramatically lower than it was for any summer during the last decade. The fourth-class cadets who completed their indoctrination during the summer of 1990 reported feeling better about their summer experience and regarded their leaders as somewhat more approachable, respected, and admired. In the long run, their leaders may be able to exert more influence on these subordinates because they are held in higher esteem. If the leaders are more highly valued and are modeling more effective behavior, their impact on the future leadership behavior of their followers may fulfill the hopes of the leaders who initiated this effort to change the culture. That remains to be seen.

References

Arvey, R. D., Davis, G. A., & Nelson, S. M. (1984). Use of discipline in an organization: A field study. *Journal of Applied Psychology, 69,* 448–460.

Arvey, R. D., & Ivancevich, J. M. (1980). Punishment in organizations: A review, propositions, and research suggestions. *Academy of Management Review, 5,* 123–132.

Bandura, A. (1971). Analysis of modeling processes. In A. Bandura (Ed.), *Psychological modeling: Conflicting theories* (pp. 1–62). Chicago: Aldine-Atherton.

Bandura, A. (1973). *Aggression: A social learning analysis.* Englewood Cliffs, NJ: Prentice Hall.

Bandura, A. (1977). *Social learning theory.* Englewood Cliffs, NJ: Prentice Hall.

Campbell, D. (1987, August). *Psychological test profiles of brigadier generals: Warmongers or decisive warriors?* Paper presented at the meeting of Division 14 of the American Psychological Association, New York.

Haimann, T., & Hilgert, R. L. (1977). *Supervision: Concepts and practices of management.* Cincinnati: South-Western.

Hollander, E. P. (1978). *Leadership dynamics: A practical guide to effective relationships.* New York: Free Press.

House, R. J. (1971). A path goal theory of leadership effectiveness. *Administrative Science Quarterly, 16,* 321–338.

House, R. J., & Mitchell, T. R. (1974). Path goal theory of leadership. *Journal of Contemporary Business, 3,* 81–97.

Ilgen, D. R., & Seely, W. (1974). Realistic expectations as an aid in reducing voluntary resignations. *Journal of Applied Psychology, 59,* 452–455.

Komaki, J. L. (1986). Toward effective supervision: An operant analysis and comparison of managers at work. *Journal of Applied Psychology, 71,* 270–279.

Komaki, J. L., Zlotnick, S., & Jensen, M. (1986). Development of an operant-based taxonomy and observational index of supervisory behavior. *Journal of Applied Psychology, 71,* 260–269.

Podsakoff, P. M. (1982). Determinants of a supervisor's use of rewards and punishments: A literature review and suggestions for future research. *Organizational Behavior and Human Performance, 29,* 58–83.

Podsakoff, P. M., Todor, W. D., & Skov, R. (1982). Effects of leader contingent and noncontingent reward and punishment behaviors on subordinate performance and satisfaction. *Academy of Management Journal, 25,* 810–821.

Preston, P., & Zimmerer, T. W. (1978). *Management for supervisors.* Englewood Cliffs, NJ: Prentice Hall.

Rootman, I. (1971). *Voluntary withdrawal from a military academy: A study in socialization outcome.* Unpublished doctoral dissertation, Yale University, New Haven, CT.

Rosebush, M. A. (1985). *Applying the positive motivation model.* Colorado Springs: U.S. Air Force Academy.

Schoen, S. H., & Durand, D. E. (1979). *Supervision: The management of organizational resources.* Englewood Cliffs, NJ: Prentice Hall.

Scott, W. E., Jr. (1977). Leadership: A functional analysis. In J. G. Hunt & L. L. Larson (Eds.), *Leadership: The cutting edge* (pp. 84–93). Carbondale, IL: Southern Illinois University Press.

Sims, H. P., Jr. (1977). The leader as a manager of reinforcement contingencies: An empirical example and a model. In J. G. Hunt & L. L. Larson (Eds.), *Leadership: The cutting edge* (pp. 121–137). Carbondale, IL: Southern Illinois University Press.

White, J. H. R. (1975). *Successful supervision.* London: McGraw-Hill.

Yukl, G. A. (1989). *Leadership in organizations.* Englewood Cliffs, NJ: Prentice Hall.

Rex J. Blake is a PhD candidate in Counseling Psychology at the University of Minnesota. He was Director of the Leadership Development Program and a member of the counseling center staff at the United States Coast Guard Academy. Earlier, he served on the faculty of the Defense Department's Equal Opportunity Management Institute.

Earl H. Potter III is Professor of Management and Associate Dean for Academic Affairs at the United States Coast Guard Academy. His research on leadership and stress has been published in the *Journal of Applied Psychology*, *Academy of Management Journal*, and *Journal of Personality and Social Psychology*. As a teacher and consultant to public and nonprofit organizations, he has focused on leadership development and team performance. He received his PhD in Organizational Psychology from the University of Washington.

Direct inquiries about this article to Rex J. Blake, c/o Counseling Psychology Program, Department of Psychology, University of Minnesota, Elliott Hall, 75 East River Road, Minneapolis, MN 55455–0344.

CHAPTER 27

Leader Abilities and Group Performance as a Function of Stress

Frederick W. Gibson

This paper extends Cognitive Resource Theory (Fiedler & Garcia, 1987) by investigating the contributions of leader intellectual resources to group performance. Leader cognitive abilities are divided into two categories: (a) generative resources, that are independent of experience and education; and (b) associative resources, that denote knowledge and skills acquired over time. These two ability types are hypothesized to interact in opposing ways with leader-felt stress in affecting group performance.

Correlational data from a laboratory study of group problem-solving tasks provide some support for the view that stress diminishes the contribution of generative resources to task performance and has the opposite effect for associative resources. Theoretical and practical implications are discussed.

For leadership theorists and practitioners alike, past research reveals a significant problem. The data show that a leader's cognitive abilities do not always guarantee effective group performance (Bass, 1981; Stogdill, 1948). Since leadership involves many intellectual tasks, such as problem recognition, strategy and plan development, and outcome evaluation, this lack of an ability-to-outcome relationship is surprising and begs explanation.

Cognitive Resource Theory

One attempt to explain this paradox is Cognitive Resource Theory, or CRT (Fiedler & Garcia, 1987). CRT seeks to identify the specific role of leader abilities, technical competence, and job-relevant knowledge in organizational performance. CRT research has consistently demonstrated that leader cognitive abilities are often unrelated, and sometimes detrimental, to effective group performance (e.g., Barnes, Potter, & Fiedler, 1983). Borrowing from Blades (1976), CRT proposes as its fundamental thesis that three uninterrupted processes must occur for the leader's cognitive abilities to translate into group performance: First, the leader must devote intellectual effort to making plans, decisions, and action strategies; second, these plans, decisions, and action strategies must be communicated to the group in the form of directions, instructions, or guidance; and third, the group must be willing and motivated to implement the leader's plans, decisions, and action strategies.

However, CRT, like other theories examining the role of leader abilities, looks at intelligence, creativity, experience and the like as separate, or at least unsystematically related, constructs. This paper offers a more systematic view of leader abilities (cognitive resources). Among other benefits, this new view will allow us to more appropriately specify the impact of leader cognitive resources on group performance.

Conceptualizing Leader Cognitive Abilities

We can think of leader cognitive abilities in rather broad terms. Laymen think of leaders as "gifted" on the basis of such broad dimensions as intelligence and creativity. In fact, research on human abilities often leads to a classification system similar to the intelligence-creativity dichotomy.

Fluid and crystallized intelligence. One of the best known theories of intelligence (Horn, 1968) argues that the primary cognitive abilities can be organized into two principal components, fluid intelligence (Gf) and crystallized intelligence (Gc). Gf includes seeing relationships among diverse stimuli, drawing inferences from relationships, and comprehending implications. This ability represents such "fundamental features" of human intelligence as reasoning, abstracting, and problem solving. These features are obtained through learning that is unique to an individual or in other ways not organized by culture (Horn, 1982).

Gc, on the other hand, indicates an individual's breadth of knowledge and experience, sophistication, comprehension of communications, judgment, understanding of conventions, and reasonable thinking. It is defined by abilities such as verbal comprehension, concept formation, and general reasoning. More importantly, crystallized intelligence represents the extent to which an individual has incorporated the knowledge and sophistication of a culture. In that sense, it represents much of what is described as general intelligence (Horn, 1988).

Thus we can distinguish between intelligence that is a form of intellectual experience (Gc) and one that is closer to a genetically influenced "native ability" (Gf). This simplification of Horn's Gf-Gc theory provides a parallel to CRT. One of the major goals of CRT, in fact, is to explain the finding that the effects of leader intelligence and experience are affected differently by leader stress, with respect to group performance. A theory of intelligence which parallels this view is a particularly relevant theoretical vantage point from which to test CRT.

Creativity. We may also think of leaders in terms of how creative they are, independent of how "smart" they may be. Studies of creativity have been influenced by Guilford's (1950) notion of divergent thinking, which refers to one's ability to generate multiple potential solutions to a problem. Mumford and Gustafson (1988) discuss creativity in relation to the production of novel, socially valued products. In their definition, creativity is a syndrome which involves a number of elements. It includes processes underlying the individual's capacity to generate new ideas or understandings, characteristics of the individual facilitating process operations, and characteristics of the individual facilitating the translation of these ideas into action. These elements constitute an interesting approximation of the causal chain Blades (1976) proposed for the translation of leader abilities into effective group performance. The similarities between this approach and the core causal process of CRT further justify integrating creativity into discussions of leadership effectiveness. In fact, recent work has begun to examine this leader cognitive resource in some detail (Gibson, Fiedler, & Daniels, 1990).

Integration. Perhaps it is prudent to concentrate on the commonalities between creativity and intelligence. This allows us to explore the dysfunctions of gifted leaders under stress by using ability measures which maintain a measurement distinction relevant to CRT. Because fluid intelligence and creativity involve generation of novel stimuli, approaches, or solutions, they may be viewed as "generative" resources and qualify as one category of giftedness in reference to leaders. When exercised, both Gf and creativity involve significant information processing, since stimulus patterns must be rearranged or novel ones produced.

Generative resources can be distinguished from crystallized intelligence and other forms of task-relevant experience, or associative abilities. Experience can be conceived traditionally (Bettin, 1983) or as Gc (intellectual experience). If the group task is a verbal one, crystallized intelligence is also task-relevant experience. Associative abilities are characterized by previously formed schemata or solutions that only need be fit to situations or problems ("framing"). Once the schema-to-problem fit is established, solutions are available with little further processing. In other words, once the leader categorizes the problem and places it in perspective, previously successful scripts for action and solutions are available automatically because they are instantly associated with the problem at hand. Chess masters do not have to spend time analyzing all the separate pieces on the chessboard and devising novel strategies to attack or counteract. They determine quickly the pattern of the pieces, frame the pattern as, for example, a Sicilian Defense, and immediately retrieve/recall the moves which are most effective against such a configuration. This re-

trieval is based on previous experience, either their own or that which is available through training. By functioning this way, experience-related resources require less processing for their effective use. This is a crucial distinction. Why is information processing an issue? Because it implies that associative resources are less subject to interference. One source of interference which is of particular interest to CRT is stress.

Stress

Boss stress. According to CRT, phenomena that disrupt the causal chain linking leader cognitive resources and group performance attenuate the relationship between the two. One such disruptive influence is stress. Several studies (Borden, 1980; Fiedler, Potter, Zais, & Knowlton, 1979) indicate that the ability to concentrate on the task is particularly weak when a relationship with important others is stressful. Fiedler and Garcia (1987) term this "boss stress" and claim that it creates evaluation anxiety or conflict that distracts the leader from focusing on the task. For this reason, the leader's cognitive abilities should correlate with group performance only when s/he is relatively free of such stress. Conversely, leader abilities should be uncorrelated with group performance when the leader reports high boss stress.

Social facilitation. Another way to view interpersonal stress is not as distraction, but as arousal. In fact, Fiedler and Garcia (1987) have also suggested social facilitation theory (Zajonc, 1965) to help explain the surprising effects of stress as a moderator of the leader abilities-group performance relationship. In Zajonc's drive theory version, persons may serve as drive-arousing stimuli; their mere presence may be enough to arouse drive in individuals performing a task. This drive produces a facilitative effect in performance on an overlearned task but decreases performance on a new or complex task. This is because the drive benefits most those responses that are already well learned or easy, since this generalized drive energizes all learned responses, whether correct or not.

A meta-analysis of social facilitation studies (Bond & Titus, 1983) found strong support for the "mere presence" view of social facilitation: Mere presence does significantly increase performance quantity and speed on simple tasks and decreases performance quantity and quality, as well as speed, on complex tasks. Therefore, the mere presence of an "audience" in a task-related situation seems enough to engender the display of dominant responses (overlearned behaviors) in individuals performing the task.

Dominant response behaviors.
How can we explain the performance deficits for gifted leaders which were noted earlier? According to social facilitation theory, leaders with high levels of generative abilities—like fluid intelligence or creativity—will tend to use these abilities under stress or when in the presence of evaluative audiences, because these abilities are the source of dominant responses. Dominant responses for these leaders will be "processual"; such leaders will feel pressed to "think" or "create" their way to solutions. This processing increase will be reflected in increased talk and less coherent verbalizations. By talking more, the leader reduces the chances for group members to talk and contribute to the group session. With a lack of experience, these leaders' verbalizations will also be relatively undirected and will therefore be seen as "babbling." Members may also tend to babble more as a function of what may be perceived by them as a lack of direction.

Leaders with substantial associative resources also resort to dominant responses under interpersonal stress. However, since these associative resources are accessed almost automatically once the problem is framed, they do not require heavy processing for their expression. Consequently, these leaders reach solutions efficiently, with less babbling and greater direction. Such efficient resource usage allows the leader to encourage more, and more directed, participation by the group members. More ideas are therefore available to help solve the group problem, and more of the comments are relevant to the problem.

In other words, to explain the performance anomalies noted in this paper, we must propose different behavioral tendencies under interpersonal stress for leaders possessing different types of cognitive resources. The major shortcoming of the Fiedler and Garcia (1987) distraction hypothesis is that it does not predict different responses for leaders with different types of abilities; if all leaders were distracted under stress, the correlation between all leader abilities and group performance would be attenuated. This is not the case. Although the distribution of these cognitive resources is probably continuous, I propose that at some level one type becomes "dominant" and its associated behavioral tendencies dominate under stress.

How do we characterize the tendencies of leaders with high levels of both generative and associative abilities? The most "effective" resource will be used so that, under stress, associative abilities—because of their reduced reliance on information processing—will be exercised. This implies that leaders with substantial generative and associative resources will enjoy relatively effective group performance under low and high stress.

Method

Participants

One hundred fifty undergraduates participated in the study. The average participant age was 19.36 years; the average age of group leaders was 19.98 years. Forty eight percent of the sample were female, and 41.2% of the group leaders were female.

Procedure

Participants were scheduled for 90-minute experimental sessions. Before reporting to the sessions, participants completed a questionnaire which assessed their demographic characteristics and included several personality measures. Next, participants completed several timed scales of intelligence and creativity, following which they were randomly assigned to 3-person groups to engage in the group problem-solving tasks. Thus, there were 50 initial task groups. The leader for each group was also randomly assigned at this point. Participants identified as leaders were told to pay special attention to the instructions that followed for information pertinent to their new position.

Once group composition and group leaders were identified, the experimenter read instructions for the first task. Embedded in some instructions were statements designed to induce interpersonal stress for the leader, as well as general statements emphasizing his or her authority. Each group performed two tasks, and the order of the tasks was counterbalanced across groups. At the end of each task, group members completed a short questionnaire describing their reactions to the task they just performed. Members were then read instructions for the second task, and they proceeded as with the first. Upon completion of the second task, the groups completed a scale identical to the scale completed after the first task.

Group task. Each group completed two creative problem-solving tasks written by the author and constructed to be similar to each other. One task required the group to write a 1-page article for the campus newspaper demanding that college athletes on an intercollegiate athletic team be paid. The other task asked the group to draft a short proposal arguing that parking should be open on campus and in the immediate vicinity. The order of presentation of the tasks was counterbalanced across groups.

Experimental manipulation. Each group performed each task under one of two experimental conditions: a control (or low stress) condition and a high stress (evaluation apprehension) condition. The order of tasks and experimental conditions was also counterbalanced across groups. Thus, there were four "scenarios," one of which was presented to each group.

In the low stress condition, the experimenter asked subjects to perform one of the group problem-solving tasks and told them the task still had some "bugs" in it to be worked out. The members were told to relax and enjoy the problem but to try to come up with the best solution. Participants were reminded that the task was a group effort but that the leader was responsible for the group's work. Once the task began, the group was left alone in the room until the time limit had elapsed, except when the experimenter entered to check for questions or problems.

In the high (interpersonal) stress condition, the experimenter told the participants that the task assessed leadership effectiveness; the leader was told that his/her performance on the task would indicate his/her leadership ability. In addition, leaders were told that each group's performance would be compared to national norms, and that especially good and poor leaders would receive later recognition. The instructions also emphasized that the leader alone was responsible for the group's work. Furthermore, the leader was informed that following the group session, he/she would be required to present the solution reached and the reason for the selection of that solution.

To further manipulate leader stress, a confederate serving as a monitor remained in the room while the group performed their task. This monitor carried a clipboard and pretended to take extensive notes during the task. The monitor spent most of the session time seated at the same table directly across from the group. Each session was limited to 15 minutes.

Measures

Pre-session questionnaire. A demographics scale asked the respondent's age, gender, prior military experience, current undergraduate year group, and leadership or management experience.

Pre-task ability measures. This battery of measures consisted of five timed ability scales used to assess generative and associative abilities.

1. Horn's (1975) Gf-Gc Sampler. Three of the five subtests from this battery (a brief measure of fluid and crystallized intelligence) were used. The vocabulary subtest ("Synonyms") consisted of eight problems which involved choosing a synonym for a target word from a list of four words. This subtest assessed crystallized intelligence, a form of associative ability.

2. The common word analogies subtest ("Analogies") consisted of 16 items asking the subject to circle a word (from a series of words) which had the same relationship to its complement as did another pair of words in the stem. This test measured both fluid and crystallized intelligence and therefore was a measure of both associative and generative abilities.

3. The letter series subtest ("Letters"). This subtest consisted of 15 sequences of letters followed by a blank. The participant's task was to determine the logical sequence underlying the series and to write the next letter in each sequence in the blank. This subtest assessed fluid intelligence, a generative ability.

4. Plot Titles. Plot Titles was developed by Guilford (1967) as a measure of creativity (a generative ability). The test consisted of two short stories for which examinees provided titles. The total number of clever responses has proved to be a measure of originality associated with remote associations or with revisions or transformations. The measure has demonstrated adequate construct validity (Guilford, Christenson, & Lewis, 1954). Test-retest reliability estimates range from .60 to .80.

5. Alternate Uses. A revised form of Unusual Uses, originally designed by Wilson, Guilford, Christenson, and Lewis (1954), was used to assess flexibility of thinking as a component of creativity, also a generative ability. Each item contained the name of a common object for which the examinee was to list as many as six other uncommon uses in the time allowed. Test-retest reliability estimates range from .75 to .85.

Post-task questionnaires. A reactions scale assessed various respondent reactions to the task. Questions included a report on the stress experienced while performing the group task.

Ratings of group performance. The written group products were evaluated by three raters using an instrument developed by the author. The instrument was an 8-item scale which required evaluators to rate the written group products on dimensions such as originality, style, persuasiveness, and elaboration. The scale was an adaptation of the scheme for describing the general properties of group-generated written passages which was developed by Hackman, Jones, and McGrath (1967).

The average interrater agreement among the three evaluators was .79 for the low stress task and .80 for the high stress task. The standardized item alpha (Cronbach, 1951) for the items and the length index was .94, an indication that the items measured a common factor. Since the coefficient alpha for the scale was so high, only one performance score was calculated. All items received equal weight in calculation of the overall score, accomplished by adding the standardized scores of each item for that group product. The items were standardized separately across the low and high stress task products.

Results

Since the purpose of the study was to examine the effects of leader stress, I chose for analysis only those groups whose leaders reported a substantial increase in stress in the experimental over the control condition (i.e., leader stress scores increased by at least one standard deviation). This left 22 cases for subsequent analyses. Although this loss in effective cases was costly, it was essential in order to make inferences about the effects of stress on the variables under study.

Tests of Hypotheses

The correlations between each leader ability score and group performance were compared under low and high stress. Correlations between subjects' leadership experience and performance are also listed. Because these correlations were attenuated by the unreliability of each measure, I corrected each coefficient for attenuation using the formula in Nunnally (1978). The corrected coefficients are listed in Table 1.

The correlations were plotted in Figure 1. Under low stress, both associative ability measures (synonyms and leadership experience) correlated near zero with performance. While all three generative ability measures (letter sequences, acceptable uses, and clever titles) correlated more strongly with performance, none of the coefficients was significant. This relationship was reversed under high stress; the

correlations between both associative measures and performance were higher than the correlations between all the generative measures and performance, although not all these differences were statistically significant.

The correlations between these generative measures and performance all decreased under stress, but again the differences were not statistically significant. Meanwhile, the difference in correlations between the associative measures and performance increased significantly: from $r = -.09$ under low stress to $r = .20$ under high stress ($t(\text{diff}) = 1.41$, $p < .10$) for the synonyms scale and from $r = .05$ to $r = .33$ ($t(\text{diff}) = 1.41$, $p < .10$) for leadership experience (see Table 1).

The correlations between all three generative measures and performance dropped from low to high stress, although none significantly so. However, one index of the reversal in the relationship among the correlations was that under low stress the differences between the associative ability (synonyms)-performance correlation and the generative ability-performance correlations were significant, while no differences between these pairings of coefficients were significant in the high stress condition. These data indicate an interaction between ability type and interpersonal stress with regard to effects on group performance. Table 2 shows the results of this analysis. Another datum supporting the general hypothesis of this study is that all five differences in correlations from low to high stress (i.e., for all the generative and associative ability measures) were in the predicted direction. The joint probability of occurrence of all these events is .03.

The correlations between leader analogies scores and performance under low and high stress were also compared. (Since the analogies subscale tapped both Gf and Gc, it was a measure of generative and associative abilities.) The correlations were positive under both low stress ($r = .17$) and high stress ($r = .27$) and increased in magnitude across the experi-

TABLE 1 Correlations between Leader Ability Scores and Group
Performance under Low and High Stress[a]

Ability Score	Low Stress	High Stress	Difference	t (diff)[b]	p value
Analogies	.17	.27	.10	− 0.51	n.s.
Synonyms	− .09	.20	.29	− 1.41	< .10
Letter Seq.'s	.25	.08	.17	0.84	n.s.
Accep. Uses	.20	.15	.05	0.25	n.s.
Clever Titles	.23	.12	.11	0.54	n.s.
Ldr. Experience	.05	.33	.28	− 1.41	< .10

Note. N = 22.

[a]N = 22.   [b]df = 19

mental conditions, but the difference between them was not significant. This analysis suggests that leaders who had both content and process abilities performed better than their less gifted counterparts under both low and high stress.

These results provide partial support for the hypotheses of this study. Although the differences among the coefficients were in the predicted direction, some differences and absolute values were not of high magnitude. Nevertheless, the data suggest that interpersonal stress seems to impair the ability of generative abilities to contribute to group performance, while it enhances the contribution of associative abilities. Leaders with high levels of both abilities seem to do relatively well in all circumstances.

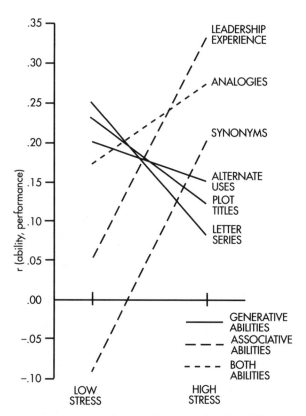

Figure 1 Correlations between leader ability scores and performance under low and high stress.

Discussion

This study sought to extend Cognitive Resource Theory (Fiedler & Garcia, 1987) by clarifying our conception of leader cognitive abilities and by examining behavioral processes proposed to underly the performance deficits suffered by gifted leaders under stress. One shortcoming of CRT is that it does not include a theory of abilities. Because of this, CRT has not yet researched the interactive effects of leader abilities and leader stress as systematically as it might. Such research could start by providing a categorization scheme which groups leader cognitive

TABLE 2 Differences in Correlations between Generative and
Associative Ability Scores and Performance under
Low and High Stress

Variable	Correlation Difference		Correlation Difference	
Pair	Low Stress	t (diff)	High Stress	t (diff)
syn–ltrs.	.34	1.69*	.12	n.s.
syn–acc. uses	.29	1.41*	.05	n.s.
syn–clev. titles	.32	1.58*	.11	n.s.

Note. N = 22.
*p < .05.

abilities into generative and associative categories.

Unfortunately, the statistical results in this study were not consistently significant, although the correlation differences were all in the predicted directions. I view the former shortfall as a result of two phenomena. First, the small sample size necessarily reduced the power of the statistical tests. Second, the stress manipulation was limited in strength for ethical reasons regarding the design of the study. Perhaps a lack of fidelity in the situation reduced the psychological strength of the manipulation for most participants. This is the "intensity" issue relating field versus laboratory settings discussed by Bouchard (1976):

> An important independent variable may display a range of intensity in the field that could not be generated in the laboratory because of ethical and other restrictions. Firings, layoffs, demotions, and transfers can produce levels of stress that would be unethical for an experimenter to simulate in a laboratory setting. (p. 365)

It would be interesting to replicate this study in a field setting. However, given the consistency of the results, if not the effect sizes, one can guardedly conclude that the correlational findings regarding leader abilities and performance are useful. This is so for several reasons. First,

they suggest that some cognitive abilities are more useful and others less so under interpersonal stress. The revised categorization system makes clear why this is so and clarifies which abilities will suffer and which will not.

The findings also imply that the "distraction hypothesis" invoked by Fiedler and Garcia (1987) to explain the effects of interpersonal stress is not adequate. If the distraction hypothesis were valid, the correlations between all ability scores and performance would decrease under stress. Obviously, this is not the case; recall that the correlations between both associative ability measures and performance increased significantly from low to high stress. An arousal hypothesis, coupled with a distinction between dominant responses of a process or content nature, seems able to account for a wider range of phenomena.

One theoretical benefit of the proposed two-resource system is that it allows us to integrate discussions of resources previously considered diverse and begin to make systematic predictions concerning their effects. CRT treats intelligence and experience as separate abilities which are affected in opposing ways by the presence of stress. This view is changing. The first step in this evolution was contributed by McGuire (1987), who demonstrated that

Gf and Gc function differently in the presence of stress. The next step, taken here, is to state that intelligence, experience, and other abilities are arbitrary distinctions which should be discarded in the context of the current theory. In fact, we may need only to distinguish between generative and associative abilities. One implication of this system is that experience and (crystallized) intelligence could be grouped together, if the task required verbal abilities such as a strong vocabulary.

Practical Implications

Cognitive Resource Theory has always stressed the importance of selection and placement, given that leader abilities translate into effective group performance only under prescribed circumstances. The findings of this study do not change the practical implications of CRT; they merely change the perspective from which the recommendations are viewed. The correlational results imply that if we can classify leaders on the basis of their general ability type, we might also be able to determine in what types of conditions they will be likely to perform effectively. Alternately, knowing the job conditions of positions we need to fill, we could select leaders on the basis of ability type. The importance of the interaction of leader ability and leader stress in predicting performance behooves us to consider jointly the individual and the job conditions, or what has been called the person-job fit.

Alternately, knowing the effects of stress on some leader abilities, we may be able to identify leaders who would benefit from stress management programs. Ethical considerations would preclude inducing stress in leaders with associative abilities, but helping leaders with high generative abilities to manage stress would seem to be beneficial. Fiedler and Chemers (1974) have already addressed such an approach as part of their "situa-tional engineering" program. This approach is particularly appropriate given the finding that some leaders are more susceptible to the effects of stressful situations, particularly those characterized by evaluation apprehension. By assessing individual differences such as trait anxiety, we can more accurately identify leaders likely to react to stressful situations and those whose behaviors will remain relatively unaffected.

References

Barnes, V., Potter, E. H. III, & Fiedler, F. E. (1983). Effect of interpersonal stress on the prediction of academic performance. *Journal of Applied Psychology, 68*(4), 686–697.

Bass, B. M. (1981). *Stogdill's handbook of leadership.* New York: Free Press.

Bettin, P. J. (1983). *The role of relevant experience and intellectual ability in determining the performance of military leaders: A contingency model explanation.* Unpublished doctoral dissertation, University of Washington, Seattle.

Blades, J. W. (1976). *The influence of intelligence, task ability, and motivation on group performance.* Unpublished doctoral dissertation, University of Washington, Seattle.

Bond, C. F., & Titus, L. J. (1983). Social facilitation: A meta-analysis of 241 studies. *Psychological Bulletin, 94,* 265–292.

Borden, D. F. (1980). *Leader-boss stress, personality, job satisfaction and performance: Another look at the interrelationship of some old constructs in the modern large bureaucracy.* Unpublished doctoral dissertation, University of Washington, Seattle.

Bouchard, T. J. (1976). Field research methods: Interviewing, questionnaires, participant observation, systematic observation, unobtrusive measures. In M.D. Dunnette (Ed.), *Handbook of industrial and organizational psychology* (pp. 363–414). Chicago: Rand McNally.

Cronbach, L. J. (1951). Coefficient alpha and the internal structure of tests. *Psychometrika, 16,* 297–334.

Fiedler, F. E., & Chemers, M. M. (1974). *Leadership and effective management*. Glenview, IL: Scott, Foresman.

Fiedler, F. E., & Garcia, J. E. (1987). *New approaches to effective leadership: Cognitive resources and performance*. New York: John Wiley.

Fiedler, F. E., Potter, E. H. III, Zais, M. M., & Knowlton, W. A., Jr. (1979). Organizational stress and the use and misuse of managerial intelligence and experience. *Journal of Applied Psychology, 64*, 635–647.

Gibson, F. W., Fiedler, F. E., & Daniels, K. M. (1990). *Stress, babble, and the utilization of leader intellectual abilities*. (Organizational Research Tech. Rep. No. 90–1). Seattle: University of Washington.

Guilford, J. P. (1950). Creativity. *American Psychologist, 14*, 469–479.

Guilford, J. P. (1967). *The nature of human intelligence*. New York: McGraw-Hill.

Guilford, J. P., Christensen, P. R., Merrifield, P. R., & Wilson, R. C. (1978). Alternate uses: Manual of instructions and interpretations. Beverly Hills: Sheridan.

Hackman, J. R., Jones, L. E., & McGrath, J. E. (1967). A set of dimensions for describing the general properties of group-generated written passages. *Psychological Bulletin, 67*, 379–390.

Horn, J. L. (1968). Organization of abilities and the development of intelligence. *Psychological Review, 75*, 242–259.

Horn, J. L. (1975). *Gf-Gc sampler*. Denver, CO: University of Denver.

Horn, J. L. (1982). Whimsy and misunderstandings of Gf-Gc theory: A comment on Guilford. *Psychological Bulletin, 91*, 623–633.

Horn, J. L. (1988). Thinking about human abilities. In J. R. Nesselroade (Ed.), *Handbook of multivariate psychology* (pp. 645–685). New York: Academic Press.

McGuire, M. A. (1987). *The contribution of intelligence to leadership performance on an in-basket test*. Unpublished master's thesis, University of Washington, Seattle.

Mumford, M. D., & Gustafson, S. B. (1988). Creativity syndrome: Integration, application, and innovation. *Psychological Bulletin, 103*, 27–43.

Nunnally, J. C. (1978). *Psychometric theory* (2nd ed.). New York: McGraw-Hill.

Stogdill, R. M. (1948). Personal factors associated with leadership: A survey of the literature. *Journal of Psychology, 25*, 35–71.

Wilson, R. C., Guilford, J. P., Christenson, P. R., & Lewis, D. J. (1954). A factor-analytic study of creative-thinking abilities. *Psychometrika, 19*, 297–311.

Zajonc, R. B. (1965). Social facilitation. *Science, 149*(3681), 269–274.

Frederick W. Gibson (Lt. Col.) is Associate Professor of Behavioral Science and Leadership at the United States Air Force Academy. His current focus is to integrate leadership research and programs conducted by his Department. His research interests include leadership, punishment and performance, and centrality of work. He received his PhD in Industrial-Organizational Psychology from the University of Washington.

Direct inquiries about this article to Frederick W. Gibson, Lieutenant Colonel, Department of Behavioral Sciences and Leadership, USAF Academy, CO 80840, 719/472–3860.

CHAPTER 28

The Impact of Personality, Gender, and International Location on Multilevel Management Ratings

Clark L. Wilson, Jane Wilson, Daniel Booth, and Frank Shipper

This paper reports on three different explorations of scores on the Survey of Management Practices (SMP): (a) their association with personality self-assessments on the Myers-Briggs Type Indicator® (MBTI™) and the Hogan Personality Inventory (HPI), (b) the differences in ratings of male and female managers by their subordinates, and (c) the differences in ratings of managers by their subordinates in Asia, Europe, and the U.S.

In these samples, self-assessments on SMP were more closely related to personality assessments than were ratings by bosses or subordinates. Ratings of men and women managers appeared to differ more by organization or occupation than by gender. Regional differences indicated higher ratings for Asian than either European or U.S. managers, while European—especially senior—managers were seen as imposing more structure or exercising more control than their U.S. counterparts.

Myers-Briggs Type Indicator is a registered trademark of Consulting Psychologists Press, Inc.

MBTI is a trademark of Consulting Psychologists Press, Inc.

The pursuit of validity is a many-faceted enterprise and the subject of historically heated discussion. We agree with Messick (1989) that, to assert validity, one must satisfactorily answer the full range of questions asked by knowledgeable people about the use and value of an assessment. Focusing on concurrent and/or predictive validity is not sufficient.

With leaders and organizations, the two most basic questions concern the extent to which an assessment relates to practical, operational criteria and the degree of change that results from feedback and follow-up programs. In a previous article (Wilson, O'Hare, & Shipper, 1990), we presented data concerning the extent to which programs based on the Survey of Management Practices (SMP) (Wilson, 1984) can satisfy these two criteria.

Here we pursue three additional practical and important questions: (a) How do managers' self-ratings on personality inventories of the type widely used in development programs relate to ratings by their bosses and others on competency-based assessments, such as those made with SMP? (b) Are women managers rated differently from men? (c) Are managers in other regions of the world rated differently from those in the U.S.?

The first question is of general theoretical interest but also carries special practical importance as an adjunct to the ever-increasing use of personality measures in development programs. The remaining two questions reflect important cultural and multinational trends and issues.

SMP provides multilevel assessments of a manager's competencies and attributes in the areas of goal clarification, planning and problem solving, work facilitation, feedback, exercise of positive control, and reinforcement of good performance. Within those six areas, 11 managerial skills and 4 interpersonal attributes are evaluated by self, bosses, and others. These evaluations are the basis for the following studies of various relationships.

Personality

Presented first are data on the association between the Survey of Management Practices (SMP) and the Myers-Briggs Type Indicator (MBTI) (Myers & McCaulley, 1985). This is followed by data on the relationship of SMP to the Hogan Personality Inventory (HPI) (Hogan, 1986). Our objective was not to evaluate either instrument as such but to explore ways in which feedback from them might be combined with that from the more operationally oriented SMP.

It should be kept in mind that the MBTI and the HPI are self-assessments. For this reason, participants in management training programs which use personality inventories often ask "What do I do next?" Their types or personality profiles describe how they feel about themselves and their preferred behaviors; they do not suggest, except by inference, what they might do to increase their effectiveness. Therefore, any association with a competency-based assessment such as SMP could provide a practical linkage for action planning and personal development.

MBTI-SMP

The data were from two sources. The first was a program conducted by psychologists (D. Johnson, R. Ochsman, & R. Webb, data supplied by personal communication, May 1990) at the University of Arkansas at Little Rock for the Army National Guard. Included were those participants on whom complete data were available for the MBTI, HPI, and SMP, a total of 924.

The second data source was a management development program in a national hotel chain (N. F. Horney, data supplied by personal communication, January 1991). Eighty-eight participants from various departments in the organization were rated on SMP by self, boss, subordinates, and peers.

The MBTI yields continuous scores for each scale ranging from less than 40 to over 150 which are dichotomized into types at a raw score of 100. The medians in the Arkansas sample were: E-I types = 99, which is close to the prescribed 100; S-N types = 84; T-F types = 80; J-P types = 76. Therefore, dividing at 100 left the scales with these breakouts: E-I 465/459; S-N 692/232; T-F 802/122; J-P 759/165. To complete the picture, the 250 ESTJs and 293 ISTJs were 59% of the total sample in these two types. There were also 89 ENTJs and 42 INTJs, for a total sample of 73% of TJ types. The hotel sample distributions were similarly unbalanced.

Methods

Our research first explored the MBTI scales as continua rather than types. Each MBTI scale distribution was divided into three parts, with 10% of cases on either side of the sample median sorted into a neutral zone. This left three categories of approximately 40%-20%-40%. ANOVA was used to assess the relationships to

SMP. These analyses revealed a substantial number of curvilinear associations with the neutral category often scoring higher on the SMP scales than did the defined types.

Upon review of the manuscript, David Saunders, who worked with Isabel Myers in shaping the original scales, and Allen Hammer of Consulting Psychologists Press, the publishers of MBTI, (personal communication, December 1991) observed that this procedure placed respondents of the same type on both sides of the neutral zone—J types on both ends, for example. They advised that this did not follow the rationale for types and that MBTI users would likely consider the method unfair.

As a result of these observations, and for the first series of analyses presented here, MBTI score distributions were split into two segments at 100. These splits were used in t-tests to probe possible differences in levels of each SMP scale.

For SMP, each participant received individual ratings by self and boss and an aggregate rating by subordinates or others. We place primary emphasis on the subordinates' ratings because we have demonstrated in previous studies (Wilson et al., 1990) that subordinate ratings are the most valid when related to performance measures.

Results

Table 1 shows the t-ratios and p-values of the tests of significance for the Arkansas sample of the E-I relationship with SMP self-scores. Similar tests were made of boss and subordinate SMP ratings to investigate how well ratings by others replicated those by self, to search for evidence of the managers' personal insights. The latter are presented only if they exceeded the .05 level of significance.

Table 1 shows significant associations between self-ratings on 13 of the 15 SMP scales; the exceptions were Control of details and Goal pressure. In all 13 cases,

the Extroverts (E) rated themselves significantly higher on the SMP scales. One subordinate rating associated significantly in the E direction, .027, with Approachability. There were no boss rating associations.

In the hotel sample, self-assessments on Encouraging participation, Recognition, Approachability, and Building trust associated positively in the E direction; Goal pressure associated with high I types. No boss or peer associations were found, but subordinates rated I types higher on Control of details. Results of tests of the other MBTI scales follow.

Sensing-Intuition (S-N). Three Arkansas SMP self-scores were significantly related to this MBTI scale in the Intuitive direction: Clarification of goals, Delegation (Permissiveness), and Interest in subordinate growth. But on Time emphasis and Control of details, the S types rated themselves significantly higher. Bosses' ratings on SMP showed the greatest number of associations (eight) of any MBTI scale, all in the Intuitive direction. These were Clarification of goals, Work facilitation, Feedback, Control of details, Recognition, Approachability, Teambuilding, and Interest in subordinate growth. No subordinate ratings associated. In the hotel sample, there were no significant associations at any level of rater on the S-N scale.

Thinking-Feeling (T-F). Four self-ratings on SMP scales related significantly in the Thinking direction: Orderly planning, Expertise, Feedback, and Time emphasis. There were no significant associations in the Feeling direction.

Among the boss SMP ratings, only Approachability significantly related, and that was with higher Feeling scores. Four subordinate ratings yielded significant associations, all in the Thinking direction: Clarification of goals, Orderly planning, Work facilitation, and Time emphasis.

In the hotel sample, several self-assessments on SMP related to the T-F

TABLE 1 Association of MBTI Extraversion–Introversion (E–I) with the
Survey of Management Practices (SMP)

SMP Scale	SMP Self-Rating by MBTI–E-I		SMP/E-I Association by Rating Groups		
	E	I	Self[a]		Subs
			t[b]	p[b]	
Clarifying goals	72.2[c]	67.9	4.79	E[d].004***	
Encouraging participation	75.5	73.2	2.90	E.004**	
Orderly planning	70.7	67.1	3.81	E.000***	
Organizational expertise	73.5	68.8	5.54	E.000***	
Work facilitation	72.1	68.6	3.63	E.000***	
Giving feedback	73.3	67.5	6.64	E.000***	
Time emphasis	79.0	76.3	2.89	E.004**	
Control of details	52.9	51.3	1.58	.115	
Goal pressure	40.7	40.7	0.05	.960	
Delegation (Permissiveness)	65.9	64.1	2.36	E.019*	
Recognition	78.5	73.5	5.22	E.000***	
Approachability	78.7	73.4	5.61	E.000***	E.027*
Teambuilding	79.2	74.9	5.24	E.000***	
Interest in subordinate growth	78.8	74.4	5.46	E.000***	
Building trust	82.8	79.5	4.36	E.000***	

Note. [a]No boss ratings were significantly related. [b]t = Critical ratio. [c]Scores are percent of maximum possible. [d]E = Extraverts scored themselves higher on SMP.

*p < .05.   **p < .01.   ***p < .001.

scale in the Thinking direction: *Clarification of goals, Encouraging participation, Time emphasis, Control of details, Recognition, Approachability, Teambuilding, Interest in subordinate growth,* and *Building trust.*

However, the five SMP scales relating to the T-F scale by subordinate ratings were all in the *Feeling* direction: *Clarification of goals, Feedback, Recognition, Teambuilding,* and *Interest in subordinate growth.* No boss or peer ratings were associated.

Judging-Perceiving (J-P). Here the self-ratings on SMP in the Arkansas study related in the *Judging* (J) direction to *Orderly work planning, Work facilitation, Feedback, Time emphasis, Control of de-* tails, *Recognition, Teambuilding, Interest in subordinate growth,* and *Building trust.*

Both boss and subordinate ratings were significantly associated with *Orderly planning* and *Time emphasis* in the *Judging* (J) direction. In addition, J types were rated higher by subordinates on *Work facilitation, Control of details,* and *Approachability.*

In the hotel sample, self-assessments on these SMP scales related in the *Judging* direction: *Clarification of goals, Encouraging participation, Orderly work planning, Expertise, Work facilitation, Feedback, Time emphasis, Control of details, Approachability, Teambuilding,* and *Building trust.* Boss's ratings on *Orderly work planning* were related, but in the P direction. Peers' ratings on *Orderly work planning*, *Work facilitation*, and *Building trust* all related in the *Judging* direction. No subordinate ratings were associated.

Further Investigation of Continuous Scores

The practice of dichotomizing continuous distributions and the curvilinear results obtained in the preliminary probing with 40–20–40 splits of MBTI scales prompted another look at the possible insights to be gained from the continuous scoring of MBTI. The data from the Arkansas sample were split to leave subsamples of at least 100 respondents centered around the 100 score level in a neutral ("?") category. ANOVA was then used to explore relationships with the SMP scales. Table 2 presents the results from the J-P scale, which produced the largest number of significant relationships.

Twelve of the 15 self-ratings on SMP scales produced significant relationships when the sample was split in this manner. Of these, 10 were curvilinear. Two self-ratings, *Orderly work planning* and *Time emphasis*, were high in the *Judging* direction; David Saunders advised that the J-P scale in one form of the MBTI includes a subscale on planning. The 10 curvilinear relationships, except for *Control of details*, tended to concentrate in scales which psychologists would usually associate with the *Consideration* factor in the Ohio State Leadership Studies (Stogdill & Coons, 1957). Examples would be *Encouraging participation*, *Work facilitation*, *Recognition*, *Approachability*, and *Interest in subordinate growth*.

However, one should note that, though they were curvilinear with the neutral (?) scores lower, the J (Judging) scores were always higher than the P (Perceiving) scores. These results prompted a further exploration, this time using Pearson product moment correlations between the 4 MBTI and the 15 SMP scales, a total of 60 correlations for each rater level. This approach resulted in 26 self-ratings significant at the .05 level. Only three boss and two subordinate correlations were significant, well within the 5% expectations. For comparison, the t-test explorations reported earlier resulted in 31 significant relationships for selves, 11 for bosses, and 9 for subordinates.

Summary of MBTI-SMP Relationships

The primary implication of the MBTI-SMP relationship is that MBTI self-ratings do associate with many self-assessments on SMP. However, our objective was to explore the relationships between self-assessments on the MBTI and ratings by relevant others on SMP to find ways to utilize the personality inventories and operationally oriented surveys in management skill training programs.

In terms of that objective, three MBTI scales, S-N, T-F, and J-P, provided some relationships with SMP scales in ratings by others. For example, high *Sensing* (S), *Thinking* (T), and *Judging* (J) scores on MBTI tended to relate to self and observer SMP scores on such skills as *Orderly work planning* and *Time emphasis*, which reflect preferences for logic and reason in combination for planful control (Myers, 1980). These scales are comparable to Ohio State's *Initiating Structure* (Stogdill & Coons, 1957). In SMP terms, these are *task-oriented* scales.

Further, self and subordinate scores on these same types also showed modest relations with some SMP scales reflecting Ohio State's *Consideration* which, in SMP terms, reflect the *tone* of one's interpersonal relations. Similarly, high *Intuitive* (N), *Feeling* (F), and *Perceiving* (P) scores tended to relate to tone-oriented ratings by others. In combination, these reflect a potential balance of tone- and task-oriented skills found by previous research (Wilson, O'Hare, & Shipper, 1990) to be most effective in management roles. This tendency may also account partially for

TABLE 2 Association of MBTI Judging–Perceiving (J–P) Scores with the Survey of Management Practices (SMP)

SMP Scale	SMP Self-Rating by MBTI J–?				SMP/J-P Association by Rating Groups		
	J	?	P	$\underline{F}^{b}$	Self	Boss[a]	Subs[a]
N =	696	104	124		p^{b}	p^{b}	p^{b}
Clarifying goals	70.8[c]	66.4	68.7	5.5	C[d].004*		
Encouraging participation	74.9	71.3	73.7	4.2	C .016*		
Orderly planning	70.8	64.2	62.2	26.4	J[e] .000*	J.010**	C.004**
Organizational expertise	71.6	68.8	71.0	2.1	.119		
Work facilitation	71.5	66.0	67.5	8.9	C .000***		C.038*
Feedback	71.2	67.3	68.5	5.2	C .006**		
Time emphasis	78.9	75.0	73.1	11.3	J .000***	J.027*	J .002**
Control of details	53.0	48.8	49.7	5.19	C .006**		C.034*
Goal pressure	40.2	41.9	42.5	1.3	.274		
Delegation (Permissiveness)	64.6	65.4	66.7	1.7	.183		
Recognition	77.0	71.4	74.3	7.6	C .001***		
Approachability	76.7	72.4	75.4	4.0	C .019*		
Teambuilding	77.9	73.0	75.6	7.7	C .000***		
Interest in subordinate growth	77.3	73.4	75.5	5.2	C .006**		
Building trust	81.8	78.5	79.8	4.6	C .010**		

[a]Boss and subordinate p-values are cited only if $F \le .05$. [b]$\underline{F}$: (2,921). [c]Scores are percent of maximum possible. [d]C = curvilinear relation. [e]J = High Judging associated with higher SMP scores.

*p < .05.   **p < .01.   ***p < .001.

the curvilinear relations in the T and J scores reported here.

Investigation of curvilinear relationships (see Table 2) raises the question of possible intervening causal factors. It is beyond the scope of this paper to investigate the reasons for curvilinearity in MBTI scales, except insofar as that characteristic might be of value in development programs.

One hypothesis could be that respondents who are decisive and consistent, although of opposing types, answer both the MBTI and SMP in a consistent positive direction. Or is it possible that respondents who have insights into their types, whether they are J or P types, also have insights into how they feel managers should behave? Is it possible that J and P types are equally disposed to be good managers, although there are reported to be substantially more J than P types in managerial roles? Myers (1980) alludes to this bipolar disposition: "To solve problems and make decisions, you need to make full use of your perception *and* [italics added] judgement" (p. 30).

It can be demonstrated that balanced management skills, as measured by SMP, are usually more effective both in terms of productivity and the quality of working life. Therefore, one training objective is to enable participants to balance their task and tone skills.

Such a training benefit might be drawn from the joint use of the MBTI and SMP in certain group problem-solving exercises. For example, suppose a trainer separates the high F and high T types into competing groups to solve a managerial interpersonal-relations problem. The tendencies reflected in the MBTI manual and the hotel data—that high F types usually project higher tone-oriented skills, such as *Feedback, Recognition, Teambuilding,* and *Interest in subordinate growth*—would give the F types opportunity to demonstrate these behaviors. This demonstration and subsequent discussions should enhance the T types understanding of how to implement their task-oriented skills in a more balanced manner. Similar exercises with high J versus high P types, or more particularly high TJ types versus others, could do the same for building task-oriented skills for those in need of better balance.

A recent experience (P. Connolly, personal communication, December 1991) gives further insights into ways to benefit from the combined use of SMP and MBTI. Connolly designed a training program involving feedback from both instruments. The trainer, who was familiar with MBTI but had only limited experience with SMP, wanted to feed back the MBTI results first, but Connolly and the client insisted on placing the SMP results ahead. After the first program, the trainer reported that participants got much more out of the MBTI feedback than at any other time in his experience. The reason, he reported, was that, having learned of their impact on their co-workers from SMP, they were more motivated to study their MBTI results for a better understanding of the reasons for that impact.

Similar experiences have been reported from the VA Medical Center in Kansas City (S. Campion, personal communication, February 1992). For several years, they have given SMP feedback the first day of an ongoing program, followed the next day with results from various psychological tests and inventories, including the MBTI. They report more favorable results by placing the SMP on-the-job observations first in the sequence.

HPI

This study was also part of the previously cited Army National Guard program conducted by psychologists at the University of Arkansas. Earlier we remarked that both the MBTI and HPI are self-reports. However, it should be noted that Hogan's interpretion of the item response process may appear to be different from others, as demonstrated by some of Hogan's (1986) relevant statements:

> People have images of themselves that they want others to accept and believe. These images organize and shape people's overt behavior. . . . This view of item responding has two major implications. First, it implies that responses to personality inventories are not self-reports (i.e., second best ways to observe behavior). Rather, the responses reveal how a person wants to be regarded. . . . The second implication . . . is that the scale scores derived from an aggregation of item responses do not necessarily reflect underlying traits in the respondent. Scale scores indicate the respondent's interpersonal style, which in turn denotes how the respondent typically is perceived by others who know him or her well. (p. 2)

Results

The Hogan *Likability* scale produced the greatest number of significant associations with SMP, especially with ratings by bosses and subordinates. According to Hogan (1986), *Likability* identifies a person as "friendly, pleasant, tolerant, and likable" (p. 11).

The data in Table 3 are evaluated by ANOVA with the Likability scores divided into thirds from low to high. The HPI includes a *Faking* scale which was not reported by the Arkansas psychologists. Results of tests of the HPI scales follow.

Likability. The first and rather striking result is the relatively large number of significant associations. Thirteen of the 15 SMP self-ratings were significantly as-

TABLE 3 Relationship of the Hogan Likability (LIK) Scale to the Survey of Management Practices (SMP) Scales

| SMP Scale | SMP Self-Ratings By LIKABILITY | | | Significance of Association | | | |
| | Low | Medium | High | Self | | Boss | Subs |
N =	330	302	292	F^a	p^a	p^a	p^a
Clarifying goals	67.7[b]	70.4	72.4	9.8	.000***		.041*
Encouraging participation	71.8	74.3	77.3	16.1	.000***	.041*	.000***
Orderly planning	67.2	69.4	70.4	3.9	.020*		
Organizational expertise	69.6	71.0	73.1	5.6	.004**		
Work facilitation	67.9	70.4	73.1	9.8	.000***		
Feedback	69.0	70.1	72.3	5.0	.007**		
Time emphasis	77.2	77.9	77.9	0.3	.780		
Control of details	52.7	52.8	50.7	1.8	.170		R.008**
Goal pressure	45.9	39.9	35.6	R^c30.4	.000***	R.000***	R.000***
Delegation (Permissiveness)	63.7	64.6	66.8	5.5	.004**		.000***
Recognition	72.8	76.0	79.7	17.5	.000***	.012**	.001***
Approachability	70.8	76.7	81.2	44.0	.000***	.000***	.000***
Teambuilding	73.9	77.0	80.6	22.9	.000***	.002**	.001***
Interest in subordinate growth	73.3	76.7	80.2	24.8	.000***	.012**	.011*
Building trust	79.5	80.3	83.9	12.8	.000***		

[a]F: (2, 921). [b]Scores are percent of maximum possible. [c]R = Direction of association is reversed from all other significant relations in which high <u>Likability</u> scores are associated with higher SMP scores.

*p < .05.   **p < .01.   ***p < .001.

sociated with *Likability*; *Time emphasis* and *Control of details* were the exceptions. Twelve associations were positive. The sole negative was high *Likability* with low *Goal pressure* with an F-ratio of (F = 30.4). Also noteworthy is the high positive association (F = 44.0) between high *Likability* and high *Approachability*. Perspective on the extreme level of these associations can be realized by noting that with these degrees of freedom (2,921), a p-value of .000 is reached at an F-value of approximately 8.0. Ratings by bosses and subordinates are also positive and significant in association with those SMP dimensions which reflect a positive tone in one's interpersonal relations: *Encouraging participation*, *Delegation*, *Recognition*, *Approachability*, *Teambuilding*, and In-

terest in subordinate growth. The negative association in both the boss and subordinate samples on *Goal pressure* reinforces this perception. Similarly, that .008 association between subordinates' ratings and *Control of details* was in the direction of higher *Likability* associated with less control.

Intellectance ("tendencies that cause people to be considered bright and cultured," Hogan, 1986, p. 9). Here, 10 of 15 SMP self-ratings were associated with *Intellectance*, the exceptions being *Encouraging participation*, *Orderly planning*, *Time emphasis*, *Goal pressure*, and *Approachability*. Most all significant associations were between higher *Intellectance* and higher SMP scores. The exceptions were *Control of details*, on which lower

Intellectance was associated with higher control, and *Teambuilding*, which was curvilinear. However, no boss or subordinate ratings were associated significantly.

Adjustment ("impress others as being well adjusted and self-confident," Hogan, 1986, p. 9). Of the 15 SMP self-ratings, 12 were associated positively with *Adjustment* although one, *Goal pressure*, was reversed with higher *Adjustment* related to lower *Goal pressure*. The SMP scales not associated were *Time emphasis* and *Control of details*. Although no subordinate ratings associated significantly, two ratings by bosses — *Delegation* and *Approachability* — both associated positively.

Prudence ("associated with hard work, conventional values, school success, and a kind of cognitive rigidity," Hogan, 1986, p. 10). Only 5 of the 15 SMP self-scores were associated with this Hogan scale and were all positively related: *Orderly planning*, *Time emphasis*, *Control of details*, *Approachability*, and *Building trust*. Among ratings by others, boss ratings were positively associated with *Orderly planning*, *Expertise*, and *Time emphasis* and were negatively associated with *Goal pressure*. No subordinate ratings were significant.

Sociability ("outgoing, exhibitionistic, and almost compulsively interactive," Hogan, 1986, p. 10). Ten of the 15 associations with self-ratings were positive and significant. Interestingly, higher *Sociability* related to higher *Goal pressure* in self, boss, and subordinate ratings. Additionally, higher *Sociability* was associated with lower *Delegation* in the bosses' ratings.

Ambition ("best interpreted as a leadership syndrome," Hogan, 1986, p. 10). *Ambition* associated significantly and positively with all 15 SMP self-ratings. These included *Goal pressure*, the only SMP scale replicated in both boss and subordinate samples with the latter missing the .05 level of significance by a narrow margin. No additional ratings by bosses or subordinates were associated significantly.

Summary of SMP-HPI Relationships

Again, self-ratings on SMP were more closely associated with HPI scores than were boss or subordinate ratings. With 6 HPI and 15 SMP scales for 90 possible relationships at each level, self-assessments were significant in 65, bosses in 15, and subordinates in 11.

The associations do ring true in a number of scales. *Likability* projects to positive tone in interpersonal relations. *Adjustment* projects to lower *Goal pressure* in self-assessments and higher *Delegation* and *Approachability* in bosses' ratings. *Prudence* relates to such task-oriented skills as *Orderly planning*, *Time emphasis*, and *Control of details*.

In development programs, the HPI could readily be used with group problem-solving exercises as suggested in the MBTI summary. Sorting a group into high and low *Likability* scores for such exercises should demonstrate the exercise of sound tone-oriented skills for those who need to strengthen those important skills. Doing the same with, say, high and low *Prudence* or *Ambition* respondents should reinforce better task-oriented skills for those in need of balancing those competencies.

Gender

Unfortunately, only occasionally does the opportunity arise to compare men and women managers. Even then the comparisons are not usually controllable with respect to occupation of the manager or gender of the respondents. The studies reported here suffer from those shortfalls but do provide an opportunity to compare women with men in two widely separated managerial situations.

The first study (A) is from a large utility in New England; the second study (B) is from a group of state employees in the Southwest (F. Shipper, personal commu-

TABLE 4 Association of Subordinate Ratings by Gender of Manager with the Survey of Management Practices (SMP) in Utility (A) and State Government (B) Samples

SMP Scale	Study[a]	F[a]	M[a]	t[b]	p[b]
Clarifying goals	A	4.74[c]	4.74	.00	.992
	B	4.83	5.07	M 2.01	.046*
Encouraging participation	A	4.88	4.91	0.29	.775
	B	5.19	5.50	M 2.84	.005**
Orderly work planning	A	4.85	4.76	.97	.332
	B	4.89	4.95	0.48	.631
Organizational expertise	A	5.02	4.96	.62	.531
	B	5.24	5.57	M 3.18	.002**
Work facilitation	A	4.91	4.71	F 1.98	.049*
	B	4.80	5.16	M 3.10	.002**
Feedback	A	4.95	4.94	.11	.910
	B	4.85	5.05	1.71	.090
Time emphasis	A	5.12	5.16	0.47	.638
	B	5.39	5.03	F 3.55	.000***
Control of details	A	4.28	4.12	1.71	.087
	B	3.94	3.58	F 3.44	.001***
Goal pressure	A	2.74	3.03	M 3.28	.001***
	B	3.06	2.53	F 4.49	.000***
Delegation (Permissiveness)	A	4.78	4.90	1.47	.143
	B	5.01	5.22	M 2.35	.020*
Recognition	A	5.19	5.19	.05	.958
	B[c]	5.33	5.54	1.61	.108
Approachability	A[c]	5.39	5.16	.21	.836
Teambuilding	A[c]	4.91	4.86	.60	.551
Interest in subordinate growth	A[c]	4.86	4.78	.80	.423
Building trust	A[c]	5.29	5.07	F 2.46	.014**

[a]Study samples: Utility (A) females = 245, males = 419; state government (B) females = 95, males = 149. [b]t-values: M = Males are rated significantly higher, F = Females significantly higher. [c]Scores are average item scores for the scale. The last four Interpersonal relations scales were not analyzed for the state government sample.

*p < .05.   **p < .01.   ***p < .001.

nication, November 1990). The results in Table 4 are from subordinate ratings only. No data are available on the types of job or gender of respondents.

Results

The first noticeable result is that there are no consistent similarities between Study A and Study B. For example, in the state government sample (B), men were rated higher than women on the SMP for *Clarification of goals, Encouraging partic-* *ipation, Expertise, Work facilitation,* and *Delegation.* Women were rated higher than their male colleagues on *Time emphasis, Control of details,* and *Goal pressure.* The combination of these highs and lows denotes the exercise of tighter control by these women. Again, however, we do not know the occupations, organization cultures, or work situations involved.

In contrast, the only subordinate ratings which differentiated men from women in the utility sample (A) were on *Work facilitation* (women rated higher than men) and *Goal pressure* (men rated higher than women). In both of these cases, the results were opposite from those in the government sample.

As for self-ratings (data not shown), in only four instances did women rate themselves differently from their male colleagues. In the utility sample (A), women said they exercised greater *Control of details* than men; their subordinates did not agree. In the government sample (B), women said they exercised more *Goal pressure* and, as noted previously, their subordinates agreed. Women rated themselves significantly higher on *Delegation (Permissiveness)*, but their subordinates rated them significantly lower. Although they rated themselves higher on *Recognition*, their subordinates did not differentiate them significantly from the men.

Summary of the Gender Studies

There are no consistent differences between men and women in these studies. This brings into question some of the writings which assert that women approach management or leadership in distinctly feminine stereotypical ways (Rosener, 1990). Rather, as we have observed in contrasting group averages, it may be that there are more differences between organizations and occupations than between genders. Since men and women are often assigned different functional roles, they may utilize managerial skills they deem appropriate to those roles.

International Comparisons

As multinational organizations increase in number and feedback-based development programs spread from country to country, the use of assessments spreads apace. We often hear, "Is this instrument useful in other countries?" The study reported here, from a multinational high-tech organization, involved managers in Asia (primarily Malaysia, the Philippines, Hong Kong, and a few managers from Ja-

pan), Europe (primarily Great Britain, France, and Germany, with a few managers from scattered other countries), and the United States (primarily from the West) (D. Booth, personal communication, November 1990). Given the international character of operations, some managers may be assigned to countries other than those of their origin.

Results of Middle-Level Managers' Ratings

Subordinate ratings were used in Table 5 because they have proved to be the most valid in previous studies (Wilson et al., 1990) and because sample sizes were larger. Ratings by self and boss will be discussed briefly.

This sample discloses clear differences in subordinates' ratings from one region to another. Fairly clearly, these differences are largely due to the higher ratings of the Asian managers. To focus on this result, the F-ratios were identified by letter to indicate the highest average rating for each scale on which there were significant differences. The Asians were rated highest on 10 of the 12 comparisons in which overall differences were significant. Two, *Encouraging participation* and *Teambuilding*, were curvilinear; in both of these cases the European managers were lowest. Although three were nonsignificant, one comparison, *Recognition*, approached significance but was curvilinear.

Analyses of self-ratings (data not shown) generally revealed the same results. Of the 15 SMP scales, significant F-ratios (p = .05) were developed on 8, with the Asian managers rating themselves noticeably higher.

However, ratings by Asian bosses (data not shown) were not as consistently high. They rated their managers significantly higher on four scales: *Clarification of goals, Expertise, Control of details*, and *Goal pressure*.

TABLE 5 Comparison of Ratings of Asian, European, and U.S.
Middle-level Managers by Subordinates

SMP Scale	Asian	Europe	US	F[a]		p[a]
N =	233	533	788			
Clarifying goals	4.96[b]	4.66	4.68	AS[c]	9.00	.000***
Encouraging participation	4.96	4.78	4.95	C[d]	5.49	.004**
Orderly planning	4.99	4.14	4.50	AS	22.50	.000***
Organizational expertise	5.09	4.88	4.84	AS	7.29	.001***
Work facilitation	4.88	4.53	4.60	AS	10.28	.000***
Feedback	4.87	4.56	4.56	AS	10.22	.000***
Time emphasis	5.25	4.84	4.89	AS	15.64	.000***
Control of details	4.32	3.89	3.81	AS	24.63	.000***
Goal pressure	3.59	3.45	3.13	AS	24.27	.000***
Delegation (Permissiveness)	4.71	4.65	4.67		0.35	.705
Recognition	5.04	4.93	5.08		2.70	.068
Approachability	5.17	5.18	5.24		0.52	.594
Teambuilding	4.97	4.68	4.81	C	7.45	.001***
Interest in subordinate growth	4.87	4.77	4.75	AS	3.09	.046*
Building trust	5.31	5.06	5.17	AS	6.09	.002**

[a]F: (2, 1551). [b]Scores are average item score for each scale. [c]AS = Asian managers
were rated highest. [d]C = curvilinear relationship.

*p < .05.   **p < .01.   ***p < .001.

Comparison of European and U.S. Managers

In addition to the middle-level managers analyzed in Table 5, there were enough senior managers in the European and U.S. samples — but not in the Asian — to permit a separate analysis. So, we repeated the analysis of the European and U.S. samples of middle managers from Table 5 to get free of the variance contributed by the Asian sample and added the senior managers from those same regions. The results are in Table 6.

Speaking first of the middle-level managers, the t-ratios are significant on only 5 of the 15 SMP scales. After omitting the Asians, the U.S. managers were rated higher than their European counterparts on *Encouraging participation, Recognition, Teambuilding,* and *Building trust* and were rated lower on *Goal pressure.*

A comparison of subordinate ratings of

senior managers produced results similar to those of the middle managers on two scales: *Goal pressure* was very significantly higher among Europeans and *Recognition* was rated higher by U.S. subordinates. Beyond that, the senior European managers' profile reflects a more task-focused, structured orientation with very significantly higher ratings on *Orderly planning, Time emphasis, Control of details,* and *Goal pressure. Feedback* is also significantly higher at the .01 level. By contrast, the U.S. managers are rated higher on *Delegation* and *Recognition.*

Summary of Regional Comparisons

In these samples, Asian managers were rated significantly higher than were their European and U.S. counterparts. This result replicated an experience of about 15 years ago when Taiwanese ratings

TABLE 6 Comparison of Ratings of Middle-Level, Senior European (EU), and U.S. Managers by Subordinates

SMP Scale	Middle			Senior		
	EU	US	p^a	EU	US	p^a
N =	533	788		81	679	
Clarifying goals	4.66[b]	4.68	.689	4.98	4.77	.058
Encouraging participation	4.78	4.95	US[c] .002**	4.77	4.95	.109
Orderly planning	4.14	4.50	.168	4.85	4.27	EU .000***
Organizational expertise	4.88	4.84	.425	5.04	4.91	.232
Work facilitation	4.53	4.60	.209	4.54	4.53	.936
Feedback	4.56	4.56	.990	4.88	4.59	EU .014**
Time emphasis	4.84	4.89	.972	5.52	4.85	EU .000***
Control of details	3.89	3.81	.154	4.08	3.63	EU .000***
Goal pressure	3.45	3.13	EU .000***	3.90	3.22	EU .000***
Delegation (Permissiveness)	4.65	4.67	.714	4.44	4.72	US .010**
Recognition	4.93	5.08	US .023*	4.79	5.10	US .014**
Approachability	5.18	5.24	.393	4.93	5.17	.094
Teambuilding	4.68	4.81	US .018*	4.75	4.80	.730
Interest in subordinate growth	4.77	4.75	.180	4.68	4.76	.489
Building trust	5.06	5.17	US .037*	5.31	5.19	.307

[a]F: Middle (1, 1391); Senior (1, 758). [b]Scores are average item scores. [c]Significant
t-ratios are tagged EU (European) or US to identify higher rated managers.

*$p < .05$.   **$p < .01$.   ***$p < .001$.

were well above the norm for another multinational corporation.

Further, the differences between European and U.S. managers at the senior level were very significantly different, with the Europeans apparently exercising greater structure in their communications. One would conclude that norms must be restandardized in moving from one international region to another unless it can be shown that one type of profile is more effective in satisfying acceptable operational criteria across cultures.

Summary

The most succinct way to present the overall results of this range of studies is to posit them in terms of a series of hypotheses:

1. *Hypothesis 1 – Personality.* Self-assessments on the MBTI and HPI are significantly related to assessments by others on a competency-based instrument such as the SMP.

2. *Hypothesis 2 – Gender.* The profiles of women managers are significantly different from those of their male counterparts when rated by their bosses or subordinates on SMP.

3. *Hypothesis 3 – International.* There are significant differences in the ratings of managers by their subordinates in different countries.

Evaluation of the Hypotheses

Within the limits of the samples and methods of these studies, one would conclude that Hypotheses 1 and 2 – personality and gender—are not fully supported. In short, personality self-assessments do not relate to SMP evaluations by others, nor do boss and subordinate ratings of managers on SMP differ consistently by gender. However, Hypothesis 3 is supported: Ratings of managers by their subordinates do differ by international region in what appears to be a systematic manner.

References

Hogan, R. (1986). *Hogan Personality Inventory*. Minneapolis: National Computer Systems.

Messick, S. (1989). Validity. In R. Linn (Ed.), *Educational measurement* (3rd ed., pp. 13–104). New York: Macmillan.

Myers, I. (1980). *Introduction to type*. Palo Alto, CA: Consulting Psychologists Press.

Myers, I., & McCaulley, M. (1985) *Manual: A guide to the development and use of the Myers-Briggs Type Indicator*. Palo Alto, CA: Consulting Psychologists Press.

Rosener, J. B. (1990, November-December). Ways women lead. *Harvard Business Review*, pp. 117–125.

Stogdill, R. M., & Coons, A. E. (1957). *Leader behavior: Its description and measurement*. (Research Monograph No. 88). Columbus: Ohio State University.

Wilson, C. L. (1984). *Survey of management practices*. New Canaan, CT: Clark Wilson Publishing.

Wilson, C., O'Hare, D., & Shipper, F. (1990). Task cycle theory: The processes of influence. In K. E. Clark & M. B. Clark (Eds.), *Measures of leadership* (pp. 185–204). West Orange, NJ: Leadership Library of America.

Clark L. Wilson is President of Clark Wilson Publishing Company, New Canaan, CT. He is the author of numerous articles on assessment of managerial, leadership, and organization skills. He received his PhD from the University of Southern California.

Jane Wilson is Vice President of Clark Wilson Publishing Company. She is a candidate for a Master's Degree at Marymount University.

Daniel Booth is President of The Booth Company in Boulder, CO, the leading distributor of Clark Wilson Publishing Company surveys since 1979. He received his EdD from the University of Colorado.

Frank Shipper is Professor of Management in the Franklin P. Perdue School of Business at Salisbury State University, with prior experience in biomechanical and structural engineering. His current research and consulting interests are leadership and social issues in management. He has authored numerous works, including *Task Cycle Management: A Competency-Based Course for Operating Managers* (Clark Wilson Publishing Company, 1990) and *Avoiding and Surviving Lawsuits: The Executive Guide to Strategic Legal Planning* (Jossey-Bass, 1989).

Direct inquiries about this article to Clark Wilson, Clark Wilson Publishing Company, Box 471—129 Woodridge Drive, New Canaan, CT 06840–0471, 203/966–3018.

CHAPTER 29

The Impact of Classroom Leadership Training on Managerial/Supervisory Job Performance

Phyllis P. Marson and Cheryl D. Bruff

The Leadership Linkages program was designed to increase the effectiveness of the Federal Aviation Administration's Leadership Development Program for newly selected/trained first-line supervisors. Leadership Linkages consists of structured projects which require on-the-job application of skills gained in training. As part of the Leadership Linkages program, the manager of the first-line supervisor was asked to take the role of a coach, providing feedback and advice to the supervisor. This study investigated the impact of this developmental strategy on both supervisory and managerial job performance.

This study investigated the impact of a Leadership Linkages program on the job performance of graduate supervisors. Managers of the supervisors were asked to coach new supervisors, providing feedback to them on the approach and outcome of each project. The impact of the manager's role was also studied.

The Leadership Linkages program consisted of 15 structured projects designed to provide supervisors with skill development opportunities on the job. The projects linked the supervisor's completion of Phase 1 (LDP-1) of the resident Leadership Development Program, with Phase 2 (LDP-2) occurring from 12 to 18 months later. The supervisor was required to select and complete at least 6 projects, most of which included working with one or more subordinates. The manager's role provided the supervisor with task background, insight gained from experience, and feedback. The supervisor and manager debriefed each project and evaluated the results, using a Project Summary Sign-Off Sheet and a Leadership Linkages Program Evaluation.

The Federal Aviation Administration (FAA) had taken a major step toward implementation of a systems approach to management development by designing and delivering the Leadership Development Program, Phases 1 and 2. This program was developed on the foundation of three major studies: (a) a Job Function Analysis of First Line Supervisors (University Research Corporation, 1986), (b) the Competency Identification Study of Successful Supervisors in the FAA (Human Technology, Inc., 1987), and (c) a study of Behavior Modeling in Management Training (Marson, 1987). A prototype of Phase 1 of the Leadership Development Program was developed in 1988, Phase 2 in 1989. Both courses are delivered in residence at the FAA's Center for Management Development in Palm Coast, Florida.

The Leadership Linkages program was aimed at increasing the on-the-job effectiveness of the Leadership Development Program by helping supervisors overcome the barriers that often exist in the work environment which interfere with the application of skills gained in training. Additionally, factors such as the failure of the supervisor to use recommended techniques with subordinates and the failure of the supervisor's manager to provide coaching and feedback were perceived as obstacles to the successful transfer of newly learned skills (Robinson, 1989). The Leadership Linkages program was designed to impact on leadership and performance, overcome these barriers, and facilitate transfer of skills from the classroom to the job.

The research attempted to determine (a) whether skills practiced in the classroom transferred more effectively to the job when structured job applications were added for learning reinforcement, and (b) whether the manager of the first-line supervisor could be used effectively as coach. It was hypothesized that the real impact of this program would be on the manager when the manager assumes the role of coach to the first-line supervisor and helps foster the same skills included in training.

Methodology

Volunteers were solicited from three LDP-1 classes graduating December 1989. The manager of each volunteer was contacted for concurrence. Only when there was commitment from both supervisor and manager were they selected to participate. The population for the study consisted of 48 supervisors and 48 managers.

The Leadership Linkages module includes hardbound notebooks containing instructions and descriptions of the projects, a videotape demonstrating feedback and coaching skills, and evaluation forms. These materials were provided to the managers of the supervisors for distribution. To aid in the evaluation of the pilot study, participants were asked to shorten the time per project from one month to one week. Each project selected was to be discussed and debriefed with the manager and evaluated by both.

Data were collected and analyzed from two sources: (a) Evaluation forms from both supervisors and managers were collected after the projects were completed, and (b) structured telephone interviews with all participants were conducted after the first data were analyzed.

Analysis of Data

Twenty-six supervisors (54%) returned their program evaluation forms following completion of the Leadership Linkages projects. Participants were offered their choice of projects. The most frequently picked project was "Task Delegation" (N = 15) and the least picked "Team Task Management" (N = 2)[1]. Participants were asked to rate 4 global factors on a 5-point

[1]Copies of project lists, their frequency of selection, evaluation forms used, and telephone survey instrument may be obtained by writing to Dr. Phyllis P. Marson, Center for Management Development, 4500 Palm Coast Parkway S.E., Palm Coast, FL 32137.

TABLE 1 Summary Table of Means and
Standard Deviations:
Global Questions (N = 26)

	Means	S.D.
Amount of Time and Effort Required	3.42	0.99
Difficulty of Projects	3.04	0.34
Usefulness of Projects	3.46	1.21
Relevancy of Debriefing Sessions	3.32	0.95

scale with 3 being "just right," 5 high, and
1 low (see Table 1).

Additionally, participants were asked
to rate specific program objectives according to the extent of accomplishment upon
completion of the projects. They were
again asked to use a 5-point scale with 5
being Very Great Extent and 1 being Not
At All (see Table 2). As part of the program evaluation, the participants were
also asked to make suggestions for program improvements and to identify the
most and the least useful aspects. The
results are listed in Table 3.

After the data from the program evaluation mail-in forms were analyzed, a telephone survey was conducted. All except
4 of the original 48 dyads were contacted
and interviewed. Forty-five percent of the

pairs indicated that time constraints, and
not being co-located in the same facility,
town, or area had prevented them from
completing all the projects. Eleven percent indicated that they had never received the Leadership Linkages program.
Forty percent (19 supervisors and 19 managers) completed all six projects and evaluations and participated in the complete
telephone survey.

Although questions were asked in the
telephone interviews about program instructions, the usefulness of the accompanying videotape, job aids/reference materials, and distribution, the primary foci
were on supervisory/managerial reaction
to the program, problems, projects, and
Changes in Supervisory Performance. See
Table 4 for the reported impacts on job
performance.

Impacts on Leadership and Recommendations

Findings from the pilot study indicate
strong field support for the concept of
managerial coaching and practical application of skills on the job. Results indicate
that the Leadership Linkages program appeared to be beneficial for providing linkage between classroom training and job
performance and for facilitating managerial coaching. Considering constraints of

TABLE 2 Summary Table of Means and Standard Deviations:
Program Objectives Accomplishment (N = 26)

	Means	S.D.
Coach Employee with Performance Problem	3.45	0.69
Manage Time (Self/Subordinates)	3.45	0.96
Foster Motivation	3.36	0.81
Use Supervisory Success Skills	3.43	0.95
Guide Subordinate with Development Plan	3.29	0.99
Support Equal Employment Policies	3.36	1.08
Apply Participative Management Skills	3.83	0.92

TABLE 3	Summary Table for Frequency: Program Improvement (N = 26)

	Frequency
Suggestions	
Keep it the Way It Is	7
Make it Optional	5
Allow More Time	3
Add Topics for Projects	2
Complete All Projects	2
Most Useful Aspects	
Generates Communication Between Supervisor/Manager	9
Reinforces LDP–1 Concepts	3
Opportunity to Practice	2
Involvement with Subordinates	2
Job Aids	2
Least Useful Aspects	
All Useful	6
Overtime and Paperwork	4

Note. Total Numbers and N differ because some participants responded more than once.

TABLE 4	Impact on Job Performance: Supervisors and Managers (N = 19)

	Frequency
Supervisors	
Better Time Management	3
Improved Interpersonal Skills	2
Coaching/Counseling Staff Better	1
New Focus on Developing/ Motivating People	1
Delegate More	1
Better Monitoring/ Observing Performance	1
Managers	
Improved Interpersonal Skills	3
Better Time Management	3
Coaching/Counseling Staff Better	2
Promotes Team Involvement	2
Delegates More	1

Note. Total Numbers and N differ because some participants responded more than once and some did not respond.

time and seemingly unusual numbers of supervisors and managers in the population who were not located at the same facility, there was overall positive reaction to the program. Even those who did not complete all the projects responded favorably to the linkages concept. It appears that the structured, planned projects served as a commitment basis for the supervisors and managers who did complete everything. Both groups reported increased communication between the two management groups as one of the outcomes with the greatest impact. Other impacts reported by both groups were improved use of interpersonal, coaching, and counseling skills.

In addition to citing a too-shortened time period for completion of the projects as an obstacle to accomplishment, many participants reported that the program could not have been initiated at a worse time of year for them operationally (January, February, March). The major recommendations from the study included: (a) Continue the use of the videotape sent to the managers which demonstrated the skills of feedback and coaching, (b) distribute the modules to supervisors while they are in residence so that clarification can be gained where needed, (c) make special provisions for those supervisors and managers who are not co-located, and (d) allow more time for completion of the projects.

Overall, recommended structural changes to the Leadership Linkages materials and process were minimal. A larger scale field study, however, is needed to insure inclusion of all technical options in the FAA as well as Headquarters representation. Many comments suggested the strong belief that a program such as Leadership Linkages should be mandatory and part of the "systems" approach to management development.

References

Human Technology, Inc. (1987). *Competency identification study for supervisors: Refined list of competencies, definitions, and behavioral clusters for first level supervisors at FAA* (Contract OPM 85-77). McLean, VA: U.S. Office of Personnel Management.

Marson, P. P. (1987). *A study of behavior modeling in management training—A case study.* Unpublished doctoral dissertation, University of Oklahoma, Norman.

Robinson, James C. (1989). *Training for impact.* San Francisco: Jossey-Bass Management Series.

University Research Corporation (1986). *Federal Aviation Administration supervisory job functions and relation to selection and training* (Contract OPM 85-74). Bethesda, MD: U.S. Office of Personnel Management.

Phyllis P. Marson, PhD, is Program Manager for all general and supervisory/managerial training conducted by the Federal Aviation Administration's Center for Management Development. Her research in the use of behavior modeling for management development is widely cited in the leadership development field, and she is a frequent presenter at international training and testing conferences.

Cheryl D. Bruff is Supervisor of Evaluation in the Research and Evaluation Department at the Federal Aviation Administration's Center for Management Development. Her interests focus on job analysis, test development and validation, the development of selection and promotion systems, and training evaluation.

Direct inquiries about this article to Phyllis P. Marson, Program Manager, Center for Management Development, Federal Aviation Administration, 4500 Palm Coast Parkway, SE, Palm Coast, FL 32137, 904/446-7258.

Taking the Measure of Leadership Impact

How Leaders Share Values in Catholic Higher Education

J. Patrick Murphy and
John F. Settich

The field study reported here examined the effect of leadership on values in Catholic colleges and the degree to which organizational members shared them. The indicators of satisfaction and dissatisfaction were used to measure the impact of leadership; a high level of satisfaction among subgroups was found. A model of value sharing is proposed.

Groucho Marx said it well. As a college president in the movie *Horse Feathers*, he expressed his values to the professorate with the words, "Members of the faculty, let's give our football team a school they can be proud of!" College presidents, and leaders in every organization, define and declare institutional values. Effective college leaders are teachers too. The best of them teach values.

Every college and university professes to have organizational values which it expresses in its mission statement, operational goals, and through the person of its leader. Many leaders in higher education claim that the transfer of institutional values significantly influences the development of seminal student values. Those who make such claims assert that these values should be observable in the leadership of the institution and its environment.

Colleges and universities are pluralistic, by their very nature. The notion of a "free republic of ideas" and a plurality of ideologies, disciplines, and sciences is essential to the business of the enterprise. Conflict, ambiguity, and the free exchange of ideas, including competing and contrasting values, must be nurtured for colleges to be successful in their educational and research missions. Conflict and ambiguity are preconditions for the generation and transmission of knowledge. Therefore, conflict is prized, and subcultures are sought. This distinguishes higher education from other organizations where the control of most conflict is necessary to achieve organizational goals. Conflict needs to be controlled in colleges too, for governing and administration purposes. This is doubly troublesome in the 1990s when it is said that knowledge doubles every 7 years.

What difference does it make that the institutions in our study all have Roman Catholic roots? Our choice was purposeful. Colleges and universities are, first of all, academic institutions and are rooted in the tradition of higher education whether they also share a Catholic, Lutheran, evangelical, or secular orientation. These Catholic academic institutions operate, as do most others, with variously powerful recollections of their original ideological origins and founder's vision and with a strong sense of continuous adjustment to contemporary realities. Catholic colleges use vision and values to focus on goals and to set aspirational standards.

Catholic institutions differ from their public counterparts and most private institutions in their missions and values. All institutions of higher education share a common mission or goal: to provide education at some measure of quality to some defined population. These Catholic institutions had additional goals such as respecting and instilling respect for the dignity of the human person, advancing the cause and service of the underprivileged, promoting social justice, providing an experience of a faith community, and providing a balanced experience of church in the modern world.

Catholic leaders seek answers to the challenge of promoting Catholic values clearly and strongly in a multicultural, faith-diverse, pluralistic society. Students are attracted to Catholic institutions for the perceived quality of academic offerings they seek. Since that academic quality can be matched, nearly always, by a local public institution at a greatly reduced cost, students must search and find other values, Catholic values, as well. Even non-Catholics can appreciate Catholic values. The challenge for Catholic leaders is to provide those distinctly Catholic values in our pluralistic society. If they fail to do so, their institutions will become secularized, even as many private universities have lost the religious ideals of their founders.

We also examined similarities among Catholic institutions of higher education and whether individual Catholic institutions were going off in their own directions, as had other church-related institutions. Because private universities, such as Harvard and Chicago, have drifted away from their denominational roots, Catholic institutions are taking the secularization issue seriously.

Roman Catholics and their observers know that religious communities have their own traditions. For instance, Jesuits have a strong esprit de corps supporting a common nickname, God's Marines. Representing schools in this study, the Sisters of Mercy, Vincentians, Dominicans, and Sisters of Providence have similarly well-developed and distinct traditions. It is important to recognize that a common religious ideology, Catholicism, coexists with six separate and distinct cultures based on the sponsoring groups' unique culture.

The Value Sharing Model

Two definitions help to explain the Value Sharing Model which is the foundation for this study. Richard L. Morrill (1980) provides three definitions of values, two of which are appropriate here:

> Value is a quality or property ascribed to something (acts, things, objects) possessing that quality.

Value is a belief about the desirable in terms of which objects, acts, events, institutions, and so forth, are considered to be valuable. (p. 147)

We rely on Carl Kaestle (1983) for a definition of ideology:

"Ideology" is used to mean a set of apparently compatible propositions about human nature and society that help an individual to interpret complex human problems and take action that the individual believes is in his or her best interest and the best interests of the society as a whole. Ideology is the aspect of culture that attempts to justify and defend a set of social relations and institutions (p. 76).

As a foundation for this research, the Value Sharing Model (see Figure 1) provides a map of where values come from, how they are communicated, and the target populations with which they are shared. Following is an explanation of the several stages of the model.

Sources of Values

In their book *Leaders: The Strategies For Taking Charge*, Bennis and Nanus (1985) state that only rarely does the leader conceive the vision alone. Primarily, visions come from the organization itself—from the values inherent in the idea and ideology of the founder, the experience of the people, and, to a degree, the experience of the leader with the ideology. Peters and Austin (1985) say that visions cannot be "concocted." Kotter (1988) found that successful general managers typically asked a lot of questions; some would literally ask hundreds of questions of subordinates in a half-hour period. Current research tells us that leaders develop compelling visions for raising organizational values by serious searching and listening. Only later, after the values have been named and agreed upon, can the vision be formulated.

In the Value Sharing Model, we show three sources of values: (a) the ideology itself, (b) the history of the institution as it

tinkers with the ideology, and (c) the personal experience of the leader with the ideology. There are many more plausible sources of values in organizations, but we focus on these three which we believe to be primary.

In the context of Catholic institutions of higher education, the likely sources of organizational values are (a) the ideology of the Roman Catholic tradition, based on scripture; (b) the experience of the college with the Catholic ideology as an academic institution; and (c) the unique contribution of the leader and the passion that grows out of personal experience with the ideologies of Catholicism and the academic community.

The Catholic tradition. The church is a multifaceted and multipurpose institution. It is represented in a hierarchy of governance; it is a community of worshipers; it is small, organic and local; it is an international conglomerate. It strives to evangelize the poor and is an agent of social justice. It is also an educational institution; medieval universities were church institutions.

Finally, the Catholic tradition is diverse in values and rich in its use of symbols and myth—the marrow of organizational culture. Academia shares this richness. The Church has developed all the ordinary tools of administration (such as structure, chain-of-command, and bureaucracy) and has an organizational culture built around worshiping groups (such as small groups, families, and the use of parables, rites, rituals, and theologies). Andrew Greeley (1991) is a frequent contributor to the discussion on the power of myth and symbol in the American Catholic Church.

Organizational experience with ideology: Catholicism and the academy. Catholic colleges and universities are primarily academic institutions; they are rooted in the traditions of higher education. To the extent that Catholic institutions develop gradually over

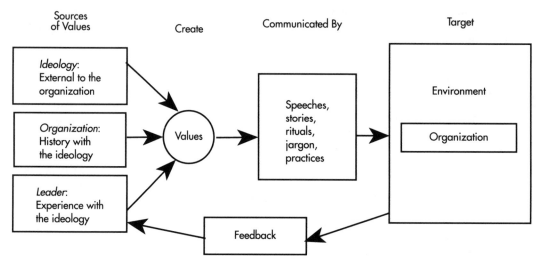

Figure 1 The value sharing model—values in Catholic higher education.

time as organizations, they express the influence of Catholic and academic ideologies in unique ways. The distinctive history of an organization embodied in its written documents, reminiscences, legends, and physical properties is influenced primarily by root ideologies.

The leader's experience with ideology. We bring our past with us into the future. We bring our experiences, good or bad. A story will illustrate. Murphy, a co-author of this study, asked Sister Jeanne O'Laughlin, O.P., one of the presidents studied, where she first learned that she wanted to be in Catholic education. She told him her story about riding a streetcar as a youth in Detroit. She spied an African-American woman with two squirming kids a few seats away (Jeanne is white). She offered to hold and soothe one of the kids, and the mother was pleased. During the course of the ride, a white woman got on the streetcar, looked at the unlikely group, and spit at Jeanne. Later that evening, she asked her parents why anybody would spit at somebody for doing the good deed of comforting a mother and child. Her wise parents explained that the spitter did not really understand, that she was uneducated. Jeanne claims

that experience as pivotal—it somehow led her to the convent and to education. She brought that personal experience with Catholic and educational values to her university and its history, and she uses it as she casts the vision for her school.

Creating Values

These three sources, the ideology itself, the organization's experience with the ideology, and the leader's experience with the ideology, are three main sources—there are certainly others—from which organizational values emerge. Organizational leaders carry the responsibility of researching these sources to distinguish the values. For instance, Sister Janice Ryan, R.S.M., President of Trinity College, grills faculty and staff in hallways.

Communicating Values

Creating a vision is merely the first half; casting it in a compelling way is the complement. Loving what you do is essential for making what you do compelling. Visionary leaders are simply passionate people. Preaching the vision with passion becomes the leader's task.

If the vision is to be compelling, not only does the deliverer of the good news have to be passionate about the news, but the leader also has to focus the vision and capture it by word or action in a simple way that demands attention. Martin Luther King's "I have a dream" speech, John Kennedy's determination to "put a man on the moon," and Ronald Reagan's use of a dollar bill to explain the budget were simple but highly effective ways of capturing the attention of the people.

Besides preaching and focusing the values, putting the vision on the road is the third way of communicating the vision. Visionaries consumed by the vision and their love for the organization pass up no opportunity to tell the world about it. They talk to anyone who will listen, inside and outside the organization, never content to target either one or the other.

Targets

There are at least two targets to which leaders and organizational members must communicate values and visions: the internal target of the college or university and the external target of the community in which they live and serve and from which they draw students. College presidents must focus on organizational members and on the local community, government agencies, sponsoring groups, and others.

The Feedback Loop

The Feedback Loop at the bottom of the model serves as a reminder that organizational members and the external environmental forces reflect and refine values and visions offered by leaders. Leaders, in turn, must observe these sources for emerging and mutating values.

Method

This study identified core values in six Catholic colleges and universities and the means used by leaders to express them. We also endeavored to learn whether the identified values were shared and, if so, by whom and to what degree.

The conceptual framework was borrowed from the literature of organizational culture for observing and measuring the degree to which values are shared. A research design and model of vision sharing developed by Murphy (1987, 1991) was followed, wherein he described how organizational "visions" are created and the degree to which they were shared in three colleges. The two-stage method called for in-depth interviews in stage one and a quantitative analysis of survey data in stage two. It combined qualitative and quantitative methodology based on prior work by Martin, Sitkin, and Boehm (1985) and Murphy (1987).

The Role of the President

Murphy once asked Warren Bennis whether he included college presidents in his study of leaders. Bennis thought about that only briefly before he replied, "No, they tend to be more like prime ministers than leaders."

Burns (1978) suggested that visions must be based on the moral principles of leaders, principles that reflect the internal values of the leader. Maccoby (1981) suggested that no single eternal model of successful leadership exists because leaders and those led differ on the bases of personal values, distinct cultures, and historical periods. What kind of people are leaders? In his classic study of leaders, Maccoby found three basic qualities modern leaders share: (a) a caring, respectful, and responsible attitude; (b) flexibility about people and organizational structure; and (c) a participative approach to management—the willingness to share

---

power. These leaders show strong identification equally with women and men. They have a sense of humor. They are students of the organizations they lead. They are willing to demystify and simplify bureaucracy, and they question both mission and structure.

Common to great leaders, however, is their ability to cast a compelling vision based on the core values of the organization. Some leaders cast that vision in noisy ways; others find quiet but moving ways to excite people. But leadership is an intuitive art; intuition is difficult to analyze.

Sample

Six Catholic institutions were selected because (a) their ideologies and values were reported to be central and readily identifiable in the dominant culture or vision of the institutional leaders, (b) they had stable leadership, and (c) they represented a variety of locales and sponsorships (see Table 1). Included were DePaul University, the College of St. Thomas, Santa Clara University, Barry University, Trinity College, and St. Mary of the Woods College. Institutions were chosen for their leaders as well: In each case, informants reported leaders to be strong and active in their roles and attuned to institutional values and the means to communicate them.

Data Gathering

The first stage of data gathering included a trip to each campus to gain a deeper understanding of each particular value system, the history of the institution, and the culture of the organization and its peculiar manifestations of values. Ethnographic observation and structured, in-depth interviews of the presidents and organizational members were used. Murphy conducted all interviews of faculty, staff, and students except at DePaul, where two graduate assistants also con-

ducted interviews. More than 90 organizational members were interviewed, resulting in more than 500 pages of transcripts.

Survey Sample and Instruments

In stage two of data gathering, the qualitative data garnered in stage one was used to construct a questionnaire to measure the degree to which organizational members recognize and share values. In each institution, all full-time faculty and staff and a stratified random sample of 800 full-time undergraduate students received surveys. In addition, surveys were sent to a random sample of 400 alums from the graduating year of 1985. The overall response rate was 30.3%.

Religious Affiliation

Among all the schools, 7 out of 10 alums and students described their religious affiliation as Roman Catholic. Of faculty and staff, 53% identified themselves as Roman Catholic, 23% Protestant, 6% Jewish, 7% other, and 12% with no affiliation.

Results

A great similarity of values was found across all institutions; each institution showed a family resemblance to each other institution (see Table 2). Five institutions ranked *high academic standards* as a premier core value. *Caring* or *respect for people* characterized each institution in some way as well.

As for specific values, five of six institutions indicated in interviews that academic quality was a core value. In each of these cases, all subgroups ranked high academic quality highest among the values identified; *friendly and personal relations* was ranked second by all groups. Students identified the same school-specific

TABLE 1 Characteristics of Selected Institutions

Institution	Location	Sponsor	Enrollment
DePaul University	Chicago, IL	Vincentians	16,000
Santa Clara University	Santa Clara, CA	Jesuits	12,000
College of St. Thomas	St. Paul, MN	Archdiocese/St. Paul	9,100
Barry University	Miami, FL	Adrian Dominicans	6,000
Trinity College	Burlington, VT	Sisters of Mercy	1,400
St. Mary of the Woods College	Terre Haute, IN	Sisters of Providence	1,000

values that emerged from on-campus interviews with leaders and organizational old-timers.

For the item "I find my values and the values of [my institution] are very similar," we found strong agreement as measured by the percentage of respondents who indicated that they agreed or strongly agreed (4 or 5 on a 5-point Likert scale). The percentage agreeing ranged from a low of 54% among Barry students to a high of 90.9% among Barry faculty and staff. The overall percentages for total respondents was 75.7% for faculty and staff, 62.8% for students, and 65.2% for alums.

The questionnaire asked the respondents whether their values and those of their college were very similar. A 5-point Likert scale was used. At all institutions the respondents reported high levels of agreement with expressions of core values as identified by leaders and organizational old-timers.

All satisfaction measures decreased significantly and in a stepwise fashion progressively from the freshman year to the senior year (see Table 3). The highest level of agreement was *proud to attend* the university. Few students volunteered for school-sponsored programs—the variable with the lowest level of agreement. This may be explained by the fact that students viewed their work in various programs as a part of the academic program or college social life rather than as a volunteer job to help the needy.

The data indicate moderately high levels of satisfaction across all groups (see Table 4). Although differences across all groups are statistically significant, ranges between high and low are quite small. In general, leaders tended to report the highest levels of agreement (true for the first five statements). This is characteristic of institutions with strong, dominant cultures. For the last three statements, alums reported the highest levels of agreement which may suggest their belief that education prepared them well for their current positions in life. More evidence for this is found in positive association between alums, contact with the university, and their willingness to encourage their children to attend the university. There are no significant differences on these measures between transfer and four-year students or between students who live on versus off campus. There is a suggestion that four-year students and those who live on campus volunteer more often for university-sponsored programs.

Students identified the same school-specific values as were identified in on-campus interviews (see Table 5). There is considerable agreement between students and alums for both the highest and lowest ranked values (see Table 6). *Friendly and personal relations* was the second highest ranked value by all groups. There are moderate amounts of agreement across all groups for lower ranked values. On two of four school-specific values, faculty are significantly different from students. The

TABLE 2 Values Ranked by Institution

Barry	DePaul	St. Thomas	S. Clara	Trinity	Woods
High Academic Standards	High Academic Standards	High Academic Standards	High Academic Standards		High Academic Standards
Caring	Vincentian Personalism	Students First	Educating Whole Person	Caring	
Respect	Respect			Respect	
Service	Service		Service		
		Community of Faith	Community of Faith	Family Community	Family Community
		Catholic Tradition			Woods Tradition
			Social Justice		Social Justice
				Challenge Individual	

Note. Values as reported by survey respondents.

TABLE 3 Mean Satisfaction with Undergraduate Program of Students

	Freshmen	Sophomores	Juniors	Seniors
Proud to attend	4.5	4.4	4.4	4.3
Satisfied with teaching & learning	4.2	4.1	4.0	3.9
Satisfied with university values	4.0	3.8	3.8	3.6
Satisfied with Catholic values	3.9	3.7	3.6	3.5
My values similar to school's	3.8	3.7	3.6	3.5
Catholic values found here	3.7	3.6	3.5	3.4
Founder's values	3.7	3.4	3.4	3.3
I volunteer	2.4	2.5	2.1	2.1

Note. The values represent mean ratings of satisfaction.

most dramatic difference is ranking of academic freedom, which ranked tenth or lower for students and alums but ranked first for leaders and faculty and fourth for staff.

A measure of dissatisfaction was designed, a calculation of the distance between the value desired and the current status of that value from the respondents' point of view (see Table 7). Respondents first rated current satisfaction with 18 values on a 5-point Likert scale and then

TABLE 4 Mean Satisfaction with School by Type of Respondent

	Students	Alums	Faculty	Staff	Leaders
Proud to attend	4.4	4.5	4.4	4.4	4.6
Satisfied with teaching & learning	4.0	4.2	3.7	3.8	3.9
Satisfied with university values	3.8	4.0	3.9	3.6	3.8
Satisfied with Catholic values	3.6	3.9	3.7	3.6	3.8
My values similar to school's	3.6	3.8	4.0	3.7	4.1
Catholic values found here	3.5	3.8	3.7	3.5	3.8
Founder's values	3.4	3.7	3.7	3.6	3.9
I volunteer	2.2	1.4	2.8	2.5	3.2

Note. The values represent mean ratings of satisfaction.

rated those same values as they would like them to be in the college. The differences were summed between means on current values and desired presence. The sum of 18 differences served as a measure of dissatisfaction, a difference of 1 equivalent to a 1-point mean difference on a 5-point Likert scale. The index of dissatisfaction across all subgroups was calculated.

There were moderately low levels of dissatisfaction for all groups (less than 1 point on a 5-point Likert scale), an indication that value expectations were being met or were attainable. There were no significant differences between men and women on their ideal versus their current ratings of the college's value system. The lower levels of dissatisfaction among freshmen and alums were probably due to

TABLE 5 School-Specific Values

Barry

A: High academic standards
B: Caring for one another
C: Social justice
D: Having a sense of purpose

Santa Clara

A: High academic standards
B: Social justice
C: Educating whole person
D: Being ethical

DePaul

A: High academic standards
B: High quality teaching
C: Education that is practical
D: Students truly want to learn

Trinity

A: Making human connection
B: Caring for the individual
C: Supporting the individual
D: Challenging the individual

St. Thomas

A: High academic standards
B: Student needs come first
C: The Catholic tradition
D: Being ethical

St. Mary of the Woods

A: High academic standards
B: Virtue & knowledge united
C: Social justice
D: A sense of tradition

Note. Values as reported by interview respondents.

TABLE 6 Current Institutional Values by Type of Respondent in Rank Order

Value	Ranking by				
	Students	Alums	Faculty	Staff	Leaders
School Specific Value A	1	1	9	1	8
Friendly & personal relationships	2	2	2	2	2
School Specific Value D	3	3	10	9	6
Service to others	4	8	6	5	5
School Specific Value C	5	5	3	4	5
Respect for others	6	4	4	8	4
Reach out to the needy	7	16	13	10	13
Become wise	8	14	17	15	16
School Specific Value B	9	7	5	7	7
A family community	10	6	8	6	9
Being a Good Samaritan	11	12	12	11	12
Following one's conscience	12	9	7	12	10
Academic freedom	13	10	1	4	1
Being a community of faith	14	11	16	14	15
Value diversity in people	15	13	11	13	11
Being children of God	16	15	15	16	14
No one is neglected	17	17	14	17	17
Spreading Gospel to poor	18	18	18	18	18

the lack of information on the front end and back end, respectively. Dissatisfaction rose significantly from freshman to senior years, possibly due to increasing familiarity with the institution's shortcomings, increasing demands in the classroom, and demands to actualize career choices.

TABLE 7 Index of Dissatisfaction[a]

All Men	14.1
All Women	14.4
Student Men	14.0
Student Women	14.6
Students	14.4
Alums	11.5
Faculty	13.8
Staff	16.6
Leaders	14.4
Freshmen	9.9
Sophomores	14.6
Juniors	16.7
Seniors	16.2

Note. The values represent mean ratings differences of dissatisfaction.

[a]Sum of (Ideal minus Current) values for all Institutional values. The potential range is −72 to +72.

Discussion

We dislike "impact of leadership" as a phrase and, rather, prefer the "influence" of leaders within the organizational culture. Colleges and universities are among the most complex organizations in this society because education, their outcome, is ambiguous and ill-defined. Out of this ambiguity we found college presidents in our sample influencing their organizational members by defining values, creating visions, and enacting them for all to see. Values are moving targets and we were describing them from a snapshot in time. As someone at Santa Clara told us, values are like getting a suntan: Both happen gradually over time.

When asked to identify people or stories that best illustrated organizational goals, survey respondents identified presidents and past presidents more often than anyone else as people who lived and communicated values. Much in the mode of "modeling the way" (Kouzes & Posner, 1987, p. 187), these leaders were recognized as people who "managed by walking around" (Peters & Waterman, 1982, p. 122), consciously and conscientiously communicating often and in a variety of ways. At Barry University, Sister Jeanne O'Laughlin, O.P., talked to students incessantly, introducing herself and quizzing them on how and what they were doing. At DePaul University, Father John Richardson, C.M., insisted that budget requests be explicitly tied to mission. One interviewee reported that DePaul employees sacrificed (she had never heard a complaint) approximately one-half percent of salary to sustain a university-sponsored tutoring program for underprivileged students from local public high schools to prepare them for college. At Trinity College, several respondents remarked that Sister Janice Ryan, R.S.M., stopped faculty and staff in public hallways to grill them on the content and meaning of the mission statement. She also instituted the Golden Banana award for organizational members who suggested novel ways to promote the mission. Her predecessor was able to call every new student by name on opening day because she studied snapshots of incoming students before they arrived. At Saint Mary of the Woods College, Sister Barbara Doherty, S.P., found time to teach theology courses during the year and brought in experts for a day-long focus on social justice issues. At Santa Clara University, Father Paul Locatelli, S.J., removed table grapes from all cafeterias when students protested unjust treatment of farm workers and sought to boycott grapes in union with them. This was a particularly significant symbolic action because some Santa Clara trustees were grape growers.

These few examples of the communication of organizational values by the use of personal example, rites, rituals, and symbols are strong evidence of what leaders do to influence followers and sustain the process of leadership through the communication of values. For the most part, followers identify with the dominant organizational culture and point to their leaders as people who understand and use cultural artifacts to strengthen the culture that nourishes Catholic values. One institution in the study suffered from a culture that we thought was too dominant, too dogmatic, too intolerant of subcultures, too *Catholic* without being *catholic*. In this case, leaders struggled with institutional mission and appropriate expressions of institutional values in a complex and pluralistic environment.

Although this research captured the sharing of values at a single point in time, some results are clear. An extreme similarity of personal values was found among all groups. Promoting racial understanding was consistently an important value for all groups. Students and alums exhibited consistent value-sharing behavior whereas faculty, staff, and academic leaders formed another group. Men and the faculty, staff, and leadership groups consistently ranked *academic freedom* higher than did women, students, and alums. All groups reported moderately high levels of satisfaction with the schools, their activities, and the shared Catholic and university values. The sharing of specific core values by students with their colleges decreased with each year of attendance from the freshman to the senior year.

People liked the stated organizational values. Some non-Catholics sought out these institutions as places to work and study because they found a good fit with their own values. An overwhelming majority of respondents were very satisfied that the fit was similar between their personal values and the institutional values.

There were differences to be noted, as well. Leaders (deans, vice presidents, presidents) and faculty ranked *academic freedom* first, whereas students, alums, and staff ranked *academic quality* first.

This may be explained as two sides of a single coin: From the viewpoint of faculty and presidents, academic freedom is the flip side of academic quality.

Not everyone liked the explicitly stated values. In the minority, and not surprisingly, a few students complained about the focus on money because of rising tuition costs, and faculty and staff complained about low salaries.

People join organizations to find values similar to their own. Most students arrived at these schools with values that matched the institution. A few came without comparable values and found themselves to be mismatched.

This study is the first of its kind to examine the links between Catholic ideologies and shared values. The Value Sharing Model explained how leaders can and do influence the sharing of values in organizations. Finally, the combination of quantitative and qualitative methodologies suited the needs of this study and put to rest for us the addressed methodological squabbles between researchers of either persuasion.

Prior to this research, it was not known if students entered with a value system; in fact, they do. Therefore, institutions need to treat their students with respect, as colleagues whose values should be nurtured, explored, deepened, and strengthened because they are the values of the institution.

Acknowledgments

We are grateful to the Lilly Endowment and DePaul University for their support of this research.

References

Bennis, W., & Nanus, B. (1985). *Leaders: The strategies for taking charge.* New York: Harper & Row.

Burns, J. M. (1978). *Leadership.* New York: Harper & Row.

Greeley, A. M. (1991, March 16). The Catholic imagination and the Catholic university. *America*, pp. 285–288.

Kaestle, C. F. (1983). *Pillars of the republic common schools and American society 1780–1860.* New York: Hill & Wang.

Kotter, J. P. (1988). *The leadership factor.* New York: Free Press.

Kouzes, J., & Posner, B. Z. (1987). *The leadership challenge: How to get extraordinary things done in organizations.* San Francisco: Jossey-Bass.

Maccoby, M. (1981). *The leader.* New York: Simon & Schuster.

Martin, J., Sitkin, S. B., & Boehm, M. (1985). Founders and the elusiveness of cultural legacy. In P. J. Frost, L. F. Moore, M. R. Louis, C. C. Lundberg, & J. Martin (Eds.), *Organizational culture* (pp. 99–124). Beverly Hills: Sage.

Morrill, R. L. (1980). *Teaching values in college.* San Francisco: Jossey-Bass.

Murphy, J. P. (1987). *College leadership: Sharing the vision.* Ann Arbor: University Microfilms.

Murphy, J. P. (1991). *Visions and values in Catholic higher education.* Kansas City: Sheed & Ward.

Peters, T. J., & Waterman, R. H., Jr. (1982). *In search of excellence.* New York: Harper & Row.

Peters, T. J., & Austin, N. (1985). *A passion for excellence: The leadership difference.* New York: Random House.

Weick, K. (1976). Educational organizations as loosely coupled systems. *Administrative Science Quarterly, 21,* 1–19.

J. Patrick Murphy, C.M., is Assistant Professor and Associate Dean of the College of Liberal Arts and Sciences at DePaul University. He teaches graduate-level courses in the Public Service Management program. He received his PhD from Stanford University and an MBA from DePaul University.

John F. Settich is Executive Director of the Illinois Podiatric Medical Association in Chicago. He holds an MS in Public Service Management.

Direct inquiries about this article to J. Patrick Murphy, Associate Dean, Management of Public Services Program, College of Liberal Arts and Sciences, DePaul University, 2323 North Seminary Avenue, Chicago, IL 60614–3298, 312/362–5608.

An Empirical Test of the Leadership-Making Model in Professional Project Teams

**Mary Uhl-Bien and
George B. Graen**

This study is an empirical test of the role of leadership-making in professional project teams. Findings of the study indicate that, as hypothesized by the model, development of mature leadership relationships between leaders and followers and between team-mates are positively and significantly related to team effectiveness and internalization of the team. Implications for professional work team functioning are discussed.

Many characteristics of leadership have been investigated to assess their impact on organizationally relevant outcomes. One characteristic, often overlooked, is the importance of the leadership relationship. Contemporary leadership theories address a panoply of issues ranging from leader traits (e.g., charismatic leadership) to substitutes for leadership, but many of these approaches fail to recognize the most basic element of leadership — its followership nature (Graen, 1976; Homans, 1950; Katz & Kahn, 1978; Zalesny & Graen, 1986). One theoretical approach developed around the leadership-followership relationship is the leadership-making model (Graen & Uhl-Bien, 1991; Uhl-Bien & Graen, 1992).

According to the leadership-making model, the impact of leadership occurs through the leader-follower relationship. Effective leadership results when high-involvement relationships, characterized by the earning and employment of incremental influence (Katz & Kahn, 1978), are developed. Within high-involvement (or mature) leadership relationship dyads, leaders and followers experience reciprocal influence, extracontractual behavior exchange, mutual trust, respect and liking, and a sense of common fate. In contrast, low-involvement (or immature) leadership relationships, in which incremental influence is not achieved, are characterized by unidirectional downward influence, contractual behavior exchange, role-defined relations, and loosely coupled fates (see Graen & Uhl-Bien, 1991, and Uhl-Bien & Graen, 1992, for in-depth discussion of this model). It is important to note that a leadership relationship is not limited to a vertical dyadic relationship; leadership may also occur among members of horizontal relationships (Graen & Uhl-Bien, 1991; Uhl-Bien & Graen, 1992). Hence, in the present investigation, the leadership-making model will be considered for examining interrelationships among team members with their leaders as well as with their coworkers.

The Three-Component Model of Leadership

The leadership-making model is based on a three-component model of leadership (see Figure 1). These three components consist of the leader, the follower, and the leadership relationship. Using the model, desirable organizational outcomes such as teamwork effectiveness (work unit outcome) and internalization of the team (team member outcome) are achieved through development of mature leadership relationships.

According to the model, leaders in mature (high involvement) leadership relationships are able to earn incremental influence with followers to enhance the effectiveness of the work unit. For example, through a "leadership-making" process, followers in high-quality leadership relationships, because they recognize the career development advantages offered them by the supervisor, agree to outgrow their formally defined job descriptions. As a result, they take on additional responsibilities and serve as cooperative teammates who aid in the design and management of the work unit. They are willing to exert extra effort in their work—to grow out of their formally

defined work roles—by engaging in activities which are not specifically prescribed by the organization. These activities may include collaborating with the leader on the vision of the team, seeking out unwritten team rules, earning team growth opportunities, enhancing team visibility, facilitating team collaboration, demonstrating initiative in terms of leadership and innovation, and working to enhance the promotability of their leader. Thus, in terms of Katz and Kahn's (1978) definition of leadership, these are the individuals with whom effective leadership processes are achieved.

In addition to earning incremental influence, the leadership-making process is also accompanied by a "transformation" in which followers internalize the goals and values of the team. This transformation process involves not only the "outgrowing" of previously described jobs but also an expansion of interests by team members from a self-focus to a team-focus. Through this transformation, team members realize that they can most effectively accomplish their individual self-interests by ensuring that the team is successful. When this occurs, team members, at least temporarily, place team interests above their individual professional interests; team problem solving becomes one of cooperation and mutual support to attain team goals, rather than a group of independent self-managers pursuing their individually focused goals (Uhl-Bien & Graen, 1992).

The leadership-making process occurs over a three-phase life cycle (Graen & Uhl-Bien, 1991). In the beginning phase, leadership-making starts out as strangers undertaking the very early stages of relationship development. These individuals engage in initial testing processes of evaluating each other's motives and abilities. Any exchanges that occur between the individuals operate on a more "transactional" or "cash and carry" basis (see Bass, 1985), and there is essentially no incremental influence between the individuals (i.e., low leader-member exchange).

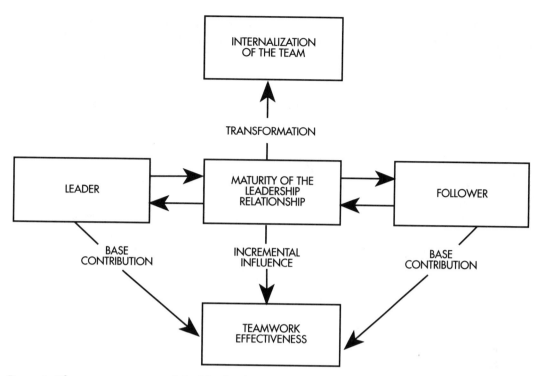

Figure 1 Three-component model of leadership.

As the leadership-making process progresses and individuals move from a lower quality leader-member exchange to one of higher quality, the relationship between the individuals becomes more "transformational" (Bass, 1985), with exchanges increasingly based on incremental influence. In these stages, leaders offer "leadership-making investments" to followers that provide them with opportunities to increase their contributions to the team; followers take advantage of these opportunities because they see them as beneficial to their career development. Leadership-making investments include activities such as the leader articulating team vision to the follower, instructing the follower in unwritten team rules, empowering team growth opportunities, promoting team visibility, inviting team collaboration, supporting team damage control, and advising team career planning.

Within the most advanced stages of leadership-making, effective dyadic relationships mature from acquaintances to established team players. The relationship is transformed from simple exchange of self-interest outcomes to one of commitment to higher level goals (e.g., team goals), with almost unlimited potential for incremental influence between the individuals. Moreover, in contrast to other models of transactional and transformational leadership (i.e., Bass, 1985), where transactional leadership is looked upon as undesirable, the leadership-making model recognizes the importance of transactional relationships in developing higher quality transformational-type relationships. In essence, without the existence of a transactional relationship in the early stages of development, individuals could never achieve transformational relationships. According to the leadership-making model, if one wants to examine the development of transformational relationships, it is necessary to consider transactions as the building blocks of transformations.

Leadership-Making in Professional Work Teams

The goals of leadership-making are twofold: first, to generate the production of incremental influence between leaders and followers which enables more effective team functioning, and second, to achieve the transformation from a work unit of individually focused, independent members to a team of team-focused, highly committed and established team players. In terms of professional work teams, this means that successful leadership-making should be positively related to teamwork effectiveness and internalization of the team by the members. The present paper tests these assumptions by examining the extent to which maturity of leadership relationships is related to (a) unit effectiveness (i.e., teamwork effectiveness) of professional work teams and (b) internalization of the team (i.e., commitment to team goals by the members, team morale, team involvement, and team-enabling conditions by teammates).

Method

Site and Sample

The data were collected within a public-sector service organization in an eastern state. In the last few years, this organization had implemented project teams in a variety of functions throughout the organization. After the implementation, top management wanted to know which teamwork and leadership processes led to the most effective work outcomes. Thus, together with top management, representatives from the human resources department, and various members working within the organization, we designed a study to analyze the impact of leadership-making on professional team functioning.

Within this organization, we asked team members to report on their leadership-making activities and team processes. From a total of 233 responses from professionals within the organization (72% response rate), we were able to generate a sample of 31 professional work teams with 184 total members (the average team size was 5.74, the minimum team size was 3 members). The individuals working within the teams consisted of relatively highly educated professionals (91% held at least a bachelor's degree, 44% had completed or were working towards completion of their Master's degree, and 13% held a doctorate or other advanced degree), were in their thirties and forties (77% were between 30 and 49, with 5% below 30, 13% between 50 and 59, and 5% over the age of 60), and were primarily white males (92% white, 77% male). Average tenure within the company was 11.71 years, and average tenure within the present position was 6.00 years.

Measures

The measures used in this study are operationalizations of the variables identified in the three-component model of leadership (see Figure 1). These measures assessed leadership-making processes (i.e., maturity of leadership relationships) and relevant organizational outcomes (i.e., measures of teamwork effectiveness and internalization of the team). Since leadership relationships are not limited to vertical dyadic relationships but may also include horizontal relationships (Graen & Uhl-Bien, 1991; Uhl-Bien & Graen, 1992), the effectiveness of the leadership-making processes between the team members with each other and with the project leader was measured. Adaptations of the leader-member and team-member exchange measures developed by Graen (Graen & Scandura, 1987) and Seers (1989) were used. These measures were the Project Leader-Member Exchange (PLMX) scale (Uhl-Bien, 1991) and the

Team-Member Exchange (TMX) scale (Seers, 1989; Uhl-Bien, 1991).

Project Leader-Member Exchange (PLMX) is the centroid question from the Leader-Member Exchange scale (Graen & Scandura, 1987; Uhl-Bien, 1991): "How would you characterize your working relationship with the project leader?" on a 5-point scale from "extremely ineffective" to "extremely effective." This measure is an adaptation of the LMX scale used by Graen (Graen, Novak, & Sommerkamp, 1982). The centroid question used in the PLMX has been shown to be a defining variable in the measurement of quality of working relationships (Graen & Scandura, 1987) and thus is an acceptable short-form measure. The Team-Member Exchange (TMX) scale (7-item) also includes this centroid question, but in addition includes items which evaluate the openness of communication and amount of trust, support, and cohesiveness among team members, as well as the amount of collaboration within the team (Cronbach alpha = .89).

The measures of team effectiveness include assessments of performance, teamwork, and team process. All are single item measures which ask raters to evaluate certain aspects of team functioning. The *Performance* measure used a 5-point scale from "very low" to "very high" for ratings of the performance of the team as a whole. *Teamwork* asked raters to indicate the effectiveness of teamwork on a 5-point scale from "extremely ineffective" to "extremely effective." *Team Process* asked evaluators to rate the extent to which team members work well together (on a 5-point scale from "no one works well together" to "everyone works well together").

The measures of internalization of the team include Goal Commitment, Team Morale, Team Involvement, and Team Enabling Conditions. *Goal Commitment* was rated on a 5-point scale (from "not at all" to "a great deal") and assessed the extent to which there was commitment to goals among project team members. *Team Morale* and *Team Involvement* measure (on a

5-point scale from "very low" to "very high") the level of morale of members of the team and the amount of interest/involvement of the members in the work of the team. *Team Enabling Conditions* is an 8-item measure based on Hackman's (1986) description of characteristics beneficial to effective team performance. This measure asks team members to report (on a 5-point scale from "not at all" to "a great deal") the extent to which they feel personal responsibility for the project, their work on the project is meaningful, their work influences the outcome of the project, expert coaching is provided when appropriate, there are adequate rewards for high performance, they receive feedback about their performance, material resources are adequate and available, and the direction of the project is clear and engaging. The Cronbach alpha for this measure is .78.

To allow for a "triangulation" of perspectives (Jick, 1979), team assessments were gathered from multiple raters. These raters included the team members themselves, project leaders, and outside raters one level above the team members who were familiar enough with the work of the team members to provide assessments of effectiveness of performance and team processes. It is also important to note that the variables used in the study consisted of team-level measures: averages of team member responses on the measures for each variable (with the exception of the ratings provided by the outside rater and project leader). Thus, the sample size is based on the numbers of teams, not on the total number of professionals who participated in the study.

Analysis

To test the assumptions of the leadership-making model, Pearson product-moment correlations (Nunnally, 1978) were computed between the leadership-making variables and the teamwork outcomes and internalization of the team measures. Positive and significant correlations between the leadership-making variables and teamwork outcome and internalization variables would indicate support for the model. Given the multiple perspectives provided by the three different raters on teamwork outcomes, correlations were computed and reported using all three ratings, and differences in findings due to different perspectives are discussed.

Results

Correlations among the leadership-making variables and team effectiveness measures are presented in Table 1. Based on these correlations, there is apparent agreement among all three raters that the quality of the project leader-member exchange (PLMX) relationship impacts positively on how well the team members work together (Team Process). Given this, high-quality leadership-making between team members and project leaders appears to be conducive to team processes by generating a work situation in which team members are able to function well together.

PLMX also correlated significantly with project leader and team member evaluations of Performance. This finding suggests that when team members develop high-quality relationships with project leaders, these relationships enable the team to perform more effectively and produce a situation in which members work well together. Moreover, PLMX correlated positively and significantly with the team members' ratings of teamwork (Teamwork: $r = .70$, $p < .001$), an indication that team members perceive high-quality relationships with the project leader as conducive to the effectiveness of teamwork on the project.

Based on these findings, the average quality of leadership-making between team members and their project leaders (PLMX) appears to contribute positively

TABLE 1 Correlations Between Leadership-making Variables and Team Effectiveness (N = 31)[a]

	PLMX	TMX
Evaluation provided by:		
Outside Rater: (N = 31)		
Performance	– .01	.04
Teamwork	.01	– .02
Team Process	.31*	.15
Project Leader: (N = 19)		
Performance	.54**	.23
Teamwork	.20	– .11
Team Process	.64***	.27
Team Members: (N = 31)		
Performance	.62***	.75***
Teamwork	.70***	.72***
Team Process	.66***	.49***

Note. PLMX is a measure of leadership relationship maturity with the project leader; TMX is a measure of teammate maturity.

[a]The sample size is based on the number of multidisciplinary project teams. However, due to missing data from the project leaders, only 19 teams with project leader ratings were available.

*$p < .05$. **$p < .01$. ***$p < .001$.

to effectiveness of team outcomes. As discussed previously, this contribution was expected to occur due to the greater feeling of trust, supportiveness, cooperation, openness of communication, and mutual exchange of resources between the project leader and team members.

In professional work teams, high involvement leadership-making between team members with each other (TMX) is also expected to be positively related to effectiveness of work outcomes for the teams. The results of the analysis conducted to test this hypothesis are also presented in Table 1. Examining these results, it appears that the strength and type of relationships uncovered between TMX and team outcome measures vary with the perspective of the individuals providing the ratings. Using outside rater and project leader criteria, no significant relationships are produced between TMX and the outcome variables. When examined using team member criterion, however, strong relationships emerge between TMX and *all* of the team outcome measures. In particular, TMX is positively and significantly related to team members' ratings of Performance ($r = .75$, $p < .001$), Teamwork ($r = .77$, $p < .001$), and Team Process ($r = .49$, $p < .001$).

Based on these findings, there is some support for the TMX hypothesis of the leadership-making model. However, this support comes only from the team members themselves. Outside rater and project leader data do not support the contribution of team-member exchanges to team outcomes, but data from team members themselves support TMX as positively affecting performance of the team, teamwork effectiveness, and team processes among the members.

The second link in the model tested in the present study involves the relationship between leadership relationships and internalization of the team. The correlations used to examine this link are presented in Table 2. As expected, these correlations reveal that both PLMX and TMX are positively and significantly related to all of the variables used to assess internalization of the team (i.e., Goal Commitment, Team Morale, Team Involvement, and Team-Enabling Conditions).

Discussion

The present paper describes a test of the leadership-making model in professional work teams. The results of the study indicate that, as expected, leadership relationship maturity (as measured

TABLE 2 Correlations Between Leadership-making Variables and Measures of Internalization of the Team ($N = 31$)[a]

	PLMX	TMX
Team-Enabling Conditions	.52***	.71***
Team Morale	.50***	.58***
Team Involvement	.40*	.56***
Goal Commitment	.68***	.76***

Note. PLMX is a measure of leadership relationship maturity with the project leader; TMX is a measure of teammate maturity.

[a]The sample size is based on the number of multidisciplinary project teams.

*$p < .05$. **$p < .01$. ***$p < .001$.

by PLMX and TMX) contributed to both team effectiveness (the leadership increment) and to the internalization of the team (the transformation).

These findings suggest that leadership-making among project leaders, followers, and teammates has critical implications for the functioning of professional work teams. By developing mature leadership relationships, leaders and members are able to increase the amount of incremental influence they exert with each other. This "expanding pie of influence" subsequently increases the total amount of resources available within the work unit. If these relationships are developed consistently between leaders, followers, and teammates, the total capability of the work team becomes greatly enhanced. In particular, as demonstrated in the present study, development of mature leadership relationships is positively related to performance, teamwork, and effective teamwork processes of the work teams.

Effective leadership-making among leaders, followers, and teammates also produces "transformations" that lead to the internalization of the team by the members. Through these leadership relationships, followers become more committed to and involved in the team, and morale of the team overall is more positive. Similarly, when transformations occur, team members feel more responsible for the project, feel their work on the project is meaningful, feel expert coaching, feedback, resources, and rewards are adequate and available, and believe the direction of the project is clear and engaging (i.e., Team-Enabling Conditions). As the present study shows, teams characterized by more mature leadership relationships (PLMX and TMX) are teams in which members report higher levels of morale and involvement in the team, greater goal commitment, and more positive evaluations of the enabling conditions of the team.

Based on these findings, it appears that project management demands the use of "leadership" beyond "managership" (Uhl-Bien & Graen, 1992). In particular, in professional project teams, directing is based on dialogue involving incremental influence (Katz & Kahn, 1978) about the relative utility of achieving team goals. Moreover, effective team outcomes cannot be ordered but do require leadership — the earning of interpersonal incremental influence. Here teamwork cannot be motivated by formal role definitions (i.e., because it's their "job"). Rather, teamwork requires that teammates be persuaded to accept and commit to the goals of the team. Thus, professional project teamwork involves more coordination and communication-facilitating activities, as well as the earning of incremental influence by leaders and team members with each other, than does managership (Graen & Uhl-Bien, 1991; Heany, 1989; Mohrman & Cummings, 1989; Sayles, 1989).

The leadership requirements for effective professional work team functioning can thus be met by the leadership-making model. Through the development of mature relationships with project leaders and teammates, team members in highly mature relationships receive the resources, support, and guidance necessary for them to effectively engage in team processes. Conversely, by establishing mature relationships with followers, project leaders ensure that the team members will feel comfortable asking for direction when necessary and will be willing to take risks to accomplish team goals because they feel confident of their leader's support (Basu, 1991). The outgrowing of roles that occurs within highly mature leadership relationships — a factor vital for effective team functioning — thus indicates that the Leadership-Making model provides a useful vehicle for the development of professional project teams.

Acknowledgments

The authors would like to thank Gayle Baugh for her work in managing the data collection process and Bernard Bass, Fred Dansereau, and Allan Wicker for their insightful comments concerning earlier developments of the leadership-making model. This article is based in part on the dissertation work of the first author.

References

Bass, B. M. (1985). *Leadership and performance beyond expectations.* New York: Free Press.

Basu, R. (1991). *An empirical examination of leader-member exchange and transformational leadership as predictors of innovative behavior.* Unpublished doctoral dissertation, Purdue University, West Lafayette, IN.

Graen, G. (1976). Role making processes within complex organizations. In M. D. Dunnette (Ed.), *Handbook of industrial and organizational psychology* (pp. 1201–1245). Chicago: Rand McNally.

Graen, G., Novak, M., & Sommerkamp, P. (1982). The effects of leader-member exchange and job design on productivity and satisfaction: Testing a dual attachment model. *Organi-*

zational Behavior and Human Performance, 30, 109–131.

Graen, G. B., & Scandura, T. A. (1987). Toward a psychology of dyadic organizing. In B. Staw & L. L. Cummings (Eds.), *Research in organizational behavior* (pp. 175–208). Greenwich, CT: JAI Press.

Graen, G., & Uhl-Bien, M. (1991). The transformation of professionals into self-managing and partially self-designing contributors: Toward a theory of leadership-making. *Journal of Management Systems, 3*(3), 33–48.

Hackman, J. R. (1986). The psychology of self-management in organizations. In M. S. Pollack & R. O. Perloff (Eds.), *Psychology and work: Productivity, change and employment* (pp. 85–136). Washington, DC: American Psychological Association.

Heany, D. F. (1989). *Cutthroat teammates: Achieving effective teamwork among professionals.* Homewood, IL: Dow-Jones-Irwin.

Homans, G. C. (1950). *The human group.* New York: Harcourt Brace.

Jick, T. D. (1979). Mixing qualitative and quantitative methods: Triangulation in action. *Administrative Science Quarterly, 24,* 602–611.

Katz, R., & Kahn, R. (1978). *The social psychology of organizations* (2nd ed.). New York: John Wiley.

Mohrman, S., & Cummings, T. (1989). *Self-designing organizations: Learning how to create high performance.* Reading, MA: Addison-Wesley.

Nunnally, J. C. (1978). *Psychometric theory* (2nd ed.). New York: McGraw-Hill.

Sayles, L. (1989). *Leadership: Managing in real organizations* (2nd ed.). New York: McGraw-Hill.

Seers, A. (1989). Team-member exchange quality: A new construct for role-making research. *Organizational Behavior and Human Decision Processes, 43,* 118–135.

Uhl-Bien, M. (1991). *Teamwork of the future: An investigation into teamwork processes of professional work teams in knowledge-based organizations.* Unpublished doctoral dissertation, University of Cincinnati, OH.

Uhl-Bien, M., & Graen, G. (1992). Self-management and team-making in cross-functional work teams: Discovering the keys to becoming an integrated team. *The Journal of High Technology Management Research, 3*(2), 225–241.

Zalesny, M., & Graen, G. (1986). Exchange theories of leadership. In A. Kieser, G. Reber, & R. Wunderer (Eds.), *Encyclopedia of leadership* (pp. 714–727). Kenstrasse, FRG: C. E. Paeschel Verlag.

Mary Uhl-Bien is Assistant Professor of Management at the University of Alaska Anchorage. She received her PhD from the University of Cincinnati.

George B. Graen is Professor of Organizational Behavior and Director of the Center for Enhancement of International Competitiveness at the University of Cincinnati. He received his PhD from the University of Minnesota.

Direct inquiries about this article to Mary Uhl-Bien, Assistant Professor, School of Business, University of Alaska Anchorage, 3211 Providence Drive, Anchorage, AK 99508, 907/786-1670.

CHAPTER 32

Beyond Situationalism
Subordinate Preferences and Perceived Leader Impact

Larry A. Pace, Diane E. Hartley, and Laura A. Davenport

Three studies were conducted using a laboratory methodology and standardized cases based on the Vroom-Yetton normative decision-making model. Analyses revealed that subordinate evaluations of leader effectiveness were most favorable when leaders used participative methods correctly. Both leaders and subordinates demonstrated awareness of the need for situationally specific leader behaviors, but subordinates preferred higher levels of participation. Role perspective (leader vs. subordinate) and the Vroom-Yetton model prescription (autocratic, consultative, or participative) affected subordinate preferences for participation. Limitations and implications of these studies are discussed.

Traditionally, organizations have relied on two primary sources of information for evaluations of the effectiveness of their leaders: supervisory ratings of subordinate leaders and the performance of the work area over which the leader is responsible. This traditional view of leadership effectiveness does not take into account directly the perceptions of subordinates or other constituencies.

Today, however, organizations are turning to nontraditional factors in the evaluation of leadership effectiveness. This movement is predicated both on dissatisfaction with the limited view of leader effectiveness afforded by traditional measures and on the increased use of constituency satisfaction measures to determine organizational effectiveness in changing and complex environments.

Nontraditional factors now being used to evaluate leader effectiveness include customer satisfaction, subordinate ratings of leader effectiveness (so-called reverse performance appraisal), peer ratings, and community participation (Deutsch, 1990; Landy & Farr, 1983; Mohrman, Resnick-West, & Lawler, 1989). Undoubtedly, most leader behaviors have consequences which affect the perceptions of the leader by various constituencies. And while leader reputation may have little direct or immediate connection to the organizational bottom line, perceptions of the effectiveness of leaders from the perspective of customers, subordinates, peers, and the community are obviously affected by the leader's behaviors. According to Bernardin (1986), managers themselves have indicated that subordinates are more qualified than anyone else to measure a manager's performance as a leader and a disseminator of information. Other research has indicated that the likability of both leaders and subordinates may cloud the accuracy of evaluations (Cardy & Dobbins, 1986; Dobbins & Russell, 1986).

These developments raise a potential dilemma for leaders. Should leaders attempt to do the right thing according to situational analysis, or should they attempt to do the thing they know will be approved by their constituents? To the extent that the "right thing" is the same in both analyses, there is no dilemma; traditional leadership models have implicitly assumed this to be so. But now, constituents, most notably subordinates, are being given increasing voice in the evaluation of leaders. Thus the issue of what is preferred versus what is correct is now of paramount importance to leaders.

In 1973, Vroom and Yetton introduced their normative model of leadership. The model prescribes the optimal decision process for different types of problem situations. Vroom and Jago (1988) cite evidence for the validity of the model that has been gathered both in the field (Bohnisch, Jago, & Reber, 1987; Margerison & Glube, 1979; Tjosvold, Wedley, & Field, 1986; Vroom & Jago, 1978; Zimmer, 1978) and in the laboratory (Field, 1982; Liddell, Elsea, Parkinson, & Hackett, 1986). The model contains seven rules designed to protect both decision quality and acceptance. These rules are used to evaluate the characteristics of the decision and to arrive at a feasible set of decision alternatives. Initially, a decision tree was used to apply the model; more re-

cently, a computer program (Vroom & Jago, 1988) has been developed as an "expert system" for the same purpose.

Decision processes range from Autocratic to Consultative to Group process. Subordinate participation in the decision-making process increases in the order of AI, AII, CI, CII, and GII. Leaders using the AI process solve the problem alone using the information available at the time. With process AII, the leader obtains any necessary information from subordinates and then makes the decision. CI is a consultative process in which the leader shares the problem with relevant subordinates individually and then makes the decision. With process CII, the leader shares the problem with subordinates in a group meeting, soliciting their ideas and suggestions, and then makes the decision. GII is a group decision process where the leader and subordinates aim to reach a group consensus on the decision.

Although subordinate commitment is included as a situational variable, the Vroom-Yetton normative model of leadership and decision making does not directly take into account subordinates' perceptions of the effectiveness of the leader who chooses various approaches according to a situational analysis.

Previous research has indicated that the affective reactions to leader behavior vary as a function of role perspective. Heilman, Hornstein, Cage, and Herschlag (1984) found a consistently more favorable response to the participative leader than to an autocratic one, no matter what the perspective of the respondent or what the circumstances. Similar results were found by Ansari (1987). In the Heilman et al. (1984) experiment, the ratings of leader effectiveness were made from the perspective of the leader in the scenario.

The present research included three studies conducted using a laboratory methodology and standardized cases taken from Vroom and Jago (1988). The first experiment extended the findings of Heilman et al. (1984) and Ansari (1987) to self-assessments of leaders, examining the effects on leader effectiveness ratings of role perspective (subordinate or leader), precision of leader behavior (correct or incorrect according to the Vroom-Yetton model), and prescription (participative or autocratic behavior chosen by the leader).

The second experiment tested subordinate preferences for participation and leaders' behavioral intentions for consistency across situations. This study was conducted to ascertain whether both leaders and subordinates recognize a key dilemma in leadership, namely that the "right" behavior may be unpopular. Rather than rate the effectiveness of a hypothetical leader's choice of decision process as was done in Experiment 1, this experiment required subjects to state their own behavioral intentions (Fishbein & Ajzen, 1975) as leader or their degree of preference for participation as a subordinate.

In Experiment 2, subjects reviewed each of three standardized cases from first, the perspective of the leader, and then from the perspective of a key subordinate. Subjects were asked to choose which decision process (AI-GII) they would select if they were the leader or which they would prefer if they were the subordinate. In the third experiment, subjects reviewed one case and were then asked to select the decision process they would use if in the leader role or in the subordinate role. Subjects then reviewed only one prescription (autocratic or participative) from only one perspective (leader or subordinate).

Experiment 1

Method

Subjects. Subjects in this study were 84 volunteers from an undergraduate management class at a large state university. Information on the age and sex of 82 subjects was available. There were 54 male and 28 female subjects with a mean age of 22.7 years (range 20–38). The subjects were naive to the Vroom-Yetton model prior to their participation in the study. At the completion of the study, subjects received an explanation of the purpose of the study and were awarded extra class credit.

Measures. Two cases from Vroom and Jago (1988) were used. After reading the scenario, subjects rated the effectiveness of the leader's decision procedure, the leader him/herself, and their projection of the likely outcome of the decision. All ratings were made on a 21-item, 9-point bipolar scale previously developed by Heilman et al. (1984). Following Heilman et al., responses were combined into six scales: Decision Process, Leader Competence, Leader Likability, Leader Dynamism, Task-Relevant Outcome, and Socio-Emotional Outcome.

Design and procedure. Subjects were divided into four groups of 21 members each. Each group read and rated two cases. In the first scenario, an autocratic decision was prescriptively correct; a participatory style was prescriptively correct in the second scenario. Group 1 members received cases in which the leader had made the prescriptively correct choice in both cases and evaluated the effectiveness of these choices by assuming the leader's role. In Group 2, subjects evaluated two prescriptively incorrect decisions from the leader's perspective. Group 3 members assumed a subordinate perspective and evaluated prescriptively correct decisions. Members of Group 4 evaluated, as subordinates, the effectiveness of a leader who had chosen prescriptively incorrect decision approaches.

Experiment 1 employed a between- and within-groups design using two levels of role perspective (leader or subordinate) crossed with two levels of precision (correct vs. incorrect approach chosen by the leader). The within-groups variable was

TABLE 1 Summary Statistics by Scenario for Experiment 1

Dependent Variable	Scenario 1			Scenario 2		
	M	SD	Alpha	M	SD	Alpha
Decision Process	5.26	1.47	.87	6.07	1.89	.93
Leader Competence	6.01	1.37	.78	6.75	1.67	.96
Leader Likability	4.49	1.32	.72	6.61	1.44	.82
Leader Dynamism	6.13	1.53	.88	5.84	1.25	.77
Task-Relevant Outcome	4.60	1.69	.80	5.84	2.09	.86
Socioemotional Outcome	3.74	1.65	.88	5.36	2.40	.89

Note. All means are on a 9-point scale with
higher scores indicating a more favorable rating.

the two levels of prescription (autocratic vs. participative) as determined by the scenarios.

Results

In Table 1 are shown the means, standard deviations, and internal consistency estimates (coefficient alpha) for the six dependent variables. Reliability estimates for the scales produced generally favorable values consistent with those reported earlier by Heilman et al. (1984).

Correlations among the dependent measures for both scenarios are presented in Table 2. Projections of task-relevant and socio-emotional outcomes were highly related for Scenario 2 (where a participative decision was prescriptively correct), but this relationship was more modest for Scenario 1. Additionally, leaders' decision-process effectiveness ratings were more strongly related to task-relevant outcome ratings in the "participative" scenario.

Since multiple dependent variables were used, a multivariate analysis of variance (MANOVA) was used to analyze the data from Experiment 1. Univariate F-ratios for each dependent measure and for the overall MANOVA are presented in

Table 3. The MANOVA detected significant main effects for perspective, prescription, and precision. Additionally, a significant interaction of prescription and precision was found.

In general, participation was evaluated more positively than autocratic decision making (for Decision Process, Leader Likability, Task-Relevant Outcomes, and Socio-Emotional Outcomes). Leaders making correct decisions were rated higher than those making incorrect decisions (on Decision Process, Task-Relevant Outcomes, and Socio-Emotional Outcomes). Subjects adopting the leader's perspective were more likely to rate Competence, Likability, and Socio-Emotional Outcomes of the leader's decision more highly than did subordinates.

The prescription by precision interaction for the separate dependent variables showed a general trend toward more positive evaluations of the correct use of participation than for any other combination. Leaders who used participation correctly (i.e., when situationally appropriate) were rated as more competent, as having used the correct approach (Decision Process), as more likable, and as having a more positive bottom-line effect on the organization.

TABLE 2 Correlations among Dependent Variables by Scenario
for Experiment 1

	Variable					
	DP	**LC**	**LL**	**LD**	**TO**	**SO**
Decision Process (DP)	—	.72*	.43*	.25*	.83*	.76*
Leader Competence (LC)	.57*	—	.55*	.34*	.71*	.61*
Leader Likability (LL)	.22*	.29*	—	.10	.54*	.57*
Leader Dynamism (LD)	.40*	.51*	−.10	—	.22*	.12
Task Outcome (TO)	.60*	.50*	.17	.30*	—	.89*
Social Outcome (SO)	.25*	.30*	.34*	−.15	.54*	—

Note. Correlations for Scenario 2 (Participative) are above the diagonal.
Correlations for Scenario 1 (Autocratic) are below the diagonal.

* $p < .05$.

TABLE 3 Multivariate and Univariate F-ratios for Between-
and Within-Groups Design (Experiment 1)

	Variable						
SOURCE	MANOVA	DP	LC	LL	LD	TO	SO
Perspective (A)	3.72	ns	10.76*	16.40*	ns	ns	7.59
Prescription (B)	11.90*	9.89*	ns	20.92*	7.29	27.52*	39.21*
Precision (C)	2.93	10.00*	ns	ns	ns	7.92	10.60*
A X B	ns	ns	ns	ns	ns	ns	ns
A X C	ns	ns	ns	ns	ns	ns	ns
B X C	21.47*	9.55*	11.00*	120.5*	ns	22.14*	38.64*
A X B X C	ns	ns	ns	ns	ns	ns	ns

Note. ns = not significant. All F-ratios are significant at $p < .05$
unless otherwise noted.

* $p < .01$.

Experiment 2

The first experiment demonstrated that both subordinate evaluations and self-evaluations of leader effectiveness are affected by the role perspective of the rater and by a combination of the precision of the leader's behavior and the specific situation. However, in Experiment 1, subjects had rated reputational consequences for predetermined leader behaviors. It remained an open question whether the behavioral intentions of subjects who adopted leader and subordinate roles would be affected by the anticipated reputational consequences of their behavior. Therefore, in Experiment 2, subjects were asked not to evaluate predetermined choices but to project their own behavioral intentions or desires into the scenario. This experiment hoped to ascertain whether subjects recognized the possibility that "appropriate" leader behaviors could have negative reputational consequences. By selecting more autocratic behaviors as leaders than they preferred as subordinates, subjects would in fact demonstrate their recognition of this key dilemma inherent in leadership.

Method

Subjects. Subjects in this study were 151 volunteers from an undergraduate class in management at a large state university. There were 90 male and 61 female subjects. The ages of the subjects ranged from 19 to 46 years with a mean of 21.9 years. Subjects were naive to the Vroom-Yetton model prior to their participation. At the completion of the study, subjects received an explanation of the purpose of the study and were awarded extra class credit.

Measures. Three standardized case scenarios were administered to each subject. After studying each case, subjects were presented the five decision processes from which they chose the style they would use if they were the leader or prefer for the leader to use if they were a key subordinate in the same scenario.

Design and procedure. Scenarios were chosen from Vroom and Jago (1988). Each subject received three scenarios: one in which the "appropriate" leader behavior was autocratic, one in which the "appropriate" leader behavior was consultative, and one in which the "appropriate" leader behavior was participative.

Subjects responded to each scenario first from the perspective of the leader in the scenario and then from the perspective of a key subordinate in the scenario. Subjects were asked first to select from the list of possible leader behaviors (AI, AII, CI, CII, and GII) their choice of what they would do if they were the leader in the given situation. Subjects were then asked

to imagine themselves in the role of a key subordinate in the scenario and to select from the possible leader behaviors the behavior they would prefer for the leader to exhibit in the situation. The design was a 2 X 3 within-groups experiment having two levels of perspective (leader vs. subordinate) crossed with three levels of prescription (autocratic, consultative, and participative).

Following Vroom and Yetton, the five possible leader behaviors were assumed to lie on a continuum from highly autocratic to highly participative (Vroom & Jago, 1988) and were assigned the values of 0, 1, 5, 8, and 10 based on Vroom and Yetton's "mean participation statistic."

Results

The within-groups analysis of variance (ANOVA) for Experiment 2 is summarized in Table 4. Inspection of Table 4 reveals the significant main effect of both prescription and perspective. There was no significant interaction of prescription and perspective. Figure 1 shows the differences in subordinate preferences for participation as a function of both role perspective and prescription. Examination of Figure 1 shows that both subordinates and leaders recognized the need for differing amounts of participation in different situations. However, subordinates uniformly preferred to be more involved than leaders indicated was appropriate. Indeed, subordinates indicated such strong preferences for participation that in the most "autocratic" scenario, subordinates requested more participation than leaders were willing to grant in even the most "participative" situation.

Experiment 3

Because of possible methodological concerns over the within-groups design in Experiment 2, a third experiment was conducted. This study was intended to

TABLE 4 Summary of Within-Groups Analysis of Variance of the Effects of Role Perspective and Model Prescription on Subordinate-Preferences for Participation (Experiment 2)

Source	df	SS	MS	F	p
Perspective (A)	1	797.5	797.5	110.7	< .001
Subject X A	150	1080.9	7.21		
Prescription (B)	2	265.0	132.5	10.4	< .001
Subject X B	300	3821.0	12.8		

determine whether the results obtained in Experiment 2 were method dependent. Experiment 3 used a completely crossed between-groups design.

Method

Subjects. Subjects in this study were 244 volunteers from an undergraduate management class at a large state university. There were 148 male and 96 female participants whose ages ranged from 18 to 48 years (mean 22.1). Subjects were naive to the Vroom-Yetton model prior to the study. After the study was completed, subjects were given an explanation of the purpose of the study. Extra class credit was awarded to each participant.

Measures. Two case scenarios taken from Vroom and Jago (1988) were used in this study. One scenario called for an au-

tocratic response, and the other scenario called for a participative response, as prescriptively "correct." After reading a case, half the subjects chose from the five decision processes the style they would choose as the leader. The remaining subjects were asked to choose the style they would prefer if they were a key subordinate in the scenario being studied.

Design and procedure. Role perspective was systematically varied by presenting half of the subjects a case from the leader's perspective and half a case from the key subordinate's perspective. The design was a 2 X 2 between-groups experiment having two levels of perspective (leader or subordinate) crossed with two levels of prescription (autocratic or participative). The dependent measure was the "mean participation statistic" of Vroom and Yetton for each subject derived from the decision process chosen.

Results

An analysis of variance (ANOVA) was performed to determine whether the decision process chosen by the subject was a function of the subordinate's role perspective, the prescriptively correct response for the scenario, or an interaction. The between-groups analysis of variance for Experiment 3 is summarized in Table 5.

As in Experiment 2, there was a significant main effect for prescription, with the amount of desired participation being

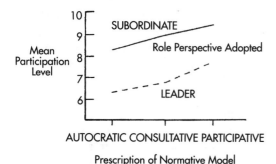

Figure 1 Preferred participation level as a function of role perspective and model prescription.

TABLE 5 Summary of Between-Groups Analysis of Variance of the Effects of Role Perspective and Model Prescription on Subject Preferences for Participation (Experiment 3)

Source	df	SS	F	p
Overall	3	286.31	8.82	< .001
Perspective (A)	1	40.98	3.79	< .05
Prescription (B)	1	240.02	22.19	< .001
A X B	1	5.31	.49	ns

greater in the "participative scenario." The main effect for perspective was significant (p = .05), indicating a tendency for subordinates to prefer more participation than leaders deemed appropriate in the same scenario. There was no significant interaction between perspective and prescription.

Discussion and Conclusions

Implications

The findings support the conclusion of Heilman et al. (1984) that participative leaders are liked more and believed to have more successful interpersonal impact than autocratic leaders. Being perceived as using the appropriate leadership style and being liked, however, do not always go hand in hand. Although these conclusions are based on data collected from undergraduate business students in the U.S., similar conclusions have been reached from such diverse populations as Pakistani engineering students (Ansari, 1987) and New York City pedestrians (Heilman et al., 1984).

The hypothesis that participation is uniformly rated more highly than autocratic decision making did not receive full support in this research. Rather, the correct (i.e., according to the model) use of participation was instrumental in leading to projections of both highly effective organizational performance and high subordinate commitment. Normative views such as that of Blake and Mouton (1964) prescribe participation coupled with concern for production (the "team approach") as the one best way for leaders. Results of this study support this conclusion if leader effectiveness is equated with subordinate satisfaction.

Experiments 2 and 3 revealed that subordinates and leaders do in fact recognize the need for situationally specific leader behaviors. However, subordinate preferences for participation were higher than leaders were comfortably willing to grant. The within-groups design of Experiment 2 and the between-groups design of Experiment 3 both clearly demonstrated that individuals recognize the dilemma that what is "right" may not be popular. At the same time, what is preferred may become "right" under conditions where subordinates expect high participation and where subordinates regularly provide feedback that may be used to evaluate leaders' effectiveness. How individuals and leaders resolve the dilemma of what is right and what is preferred is a crucial question.

The findings of this study could have substantial impact for people in leadership roles. In circumstances when positive evaluations from their subordinates are important to leaders, it may be to the leader's advantage to manage the characteristics of the situation in such a way that participation would be appropriate.

Avoiding or intentionally changing situations calling for autocratic decision making may prevent or reduce unfavorable evaluations of leader effectiveness.

The results of this research clearly indicate that normative models which fail to take into account the strong bias toward participation that subordinates bring to the evaluation of leaders will underprescribe participation. Leaders who are evaluated by their subordinates should attend to the amount of participation they use in their decision processes. Leaders who behave autocratically, even when such behavior is appropriate given a normative situation analysis, are likely to suffer.

Possible Limitations of the Present Studies

In Experiment 2, the order of the scenarios and the order of perspective were constant. Each subject responded to the scenarios first from the leader perspective and then from the subordinate perspective. Possible order effects were controlled in Experiment 3, which used a completely crossed design.

The present studies are potentially limited in generalizability because of the subject population and the laboratory methodology employed. For these reasons, it is perhaps best to conceive of these findings as a first step in the development of an integrative view of leadership that recognizes, simultaneously, the need for some situation specificity and the bias toward involvement that subordinates bring to the evaluation of their leaders. Future research should attempt to replicate these findings in organizational settings. While experimental research using "paper people" and employing undergraduate students as subjects is currently the subject of much criticism because of its possible external invalidity, discarding experimental methods and the use of student subjects to study organizational processes may be an overreaction. One trio of researchers (Dobbins, Lane, & Steiner, 1988) likened such a reaction to throwing out the baby with the bathwater. In the final analysis, of course, generalizability is an empirical question that should be answered empirically, not rhetorically.

Acknowledgments

This research was conducted while all three authors were affiliated with the University of Tennessee, the financial support of which is acknowledged.

The authors are grateful to Professors R. T. Ladd, J. Philpot, and G. H. Dobbins for their assistance and advice in statistical analysis and interpretation and for their comments on previous drafts of this article.

References

Ansari, M. A. (1987). Effects of leader persistence and leader behavior on leadership perceptions. *Pakistan Journal of Psychological Research*, 2(3–4), 1–10.

Bernardin, H. J. (1986). Subordinate appraisal: A valuable source of information about managers. *Human Resource Management*, 25, 421–439.

Blake, R. R., & Mouton, J. S. (1964). *The managerial grid*. Houston: Gulf.

Bohnisch, W., Jago, A. G., & Reber, G. (1987). Zur interkulterellen validatat des Vroom/Yetton modells. *Die Betriebswirtschaft*, 47, 85–93.

Cardy, R. L., & Dobbins, G. H. (1986). Affect and appraisal accuracy: Liking as an integral dimension in appraising performance. *Journal of Applied Psychology*, 71, 672–678.

Deutsch, C. H. (1990, June 3). Firms use money to change behavior. *Knoxville News-Sentinel*, p. 10.

Dobbins, G. M., Lane, I. M. & Steiner, D. D. (1988). A note on the role of laboratory methodology in applied behavioral research. Don't throw out the baby with the bath water. *Journal of Organizational Behavior*, 9, 281–286.

Dobbins, G. H., & Russell, J. (1986). The biasing effects of subordinate likableness on leaders' attributions and corrective actions. *Personnel Psychology, 38,* 759–777.

Field, R. H. G. (1982). A test of the Vroom-Yetton normative model of leadership. *Journal of Applied Psychology, 67,* 523–532.

Fishbein, M., & Ajzen, I. (1975). *Belief, attitude, intention, and behavior: An introduction to theory and research.* Reading, MA: Addison-Wesley.

Heilman, M. E., Hornstein, H. A., Cage, J. H., & Herschlag, J. (1984). Reactions to prescribed leader behavior as a function of role perspective: The case of the Vroom/Yetton model. *Journal of Applied Psychology, 69,* 50–60.

Landy, F. J., & Farr, J. L. (1983). *The measurement of work performance: Methods, theory, and applications.* Orlando, FL: Academic Press.

Liddell, W. W., Elsea, S. W., Parkinson, A. E., & Hackett, A. M. (1986). *A replication and refinement of "A test of the Vroom-Yetton normative model of leadership."* Unpublished manuscript.

Margerison, C., & Glube, R. (1979). Leadership decision-making: An empirical test of the Vroom and Yetton model. *Journal of Management Studies, 16,* 45–55.

Mohrman, A. M., Jr., Resnick-West, S. M., & Lawler, E. E. (1989). *Designing performance appraisal systems.* San Francisco: Jossey-Bass.

Tjosvold, D., Wedley, W. C., & Field, R. H. G. (1986). Constructive controversy, the Vroom-Yetton model, and managerial decision-making. *Journal of Occupational Behaviour, 7,* 125–138.

Vroom, V. H., & Jago, A. G. (1978). On the validity of the Vroom/Yetton model. *Journal of Applied Psychology, 63,* 138–151.

Vroom, V. H., & Jago, A. G. (1988). *The new leadership: Managing participation in organizations.* Englewood Cliffs, NJ: Prentice-Hall.

Zimmer, R. J. (1978). *Validating the Vroom-Yetton normative model of leader behavior in field sales force management and measuring the training effects of TELOS on the leader behavior of district managers.* Unpublished doctoral dissertation, Virginia Polytechnic Institute and State University, Blacksburg.

Larry A. Pace is Associate Professor of Management at Louisiana State University in Shreveport. He teaches, conducts research, and consults in Total Quality, leadership, and human resource management. He has published over 50 articles, chapters, and reviews and is currently working on a series of textbooks. He earned his PhD in Industrial Psychology from the University of Georgia.

Diane E. Hartley is a PhD candidate in Industrial-Organizational Psychology at the University of Tennessee, Knoxville. Her dissertation focuses on an individual's intention to behave ethically when personal and organizational norms or values conflict. She is currently an intern in the Management and Organization Development Group at Martin Marietta Energy Systems, Oak Ridge, Tennessee.

Laura A. Davenport is a PhD candidate in Industrial-Organizational Psychology at the University of Tennessee, Knoxville. She teaches courses in Human Resource Management and Organizational Behavior at the University of Tennessee and Maryville College. She held a graduate assistantship at ALCOA, Tennessee Operations' training department, working in the areas of training evaluation, survey development, and selection system design and administration.

Direct inquiries about this article to Larry A. Pace, Associate Professor, Department of Management and Marketing, Louisiana State University, One University Place, Shreveport, LA 71115, 318/797-5276.

Leadership within the "Discontinuous Hierarchy" Structure of the Military

Are Effective Leadership Behaviors Similar within and across Command Structures?

**Peter W. Dorfman,
Jon P. Howell,
Benjamin C. G. Cotton,
and Uday Tate**

The primary goal of this project was to compare the impact of specific leadership behaviors within the commissioned officer (CO) ranks of the U.S. military with those *between* the commissioned and high-level noncommissioned officer (NCO) ranks. When analyzed separately, most leader behaviors impacted attitudes and several impacted job performance both within and across hierarchies. The causal model analysis (considering all leader behaviors simultaneously) showed that supportive and participative leader behaviors were impactful for both COs and NCOs; other leader behaviors had differential impacts in the two samples. Several individual and organizational factors were found to enhance, neutralize, or substitute for specific leadership behaviors. Each of these factors served to empower the individual job holder—leader or subordinate.

The importance of leadership in the military is evidenced by extensive training programs focused on leadership excellence and by the prominence of effective leadership in the recent (1990–1991) Mideast war. Research scholars continue to find the military a rich and fruitful area to examine in terms of both practical and theoretical issues of leadership (Bass, 1990; Yukl & Van Fleet, 1982). A recent text on leadership (Clark & Clark, 1990) contains many studies conducted in the military with research samples from Air Force Academy cadets (Clover, 1990) to General Officers in the Army (Jacobs & Jaques, 1990). From a practical perspective, there is an abundance of "how to effectively lead" manuals developed and used at various military training centers. Yet, there is an apparent void in the military leadership literature comparing effective leadership by commissioned officers (COs) of other COs with leadership by COs of noncommissioned officers (NCOs).

Considering the differences in background, training, duties, and responsibilities between COs and NCOs (Huntington, 1957, referred to these as "discontinuous hierarchies"), it seems important to determine whether the most effective leadership behaviors for supervising within a hierarchy (e.g., commissioned officer ranks) are similar to supervising across ranks (e.g., COs supervising NCOs). With this in mind, the primary goal of this project was to compare the impact of specific leadership behaviors within the commissioned officer ranks with those between the commissioned and high-level noncommissioned officer ranks.

Leaders in certain types of nonmilitary organizations also face problems involving dual or discontinuous hierarchies, though these organizations are often quite different from the military. Managers in health service organizations often use different strategies in dealing with the medical staff than in dealing with the administrative staff. Administrators in colleges and universities confront administrative and academic hierarchies. Other professional organizations, such as public accounting and legal service organizations, often have dual hierarchies. These are not simply line-staff distinctions; they include the existence of separate graded hierarchies with different (but related) purposes.

In the army, commissioned officers obtain their initial position primarily through schooling (ROTC or West Point); a minority come from enlisted personnel through Officer Candidate School. Their schooling emphasizes planning, organizing, leading, and training of military units with an emphasis on unit performances and the "big picture." They are taught to regard themselves as professional managers of violence, and the term "officer" remains a high-status personnel category in the military.

Noncommissioned officers obtain their position from demonstrated competence and performance—they rise through the ranks. As they are promoted, they are highly schooled in individual soldier training and development, maintenance, readiness, and performance, with a strong emphasis on technical issues. NCOs are the linkage between COs and small groups of enlisted personnel. They prepare for and execute plans and policies developed primarily by COs.

Given these differences between COs and NCOs and the evidence favoring situational/contingency approaches to leadership (cf., Indvik, 1986; Yukl, 1989), one would be surprised if the same leadership patterns would be effective with both COs and NCOs. In fact, what little research evidence does exist points to differences in effective leadership patterns as rank increases (Rogers, 1983; Van Fleet & Yukl, 1986).

A common image of the U.S. military is that of a "Command Bureaucracy" (Jermier & Berkes, 1979) where authoritative and directive leadership behaviors are predominant and required for success. Yet, the emphasis on speedy decisions by directive, task-oriented leaders will not always lead to the most effective solutions (Bass, 1990). Recent research shows that numerous leader behaviors are prevalent and necessary for effectiveness at all levels of the military (Van Fleet & Yukl, 1986). The particular "mix" and pattern of behaviors deemed important to effective leadership is often situationally determined (combat versus noncombat is an obvious situational moderator). The issue of which leader behaviors have an optimal impact in a given military situation is changing. Military leaders are required to operate under conditions vastly different from those existing in World War II and Vietnam. The recent fighting in the Middle East was more intense, lethal, and destructive than ever before. Everything about the modern military is more complex, including technological sophistication of the military hardware, maintenance requirements, and political consequences of various actions. Effective leadership in politically complex conflicts like the Middle East is critical and is becoming increasingly more difficult.

Researchers in the past several years have been interested in viewing leadership from the new perspective of Transformational or Charismatic Leadership (Bass, 1985). Perhaps somewhat unfortunately, a new trend among leadership researchers is the dichotomization between transformational and transactional leadership. Yukl's (1989) caveat seems appropriate: Be careful about viewing leadership using a simple dichotomous model. Simple models of leadership are seductive because they are easily explained and understood, but they do not reflect the complex necessities of large modern organizations such as the U.S. military. This study incorporates several leader behavior patterns including charismatic, directive, supportive, contingent punishment, contingent reward, participative, and representative leadership. The first four behaviors represent the key leader behaviors identified by Van Fleet and Yukl (1986) in their multimethod study of leadership in the U.S. military. The last three behaviors have been prominent in other contingency studies of leaders' behavior (Yukl, 1989). Given that the military is much more complicated now than it was 20 to 40 years ago, a situational/contingency approach to leadership seems especially appropriate. Several important situational variables are included in the analysis to reflect the complexity of modern military life.

We examined multiple leader behaviors found to be effective in both military and nonmilitary situations as well as leadership within and across the discontinuous hierarchy dealt with by military officers. We also explored the impact of specific substitutes, neutralizers, and enhancers of leadership within and across hierarchies. Substitutes are factors which at the same time neutralize (negate) and replace specific leader behaviors. Enhancers increase the impact of specific leader behaviors. An example of the former is professionalization of the subordinate; an example of the latter is expertise of the supervisor (Howell & Dorfman, 1981, 1986). We analyzed the impact of leadership on both attitudinal and job performance measures.

Method

Data were collected from two samples comprised of active duty commissioned and noncommissioned officers stationed at a major U.S. Army facility in the southwest. Survey questionnaires were administered at the soldier's place of duty. Performance evaluation data were obtained by placing a blank copy of the evaluation report forms at the end of the questionnaire. Participants reproduced their evaluations on this form or xeroxed their evaluations and turned them in with the questionnaires. Although we relied on the soldier's recollection and accurate reporting of these data, no respondent reported any problem in recalling these data which are critical to their career. All data were collected 3 to 6 months prior to the Mideast war.

Samples

The commissioned officer sample was comprised of 146 individuals from Second Lieutenant to Colonel with the majority being company grade officers (Lieutenants and Captains). The mean years in the Army for officers was 6.8 years (range of 1 to 26 years), and the mean age was 30 years (range of 23 to 53 years). All but 1% of the officers in this sample were college graduates with an average 16.2 years of formal education. All were active duty Air Defense Artillery Officers with varying levels of expertise and leadership training. The majority had led platoons and/or batteries of soldiers numbering from 30 to 120 individuals. Technical army experience for this sample primarily consisted of surface-to-air missiles systems, communications systems, electronics, and computers.

The noncommissioned officer sample was comprised of 102 individuals from Staff Sergeant (E-6) to Sergeants Major (E-9). The majority were Master Sergeants and First Sergeants, both of grade E-8. The mean years of service in the Army for NCOs was 20 years (range of 9 to 32 years), and the mean age was 41 years (range of 33 to 51 years). All but 1% of the NCOs were high school graduates, with an average 14 years of formal education. All were active duty noncommissioned officers with varying areas of expertise and with at least the minimum required Army leadership training commensurate to their rank. The majority led squads, teams, platoons, companies, and/or battalions of soldiers numbering from 5 to 600 individuals. The NCOs represented a wide degree of technical diversity within the Army.

Measures

The leadership behaviors utilized in this study included:

1. Directiveness—clarifying performance expectations, assigning tasks, specifying methods to be used. This scale was developed by Schriesheim (1978) for use in Path-Goal Theory testing.

2. Supportiveness—showing a concerned and caring attitude to followers. This scale was also developed by Schriesheim (1978).

3. Participativeness—obtaining input from followers for important decisions. This scale was modified from scales developed by Yukl (1982) and R. J. House (personal communication, 1984).

4. Contingent Rewards—providing social rewards to followers (e.g., compliments) for good performance. This was derived from the Leader Reward and Punishment Questionnaire developed by Podsakoff and Skov (1980).

5. Contingent Punishment—providing aversive social consequences to followers for poor performance. This was also derived from Podsakoff and Skov (1980).

6. Charisma—inspiring and developing confidence among followers. This was modified from scales developed by House (personal communication, 1984) and Yukl (1982).

7. Representativeness—supplying, networking, and buffering followers from unreasonable demands. This was modified from a scale developed by Yukl (1982).

Measures of two potential substitutes for leadership were modified from Kerr and Jermier's (1978) Substitutes for Leadership Scale. They were subordinate's ability, experience, training and knowledge, and organizational formalization (standard operating procedures). Also measured on the questionnaire for this study as possible leadership neutralizer/substitutes or enhancers respectively were years of service and perceived leader expertise. Attitudes, classified as mediators or intervening variables in this study (Yukl, 1989), included satisfaction with supervision and satisfaction with work, measured by the Minnesota Satisfaction Questionnaire (Weiss, Dawis, England, & Lofquist, 1967); organizational commitment was assessed through the Porter and Smith (1970) questionnaire; and role ambiguity was measured by the Rizzo, House, and Lirtzman (1970) scale.

A single performance measure for each CO and NCO was obtained by combining various measures of job performance found in each soldier's performance evaluation report. For COs, we combined and then standardized the overall evaluation and potential-for-promotion ratings (two separate ratings) found in the officer evaluation report. This measure was added to a senior evaluator rating which was also standardized. For NCOs, we standardized the total rating of each soldier and summed this score with a standardized rating score completed by a senior rater. Thus for both groups, the performance measure was an index that assessed two levels of performance evaluation: that of the supervisor and that of a second-level senior rater.

Research Questions

This research effort explored the impacts of CO leadership on other (lower level) COs and on NCOs. While all the leader behaviors had potential impacts on follower attitudes and performance, we did expect differences in the degree and possibly the direction of impact between the two samples. The overall research questions were as follows:

1. Which leader behaviors have the strongest impact when high-level COs supervise lower level COs?

2. Which leader behaviors have the strongest impact when COs (aggregated together) supervise NCOs?

3. Are the same set of leader behaviors effective (impactful) when high-level COs supervise low-level COs compared to COs supervising NCOs?

4. Are the same set of leader behaviors effective when high-level COs supervise NCOs compared to when low-level COs supervise NCOs?

5. Do these military samples contain leadership substitutes, neutralizers, or enhancers like those found in other organizational situations?

Analytical Strategy

Data analysis proceeded in stages. First, we assessed the similarities and differences between the samples in the amount (i.e., level) of leadership provided to the subordinates. Second, we assessed the impact of specific leader behaviors for each sample by conducting correlation and regression analyses. As a third analytical strategy, causal modeling methodology (LISREL VI) (Jöreskog & Sörbom, 1984) was used to assess the simultaneous impact of all leader behaviors on mediators and job performance. This technique helped us to determine the viability of a graphic causal model linking specific leadership behaviors to job performance through various hypothesized mediators such as job satisfaction. We developed two models, one for COs supervising lower level COs and the other for COs supervising NCOs. Similarities and differences between the models were examined. Significant causal paths in the causal models were further analyzed to determine the presence of substitutes for leadership. This technique involves the use of hierarchical multiple regression to identify the presence of the type of moderator—substitute, neutralizer, or enhancer. (See Howell and Dorfman, 1986, for a complete description of this technique.)

Results

Amount of Leadership

Table 1 presents the means, standard deviations, and reliabilities for both samples. Significant differences were found between the two samples on the amount of leadership shown and the level of subordinate satisfaction, commitment, and role ambiguity. The pattern was quite clear. COs supervising lower level COs were significantly more directive and used more contingent punishment than COs supervising NCOs. Conversely, COs supervising NCOs were significantly more supportive, used more contingent reward, were more charismatic, and exhibited more representative leadership than when supervising lower level COs. COs supervising NCOs were only slightly more participative than COs supervising low-level COs.

A clear pattern also emerged with respect to the attitudes of subordinates of COs. Consistent differences emerged between NCOs being supervised by COs and lower level COs being supervised by higher level COs. NCOs experienced significantly less role ambiguity, more satisfaction with work, satisfaction with supervision, and organizational commitment than did lower level COs being supervised by higher level COs.

Differences in the amount of leadership provided also were evident when comparing NCOs supervised by high- or by low-level COs. As shown in Table 2, lower level COs supervising NCOs were significantly more supportive, charismatic, and representative and used more contingent reward than higher level COs supervising NCOs. Although no significant differences were found for leader contingent punishment or directiveness, lower level COs were slightly more participative than higher level COs. In general, all of these differences were also accompanied by differences in subordinate attitudes. Supervision by lower level COs resulted in higher level satisfaction with work and organizational commitment and less role ambiguity than did supervision by higher level COs. Somewhat surprising, given the more facilitative leadership behaviors from lower level COs, was the finding that there were only slight differences for satisfaction with supervision.

Impact of Leadership

Correlations between the leader behaviors and criteria are shown in Table 3 for both samples. This table also presents the regression results. By examining the data in this table, we can view the relative impact of each leader behavior on the criteria and also note significant differences between the two samples.

COs supervising low-level COs and COs supervising NCOs. Overall, when considering both samples simultaneously, we find more than 80% of the correlations between leader behaviors and criteria are significant. For COs supervising lower level COs, all of the "facilitative leader behaviors" (support, contingent reward, charismatic, participative, and representative leadership) had strong positive impacts on attitudinal criteria and mostly moderate impacts on job performance. The "controlling leadership behaviors" (directive and contingent punishment) had moderate impacts on attitudinal criteria and weak impacts on job performance.

For COs supervising NCOs, facilitative leader behaviors had significant impacts on attitudinal criteria and generally moderate impacts on job performance. However, neither directive leadership nor contingent punishment had consistent impacts on either the attitudinal or job performance criteria (one exception was a significant correlation between directive leadership and satisfaction with supervision).

Prior studies would lead us to predict *differential* effects of leadership between and across hierarchies. Hierarchical multiple regression has proven to be more sensitive than correlations in determining differences between samples such as those in the present study. Regression results are also presented in Table 3. The differential impacts (shown by boxes in Table 3) of leadership were generally concentrated in two leader behaviors: Directive leadership and contingent punishment generally had stronger favorable impacts for COs supervising low-level COs.

For both samples, the LISREL analysis (Figures 1 and 2) provides strong support for the indirect impact of leadership on job performance. In both models, either contingent punishment or contingent reward reduces role ambiguity (resulting in increased satisfaction with work), supportive leadership increases satisfaction

TABLE 1 Means, Standard Deviations, and Reliabilities of All Variables

	Low Level COs Supervised by High-Level COs (N = 146)			NCOs Supervised by COs (N = 102)			Significance between Means
	Mean	S.D.	Reliability	Mean	S.D.	Reliability	
Leader Behaviors							
Directive	4.72	1.03	.87	4.30	1.15	.85	p < .01
Supportive	4.86	1.29	.95	5.69	1.14	.93	p < .01
Contingent Reward	4.59	1.38	.95	5.41	1.31	.96	p < .01
Contingent Punishment	5.47	1.11	.94	5.11	1.13	.85	p < .01
Charismatic	3.69	.82	.92	4.16	.77	.94	p < .01
Participative	3.51	.93	.93	3.72	.93	.92	p < .10
Representative	3.78	.80	.87	4.10	.84	.93	p < .01
Mediators							
Role Ambiguity	1.97	.60	.82	1.60	.58	.85	p < .01
Satisfaction With Work	4.05	.68	.86	4.40	.50	.82	p < .01
Satisfaction With Supervisor	3.34	1.02	.96	3.91	.90	.96	p < .01
Organizational Commitment	5.28	1.16	.93	5.81	.93	.88	p < .01
Outcome Variable							
Job Performance[a]	—	—	.74	—	—	.82	

Note. Charismatic, Participative, and Representatve Leader Behaviors were measured using 5-point Likert scales. All other Leader Behaviors were measured on 7-point Likert scales.

[a]Job Performance scores were standardized: M = 0; STD = 1.00.

TABLE 2 Means, Standard Deviations, and Reliabilities of All Variables

	NCOs Supervised by High-Level COs (N = 46)		NCOs Supervised by Low-Level COs (N = 56)		Significance between Means
	Mean	S.D.	Mean	S.D.	
Leader Behavior					
Directive	4.09	1.08	4.47	1.18	NS
Supportive	5.22	1.34	6.08	.77	p < .01
Contingent Reward	4.95	1.38	5.79	1.13	p < .01
Contingent Punishment	4.93	1.15	5.25	1.10	NS
Charismatic	3.79	.83	4.46	.57	p < .01
Participative	3.55	1.01	3.86	.84	p < .10
Representative	3.83	.93	4.33	.70	p < .01
Mediators					
Role Ambiguity	1.75	.52	1.47	.60	p < .01
Satisfaction With Work	4.21	.57	4.56	.37	p < .05
Satisfaction With Supervisor	3.73	.98	4.05	.80	p < .10
Organizational Commitment	5.48	1.07	6.09	.69	p < .01
Outcome Variable					
Job Performance[a]	.22	1.91	− .16	1.85	NS

Note. Charismatic, Participative, and Representative Leader Behaviors were measured using 5-point Likert scales. All other Leader Behaviors were measured on 7-point Likert scales.

[a]Job Performance scores were standardized within NCO ranks: M = 0; STD = 1.00.

with supervision, and participation increases satisfaction with work. These three mediators, in turn, impact organizational commitment which then influences job performance. Differences between the models are also apparent. For COs supervising COs (see Figure 1), contingent punishment was more important than contingent reward in influencing attitudes. In addition, charismatic leadership had a significant influence on satisfaction with supervision. For COs supervising NCOs (see Figure 2), directive leadership significantly influenced satisfaction with supervision. Representative leadership played an important role for this NCO

sample, but the LISREL analysis did not capture the impact of charismatic leadership found in the correlation and regression results. (For the NCO sample, it appeared that the large shared variance between support and charismatic leadership prevented both impacts from occurring simultaneously. For the CO sample, a similar shared variance between participation and representation caused the latter leader behavior to drop out.)

High-level COs supervising NCOs and low-level COs supervising NCOs. Contrasting high-level COs supervising NCOs with low-level COs su-

TABLE 3 Correlation and Regression Results: COs Supervising Low-Level COs and COs Supervising NCOs

Leader Behavior		Role Ambiguity		Satisfaction with Work		Satisfaction with Supervision		Organizational Commitment		Job Performance	
		CO	NCO	CO	NCO	CO	NCO	CO	NCO	CO	NCO
Directive	$r =$	−.26	ns	.25	ns	.44	.42	.19	−ns	ns	ns
	$\beta =$	−.15	ns	.16	ns	.43	.34	.21	ns	ns	ns
Contingent Punishment	$r =$	−.27	ns	.38	ns	.20	ns	.21	ns	−ns	+ns
	$\beta =$	−.14	ns	.23	ns	.18	ns	.22	ns	−ns	+ns
Supportive	$r =$	−.33	−.43	.38	.51	.70	.60	.35	.44	.36	.24
	$\beta =$	−.15	−.23	.20	.23	.55	.46	.32	.36	.50	.39
Contingent Reward	$r =$	−.35	−.39	.43	.47	.63	.62	.38	.27	.27	.32
	$\beta =$	−.15	−.17	.21	.19	.47	.42	.32	.19	.35	.45
Charismatic	$r =$	−.33	−.32	.47	.52	.65	.68	.33	.50	.21	.37
	$\beta =$	−.24	−.25	.39	.35	.81	.78	.47	.60	.44	.91
Participative	$r =$	−.28	−.22	.47	.45	.56	.44	.40	.35	.19	.22
	$\beta =$	−.18	−.14	.34	.26	.64	.43	.50	.36	.37	.46
Representative	$r =$	−.33	−.20	.41	.44	.52	.63	.38	.35	ns	.24
	$\beta =$	−.24	−.14	.35	.27	.67	.65	.57	.38	ns	.54

Note. Only significant correlation and regression coefficients are presented. $N = 146$ for COs, $p < .05$ if $r \geq .16$; $N = 102$ for NCOs, $p < .05$ if $r \geq .20$. Regression coefficients are presented below the correlation coefficients. Significant differences between correlations or regression coefficients are indicated by enclosing the appropriate numbers with a box.

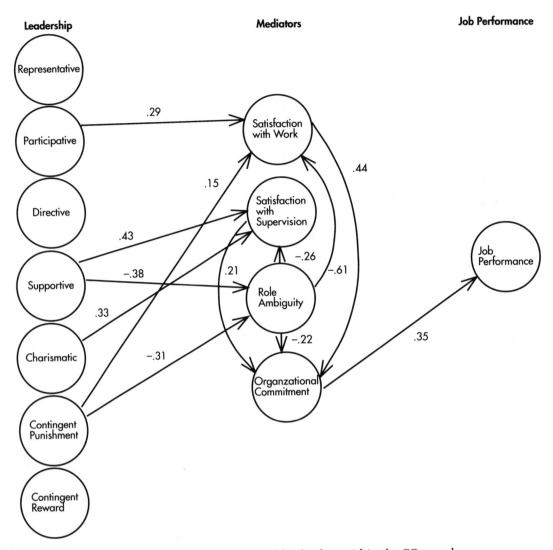

Figure 1   LISREL Model indicating the impact of leadership within the CO sample.

pervising NCOs (see Table 4) yields differences which were not as large as expected. The only significant difference concerns the effects of participative leadership on attitudes (shown in boxes in Table 4) and a marginally significant difference on job performance. Participative leadership was most impactful for high-level COs supervising NCOs, not low-level COs supervising NCOs. For representative leadership, one of the largest correlations for satisfaction with supervision and one of the largest regression coefficients for job performance occurred with low-level COs supervising NCOs.

We were not able to conduct a LISREL analysis to examine Hi/Lo COs supervising NCO similarities and differences due to the relatively small sample sizes. However, summary information from Tables 2 and 4 are presented in Table 5 and will be discussed in the last section of this paper.

Substitutes, Neutralizers, and Enhancers

The significant causal paths shown in the LISREL causal models were analyzed to determine if they were affected by po-

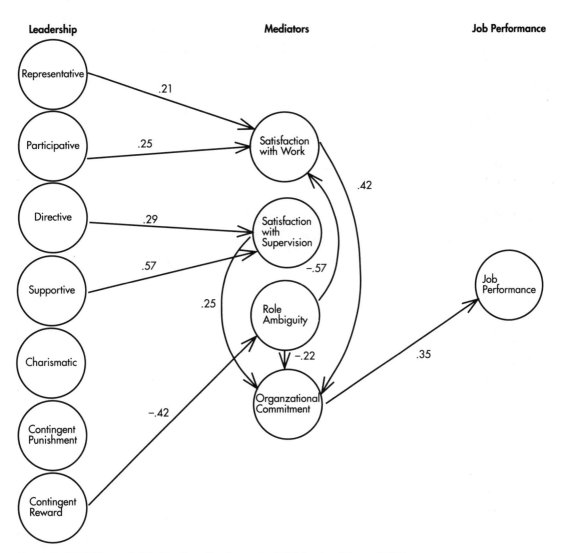

Leadership   **Mediators**   **Job Performance**

Figure 2   LISREL model indicating the impact of CO leadership on NCOs.

tential leadership substitute variables. In the causal model for COs (see Figure 1), the two paths from leaders' contingent punishment behavior (impacting satisfaction with work and role ambiguity) were not affected by either the substitute variables or the potential enhancer (perceived leader expertise). Contingent punishment appears to be a powerful and robust leader behavior within the CO hierarchy. The path from participative leadership to satisfaction with work was also not affected by the substitutes or the enhancer variables. Participation seems to be another robust leader behavior for COs.

The two paths from supportive leadership (impacting satisfaction with supervision and role ambiguity) were affected by the substitutes and the enhancer. Subordinate years of service *neutralized* the impact of support on both mediators, and subordinate rank *neutralized* the impact of support on role ambiguity. The longer the subordinate has served in the Army and the higher his/her rank, the less impact the supportive leader has on the subordinate. Conversely, the same two paths from leaders' supportiveness were *enhanced* by perceived leaders' expertise. The more the leader is seen as capable and

TABLE 4 Correlation and Regression Results: High-Level COs Supervising NCOs and Low-Level COs Supervising NCOs

Leader Behavior		Role Ambiguity		Satisfaction with Work		Satisfaction with Supervision		Organizational Commitment		Job Performance	
		Hi	Low	Hi	Low	Hi	Low	Hi	Low	Hi	Low
Directive	r =	ns	ns	ns	ns	.33	.48	ns	ns	ns	ns
	β =	ns	ns	ns	ns	.31	.33	ns	ns	ns	ns
Contingent Punishment	r =	ns	ns	ns	ns	ns	ns	ns	ns	ns	ns
	β =	ns	ns	ns	.09	ns	.18[a]	ns	ns	ns	ns
Supportive	r =	-.40	-.41	.51	.27	.65	.49	.39	.28	.33	ns
	β =	-.17	-.33	.21	.16	.46	.50	.30	.27	.48	ns
Contingent Reward	r =	-.33	-.36	.48	.30	.66	.52	.29[a]	ns	.41	ns
	β =	-.13	-.20	.19	.13	.46	.37	ns	ns	.58	ns
Charismatic	r =	ns	-.30	.48	.37	.62	.77	.42	.43	.35	.40
	β =	ns	-.33	.33	.24	.71	1.13	.52	.47	.83	1.30
Participative	r =	-.36	ns	.63	ns	.51	.33	.49	ns	-.26[a]	ns
	β =	-.19	ns	.36	ns	.51	.30	.51	ns	.52[a]	ns
Representative	r =	ns	ns	.46	.25[a]	.54	.70	.33	ns	ns	.31
	β =	ns	ns	.28	.15	.56	.80	.35	ns	ns	.81

Note. N = 46 for Hi Level COs, p < .05 if r ≥ .30; N = 56 for Low Level COs, p < .05 if r ≥ .27. Regression coefficients are presented below the correlation coefficients. Significant differences between correlations or regression coefficients are indicated by enclosing the appropriate numbers with a box.

[a] p < .10.

TABLE 5 Summary Results: Leader Behavior Level and Impact (High- versus Low-Level COs Supervising NCOs)

	High-Level CO			Low-Level CO		
	Amount of Leader Behavior Shown	Impact on 4 Mediators	Impact on Performance	Amount of Leader Behavior Shown	Impact on 4 Mediators	Impact on Performance
Directive	Low/Medium	Weak	Weak	Medium	Weak	Weak
Contingent Punishment	Medium	Weak	Weak	Medium/High	Weak	Weak
Supportive	Medium/High	Strong	Moderate	Very High	Moderate	Weak
Contingent Reward	Medium	Moderate	Moderate/Strong	High	Moderate	Weak
Charismatic	Medium/High	Moderate/Strong	Strong	Very High	Strong	Strong
Participative	Medium	Very Strong	Weak/Moderate	Medium/High	Weak	Weak
Representative	Medium/High	Moderate	Weak	Very High	Weak[a]/Strong	Moderate

[a]Weak effects for all attitudes with the exception of strong effects on satisfaction with supervision.

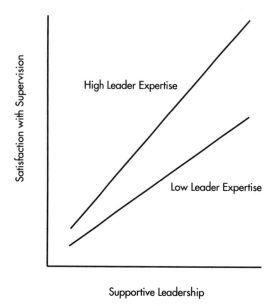

Figure 3 Leadership expertise as an enhancer of supportive leadership.

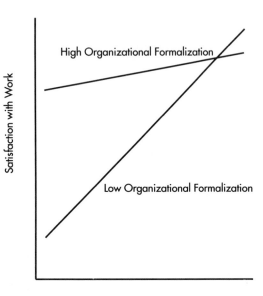

Figure 4 Organizational formalization as a substitute for participative leadership (COs supervising NCOs).

knowledgeable about the job, the stronger the impact of his/her supportiveness on the subordinate (see Figure 3 for a graphical representation of this enhancer). The path from charismatic leadership to satisfaction with supervision was *enhanced* by organizational formalization. That is, the greater the number of formalized plans and procedures facing the subordinate in his/her job, the stronger the impact of charismatic leadership on satisfaction with supervision.

In the causal model for NCOs (see Figure 2), the path from leaders' contingent reward to subordinates' role ambiguity was neither substitutable nor enhanced by the variables studied. Contingent reward appears to be another robust leader behavior. The impact of leader supportiveness on satisfaction with supervision was *enhanced* by subordinates' ability, experience, training, and knowledge. The most capable subordinates were more appreciative of a supportive leader than were less capable subordinates. The impact of di-

rective leadership on satisfaction with supervision was *substituted* for by organizational formalization. Subordinates derive guidance from formalized plans and procedures when available, and a directive leader has little impact in this situation.

The other two significant causal paths were highly substitutable. The impact of leader participativeness on satisfaction with work was *substitutable* by organizational formalization. A high degree of formalized plans and procedures prevented a participative leader from affecting the subordinate and made that leadership behavior unnecessary (see Figure 4 for a graphical representation of this substitute). And the impact of leader representativeness on satisfaction with work is *neutralized* by subordinates' years of service and subordinate rank. This leadership behavior is also substituted for by organizational formalization. The presence of a high degree of formalization, high subordinate rank, or years of service in the Army all decrease and may substitute for the impact of the leader's representative behavior.

Discussion

Leadership of commissioned officers in this study seemed to approximate the "command bureaucracy" described in the introduction, with high levels of directive and contingent punishment leadership behaviors being evident. Leadership of NCOs was more "facilitative"—creating conditions where experienced and capable individuals can implement plans and policies with the freedom they need. This freedom and facilitation was reflected in high levels of NCO organizational commitment, job satisfaction, and satisfaction with supervision. Low-level COs seemed especially facilitative in dealing with NCOs, perhaps recognizing the symbiotic relationship which must exist between a lieutenant or captain and his/her head NCO. We might also note that in contrast to Grundstad (1976), who found that satisfaction with supervision increases linearly with rank throughout the military system, the NCOs in our project were more satisfied and generally had more positive attitudes than the COs.

Many leader behaviors affected attitudes; several impacted performance. However, leader directiveness and contingent punishment behaviors had a greater affect on the attitudes of COs than on NCOs. The potential for contingent punishment (supervisors pointing out substandard work) is ever present in the military. The substitutes analysis showed that organizational formalization substituted for directive leadership with NCOs. It may be that other variables not included in this study neutralized or substituted for the leaders' contingent punishment behavior with NCOs. It may also be that the lower level COs expected to be treated in a controlling manner and reacted positively to this style. Yet, these command-type behaviors were not impactful of *performance* in either sample. Whereas COs (at both high and low levels) may still view a "good leader" as one who emphasizes command-type leader behaviors, the modern peacetime military may be outgrowing this as a predominant leadership style. Other facilitative leader behaviors seem to be more impactful on subordinate performance.

The LISREL model provided a good look at probable causal effects of key leader behaviors when they were all assessed simultaneously for impacts on attitudes and performance of subordinates. It is clear from these models that the emphasis on leadership training in the U.S. military is not misplaced. However, the effect of leadership on performance in this peacetime sample is indirect; it influences performance via improvements in subordinate attitudes and perceptions. Leadership causes improved attitudes and perceptions regarding work tasks and the organization which, in turn, result in improved subordinate performance.

For both the CO and NCO models, numerous leader behaviors were important. Both models included command and facilitative leader behaviors. All the leader behaviors studied appeared as important causal variables in at least one model. Supportive and participative leadership appeared in both models, perhaps indicating that these facilitative leadership behaviors are more generalizable across hierarchies in this military sample. Van Fleet and Yukl (1986) also found that supportive leadership was an important leader behavior in the military. It was, as might be expected, somewhat less important in combat situations than in noncombat situations. In contrast to our findings, participative leadership had no impact on leadership effectiveness in their research.

Enhancers and Substitutes

An important general pattern emerged when comparing the supervision of NCOs by high- and low-level COs. Low-level

COs showed more leadership behavior but had less impact than high-level COs (see Table 5). For example, supportive and participative behaviors by a high-level CO resulted in large increases in follower attitudes; not so when low-level COs were supportive and participative. Leader rank clearly enhances the impact of leadership in this sample.

Perceived leader expertise (for COs), and subordinates' ability, expertise, training, and knowledge (for NCOs) were *enhancers* of the impact of supportive leadership. The enhancing effect of a leader's rank and expertise was expected, but military leaders might be surprised to find that increasing a subordinate's capabilities will also make those subordinates *more* responsive to supportive leadership.

In this study, organizational formalization was the major *leadership substitute*, decreasing and replacing the impact of directive, participative, and representative leader behaviors on specific subordinate attitudes. All of these substitution effects occurred with COs supervising NCOs. This finding should not be surprising since Wojdakowski (1988) recently reported in the *Military Review* that formal *written* guidance provided by the staff plays an increasingly important role in specifying job requirements. For these NCOs, formal written guidelines improved attitudes and perceptions *and* relieved the leader of the need to provide several types of leadership, leaving him/her free to address other subordinates whose tasks are less formalized.

Subordinate rank was the strongest leadership *neutralizer*, decreasing the impact of supportive leadership (for COs) as well as representative leadership (for NCOs). Another important neutralizer of leader supportiveness was the subordinate's years of service in the military. It should be interesting to military leaders that two clearly identifiable subordinate characteristics (rank and years of service) have such strong neutralizing effects on supportive leadership.

The substitute/enhancer/neutralizer variables which were important in this study all have a common element: *All serve to empower the individual job holder — leader or subordinate.* Increased CO rank clearly adds power to the leader, but increased rank or years of service does the same for a subordinate. In the first case, rank enhances the leader's impact; in the second case, rank or years of service allow the subordinate to resist certain types of leader influence. Sources of empowerment at all levels (including rank, years of service, leader and subordinate expertise, and knowledge of organizational procedures) are clearly major sources of substitutes, enhancers, and neutralizers in the military.

In summary, leadership behaviors were quite impactful in this study, with some differences and some similarities between the two samples. When leadership substitutes or neutralizers were not present, leaders' supportive, charismatic, representative, and contingent reward behaviors were effective with both COs and NCOs. Controlling-type leadership behaviors (directive and contingent punishment) were more effective by high-level COs supervising low-level COs than with NCOs. Participative leadership with NCOs was more effective by high-level COs than by low-level COs.

Leadership enhancers are obviously factors which leaders would like to identify. Leadership enhancers often come from the leaders themselves (e.g., expertise), or they may derive from characteristics of the subordinate (e.g., high ability). A word of caution is in order, however, when interpreting the results regarding leadership neutralizers and substitutes: The presence of neutralizers and substitutes does *not* mean that all leadership is unimportant in these situations. It does mean, however, that certain leader behaviors are less impactful (neutralized) or unnecessary (substituted), allowing the leader to place his/her attention elsewhere to achieve maximum effectiveness.

References

Bass, B. M. (1985). Leadership: Good, better, best. *Organizational Dynamics, 13,* 26–40.

Bass, B. M. (1990). *Bass & Stogdill's handbook of leadership* (3rd ed.). New York: Free Press.

Clark, K. E., & Clark, M. B. (1990). *Measures of leadership.* West Orange, NJ: Leadership Library of America.

Clover, W. H. (1990). Transformational leaders: Team performance, leadership ratings, and firsthand impressions. In K. E. Clark & M. B. Clark (Eds.), *Measures of leadership* (pp. 171–184). West Orange, NJ: Leadership Library of America.

Grundstad, N. L. (1976). Overview, USAWC study of leadership for the 1970s. In The Associates, Office of Military Leadership, United States Military Academy, *A study of organizational leadership.* Harrisburg, PA: Stackpole Books.

Howell, J. P., & Dorfman, P. W. (1981). Substitutes for leadership: Test of a construct. *Academy of Management Journal, 24,* 714–728.

Howell, J. P., & Dorfman, P. W. (1986). Leadership and substitutes for leadership among professional and nonprofessional workers. *Journal of Applied Behavioral Science, 22,* 29–46.

Huntington, S. P. (1957). *The soldier and the state.* Cambridge, MA: Harvard University Press.

Indvik, J. (1986). Path-goal theory of leadership: A meta-analysis. *Proceedings of the Academy of Management Meetings,* 189–192.

Jacobs, T. O., & Jaques, E. (1990). Military executive leadership. In K. E. Clark & M. B. Clark (Eds.), *Measures of leadership* (pp. 281–295). West Orange, NJ: Leadership Library of America.

Jermier, J. M., & Berkes, L. J. (1979). Leader behavior in a police command bureaucracy: A closer look at the quasi-military model. *Administrative Science Quarterly, 24,* 1–23.

Jöreskog K. G., & Sörbom, D. (1984). *LISREL VI: Analysis of linear structural relationships by the method of maximum likelihood.* Chicago: National Educational Resources.

Kerr, S., & Jermier, J. (1978). Substitutes for leadership: Their meaning and measurement. *Organizational Behavior and Human Performance, 22,* 375–403.

Podsakoff, P. M., & Skov, R. (1980). *Leader reward and punishment behavior scales.* Unpublished research, Indiana University, Bloomington, IN.

Porter, L. W., & Smith, F. J. (1970). *The etiology of organizational commitment.* Unpublished manuscript, University of California—Irvine.

Rizzo, J. R., House, R. J., & Lirtzman, S. I. (1970). Role conflict and ambiguity in complex organizations. *Administrative Science Quarterly, 15,* 150–163.

Rogers, G. L. (1983). The leader as a teacher. *Military Review, 58,* 2–13.

Schriesheim, C. A. (1978). *Development, validation, and application of new leader behavior and expectancy research instruments.* Unpublished doctoral dissertation, Ohio State University, Columbus.

Van Fleet, D. D., & Yukl, G. A. (1986). *Military leadership: An organizational perspective.* Greenwich, CT: JAI Press.

Weiss, D. J., Dawis, R. V., England, G. W., & Lofquist, L. H. (1967). *Manual for the Minnesota Satisfaction Questionnaire* (Minnesota Studies on Vocational Rehabilitation Vol. 22). Minneapolis: University of Minnesota Industrial Relations Center.

Wojdakowski, P. W. (1988, November). A staff philosophy. *Military Review,* pp. 43–52.

Yukl, G. (1982). *Managerial Behavior Survey.* Copyrighted instrument received through personal communication.

Yukl, G. A. (1989). *Leadership in organizations* (2nd ed.). Englewood Cliffs, NJ: Prentice Hall.

Yukl, G. A., & Van Fleet, D. D. (1982). Cross-situational, multimethod research on military leader effectiveness. *Organizational Behavior and Human Performance, 30,* 87–108.

Peter W. Dorfman is Professor of Human Resources Management at New Mexico State University's College of Business Administration and Economics and formerly taught at Rice University and Montana State University. His research interests include the impact of cultural influences on managerial behavior and leadership styles, human resources management, and organizational behavior. He has published articles on leadership and performance appraisals. He received his PhD from the University of Maryland.

Jon P. Howell is Professor of Management and Organizational Behavior in the College of Business Administration and Economics at New Mexico State University and the President of two California corporations. His primary research interests are leadership, substitutes for leadership, and international management. He has published several book chapters and articles and is currently writing a book, tentatively titled *Leadership and Its Substitutes*. He received his PhD from the University of California at Irvine.

Benjamin C. G. Cotton, Captain, is an active duty Army Officer of 12 years. He is currently a full-time, Army-sponsored graduate student in Industrial Engineering at New Mexico State University. He has held a variety of troop leadership and management positions, including command of an Air Defense Vulcan gun platoon and a Patriot missile battery.

Uday Tate is Associate Professor of Marketing at Southeastern Louisiana University. He has published several articles and papers on consumer attitudes, health care marketing, and organizational behavior in cross-cultural and sales management settings. He received his PhD in Business Administration from the University of Tennessee-Knoxville.

Direct inquiries about this article to Peter W. Dorfman, Department of Management, Dept. 3DJ/Box 30001, New Mexico State University, Las Cruces, NM 88003–0001, 505/ 646–1294.

CHAPTER 34

Preliminary Report on Development and Validation of the Influence Behavior Questionnaire

Gary Yukl,
Rick Lepsinger,
and Toni Lucia

This report describes the development and validation of the Influence Behavior Questionnaire (IBQ). The IBQ is designed to measure a manager's use of nine tactics to influence subordinates, peers, and superiors. The influence tactics are based on previous research and theory, on our own research with diaries and critical incidents, and on the developmental research with the questionnaire. The psychometric evidence supports the reliability and validity of the IBQ scales. The research has been integrated closely with practical applications of the IBQ for management development.

Influence is the essence of managing. To be effective as a manager, you must influence people to support your proposals and plans, and you must motivate others to implement your decisions. The mere possession of power and authority is not enough to ensure that a manager will successfully exercise influence over other people (Yukl, 1989, 1990). Power is exercised through influence behavior, and different forms of influence behavior can be classified into behavior categories called "influence tactics."

Researchers in several disciplines have proposed taxonomies of influence tactics. The work by Kipnis, Schmidt, and Wilkinson (1980) is one example. They asked students to write descriptions of "how I get my way" with people at work, grouped these descriptions of influence behavior into categories based on similarity, then developed a questionnaire called the Profiles of Organizational Influence Strategies (POIS) with scales to measure several distinct categories. The current version of the POIS is based on the single factor analysis study by Kipnis et al. Unfortunately, the questionnaire has serious limitations, such as the inclusion of some marginally relevant tactics and exclusion of some important tactics (Schriesheim & Hinkin, 1990; Yukl & Falbe, 1990).

This paper describes research conducted over the past 4 years to develop and validate a new, more comprehensive measure of influence behavior called the Influence Behavior Questionnaire (IBQ). To date, several studies have been conducted with a variety of research methods to identify relevant influence tactics. The paper begins with a description of the development of the questionnaire, followed by a report of psychometric analyses and, finally, by a discussion of our attempts to achieve mutual facilitation between the validation research and practical applications.

Development of the IBQ

The IBQ was developed to measure influence behaviors that are relevant for managerial effectiveness. Although most aspects of managerial behavior have some implications for influencing people, we focused on proactive behaviors used primarily to influence compliance with a manager's requests and commitment to a manager's plans and proposals. Behaviors primarily intended to guide target behavior (e.g., giving instructions, explaining procedures), and behaviors that are reactive rather than proactive (e.g., rewarding effective performance, criticizing inappropriate behavior), were not included in the item pool. These types of behaviors are already measured by existing questionnaires, such as the Managerial Practices Survey (Yukl, Wall, & Lepsinger, 1990). We used several sources of ideas about relevant forms of influence behavior to include in the IBQ. We considered results of prior research on influence tactics and power, descriptions of successful influence episodes from the management literature, and descriptions of influence behavior in diaries and critical incidents collected in our own research. Four methods were used to identify relevant categories of influence behavior: (a) factor analysis and item analysis of questionnaires, (b) Q-sorts of influence behavior examples by subject matter experts, (c) revision of categories after experience with them in coding descriptions of influence attempts from diaries and critical incidents, and (d) examination of the outcomes of various tactics used by managers. These methods have resulted in the current taxonomy of nine influence tactics shown in Table 1.

Several of our influence tactics correspond to those used in earlier questionnaire studies by Mowday (1978) and Kipnis et al. (1980). Rational persuasion corresponds to "reason" in the POIS and to Mowday's "persuasive arguments." Exchange tactics are similar to "bargaining" in the POIS and to Mowday's "exchange of favors." Pressure tactics are similar to "assertiveness" in the POIS and to Mowday's "threats." Ingratiation is similar to "friendliness" in the POIS. Coalition tactics are similar to "coalition" in the POIS. Legitimating tactics are similar to Mowday's "appeals to legitimate authority." Aspects of these tactics also can be found in the influence behaviors reported in research with critical incidents (Keys & Case, 1990; Schilit & Locke, 1982).

Not all of our influence tactics correspond to those in earlier studies; our taxonomy goes further in some important respects. Prior questionnaire studies did not include consultation, inspirational appeals, and personal appeals as explicit tactics. Research on participative leadership has found that consultation with subordinates is effective in some contexts for increasing decision acceptance (Bass, 1990; Vroom & Jago, 1988). The importance of inspirational appeals is suggested by research on transformational leadership (Bass, 1985; Conger, 1989; Tichy & Devanna, 1986) and by some research on military leadership (Van Fleet & Yukl, 1986). Leaders who obtain commitment by subordinates to implement major strategies or innovations typically present a

TABLE 1 Definition of Influence Tactics

Rational Persuasion: The person uses logical arguments and factual evidence to persuade you that a proposal or request is viable and likely to result in the attainment of task objectives.

Inspirational Appeals: The person makes a request or proposal that arouses enthusiasm by appealing to your values, ideals, and aspirations, or by increasing your confidence that you can do it.

Consultation: The person seeks your participation in planning a strategy, activity, or change for which your support and assistance are desired, or is willing to modify a proposal to deal with your concerns and suggestions.

Ingratiation: The person seeks to get you in a good mood or to think favorably of him or her before asking you to do something.

Personal Appeals: The person appeals to your feelings of loyalty and friendship toward him or her when asking you to do something.

Exchange: The person offers an exchange of favors, indicates willingness to reciprocate at a later time, or promises you a share of the benefits if you help accomplish a task.

Coalition Tactics: The person seeks the aid of others to persuade you to do something, or uses the support of others as a reason for you to agree also.

Pressure: The person uses demands, threats, frequent checking, or persistent reminders to influence you to do what he/she wants.

Legitimating Tactics: The person seeks to establish the legitimacy of a request by claiming the authority or right to make it, or by verifying that it is consistent with organizational policies, rules, practices, or traditions.

---

clear and inspiring vision that appeals to the values, ideals, and emotions of subordinates. Personal appeals are based on referent power, which is the identification of subordinates with their leader. Referent power is one of the most important sources of leader influence (Hinkin &

Schriesheim, 1989; Podsakoff & Schriesheim, 1985; Yukl & Falbe, 1991).

Description of the IBQ

Unlike the POIS, which has only an agent version, the IBQ has both agent and target versions. However, our developmental research has emphasized the target version. Based on findings in research on leadership behavior questionnaires, we expected that target reports would be more accurate than agent reports for most forms of influence behavior. In addition, target reports are essential for providing feedback to managers about the way others view their influence behavior.

The current version of the IBQ (now in its third revision) has scales measuring the nine influence tactics described earlier in Table 1. Each scale has five to seven items. The target version has the following response choices:

1. I cannot remember him/her ever using this tactic with me.

2. He/she very seldom uses this tactic with me.

3. He/she occasionally uses this tactic with me.

4. He/she uses this tactic moderately often with me.

5. He/she uses this tactic very often with me.

Following is a sample item from each scale in the target version:

1. Uses facts and logic to make a persuasive case for a proposed plan of action that he/she wants you to support or implement (rational persuasion).

2. Describes a proposed task or project with enthusiasm and conviction that it is important and worthwhile (inspirational appeal).

3. Tells you what he/she is trying to accomplish and asks if you know a good way to do it for him/her (consultation).

4. Says that his/her request is consistent with organization rules and policies (legitimating tactic).

5. Compliments you on past accomplishments before asking you to do another task (ingratiation).

6. Explains that he/she is in a difficult situation and would really appreciate your help (personal appeal).

7. Indicates that he/she will do a favor for you in return for doing what he/she wants (exchange).

8. Confronts you and demands that you carry out a requested action promptly (pressure).

9. Asks other people to provide evidence to you supporting a plan or proposal that he/she wants you to help implement (coalition).

The agent version has parallel items and similar response choices with slightly different wording to make them suitable for describing one's own influence behavior rather than the behavior of another person. The agent version can be used to describe influence behavior toward an individual target person (e.g., one's boss, a particular subordinate or peer) or behavior toward a defined category of target persons (e.g., subordinates). The agent version makes it possible for managers to compare their self-perception of influence behavior with feedback about the way others perceive their influence behavior.

Psychometric Analyses of the IBQ

As noted earlier, development and validation of the IBQ has been focused on the target version. Factor analyses and assessment of scale reliability and validity have been done with the target version rather than the agent version. Several types of psychometric analyses have been conducted for the target version of the IBQ scales, including factor analysis, content validity, internal consistency, retest stability, and criterion-related validity.

Factor Analysis

Factor analyses of agent-reported influence behavior in the POIS (Kipnis et al., 1980; Schriesheim & Hinkin, 1990) have found fairly consistent evidence for six influence tactics, including rational persuasion, exchange, pressure, coalition, ingratiation, and upward appeals. When we began our research on target reports of influence behavior, we did not know whether the factor patterns would be similar to those found earlier for agent self-reports, because some tactics may be perceived differently by targets than by agents.

Two target versions of the IBQ have been factor analyzed, with several hundred respondents used in each study. The factor analyses yielded orthogonal factors for nine factors. Six of the factors correspond to the ones found in the research by Schriesheim and Hinkin (1990) on the agent-report POIS, namely rational persuasion, exchange, pressure, ingratiation, coalition, and upward appeals. Our factor analyses also yielded orthogonal factors for three influence tactics not included in the POIS, namely consultation, inspirational appeals, and legitimating tactics. As in research on the POIS, the factor structure in our research varied somewhat for different types of respondents and for influence attempts in different directions. Development of the IBQ scales continues in order to refine the scales, strengthen weak factors, and improve their stability from sample to sample.

Factor analysis can be used to provide evidence of discriminant validity for different types of constructs. The second factor analysis study included data from a power inventory described in Yukl and Falbe (1991), in addition to the IBQ data. The analysis yielded separate factors for power sources and influence tactics, providing additional evidence that the IBQ scales measure influence behavior rather than perception of agent power.

Each time the IBQ was revised, factor analysis was used to aid in selecting items. However, our approach differed somewhat from the more traditional psychometric approach represented by the efforts of Schriesheim and Hinkin (1990) to refine the POIS. By eliminating all items except those with very high factor loadings, Schriesheim and Hinkin limited the scope of each tactic category to a narrow range of influence behaviors. Their procedure also eliminated behaviors that involved two or more tactics at the same time. In contrast, we attempted to develop tactic categories with a broader range of influence behaviors. Multidimensional items were retained if they seemed to be especially relevant and appeared frequently in our critical incidents research. An example is the item "says you are the most qualified person for a task he/she wants you to do," which loads on both ingratiation and inspirational appeals. Another example is the item "explains how his/her proposal or plan would benefit you," which loads on both rational persuasion and exchange. Our strategy increased the overlap among tactics a little, but we believe it also improved the content validity and relevance of the scales.

Even though the factor structure for influence behavior has been found to vary somewhat depending on the direction of influence (Erez, Rim, & Keider, 1986; Kipnis et al., 1980), we sought to develop a single measure of influence tactics for use with subordinates, peers, or superiors. We did not want to have different versions for different directions of influence. However, identification of generic behavior examples was difficult, because the most relevant examples of influence behavior in a particular direction are not always appropriate for another direction. The content of the current scales reflects a compromise between the two competing objectives. Some of the items in our scales are equally applicable in all three directions, whereas other items are more relevant in one direction or another. The strategy of developing widely applicable scales made it unlikely that our factor results would be as clear as those found by Schriesheim and Hinkin (1990), who focused only on tactics used in upward influence.

Content Validity

One test of content validity is to have judges assess the extent to which the items in a scale are relevant and representative examples of the influence tactic measured by the scale. Two studies of judgmental classification will be described. The first study had 41 judges who were graduate students in business. Items from the IBQ were presented in random order, and judges familiar with the definitions of the influence tactics coded each item into the most relevant tactic category. If an item did not appear to fit any of the categories, it was coded as "miscellaneous." The second study, which used 27 undergraduates as judges, allowed the judges to indicate a secondary category if an item represented dual categories. The results from both studies (see Table 2) indicate clearly that most items in the IBQ are perceived by most judges as relevant defining examples for the nine tactics.

Most items coded into the miscellaneous category involved aspects of influence behavior that are clearly different from the nine primary tactics, such as distortion of information, appeals to expertise, and some forms of upward appeal. Although the nine primary tactics do not include all possible forms of influence behavior, we believe that behaviors not represented in the IBQ are of only marginal relevance for a target questionnaire designed for managers. Information distortion is measured

TABLE 2 Mean Coding Accuracy for Items in IBQ Scales

Influence Tactic	Study 1		Study 2	
	Accuracy	Items	Accuracy	Items
Inspirational Appeals	.99	5	.91	6
Consultation	.95	5	.97	6
Rational Persuasion	.85	5	.84	6
Ingratiation Tactics	.88	4	.84	6
Exchange Tactics	.96	5	.98	7
Personal Appeal	.88	4	.90	6
Coalition Tactics	.84	5	.92	7
Legitimating Tactics	.88	5	.89	5
Pressure Tactics	.91	5	.96	7

Note. Accuracy score is the mean across items in a scale on the percentage of judges who coded an item correctly.

more appropriately from the perspective of the agent than the target and is a tactic that usually involves unethical behavior. Appeals to expertise ("trust me, I know") and upward appeals to the target's boss have a low frequency of use, and they are usually ineffective for increasing target task commitment or even compliance.

Internal Consistency

Internal consistency is the degree of intercorrelation among items in a scale. High internal consistency is evidence that a scale is measuring a category of interrelated behaviors, although it is not necessary for all of the defining examples in a category of behavior to be highly intercorrelated or to be used with equal frequency. Yukl and Falbe (1990) reported moderate internal consistency for the scales in the initial agent and target versions of the IBQ used in that study. Since then, the questionnaire has been revised three times; data on internal consistency for the target version of the IBQ is available from three studies.

The sample in the first study included 709 respondents who used the IBQ to describe the influence behavior of a subordinate, peer, or boss. The sample in the sec-

ond study (from research by Leanne Atwater) included 208 subordinates of managers from a variety of companies; each respondent used the IBQ to describe the influence behavior of his or her boss. The sample in the third study included 45 MBA night students, with regular jobs during the day, who also used the IBQ to describe the influence behavior of their immediate superior. Results for internal consistency of IBQ scales in the three studies are shown in Table 3. In most cases, internal consistency has improved with each revision of the questionnaire and is now high or moderately high for all of the IBQ scales.

Retest Stability

Evidence for reliable measurement also is provided by demonstrating stable scale scores over a time interval in which the influence behavior of the agent should remain unchanged. Retest stability was assessed in the same sample of 45 MBA night students described earlier. Each student was asked to fill out the 1990 target-subordinate version of the IBQ on two occasions separated by an interval of 5 weeks. A second sample of 29 MBA night students with regular daytime jobs filled

TABLE 3 Reliability of IBQ Scales

Influence Tactic	Internal Consistency			Retest Stability	
	Study 1	Study 2	Study 3	Study 1	Study 2
Inspirational Appeals	.84	.86	.77	.76	.85
Consultation	.85	.88	.90	.87	.68
Rational Persuasion	.79	.82	.84	.84	.72
Ingratiation Tactics	.63	.84	.84	.76	.67
Exchange Tactics	.74	.78	.85	.79	.69
Personal Appeal	.56	.75	.88	.75	.79
Coalition Tactics	.76	.68	.76	.77	.75
Legitimating Tactics	.77	.78	.86	.59	.64
Pressure Tactics	.89	.89	.83	.60	.78
Sample Size	709	206	45	45	29

Note. All results are for the target version of the IBQ.

out the 1991 target-subordinate version of the IBQ twice over a 4-week interval. Table 3 shows the correlation between corresponding scale scores for each respondent for the two studies. Retest stability was adequate for all scales.

Criterion-Related Validity

The most important indicator of utility for a measure of influence behavior is its capacity to predict outcomes of influence attempts and explain managerial effectiveness. Two studies have examined the correlation between IBQ scales and various criteria of leadership effectiveness.

The first study was conducted with 506 subordinates and 496 peers of 118 managers from three large companies: a pharmaceuticals company, a chemicals and manufacturing company, and a financial services company. Managers who participated in a management development workshop conducted by a consulting company were asked to distribute questionnaires to a representative set of subordinates and peers who had known the manager at least 6 months. Each respon-

dent returned the questionnaire directly to the consulting company in a self-addressed, stamped envelope provided for that purpose. The questionnaires included the IBQ and two criterion measures: a single-item rating of target task commitment (on a 6-point scale) and a single-item rating of the quality of relations between the manager and the respondent (on a 4-point scale). Respondents were anonymous and were assured that the managers would see only the composite results on the influence tactics. The ratings of task commitment and quality of relations were for research purposes only, and managers did not receive any feedback on these measures.

The second study (Yukl & Tracey, in press) was conducted with respondents from five large companies: a pharmaceuticals company, a chemicals and manufacturing company, a financial services company, and two insurance companies. The procedure was the same as in Study 1, except that quality of relations was not included as a criterion measure in the questionnaire. Instead, the boss of each manager rated the manager's overall effectiveness on a 9-point scale. A manager was included in the final data set only if questionnaires were received from the manager's boss and at least three peers and three subordinates. The final sample included 526 subordinates and 543 peers of 128 managers. The number of respondents describing each manager ranged from 6 to 10, with a median of 8.

As in Study 1, analyses of the relation between each influence tactic and target task commitment were conducted at the individual level because data on the predictors and the criterion were from the same respondents. However, the ratings of managerial effectiveness were obtained from a different source than the ratings of influence behavior, and a group level of analysis was used for correlations involving this independent criterion. For downward influence, the group mean score on each influence tactic from a manager's subordinates was correlated with the effectiveness rating made by a manager's boss. For lateral influence, the group mean score on each influence tactic for a manager's peers was correlated with the effectiveness rating made by a manager's boss.

The correlations between IBQ scales and the criterion measures for both studies are shown in Table 4. Results for task commitment were stronger in Study 2 than in Study 1, probably due to improvements in some of the IBQ scales between the two studies. As expected, a manager's use of rational persuasion, consultation, and inspirational appeals correlated in a positive direction with target task commitment, indicating that these three tactics were generally the most effective for influencing subordinates and peers. In addition, the same three tactics correlated positively with quality of agent-target relations and boss ratings of managerial effectiveness. Pressure, coalition, and legitimating tactics usually had a negative or nonsignificant correlation with the criteria, indicating that these three tactics are usually ineffective. Results for ingratiation, exchange, and personal appeals

were sometimes positive and sometimes nonsignificant, indicating that these tactics are intermediate in effectiveness. Overall, the results indicated strong criterion-related validity for the nine scales in the target version of the IBQ.

Applications for Management Development

The process of mutual facilitation between research and application for the IBQ can be described as an extension of more traditional validation processes. Practicing managers have been involved in the development of the IBQ from the beginning of the research program. The initial item pool was reviewed by a panel of managers who evaluated their relevance and suggested important behaviors that were missing. Another group of managers kept diaries for several weeks, describing their influence behavior toward subordinates, peers, and superiors. These diaries served as another check on the relevance and comprehensiveness of the IBQ items and scales.

The early research on the IBQ was conducted with random samples of individual respondents who answered either the agent or the target version of the questionnaire. After the early research was completed, we began using the IBQ in management development workshops to help middle managers and executives gain a better understanding of their influence behavior. The management development activities conducted in several companies have contributed to the improvement of the questionnaire.

In the workshops, the IBQ provides a source of feedback to managers about the way their influence behavior is perceived by subordinates, peers, and their boss. Feedback is presented at the item level as well as at the scale level to make it more useful to the managers. Discussion of the

TABLE 4   Criterion Related Validity of IBQ Scales in Two Studies

Influence Tactic	Study 1 Commitment		Study 1 Quality Relat.		Study 2 Commitment		Study 2 Effectiveness	
	Subs.	Peers	Subs.	Peers	Subs.	Peers	Subs.	Peers
Persuasion	.34*	.20*	.20*	.15*	.38*	.43*	.39*	.33*
Inspiration	.37*	.33*	.27*	.17*	.51*	.52*	.20*	.19*
Consultation	.22*	.24*	.23*	.23*	.42*	.47*	.26*	.24*
Ingratiation	.18*	.19*	− .03	− .05	.34*	.31*	− .01	.08
Exchange	.07	.14*	− .04	− .02	.26*	.24*	.10	.07
Personal	.13*	.17*	− .04	− .06	.15*	.19*	.03	.01
Coalition	.00	.02	− .19*	− .24*	.00	− .09	.04	.03
Legitimating	.12*	− .01	− .16*	− .21*	− .05	− .17*	− .08	− .01
Pressure	.03	.01	− .39*	− .31*	− .23*	− .12*	− .20*	− .08
Sample Size	506	495	506	495	526	543	128	128

* p < .01 for large samples and .05 for small samples.

feedback with managers revealed problems with some of the items in an earlier version of the questionnaire. For example, many of the pressure items described coercive forms of pressure, many of the ingratiation items appeared manipulative and insincere, and many of the exchange items seemed like bribes. Managers usually responded very negatively to these items. Agents said they rarely used them and targets reported that they were rarely used. As a result, we identified more subtle and effective examples of these tactics to replace the original items. The workshop discussions also confirmed that upward appeals is an influence tactic avoided by most managers in business organizations because it is seldom effective. Thus, we had additional justification for deleting this tactic as an IBQ scale, although a few items on upward appeals were retained for research purposes in the current version.

Since 1990, the management development workshops have also included feedback about the way a manager's power is perceived by peers and subordinates. Dis-cussion of the relationship of power and influence in a manager's daily activities has provided insights into the way power is exercised effectively. We are now developing and testing a model to predict the choice of influence tactics and their outcomes in different situations.

Summary

The research to date on the IBQ has been very promising. The initial psychometric results suggest that the scales are reliable and valid, although more research is clearly needed before any firm conclusions can be reached. Parallel research with critical incidents (Falbe & Yukl, in press) provides multimethod convergence with the results from the questionnaire study; together the two types of research demonstrate the relevance of the tactics measured by the IBQ. Finally, managers in the feedback workshops report that feedback based on the IBQ scales is very relevant and helpful. We will continue to refine and improve the scales, and we hope to extend the research to include other types of validity studies.

References

Bass, B. M. (1985). *Leadership and performance beyond expectations.* New York: Free Press.

Bass, B. M. (1990). *Handbook of leadership: A survey of theory and research.* New York: Free Press.

Conger, J. A. (1989). *The charismatic leader: Behind the mystique of exceptional leadership.* San Francisco: Jossey-Bass.

Erez, M., Rim, Y., & Keider, I. (1986). The two sides of the tactics of influence: Agent vs. target. *Journal of Occupational Psychology, 59,* 25–39.

Falbe, C. M., & Yukl, G. (in press). Consequences for managers of using single influence tactics and combinations of tactics. *Academy of Management Journal.*

Hinkin, T. R., & Schriesheim, C. A. (1989). Development and application of new scales to measure the French and Raven bases of social power. *Journal of Applied Psychology, 74,* 561–567.

Keys, J. B., & Case, T. L. (1990). How to become an influential manager. *The Executive, 4,* 38–51.

Kipnis, D., Schmidt, S. M., & Wilkinson, I. (1980). Intra-organizational influence tactics: Explorations in getting one's way. *Journal of Applied Psychology, 65,* 440–452.

Mowday, R. T. (1978). The exercise of upward influence in organizations. *Administrative Science Quarterly, 23,* 137–156.

Podsakoff, P., & Schriesheim, C. (1985). Field studies of French and Raven's bases of power: Critique, reanalysis, and suggestions for future research. *Psychological Bulletin, 97,* 387–411.

Schilit, W. K., & Locke, E. (1982). A study of upward influence in organizations. *Administrative Science Quarterly, 27,* 304–316.

Schriesheim, C. A., & Hinkin, T. R. (1990). Influence tactics used by subordinates: A theoretical and empirical analysis and refinement of the Kipnis, Schmidt, and Wilkinson subscales. *Journal of Applied Psychology, 75,* 246–257.

Tichy, N. M., & Devanna, M. A. (1986). *The transformational leader.* New York: Wiley.

Van Fleet, D., & Yukl, G. (1986). *Military leadership: An organizational behavior perspective.* Greenwich, CT: JAI Press.

Vroom, V. H., & Jago, A. G. (1988). *The new leadership: Managing participation in organizations.* Englewood Cliffs, NJ: Prentice-Hall.

Yukl, G. (1989). *Leadership in organizations.* Englewood Cliffs, NJ: Prentice-Hall.

Yukl, G. (1990). *Skills for managers and leaders: Text, cases, and exercises.* Englewood Cliffs, NJ: Prentice-Hall.

Yukl, G., & Falbe, C. M. (1990). Influence tactics in upward, downward, and lateral influence attempts. *Journal of Applied Psychology, 75,* 132–140.

Yukl, G., & Falbe, C. M. (1991). The importance of different power sources in downward and lateral relations. *Journal of Applied Psychology, 76,* 416–423.

Yukl, G., & Tracey, B. (in press). Consequences of influence tactics used with subordinates, peers, and the boss. *Journal of Applied Psychology.*

Yukl, G., Wall, S., & Lepsinger, R. (1990). Preliminary report on validation of the Managerial Practices Survey. In K. E. Clark & M. B. Clark (Eds.), *Measures of leadership* (pp. 223–237). West Orange, NJ: Leadership Library of America.

Gary Yukl is Professor of Management at the State University of New York in Albany. He has written numerous articles and papers on leadership and is the author of *Leadership in Organizations* (Prentice-Hall, 1989) and *Skills for Managers and Leaders* (Prentice-Hall, 1990). He received his PhD in Industrial-Organizational Psychology from the University of California at Berkeley.

Rick Lepsinger is Managing Partner with Manus Associates, a Connecticut-based consulting firm that specializes in strategic management and leadership development. He has extensive experience in developing and using feedback-based technology to help managers identify their strengths and weaknesses. He has a Master's Degree in Planning, with an emphasis on strategic and economic planning, from the University of Southern California.

Toni Lucia is Managing Partner of Manus Associates. Her consulting work has included linking human resource plans to strategic plans and using feedback instruments to help managers become more effective. She is co-author of several chapters in *The Practice of Management Development* (Praeger Press, 1988) and earned degrees from Hood College and the University of Florida.

Direct inquiries about this article to Gary Yukl, Professor, Management Department, School of Business, State University of New York, 1400 Washington Avenue, Albany, NY 12222, 518/442–4932.

Breadth, Focus, and Content in Leader Priority-Setting

Effects on Decision Quality and Perceived Leader Performance

**Ariel S. Levi and
Larry E. Mainstone**

Leaders provide purpose and direction to their organizations largely through priority-setting. Numerous management scholars have therefore proposed a connection between leader priority-setting and organizational effectiveness. In this paper, we differentiate two aspects of priority-setting, breadth and focus, and investigate their effects on decision quality and perceived leader performance in a complex and realistic management simulation.

In his recent book, *Managing as a Performing Art*, Peter Vaill (1990) used the metaphor of "permanent white water" to represent the uncertainty and chaos inherent in today's managerial environment. In this environment, an endless stream of problems forces leaders to set priorities by allocating attention and resources among competing demands. Selecting the right "portfolio" of issues is thus an inescapable necessity of organizational leadership.

In addition to being a necessity, however, priority-setting serves a crucial leadership function of providing purpose and direction to organizational members. This is a theme that appears repeatedly in the management literature, extending back to Barnard (1939) and Selznick (1957). More recently, Bennis and Nanus (1985) found that a major characteristic of successful executives is their ability to communicate a clear mission, or set of priorities, to organizational members. Similarly, Peters and Waterman (1982) characterized effective organizations as having "simultaneous loose-tight controls," permitting leaders to push for close monitoring and high achievement on priority issues while allowing loose control on others. Finally, Vaill's (1982) model of leadership in high-performing systems emphasized the "purposing" of leaders' priorities which unite the organization in a common direction and reduce the "centrifugal forces" that occur when individuals pursue personal, at the expense of organizational, goals.

Purposing—and the related concepts of direction and mission—entails a narrowing of attention that can promote unity and goal attainment. However, a narrowing of attention does not necessarily have a uniformly positive effect on organizational outcomes. Sometimes its effects can be detrimental, as when attention is directed toward an inappropriate or too narrow set of goals. For example, some university athletic programs have placed such a high priority on winning and generating revenue that they have neglected the academic progress of their athletes and inadvertently encouraged illegal recruiting practices. The sanctions subsequently imposed by the National Collegiate Athletic Association have harmed these programs' reputations and reduced their chances of athletic success.

The double-edged nature of narrowing of attention suggests that its main source—leader priority-setting—be investigated. In this paper, we refine the notion of leader priority-setting and relate it to organizational outcomes. Specifically, we (a) offer a conceptualization of leader priority-setting in terms of allocation of attention and (b) test predictions concerning the effect of attention allocation on organizational decision quality and perceived leader performance.

Patterns of Leader Priorities

In our conceptualization, priority setting is characterized by two dimensions: *breadth* and *focus*. Breadth refers to the number of issues in the leader's "portfo-lio," the number of issues the leader deems worthy of attention. Focus refers to the extent to which the leader accords different levels of importance to the various issues in his or her portfolio. Leaders who accord much more importance to some issues than to others are higher in focus than are leaders who accord more similar levels of importance to all issues. In general, the importance a leader accords an issue is reflected in the amount of attention he or she allocates to that issue (Vaill, 1982; cf. Peters, 1982).

Figure 1 illustrates four possible combinations of breadth and focus. The horizontal axis represents the number of issues; the vertical axis, the *percent of total attention* allocated to each issue by the leader. To simplify presentation, the issues (represented by letters) are shown in descending order of attention allocated. In graphs (a) and (b), the leader is concerned with only 7 issues, representing low breadth; in graphs (c) and (d), with 14 issues, representing high breadth. Graphs (a) and (c) represent cases of high focus, in which a few issues receive a great deal more attention than others; graphs (b) and (d) represent low focus, in which all issues receive similar amounts of attention.

Breadth and focus serve different signalling functions. Breadth reflects the leader's receptivity to information concerning a wide number or variety of issues. A high-breadth priority pattern will typically indicate to subordinates that scanning for and communicating information about a wide range of issues will be valued. In contrast, a low-breadth pattern will typically indicate to subordinates that they should ignore information concerning all but a few issues. Other things being equal, receptivity to a wide range of information and free flow of information through an organization should promote decision quality (Janis & Mann, 1977). Thus, leaders with high-breadth priority patterns should have higher decision quality within their units than should leaders with low-breadth priority patterns.

In addition, a high-breadth pattern will

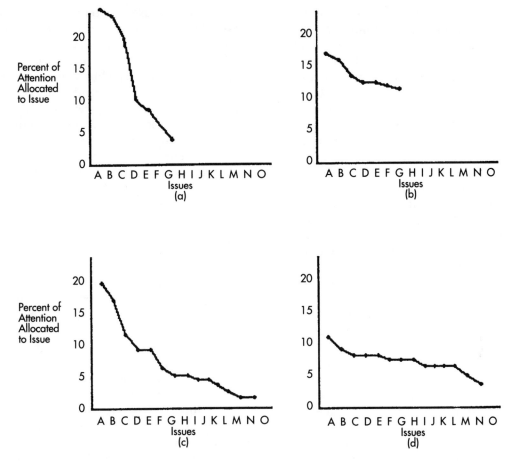

Figure 1 Patterns of priorities: (a) low breadth, high focus; (b) low breadth, low focus; (c) high breadth, high focus; (d) high breadth, low focus.

usually be associated with the leader's use of a large network of contacts at different levels in the organization: The more issues one is dealing with, the more sources of information and opinion one needs (Kotter, 1982). Such conditions promote greater receptivity to subordinates' communications. Leader activity and receptivity to upward communication have been shown to be associated with perceptions of leader effectiveness (e.g., Hollander, 1978). Thus, leaders with high-breadth priority patterns should be perceived as higher performers than should leaders with lower breadth patterns.

Let us now consider the second dimension of priority-setting, focus. A high-focus priority pattern indicates to subor-

dinates the direction in which they should be placing their efforts. High focus reduces ambiguity and provides a manageable number of goals to work toward. This should promote goal clarity and unity of effort among subordinates (cf. House & Mitchell, 1974) which, in turn, should improve decision quality (e.g., Huber, 1980).

However, too narrow a focus can lead to organizational "tunnel vision": obliviousness to other potentially important issues and goals, receptivity to only a narrow range of information, and the discouragement of lateral and upward communication about "nonfocal" issues. By including a wider range of issues in their priority set while maintaining focus on a subset of these issues, leaders can avoid the tunnel vision symptoms. Thus, from the standpoint of decision quality, we predict an interaction between breadth and focus: a high-breadth, high-focus priority pattern (Figure 1c) should be more effective than other patterns. Such a pattern encourages subordinates to remain open to new information and issues, yet still signals which issues warrant the most attention.

We expect breadth and focus to interact in the same manner for perceptions of leader performance. As previously discussed, leaders with high-breadth patterns, which encourage open communication, should be perceived as more effective than leaders with low-breadth patterns. In itself, however, a high-breadth pattern may not sufficiently fulfill a major aspect of the leadership role: providing direction and purpose for subordinates. A high-focus pattern does fulfill this aspect. Thus, leaders with high-breadth, high-focus patterns should be perceived as higher performers than leaders with other patterns.

To summarize our predictions, we expect breadth to have a main effect on both decision quality and perceived leader performance. We also expect breadth and focus to interact: Focus should have positive effects on decision quality and perceived leader performance, but only when breadth is high.

Content of Leader Priorities

Breadth and focus are abstract concepts that ignore content. However, the content of priorities — what they are about — matters. Some issues are more appropriate for inclusion in leaders' sets of priorities. Leaders are expected, for example, to focus on strategic and long-term issues and delegate more mundane issues to subordinates.

One widely used scheme classifies issues along a continuum of *crises*, *problems*, and *opportunities* (Mintzberg, Raisinghani, & Theoret, 1976). Crisis decisions, which are evoked by strong and urgent threats, and opportunity decisions, which are initiated to improve an existing situation, tend to be longer term and more strategic than problem decisions, which are evoked by relatively mild pressures. In addition, crisis and opportunity decisions tend to be more uncertain and less "programmable" than problem decisions (cf. Nutt, 1984). Leaders' strategic position and awareness of the "big picture" should therefore produce a greater payoff for attending to crises and opportunities than to problems. Thus, to the extent that leaders allocate more attention to crises and opportunities than to problems, decision quality should be higher.

Subordinate perceptions of leader performance should also be affected by the content of leaders' priorities. To the extent that leaders' priorities address crucial organizational needs, the leaders should be perceived as more effective. Therefore, leaders who allocate proportionately more attention to crises and opportunities, as compared to problems, should be perceived as more effective.

This generalization rests on three assumptions: (a) Crises and opportunities involve more crucial issues than do problems, (b) subordinates are aware of their leaders' priorities, and (c) subordinates have a reasonably accurate perception of the actual importance to the organization of different issues. Events that evoke crisis decisions are likely to be more dramatic, obvious, and threatening than events that evoke opportunity decisions; therefore, subordinates may underestimate the importance of opportunity decisions. This may occur even when crisis and opportunity decisions are of equal urgency and strategic importance. As a result, under many circumstances subordinates may not perceive accurately the importance of the issue to the organization. In this case, leaders who attend more to crises will be perceived as more effective than leaders who attend more to opportunities (assuming, of course, that the crises themselves are not attributed to the leader).

Setting and Participants

The Looking Glass, Inc., Simulation

Our research setting was a complex, realistic management simulation, the University Edition of Looking Glass, Inc. (LGI) (Lombardo, McCall, & DeVries, 1983). LGI, developed by the Center for Creative Leadership, is an example of a large-scale behavioral simulation in which participants assume the roles of managers in a realistic organizational structure. Recently, several researchers have demonstrated the feasibility of using large-scale behavioral simulations, including LGI, to investigate leadership and decision making (Dutton & Webster, 1988; Mullen & Stumpf, 1987).

LGI is designed to recreate a day in the lives of the top 20 managers of a medium-sized glass manufacturing company. During the day-long simulation run, participants must sort through a heavy load of information, identify threats and opportunities, set priorities, and make decisions. LGI contains over 30 decision issues, ranging from the relatively trivial (e.g., deciding on company press releases) to the crucial (e.g., how to deal with a severe plant overcapacity problem).

LGI has four levels in its management hierarchy: President, Vice President, Director, and Plant Manager. The company has three divisions, Advanced Products Division (APD), Industrial Glass Division (IGD), and Commercial Glass Division (CGD), each of which manufactures and markets its own product lines. The three divisions differ in the amount of environmental uncertainty they face, with APD facing the most and CGD the least.

About 10 days before the run, each participant received an in-basket folder—specific to his or her LGI role—containing extensive information about LGI, its products, market conditions, personnel, financial status, and so on. Participants prepared themselves by examining the contents of their folders. During each run, participants remained in role about 6 hours.

The simulation site was a large behavioral laboratory with four small rooms surrounding a central room. Each room was equipped with a video camera which remained on during the entire run. These cameras, in addition to a mobile camera, were used to videotape all group decision-making meetings during the LGI run.

Participants and Role Assignments

Participants were 165 graduate and undergraduate business students who volunteered to take part in LGI. One hundred and nine (66%) of the participants were male, and 120 (73%) had previous managerial experience. Participants' ages ranged from 21 to 64, with a mean of 30 and a median of 29 years. Nine runs of LGI were conducted. One of these runs included 13 participants; the others included between 16 and 20.

Participants with the most managerial experience were assigned to the top two levels; assignment to the other positions was random, with the constraint that the proportion of males and females remain constant across divisions.

In the present study, our sample of primary interest consisted of all participants in the Presidential and Vice Presidential positions in LGI. These positions constitute the key leadership roles in LGI. Each Vice President heads one of the three LGI divisions and reports to the President. Our sample (N = 35) consisted of 27 males and 8 females, with a mean of 36 and a median age of 34 years. Thirty-four (97%) had at least 1 year of managerial experience; 31 (89%) had 3 or more years of managerial experience.

Data Collection

Two methods of data collection were used. The first method was videotaping. Videotaped meetings were transcribed and entered into a database. Each row in the database contained a single statement by a participant and included information pertaining to that statement: who made it; the issue to which it pertained; and, based on the LGI Administrator's Guide (Lombardo et al., 1983) and our familiarity with LGI, whether that issue was a crisis, problem, or opportunity. Each run's transcripts were stored in a separate database file. The average number of statements per file was 2,284.

Questionnaires served as the second method of data collection. Participants received postsimulation questionnaires containing items on their perception and handling of LGI decision issues. In addition, each participant rated from four to six other participants on 11 performance dimensions commonly used in assessment centers (energy, problem analysis, initiative, planning and organizing, decisiveness, sensitivity to people, leadership, impact, oral communication and presentation, management control, and creativity; Thornton & Byham, 1982).

Videotape transcription and coding was conducted for four runs (N = 73). Questionnaire and observational data were collected for all runs (N = 165).

Variables and Measures

The following three variables pertain to the breadth, focus, and content of priorities:

1. *Breadth of attention* was defined by the *number* of issues dealt with by the participant. This number was obtained by querying the database or by counting the number of issues (of the 24 listed on the questionnaire) in which the participant had claimed involvement.

2. *Focus of attention* was defined by how unevenly the participant's attention was distributed across the issues in which he or she was involved. For each participant, the percent of total statements made regarding each of the issues he or she handled was obtained from the database. For example, suppose that a participant dealt with 10 issues and made a total of 150 statements. If the participant devoted 30 statements to issue A and 15 to issue B, then the percentages for these two issues would be 20 and 10, respectively. Once the percentages were obtained, the Ray and Singer (1973) index of concentration was calculated for each participant (Taagepera & Ray, 1977). This index, which ranges from 0 to 1, indicates the variance in the percent of attention allocated across different issues. The closer the index is to 0, the lower the variance and the more the issues in the set received the same amount of attention from the individual. An index near 1 indicates that the individual allocated very different amounts of attention to the different issues.

3. *Content of priority* was defined as the participant's relative distribution of attention across crises, problems, and opportunities. Of the 24 issues, 4 were classified as crises, 15 as problems, and 5 as opportunities. As examples, one of the crises was what to do about an increasingly unprofitable integrated circuits plant; one of the problems was how to deal with an increased number of defects in auto glass products; one of the opportunities was whether to purchase a bottling plant to expand LGI into a new market area. For each participant, the percent of statements pertaining to each of the three categories

(crises, problems, opportunities) was obtained from the database.

The following two variables pertain to the potential impact of leadership in LGI:

1. *Decision quality* was measured by means of the scoring guide in the *Supplement to the Administrator's Guide* (Center for Creative Leadership, 1983). This guide scores each division on its handling of key issues. Points are awarded for good decisions and subtracted for poor decisions. Good decisions are defined as those that are appropriate to the needs of the division, that make full use of the available and relevant information, and that are likely to be financially successful. Scoring can range from 0 to 100 for each division. The overall decision quality for each LGI run was measured by averaging the scores of the three divisions within that run. Participants received feedback on their decision quality at the very end of the run.

2. *Perceived leader performance* was measured by averaging ratings. On average, each participant was rated by approximately five other participants. The ratings received by each participant were averaged, first across raters and then across the 11 dimensions (Cronbach's alpha for the scale combining all dimensions was .88; for overall interrater reliability, .55). The resulting overall average score was used as the measure of perceived performance.

Results

Table 1 presents the descriptive statistics and correlations among the variables based on data from the top two levels of the LGI hierarchy, President and Vice President. Included in the table is the variable LGI division (1 = APD, 2 = IGD, 3 = CGD), which can be considered a surrogate for environmental uncertainty. Previous research on LGI suggests that this variable can affect communication and decision making in the simulation (Dutton & Webster, 1988).

General Tendencies in Priority-Setting

The descriptive statistics reveal some general tendencies in leaders' priority-setting. First, on average the leaders became involved in approximately 14 issues. This represents a moderately high level of breadth, as it exceeds the average number of 12 issues included in the leaders' inbaskets. The fewest number of issues dealt with by a leader was 5; the most was 18.

Second, the average level of focus (.29 on the Ray & Singer index) was moderately low. This index would correspond to a graph intermediate between (c) and (d) in Figure 1. The focus index ranged from .21 to .52, indicating that at least some leaders approximated graph (1c) in their pattern of priorities. However, extreme focus, corresponding to a "tunnel vision" pattern, was not observed.

Third, the leaders on average allocated proportionately more attention to crises and opportunities than to problems. Crises and opportunities made up 38% of the key issues in LGI, yet received 59% of the leaders' attention. By comparison, the lower levels in LGI (Directors and Plant Managers) allocated only 46% of their attention to crises and opportunities. Crises, in particular, captured a disproportionate amount of the leaders' attention: Only 16% of the issues were crises, yet they received 34% of the leaders' attention. However, large differences among the leaders were found. Across leaders, the percent of attention allocated to crises ranged from 7 to 65.

LGI division was significantly associated with leaders' priorities. The greater the environmental certainty of the division, the greater the attention allocated to

TABLE 1 Means, Standard Deviations, and Correlations of Variables

Variable	M	SD	1	2	3	4	5	6	7	8	9
1. LGI division	2	.85	X								
2. Breadth	13.7	3.0	07	X							
3. Focus	.29	.09	03	-41*	X						
4. % attention to crises	34	12	34	58***	19	X					
5. % attention to problems	39	12	-26	13	-45**	-31	X				
6. % attention to opportunities	25	12	23	-52***	-19	-56**	-27	X			
7. % attention to crises and opportunities	59	11	63***	12	01	45**	-62***	49**	X		
8. Decision quality	59.9	16.1	55***	65***	-09	54**	-10	-23	31	X	
9. Perceived leader performance	5.37	.53	-06	52***	-41*	51**	31	-35	16	06	X

Note. LGI Division = 1–3, higher scores indicating less environmental uncertainty. Breadth = number of issues handled. Focus = 0–1, higher scores indicating more focus. Decision quality = 0–100, higher scores indicating higher decision quality in the leader's unit. Perceived leader performance = 1–7, higher scores indicating higher perceived performance. $20 \leq N \leq 35$. Correlations are presented without decimal points. Significance levels are two-tailed.

*p < .10.   **p < .05.   ***p < .01.

crises and opportunities. Although somewhat surprising, this result does not necessarily mean that environmental certainty *causes* leaders to attend more to crises and opportunities. Instead, a *correlational* explanation may be more valid: The three divisions (used as a surrogate measure of environmental uncertainty) were associated with different sets of issues, and these differences in issue sets, rather than level of uncertainty per se, led to the leaders' attention patterns.

Our observations suggest that the leaders in LGI exerted substantial control over both the breadth of their priority sets and their degree of focus on particular issues. Some leaders decided early during the run, or even prior to it, which issues they would handle. For example, one President announced at the beginning of the run that he would deal "only with capitalization decisions." During the run, he met almost exclusively with the Vice Presidents, while problem-solving activity took place autonomously at the Director and Plant Manager level. This leader had a low-breadth, moderate-focus priority pattern.

Other leaders took a more open approach to priority-setting. For example, one President spent the early part of the run listening to his Vice Presidents and Directors describe their key issues and potential solutions. He then developed an extensive list of issues and questions, which he posted on his office wall. As new information and alternatives were discussed in a series of meetings, he revised the list repeatedly, clustering the issues into different groups alongside descriptions of potential solutions. This leader had a high-breadth, low-moderate focus priority pattern.

Effects of Priority Patterns: Breadth and Focus

Breadth and focus were conceptualized as independent dimensions. However, the correlation of -.41 between the two variables suggests that this assumption may not hold true. Leaders who included more issues in their priority sets tended to exhibit less focus, suggesting that patterns (b) and (c) in Figure 1 may be empirically quite rare.

Interestingly, decision quality and perceived leader performance were uncorrelated. The ambiguity of LGI, which made it difficult for participants to evaluate the quality of decisions, and the fact that participants rated each others' performance before learning of their division's decision quality, probably contributed to this result. In addition, participants may have given heavier weight to decision processes, including leader style, than to decision outcomes.

The strong and significant correlation between breadth and decision quality supports the prediction that leaders who include more issues in their priority set would have higher decision quality within their units. This correlation remained significant after the effect of focus was partialled out (partial correlation = .74, p < .01).

The expected relationship between breadth and perceived performance was also supported: The more issues in the leader's priority set, the higher his or her performance rating. This correlation remained significant after the effect of focus was partialled out (partial correlation = .53, p < .01).

More than any of the other patterns, we expected that the high-breadth, high-focus priority pattern would be associated with higher decision quality and perceived leader performance. These expectations were tested by running separate hierarchical regression analyses, with decision quality and perceived leader performance as the dependent variables and breadth, focus, and the interaction term, breadth x focus, as the predictor variables.

Breadth and focus were entered into the equation first, followed by the interaction term. For decision quality, the

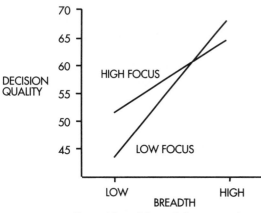

Figure 2 Effect of breadth and focus on decision quality (Breadth: R^2 increment = .45, p < .008; Breadth × Focus: R^2 increment = .30, p < .004).

squared multiple correlation increments were significant for breadth (.45, p < .007) and for the interaction term (.30, p < .004). An examination of decision quality based on a median split of breadth and focus revealed that focus had a greater effect on decision quality for leaders who had low-breadth priority patterns than for those who had high-breadth patterns. This interaction effect is evident in Figure 2, which presents the results of the analysis. The means for the four cells were: low breadth, low focus, 44.5; low breadth, high focus, 50.9; high breadth, low focus, 67.7; high breadth, high focus, 64.2. Thus the form of the interaction differed from our predicted pattern.

The predicted interaction effect of breadth and focus on perceived leader performance was not supported. The squared multiple correlation increment was significant only for breadth (.48, p < .005).

Effects of Priority Content: Crises, Problems, and Opportunities

The correlations in Table 1 show that the combined percent of leader attention allocated to crises and opportunities was positively, though nonsignificantly, associated with decision quality (r = .31) and

perceived leader performance (r = .16). Considered separately, however, the percent of crisis attention was positively and significantly associated with decision quality and perceived leader performance (r = .54 and .51, respectively), whereas the percent of opportunity attention was negatively (though nonsignificantly) associated with these two outcomes (r = -.23 and -.35, respectively).

We explored these associations further by conducting hierarchical regression analyses. In one analysis, we included LGI division, followed by crisis-opportunity attention, as predictors of decision quality. LGI division was a significant predictor of decision quality (R square = .33, p < .03), but crisis-opportunity attention did not account for additional variance in decision quality. A second analysis, including the same two variables as predictors, revealed no effect of either variable on perceived leader performance.

Two other regression analyses examined the effects of attention to crises on decision quality and perceived leader performance. Attention to crises did not account for a significant amount of variance in decision quality after the effects of LGI division were taken into account. However, attention to crises did account for a significant amount of variance in perceived leader performance (increment in R square = .30, p < .03) after the effects of LGI division, breadth, and focus were taken into account.

Discussion

Providing purpose and direction to organizational members is a crucial function of leadership. Leaders accomplish this function largely through priority-setting, that is, allocating attention to some issues at the expense of others. Numerous management scholars have proposed a close connection between leader priority-setting and organizational effectiveness, but few empirical studies in this area have been conducted. In this paper, we differentiated two aspects of priority-setting—breadth and focus—and investigated their effect on decision quality and perceived leader performance. We also examined the effects of priority content on these two outcome variables.

Our predictions for the positive effects of breadth (i.e., the number of issues a leader includes in his or her set of priorities) were supported. Several explanations for these effects are possible. A high-breadth priority pattern may have (a) promoted the active search, processing, and communication of a wide range of information throughout the organization; (b) increased leaders' use of large networks of contacts, facilitating the sharing of information and alternative solutions to problems; and (c) increased the chances of leaders and subordinates seeing connections among issues and thus generating more efficient or creative solutions.

Additional analyses of LGI process data supported these possibilities. Breadth of leader priorities was correlated with breadth of subordinate priorities (r = .39), average number of statements made by subordinates (indicating overall communication and activity level, r = .32), and percent of meetings that included members from more than one division (indicating extent of information sharing and interpersonal networks, r = .39). Although these correlations did not reach conventional levels of statistical significance and allowed more than one causal interpretation, they are nevertheless consistent with the expected effects of leader priority breadth on both decision quality and perceived leader performance.

We had predicted that the high-breadth, high-focus priority pattern would lead to more favorable outcomes than would other patterns. The results, however, show that the two high-breadth patterns were similar in decision quality and that focus had a greater effect on decision quality for leaders who had low-breadth patterns than for those who had high-breadth patterns. Decision quality suffered most under the low-breadth, low-focus priority pattern.

Given the small sample size, these results are striking. A potential explanation for the interaction pattern lies in the interpretation of breadth and focus. Breadth can be interpreted as degree of leader activity and openness to new information; focus can be interpreted as leader ability and willingness to differentiate among issues and set direction for subordinates. Given these interpretations, a low-breadth pattern restricts information flow and communication, generally reducing decision quality. Under such conditions, providing focus may increase the coordination among subordinates so that the decisions they make are more thorough and therefore of higher quality. In contrast, information flow and communication may be sufficiently high under high breadth that subordinates can more readily perceive which issues warrant more attention, thus reducing the need for leader direction (i.e., focus). In essence, this explanation assumes that subordinate knowledge can function as a "substitute for leadership" (Kerr & Jermier, 1978).

The results failed to support the expected interaction effect for perceived leader performance. The regression analysis revealed that once the significant effect of breadth was taken into account, the effects of focus and the interaction term (breadth x focus) were nonsignificant. The correlation between breadth and focus makes it difficult to determine whether participants were responding positively to high breadth, negatively to high focus, or both. In general, though, breadth appears to have had a more powerful effect on both decision quality and perceived leader performance.

With respect to priority content, the percent of leader attention allocated to crises was positively and significantly associated with decision quality. However, once the effects of LGI division were controlled for, this relationship became nonsignificant. Thus, LGI division accounted for both the percent of leader attention allocated to crises and the level of decision quality. We therefore cannot conclude that higher decision quality resulted from a higher proportion of leader attention allocated to crises.

In contrast, even after potential confounding variables (LGI division, breadth, and focus) were controlled for, the association between percent of crisis attention and perceived leader performance remained significant. This result supports our prediction that subordinates would perceive leaders as effective to the extent that they focused on issues crucial to the organization. It is also consistent with the expectation that subordinates would tend to consider crises (i.e., salient and urgent issues that threaten loss) to be more crucial than opportunities (i.e., less salient, longer term, and less urgent issues that promise gain), even though both types of issues are strategically important to the organization.

Methodological Comments

This study demonstrates three advantages of the use of simulations for investigating complex organizational phenomena: (a) providing a realistic, complex setting; (b) permitting multiple simulation runs as replications; and (c) permitting multiple methods of measurement to capture simulation processes and outcomes.

Our study also illustrates one limitation of our approach for using simulations to investigate leadership: the problem of inferring cause and effect. In general, using correlational techniques to analyze simulation data makes it difficult to establish causality (e.g., did the high-breadth priority pattern cause higher decision quality?). There is also the related potential for spurious correlation. For example, high-breadth and high-perceived performance may have no causal connection but may instead reflect the effects of an unmeasured third variable (e.g., cognitive

complexity). Although plausible alternative explanations can be ruled out by the appropriate techniques, as we have attempted to do in this study, caution is still advisable in interpreting the results.

Implications for Leadership

In this study, we examined leader priority-setting in terms of breadth, focus, and content. In spite of the relatively small sample and the inherent "noisiness" of simulation data, we found that breadth, focus, and content had effects on decision quality and perceived leader performance.

One implication of the study is that leaders who are involved in a wide, rather than a narrow, range of organizational issues will generally be perceived by subordinates as more effective. The content of these issues, however, also matters a great deal. Leaders who allocate attention disproportionately to crises, as compared to opportunities, will be perceived as more effective. This finding is consistent with previous findings that managers who are willing to act, accept risk, and take action in response to immediate problems are often more successful than those who are more deliberate and analytical (e.g., McCall & Kaplan, 1985; cf. Kotter, 1982). It is also consistent with the classic leadership tactic of manufacturing crises to gain the support and admiration of followers. Because crises provide a forum for decisive action, leaders who deal with them successfully often gain in credibility and stature.

Because opportunities often—though not always—provide less of a forum for decisive action, leaders who allocate attention primarily to opportunities may be viewed as less "leaderlike." It is natural, of course, for people to be more concerned with potential losses than potential gains (Tversky & Kahneman, 1981) and therefore accord higher importance to crises. However, from a long-term perspective, it may be just as crucial for leaders to foresee new developments and take the initiative to improve the competitive position of their organizations. In fact, crises are often the end result of a persistent failure to make improvements in the absence of direct threats. This suggests that leaders may need to communicate to their organizations the importance of proactively developing and responding to opportunities, in addition to reacting to external threats.

With regard to decision quality, the results suggest that a low-breadth, low-focus priority pattern may be the least likely to promote high decision quality. In practice, this suggests that leaders who are concerned with a narrow set of issues, and who fail to distinguish among these in terms of importance, will not provide sufficient scope or direction for their units. This pattern may represent a case of "the worst of both worlds": low breadth, which restricts information flow and communication, and low focus, which leaves subordinates unclear about where they should place their efforts.

The findings from this study, based on a sample of MBA students in an organizational simulation, point out the importance of priority-setting. Although leaders do not have complete control over their priorities, they can exert considerable control over them. By deliberately selecting their portfolio of issues, including the number and types of issues and which issues should receive the most attention, leaders can not only affect how they are perceived by subordinates but affect organizational communication patterns and decision quality as well.

References

Barnard, C. (1939). *The functions of the executive*. Cambridge, MA: Harvard University Press.

Bennis, W. G., & Nanus, B. (1985). *Leaders*. New York: Harper & Row.

Center for Creative Leadership. (1983). *Looking Glass, Inc.: Supplement to the Administrator's Guide*. Greensboro, NC.

Dutton, J. E., & Webster, J. (1988). Patterns of interest around issues: The role of uncertainty and feasibility. *Academy of Management Journal*, 31, 663–675.

Hollander, E. P. (1978). *Leadership dynamics*. New York: Free Press.

House, R. J., & Mitchell, T. R. (1974). Path-goal theory of leadership. *Journal of Contemporary Business*, 3, 81–97.

Huber, G. P. (1980). *Managerial decision making*. Glenview, IL: Scott, Foresman.

Janis, I. L., & Mann, L. (1977). *Decision making*. New York: Free Press.

Kerr, S., & Jermier, J. M. (1978). Substitutes for leadership: Their meaning and measurement. *Organizational Behavior and Human Performance*, 22, 375–403.

Kotter, J. P. (1982). *The general managers*. New York: Free Press.

Lombardo, M. M., McCall, M. W., Jr., & DeVries, D. L. (1983). *Administrator's Guide, University Edition, Looking Glass*. Greensboro, NC: Center for Creative Leadership.

McCall, M. W., Jr., & Kaplan, R. E. (1985). *Whatever it takes: Decision makers at work*. Englewood Cliffs, NJ: Prentice-Hall.

Mintzberg, H., Raisinghani, D., & Theoret, A. (1976). The structure of "unstructured" decision processes. *Administrative Science Quarterly*, 21, 246–275.

Mullen, T. P., & Stumpf, S. A. (1987). The effect of management styles on strategic planning. *The Journal of Business Strategy*, 7, 60–75.

Nutt, P. (1984). Types of organizational decision processes. *Administrative Science Quarterly*, 29, 414–450.

Peters, T. J. (1982). Symbols, patterns and settings: An optimistic case for getting things done. In D. A. Nadler, M. L. Tushman, & N. G. Hatvany (Eds.), *Managing organizations: Readings and cases* (pp. 460–475). Boston: Little, Brown.

Peters, T. J., & Waterman, R. H., Jr. (1982). *In search of excellence: Lessons from America's best-run companies*. New York: Harper & Row.

Ray, J. L., & Singer, J. D. (1973). Measuring the concentration of power in the international system. *Sociological Methods and Research, 1*, 403–437.

Selznick, P. (1957). *Leadership in administration.* New York: Harper & Row.

Taagepera, R., & Ray. J. L. (1977). A generalized index of concentration. *Sociological Methods and Research, 5*, 367–384.

Thornton, G. C., III, & Byham, W. C. (1982). *Assessment centers and managerial performance.* New York: Academic Press.

Tversky, A., & Kahneman, D. (1981). The framing of decisions and the psychology of choice. *Science, 211*, 453–458.

Vaill, P. B. (1982). The purposing of high performing systems. *Organizational Dynamics, 11*(2), 23–39.

Vaill, P. B. (1990). *Managing as a performing art: New ideas for a world of chaotic change.* San Francisco: Jossey-Bass.

Ariel S. Levi is Assistant Professor in the Department of Management and Organization Sciences at Wayne State University. His research interests include judgment and decision-making processes at the individual, group, and organizational levels and the effect of leadership style on these processes. He received his PhD in Social Psychology from Yale University.

Larry E. Mainstone holds the Richard E. Meier Professorship in Management at Valparaiso University. He has published numerous articles and has been a consultant for several organizations. His recent research has focused on decision making and judgment. He received his PhD in Organizational Behavior from Michigan State University.

Direct inquiries about this article to Ariel S. Levi, School of Business Administration, Department of Management, Wayne State University, Detroit, MI 48202, 313/577–4518.

CHAPTER 36

In-Situ Team Evaluation

A New Paradigm for Measuring and Developing Leadership at Work

Mark R. Edwards

Leadership assessment represents a critical element in organizational success. Unless the correct people are identified, promoted, and given other organizational rewards such as special training, pay, choice assignments or jobs, organizational motivation wanes. A new procedure called in-situ (in place) assessment offers a new model for measuring and developing leadership at work and provides advantages not available with such traditional assessment procedures as assessment centers. In-situ team evaluation offers a "full view" of performance rather than a "single view" from one source or multiple views from "expert assessors." The in-situ model uses (a) on-the-job assessments rather than off-the-job tests or simulations, (b) includes everyone rather than only a few "high potentials," (c) occurs annually rather than only once in a career, (d) allows employee participation, and (e) captures performance (merit) information as well as promotability information. In-situ team evaluation holds promise for reducing assessment bias since the data reported here show positive gender and age association with leadership performance and neutral ethnicity scores.

Some things — like winds aloft, deep ocean currents, and leadership talent — are best measured in-situ, in the place where they occur.

Effective leadership assessment identifies those employees who will most likely succeed in higher level management or professional positions. Employee career and leadership growth, as well as organizational success, depend on accurately identifying those who most deserve differential organizational rewards such as training, merit pay, and promotion.

The continuing search for improvements in assessment methods has produced a new type of measurement technique called in-situ team evaluation. In-situ, in the place of, creates an assessment which is essentially an in-place assessment center, without:

1. The simulated exercises and tests (replacement: real job behaviors).

2. Taking the assessee off the job to an artificial setting (replacement: assessment occurs on the job, in-situ).

3. The use of highly trained assessors (replacement: lightly trained work associates).

4. High time and use costs (replacement: fast assessment procedures applied at low cost).

The in-situ assessment model uses team evaluation from multiple work associates that takes advantage of three well-established factors:

1. A confidential, multiple-rater consensus decision process produces a better result, on average, than a single judgment, no matter how well trained the judge (Bayroff, Haggerty, & Rundquist, 1954).

2. Lateral associates (work contacts near the organizational level of the assessee) provide the most reliable and most predictably valid assessment of future advancement—significantly better than supervisory ratings (Korman, 1968; Latham & Wexley, 1981).

3. Direct reports (subordinates) offer highly reliable assessment information that may yield higher predictive validities than assessment centers (Bernardin & Beatty, 1987).

Team evaluation creates an in-situ, in-place, leadership assessment by capturing the collective wisdom of those directly involved with each organization member in a manner that minimizes distortion or bias. Tapping the most reliable and valid source of relevant decision information—lateral associates—develops a minimum bias, "full view" picture of each performer's leadership behaviors and managerial skills. Such a process improves *competitive equity* and assures more equal rules of competition for all organizational rewards, including pay and promotions.

Employees know that a *high leadership rating translates into more value to the employee than a high merit rating.* High performance appraisal ratings often result in relatively small (1–10%) merit increases. In contrast, high talent ratings

provide many valuable opportunities, including:

1. **Promotion:** Salary increases (8–20%) larger than merit awards usually accompany advancement.

2. **Compounded monetary rewards:** All future merit increases are calculated on a larger base salary derived from prior promotion increases to salary.

3. **Recognition** by relevant people, including work associates.

4. **Rich job activities,** such as special assignments and increased authority.

5. Improved **training opportunities:** "High leadership potentials" often get special treatment and training exposure.

6. Enhanced **access to mentors:** Higher level managers prefer fast-track stars.

From an individual perspective, *leadership ratings may be the most important activity at work.* It is difficult to identify any process within a firm that has more impact on an employee's career than the power of a high (or low) leadership talent-level prophecy. The relative strengths and weaknesses identified in a credible leadership assessment process provide a driver for training, development, and career planning.

Leadership assessment information may be just as important from the perspective of the organization as a whole. Firms are facing increasingly competitive environments which require the selection of the most capable members for higher level managerial and professional positions. Organizations that suboptimize the talent assessment process by compromising with weak assessment procedures (such as clinical, intuitive, or supervisory judgment processes) are likely to face two significant problems. First, such organizations will find it increasingly difficult to maintain marketplace competitiveness because *too many leadership positions will be assumed by the wrong people*. Second, these organizations can expect *indefensible* claims of discriminatory or otherwise unfair employment practices from organization members who may, legitimately or otherwise, believe their leadership talent has been unfairly assessed (Field & Holley, 1981). Such claims of improper treatment practices are especially likely in organizations where many highly trained and talented people vie for increasingly fewer higher level positions.

Contemporary Organization Environments

Contemporary firms are characterized by such features as highly trained professionals, rapidly changing technology and market needs, extensive investment in people, ample opportunities for competitors to raid skilled personnel, and a wide variety of talents and experiences within the organization. Many organizations are also typified by matrix management designs that temporarily assign employees to special projects outside the direct supervision of an immediate boss (Cleland, 1981). Matrix management designs may include temporary project team assignments, special training assignments, and cross-functional or interdisciplinary job rotations. These special characteristics of contemporary firms make them unsatisfactory for traditional assessment methods (DeVries, Morrison, Shullman, & Gerlach, 1981).

Traditional businesses could employ competent young people and expect many years of apprenticeship and observation to shape a knowledge base regarding who had the relative competencies required for higher positions. Today, employee expectations about apprenticeship and "waiting for the right opportunity" have changed. Further, time, size, and market constraints give higher level management less and less opportunity to observe the performance of lower organization level personnel. The changes in employee expectations, combined with lowered visibility to management and increasing competitive pressures, increase the requirement for effective talent assessment.

An equally difficult problem shared by organizations occurs because the half-life of technical knowledge has diminished to less than ten years. Therefore, leadership assessment must measure not only potential for future contribution and leadership but also capacity for career (life-long) learning and *sustained performance*.

The focus here is on assessment designed to identify leadership from organizational judgment procedures. Other sources provide excellent reviews of alternative assessment methods such as psychological tests (Gough, 1983), biographical data (Owens, 1983) and interviews (Arvey, 1988; Ulrich & Trumbo, 1965; Wagner, 1949).

Supervisory Ratings

Certainly the most commonly used form of talent identification is the supervisory promotion list. Most organizations, including IBM, Exxon, and Xerox, primarily use supervisory recommendations for promotion (Bolt, 1982). Nevertheless, problems identified by research on supervisory ratings include high visibility performers who emerge on such lists independent of their performance, while low visibility performers tend to be overlooked. With such a system, it is often possible to predict promotions based on who sits closest to the boss or who is most visible. Research and common sense indicate supervisor-only ratings are sometimes more a function of the rater, the supervisor, than of the ratee's actual performance (Bedeian, 1976; Borman, 1979). A commonly recommended alternative to the deficiencies of supervisory assessment is a combination of supervisory nomination and the assessment center (Joiner, 1984).

The Assessment Center

The assessment center, AC, has been a popular procedure for identifying organizational talent and has claimed the most predictive validity for leadership talent assessment (Moses & Byham, 1977; Thornton & Byham, 1982). An AC simulates the job setting with multiple synthetic activities performed in front of or scored by trained assessors who are objective, independent, and do not know the assessees (Keil, 1981). However, ACs have been challenged because they tend to lack job relatedness (content validity) in that artificial or simulated work tasks serve as surrogates of actual work performance (Dreher & Sackett, 1981).

A common AC rule is that assessors *not know assessees personally* in order to minimize favoritism bias. Unfortunately, this constraint insures that *assessors have no opportunity to observe assessees' actual responses to real problems in the context of the actual work environment.* Assessors must infer such responses from assessees' performance on synthetic work tasks.

Simulation outside the normal work environment makes ACs expensive. Per-assessee cost may range from $500 to $5,000 when assessee and assessor training, observation, participation, analysis, and debriefing time are calculated. Analysis by the author of actual AC costs in seven firms resulted in the conservative average cost calculation of $3,500 per assessee. Therefore, in many firms only a select few employees, possibly 0.5 to 2%, have an opportunity to participate. These limitations pose some important questions:

1. How should the special people who receive an opportunity to enter an AC be fairly and accurately selected from the total employee population?

2. Should the organization ignore the possibility of extraordinary talent in the nonassessed group?

3. What about late bloomers (performers who develop superb talents in mid-life)?

4. What about employees who perform well at work and have outstanding potential but experience debilitating test anxiety in AC settings?

Another problem may be even more significant. Since ACs are so expensive, employees who do participate may only be assessed once in their career—hardly acceptable when technologies and market opportunities change rapidly.

In addition to the identified problems, time costs make ACs unacceptable for many organizations. A common rule is one assessor for each one or two assessees. The AC process of training one set of assessors—before any assessments begin—could cost a week of expensive management time under a two- or three-day assessment center program (with possible travel time, a day or two preparation time, a day or two for assessment analysis, and another day for assessment feedback). Beyond the expense factor, assessor-managers have a significant opportunity cost in serving on repeated assessment centers.

A Solution: In-Situ Team Evaluation

Beginning in the mid-1970s, some firms initiated a new type of leadership assessment procedure called in-situ or team evaluation (TE) that overcame some of the problems associated with assessment centers (Edwards, 1983). The change was prompted by the desire to improve cost effectiveness yet capitalize on the accuracy derived from multiple raters in talent identification.

Firms using various forms of the TE procedure described here include R.J.

Reynolds, Bank of America, Dow Agrichemical, Florida Power and Light, Westinghouse STGD, Lawrence Livermore Laboratories, Gulf Oil, G.A. Technologies, American Airlines, McDonnell Douglas, Rolls-Royce, Bausch & Lomb, Ciba-Geigy, Disney, Syntex, and Levi Strauss. Some have publicly reported at least partial results from their projects (Edwards, 1990a). These firms have used the generic consensus evaluation process in many different formats and for a variety of selection decisions such as merit appraisal, training needs analysis, career development, and retention decisions (Edwards, 1990b). In most cases the TE consensus process provided **additional** information to managers rather than replacing existing management systems (Edwards, 1990a). *Team Evaluation systematically captures—and provides to management —information from the highest quality information source available regarding merit and promotability: lateral associates or peers.*

Positioning Team Evaluation

Team evaluation may be appropriately positioned on the spectrum between supervisor-only ratings and assessment centers. The immediate supervisor serves as one of the raters on the Evaluation Team. The other three to seven raters are chosen by the assessee. Experience indicates the lowest rater variance (maximum interrater agreement) occurs where the organizational distance between the assessee and the raters is minimized (Edwards & Sproull, 1985). One organization has aptly termed its team evaluation process an in-place assessment center because the network of near-lateral work associates who are in regular contact with the assessee provides the primary information for the TE process.

Every published review of empirical assessment research concludes that peer ratings have higher reliability than supervisory ratings (Glueck & Milkovitch, 1982;

Korman, 1968; Landy & Farr, 1980). Multiple perspectives provided by peer evaluations reflect how the employee interacts with the boss as well as with other organizational members. Lateral associates have a comprehensive view of an employee's performance and have more relevant job information upon which to make an evaluation than do other sources (Latham & Wexley, 1981).

In addition to being reliable, peer appraisals are valid predictors of job performance. In fact, they have higher predictive validities than supervisors' appraisals (Wherry & Fryer, 1949; Williams & Leavitt, 1947). Literature reviews, such as Korman (1968) and Glueck and Milkovich (1982), also conclude that peer ratings are among the best predictors of performance in subsequent jobs.

The validity of peer ratings as predictors of both objective and subjective performance criteria has been investigated extensively in military settings (Armir, Kovarsky, & Sharan, 1970; Hollander, 1954; Wherry & Fryer, 1949; Williams & Leavitt, 1947). Peer ratings have also been shown to be valid for predicting the success of medical students (Kubany, 1957), insurance agents (Mayfield, 1970; Weitz, 1958), industrial managers (Roadman, 1964), salespeople (Mayfield, 1972; Waters & Waters, 1970), and police officers (Landy, Farr, Saal, & Freytag, 1976).

Empirical research (Hollander, 1956; Waters & Waters, 1970; Wherry & Fryer, 1949) shows that friendship does not bias peer evaluations. Even if such bias should occur, the multiple safeguards designed into the TE process minimize the impact of all types of bias, including friendship bias (Edwards, 1990b). At such organizations as Walt Disney Productions, Arizona State University, and Arizona Public Service, skeptical first-time participants were allowed to choose dual evaluation teams, one composed of "friends" and the other composed of "non-friends." In these projects, over 90% of the dual evaluation teams provided nearly identical TE consensus results for individual evaluation criteria as well as for the composite score. One engineering manager chose three unique evaluation teams. The range of his three TE composite scores was 3%—indicating no difference among the different evaluation teams.

Additional research indicates that the perspective of other work associates may differ from that of the immediate supervisor, partially because some individuals behave differently when the boss is present (Wexley, 1979). A supervisor may have a limited view of total performance, yet still be the only one in position to determine accomplishment of performance results. Behavioral observation of lateral associates provides a full view of behaviors that usually, but not always, correspond with performance results. In effect, the multirater measure assesses if the target person is performing job functions effectively, while the supervisor provides the measure of whether the "right things" get done.

In order to capture supervisor as well as lateral perspectives, the TE design includes the supervisor as one of the members of the evaluation team. In addition, TE results are commonly combined with the supervisor's judgment on performance results against objectives. Thus, the TE measure provides an *additional* piece of highly reliable and valid assessment information that contributes to the supervisor's own judgments. Since rater feedback nearly always (over 95% of the time) demonstrates the supervisory judgment to be similar to the consensus of the evaluation team, the TE results have credibility to both the supervisor and the assessee.

Subordinate Behavior Feedback

Another group with considerable observation opportunity for leadership behaviors, subordinates or direct reports often have an even greater opportunity for interaction with in-situ leadership assessees than colleagues (Mount, 1984). Who knows more about leadership behaviors than those on whom those skills are prac-

ticed? Direct reports have opportunity, presence, and motivation to appraise upward. However, relatively little is known regarding the efficacy of subordinate appraisal management (McEvoy, Buller, & Roghaar, 1988).

When asked about providing input from direct reports to supervisors, managers often react with three questions:

1. Are subordinates **willing** to provide evaluation input?

2. Are subordinates **able** to provide accurate information?

3. Do subordinates **inflate** leadership ratings of their supervisors?

The focus here will be on the **willingness** and **ability** of subordinates to appraise the leadership behaviors and skills of management.

The Present Studies

The studies reported here represent two sets of information:

1. Upward evaluation readiness surveys across five private sector corporations totalling over 600 participants. Each of these six organizations subsequently used multiple rater evaluation, with subordinates included in the evaluation process, for the purpose of performance appraisal or career development.

2. A leadership behavior feedback project for an industry leader customer service organization that covered 5,640 participants with 5,233 usable score sets.

Are Subordinates Willing Appraisers of Leadership?

Surveys of over 650 employees across 5 organizations using subordinates in the evaluation process provided results as follows:

1. Over 93% of subordinates said they wished to give input to the evaluation process. Of course, subordinates were assured of rating confidentiality.

2. Supervisors reflected a similar level of interest with more than 86% stating a desire for subordinate input on leadership behaviors.

As has been reported elsewhere, respondent age and willingness to participate in a subordinate review process, either as a rater or as a ratee, were inversely related to age. Older leaders were especially reluctant to have very junior subordinates rating their leadership behavior.

The response rates for subordinates, those who actually completed the leadership feedback survey, was 80.5% compared with 83.7% for colleagues. Higher level jobs had a higher response rate for subordinates, indicating greater willingness to participate in the evaluation of leadership at higher organization levels.

Hence, subordinates say they are willing to rate leadership and most leaders desire feedback, at least for development purposes. When asked to actually rate, subordinates respond at about the same level as colleagues.

The Leadership Initiative

The leadership behavior feedback project provided input to over 5,000 executives, managers, and supervisors from self, 5 colleagues, and 5 subordinates (direct reports). Supervisors may have been included in the colleague feedback but were not reported separately. Each participant was given 11 precoded leadership behavior surveys with instructions to complete 1 self-assessment and to distribute the others to five colleagues and five direct reports. The surveys were rated anonymously, returned via company mail, and then sent to an outside vendor for scoring.

The 35 leadership behaviors shown in Figure 1 represent the critical success behaviors for one organization's management in the 1990s. The leadership behavior survey was developed through a two-day systematic focus group. The instrument was revised through a pretesting process that included wide participation throughout the corporation. The behavior survey asked raters to rate each of 35 leadership behaviors using a 10-point scale on the **importance** of the behavior to those who interact with the target person and on that person's actual **performance** on that behavior. Completing the two-page, 35-item leadership behavior feedback survey required 12 to 20 minutes.

In order to assure confidentiality to raters, the surveys were scored **only when three or more were returned by colleagues or direct reports**. Over 60,000 surveys were sent out; over 47,000 usable surveys were returned in 1990. Participants with an insufficient number of responses (less than three respondents in either colleague or direct report rater set) were given additional surveys to distribute so that they could receive behavior feedback.

The project assured anonymity to both raters and ratees. **The behavior feedback was for career development purposes and provided only to the person rated.** The individual scores on behavior feedback were not available to supervisors, management, or the personnel staff. An outside firm completed the scoring and produced reports in order to insure confidentiality.

Each participant received 13 pages of behavior feedback, in graphic and descriptive formats, which are available from the author. A summary report for one participant is shown in Figure 1. The graphic summary report shows scores on every behavior and for each factor. Behavior scores represent the mean score for the five colleagues or the five direct reports for each behavior. Factor scores, such as

	Coll.	Dir.
Creating a Vision	**6.9**	**4.3**
Thinks like an owner	7.7	5.5
Focuses on "core" business issues	7.3	4.3
Visualizes possibilities beyond today	6.3	5.0
Visualizes like a customer	5.7	3.3
Goes beyond the traditional boundaries	6.3	3.3
Gathers information effectively	7.7	5.0
Effective listening	7.3	3.5
Dev. Comm. to a Shared Vision	**6.9**	**4.4**
Communicates long-range goals	6.0	3.0
Involves subordinates	6.7	3.8
Provides specific and frequent feedback	6.0	4.3
Supports open communication	6.7	4.0
Encourages feedback	6.0	3.5
Supports organizational goals	8.0	6.5
Shows integrity	8.7	5.8
Taking Initiative	**6.8**	**4.3**
Takes calculated risks	6.7	5.0
Pursues opportunity	7.3	5.0
Takes responsibility	6.0	4.8
Shows involvement	5.3	4.0
Implements required actions	6.0	2.5
Anticipates and initiates positive change	8.0	4.0
Makes hard decisions	8.0	5.0
Delegating Ownership	**6.5**	**5.2**
Identifies opportunities for compet. adv.	6.7	6.7
Communicates high performance stds.	7.3	4.8
Selects effective team members	6.0	5.8
Encourages others to take calc. risks	6.3	4.5
Can accept failure	6.0	4.3
Gives employees authority	6.7	6.0
Acts as a coach versus a player	6.7	4.3
Giving and Gaining Support	**6.6**	**4.4**
Eliminates dumb rules	7.0	2.8
Supports team even during failure	6.0	4.8
Rewards and recognizes employees	5.3	3.5
Allocates and shares resources	5.7	4.0
Stands up for what's right	7.0	4.5
Pursues proposals	7.0	4.3
Encourages dec. based on knowledge	8.0	7.0

Scale: 0   2   4   6   8   10

Key: Colleagues ————————
Direct reports — — — — — — —

Note. The first two bars in each cluster represent composite or summary scores.

Figure 1   Graphic summary report of performance ratings by colleagues and direct reports.

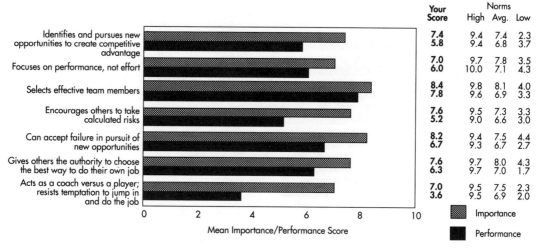

	Your Score	Norms High	Avg.	Low
Identifies and pursues new opportunities to create competitive advantage	7.4 / 5.8	9.4 / 9.4	7.4 / 6.8	2.3 / 3.7
Focuses on performance, not effort	7.0 / 6.0	9.7 / 10.0	7.8 / 7.1	3.5 / 4.3
Selects effective team members	8.4 / 7.8	9.8 / 9.6	8.1 / 6.9	4.0 / 3.3
Encourages others to take calculated risks	7.6 / 5.2	9.5 / 9.0	7.3 / 6.6	3.3 / 3.0
Can accept failure in pursuit of new opportunities	8.2 / 6.7	9.4 / 9.3	7.5 / 6.7	4.4 / 2.7
Gives others the authority to choose the best way to do their own job	7.6 / 6.3	9.7 / 9.7	8.0 / 7.0	4.3 / 1.7
Acts as a coach versus a player; resists temptation to jump in and do the job	7.0 / 3.6	9.5 / 9.5	7.5 / 6.9	2.3 / 2.0

Mean Importance/Performance Score

▨ Importance
■ Performance

Figure 2   Ratings on delegating ownership by colleagues.

"Taking Initiative," represent the average of the seven behavior means that make up the factor. A profile of 7 of the 35 leadership behaviors associated with delegating ownership for one participant from the perspectives of colleagues and from direct reports are shown in Figures 2 and 3.

These leadership feedback reports were provided to participants as segments of the leadership model and were discussed during the 4 1/2 day leadership training. The leadership feedback made the session content highly relevant since after discussing delegation, for example, participants received feedback on their delegation skills from colleagues and from direct reports. They then created action plans based on their results.

Are Subordinates Able Raters of Leadership?

The leadership initiative presented a unique opportunity to compare subordinate raters with colleagues who also rated the 35 leadership behaviors. The analysis of both range and variance for ratings of each ratee indicated subordinates were more consistent in their view of each leader than were the separate set of colleagues. The degree of agreement was significantly higher for direct reports than for colleagues, as indicated by the tighter range of their ratings for each supervisor. For example, for criterion 2, "Clearly communicates goals" for colleagues and direct reports respectively, the mean standard deviation for the score ranges were 1.65 versus 1.38. These findings indicate that for this behavior, subordinates were in higher agreement with less range in their ratings. The degree of agreement for both direct reports and for colleagues stayed fairly constant across the 35 behaviors.

The standard deviation from each consensus score was consistently lower for direct reports than for colleagues: 1.74 versus 2.06. Hence, measures of variance, both the range of ratings and the standard deviation, show evidence that subordinate raters are more consistent with one another than are colleagues.

Direct reports rated their managers, on average, 0.14 lower on the 10-point scale than did colleagues. Hence, not only do direct reports not inflate ratings, they are actually more rigorous than colleagues on many leadership behaviors.

An interesting finding was the similarity of the "shape of the leadership profile." Colleagues and direct reports agreed far more than they disagreed on the strongest

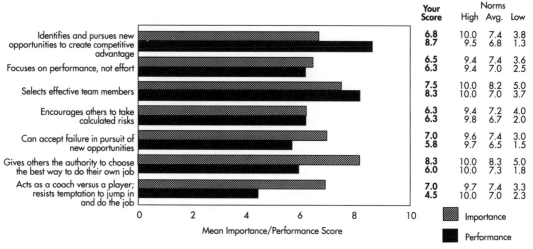

	Your Score	Norms High	Avg.	Low
Identifies and pursues new opportunities to create competitive advantage	6.8 / 8.7	10.0 / 9.5	7.4 / 6.8	3.8 / 1.3
Focuses on performance, not effort	6.5 / 6.3	9.4 / 9.4	7.4 / 7.0	3.6 / 2.5
Selects effective team members	7.5 / 8.3	10.0 / 10.0	8.2 / 7.0	5.0 / 3.7
Encourages others to take calculated risks	6.3 / 6.3	9.4 / 9.8	7.2 / 6.7	4.0 / 2.0
Can accept failure in pursuit of new opportunities	7.0 / 5.8	9.6 / 9.7	7.4 / 6.5	3.0 / 1.5
Gives others the authority to choose the best way to do their own job	8.3 / 6.0	10.0 / 10.0	8.3 / 7.3	5.0 / 1.8
Acts as a coach versus a player; resists temptation to jump in and do the job	7.0 / 4.5	9.7 / 10.0	7.4 / 7.0	3.3 / 2.3

Mean Importance/Performance Score

▦ Importance
■ Performance

Figure 3 Ratings on delegating ownership by direct reports.

and weakest behaviors among the seven behaviors in each of the five components of the leadership model. Even though they clearly have different perspectives, they share considerable agreement on the **extreme**s of leadership behaviors.

Age and Ethnicity Findings

In-place leadership behavior feedback gives a 360 degree look, essentially a quality control check for each leader. Such a process changes the rules since, instead of catering to one boss to receive a good performance rating, those receiving high ratings using team evaluation feedback must perform well upward, sideways, and, in some cases, even downward. Multirater feedback creates a different measure of performance than the traditional supervisor-only look downward. Therefore, it is important to consider if the results have unusual impact on older leaders or leaders who represent ethnically diverse groups.

Analysis of 6,455 ratings indicate an association between age and performance. Performance increases slightly with age, as shown in Figure 4. Analysis of the same group, as shown in Figure 5, shows essentially no difference across ethnic status: anglo, black, hispanic, oriental, and other.

Analysis of a second group of 5,083 participants in first-line supervisory jobs, shown in Figure 6, indicates no ethnic differences in leadership scores.

Gender Findings

Women were rated higher than men on all 35 leadership behaviors by both colleagues and direct reports. Figure 7 shows the slightly higher performance scores for women compared with men for leadership behavior number 27, "Makes Hard Decisions." While both colleagues and direct reports rated women higher than men, women were rated higher by direct reports than by colleagues on 74% of leadership behaviors. Table 1 reports the percentage of the 35 leadership behaviors rated higher by colleagues and by direct reports for both men and women. These results show that direct reports tend to rate women slightly higher than their male colleagues on most **but not all** leadership behaviors. Rater gender was not tracked in this project, but a majority of both colleagues and direct reports were male. The gender proportion of ratees, those rated, was 22% women and 78% men.

Another interesting finding was that raters were in closer agreement for

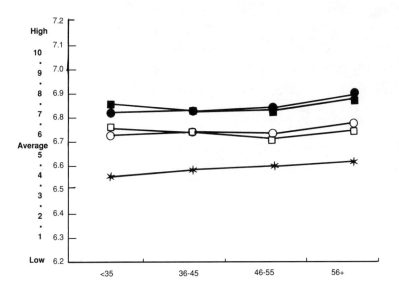

Figure 4   Ratings of leadership performance by age of leader.

women than for men, as indicated by Table 2. When the target person was a woman, the standard deviation of ratings was lower when the raters were direct reports than when the raters were colleagues. The highest leadership behavior rating agreement occurred for direct reports rating women. Evidently, direct reports are highly sensitive and in high agreement to leadership behaviors for women.

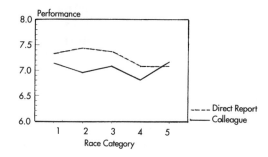

Figure 5   Ratings of leadership performance "Makes decisions" by race of leader.

Discussion

These studies provide strong evidence that subordinates are quite **willing** to participate in assessing leadership. They report that they want to rate; they are often upset when others are asked and they are left out of the supervisory evaluation process.

The empirical evidence from this project indicates direct reports are more **reliable** as raters than are colleagues. A subordinate rater tends to be in higher agreement with other subordinate raters than colleagues are with one another. The interrater agreement advantage for direct reports was demonstrated by the tighter range of ratings around each consensus and by the standard deviation of the rating by each rater.

An important caution in these findings is that interrater agreement shows **reliability** but not **validity**. Hence, these data do not indicate the validity of subordinate ratings. However, since these data are captured and stored electronically, the predictive validity test—in terms of eventual organization success for these

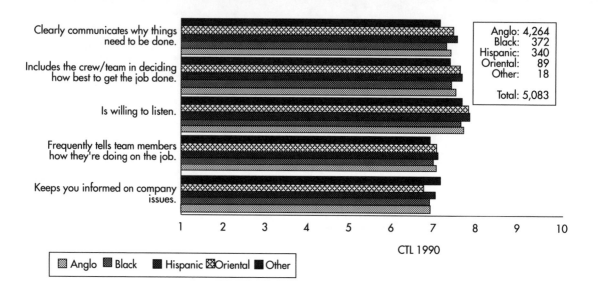

Figure 6 Ratings of leadership performance "Developing a commitment to a shared vision" by ethnic status of leader.

participants—can be determined at a later time.

The age, ethnicity, and gender findings are unusual. The author has completed

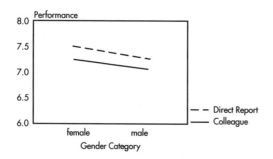

Figure 7 Ratings of leadership performance "Makes decisions" by gender of leader.

over 400 multirater field projects and reported previously that women are usually benefitted by higher ratings with the use of multiple raters as compared to supervisor-only ratings (Edwards & Cook, 1988). It appears that both colleagues and subordinates have a higher estimate of the leadership capability for women than do their supervisors when rating alone. An interesting note is that, when supervisors rate confidentially as part of an evaluation team, there is no difference between their ratings of women and the ratings of colleagues and direct reports. The gender advantage seems to occur when raters, supervisors, colleagues, and direct reports feel they can be honest due to anonymity within the assessment and feedback process.

TABLE 1 Ratings on Women by Colleagues and Direct Reports by Percentage of the 35 Leadership Behaviors

	Colleagues	**Direct reports**	**No difference**
Men	28%	60%	12%
Women	17%	74%	9%

TABLE 2 Rater Agreement for Men and Women Raters Reported in Average Standard Deviation

	Colleagues	Direct reports
Men	2.16	1.88
Women	2.05	1.79

Assessor-Assessee Distance

The empirical research indicates that the organizational closeness or distance of evaluators plays an important role in assessment accuracy. Significantly, analysis of raters in TE projects totalling over 16,000 participants indicates subordinates have the highest interrater reliabilities, with immediate supervisors and colleagues (peers) a close second. The second-level supervisors, when used, are a far-distant fourth and actually make very poor raters of leadership behaviors since they are highly variant with other sources of leadership information. These findings correspond with Sawyer's research regarding the value of statistical versus clinical prediction. Distant raters essentially make a clinical prediction with relatively little information. Such findings suggest the need to equalize assessee visibility by allowing each assessee to choose a personal evaluation team composed of those with maximum work interaction. Selection and choice of the team minimize distortion in the assessment process.

The assessment distance phenomenon suggests that assessment boards, assessment center review panels, or interviews by managers far distant from the performer tend to suboptimize the quality of assessment compared to the results that could be obtained from those in regular work contact with the assessee. When normally far distant organization assessors are brought together at high cost for the purpose of the assessment center, they may provide lower quality assessment judgments because they have weaker information than those in regular work contact with the assessee.

TE Limitations

TE is not without limitations. Only a relatively few human resource professionals have used a TE process. Another problem is that there are currently only a few sources for effective computerized solutions for the Team Evaluation Consensus. Current methods include application programs using spreadsheets like Lotus 1,2,3 or EXCEL and relational databases like Paradox, Oracle, Revelation, or dBase IV. A few specialized programs are designed specifically for the purpose of small sample consensus decisions such as TEAMS, Inc.'s "TEAMS Survey Software" or "BrainTrust," Strategic Decision Data's "Scaled Comparison," and Westinghouse's "Choice." A number of vendors offer fixed criteria multirater surveys such as Personnel Decisions, Inc.'s "Management Skills Profile" and "The Profilor," the Center for Creative Leadership's "Benchmarks" and **"SKILL**SCOPE," and Harbridge House's surveys on leadership, innovation, and culture. Alternative data analysis procedures are certain to be available in the near future as more organizations adopt multirater processes.

On-the-job assessment using multiple raters may conflict with a single supervisory control culture that views multiple raters as a threat to supervisory power. Another obvious disadvantage is that the TE assessment has not yet been adequately tested in formal long-term validation studies. However, since in-situ TE taps the knowledge network around each leader, TE is likely to equal or out-perform the predictive validates associated with assessment centers and to demonstrate a considerably higher cost/benefit.

Summary

Organizations need improved methods for identifying highly skilled leaders. Traditional methods such as longevity, interviews, and supervisory promotion lists are inappropriate due to their inaccuracies and low relationship with actual performance. Increasing competitive pressures and values and expectations among new employees have accelerated the search for effective leadership talent assessment procedures.

In-situ, in place, team evaluation offers an efficient solution that taps the best source of leadership knowledge — the collective intelligence surrounding the leader at work. The studies reported here indicate that in-situ assessment systems should include assessment information from subordinates because, as a group, they are both willing and able assessors of leadership. They are more consistent assessors, with one another, than are colleagues.

Multirater, in-situ feedback systems in the large field study reported here show positive association with age and gender and are nearly neutral to ethnicity. Such assessment systems offer hope for moderating the high social costs of individual biases.

The positive gender finding reported here opens an argument that the "glass ceiling" that limits women's ascension up the organizational ladder may be simply an artifact of using the wrong mode of assessment. Single rater, supervisory-only measures perpetuate cronyism and impose gender, age, and ethnicity biases. Change the assessment paradigm and change the assessment answers. Which are the true scores, the old or the new?

Assessment centers offer a multirater assessment model but retain the negative impacts of a political gamesmanship: Rather than using a competence-based reward system, supervisors alone are typically used to select participants. ACs are useful but represent off-the-job tests; simulations are an expensive forum for exploring the nuances of leadership talent.

The numerous advantages offered by the in-situ TE process over assessment centers include:

1. Provides accurate assessment information at substantially less cost in terms of both dollars and management time.

2. Allows all organization members to participate in the talent assessment process, rather than allowing participation by only a select few.

3. Allows the organization to reward members fairly for displaying the behaviors that lead to productivity — such as problem-solving, efficiency, and goal accomplishment.

4. Provides leaders with valuable, relevant, and specific information about their **relative** standing on job-related performance criteria.

5. Provides not only talent assessment information but also a multidimensional and accurate measure of current performance.

6. Allows involvement by managers and employees in system development and use.

7. Gives a simple and credible behavior feedback to participants.

8. Incorporates multiple safeguards, such as rater feedback, designed to insure individual fairness.

An organization that uses a leadership assessment process which is accepted and supported by organization members can insure that organizational rewards go to the correct performers. Further, the organization can expect to gain the maximum benefit for the limited rewards through improved motivation and productivity. Employees who recognize that their productive efforts will be rewarded with promotions are highly motivated to maximize their contribution to organization productivity.

References

Armir, Y. Y., Kovarsky, K., & Sharan, S. (1970). Peer nominations as a predictor of multistage promotions in a ramified organization. *Journal of Applied Psychology, 54*, 462–469.

Arvey, R. D. (1988). *Fairness in selecting employees.* Menlo Park, CA: Addison-Wesley.

Bayroff, A. G., Haggerty, R. H., & Rundquist, E. A. (1954). Validity of ratings as related to rating techniques and conditions. *Personnel Psychology, 7*, 92–113.

Bedeian, A. (1976). Rater characteristics affecting the validity of performance appraisals. *Journal of Management, 2*, 37–45.

Bernardin, H. J., & Beatty, R. W. (1987). Can subordinate appraisals enhance managerial productivity? *Sloan Management Review, 28*(4), 63–73.

Bolt, James F. (1982). Management resource planning: Keys to success. *Human Resources Planning, 5*(4), 185–196.

Borman, W. C. (1979). Individual differences correlate of rating accuracy using behavior scales. *Applied Psychological Measurement, 3*, 103–115.

Cleland, D. I. (1981). Matrix management: A kaleidoscope of organizational systems. *Management Review, 17*, 48–56.

DeVries, D. L., Morrison, A. M., Shullman, S. L., & Gerlach, M. L. (1981). *Performance appraisal on the line.* New York: Wiley.

Dreher, G. F., & Sackett, P. R. (1981). Some problems with applying content validity evidence to assessment center procedures. *Academy of Management Review, 6*, 551–560.

Edwards, M. R. (1983). Productivity improvement through innovations in performance appraisal. *Public Personnel Management, 12*(1), 13–24.

Edwards, M. R. (1990a). Sustaining culture change with multiple rater systems for career development and performance appraisal. *The Corporate Culture Sourcebook,* 194–205.

Edwards, M. R. (1990b). Assessment: Implementation strategies for multiple rater systems. *Personnel Journal, 21*(6), 130–139.

Edwards, M. R., & Cook, S. H. (1988). A comparative evaluation of the accuracy of team and supervisor-only evaluations of female job performance. *International Journal of Management, 5*(4), 400–411.

Edwards, M. R., & Sproull, J. R. (1985). Team talent assessment: Optimizing assessee visibility and assessment accuracy. *Human Resources Planning, 8*(3), 157–171.

Field, H. S., & Holley, W. H. (1981). The relationship of performance appraisal characteristics to verdicts in selected employment discrimination cases. *Academy of Management Journal, 2*, 392–406.

Glueck, W. F., & Milkovich, G. T. (1982). *Personnel: A diagnostic approach* (3rd ed.). Plano, TX: Business Publications.

Gough, H. (1983). Personality & personality assessment. In M. D. Dunnette (Ed.), *Handbook of industrial and organizational psychology* (2nd ed., pp. 521–608). New York: McGraw-Hill.

Hollander, E. P. (1954). Buddy ratings: Military research and industrial implications. *Personnel Psychology, 7*, 385–393.

Hollander, E. P. (1956). The friendship factor in peer nominations. *Personnel Psychology, 9*, 425–447.

Joiner, D. A. (1984). Assessment centers in the public sector: A practical approach. *Public Personnel Management, 13*(4), 435–450.

Keil, E. C. (1981). *Assessment centers: A guide for human resource management.* Reading, MA: Addison-Wesley.

Korman, A. K. (1968). The prediction of managerial performance: A review. *Personnel Psychology, 21*, 295–322.

Kubany, A. J. (1957). Use of sociometric peer nominations in medical education research. *Journal of Applied Psychology, 41*, 389–394.

Landy, F. J., & Farr, J. L. (1980). Performance rating. *Psychological Bulletin, 87*, 72–107.

Landy, F. J., Farr, J. L., Saal, F. E., & Freytag, W. R. (1976). Behaviorally anchored scores for rating the performance of police officers. *Journal of Applied Psychology, 61*, 750–758.

Latham, G. P., & Wexley, K. N. (1981). *Increasing productivity through performance appraisal.* Reading, MA: Addison-Wesley.

Mayfield, E. C. (1970). Management selection: Buddy nominations revisited. *Personnel Psychology, 23*, 377–391.

Mayfield, E. C. (1972). Value of peer nominations in predicting life insurance sales performance. *Journal of Applied Psychology, 56*, 319–323.

McEvoy, G. M., Buller, P. F., & Roghaar, S. R. (1988). A jury of one's peers. *Personnel Psychology, 41*, 94–101.

Moses, J. L., & Byham, W. C. (Eds.). (1977). *Applying the assessment center method.* New York: Pergamon Press.

Mount, M. K. (1984). Psychometric properties of subordinate ratings of managerial performance. *Personnel Psychology, 37*, 687–701.

Owens, W. A. (1983). Background data. In M. D. Dunnette (Ed.), *Handbook of industrial and organizational psychology* (2nd ed., pp. 609–644). New York: McGraw-Hill.

Roadman, H. E. (1964). An industrial use of peer ratings. *Journal of Applied Psychology, 48*, 211–214.

Thornton, G. C., III, & Byham, W. C. (1982). *Assessment centers and managerial performance.* New York: Academic Press.

Ulrich, L., & Trumbo, D. (1965). The section interview since 1949. *Psychological Bulletin, 63*, 100–116.

Wagner, R. (1949). The employment interview: A critical summary. *Personnel Psychology, 2*, 17–46.

Waters, L. K., & Waters, C. W. (1970). Peer nominations as predictors of short term sales performance. *Journal of Applied Psychology, 54*, 42–44.

Weitz, J. (1958). Selecting supervisors with peer ratings. *Personnel Psychology, 11*, 25–35.

Wexley, K. W. (1979). Roles of performance appraisal in organizations. In S. Kerr (Ed.), *Organizational behavior* (pp. 84–86). Columbus, Ohio: Grid Publishing.

Wherry, R. J., & Fryer, H. (1949). Buddy ratings: Popularity contest or leadership criteria? *Personnel Psychology, 2*, 147–159.

Williams, S. E., & Leavitt, H. J. (1947). Group opinion as a predictor of military leadership. *Journal of Consulting Psychology, 11*, 283–391.

Mark R. Edwards, PhD, is a Professor and the Director of the Laboratory for Innovation and Decision Research in the College of Engineering at Arizona State University. He was formerly Personnel Director for a Fortune 50 firm and has done extensive personnel systems research and consulting. He has published over 70 academic and professional articles on human productivity, performance measurement, talent assessment, creativity, and health promotion.

Direct inquiries about this article to Mark R. Edwards, Laboratory for Innovation and Decision Research (LIDR), College of Engineering, Arizona State University, Tempe, AZ 85287, 602/968-2272.

The Dual Impact of Leadership on Performance Appraisal

A Levels-of-Analysis Perspective

Steven E. Markham, William D. Murry, and K. Dow Scott

The key to improving performance appraisals in organizations may be the leadership exchange processes that occur between managers and subordinates. We suggest two ways in which this might unfold: (a) the direct relationships among leadership attention, tenure with supervisor, and actual performance appraisal rating and (b) the configuration of these three variables around the organization's structure in which differences between supervisory groups are highlighted. Our findings suggest that all three variables are significantly related. For leadership attention and performance appraisal, an individual-level model best applies. A group model is implied for leadership attention and tenure with supervisor, whereby entire supervisory groups that have longer tenure with their supervisor also receive, on average, higher amounts of leadership attention.

Both practitioners and researchers are very concerned with understanding and improving the performance appraisal process in organizations (Dansereau & Markham, 1987; Murphy & Cleveland, 1991). Inherent in most organizational compensation systems is the need for a reliable method of appraising an individual's performance. Generally, this occurs in the form of a supervisor's periodic evaluation of each employee's work habits, behaviors, or results. Most of the early research on performance appraisal focused on problems of measurement, with little conceptualization from a social-psychological framework (Murphy & Cleveland, 1991). However, the underlying assumption of this paper is that the key to understanding performance evaluations lies with the supervisor who gives the actual appraisal rather than with the format of the rating instruments (cf. Hills, 1979, 1987).

Leadership Impact

We are interested in the direct impact of three variables: leadership attention received by the subordinate, the performance appraisal rating given by the supe-

---

rior, and the amount of time that a subordinate has reported to his or her superior. We use the term direct impact to refer to the possible existence of a relationship between variables *without* considering how these variables might be configured around the organization's structure. These variables conceptually fit into a social-psychological framework of exchange between supervisor and subordinate as outlined by Murphy and Cleveland (1991). They suggest that exchanges between leaders and their group members affect the leaders' goals in administering the appraisal as well as the manner in which leaders treat their subordinates during the appraisal process. The importance of leader-member relations to the performance appraisal process has been echoed in similar research on perceptual congruence in two studies by Wexley and Pulakos (1983) and Pulakos and Wexley (1983). From the vantage of both superior's ratings of subordinate performance and subordinate's ratings of superior's performance, they found that perceptual similarity had a significant effect on the ratings given by either party. They concluded in these studies that performance appraisal research has neglected the nature of leader-member relationships. Thus, rather than being viewed solely as a function of subordinate performance, performance appraisal may be regarded as part of a larger nomological network that includes leadership constructs in addressing our underlying concern: Can we find evidence linking leadership and performance appraisal processes?

To the extent that leadership processes and performance appraisal ratings together might reflect an underlying social exchange process, we expect the *perceived amount of received leadership attention*, as reported by the subordinate, will be significantly related to the *performance appraisal rating* assigned by the superior. Given the realities of dealing with different subordinates, we suspect that this leader-member exchange does not unfold equally for all subordinates.

The nature of leadership attention, as defined by Dansereau, Alutto, and Yammarino (1984), focuses on giving interpersonal consideration as a form of return on the investments made by the subordinate who, in turn, engages in mutually satisfying work. Thus, a new member of a supervisory group would require some time in his or her role to prove that the superior should invest in such a relationship. This is not to say that the new recruit will not be given direction and guidance; rather, the role-making phase of the relationship needs to be established before a full exchange relationship can take place.

Dansereau, Graen, and Haga (1975) examined the longitudinal unfolding of this exchange process. They found that, in fact, a period of time is required for new superior-subordinate relationships to become clear and for an exchange relationship to fully develop. Thus, we expect that the *amount of time (or tenure)* the subordinate has served with the same supervisor will be related to both the amount of leadership attention he or she reports and the performance appraisal ratings he or she receives.

The Configurational Impact of Leadership

Configurational impact refers to the effect of the organizational structure on any of the relationships between the variables described. This configurational issue is inherent within the leadership-performance appraisal domain regardless of which specific variables are selected. Indeed, Graen and Schiemann (1978) indicate that an understanding of leader-member exchanges is intimately tied to a level of analysis problem. In other words, should individuals, dyads, supervisory work groups, or some larger collectivity be studied as the unit of analysis around which a set of variables are configured? We can extend this issue by asking if the leadership-performance appraisal relationship reflects a process of differentiation whereby superiors recognize relative differences within the group or if they stress the "sameness" of the group by downplaying differences within the group, thereby treating all members homogeneously. This is the configuration issue in performance appraisal (see Dansereau & Markham, 1987).

Dansereau, Alutto, and Yammarino (1984) and Dansereau and Markham (1987) illustrated four ways in which the variables might be configured with respect to a single level of analysis built around the work group. First, entire supervisory units can be characterized by (a) similar average levels of leadership attention and performance ratings and (b) a significant correlation among these unit scores. This is termed a between-unit model because it focuses on differences between groups, thereby implying similarity inside units. In the leadership research literature, it has also been called the Average Leadership Style (ALS) (Dansereau et al., 1975) because it uses averaged reports about one supervisor from many subordinates. For one organization, Markham (1988) found that differences between supervisory groups were crucial to understanding the pay-for-performance system whereby pay and performance ratings were significantly correlated at the supervisory unit level but not at the individual level.

Second, supervisory units can be characterized by (a) high variability within groups on both variables and (b) a significant correlation based on this source of variation, such that a subordinate who is high on leadership attention compared to the group's average is also given a relatively high performance rating. This is called a within-group configuration. At times, this configuration has been associated with the Leader-Member Exchange model (LMX) (Dansereau et al., 1984). (See Markham, Dansereau, Alutto, & Dumas, 1983, for an example of this effect in the leadership area.)

Third, it may well be that variables de-scribing the leadership exchange process are independent of supervisory groups. In other words, there may be important variance and covariance between and within units. In such a case, it would be faulty logic to state that both models mentioned are operating. Since they are mutually exclusive, it is more parsimonious to suggest that because the imposition of supervisory units as statistical cells does not help in understanding the configuration of the data, another level of analysis might be more powerful. Thus, this type of *equivocal* model might best be interpreted as a function of individual differences that could arise from the dyadic level of analysis in which high- and low-rated dyads are evenly scattered across supervisory groups.

A fourth and final model corresponds to the traditional null model. In this model, no statement can be made about configuration because no relationships can be found among the variables.

We do not imply that all leadership-performance appraisal processes are configured the same way and at the same level of analysis. Rather, different leadership processes may unfold at different levels of analysis, as noted by Schriesheim (1980).

> It makes little sense to see these approaches [average leadership style (ALS) and leader-member exchange (LMX)] . . . as mutually exclusive. It makes much more sense to study individual and group-directed leadership in combination and within a particular group context (p. 192).

While Graen, Liden, and Hoel (1982) found the LMX to be a better configuration than the more traditional ALS approach, Dansereau, Alutto, Markham, and Dumas (1982) found that these models, although distinct in terms of different variables, can operate on a simultaneous basis.

The empirical question, according to Dansereau et al. (1982), is whether a specifically identified nomological network of variables is more compatible with the

ALS model or with the LMX model. This study, therefore, tests the relationships among leadership attention, tenure with supervisor, and performance rating at both the individual level of analysis and at the supervisory-group level of analysis.

Methods

The research site for this study was a large transit authority located in the United States. This authority had over 5,000 employees; about 1,000 participated in the transit system's merit pay plan. Performance appraisal ratings and supervisory-group membership information were collected from the archival records of approximately 1,000 employees who participated in the plan. In conjunction with the collection of the archival data, approximately 800 employees completed a questionnaire designed to tap their attitudes toward the pay-for-performance system. Because employees were asked to identify themselves on the questionnaires in order to match their responses with archival records, confidentiality of information was stressed.

Subjects

Of the 1,000 employees on whom archival data were collected, approximately 455 provided identification numbers which could be matched with archival records in order to compile supervisory groups. These employees were embedded within 191 supervisory units. The age of the respondents ranged from 26 to 67 years, with an average of 44.25 years. Respondents had an average length of service of 12.6 years, with a range of 1 to 44 years. Of the respondents, 78% were male and 22% were female.

Measures

Leader-member exchange. The quality of the exchange between superior and subordinate was measured using a shortened version of the subordinate self-report scale previously used by Dansereau et al. (1984). The full scale has 11 items with a coefficient alpha (Cronbach, 1951) score of .92, while the shortened scale has 4 items with a satisfactory coefficient alpha of .88. The mean for this scale was 4.34, with a standard deviation of 1.38 and a range of responses from 1 to 6. It contained items such as "Assurance by my superior that he has confidence in my integrity, motivation, and ability."

Tenure with supervisor. Because previous research (Dansereau et al., 1975) suggests that the first year or two is critical in developing leader-member exchanges, we assigned subordinates to one of three categories. If subordinates had been with their supervisor 1 year or less, they were assigned a "1." About 43% of the respondents were in this category. If subordinates had been with their supervisor 1 to 2 years, they were assigned a "2." This category contained 28% of the respondents. If subordinates had been with their supervisor 3 or more years, they were assigned a "3." This category contained 29% of the respondents. The average for this variable was 1.86, with a standard deviation of .84.

Performance appraisal. The performance appraisal evaluation was an elaborate document comprised of separate supervisory ratings of the employee on work habits, task behaviors, and results. The supervisor was required to combine all of this information into an overall judgment of performance which was then used in conjunction with guide charts for the determination of individual pay increases. The actual performance appraisal rating was formally reviewed by upper management. For this study, the overall evaluation was used as the measure of performance level. The scaling, which was converted to a numeric system by assigning values of 1 through 5 to the performance levels, corresponded to "unsatisfactory," "needs improvement," "competent," "superior," and "outstanding," respectively. Overall mean score for the respondents was 3.65, with a standard deviation of 0.66 and a range from 2 to 5.

Data analysis procedure. Within and between analysis (WABA), derived from Dansereau et al. (1984) and utilized by Markham (1988) and Markham and McKee (1991), was the statistical technique employed for this study. This inferential/statistical method simultaneously examines sources of variation and covariation within and between supervisory units. This technique has been further utilized in drawing inferences within the leadership area by Dansereau et al. (1982) and Markham et al. (1983).

The logic behind WABA requires the explicit linking of a supervisory group with statistical cells in an ANOVA sense. To strongly infer an ideal entire group effect, we must demonstrate that (a) there are significant differences between groups on both variables, (b) the weighted unit averages of leadership attention correlate with the average unit scores on the performance appraisal rating, (c) the within-unit (or partial) correlations of the same variables are not significant, and (d) there is a significant difference between the correlation based on the unit averages (derived from between-unit differences) and the correlation based on within-unit differences (derived from individual deviation scores after between-unit differences were held constant).

In order to infer that a within-unit configuration exists, we must find that the within-unit correlation is significantly larger than zero and larger than the corresponding correlation based on weighted unit averages. An equivocal condition exists when both correlations are significant but not different from each other. A null condition exists when neither correlation is significant. For a complete explanation of this technique, see Dansereau et al. (1984).

Results

The results of aligning the supervisory units as statistical cells showed significant differences for *leadership attention* ($F = 1.33$; df = 190, 383; $R^2 = .57$, $p < .05$) and for *performance rating* ($F = 1.25$; df = 190, 383; $R^2 = .55$, $p < .05$). These initial results supported the notion of differences between groups. However, these differences might not covary. As shown in Figure 1, leadership attention was significantly related to the performance appraisal measure using the total correlation ($r_t = .26$, $p < .01$) based on an N of 383 individuals. Notice also in Figure 1 that the correlation based on group averages was significant ($r_b = .25$, $p < .01$ with J = 191 supervisory units), as was the within-unit correlation ($r_w = .26$, $p < .01$). It is tempting to infer that a clear, group-based effect had been identified. However, this inference cannot be made because of the significant within-unit correlation, which shows that individuals who reported high levels of leadership attention when compared to the group's average also received high performance appraisals. Thus, the most parsimonious interpretation of these data according to Dansereau et al. (1984) would be that the imposition of supervisory groups as statistical cells does not aid our understanding of the data. It appears that some version of an individual level of analysis best models the configuration of these data. This version could include either a dyadic model or a full individual model, both of which are lower levels of analysis than the supervisory work group. This equivocal condition can be interpreted by Dansereau et al. (1984) as an indication of the possibility that a level of analysis, such as

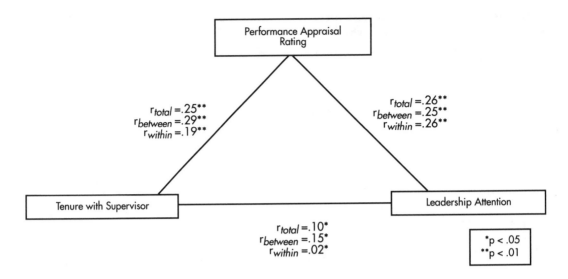

Figure 1 The configuration correlations for leadership attention, tenure with supervisor, and performance appraisal rating.

the dyad, should be investigated to obtain a clear configuration effect.

The inference regarding the relationship of *leadership attention* and *tenure with supervisor* is different from the preceding inference. In this case, as they did with leadership attention, the results of aligning the supervisory units as statistical cells also showed significant differences for tenure with supervisor (F = 1.92; df = 190, 383; R^2 = .64, p < .01). Figure 1 shows that the correlation based on group averages was significant (r_b = .15, p < .05 with J = 191 supervisory units). However, the within-unit correlation was not significant (r_w = .02, n.s.). We infer a weak between-unit condition in which groups that have, on average, a longer tenure with their supervisor also receive, on average, more attention. (This is a weak inference because the difference between r_b and r_w was marginal, using a Z test [Z = 1.26] to compare significant differences between the two correlations.)

The inference regarding the relationship of *performance appraisal* and *tenure with supervisor* also appears equivocal. This is reflected in the previously mentioned univariate 'F' test for significant differences

between units on these variables. Note in Figure 1 that the correlation based on group averages was also significant (r_b = .29, p < .01 with J = 191 supervisory units), as was the within-unit correlation (r_w = .19, p < .01). Thus, the individual correlation of r_t = .25, p < .01, representing the individual level of analysis, seemed the most parsimonious.

Post-hoc analysis. In order to shed more light on this network of variables, we investigated the possibility that the tenure variable might serve as a potential boundary condition. We identified three categories into which entire supervisory groups were placed: (a) those in which most of the members had been with their supervisor 1 year, (b) those who had been with their supervisor 2 years, and (c) those who had been with their supervisor 3 or more years. We then ran a one-way ANOVA on leadership attention and performance appraisal. The results are presented in Figure 2.

There was a significant difference in leadership attention received by subordinates across the three levels of time with supervisor (F = 3.71; df = 2, 383; p < .03). A Duncan's test (Miller, 1981) isolated this

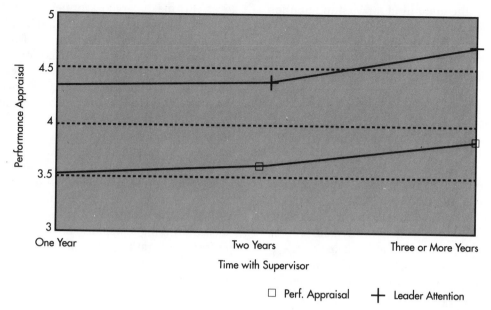

Figure 2 One-way ANOVA of time with supervisor on performance appraisal and leadership atten-tion.

effect to the most senior level. In other words, there was no detectable difference between the first-year subordinate's ($\bar{x}$ = 4.35) and second-year subordinate's ($\bar{x}$ = 4.38) reported levels of leadership attention. However, if the individuals in a group had remained with their supervisor 3 years or more, they received significantly higher levels of leadership attention ($\bar{x}$ = 4.71). Exactly the same pattern was found for the performance appraisal measure (overall F = 8.72; df = 2, 383; p < .0002). Subordinates in first-year supervisory groups ($\bar{x}$ = 3.52) and second-year supervisory groups ($\bar{x}$ = 3.61) had significantly lower performance appraisal ratings than did the third-year groups ($\bar{x}$ = 3.83). The difference between the first year and second year was nonsignificant.

Discussion

We can affirm the research question posed at the beginning of this paper: There appears to be evidence of the dual impact of leadership on performance appraisals,

despite the rather low magnitude of the bivariate correlations. Although research with a nomological network of variables using multiple regression could increase the amount of explained variance, variables must be used that operate at the same level of analysis (Dansereau et al., 1984).

The empirical results of this study provide evidence for two important themes. First, there is support for the basic notions from Murphy and Cleveland (1991) that leadership can have an impact upon performance ratings, a process which can be understood within the social-psychological framework of exchange theory.

Second, from an organizational-configuration perspective, the evidence suggests at least two different types of processes. In the "entire group" process, entire supervisory groups are characterized by their average tenure with their supervisor which is, in turn, correlated with the group's average amount of leadership attention. In the "individualized" process, supervisors appear to provide leadership attention to subordinates independently of their membership in the groups. In other words, the amount of leadership attention is a function of the individual employee's relationship with the subordinate, independent of membership in the work unit. At the same time, individuals with longer tenure with their supervisor also receive higher performance-appraisal scores. Surprisingly, the relationship between tenure and leadership attention appears to operate at a different level of analysis.

In conjunction with Markham's (1988) group-level findings, the identification of between-group phenomena for some of these variables invites speculation about the underlying leadership dynamics in organizations. For example, it may well be that supervisors engage in an exchange process with subordinates and that performance appraisal ratings are really a surrogate indicator of a superior's satisfaction with this relationship (Dansereau et al., 1984; Graen, Dansereau, Minami, & Cashman, 1973).

This model presupposes that the supervisor is in that role first and in some manner helps select or even recruit the subordinate. What happens when a new supervisor, through succession, inherits an entire group of incumbents? In such a case, the supervisor might deal with incumbents as an entire group to keep the group intact. It is conceivable that this process continues throughout the life of the group, even as new members are socialized into the group. Thus, it is possible that two different processes operate in mature groups.

While this exchange seems to be reflected in the performance appraisal scores, this process might unfold at the dyadic level. A study using matched superior-subordinate reports would be needed to determine if the dyadic level of analysis would best model the data.

Given the dearth of studies that have investigated the relationship between leadership and performance appraisal, these results are encouraging as a step into future studies of configuration. From an applied perspective, they also suggest (a) the use of the superior-subordinate dyad as a lever to make organizational improvements in performance and (b) the need to consider explicitly what types of configurations might result in maximum organizational-level performance. As organizations face dwindling capital resources in the 1990s, they must turn to their human capital for long-term increases in performance. The configuration of the leadership exchange process may well hold the key to understanding this effect.

In summary, this research has continued the effort to determine not only the key variables that comprise the nomological network linking leadership behaviors with performance ratings, but also the ways variables are configured around the structure of an organization.

Acknowledgments

We wish to thank Michael Vest and Beverly Little for their timely assistance. Funding was provided through the Barringer Research Center at Virginia Tech.

References

Cronbach, L. J. (1951). Coefficient alpha and the internal structure of tests. *Psychometrika, 16*, 297–334.

Dansereau, F., Alutto, J., Markham, S. E., & Dumas, M. (1982). Multiplexed supervision and leadership: An application of within and between analysis. In J. G. Hunt, U. Sekaran, & C. Schriesheim (Eds.), *Leadership: Beyond establishment views* (pp. 81–103). Carbondale, IL: Southern Illinois University Press.

Dansereau, F., Alutto, J., & Yammarino, F. (1984). *Theory testing in organizational behavior: The varient approach.* Englewood Cliffs, NJ: Prentice-Hall.

Dansereau, F., & Markham, S. E. (1987). Levels of analysis in personnel and human-resource management research. In K. M. Rowland & G. M. Ferris (Eds.), *Research in personnel and human resources management: A research annual* (pp. 1–50). Greenwich, CT: JAI Press.

Dansereau, F., Graen, G., & Haga, W. J. (1975). A vertical dyad linkage approach to leadership within formal organizations: A longitudinal investigation of the role-making process. *Organizational Behavior and Human Performance, 13*, 46–78.

Graen, G. B., Dansereau, F., Minami, T., & Cashman, J. (1973). Leadership behaviors as cues to performance evaluation. *Academy of Management Journal, 16*, 611–623.

Graen, G. B., Liden, R. C., & Hoel, W. (1982). Role of leadership in the employee withdrawal process. *Journal of Applied Psychology, 67*(6), 868–872.

Graen, G., & Schiemann, W. (1978). Leader-member agreement: A vertical dyad linkage approach. *Journal of Applied Psychology, 63*(2), 206–212.

Hills, F. (1979). The pay-for-performance dilemma. *Personnel, 56*(5), 23–31.

Hills, F. (1987). *Compensation decision making.* New York: Dryden.

Markham, S. E. (1988). Pay-for-performance dilemma revisited: Empirical example of the importance of group effects. *Journal of Applied Psychology, 73*(2), 172–180.

Markham, S. E., Dansereau, F., Jr., Alutto, J. A., & Dumas, M. (1983). Leadership convergence: An application of within and between analysis to validity. *Applied Psychological Measurement, 7*(1), 63–72.

Markham, S. E., & McKee, G. H. (1991). Declining organizational size and increasing unemployment rates: Predicting employee absenteeism from a within- and between-plant perspective. *Academy of Management Journal, 34*(4), 952–965.

Miller, R. G., Jr. (1981). *Simultaneous statistical inference.* New York: Springer-Verlag.

Murphy, K. R., & Cleveland, J. N. (1991). Performance appraisal: An organizational perspective. Boston, MA: Allyn & Bacon.

Pulakos, E. D., & Wexley, E. D. (1983). The relationship among perceptual similarity, sex, and performance ratings in manager-subordinate dyads. *Academy of Management Journal, 26*(4), 129–139.

Schriesheim, J. F. (1980). The social context of leader-subordinate relations: An investigation of the effects of group cohesiveness. *Journal of Applied Psychology, 65*(2), 183–194.

Wexley, K., & Pulakos, E. D. (1983). The effects of perceptual congruence and sex on subordinates' performance appraisals of their managers. *Academy of Management Journal, 26*(4), 666–676.

Steven E. Markham is Associate Professor in the Department of Management at Virginia Polytechnic Institute and State University. His research interests include leadership, gainsharing, team building, absenteeism, and the application of Within and Between Analysis to issues of organizational configuration.

William D. Murry is a PhD candidate and an Instructor at Virginia Polytechnic Institute and State University in the Department of Management. His research interests include leadership, performance appraisal, organizational culture, and the psychometric qualities of standardized personality assessment instruments.

K. Dow Scott is Associate Professor in the Department of Management at Virginia Polytechnic Institute and State University. His research interests include merit compensation plans, performance appraisal, absenteeism, and gainsharing.

Direct inquiries about this article to Steven E. Markham, Associate Professor, Department of Management, Virginia Polytechnic Institute and State University, Blacksburg, VA 24061–0233, 703/231–7381.

The Impact of Personality Characteristics on Leadership Effectiveness Ratings

Peter K. Hammerschmidt and Andrew C. Jennings

The findings are presented of a study of the relationship of specific personality characteristics to leadership effectiveness ratings. The dependent variables were two leadership effectiveness measures, the Leadership Style Indicator (LSI) and the Leadership Style and Influence subscale of the Management Skills Profile (MSP). The California Psychological Inventory (CPI), other personality measures, and biographical characteristics served as independent variables. It was found that (a) the LSI and the MSP were highly correlated, (b) specific scales on the CPI and biographical variables were related to leadership effectiveness, and (c) a leadership effectiveness profile could be constructed from the variables in this study.

The search for personality characteristics related to leadership is as old as the study of leadership itself. Indeed, prior to 1945, trait theories provided the primary avenue for the study of leadership. However, as demonstrated by situational leadership models, a trait considered positive in one situation could be a flaw in another. As a result, trait theories have offered few significant or consistent findings (Gibb, 1954; Stogdill, 1948). Jennings (1961) summarized trait research by concluding that "fifty years of study have failed to produce one personality trait or set of qualities that can be used to discriminate leaders and non-leaders" (p. 2). However, recent studies have renewed interest in personality characteristics by suggesting that "certain traits increase the likelihood that a leader will be effective, but they do not guarantee effectiveness, and the relative importance of the different traits is dependent upon the nature of the leadership situation" (Yukl, 1981, p. 70).

With this caution in mind, the present study attempts to determine which, if any, measurable personality characteristics are associated with leadership effectiveness as measured by peer, subordinate, and superior observers in the workplace using the Leadership Style Indicator (LSI) (Bailey, 1990) and the Leadership Style and Influence subsection of the Management

Skills Profile (MSP) (Personnel Decisions, Inc., 1985).

Most prior studies of trait theory are descriptive or observational with few attempts to quantify the relationship of these characteristics to leadership effectiveness in an objective fashion. Some notable exceptions include Kouzes and Posner's (1987) survey of 2,615 managers which revealed preferred leadership characteristics. Conversely, McCall and Lombardo (1983) found "fatal flaws" or missing characteristics that reduced leadership effectiveness. Finally, Gough (1990) found that CPI variables in the interpersonal domain were positively related to leadership.

The California Psychological Inventory (CPI) (Gough, 1957) has been used extensively to investigate the role of personality characteristics in leadership. The CPI measures 20 personality characteristics that attempt to give a psychological description of the person tested. A few of the 20 scales on the CPI are "Dominance," "Empathy," "Intellectual Efficiency," and "Tolerance." The goals for each of these measures are: "(1) to predict what people will say and do in specified contexts and (2) to identify individuals who will be evaluated and described in particular and interpersonally significant ways" (Gough, 1987, p. 4).

First, this study examines the relationship between the LSI and the MSP in leadership effectiveness ratings. Secondly, the LSI and the MSP are treated as dependent variables to determine if a relationship exists between certain personality and biographical characteristics. Finally, a leadership effectiveness profile is constructed from the independent variables used in the study.

Method

The participants in this study attended the Leadership Development Program at Eckerd College (LDPEC). The subjects were 187 mid- to upper-level managers who attended one of the 1-week sessions between January through June, 1990. This group was primarily white (93%), the average age was 42 years (68% were between 35 and 49), and 16% were female. Male/female differences were not examined in this study.

Procedure

The LSI is an evaluation instrument designed to be completed by subordinates who rate the leadership effectiveness of their "superiors." The subordinate selects up to 48 adjectives that apply to the superior being rated. The rater then determines whether the adjectives selected have a positive or negative influence on the rater. The number of positive adjectives is divided by the total number of adjectives selected to provide an overall leadership rating on a scale of 0–1. A score of 0 indicates that none of the total adjectives selected were positive; conversely, a score of 1 would indicate that all of the selected adjectives were positive. Therefore, the higher the score, the more favorable the leadership rating.

The MSP leadership score is based on ratings by peers, superiors, and subordinates combined in equal weight per category, not per person. The scores are based on a scale of 1–5, with 1 being a very low score and 5 being a very high score on the extent to which leadership skills are perceived by observers. Specifically, this score is designed to give feedback on the individual's effectiveness at "taking charge and initiating actions, directing the activities of individuals and groups toward the accomplishment of meaningful goals and commanding the attention and respect of others" (Personnel Decisions, Inc., 1985, p. 2).

The independent variables, which came from a variety of sources used at the Eckerd College Leadership Development Programs, primarily consisted of the 20 scales that comprise the CPI. Two additional instruments were used to gauge independently the influence of introversion/extroversion (I/E) on leadership. One variable was the introversion/extroversion measure of the Strong Campbell Interest Inventory (SII) (Strong, Campbell, & Hansen, 1985); the other was the introversion/extraversion measure provided by the Myers-Briggs Type Indicator® (MBTI™) (Myers & McCaulley, 1985).

The Kirton Inventory (K) (Kirton, 1976), a measure of a person's preference in defining and solving problems, was also included. Essentially, the Kirton measures how a person likes to use their creativity: High scorers are seen as innovative with a preference to do things "differently," whereas low scorers are adaptive with a preference to do things "better." The remaining independent variables were primarily biographical and included sex (S), educational level (ED), salary ($), and age (A). In functional form, LSI and MSP = f (CPI, I/E, K, S, ED, $, A).

Results

MSP and LSI Correlation Results

On 173 LSIs compared to 166 MSPs, a correlation coefficient of .49 was significant at the 99% confidence level. That is, managers who scored high on the LSI also tended to be rated high on the MSP.

Regression Results

Using the SPSS-X statistical package for the social sciences, linear, quadratic, and cubic regressions of the data were performed using all variables specified. The MSP and the LSI were treated as the dependent variables in separate equations. The stepwise function was em-

Myers-Briggs Type Indicator is a registered trademark of Consulting Psychologists Press, Inc.

MBTI is a trademark of Consulting Psychologists Press, Inc.

ployed to delete the less significant variables. The results of the best-fitting final MSP regression are illustrated in Table 1. The R^2 (Coefficient of Determination) value was .23, which means that 23% of the variance in the MSP can be explained by the full set of independent variables. The F statistic is 9.90, high enough to ensure a significant regression at the 95% confidence level.

Table 2 illustrates the best-fitting final regression with the LSI as the dependent variable. The R^2 for the MSP regression is much higher than that for the LSI, which has a coefficient of determination value of .06, indicating that only 6% of the variance in the LSI is predicted by the full set of independent variables. Again, the F statistic value of 5.010 is high enough to show a significant regression at the 95% confidence level.

Regression Conclusion

Overall, the entire set of independent variables did a better job of predicting the MSP than did the LSI. This held true for linear, as well as nonlinear, models. The MSP also illustrated a much higher correlation to several of the independent variables than did the LSI; most notably, Dominance (DO), Capacity for Status (CS), Educational Level (ED), Responsibility (RE), and Communality (CM). The MSP leadership rating exhibited a positive relationship with DO, ED, and RE and was inversely related to CS and CM in the best-fitting nonlinear model. It is not surprising to see a high positive relationship between DO and the MSP. High dominance indicates a willingness and ability to take charge in a group and act in a leadership capacity. Indeed, the dominance "scale was intended to measure dimensions of leadership ability" (Rodgers et al., 1983, p. 58) and appears to do so.

Also, the positive correlation of the Responsibility (RE) scale indicates that higher rated leaders are perceived as conscientious, socially responsible, and de-

TABLE 1 Nonlinear Regression of Leadership Data Using All Variables with the MSP as the Dependent Variable

$$MSP = 3.3869 + .0167 \text{ DO} - .00000208 \text{ (CS)}^3 + .052 \text{ ED}$$
$$(8.088)^a \qquad (4.657) \qquad (4.438) \qquad (1.911)$$
$$+ .0000012429 \text{ (RE)}^3 - .01311 \text{ CM}$$
$$(2.391) \qquad (2.032)$$
$$F \text{ statistic} = 9.90 \quad R^2 = .2307$$

Variables Remaining in the Equation: MSP—Management Skills Profile; DO—Dominance; CS—Capacity for Status; ED—Educational Level; RE—Responsibility; CM—Communality.

[a]Values in parentheses are t values

pendable. Moreover, the positive relationship to Educational Level (ED) may illustrate, to an extent, that education does what we want it to do: prepare leaders through providing better verbal, writing, and analytical skills.

It is interesting to note that, in all of the regression models, Capacity for Status (CS) was inversely related to leadership ratings. The purpose of the CS scale is "to serve as an index of an individual's capacity for status (not his actual or achieved status). The scale attempts to measure the personal qualities and attributes which lead to status" (Gough, 1975, p. 10). This is not to say that highly rated leaders rate low in CS (see Table 3), but rather that higher CS ratings are not likely to lead to increased leadership ratings.

The Communality (CM) score also exhibited an inverse relationship to leader-

ship ratings. This result is difficult to interpret since CM is primarily a validity scale in the CPI. However, it may suggest that perceived leaders have some traits that set them apart from how the "average" person answers the CPI; that is, leaders may be seen as being slightly different from others.

For comparative purposes, Table 3 provides an overall summary of the means and standard deviations of the low- and high-rated leadership scores as they pertain to the independent variables used in the study.

Discussion

This study investigated several key points regarding the measurement of leadership and the factors that may influence leadership effectiveness ratings. Findings indicate that the LSI and the MSP have a high degree of positive correlation in terms of leadership effectiveness ratings. However, the MSP was much more predictable in terms of its relationship to the CPI and certain biographical variables than was the LSI. This does not suggest that the MSP is a better measure of leadership than is the LSI, but it does indicate that it correlates more highly with certain psychological characteristics, such as Dominance and Responsibility. Overall, two key questions surface:

TABLE 2 Linear Regression of Leadership Data Using All Variables with the LSI as the Dependent Variable

$$LSI = .674425 + .0058 \text{ IE} - .00343 \text{ PY}$$
$$(6.773)^a \qquad (3.087) \qquad (2.073)$$
$$F \text{ statistic} = 5.010 \quad R^2 = .0569$$

Variables Remaining in the Equation: LSI—Leadership Style Indicator; IE—Intellectual Efficiency; PY—Psychological Mindedness.

[a]Values in parentheses are t scores

TABLE 3 Comparison of High and Low Scores on the MSP and LSI

Characteristics			LSI High/Low Comparison					MSP High/Low Comparison					
Indep. Means Variable	Total Sample N = (187)		Low Scores (L$_L$) LSI ≤ .6 N = 22		High Scores (H$_L$) LSI ≥ .93 N = 27		Dir. of Signif. Differ. Between LSI Means (t-test) (α = .05)	Low Scores (L$_M$) MSP ≤ 3.3 N = 19		High Scores (H$_M$) MSP ≥ 4.3 N = 27		Dir. of Signif. Differ. Between MSP (t-test) (α = .05)
	Mean	Std. Dev.	Mean	Std. Dev.	Mean	Std. Dev.		Mean	δ	Mean	δ	
DO	64.0	(9.0)	62.4	(8.4)	65.2	(8.1)	=	59.6	(10.6)	69.0	(7.0)	L$_M$ < H$_M$
CS	54.8	(7.4)	55.3	(8.2)	54.7	(5.0)	=	57.8	(7.1)	53.9	(5.7)	L$_M$ > H$_M$
SY	53.1	(7.8)	54.1	(8.4)	54.0	(8.0)	=	53.2	(8.4)	55.7	(6.6)	=
SP	52.9	(11.5)	53.5	(14.6)	52.4	(11.3)	=	53.5	(12.9)	52.6	(9.9)	=
SA	56.6	(8.6)	57.2	(10.1)	59.3	(5.2)	=	55.4	(10.2)	58.3	(6.4)	=
IN	58.4	(6.2)	58.8	(6.7)	59.3	(5.9)	=	54.8	(7.7)	59.9	(9.2)	=
EM	54.0	(9.5)	53.9	(9.5)	56.0	(8.5)	=	54.8	(9.7)	54.3	(9.2)	=
RE	55.8	(6.8)	54.6	(5.2)	57.6	(5.8)	=	53.8	(7.0)	58.6	(6.2)	L$_M$ < H$_M$
SO	54.6	(7.2)	51.6	(7.5)	55.4	(7.5)	=	50.9	(5.2)	56.6	(6.1)	L$_M$ < H$_M$
SC	53.6	(7.5)	52.2	(8.0)	54.5	(5.8)	=	52.8	(6.0)	55.2	(7.2)	=
GI	53.1	(7.4)	54.4	(7.2)	53.2	(5.8)	=	52.8	(6.5)	54.3	(8.0)	=
CM	55.6	(4.8)	54.3	(4.6)	56.6	(4.0)	=	54.5	(4.2)	54.1	(5.0)	=
WB	54.6	(7.6)	54.5	(6.6)	55.3	(6.2)	=	54.3	(7.0)	55.0	(6.3)	=
TO	56.2	(6.2)	55.4	(6.7)	56.8	(3.9)	=	56.2	(6.3)	57.6	(6.5)	=
AC	58.3	(6.2)	57.4	(5.6)	59.8	(7.2)	=	54.6	(7.2)	60.8	(6.0)	L$_M$ < H$_M$
AI	57.4	(5.5)	58.0	(6.0)	58.9	(4.4)	=	58.1	(6.0)	56.6	(5.6)	=
IE	53.3	(6.4)	50.5	(7.0)	55.4	(5.1)	L$_L$ < H$_L$	52.3	(7.1)	54.9	(6.0)	=
PY	56.1	(7.2)	56.5	(8.5)	57.1	(7.5)	=	56.9	(7.5)	56.9	(6.7)	=
FX	48.8	(9.2)	50.0	(9.3)	49.8	(9.7)	=	54.1	(9.1)	45.9	(10.5)	L$_M$ > H$_M$
FM	46.8	(9.3)	48.0	(13.5)	47.0	(7.0)	=	45.9	(7.6)	45.0	(7.5)	=
SII I/E	49.1	(10.6)	46.7	(10.6)	48.1	(9.7)	=	52.1	(12.5)	46.4	(12.4)	=
MBTI I/E	5.88	(24.1)	4.2	(21.7)	6.6	(20.3)	=	.6	(28.3)	.6	(21.0)	=
Sex	1.1	(.31)	1.1	(.4)	1.1	(.4)	=	1.1	(.3)	1.1	(.3)	=
Education	4.3	(1.2)	4.5	(1.2)	4.6	(1.3)	=	4.3	(1.5)	5.0	(.7)	L$_M$ < H$_M$
$ Salary	7.4	(2.6)	7.1	(2.4)	6.7	(1.5)	=	6.7	(2.1)	7.7	(2.0)	=
Age	42.4	(6.6)	41.2	(6.8)	41.7	(6.7)	=	42.3	(7.8)	46.0	(4.5)	L$_M$ < H$_M$
Kirton	103.5	(14.8)	103.5	(15.4)	101.5	(16.2)	=	107.4	(11.3)	106.1	(14.4)	=

First, why is the CPI a much better predictor of the MSP than it was of the LSI?, and second, why did so many of the independent variables which were selected have no significant relation to the MSP or the LSI?

One reason the MSP was better correlated with the CPI than was the LSI could be attributed to the observation of leadership skills in their managers by MSP raters, whereas the LSI raters often listed adjectives they wanted from their managers. That is, the MSP may give more insight into the person being rated while the LSI may actually provide more information on the values of the person doing the rating. Therefore, the MSP of the person being rated would be better correlated with his or her CPI than would the LSI. It should also be noted that the LSI respondents were usually subordinates, whereas the MSP respondents comprised the entire corporate hierarchy.

In response to the second question, one reason why so few variables seemed to be significant could be the nature of the group selected for this study. As noted earlier, this group, which consisted of primarily mid- to upper-level managers, may not have offered as much diversity as would a group from the general population.

In sum, the results of this study do not support the notion that personality characteristics are solely responsible for leadership effectiveness. However, it does suggest a profile of highly rated managers as leaders. This profile, which is appropriately dominant, is not necessarily one that pursues socioeconomic status but rather accepts or enjoys it as a by-product of leadership effectiveness. Further, the characteristics that emerge imply high responsibility and socialization into appropriate behavior, as demonstrated by agreement between the MSP and LSI. Intellectual efficiency, age, and education also play a role in leadership effectiveness. It is interesting to note that Introversion/Extroversion had no noticeable influence on any of the leadership effectiveness ratings. Further, creativity style had no measurable impact on leadership effectiveness.

The findings of the present study demonstrate that discrete scales of the CPI, coupled with particular biographical characteristics, are predictive of leadership effectiveness. Perhaps future studies should include a larger, more heterogeneous sample in an attempt to clarify the nature of the relationship between personality characteristics and leadership.

Acknowledgments

We would like to give special thanks to all who helped with this paper. Specifically, thanks to Mike Dillon for the help with EMACS, the text editor, and SPSS-X; Dr. Jeff Howard for his knowledge of SPSS-X; Dr. Walter Walker for his help with the nonlinear data manipulations; and all the people in the Eckerd College Management Development Institute for their help with the data collection. A very special thank you to Dr. Sal Capobianco for his insightful suggestions and helpful review of this paper.

References

Bailey, R. S. (1990). *Leadership Style Indicator*. Greensboro, NC: Center for Creative Leadership.

Gibb, C. A. (1954). Leadership. In G. Lindsey (Ed.), *Handbook of social psychology*. Cambridge, MA: Addison-Wesley.

Gough, H. G. (1957). *Manual for the California Psychological Inventory*. Palo Alto, CA: Consulting Psychologists Press.

Gough, H. G. (1987). *California Psychological Inventory: Administrators guide*. Palo Alto, CA: Consulting Psychologists Press.

Gough, H. G. (1990). Testing for leadership with the California Psychological Inventory. In K. E. Clark & M. B. Clark (Eds.), *Measures of leadership* (pp. 355–379). West Orange, NJ: Leadership Library of America.

Jago, A. G. (1982). Leadership: Perspectives in theory and research. *Management Science, 28,* 315–336.

Jennings, E. E. (1961). The anatomy of leadership. *Management of Personnel Quarterly,* 1(1), 2–9.

Kirton, M. J. (1976). Adaptors and innovators: A description and measure. *Journal of Applied Psychology, 61,* 695–698.

Kouzes, J. M., & Posner, B. Z. (1987). *The leadership challenge: How to get extraordinary things done in organizations.* San Francisco: Jossey-Bass.

McCall, M. W., Jr., & Lombardo, M. M. (1983, February). What makes a top executive? *Psychology Today,* pp. 26–31.

Myers, I. B., & McCaulley, M. H. (1985). *Manual: A guide to the development and use of the Myers-Briggs Type Indicator.* Palo Alto, CA: Consulting Psychologists Press.

Personnel Decisions, Inc. (1985). *Management Skills Profile/MSP: Definitions and development priorities.* Minneapolis, MN.

Rodgers, D. A., Webb, J. T., & McNamara, K. M. (1983). *Configural interpretations of the MMPI and CPI.* Columbus: Ohio Psychology Publishing.

Stogdill, R. M. (1948). Personal factors associated with leadership: A survey of the literature. *Journal of Psychology, 25,* 35–71.

Strong, E. K., Campbell, D. P., & Hansen, J. C. (1985). *Strong Campbell Interest Inventory.* Palo Alto, CA: Consulting Psychologists Press.

Yukl, G. A. (1981). *Leadership in organizations.* Englewood Cliffs, NJ: Prentice-Hall.

Peter K. Hammerschmidt is Professor of Economics at Eckerd College. Recognized in 1984 as the Robert A. Staub Distinguished Professor of the Year, he has been a developer, lead instructor, and researcher in several leadership programs sponsored by the Eckerd College Management Development Institute.

Andrew C. Jennings is a law student at the University of Washington. While at Eckerd College as an undergraduate, he was awarded a Ford Foundation Scholarship which provided the grant money for this research paper.

Direct inquiries about this article to Peter K. Hammerschmidt, Professor of Economics, Eckerd College, P.O. Box 12560, St. Petersburg, FL 33733, 813/867–1166.

The Impact of Leaders on Group and Intergroup Dynamics in Teleconferences between Interdependent Work Teams

Larry W. Penwell

This paper explores the impact of leaders on group and intergroup dynamics in audio-only teleconferences. The study compared audio-only teleconferences with leaders to teleconferences without leaders on group dynamics, intergroup competition, task performance, and participant satisfaction. The research is discussed in relation to work groups in exotic environments.

What impact does the leader have on individual and group interactions in teleconferencing? For many geographically distant yet interdependent work teams, teleconferencing is a primary means of communication and interaction. In large businesses, teleconferencing often supplements travel between different plant sites, and a growing portion of daily business decisions are made using teleconferencing technologies.

Various forms of teleconferencing exist, ranging from the transmission of the written word (e.g., computer conferencing or other forms of electronic mail) to full motion interactive audio-video conferences, where participants in one location can see and talk with participants at another location. Of these various forms, audio-only (voice) is the most accessible, the least expensive, and currently the most widely used form of teleconferencing (Dickey, 1986; Johansen, 1984).

In spite of the widespread use of these technologies, psychological investigations which compare the various forms of teleconferences suggest a variety of "costs" which may be associated with audio-only teleconferences that deserve attention. For example, research by Weston and his colleagues (Weston & Kristen, 1973; Weston, Kristen, & O'Connor, 1975) found that audio-only teleconferencing between small groups (three people at each of two sites) created significantly more intergroup conflict than did two-way full motion audio/video teleconferencing. In the audio-only teleconferences, almost all antagonistic remarks were directed at the other site, while in the audio/video mode, antagonistic remarks were as likely to be directed at participants at one's own site. Also, the use of "we" to refer to participants at one's own site and "you" to refer to participants at the other site was much more common in the audio-only condition than in the audio-video condition. Further, Weston's research found that task performance was significantly worse in the audio-only teleconference condition.

Additionally, site-dependent coalition formation (interpretable as a form of intergroup conflict) was found in a study of audio-only teleconferencing using only two subjects at each site (Williams, 1975). People at each site rated each other as more intelligent, constructive, competent, trustworthy, and sensible than they rated the participants at the "other" site. Conversely, the subjects rated participants at the other site as more impersonal, more boring, and more unreasonable than participants at their own site. Further, ideas generated by those at their own site were supported more often; they more often opposed ideas proposed by the other site.

An implication that can be drawn from these studies is that the medium may contribute to the development of intergroup conflict. There is also evidence from field studies to support this contention.

In hazardous and isolated environments, such as missions to outer space, Antarctic scientific missions, submarines, and mountain climbing expeditions, groups are often totally dependent upon telecommunications and teleconferencing as the means of communication with their distant support teams. Research and anec-dotal accounts suggest that a norm against outsiders (out-group discrimination) may emerge among group members in these exotic environments and that intergroup conflict between these isolated groups and their "outside" support team is inevitable (Bluth, 1981; Kanas, 1985, 1987; Oberg, 1981; Penwell, 1990). As in laboratory studies, there are many possible explanations for this emergent intergroup conflict. Two that have been proposed are displacement of intragroup hostilities (Kanas, 1985) and authority struggles between the leaders of the two groups (Bluth, 1981).

Coser (1966) argued that displacement of intragroup hostilities to an outside group occurred only when the group displays minimal cohesiveness. A repeated finding in studies of long-term missions in exotic environments is a gradual withdrawal by team members and an increase in interpersonal conflict, that is, decreased cohesiveness (Nicholas, 1987). Authority conflicts between leaders of space-based crews and ground control personnel have been documented (Bluth, 1979, 1981). Clearly, the communication medium may be one factor contributing to the evident intergroup conflicts.

Leaders and Intergroup Conflict

Pursuing Coser's (1966) argument about intragroup cohesiveness and the notion of unclear authority, Bekkers (1976) found that leaders in precarious leadership situations—when their intragroup authority was unclear—tend to exacerbate intergroup conflicts if they believe they stand a good chance of winning. This finding has historical antecedents. History has repeatedly shown that an external adversary presenting a perceived threat provides an excellent rallying point for group unification.

Intergroup competition or conflict may have some identifiable benefits for a group leader. For example, Schein (1978) noted that among the effects of intergroup conflict are increased intragroup cohesiveness, increased demand for conformity, and a shift from democratic to autocratic leadership.

Since previous studies of teleconferences did not differentiate roles, that is, no leader was present, and most applications of teleconferencing in business and in exotic environments exist in the context of an authority structure, the following research investigated the impact of introducing the role of a leader on group and intergroup dynamics, task performance, and participant satisfaction in two-site, audio-only teleconferences. It was designed as an analogue to a typical business use of audio-only teleconferencing between interdependent work teams and therefore is not a precise analogue to the use of audio-only teleconferences between groups in exotic environments and their support teams. However, some of the findings may still generalize to this situation.

Methods

A total of 27 conferences were conducted: 13 conferences without leaders and 14 conferences with leaders. A total of 309 students from the University of Cincinnati participated: 124 women and 185 men. Their ages ranged from 17 to 37, with a mean of 19.5 years.

The task was a modified version of Maier's (1973) new truck problem, a resource allocation problem that might be faced routinely in business. In the present version of this role-play exercise, two geographically distant work teams were asked to engage, via audio teleconferencing, in a resource allocation decision. Only one of the teams could receive the resource, a new truck. A set of voice activated intercoms was used as the teleconferencing system.

Except for the "leaders," all participants in both conditions were recruited for an experiment on "group problem solving"

and were randomly assigned to 1 of 12 roles. Each role, and therefore the participant assigned to that role, was assigned to one of the two different work teams, located in one of two different rooms.

For the conferences with leaders, the leaders were recruited separately for an experiment on "leadership training." They were given a minimal training experience just prior to the beginning of the problem-solving/decision-making exercise which consisted of reading two articles on leading meetings and the potential for intergroup conflict; they also were instructed to "collaborate." The only designation of authority evident to all conference participants in the with-leaders condition was that one of the roles in each group (titled "salesperson" in the without-leaders condition) was titled "salesperson/supervisor" in the with-leaders condition.

After the exercise, each subject completed a questionnaire that assessed her/his views of the relative friendliness, task orientation, and dominance of each of the roles during the exercise. The quality of solution, complexity of solution, and time to solution were used to measure task performance. Participants' satisfaction with the solution was assessed using a 5-point Likert scale.

Measures of Group and Intergroup Dynamics

The measures used to ascertain differences between conditions in participants' perceptions of the group and intergroup dynamics were constructed from Bales and Cohen's (1979) 26-item SYMLOG adjective rating scale. SYMLOG, the SYstematic Multiple Level Observation of Groups, is a system for the observation, measurement, and theoretical conceptualization of individual and interpersonal behavior in the context of a group of individuals. The SYMLOG system, based on a multiple-level field theory (Bales, 1985), includes: a three dimensional spatial model, two different behav-

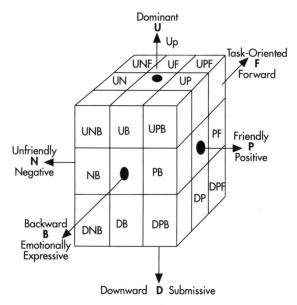

Figure 1 The SYMLOG cube diagram (adapted: from Bales & Cohen, 1979).

ioral measurement methods, and various data conversion and analysis tools for converting the measurements into useful data.

Figure 1 is a graphic representation of the SYMLOG space. The three bipolar dimensions that define the space are, in the parlance of the system, Up/Down (UD), Positive/Negative (PN), and Forward/ Backward (FB). Each dimension in the SYMLOG space represents some quality of human behavior that may be viewed as a continuous variable on a bipolar scale. The UD dimension represents the quality of behaviors that can be described as relatively dominant (Up) or relatively submissive (Down). The PN dimension represents the quality of behaviors that can be described as relatively friendly (Positive) or relatively unfriendly (Negative). The FB dimension represents the quality of behaviors that can be described as relatively task oriented (Forward) or relatively emotionally expressive (Backward).

Each participant retrospectively rated, on a 5-point Likert-type scale, the extent to which he/she and the other members of the conference had manifested the characteristics described in each of 26 items.

The individual items corresponded to 1 of 26 vectors in the three-dimensional SYMLOG space. This adjective rating scale approach requires no prior training for the individuals completing the ratings and has been shown to correlate highly with the more detailed interaction scoring method (Bales & Cohen, 1979). The scores produced by each of the participants in a given conference were combined in several different ways to produce the specific measures used to test the hypotheses regarding the participants' perceptions of group and intergroup dynamics.

Measures Derived from SYMLOG

The first measure was designed to test for differences between conditions in the overall ratings of total conference (group) dynamics. Average scores for each role were calculated in accord with the data synthesis methods prescribed by Bales and Cohen (1979) based on the ratings made of that role by all participants in a given conference. This yielded a "conference level" rating for each role on each of the three SYMLOG scales.

Two different measures were developed from the SYMLOG ratings to test the hypotheses regarding differences between conditions in intergroup discrimination. First, in accord with Bales and Cohen's (1979) method for synthesizing group ratings, the ratings by members of themselves at one site and of the other members at that same site were reduced to create an in-group rating on the three SYMLOG scales for each of the in-group roles. Next their ratings of the participants at the other site were reduced to create an out-group rating for each role on the three SYMLOG scales. From these two ratings on each of the three SYMLOG scales for every role, two intergroup measures were created.

The first intergroup measure ($Ingroup_{avg}$-$Outgroup_{avg}$) was designed to assess in-group bias and/or out-group discrimination. It was the absolute value of the differences between the average of the ratings summing across all of the in-group roles (average in-group) and the average of the ratings summing across all of the out-group roles (average out-group), on each of the SYMLOG scales in each conference.

The second intergroup measure (Role n $_{\text{In-Out}}$) was designed to assess the degree of differentiation of individuals in the out-group. It was the absolute value of the differences between the in-group rating of an individual role and the out-group rating of that same role, on each of the SYMLOG scales.

Results

The conferences were viewed from two different perspectives. The first perspective was to view each conference as a single group. The second perspective was to view each conference as two interacting groups.

Group (Conference) Dynamics

It was expected that participants in conferences with leaders would, on the average, rate themselves and others in their conferences higher than would the participants in the conferences without predesignated leaders on all three SYMLOG scales: Friendliness, Task-Orientation, and Dominance. ANOVAs were run on each SYMLOG scale independently (see Table 1). Participants in conferences with leaders were, on the average, rated as friendlier —but neither more task oriented nor more dominant— than the participants in conferences without leaders.

The variance among roles was greater in conferences with leaders than in the conferences without leaders on all three scales. This suggests that greater role differentiation occurred when leaders were present (see Table 2).

Intergroup Dynamics

The second perspective was to view the conferences as two interacting groups. Two different approaches to measuring intergroup dynamics were used in the present study: (a) in-group bias/out-group discrimination and (b) in-group/out-group differentiation.

In-group bias/out-group discrimination. According to numerous authors (see Tajfel, 1982), in intergroup conflict situations, the in-group is more likely to view its members as more desirable (in-group bias) and the members of the out-group as manifesting characteristics that are less desirable (out-group discrimination). Since the conferences with leaders were expected to be more secure as groups and therefore manifest relatively less intergroup conflict, the amount of in-group bias or out-group discrimination, as measured by the difference between the average in-group rating and the average out-group rating (Ingroup$_{\text{avg}}$-Outgroup$_{\text{avg}}$), was expected to be significantly less in conferences with leaders.

Contrary to these expectations, the differences between the average of the in-group ratings and the average of the out-group ratings were larger in the conferences with leaders than in the conferences without leaders on all three SYMLOG scales. In the case of the task-orientation (FB) scale, the apparent difference between the conditions proved to be statistically significant (see Table 3).

In-group/out-group differentiation. Since the conferences with leaders were expected to produce the least amount of intergroup conflict, they were also expected to more accurately differentiate individual roles in both the in-group and the out-group. Out-group ratings of a particular individual, in a given role, were expected to coincide more closely with the in-group's rating of that individual and thereby manifest the

TABLE 1 ANOVAs on SYMLOG's Friendliness (PN), Task-Orientation (FB), and Dominance (UD) Scales by Condition and Role

		SS	df	MS	F	p
Friendliness	Condition (C)	826.46	1	826.46	9.64	< .005
(PN)	Error	2142.46	25	85.70		
	Role (R)	110667.85	11	10060.71	96.77	< .0001
	RxC	8152.58	11	741.14	7.13	< .0001
	Error	28589.13	275	103.96		
Task =	Condition (C)	3.35	1	3.35	0.03	n.s.
Orientation	Error	2937.83	25	117.51		
(FB)	Role (R)	94371.44	11	8579.22	92.05	< .0001
	RxC	6695.14	11	608.65	6.53	< .0001
	Error	25630.83	275	93.20		
Dominance	Condition (C)	1217.59	1	1217.59	0.61	n.s.
(UD)	Error	50124.40	25	2004.98		
	Role (R)	25912.75	11	2355.70	41.72	< .0001
	RxC	1907.92	11	173.45	3.07	< .001
	Error	15529.12	275	56.47		

TABLE 2 Means & Standard Deviations of SYMLOG Measures across Roles by Scale and Condition; F Test Results for Differences between Variances on Each of the SYMLOG Scales

Scale		Without Leaders	With Leaders	F	p
Friendliness	M	3.96	7.16		
(PN)	SD	14.14	24.52	3.01	< .05
Task-	M	− 1.31	− 1.11		
Orientation (FB)	SD	13.22	22.51	2.90	< .05
Dominance	M	0.56	4.44		
(UD)	SD	6.92	11.82	2.92	< .05

smallest differences between the in-group's rating of a particular participant and the out-group's rating of that participant. To measure out-group differentiation, the difference between the in-group's rating of a role and the out-group's rating of that same role (Role n $_{In-Out}$) was calculated. Only on the dominance scale did the difference between an in-group's rating of a role and the out-group's rating of that role prove to be statistically smaller in conferences with leaders than in conferences without leaders (see Table 4).

TABLE 3 Means, Standard Deviations, and t-Test Results on Differences between Average In-Group Rating and Average Out-Group Rating by Condition for Each SYMLOG Scale

	Without Leaders		With Leaders				
	M	SD	M	SD	t	df	p
Friendliness (PN)	2.97	1.20	4.04	1.54	− 1.98	25	n.s.
Task-Orientation (FB)	3.33	1.70	5.75	1.37	− 4.10	25	< .001
Dominance (UD)	3.91	2.04	4.68	1.34	− 1.17	25	n.s.

TABLE 4 ANOVAs on Absolute Value of Differences between In-Group's Rating and Out-Group's Rating of the Same Role on Each of the SYMLOG Scales

		SS	df	MS	F	p
Friendliness (PN)	Condition (C)	532.69	1	532.69	0.6	n.s.
	Error	22378.62	25	895.14		
	Role (R)	8542.19	11	776.56	8.46	< .0001
	RxC	212.19	11	19.29	0.21	n.s.
	Error	25.83	275	91.77		
Task-Orientation (FB)	Condition (C)	961.95	1	961.95	1.58	n.s.
	Error	15188.82	25	607.55		
	Role (R)	6186.84	11	562.44	6.22	< .0001
	RxC	187.36	11	17.03	0.19	n.s.
	Error	24847.44	275	90.35		
Dominance (UD)	Condition (C)	21179.94	1	21179.90	6.74	< .05
	Error	78581.81	25	3143.27		
	Role (R)	1372.10	11	124.74	1.55	n.s.
	RxC	1251.84	11	113.80	1.41	n.s.
	Error	22171.47	275	80.62		

Task performance. Contrary to prediction, the conferences with leaders did not perform better than the conferences without leaders on the measures of quality of solution, complexity of solution, or time to solution.

Satisfaction. Also contrary to prediction, the conferences with leaders were not more satisfied with the decisions reached. Instead, groups that acquired the limited resource (a new truck) were consistently more satisfied with the decision than groups which did not receive a new truck, regardless of leader condition.

Discussion

From these results, it appears that although the leaders did not contribute to performance or satisfaction in the decision-making exercise, they did: (a) increase the perceived friendliness of the conferences, (b) increase role differentiation on all three SYMLOG dimensions, (c) increase agreement between the two sites on the relative dominance of each role, and (d) increase each site's perception that it was more task oriented than the other group. The first three findings support the contention that leaders may have reduced intergroup conflict; the fourth finding, however, suggests that leaders actually exacerbated in-group bias and possibly introduced a little "friendly" competition. Observation of the teleconferences suggested that, in both conditions, the two sites typically developed bargaining positions and gradually reached a negotiated solution. In all conferences, the initial position taken by each site was a competitive one. As is evident from the satisfaction scores, winning the new truck for the in-group was important.

There are several limitations to the present study as an analogue to a typical business application of audio-only teleconferencing. First, the subjects were all students with limited business experience, limited leadership experience, and limited investment in the actual outcome of the exercise. In addition, the exercise had no real-world consequences for the students, yet the degree of anger generated in a couple of the conferences was, frankly, quite surprising. Second, the "leaders" had limited real-world leadership experience, their authority in the exercise had been limited by design to a facilitating/helping role, and they had neither history nor future with the group.

Drawing analogies to groups in exotic environments is even more difficult. However, some conclusions can be drawn from this study which may generalize to teleconferences in any context: (a) It is useful to view interdependent work teams, using audio teleconferences as an intergroup event instead of as a single group event; (b) as such, they are susceptible to intergroup conflict; (c) leaders do not necessarily reduce intergroup conflict and may consciously or unconsciously increase it by introducing intergroup competition, even when instructed to collaborate; and (d) reading about the potential for intergroup conflict in teleconferences (making the unconscious conscious) is not sufficient to reduce competition between teleconferencing groups.

These findings suggest some possible prevention/intervention techniques. First, in situations involving interdependent work groups, both teams can be made aware of the probable occurrence of intergroup conflict. Training on group and intergroup dynamics might help members of both teams recognize and respond to emerging maladaptive facets of group and intergroup conflict.

Second, according to other studies (Weston & Kristen, 1973; Weston et al., 1975), televideo conferences produce less coalition formation and less in-group bias/out-group discrimination. Therefore, the use of televideo conferencing whenever possible and/or practical to increase the "social presence" (Short, Williams, & Christie, 1976) of the other team should diminish the probability of intergroup conflict disrupting a mission. Soviet efforts to use two-way video extensively in their space program may reflect their awareness of these problems with audio-only teleconferences (Oberg, 1981).

Third, careful analogue and "real life" studies of these interactions as intergroup events would increase our understanding and potentially our ability to diminish the negative effects of intergroup conflict.

Fourth, training leaders in intergroup dynamics and intergroup conflict-resolution methods might be useful. With the growth in this culture of decentralization of authority, Klein (1984) has noted the more general need to train leaders in intergroup dynamics.

Fifth, training the interdependent teams together should decrease the initial intergroup differentiations. An established history of collaborative relationships and similar experiences might prove useful if intergroup conflict begins to emerge.

Sixth, well-defined authority relations and mature, secure leaders may help diminish the probability of disruption of a mission by intergroup conflict. Although the leader condition in the present research was, by design, a minimal leadership condition, the role of leader did have some potentially positive effects. Research with real leaders might prove interesting.

Given experiences with groups in isolation, the critical role played by leaders in exotic environments, and the problems evident in the teleconferencing literature, the need seems evident for further research on the impact of group leaders on intergroup conflict. The adaptation of the SYMLOG system presented in this paper may be a useful tool for future studies.

Note

The research described in this paper was conducted as part of the author's dissertation at the University of Cincinnati.

References

Bales, R. F. (1985). The new field theory in social psychology. *International Journal of Small Group Research, 1*(1), 1–18.

Bales, R. F., & Cohen, S. P. (1979). *SYMLOG: A system for the multiple level observation of groups.* New York: Free Press.

Bekkers, F. (1976). A threatened leadership position and intergroup competition (A simulation exercise with three countries). *International Journal of Group Tensions, 6* (1–2), 67–94.

Bluth, B. J. (1979, September). The truth about the Skylab "revolt." *L-5 News,* p. 13.

Bluth, B. J. (1981). Soviet space stress. *Science 81, 2,* 30–35.

Coser, L. (1966). *The functions of social conflict.* Glencoe, IL: Free Press.

Dickey, S. (1986, July). Electronic meetings: Substitutes with substance. *Today's Office,* pp. 41–46.

Johansen, R. (1984). *Teleconferencing and beyond: Communication in the office of the future.* New York: McGraw-Hill.

Kanas, N. A. (1985). Psychosocial factors affecting simulated and actual space missions. *Aviation, Space and Environmental Medicine, 56,* 806–811.

Kanas, N. A. (1987). Psychological and interpersonal issues in space. *American Journal of Psychiatry, 144*(6), 807–809.

Klein, E. B. (1984). Group work: 1985 and 2001. *Journal for Specialists in Group Work, 10,* 108–111.

Maier, N. R. F. (1973). *Psychology in industrial organizations.* Boston: Houghton Mifflin.

Nicholas, J. M. (1987). Small groups in orbit: Group interaction and crew performance on Space Station. *Aviation, Space and Environmental Medicine, 58,* 1009–1013.

Oberg, J. E. (1981). *Red star in orbit.* New York: Random House.

Penwell, L. W. (1990). Problems of intergroup behavior in human spaceflight operations. *Journal of Spacecraft and Rockets, 27, 5,* 464–470.

Schein, E. H. (1978). Intergroup problems in organizations. In W. L. French, C. H. Bell, & R. A. Zawacki (Eds.), *Organizational development: Theory, practice and research* (pp. 80–84). Dallas, TX: Business Publications.

Short, J. A., Williams, E., & Christie, B. (1976). *The social psychology of teleconferencing.* London: Wiley.

Tajfel, H. (1982). Social psychology of intergroup relations. *Annual Review of Psychology, 33,* 1–39.

Weston, J. R., & Kristen, C. (1973). *Teleconferencing: A comparison of attitudes, uncer-*

tainty and interpersonal atmospheres in mediated and face to face group interaction — Report #1 (Contract No. OGR2–0152/0398). Ottawa, Canada: The Social Policy and Programs Branch of the Department of Communications.

Weston, J. R., Kristen, C., & O'Connor, S. (1975). *Teleconferencing: A comparison of group performance in mediated and face to face interaction — Report #3* (Contract No. OSU4–0072). Ottawa, Canada: The Social Policy and Programs Branch of the Department of Communications.

Williams, E. (1975). Coalition formation over telecommunications media. *European Journal of Social Psychology, 5,* 503–507.

Larry W. Penwell is on the faculty of the Psychology and Business Administration Departments at Mary Washington College. He worked previously in the aerospace industry as an Organizational Development and Change Consultant. He received his PhD from the University of Cincinnati.

Direct inquiries about this article to Larry W. Penwell, Assistant Professor, Department of Psychology, Mary Washington College, Fredericksburg, VA 22401–5358, 703/ 899–4595.

CHAPTER 40

The Impact of Personal Style on the Effectiveness of Latin American Executives

**T. Noel Osborn and
Diana B. Osborn**

Latin American executives participating in a leadership development program completed the Leadership Styles Inventory (LSI) as a measure of leadership effectiveness and the California Psychological Inventory (CPI) as a measure of personal style. Significant differences in personal style were noted between leaders who impact positively and negatively in their management environment.

Tecnología Administrativa Moderna (TEAM) has collected data on leadership and personality characteristics of personnel in Latin American organizations since 1982. Prior publications have dealt with comparative data on certain personality characteristics between Latin American and U.S. samples. Osborn and Osborn (1986) compared Myers-Briggs Type Indicator and FIRO-B profiles of mid-level managers. Osborn and Osborn (1990) added to this database a sample of 100 Mexican secretaries and administrative assistants. The comparisons resulted in a "profile" with combined management and support levels of Latin American and U.S. organizations.

Since 1984, TEAM has collected data on high-level Latin American executives. This total database sample consists of 282 managers who attended the Center for Creative Leadership's "Leadership Development Program" conducted in Spanish in Mexico.

Table 1 lists the demographics of this sample. They are principally executive to upper-middle level managers, largely Mexican but with representation from other countries. Nearly 90% are males, and the average age is about 40. The U.S. subgroup is principally expatriate Americans working in Latin America. Nearly all are employed in industrial and service companies, mostly U.S. subsidiaries, in Latin America.

The primary focus of the research reported here is on the effectiveness of Latin American executives, to distinguish between highly effective and less effective leaders in Latin American management contexts.

Methodology

The chosen measurement tool is the Leadership Style Indicator (LSI), a leadership effectiveness inventory developed by Robert Bailey at the Center for Creative Leadership. Developed out of the Ohio State models of task and relationship behaviors, the LSI uses a set of 48 adjectives to describe leadership behaviors as they impact on others, especially subordinates. Respondents are asked to indicate whether or not each of the 48 adjectives describes the subject's behavior in a leadership situation, and if so, whether or not the behavior positively or negatively affects the person's performance. Colleagues may also respond, as long as their responses are not mixed with those of subordinates. (A minimum of 3 in either category is required in order to produce a report.) The subject is also asked to respond to the 48 adjectives, so that a self-report on leadership effectiveness can be produced.

Thus, the output of the LSI is a "180 degree" feedback (or "270 degrees" if both colleagues and subordinates are reported) on how the leader is perceived by others, as compared to self-perception.[1] For the participant, the richness of the feedback comes from the behaviorally oriented adjectives and from a section of the report which suggests what the subject can change in his or her behavior to be more effective.

The LSI gives a measure of effectiveness of leadership style through the calculation of an "Overall Leadership Ratio" (OLR). The OLR results from dividing the sum of positively reported adjectives by

the total number of adjectives marked. The possible range, then, is from 1.00, indicating all adjectives were marked positively, to .00, indicating all were considered to have a negative impact.

The leader receives an overall global evaluation of the perception of his/her effectiveness regardless of the particular style(s) the individual is perceived to use, for example, more task or more relation-

TABLE 1 Biographical Data
Total Sample n = 282

	Mean	S.D.
Average Age	40.6	7.45
Age Range	23–61	

	n	%
# Men	251	89
# Women	31	11

Nationality

	n	%
Mexico	174	62
U.S.A.	18	6
Ecuador	9	4
Colombia	17	6
Puerto Rico	1	< 1
Guatemala	8	3
Peru	2	1
Argentina	10	4
Panama	14	5
Chile	3	1
Venezuela	3	1
Salvador	1	< 1
Costa Rica	4	1
Other	18	6
Total	282	100

Organizational Level	n	%
Top Level	23	8
Executive Level	111	39
Upper Middle Level	120	43
Middle Level	17	6
Other	11	4

TABLE 2   Biographical Data

	Group A			Group B		
	Most Effective $n = 43$			**Least Effective** $n = 46$		
Average Age	39.7			40.6		
SD	7.3			8.1		
Age Range	28–55			23–59		
	n	**%**		**n**	**%**	
# Men	36	84		43	93	
# Women	7	16		3	7	
Nationalities	**n**	**%**		**n**	**%**	
Mexico	29	68		24	53	
U.S.A.	3	7		5	11	
Ecuador	2	5		1	2	
Colombia	4	9		1	2	
Puerto Rico	1	2		—	—	
Guatemala	—	—		5	11	
Peru	—	—		—	—	
Argentina	1	2		4	9	
Panama	2	5		2	4	
Chile	—	—		1	2	
Venezuela	—	—		1	2	
Salvador	—	—		—	—	
Costa Rica	—	—		—	—	
Other	1	2		2	4	
	43	100		46	100	
Organizational Level	**n**	**%**		**n**	**%**	
Top Level	1	2		4	9	
Executive Level	15	35		21	46	
Upper Middle Level	22	51		17	37	
Middle Level	3	7		3	7	
Other	2	5		1	4	

ship. An OLR of above .60 is desirable, indicating that the impact of the leader is perceived as more positive than negative.

This sample had a distribution of OLR with a mean of .79 and a standard deviation of .12. The sample was divided into 3 groups: (a) Group A was considered a "positive impact" group with OLR at $\geq$ 1 s.d. above the mean, (b) Group B was a "negative impact" group with OLR at $\geq$ 1 s.d. below the mean, and (c) Group C was a "middling" group whose impact was seen as sometimes positive, sometimes not. Groups A and B, each of which included about 45 leaders (n_A = 43, n_B = 46), were focused on as more extreme clusters.

Table 2 lists the demographics for each of these two subgroups. The groups are

Subscale	Scores: Std.	Raw	SD
Dominance	62	33	4.9
Capacity for Status	54	21	3.8
Sociability	51	25	4.6
Social Presence	52	35	6.1
Self-Acceptance	55	21	3.2
Well-Being	49	37	4.7
Responsibility	50	31	4.4
Socialization	53	39	5.1
Self-Control	51	32	6.8
Tolerance	50	23	4.7
Good Impression	52	22	6.1
Communality	45	25	2.3
Ach. Conformity	53	29	4.4
Ach. Independence	52	20	3.8
Intel. Efficiency	46	38	5.3
Psych. Mindedness	55	13	2.7
Flexibility	45	7	3.9
Femininity	52	17	3.6

TABLE 3 California Psychological Inventory Data on Spanish Language Participants in the Leadership Development Program, 1984–1990: n = 282

scale interpretation of the CPI, see Gough (1968) or McAllister (1988).

CPI data were collected on all 282 Latin American executives. Table 3 projects the resulting measures. While there are some interesting differences, the profile is similar to that of U.S. executives who participated in the Center for Creative Leadership's executive development programs.

Of importance to this study is an examination of the CPI profiles for the "positive impact" (A) group as compared to the "negative impact" (B) group. Table 4 and Figure 1 indicate the differences in scores between the two groups. Statistically significant differences exist at the 95th percentile or higher on 12 of the 20 scales. "Successful" managers in Latin America scored significantly higher in Dominance, Sociability, Self-acceptance, Sense of Well-being, Responsibility, Socialization, Self-control, Tolerance, Good Impression, Achievement via Conformance, Intellectual Efficiency, and Femininity. As Figure 1 indicates, the curve for the 43 successful executives lies consistently above that of the 46 less-positively impacting executives except in Flexibility, which is not one of the significant differences[3].

Compatible results on CPI personality comparisons have been reported in research on groups in the U.S. In a study of 30 "highly successful" and 30 "less successful" U.S. executives, Rawls and Rawls (1974) found significant differences on 10 of the CPI scales. Four of their scales coincide with the findings of this study in the same (positive) direction: Dominance, Sociability, Self-acceptance, and Intellectual Efficiency. Two of their scales significant in the opposite direction are Self-control and Femininity; these were lower in Rawls' more successful groups and higher in the sample for this study.

In their study of "more effective" and "less effective" managers (n = 73 and 78, respectively), Mahoney, Jerdee, and Nash (1960) also identified characteristics which separated their groups. The one CPI scale that significantly discriminated was Dominance[4].

similar, with a slightly heavier (but not statistically significant) weighting of Mexicans in the "more effective" group.[2]

Results

What kinds of people are these positive and negative impacters? Are there differences in personal style between the two groups? Chosen for this analysis was a broad measuring instrument of inter- and intrapersonal function, the California Psychological Inventory (CPI). Originally developed in the 1950s by Harrison Gough and recently updated, the CPI provides a comprehensive view of overall personal profiles using 20 scales of personality measurement. For a scale-by-

TABLE 4 California Psychological Inventory Data on Spanish Language
Participants in the Leadership Development Program,
1984–1990

| | **Most Effective Mgrs.** | | | **Least Effective Mgrs.** | | | |
| | *n* = 43 | | | *n* = 46 | | | |
Subscale	Std	Raw	sd	Std	Raw	sd	p
Dominance	65	34.3	3.6	60	32.0	4.9	< .05
Capacity for Status	55	21.5	3.3	52	20.0	4.2	ns
Sociability	53	26.0	4.0	47	23.9	4.2	< .05
Social Presence	54	36.3	5.7	50	34.0	6.4	ns
Self-Acceptance	56	21.6	2.5	52	20.0	2.6	< .01
Well-Being	54	38.6	3.3	46	36.0	5.1	< .01
Responsibility	53	32.4	4.0	48	30.4	4.5	< .05
Socialization	58	41.2	3.4	52	38.0	5.1	< .01
Self-Control	54	34.0	6.1	49	30.4	7.1	< .05
Tolerance	51	23.9	4.1	47	21.7	5.2	< .05
Good Impression	57	24.1	5.9	50	20.4	6.2	< .01
Communality	48	24.7	1.3	46	24.6	2.0	ns
Ach. Conformance	57	31.0	3.9	49	27.4	4.1	< .01
Ach. Independence	53	20.2	3.3	51	19.2	3.7	ns
Intellec. Efficiency	50	39.6	3.8	44	36.5	5.2	< .01
Psych. Mindedness	56	12.8	2.0	54	12.2	2.7	ns
Flexibility	43	6.8	4.2	46	7.6	4.1	ns
Femininity	54	17.7	3.5	50	16.1	3.1	< .05

Conclusion

It appears that executives perceived as more successful in Latin America have an upward bias in the CPI towards more positive scores on most scales. Given the generally "positive bias" of the CPI, where higher scores are associated with more socially positive interpersonal and intrapersonal characteristics, it appears that more successful managers demonstrate to subordinates and colleagues a more positive set of personal styles. Latin American leaders appear to exhibit these styles in behaviors that elicit a more positive view of their leadership impact.

Considerable work has been done over the years on personality characteristics and leadership. Clark and Clark (1990) collected a summary of current attempts to measure leadership characteristics, especially in a U.S. context. Instruments such as the LSI and CPI may be appropriately used to predict successful leadership characteristics across cultural boundaries as well as in U.S. groups.

Acknowledgment

The authors wish to thank Liviere De la Vega for assistance in data preparation.

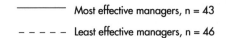

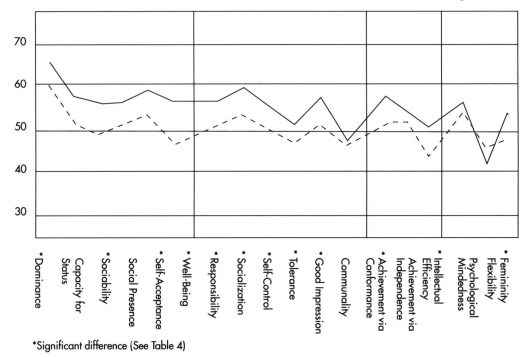

*Significant difference (See Table 4)

Figure 1 California Psychological Inventory data on Spanish language participants in the Leadership Development Program, 1984–1990.

Endnotes

1. A new version of the LSI also includes the possibility of including supervisors' viewpoints so that the output can be "360 degrees."

2. Although there are some differences in additional parameters such as age, gender, and organizational level between A and B groups, none was statistically significant. There were more women in the effective group, who tended to work at lower organizational levels; the total number of females in both groups is so small as to make comparisons inconclusive.

3. When men are separated from women in the sample, "A" men are significantly different from "B" men on the same scales as the combined groups, except for three: Sociability, Responsibility, and Tolerance. The women in the A and B samples showed more difference from each other on these three scales than did their male counterparts, thus affecting the statistics of the combined groups. In addition, there were significant differences for women on 3 further scales: Capacity for Status, Social Presence, and Achievement via Independence. However, A and B women did not differ significantly on Well-being, Self-control, and Good Impression. Conclusions on women are severely limited due to the small number in each group (N_A = 7, N_B = 3). More research is needed on the styles and impact of Latin American executive women.

4. However, another of their distinguishing variables was the (IQ) score on the Wonderlik Personnel Test. The A and B groups of this study had exactly the same score average on this instrument.

References

Clark, K. E., & Clark, M. B. (Eds.). (1990). *Measures of leadership*. West Orange, NJ: Leadership Library of America.

Gough, H. G. (1968). An interpreter's syllabus for the California Psychological Inventory. In Paul McReynolds (Ed.), *Advances in Psychological Assessment* (Vol. 1, pp. 55–79). Palo Alto, CA: Science & Behavior Books.

Mahoney, T. A., Jerdee, T. N., & Nash, A. N. (1960). Predicting managerial effectiveness. *Personnel Psychology, 13*, 147–163.

McAllister, L. W. (1988). *A practical guide to CPI interpretation* (2nd ed.). Palo Alto, CA: Consulting Psychologists Press.

Osborn, T. N., & Osborn, D. B. (1986). Leadership training in a Latin context. *Issues & Observations, 6*(2). Greensboro, NC: Center for Creative Leadership.

Osborn, T. N., & Osborn, D. B. (1990). Leadership in Latin American organizations: A glimpse of style through personality measures. In K. E. Clark & M. B. Clark (Eds.), *Measures of leadership* (pp. 449–454). West Orange, NJ: Leadership Library of America.

Rawls, J. R., & Rawls, D. J. (1974). Toward earlier identification and development of managerial success. *Psychological Reports, 35*, 819–822.

T. Noel Osborn is President of TEAM, S.C. Twice a Fulbright grantee to Mexico, he became a tenured Professor at the Business College of the National University of Mexico (UNAM) and was later Director (Dean) of the Mexico Campus of U.S. International University. He holds a PhD in Economics from the University of Colorado-Boulder.

Diana B. (Dede) Osborn is a founding partner of TEAM, S.C. and Director of the Leadership Development Program in San Antonio, TX. She has an M.A. in Clinical Psychology and is responsible for program design, training, and research in TEAM's programs both in Latin America and the U.S.

Direct inquiries about this article to T. Noel Osborn, President, TEAM, S.C., 14206 Arbor Oak, San Antonio, TX 78249, 512/493–1452.

The Impact of Institutional Financial Performance on Executive Succession in Higher Education

Patricia K. Fullagar

The relationship between institutional financial performance and presidential succession in U.S. colleges and universities was studied for a large national sample of institutions for the period 1980 to 1988. The higher education sector was selected because (a) it contains a large population of organizations with relatively similar characteristics on which data are collected annually, (b) the succession question is less well studied in this sector than in the corporate sector, and (c) perceptions of college and university presidents support the importance of examining financial factors relative to executive succession.

Financial performance of institutions experiencing succession were statistically compared to those that did not have such an occurrence. Results indicated that financial performance was differentially related to presidential succession by type of college or university.

Results suggest that the antecedents of presidential succession are less straightforward than in the corporate or athletic sectors where the bottom line of profits or winnings are clear determinants.

The conventional view of the relationship between U.S. colleges and universities and their presidents is that institutions of higher education remain relatively unchanged as their presidents are replaced (Birnbaum, 1989; Cohen & March, 1986). Only recently has the reverse been studied (Anderson, 1989): Are presidents replaced when institutional performance changes?

Despite recent emphasis in the higher education literature on relationships between institutional performance and effectiveness (Cameron, Whetten, Kim, & Chaffee, 1987; Chaffee, 1984; Parker & Zammuto, 1986), the relationship between organizational performance and executive leadership has received relatively little attention in higher education empirical research. This relationship is particularly intriguing, however, and is studied extensively in other sectors of society. Succession of an executive provides a specific point in time before and after which various organizational characteristics, including organizational performance, can be observed and measured. Moreover, an understanding of factors related to executive succession can be helpful to successors as they seek to formulate and implement effective organizational strategy. The study reported here sought to (a) extend empirical research on this relationship in the higher education sector by employing a large national sample of colleges and universities and (b) focus on parameters related to the measurement and interpretation of institutional performance with recommendations for future research.

Background: Executive Leadership

Earlier works, such as Cohen and March's (1986) seminal exploration of the university presidency, *Leadership and Ambiguity*, described presidents as interchangeable as light bulbs. More recently, Birnbaum (1989) examined the consequences on institutional performance of presidential succession in higher education and concluded that presidents had little, if any, impact on institutional performance. Yet elsewhere, university presidents are described as making significant differences in such diverse areas as acquisition of resources (e.g., monetary gains, capital gifts, faculty hires) and definition of institutional mission (Chaffee, 1984; Kerr & Gade, 1986). Burton Clark's (1970) *The Distinctive College* contributed immeasurably to higher education literature with rich descriptions of dramatic changes in three colleges, each under the leadership of a forceful president. Inconsistencies among the findings and perceptions in the study of the organizational and leadership behavior of the higher education sector may reflect the lack of an extensive and cumulative empirical base (Cameron, Kim, & Whetten, 1988).

Context: Institutional Performance

There are many measures of institutional performance in higher education. Among them are quality of faculty and students, levels of faculty scholarship and research, financial health of the institution, and enrollment patterns of students. In recent years, empirical research that focused on institutional performance in higher education relied heavily on financial and enrollment factors (Anderson, 1985; Cameron, Kim, & Whetten, 1987; Milliken, 1990; Parker & Zammuto, 1986). Indeed, no less a scholar of higher education than Robert Maynard Hutchins (1963) argued that there was an inextricable link between the financial health of an institution and effectiveness in all realms, including scholarship and instruction. Recent empirical research by Anderson (1985) demonstrated that this link was questionable, but his findings did suggest that institutional financial health had profound implications for actions and behaviors of administrators, including presidents. Moreover, surveys of college and university presidents (Cole, 1976; Cote, 1985) indicated the importance of financial factors on the presidency in higher education. Cote's (1985) research examined the importance for presidents of 20 roles that ranged from articulating the institutional vision to being an overseer of the physical plant and a specialist for labor relations. He found that 2 financial roles, fund raiser and financial manager, ranked fourth and fifth, respectively, out of the total of 20. Only the roles of articulating an institutional vision, maintaining rapport with trustees, and being a public relations specialist ranked higher in importance for presidents. In his study of the "reeling presidency," Cole found that institutional financial exigencies accounted for 60% of the reasons given by presidents for their resignation. Indeed, Cole found that poor financial health, as well as the relative state of declining financial health, became overwhelming preoccupations among college and university presidents.

The present study examined the relationship between institutional financial performance and presidential succession. Moreover, it examined the relationship directly, rather than through the perceptions of presidents or third-party observers that might be obtained through surveys or interviews.

The higher education sector in the United States was selected for this study for several reasons. It contains a large population of organizations with relatively similar characteristics. The Higher Education General Information Survey (HEGIS) (1981, 1982, 1983, 1984, 1985, 1986) provides data on numerous variables from all organizations in this population. Since they extend back in time over many years, these data permit longitudinal analysis. Additionally, the HEGIS data bank is available in electronic format suitable for extensive analysis through appropriate statistical computer software programs (e.g., SAS, SPSS-X). The higher education sector provides a well-established structural framework that divides colleges and universities by organizational control (i.e., public and private) and function (i.e., research universities, doctorate-granting universities, comprehensive universities, and liberal arts colleges). In recent years, empirical literature has focused on the organizational performance of this population and the turbulence of its environment (Anderson, 1985; Anderson, 1989; Baltes, 1988; Birnbaum, 1989; Cameron, Kim, & Whetten, 1987; Cameron, Whetten, Kim, & Chaffee, 1987; Parker & Zammuto, 1986; Rusk, Leslie, & Brinkman, 1982; Zammuto, 1986). The relationship between organizational performance in higher education and leadership, however, has not been studied in a comprehensive manner within the empirical literature.

The context for the study was the population of colleges and universities that grant at least the baccalaureate degree and included those that grant advanced degrees, such as the masters and doctorate degrees. Excluded were community, technical, and junior colleges and highly specialized institutions, such as theological seminaries and music schools. This distinction parallels earlier studies that measured organization performance in higher

education (Anderson, 1985; Cameron, Kim, & Whetten, 1987).

Method

Data

All institutions that grant at least the baccalaureate degree (N = 1365) were examined to determine (a) whether presidential successions occurred between the academic years 1980–1981 through 1985–1986 and (b) whether complete sets of revenue data were available. Succession was defined as a change in the individual who held the office of an institution's chief administrative or executive position, whether that office was titled president, chancellor, headmaster, or otherwise designated. In this study, the term "president" is used exclusively to refer to this primary administrative office. Institutional performance in this study was measured using revenue data collected annually by the U.S. Department of Education through the Higher Education General Information Survey (HEGIS) (1981, 1982, 1983, 1984, 1985, 1986). Revenue was defined as the total, aggregated, annual income from all sources for each institution. All revenue figures were converted to 1967-constant-dollars prior to computing annual percent change for each institution. As is the practice in the empirical literature, annual percent changes in revenue, rather than actual revenue, were used in the analyses (Cameron, Kim, & Whetten, 1987).

Institutions with incomplete HEGIS revenue data (n = 10), and those experiencing presidential succession during the time period from 1980–1981 through 1985–1986 (n = 646), were excluded from this study. In measuring revenue trends, previous researchers noted the importance of establishing time periods of sufficient length for patterns of development (e.g., growth, decline, stability) to be apparent to the institution, its leadership, and outside evaluators (Anderson, 1985; Cameron, Kim, & Whetten, 1987; Parker & Zammuto, 1986; Rusk, Leslie, & Brinkman, 1982). Time periods of at least 5 consecutive years were recommended and used by these researchers. Therefore, exclusion of the institutions experiencing succession during the interim in which organizational performance was measured (1980–1981 through 1985–1986) was necessary in order to establish performance trends over multiyear periods in a consistent manner that would not confound the results (Anderson, 1985; Cameron, Kim, & Whetten, 1987; Parker & Zammuto, 1986; Rusk, Leslie, & Brinkman, 1982).

The remaining institutions were examined for occurrence of presidential succession during either of the academic years 1986–1987 or 1987–1988. Those that experienced succession during either year were screened to determine if the cause of succession was due to either death or retirement (n = 72). These were dropped; inclusion of successions that occurred as a function of time or life expectancy (i.e., retirement or death) would confound results of a study designed to examine succession as a function of organizational performance.

Rather than using a much shorter period (e.g., only those successions occurring once during the summer or fall of 1986), succession was measured once during the 2-year time period of 1986–1987 or 1987–1988. Institutions of higher education, thought to be more protected from immediate environmental impacts than are many other types of institutions or businesses (Blau, 1973), may take longer to react to change than those with a "bottom-line" or clear record of team winnings. Such a long period of time increased risks that could confound the results (e.g., multiple successions); each institution was screened carefully in an effort to avoid this possibility.

Institutions remaining in this study (see Table 1), and therefore included in the analyses which follow, constituted the population of U.S. colleges and universities (n = 637) that met the following characteristics:

1. Complete HEGIS revenue data, and

2. Either no presidential succession between the academic years 1980–1981 through 1985–1986 or presidential succession due to reasons other than death or retirement during 1986–1987 or 1987–1988 (i.e, succession group, n = 112), or

3. No presidential succession between the academic years 1980–1981 through 1987–1988 (i.e., non-succession group, n = 525).

The listing of colleges and universities maintained by the Carnegie Commission on Higher Education (Carnegie Foundation, 1987) is categorized by institutional control and institutional function or mission. Control refers to the institution's public or private status. Function distinguishes between those institutions that grant doctorate degrees (research universities, plus doctorate-granting universities) and those that do not (comprehensive universities and liberal arts colleges). These distinctions were used in this study. Indeed, one purpose of the study was to determine if there were differences by institutional type (control and function) in the relationship between performance and succession.

Research Design

Use of multiple regression analysis with succession as the dependent variable and institutional performance data (i.e., percent change in revenue across 5 consecutive years) as independent variables formed the model. Type I sums of squares (SAS, 1985) was used because of the temporal nature of the financial variables.

A significant strength of this approach was that it permitted exploration of the influence of performance and structure

TABLE 1 U.S. Colleges and Universities: Adjusted Population, 1988

Institutional Function	Institutional Control		
	Public	Private	Total
Doctorate-Granting	51	40	91
Nondoctorate-Granting	152	394	546
Total	203	434	637

year by year through examination of individual sums of squares and correlations. Earlier studies that advocated use of longitudinal models (Cameron, Kim, & Whetten, 1987; Parker & Zammuto, 1986) did not report empirical evidence of the significance of the overall 5-year time period, nor of the intervening years. The present study examined the significance of the relationship between percent change in revenue and succession for each year in the analysis for all the institutions experiencing succession.

Results

Public Colleges and Universities

Noting Type I sums of squares, the full 5-year time period was necessary for emergence of a statistically significant relationship between revenue change and succession in public universities (see Table 2, Revenue 1981). Furthermore, the zero-order correlation between succession and revenue change was significant and positive at the fifth year prior to succession. This finding suggested that public institutions that experienced executive succession tended to experience greater financial growth than those that did not experience succession.

Private Colleges and Universities

Type I sums of squares for this regression analysis indicated a statistically significant relationship between revenue and succession in the year closest to succession (see Table 3, Revenue 1985). In addition, the correlation between succession and revenue for the year closest to succession was negative and significant. In private colleges and universities, therefore, results suggested a relationship between revenue decline and presidential succession and that this relationship may develop relatively quickly.

Doctorate-Granting Colleges and Universities

Revenue changes and presidential succession were not statistically related for this group of institutions.

Nondoctorate-Granting Colleges and Universities

Results of testing the relationship between revenue performance and succession were significant ($p < .05$), and examination of Type I sums of squares suggested that the first 2 years prior to succession were critical (see Table 4). Furthermore, similar to the analysis of private colleges and universities reported in Table 3, zero-order correlations suggested

TABLE 2   Succession and Revenue Change in Public Institutions

Multiple Regression: [R² = .05, F(5,197) = 1.99, p < .10]

Source	SSI	df	F	r
Revenue 1985	0.00	1	0.00	− .00
Revenue 1984	0.36	1	2.54	− .09
Revenue 1983	0.00	1	0.03	− .01
Revenue 1982	0.01	1	0.08	− .00
Revenue 1981	1.04	1	7.31*	.20*

*p < .01

TABLE 3   Succession and Revenue Change in Private Institutions

Multiple Regression: [R² = .02, F(5,28) = 1.54, p < .10]

Source	SSI	df	F	r
Revenue 1985	0.75	1	5.21*	− .10*
Revenue 1984	0.17	1	1.21	− .07
Revenue 1983	0.16	1	1.11	− .04
Revenue 1982	0.01	1	0.11	− .03
Revenue 1981	0.00	1	0.05	.00

*p < .05

TABLE 4   Succession and Revenue Change in Nondoctorate-Granting Institutions

Multiple Regression: [R² = .02, F(5,540) = 2.54, p < .05]

Source	SSI	df	F	r
Revenue 1985	0.83	1	5.86**	− .10**
Revenue 1984	0.53	1	3.74*	− .08*
Revenue 1983	0.22	1	1.55	− .04
Revenue 1982	0.05	1	0.39	− .03
Revenue 1981	0.16	1	1.15	.04

*p < .05.   **p < .01.

that nondoctorate granting institutions that had less growth in these years were more likely to experience presidential succession than were those with greater growth.

Summary of Results

In two of the four categories of higher education institutions (i.e., private and nondoctorate-granting) results were in the direction expected: Revenue decline, in private as well as nondoctorate-granting institutions, appeared to be related to executive succession. In each of these groups, however, the relationship occurred in the period immediately prior to succession rather than requiring the predicted longer period of 5 years (see Tables 3 and 4).

Relationships between performance and succession in public colleges and universities, on the other hand, were in marked contrast to those in private and nondoctorate-granting institutions. In public institutions, the correlation between revenue and presidential succession suggested that growth, not decline, occurring 5 years previously was significant (see Table 2). The time period required for a discernible trend leading to a statistically significant relationship was predicted; not anticipated was the positive direction of revenue change.

Discussion

A primary implication of this study was that antecedent effects on subsequent presidential succession should not be generalized either across sectors of organizations (e.g., corporate, athletic, and education) or across different types of institutions within the higher education sector. Research results from other sectors (e.g., athletic and corporate) clearly indicate that performance decline is associated with subsequent executive succession. An assumption prior to this study was that this would hold true in the higher education sector as well. However, in this national study of higher education institutions, results were mixed.

In two categories of institutions, nondoctorate-granting and private, results quite closely paralleled the corporate sector. In these two instances, not only was revenue decline related to succession as predicted, but the decline occurred just prior to succession, rather than 5 years before. Moreover, the relationship between revenue performance and succession in private institutions became progressively weaker with greater intervals of time (see Table 4). Examination of the types of institutions that constitute these two groups may provide insight into this unexpected finding. Nondoctorate-granting colleges and universities, as well as those that are private, are dominated by liberal arts colleges (44% and 55%, respectively). Many of these institutions have very little financial slack and thus may be far more responsive to the exigencies created by resource scarcity than previously thought (Blau, 1973). Therefore, decline, even of a modest nature, may have immediate and profound effects resulting in patterns that closely mirror the corporate sector. And, indeed, the lack of a statistically significant relationship between organizational performance and executive succession in the most complex of all higher education institutions (Blau, 1973), those that are doctorate-granting, lends credence to the possibility that presidents may be more closely associated with institutional financial performance in small colleges and universities than in institutions that are larger or more complex.

In the category of public institutions, where revenue growth signaled executive succession, comprehensive universities comprised 61% of the total. In this group, the relation of growth, rather than decline, to presidential succession can be examined through multiple perspectives. Revenue growth, for instance, may present new opportunities that affect institutional purpose or mission. Comprehensive universities experiencing pecuniary largess may seek to expand their facilities and programs to include doctorate-granting programs. Since the president is symbolically the embodiment of organizational mission and purpose (Birnbaum, 1989), such growth may signal a need for leadership change (e.g., a president familiar with research programs).

The presidency itself is another perspective through which to explore this unexpected finding. Presidents associated with performance growth are considered successful by others, as well as by themselves. Such persons likely are in high demand and may receive offers from other institutions in higher education, or even from other sectors. It is estimated, for instance, that 25% of those presidents who resign each year go to other sectors, such as private corporations, foundations, or research units, or to federal or state government service (Kerr & Gade, 1986).

Conclusion

This study represented a comprehensive examination of revenue performance antecedent to presidential succession in U.S. colleges and universities. Major strengths included its utilization of the population of U.S. colleges and universities that grant at least the baccalaureate degree and its longitudinal approach, with results reported by chronological sequence. Although other researchers have reported results using longitudinal performance measures, there had been no report of the relative significance of different years. Results from this study suggest that performance measures may be differentially significant depending on institutional control and function.

The total aggregated revenue in this study never accounted for more than 5% of the variance in succession (see Tables 2, 3, and 4). Future research might consider disaggregating revenue items. The relationship between forms of revenue under more direct purview of presidents (e.g., gifts and endowments) might provide a more valid test of the logic of studies that examine the interaction between financial performance of institutions and the leadership of those institutions. Such a study might produce greater variations among succession and nonsuccession groups as well as among public and private, or doctorate-granting and nondoctorate-granting, institutions.

The perceptions of college and university presidents support the importance of including financial factors (Cole, 1976; Cote, 1985) when defining institutional performance. The results of this study support the reality that there are many factors that define institutional performance in higher education. Financial health is but one factor that can influence presidential actions, including succession. For governing boards, presidents, and their institutions of higher education, these results suggest that antecedents of presidential succession are less straightforward than in the corporate or athletic sectors where the bottom line of profits or winnings are clear determinants.

References

Anderson, K. S. (1989). Turnover in the top organizational position: A sociological analysis (Doctoral dissertation, University of Nebraska, 1988). *Dissertation Abstracts International, 49*(8).

Anderson, R. E. (1985). Does money matter? *Journal of Higher Education, 56,* 623–639.

Baltes, P. C. (1988). Fiscal stress and implications for planning. *Planning for Higher Education, 16,* 3–18.

Birnbaum, R. (1989). Presidential succession and institutional functioning in higher education. *Journal of Higher Education, 60,* 123–135.

Blau, P. M. (1973). *The organization of academic work.* New York: John Wiley.

Cameron, K. S., Kim, M. U., & Whetten, D. A. (1987). Organizational effects of decline and turbulence. *Administrative Science Quarterly, 32*, 222–240.

Cameron, K. S., Kim, M. U., & Whetten, D. A. (1988). Organizational effects of decline and turbulence. In K. S. Cameron, R. I. Sutton, & D. A. Whetten (Eds.), *Readings in organizational decline: Frameworks, research, and prescriptions.* Cambridge, MA: Ballinger.

Cameron, K. S., Whetten, D. A., Kim, M. U., & Chaffee, E. E. (1987). The aftermath of decline. *The Review of Higher Education, 10*, 215–234.

Carnegie Foundation. (1987). *A classification of institutions of higher education* (Technical Report). Princeton, NJ: The Carnegie Foundation for the Advancement of Teaching.

Chaffee, E. E. (1984). Successful strategic management in small private colleges. *Journal of Higher Education, 55*, 212–241.

Clark, B. R. (1970). *The distinctive college: Antioch, Reed, and Swarthmore.* Chicago: Aldine.

Cohen, M. D., & March, J. G. (1986). *Leadership and ambiguity: The American college president* (2nd ed.). Boston: Harvard Business School Press.

Cole, C. C., Jr. (1976). Reeling of the presidency. *Educational Record, 57*, 71–78.

Cote, L. S. (1985). The relative importance of presidential roles. *Journal of Higher Education, 56*, 664–676.

Higher Education General Information Survey. (1981, 1982, 1983, 1984, 1985, 1986). *Financial statistics of institutions of higher education for fiscal year ending 1981 (1982, 1983, 1984, 1985, 1986).* Washington, DC: National Center for Education Statistics.

Hutchins, R. M. (1963). *Addresses on the role of government in education.* Houston: Rice University Press.

Kerr, C., & Gade, M. L. (1986). *The many lives of academic presidents.* Washington, DC: Association of Governing Boards of Universities and Colleges.

Milliken, F. J. (1990). Perceiving and interpreting environmental change: An examination of college administrators' interpretation of changing demographics. *Academy of Management Journal, 33*, 42–63.

Parker, B., & Zammuto, R. F. (1986). Enrollment decline: Perceptions and responses. *The Review of Higher Education, 10*, 63–84.

Rusk, J. J., Leslie, L. L., & Brinkman, P. T. (1982). The increasing impact of economic conditions upon higher education enrollments. *Economics of Education Review, 2*, 25–48.

SAS Institute, Inc. (1985). *SAS User's Guide: Statistics, Version 5 Edition.* Cary, NC: SAS Institute.

Zammuto, R. F. (1986). Managing decline in American higher education. In J. C. Smart (Ed.), *Higher education: Handbook of theory and research* (Vol. 2). New York: Agathon Press.

Patricia K. Fullagar, PhD, holds a research position with the Carolina Policy Studies Program at the University of North Carolina at Chapel Hill. Her research interests include issues that affect policy at institutional and governmental levels.

Direct inquiries about this article to Patricia K. Fullagar, Research Investigator, The Carolina Institute for Child and Family Policy, CB# 8040, 300 NCNB Plaza, The University of North Carolina, Chapel Hill, NC 27599-8040, 919/962-7374.

CHAPTER 42

Perceptions of Leadership Gender and Situational Effects on Rater Policies

Nina Wrolstad,
Joy Fisher Hazucha,
Charles Huff, and
Keith M. Halperin

This study investigated leadership from the perceiver's point of view, with situation (competitive or cooperative) and gender of the rater as moderator variables. It analyzed the relationship between the leaders' personality (measured by the California Psychological Inventory) and skills (measured by peer ratings on the Management Skills Profile) and the rankings they received from peers in an interactive group. The participants were managers who attended a development program. Results indicate that verbal ascendancy is an asset in being perceived as a leader in all situations, regardless of the gender of the rater. However, situation and gender of rater had some effect on the policies used, some of which are in gender-stereotypical directions. The results suggest that people who communicate effectively and who interact with group members are seen as effective leaders across situations but that leaders should also adjust their behavior according to the situation and the gender of the followers.

The objective of this study was to capture the policies that raters use to rank order leaders, contrasting male and female policies and those applied in competitive versus cooperative contexts. Two questions posed were (a) whether gender or situation affect the policies applied by rankers, and (b) what is the size of the effect. These questions are important because of the interactive nature of the leadership process: A leader is a person to whom another person has attributed leadership qualities. The results of the study have implications for whether leaders will be seen as equally effective across situations and by male and female perceivers.

Leadership has long been considered an attribute of the individual being observed. Thus, initial research focused on identifying traits and behaviors of leaders as well as situational variables that influence leaders (Fiedler, 1967; Fleishman, 1967; Mann, 1959; Stogdill, 1948). Calder (1977) noted that much research on leadership has been vague and more reliant on general assumptions than scientific principles. As a result, the debate concerning "one best way" to lead and situational constraints on leadership has continued.

Consequently, past research on gender

and leadership also has focused largely on the characteristics of female and male leaders as identified by a variety of tests, questionnaires, and exercises (Adams & Hicks, 1980; Brenner & Bromer, 1981; Carli, 1989). Women's performance as leaders has been characterized as more accommodating and tension reducing (Bond & Vinacke, 1961; Strodtbeck & Mann, 1956). More recent studies have also supported the gender-stereotypical notion that the female leader's behavior is one of less control and more collaboration between managers and subordinates, while male leadership behavior is characterized by competitiveness, a preference for hierarchical authority, and high control (Loden, 1985). However, some theorists have argued that these reported differences are really caused by the gender stereotypes of the raters; the actual behavior of male and female leaders may be the same, but raters may report only what fits their stereotype, resulting in apparent differences (Bartol & Wortman, 1975; Hollander & Julian, 1969).

In support of this notion of possible rater bias, there is evidence that differences in leadership behavior between males and females are relatively small. In a meta-analysis of past leadership studies, Eagly and Johnson (1990) found that gender differences have been found mostly in laboratory settings, while field settings are much less likely to uncover gender differences. In fact, managers, male or female, given equivalent levels of responsibility within an organization usually exhibit the same leadership behavior. Eagly and Johnson hypothesized that this phenomenon may be explained by socialization into rules and governing values that occurs for both males and females within an organization. Self-selection may also be a factor: Men and women who choose management may be more similar than men and women in general. In addition, the specific duties and constraints of a manager's responsibilities may override any adherence to general sex-differentiated styles of behavior. Thus, it is possible that gender differences in leadership are relatively small and that reported differences may be an artifact of rater bias (Eagly, 1991).

As mentioned, most research on leadership has focused on the leader, ignoring the characteristics of the individual making judgments about that leader. Yet, there is evidence that the perceiver may maintain internal rules for assessing a leader which may interact with actual leader behavior when the perceiver is forming leadership judgments (Lord, 1977). This approach recognizes the interactive process of leadership as influenced by both the leader's actual behavior and the expectations and implicit theories held by those who work with the leader. Work in the area of implicit personality prototypes indicates that people do, in fact, have rules for assessing personality types in other people (Cantor & Mischel, 1979). Further, research has shown that people often base their judgments on expectations about the kinds of behaviors and persons "best suited" and "worst suited" for different situations (Magnussen & Endler, 1972).

Studies of perceptions of leadership have uncovered influences that may mediate a rater's perception of leadership. External outcome is one factor found to impact a rater's perception of a leader. For example, research on political leaders has indicated that even when the behavior of a politician remains stable, voters' perceptions of the candidates' leadership qualities change as a result of the outcome of the election (Foti, Fraser, & Lord, 1982). A second factor which influences raters' perceptions is the salience of the leader. When Phillips (1981) concurrently videotaped a leader from two different camera angles, the leader was evaluated differently by people viewing the two resulting videotapes. In addition, rater personality has been found to affect interpersonal perceptions, even when the behavior observed is constant for all observers (Lord, Phillips, & Rush, 1980). Thus, there is evidence that both rater characteristics (personality) and situational variables (election outcome, leader salience) may affect the ways in which leadership behavior and traits are interpreted.

Gender—as a characteristic of the rater—has received very little attention. Bartol and Butterfield (1976) asked women to evaluate descriptions of managers and found that women rated all of the managers higher overall than did the male raters. Despite the fact that the described leadership behavior was identical, females and males evaluated the behavior differently. Holt and Mount (1991) examined coworker ratings of managers who had been rated by one male and one female peer and one male and one female subordinate. They found that gender of the rater affected (a) the mean skill ratings and (b) the relationship between these skills and overall performance. This suggests that men and women may have different standards for leadership behavior and may use different information to draw conclusions about overall performance.

Much research in these areas has been conducted in the laboratory. However, two meta-analyses of gender differences (Eagly & Johnson, 1990; Smith, Falgout, & Olsen, 1991) have found that conclusions drawn from lab studies do not generalize to organizational settings. Therefore, it is important to study real leaders and managers in naturalistic settings.

This study investigated the personality and skill information taken into account by male and female raters when making decisions about leadership in competitive and cooperative situations. The situation is a "live" one, where the raters interact with the ratees. In addition, the participants are real managers from a number of organizations.

The implications of research on gender and situational influences on perceptions of leadership are plentiful. If, in fact, perceptions of leadership behavior are affected by gender or situation, leaders aware of these differences may be able to adjust their behavior to elicit a more favorable response and better relations with their followers. Further, in evaluating ratings of their own leadership, managers should consider whether they were rated by a male or a female and whether the situation was competitive or cooperative. Finally, leaders can be chosen for different positions based on how well their skills fit the competitiveness or cooperativeness required in those positions.

Method

Sample

The sample consists of 234 people who attended a management development program in 1990. Each "class" was a week long and included 15 to 21 participants. Of the 12 classes, 7 were offered on an open-enrollment basis, with a maximum of 2 people from the same organization. Five were "in-house" centers, where all of the participants were from the same organization. Each participant was sponsored by his or her employer, and attendance was usually viewed as a perquisite.

The participants were from a variety of industries and functions. Seventy-eight percent were male, 93.5% were white, and the median age was 40. All but 10% had a college degree, and 35% also had a graduate degree. The median organizational level was middle management, but the range was from nonmanagement to executive management. The median number of direct subordinates was 4, and the median number of indirect subordinates (people reporting through the direct subordinates) was 12.

Data Collection

The answers to the questions posed by this study rely on three sets of data: leadership rankings—the dependent variable—and two sets of independent variables—the California Psychological

Inventory (CPI) (Gough, 1987) and the Management Skills Profile (MSP) (Sevy, Olson, McGuire, Fraser, & Paajanen, 1985). The independent variables differ from past research: They were collected before, rather than during, the leadership situation. In addition, the CPI is a self-report instrument completed by the ratee, and the MSP was completed by peers from the work setting. Therefore, this study tests the assumption that there is a relationship between self-reported personality, peer ratings from the work setting, and leadership rankings by peers in a novel situation. Each of the data sets will be described.

Leadership rankings. Leadership rankings were obtained from participants at the end of each of two "leaderless group discussion" (LGD) exercises. These LGDs occurred in small groups with five to seven members each. These group exercises took place on the first full day of the 5-day program and provided the first opportunity for the participants to work together.

In assigning people to groups, attempts were made to place together strangers from similar organizational levels. To this end, two rules were followed: First, if people from the same organization attended the same class, they were placed in different groups for the LGDs; and second, participants' organizational levels were roughly matched, so that first-line supervisors and CEOs were not assigned to the same group. In addition, at least one female participant was assigned to each group. The groups were reshuffled between the two exercises, so that only two or three people together for group one remained together for group two. This reshuffling minimized the carry-over effect from one group to the other.

The first exercise was competitive and creative. Working independently, participants were given 30 minutes to prepare a resumé for an ideal fictitious candidate to lead a challenging and risky expedition. When the group convened, each partici-

pant was given 3 minutes to present his or her candidate to the group, after which the group had 45 minutes to rank the candidates in order of merit. The group was free to choose whatever method they wished to accomplish this task. This exercise, Earth II©, was developed in 1975 by the Center for Creative Leadership, Greensboro, North Carolina.

The second exercise was cooperative and logical. Each group was given 45 minutes to select a person from a list of candidates to fill a specific position. Only one candidate fit the position requirements, which were scattered throughout five booklets. Because each participant had only one booklet, the group first needed to discover that they each had different information. They then needed to obtain all of the relevant information, deduce the rules, and apply them to eliminate the unqualified candidates. This exercise, Energy International, is taken from the *1972 Annual Handbook for Group Facilitators* (Pfeiffer & Jones, 1972) and was revised in 1986.

At the end of each exercise, each group member was asked to rank order all participants in the group (including him- or herself) according to each individual's contribution to the group.

The Management Skills Profile.
The Management Skills Profile (MSP) (Sevy et al., 1985) is an instrument developed to provide managers with feedback from co-workers, typically including the boss, three peers, and three subordinates. It consists of 122 items grouped into 19 skills, abilities, and other attributes (dimensions). For each item, respondents are asked "to what extent does this manager . . ."; the response scale is a Likert scale ranging from 1 (Not at all) to 5 (To a very great extent). The dimensions are organized around eight larger areas which include Administrative Skills, Leadership Skills, and Personal Motivation. Alphas for the dimensions range from .70 (Conflict Management) to .91 (Human Relations) (Sevy et al., 1985). This indicates

that the dimensions are internally consistent. Sevy et al. found interrater reliabilities (intraclass correlations) ranging from .52 (Managing Conflict) to .73 (Personal Organization, Financial and Quantitative) for groups of three peers. This indicates that peers agree fairly well about an individual manager's skill levels.

Participants distributed the questionnaires several weeks before the program and received feedback on their results at the end of the first full day of the program (after the group exercises). For this study, only peer ratings and a subset of the items were chosen. Peer MSP ratings were chosen because the dependent variable is peer rankings, and correlations within rater type are larger than those between rater types (Davis & Hazucha, 1991). To select the items, experienced LGD assessors were asked to indicate which items they thought would be related to LGD performance. In addition, some items not chosen as important to performance in these groups (mostly Administrative and Financial/Technical) were also included.

The California Psychological Inventory.

The California Psychological Inventory (CPI) was developed by Gough (1987) to measure "folk concepts" of personality. It includes interpersonal scales (e.g., Dominance, Sociability), intrapersonal scales (e.g., Responsibility, Socialization), achievement, and "other." Participants completed the CPI before the development program and received feedback on day four.

Data Analysis

The first step in data analysis was a reduction of the MSP and CPI data. A factor analysis of the CPI yielded the two traditional factors (intrapersonal and interpersonal), plus Femininity. Therefore, three composite variables were created by summing the raw scores for the CPI scales shown in Table 1, resulting in three CPI

TABLE 1 California Psychological Inventory—Groups of Scales

CPI 1. Intrapersonal
    Sc Self-Control
    Gi Good Impression
    Wb Well-Being
    Ac Achievement via Conformance
    Re Responsibility
    Ie Intellectual Efficiency
    Py Psychological-Mindedness

CPI 2. Interpersonal
    Do Dominance
    Cs Capacity for Status
    Sy Sociability
    Sp Social Presence
    Sa Self-Acceptance
    Ai Achievement via Independence

CPI Fe. Femininity
    Fe Femininity

independent variables: intrapersonal (CPI 1), interpersonal (CPI 2), and Femininity (CPI Fe). The MSP items were factor-analyzed, yielding five factors: Communication (Com), Impact (Impct), Human Relations (Rels), Financial/Technical (Fin/Tec), and Administrative (Admin). The factors, the items, and their loadings are shown in Table 2.

The procedure used to capture the rankers' policies was a stepwise discriminant function analysis. The dependent variable was rank (first vs. last), and the independent variables were the gender, MSP, and CPI factor scores of the person being ranked. The moderator variables were gender of rater and type of exercise.

Eight analyses were performed, and in each case the functions were computed and saved for further analyses. These analyses were:

1. competitive (ignoring gender of rater)

2. cooperative (ignoring gender of rater)

3. males (ignoring exercise type)

4. females (ignoring exercise type)

TABLE 2   Management Skills Profile—Item Text and Factor Loadings

Factor Loading   Item Text

1. Communication (MSP Com)

.678   states views concisely and logically when speaking with individuals or groups
.641   gets point across when talking
.763   is clear and understandable in oral communications
.761   clearly expresses ideas and concepts in writing
.652   uses incorrect grammar in written communications

2. Human Relations (MSP Rels)

.548   involves others in the planning process
.78   listens well to others in a group situation, conveying understanding and acceptance of the comments of others
.695   does not interrupt others
.441   makes decisions based on adequate and accurate information
.846   considers the opinions and feelings of others when presenting own ideas
.781   develops and maintains good, cooperative working relationships with others
.601   recognizes and deals with problems between individuals and groups

3. Financial/Technical (MSP FinTec)

.869   quickly analyzes financial information
.860   is able to identify key factors when reviewing budgets and financial statements
.464   keeps up to date on technical developments related to his/her work

4. Impact (MSP Impct)

.773   seems comfortable in a leadership position, exercising authority and control
.650   when in a group, readily commands the attention and respect of others
.431   persists at a task despite unexpected difficulties

5. Administrative Skills (MSP Admin)

.719   establishes effective and efficient procedures for getting work done
.666   makes good use of his/her time
.719   handles detail without getting bogged down
.685   makes timely decisions based on adequate information

---

5. competitive, males

6. competitive, females

7. cooperative, males

8. cooperative, females

To compare the policies used in each analysis, the independent variables entered in each function were compared, and the functions resulting from these analyses were intercorrelated. A zero correlation between function A and B would mean that group A (e.g., males) and group B (e.g., females) used totally different policies to rank order the group members. For example, each participant may have rated him/herself first and the person to his/her left last. A correlation of 1.0 between functions C and D would mean that all groups and all persons within a group used exactly the same policy to rank order the group members, such as ranking them from tallest to shortest. A moderate correlation between functions E and F would indicate that these two groups showed some similarities and some differences in the variables they took into account when they rank ordered people in their group.

To contrast gender and exercise-type effects on rater policy, pairs of correlations were contrasted. First, the competitive (function 1) and cooperative (function 2) functions were correlated. Second, the male (function 3) and female (function 4) functions were correlated. Next, the within-gender across-exercise correlations were computed: male cooperative versus competitive (function 5 correlated with 7) and female cooperative versus competitive (function 6 with 8). Then, the within-exercise across-gender correlations were computed: cooperative male versus female (function 7 with 8) and competitive male versus female (function 5 with 6). The latter two pairs of correlations were contrasted, using Fisher's z' transformation for comparing independent rs ($z = z'_s - z'_h / sd_{z'}$; $sd_{z'} = 1 / \sqrt{n-3}$). This was chosen as the most appropriate statistic, because each function was developed on a sample which was independent of the sample used to develop the comparison function. For example, the male equation was developed on males, the female equation on females.

Results

Table 3 shows the independent variables which entered each equation, along with the Chi-squares, all of which are significant. The significant Chi-squares indicate that, in each analysis, the first- and last-ranked participants were distinguishable based on their gender, CPI, and/ or MSP scores.

There were commonalities and differences in the independent variables entering each function. MSP Communication and CPI Interpersonal entered each of the eight equations. MSP Financial and Technical skills entered all three male equations (competitive, cooperative, and total). MSP Impact entered all three competitive equations (male, female, and total). Leader (ratee) gender and CPI Femininity had interesting relationships: Females tended to be ranked higher in the cooperative exercise (by males and total). However, in several equations CPI Femininity (on which females score higher) received a positive weight, and gender (on which females also score higher) a negative weight. This indicates a complex relationship: Males with higher Femininity scores were more likely to receive higher leadership rankings. MSP Administrative Skills and MSP Human Relations were not entered into any of the equations.

The similarities and differences between functions are illustrated by the correlations in Table 4. (The large Ns are due to the multiple records per rater and refer to the number of ratees included in that correlation, rather than the number of raters.) Both the competitive-cooperative and the male-female correlations are quite high ($r = .85$ and $.79$, both $p < .001$). This signifies that context of leadership and gender of rater do not have a large effect on leadership rankings; there is more similarity than difference. As shown in Table 3, all four of these equations include CPI Interpersonal and MSP Communication and Financial/Technical. It would be inappropriate to contrast these two correlations statistically, as one correlation (competitive-cooperative) is between functions derived from the same sample, while the other (male-female) is between functions from independent samples.

Table 4 also shows the correlations between the competitive and cooperative policies, within gender (males $r = .68$, females $r = .62$, both $p < .001$). These two correlations are quite high and not significantly different from each other ($t = 1.29$), which indicates that cooperative and competitive policies tend to be equally similar within gender. However, a look at Table 3 shows that male cooperative and competitive policies share three

TABLE 3 Variables in Each of the Discriminant Functions:
Male, Female, Competitive, Cooperative
(in order of entry)

Exercise	Competitive	Cooperative	Total
Gender	(function 5)	(function 7)	(function 3)
Male	CPI 2 MSP Com MSP Impct Gender[a] (–) CPI Fe MSP FinTec	CPI 2 MSP Com Gender[a] CPI 1 MSP FinTec	CPI 2 MSP Com MSP FinTec MSP Impct CPI Fe CPI 1
Chi-sqr	44.39***	40.661***	71.34***
	(function 6)	(function 8)	(function 4)
Female	MSP Com CPI 2 MSP Impct CPI Fe	CPI 2 CPI 1 (–) MSP Com	CPI 2 MSP Com CPI 1 CPI Fe MSP FinTec
Chi-sqr	12.86*	11.55*	22.23**
	(function 1)	(function 2)	
Total	CPI 2 MSP Com MSP Impct MSP FinTec CPI Fe Gender[a] (–)	Gender[a] CPI 2 MSP Com MSP FinTec	
Chi-sqr	52.70***	42.68***	

Note. (–) indicates negative weight.

[a]1 = male, 2 = female.

*$p < .01$. **$p < .001$. ***$p < .0001$

independent variables, CPI Interpersonal (CPI 2), MSP Communication, and MSP Financial/Technical, while only the first two are shared by the corresponding female policies.

The third pair of correlations compares male and female policies within exercise type. Again, each is quite certainly different from 0 (cooperative $r = .42$, competitive $= .70$, both $p < .001$). However, the two correlations are also signi-

ficantly different from each other ($t = 9.0302$, $p < .001$), an indication that male and female competitive policies are more similar than their cooperative policies. Table 3 sheds some light on the differences between these policies. The most striking cooperative difference is that the CPI Intrapersonal factor (CPI 1) is positively weighted in the male equation but negatively weighted in the female equation. On the other hand, the competi-

TABLE 4 Correlations among Functions (1–8)

	r	N	t
Main Effects			
Cooperative (2) with Competitive (1)	.85	936	
Female (4) with Male (3)	.79	936	
Interactions			
Male: Coop. (7) with Competitive (5)	.68	736	1.29
Female: Coop. (8) with Competitive (6)	.62	200	
Cooperative: Male (7) with Female (8)	.42	468	9.03*
Competitive: Male (5) with Female (6)	.70	468	

*p < .001

tive policies share four variables: CPI Interpersonal (CPI 1), MSP Communication, MSP Impact, and CPI Fe.

Discussion

We begin the discussion with a methodological conclusion. The relationship between self-reported personality and peer ratings is sufficiently related to peer rankings in a novel setting to allow significant prediction. This is evidence of the convergent validity of personality, peer ratings from the work setting, and leaderless group discussions with relative strangers in identifying leaders. Thus, there is hope for the study of perceptions of leadership in naturalistic settings.

The most general substantive conclusion is that a large portion of perceptions of leadership seems to be constant across situations and raters. A high level of communication and interaction activity is related to higher ratings across competitive and cooperative situations, as perceived by male and female raters. This is consistent with Eagly's (1991) suggestion that leadership role expectations are stronger than gender role expectations in organizations.

Two independent variables were not entered into any of the discriminant functions: MSP Administrative and Interpersonal. We did not expect Administrative, which includes making good use of one's time, handling detail, and making timely decisions, to be a good predictor of group leadership. However, we did expect Interpersonal, which includes involving others, listening, not interrupting, developing good relationships, and conflict management, to be important. This finding is consistent with Eagly's (1991) finding that task-oriented behavior was more strongly related to leader emergence than was interpersonal behavior.

There are also predictable differences between policies used in different settings and by different raters. In situations which require a formal presentation and where the group task is competitive, behaviors which establish dominance and impact are viewed as characteristic of leaders.

There was a tendency for raters to prefer people who are warm and supportive (as indicated by high CPI Femininity), regardless of situation and gender.

Two of the gender-related findings support stereotypes of male and female leadership behavior. First, across situations, male raters view technical skill and logical analysis as important. This finding was surprising, as the exercises did not require using financial or technical information. Second, males tend to rank women higher in cooperative exercises; they ranked supportive (high Fe) males with high impact as better leaders in competitive situations.

A third gender-related finding was unexpected: Men view high intrapersonal CPI scores as positive, while women view them as negative in the cooperative situation. Our best post hoc explanation for this is that women respond more positively to leaders who are less conventional and more spontaneous, while men prefer those who are more controlled and predictable. This does, in fact, fit with other findings about how women and men lead (Loden, 1985) and indicates that raters, male and female, may prefer leaders who are more similar to them.

One more gender difference is noteworthy. Men took gender into account in both exercises: Women were ranked higher in the cooperative group, men in the competitive situation. However, the gender of the ratee did not enter the female equations. This finding fits with Eagly's (1991) summary of research on the interaction between rater and ratee gender, which found that women rated men and women about the same. However, Eagly found that men tended to rate men higher, while this study found that the direction of the effect was moderated by the situation.

The implications for leaders are the following. First, verbal ascendancy is more important to perceptions of leadership than are the situation or the gender of the perceiver. Therefore, any leader in any situation can benefit from honing these skills, including stating views concisely, getting the point across, and writing clearly. Second, an awareness of followers' expectations and preferences may help people to be more effective leaders. Team-building strategies may be helpful in clarifying these expectations. Third, people can choose and modify leadership situations to play to their strengths. For example, leaders with weaker interpersonal impact will be more effective in cooperative situations, and female leaders will be better received by a group of males if the situation is cooperative.

Further research in this area should seek to better understand the dynamics of the process of making leadership judgments. In addition, other moderators of gender-based differences may include salience and tokenism and should be investigated. This study has shown that it is possible to investigate these dynamics in a field setting, and it is important to do so.

Acknowledgment

We wish to thank Tim Hansen for his assistance with data collection and cleaning.

References

Adams, J., & Hicks, J. M. (1980). Leader sex, leader descriptions of own behavior, and subordinates' description of leader behavior (Project Athena: West Point). *International Journal of Women's Studies, 3*, 321–326.

Bartol, K. M., & Butterfield, D. A. (1976). Sex effects in valuating leaders. *Journal of Applied Psychology, 61*(4), 446–454.

Bartol, K. M., & Wortman, M. S. (1975). Male versus female leaders: Effects on perceived leader behavior and satisfaction in a hospital. *Personnel Psychology, 28*, 533–547.

Bond, J. R., & Vinacke, W. E. (1961). Coalitions in mixed sex triads. *Sociometry, 24*, 61–75.

Brenner, O. C., & Bromer, J. A. (1981). Sex stereotypes and leader's behavior as measured by the agreement scale for leadership behavior. *Psychological Reports, 48*, 960–962.

Calder, B. J. (1977). An attribution theory of leadership. In B. M. Staw & G. R. Salancik (Eds.), *New directions in organizational behavior* (pp. 179–204). Chicago: St. Clair Press.

Cantor, N., & Mischel, W. (1979). Prototypes in person perception. In L. Berdowitz, (Ed.), *Advances in experimental social psychology, 12*, 3–52.

Carli, L. L. (1989). Gender differences in interaction style and influence. *Journal of Personality and Social Psychology, 56*, 565–576.

Davis, B. L., & Hazucha, J. F. (1991, August). *Practical and methodological issues in using the Management Skills Profile.* In M. D. Dunnette (Chair), *Multi-rater feedback: Lessons learned.* Symposium presented at the 99th meeting of the American Psychological Association, San Francisco.

Eagly, A. H. (1991, August). *Gender and leadership.* Paper presented at the 99th meeting of the American Psychological Association, San Francisco.

Eagly, A. H., & Johnson, B. T. (1990). Gender and leadership style: A meta-analysis. *Psychological Bulletin, 108*, 233–256.

Fiedler, F. E. (1967). *A theory of leadership effectiveness.* New York: McGraw-Hill.

Fleishman, E. A. (1967). The development of a behavior taxonomy for describing human tasks: A correlational-experimental approach. *Journal of Applied Psychology, 51*, 10.

Foti, R. J., Fraser, S. L., & Lord, R. G. (1982). Effects of leadership labels and prototypes on perceptions of political leaders. *Journal of Applied Psychology, 67*, 326–333.

Gough, H. G. (1987). *California Psychological Inventory administrator's guide.* Palo Alto, CA: Consulting Psychologists Press.

Hollander, E. P., & Julian, J. W. (1969). Contemporary trends in the analysis of leadership perceptions. *Psychological Bulletin, 71*, 387–397.

Holt, K. E., & Mount, M. K. (1991, August). Behavior, performance, and effectiveness of female managers and executives. In C. E. Marsh (Chair), *Women's management careers: Issues in effectiveness, advancement, and derailment.* Symposium conducted at the 99th meeting of the American Psychological Association, San Francisco.

Loden, M. (1985). *Feminine leadership or how to succeed in business without being one of the boys.* New York: Time Books.

Lord, R. G. (1977). Functional leadership behavior: Measurement and relation to social power and leadership perceptions. *Administrative Science Quarterly, 22*, 114–133.

Lord, R. G., Phillips, J. S., & Rush, M. C. (1980). Effects of sex and personality on perceptions of emergent leadership, influence, and social power. *Journal of Applied Psychology, 65*, 176–182.

Magnussen, D., & Endler, N. S. (Eds.). (1972). *Personality at the crossroads: Current issues in interactional psychology.* Hillsdale, NJ: Erlbaum.

Mann, R. D. (1959). A review of the relationships between personality and performance in small groups. *Psychological Bulletin, 56*, 241–270.

Pfeiffer, J. W., & Jones, J. E. (Eds.). (1972). *The 1972 Annual Handbook for Group Facilitators.* San Diego: University Associates.

Phillips, J. S. (1981). *Leadership as attribution: The relationships of causal ascriptions to perceptions of leadership.* Unpublished doctoral dissertation, University of Akron, OH.

Sevy, B. A., Olson, R. D., McGuire, D. P., Fraser, M. E., & Paajanen G. (1985). *Management Skills Profile research report and technical manual.* Minneapolis, MN: Personnel Decisions.

Smith, C. S., Falgout, K., & Olsen, H. (1991, April). *A career path framework for examining sex differences in job-related attitudes and behavior.* Paper presented at the annual meeting of the Society for Industrial and Organizational Psychology, St. Louis, MO.

Stogdill, R. M. (1948). Personal factors associated with leadership. *Journal of Psychology, 25*, 35–71.

Strodtbeck, F. L., & Mann, R. D. (1956). Sex role differentiation in jury deliberations. *Sociometry, 19*, 3–11.

Nina Wrolstad is a candidate for a Master's Degree from the School of Labor and Industrial Relations at Michigan State University. Her project involvements include sponsored child care, organizational socialization, total quality management, and a summer position with IBM working on issues of diversity management and organizational development. The study for this article was conducted as a senior project in Psychology at St. Olaf College, Northfield, MN.

Joy Fisher Hazucha is Director of Research at Personnel Decisions, Inc. Her research interests include management and executive effectiveness, career development, management development, and multirater feedback. She holds a PhD in Industrial-Organizational Psychology from the University of Minnesota.

Charles Huff is Assistant Professor of Psychology at St. Olaf College. His research interests include computing and society and attribution of responsibility. He has published works on gender and computing and on an attributional model of damage assessment.

Keith M. Halperin is Senior Vice President at Personnel Decisions, Inc. and the head of PDI's Training and Development Division, which designs and delivers management development programs. His experience is in management consulting and human resource development. He received his PhD in Clinical Psychology from the University of Kansas.

Direct inquiries about this article to Joy Fisher Hazucha, Personnel Decisions, Inc., 2000 Plaza VII Tower, 45 South Seventh Street, Minneapolis, MN 55402–1608, 612/339–0927.

CHAPTER 43

Leadership Styles of Successful Women Administrators in Higher Education

Charlotte Jacobsen Weddle

*The Myers-Briggs Type Indicator® (MBTI™)
is used to examine the personality characteristics of 371 women administrators in higher
education in order to understand the leadership styles of women in responsible positions. This study explored whether their
styles in a male-dominated structure affected
their advancement to senior positions.*

Myers-Briggs Type Indicator is a registered trademark of Consulting Psychologists Press, Inc.

MBTI is a trademark of Consulting Psychologists
Press, Inc.

Women increasingly hold responsible
leadership positions in a variety of career
fields. However, the overall percentage of
women promoted to CEO or college president remains small in spite of special
training and equal opportunity efforts.
Paradoxically, the literature suggests that
women managers are similar to their male
counterparts in key leadership attributes
and are generally evaluated by superiors
and subordinates as performing effectively. The contrast between performance
and advancement raises questions about
possible special contextual factors related
to the leadership style of women which
may have a negative impact on evaluation
of their performance and their potential
for promotion. This may suggest an interaction between gender expectations and
personal style.

In light of the urgent call for a new kind
of empowering leader whose practices
motivate followers and create sustained
change through a shared vision and a participatory process (Bennis, 1990; Heller &
Van Til, 1982; Kanter, 1989; Kotter, 1990)
there is a pressing need to learn more
about the potential contribution of
women as change-oriented leaders and
the impact of their leadership styles on
male-dominated organizations. This
study of 371 women administrators in
higher education who attended a highly
selective professional development insti-

tute answered some questions that continue to be posed in the literature. It revealed individual similarities and differences in the predicted style of women leaders in addressing problems, innovating change, interacting with colleagues, organizing tasks, and handling authority. This preliminary profile is part of an ongoing research project by the investigator in cooperation with the Bryn Mawr Summer Institute.

Gender Differences in Leadership

Bass's (1990) literature review documents the dramatic increase in the number of women moving into responsible leadership positions in the corporate sector, where they have demonstrated their competence in a wide range of fields. Despite their increased presence in middle management and generally satisfactory performance, Bass reports the numbers of women reaching top corporate positions or college presidencies remains extremely low. One reason for this surprising lack of advancement is speculated to be a "glass ceiling," described by Morrison, White, and Van Velsor (1987) as a seemingly impermeable barrier blocking promotion of highly competent midlevel women executives. Male attitudes and unreasonable expectations for women executives appear to create the promotion barrier.

Reviews of the literature fail to identify any significant differences in personality attributes, training, or management behavior between male and female leaders (Bass, 1990; Denmark, 1977; Statham, 1987). Although Denmark and Kanter (1977) document myriad ways in which women are subjected to differential treatment by groups and by corporations due to their social marginalization, relative lack of power, deferential communication patterns, and sex stereotyping, the literature largely overlooks the impact of stylistic differences and the potential impact of gender typing on advancement.

It is ironic to note that even as women struggle in the workplace to be evaluated as individuals with differences rather than as members of a gender group, a distinctive "feminine leadership style" is being propounded (Helgesen, 1990; Loden, 1985; Rosener, 1989; Schwartz, 1989). These researchers hold that shared socialization experiences of women as a group, with emphasis on sensitivity to relationships and collaboration, predispose women to be participatory leaders who prefer nonhierarchical structures and sharing of information and power. Morrison and colleagues (1987) warn against the new form of gender stereotyping which ignores individual differences. This controversy underscores the need for qualitative and quantitative data on differences in leadership styles of women in the workplace.

Denmark (1977) suggests that higher education represents a model of a nonhierarchical structure with its dynamic, politically liberal climate, collegially shared decision-making patterns, information sharing, and dispersion of power. She proposes that this climate is receptive to a participatory leadership style among administrators and faculty leaders where women are more likely to be advanced as leaders than in hierarchically structured corporations. No studies were found which explored this interesting hypothesis.

Bass (1990) documents the long history of sex discrimination and unfair treatment faced by working women which have historically limited their effectiveness and functioning. He asserts that women have been negatively stereotyped as leaders due to gender-biased perceptions; important leadership qualities such as toughmindedness, critical ability, logic, high organizational ability, decisiveness, and resistance to emotionality were considered more typical of men than women as a group. The literature indicates that women managers are often negatively evaluated when judged to be displaying "unfeminine" behaviors such as assertiveness and directiveness; women are judged more harshly than males for using the same stylistic approach (Bass, 1990; Kushell & Newton, 1986).

Rather than differing markedly from comparable males as leaders, Bass (1990) reports that women who become leaders tend to be more similar in personality to their male counterparts than to women in general. Earlier, Denmark (1977), who had reached the same conclusion, also found that women managers tend to demonstrate a greater concern for relationships than did men. She theorized that the stronger relationship orientation of women was an adaptive response of women to the male-generated stereotype of them as more nurturant and less powerful when working in groups, rather than an indication of biological differences.

Statham (1987) also found no differences in leadership behavior of males and females, but she highlighted the difficulty of separating behavioral outcomes from stylistic differences. Statham speculated that women may be perceived as less effective leaders because of their style, either feminine/nurturing or masculine/ aloof, even though they may be demonstrably effective in achieving organizational goals. The possibility of gender-specific response to differing leadership styles may account for the glass ceiling faced by women if their behavior is not in accord with gender-expected norms.

Underrepresentation of Women in Higher Education

Women have struggled to achieve leadership roles in higher education; they have been underrepresented and discriminated against (Pearson, Shavlik, & Touchton, 1989; Sandler & Hall, 1986; Shavlik & Touchton, 1983; Touchton & Davis, 1991). Sandler and Hall detail the subtle and less than subtle ways in which women have been negatively affected by the "chilly climate" of higher education, even as their representation has increased.

The virtual exclusion of women from top academic leadership is attributed by Shakeshaft (1987) to the male-dominated nature of higher education and its traditional stereotyping of women. Shakeshaft's research indicates that a competent woman seeking a position is at a greater disadvantage than women of lesser ability and is more likely to lose her job than an equally performing male: her competence threatens male supervisors.

Hoferek (1986) reports evidence of a tendency of male colleagues to resent successful women and verbally "trash" high-achieving women. Pearson et al. (1989) report that women leaders remain isolated in their institutions due to low numbers of high status women; they feel like aliens in a male-dominated academy which has strongly resisted making fundamental changes to meet the needs of women as students and staff.

Myers-Briggs and Leadership Styles Assessment

The Myers-Briggs Type Indicator (MBTI) is increasingly used in human resource development and leadership training (Bass, 1990) to measure individual differences in personal style, decision making, and approaches to interpersonal relationships. The MBTI (Myers & McCaulley, 1985) assesses differences in how people perceive, organize, and act upon information, solve problems, structure their lives, interact with others, respond to authority, and express their personal values. Based on Jung's theory of personality as expanded and applied by Myers and Briggs, the MBTI measures personal preferences for the following four separate bipolar dimensions of personality: (a) Extraversion (E) and Introversion (I); (b) Sensing (S) and Intuition (N); (c) Thinking (T) and Feeling (F); and (d) Judging (J) and Perceiving (P). (See Myers and Mc-Caulley, 1985, for a full history and description of the theory and instrument.) These personality dimensions are considered to be independent of each other and of general intelligence. A slight but consistent sex difference, found only on the Thinking/Feeling scale, shows a male preference for Thinking and a female preference for Feeling. However, there is wide variation among men and women in each direction, and the overall difference is not great. The instrument creates forced choices which result in assignment of the respondent to 1 of 16 clusters of personality characteristics referred to as "psychological types."

In applying type theory to work settings, Keirsey and Bates (1978) distinguish four clusters of MBTI types as constituting distinctive Management/Leadership Styles: (a) NT Rational/Visionary style with a strong preference for creating new theories and structures to organize ideas and organizations; (b) NF Feeling/Catalyst style with strength in communicating feelings and working harmoniously with others; (c) SP Troubleshooter/Artisan style characterized by high flexibility and improvisational strength; and (d) SJ Guardian/Traditionalist style with careful attention to maintaining standards and dealing with problems in a practical and responsible manner.

According to McCaulley (1990), there is no single best leadership profile, and leaders are distributed across all 16 types. However, leaders in senior positions in all kinds of organizations include an excess of Sensing/Thinking (ST) and Intuition/Thinking (NT) types. The Thinking/Judging (TJ) combination is also overrepresented in top leadership, including approximately 60% of top executives in that structured, analytical style (Kroeger & Thuesen, 1988). While an excess of Extraversion types is also reported by persons in leadership positions, the difference is not significant. ESTJ is the most frequently reported single MBTI type for leaders in the corporate world and military.

Gender Differences in Leadership Style

In her comprehensive review of MBTI literature on leadership, McCaulley (1990) compares mean scores on Extraversion, Sensing, Thinking, and Judging for 59 diverse groups of leaders drawn from the CAPT databank (Macdaid, McCaulley, & Kainz, 1986) and creates an overall ranking for all groups on those preferences. It is difficult to assess gender differences, as only 4 all-female samples are reported in the 59 leader groups. McCaulley compared the largest sample of women leaders who attended Leadership Development programs sponsored by the Center for Creative Leadership (CCL) with males attending similar programs. Predictable differences, consistent with previous findings, show women scoring higher on Intuition and Feeling while the male leaders are stronger in Thinking and Sensing. McCaulley draws no conclusions on gender differences among the leadership samples.

Cross-Gender Typing for Women Leaders

Stokes, (1987a, 1987b) explores a possible negative interaction between gender and psychological styles, particularly for "atypical combinations" of women high in Thinking and Judging and men who prefer Feeling. Surveying 19 experts who have applied the MBTI extensively in various contexts, Stokes (1987a) finds a strong consensus. If a woman's dominant style features analytical thinking and the assertive TJ decision-making combination traditionally related to masculinity, she is likely to be negatively evaluated by others for behaving in ways not traditionally associated with women, in spite of her demonstrated competence in performance. Kroeger and Thuesen (1988) support the view that Thinking Dominant women are likely to be perceived by colleagues as hard, unfeminine, insensitive, competitive, and manipulative due to their independent and assertive style. Competent women with these characteristics tend to be perceived as threats by superiors and insecure colleagues; their assertive "take charge" style subjects them to criticism, even when their style is effective in a particular work context or when used by males in similar positions. NT women, in particular, may have difficulty relating to men who hold traditional views about feminine behavior, such as the ESTJs who are highly represented in supervisory positions. Thinking Dominant women may be criticized as intimidating and unfeeling if their style does not meet the emotional needs of male and female coworkers in traditionally "feminine" ways. It may be that cross gender-typed women leaders face a "no win" situation; women strong in Feeling are vulnerable to criticism for being too emotional and softhearted as leaders, while highly analytical and tough Thinking women whose style does not conform to traditional cultural expectations for women may face barriers to advancement for not being feminine enough.

The 371 women administrators in this study represent a diverse group. They were nominated and generally financially supported by their institutions to attend the Summer Institute for Women in Higher Education Administration jointly sponsored by Bryn Mawr College and HERS Mid-America (University of Denver). Participants were selected on the basis of their leadership performance and their demonstrated potential for advancement to top administrative positions. The Summer Institute women provided a sample of competent women managers achieving at a high level in a competitive academic environment.

Method

Subjects

The 371 women attended a one month Summer Institute (SI) professional development program at Bryn Mawr College between 1986 and 1990. The groups averaged 75 women each summer and represented a variety of colleges and universities from the United States, Canada, and a few foreign countries. Seventy-four percent came from public institutions, and 71% came from institutions with student enrollments greater than 5,000.

More than half were academic administrators and faculty members; the next largest areas represented were student services (17%) and administrative services (16%). Range of experience varied from less than 2 years to more than 20 years. Subjects ranged in age from early 20s through late 50s, with the largest percent in their 40s. More than 86% had graduate degrees; 56% held doctorates or terminal degrees. The group was 77.2% Caucasian, 16.7% black/African-American, 2.8% Hispanic and Latina, and 1.8% Asian-American.

Measures

All subjects completed the Myers-Briggs Type Indicator in one of two forms, either the full G form or the Abbreviated G Form. Scores were confidential unless permission to reveal them to fellow participants was obtained. No individually identifiable data were used in this study.

Procedures

Following a presentation by the investigator about the instrument, the meaning of scores, a group profile, and applications to leadership for women, participants were divided into same style groups for discussion of behavioral patterns and values in work settings of the four styles of Keirsey and Bates (1978).

Results

Analysis of Data

MBTI scores were analyzed using the Selection Ratio Type Table program (SRTT), developed by Allen, Myers, and Kainz (1976) and described by McCaulley (1985). Preference scores and distribution within the 16 types and 4 leadership styles for SI subjects were compared with samples of leaders and educators using data available in published rankings of MBTI scores on leadership samples (McCaulley, 1990) and the databank maintained by the Center for the Advancement of Psychological Type (Macdaid et al., 1986).

MBTI Preferences of SI Women

Table 1 reports the number and percentage of SI women preferring each type and their distribution in each of the 16 MBTI types. Self-Selection Index scores are reported using the SRTT program. The Self-Selection Index scores (I) are computed as a basis of comparison of the ratio of obtained responses by the SI group to a comparison sample of 16,880 Females completing the G Form of the MBTI between 1978–82 (Macdaid et al., 1986). Index scores represent the calculated ratio of percent of type in a comparison reference group to obtained percent in the SI sample. The calculated values of Chi-square (or Fisher's exact probability with limited cell size) were used to ascertain levels of statistical significance.

Inspection of Table 1 reveals that SI subjects differ significantly from the comparative reference group of all Females completing Form G. SI women define themselves as much more strongly Thinking-oriented in personal style than Form G females (76.01%, Index score =

1.82, $p < .001$) and also present very high scores on Intuition (74.12%, Index score = 1.69, $p < .001$ level) and on Judging (75.74%, Index score = 1.24, $p < .001$ level). A slight majority of the women administrators were Extraverted (54.72%), which is not significantly different than the female norm group.

For SI women leaders, the ENTJ profile was the single largest type preference of the 16 types, accounting for 26.42% of the total sample, which is significantly greater than the female norm group (Index score = 5.11, $p < .001$ level). The next largest single type grouping was INTJ with 16.98% of the subjects (Index score = 4.24, $p < .001$ level). The combined four NT types accounted for 56.60% of the sample (Index score = 3.43, $p < .001$ level), indicating that the dominant Leadership Style for these women administrators was the NT Rational/Visionary style, an atypical style for women in studies published previously. SI participants also reported a much stronger preference for the Thinking/Judging combination than Form G females (61.19%, Index score = 2.11, $p < .001$ level).

Overall, Table 1 indicates wide variation in MBTI scores and distribution across MBTI types. However, the sample has an excess of Intuition, Thinking, and Judgment types at a significantly higher level than is true of the CAPT female sample. Profiles for the five SI groups between 1986 and 1990 showed little variation in distribution or strength of preference for cohort groups.

Comparison with Other Groups of Leaders

In order to compare the relative strength of preference of SI women with other published leadership samples, an analysis was made of the 59 groups presented by McCaulley (1990, pp. 402–405). McCaulley rank ordered the groups on the basis of percentage preferring Extraversion, Sensing, Thinking, and Judging (the

TABLE 1 Comparison of Self-Selection Index Scores and Type
Distribution of SI Women and CAPT Female Reference Group
on MBTI Types

MBTI Type	Number	Percent	Index Score
Extraversion	203	54.72	1.00
Introversion	168	45.28	1.00
Sensing	96	25.88	0.46***
Intuition	275	74.12	1.69***
Thinking	282	76.01	1.82***
Feeling	89	23.99	0.41***
Judging	281	75.74	1.24***
Perceiving	90	24.26	0.62***
ST	72	19.41	0.77**
SF	24	6.47	0.21***
NF	65	17.52	0.64***
NT	210	56.60	3.43***
TJ	227	61.19	2.11*
ISTJ	42	11.32	1.16
ISTP	4	1.08	0.40
ESTP	2	0.54	0.19**
ESTJ	24	6.47	0.64*
ISFJ	7	1.89	0.18***
ISFP	2	0.54	0.13***
ESFP	3	0.81	0.14***
ESFJ	12	3.23	0.30***
INFJ	16	4.31	0.90
INFP	8	2.16	0.32**
ENFP	22	5.93	0.60*
ENFJ	19	5.12	0.80
INTJ	63	16.98	4.24***
INTP	26	7.01	2.19***
ENTP	23	6.20	1.51*
ENTJ	98	26.42	5.11***
Total	371		

Note. Self-Selection Index scores represent the calculated ratio of percent of a
selected reference group preferring each type compared with the obtained
percent of the sample under study (SI women). Index scores indicate the
degree to which SI women differ positively (above 1.0) or negatively (less
than 1.0) from the CAPT reference group of 16,880 female taking Form G of
the MBTI between 1978–82 as drawn from the CAPT databank. (Source:
Macdaid, McCaulley, and Kainz, 1986).

*$p < .05.$ **$p < .01.$ ***$p < .001.$

most frequently reported leadership profile). It was difficult to assess gender differences, as there were only four female groups comprised of 181 women attending Center for Creative Leadership programs, 18,070 female college students, and two samples of college student government leaders totaling 100 women.

Analysis of the 59 groups revealed that SI women leaders differ markedly from the 4 other all-female leader samples, being more strongly Introverted (5th of the 5 groups on Extraversion) and higher on Intuition (5th of 5 on Sensing). SI subjects had a much stronger preference for Thinking and Judging, ranking at the top of the five female samples on both dimensions. The nearest group to the 76.01% of the SI group who preferred Thinking included only 63.54%, while 64.99% preferred Judging compared with 75.74% for SI women. In comparison with the remaining all-male and mixed gender leader groups analyzed by McCaulley, SI women ranked just below the median on Extraversion (32/60), near the bottom on Sensing (59/60), well above the median on Thinking (21/60), and quite high on Judging (17/60).

Comparison of Leadership Style Distribution

Table 2 presents Self-Selection Index ratio scores on MBTI Leadership Styles and type combinations for SI subjects compared with five sample groups chosen from the CAPT database for similarity in key aspects.

Group A is Females completing the MBTI G (N = 16,880); Group B is Women attending CCL programs (N = 181); Group C is a mixed gender group of Educational Administrators (N = 1,857); Group D is a mixed gender group of Administrators: Managers and Supervisors (N = 3.677); Group E is a mixed gender sample of Managers and Administrators (N = 7,463); and Group F is a mixed gender sample of University Teachers (N = 2,282). Index scores are reported for SI women on the four Kiersey-Bates leadership styles and the TJ combination in comparison with each sample group.

SI women differ significantly in their leadership styles from all comparison samples. In particular, SI women are significantly more NT Rational/Visionary in style than any of the comparative groups. They are characterized by the hard-driving, decisive TJ leadership combination to a greater degree than any of the all-female or mixed gender samples. SI participants have less preference for Feeling than the two female samples and University teachers but they are roughly similar to Feeling scores of the mixed gender managers in Groups D and E. As indicated by the high Index scores for the NT style, these women administrators are markedly greater Visionary planners of change than are Females in Group A and the mixed gender samples of Educational Administrators and Managers/Supervisors in Groups D and E.

Discussion

As illustrated by the results presented in Tables 1 and 2, the 371 women leaders who attended the Summer Institute over the five-year period were highly Thinking Dominant and decisive in their leadership and personal style, demonstrating a strong preference for innovation of change using Intuition, dispassionate analytical problem-solving techniques using Intuition, and organizational structure and comfort with authority using Judgment. Extraverts outnumbered Introverts in the sample, but the difference is not significant. The dominant leadership style is Rational/Visionary (NT), with an emphasis on creative planning for structural change in a highly logical and unemotional way.

As leaders, the women administrators in this study are similar to previous studies of leaders in their preference for Thinking, Judging, and Extraversion. They are more Intuitive than leaders in corporate and general samples which is consistent with previous profiles of University administrators and faculty working in the academy where theoretical and ideational fluency are valued.

In comparison with other female leaders for whom MBTI scores are available, SI women are dissimilar in their strong preference for Thinking over Feeling, are lower on Extraversion, and have a strong preference for Judgment over Perception. They are similar to women leaders attending programs at CCL on Intuition rather than Sensing, and somewhat similar to them on Thinking over Feeling.

TABLE 2 Self-Selection Index Scores of SI Women Compared with Selected Reference Samples on Keirsey–Bates/MBTI Leadership Styles

Reference Group	NT Rational Visionary	NF Feeling/ Catalyst	SP Trouble- shooter	SJ Guardian	TJ Driver
A: CAPT Females[a]	3.43***	0.64***	0.19***	0.56***	2.11***
B: CCL Females[b]	1.37***	0.61**	0.38*	1.04	1.56***
C: Edn'l Admins.[c]	2.34***	0.66***	0.35***	0.56***	1.42***
D: Mgrs./ Supvsrs.[d]	2.31***	1.00	0.25***	0.50	1.25***
E: Mgrs./ Admins.[e]	2.34***	0.90	0.28***	0.50***	1.28***
F: Univ. Tchrs.[f]	1.81***	0.54***	0.48*	0.77**	1.54***

Note. [a]Represents all Females completing Form G of the MBTI between 1978–82 from the CAPT databank (N = 16,880). [b]Represents Females participating in leadership programs of the Center for Creative Leadership between 1979–83 (N = 181). [c]Represents a mixed gender sample of Educational Administrators drawn from the CAPT database (N = 1,857). [d]Represents a mixed gender sample of Administrators (Managers and Supervisors) drawn from the CAPT databank 1971–84 (N = 3,678). [e]Represents a mixed gender sample of Business Managers and Administrators drawn from the CAPT databank, 1971–84 (N = 7,463). [f]Represents a mixed gender sample of University Teachers drawn from the CAPT databank 1971–84 (N = 2,282). Source: Macdaid, McCaulley, & Kainz, 1986.

$*p < .05$. $**p < .01$. $***p < .001$.

Implications

Caution must be used in drawing inferences due to the limited nature of this study and the general paucity of psychological data on women leaders in other settings. The predominant NT style suggests these women are comfortable taking risks, innovating change, and handling conflicts with primarily male supervisors and colleagues. Collegiality may be easier for them because they are highly similar to their male colleagues in intellectual orientation and have been able to adapt themselves to male-dominant values and power structures. They have the competence to deal with diverse administrative tasks, the intensely political climate, and

social isolation in senior positions. The predominance of tough-minded NT and ST types may reflect both their willingness to persist against adverse conditions and their recognized competence by male colleagues in an environment where knowledge and analytical thinking are valued. The fact that they have successfully advanced in the informal, collaborative culture of dispersed power in higher education suggests that they work well as group members. Further specific study of women's leadership styles is needed to assess any tendency toward participatory or "feminine" leadership style by women leaders in general.

In light of the strongly cross-gender typed profile of these women administrators who have attained academic leadership, the possibility of an interactive effect between leadership style and gender for Thinking Dominant women merits further thought and investigation. These successful women are strongly atypical of cultural expectations for women in their preference for analytical decision making and high structure and control. Data now being analyzed in the ongoing study of Summer Institute participants may reveal whether their style and gender are seen by these women as influencing their advancement and effectiveness.

In conclusion, this study demonstrates that women leaders represent a wide range of personal abilities and psychological styles which are effectively applied in a work environment not generally considered supportive of women. More research is needed to identify attitudes and contextual factors which continue to inhibit women from applying all their natural abilities and leadership potential to senior positions in higher education.

Acknowledgments

Research for this study was supported by Bucknell University where the author was chief student affairs officer and adjunct member of the Psychology Department. Bryn Mawr College and HERS Mid-America (University of Denver) cosponsored the project and assisted with the data collection. The author extends special thanks to Gary Sojka, Bob Midkiff, Susan Wallace, and Patricia Witkowski of Bucknell University for their invaluable support, to Cynthia Secor and Betsy Metzger of HERS for their encouragement and assistance, and to Janet Heckman and Patricia Lawlor for their advice.

References

Allen, J., Myers, I. B., & Kainz, R. I. (1976). *The Selection Ratio Type Table Program.* Gainesville, FL: Center for the Applications of Psychological Type.

Bass, B. M. (1990). *Bass and Stogdill's handbook of leadership theory, research, and managerial applications* (3rd ed.). New York: Free Press.

Bennis, W. (1990). *Why leaders can't lead: The unconscious conspiracy continues.* San Francisco: Jossey-Bass.

Denmark, F. L. (1977). Styles of leadership. *Psychology of Women Quarterly, 2*(2), 99–113.

Helgesen, S. (1990). *The female advantage: Women's way of leadership.* New York: Doubleday.

Heller, T., & Van Til, J. (1982). Leadership and followership: Some summary propositions. *Journal of Applied Behavioral Sciences, 18*(3), 405–414.

Hoferek, M. J. (1986). *Going forth: Women's leadership issues for women in higher education and physical education.* Princeton, NJ: Princeton Book Co.

Kanter, R. M. (1977). *Men and women of the corporation.* New York: Basic Books.

Kanter, R. M. (1989). The new managerial work. *Harvard Business Review, 67*(6), 85–92.

Keirsey, D., & Bates, M. (1978). *Please understand me.* Del Mar, CA: Prometheus Nemesis.

Kotter, J. P. (1990). What leaders really do. *Harvard Business Review, 68*(3), 103–111.

Kroeger, O., & Thuesen, J. (1988). *Type talk: The 16 personality types that determine how we live, love, and work.* New York: Delta Books.

Kushell, E., & Newton, R. (1986). Gender, leadership style, and subordinate satisfaction: An experiment. *Sex Roles, 14*(3/4), 203–209.

Loden, M. (1985). *Feminine leadership: Or how to succeed in business without being one of the boys.* New York: Times Books.

Macdaid, G. P., McCaulley, M. H., & Kainz, R. I. (1986). *Myers-Briggs Type Indicator atlas of type tables.* Gainesville, FL: Center for the Applications of Psychological Type.

McCaulley, M. H. (1985). The Selection Ratio Type Table: A research strategy for comparing type distributions. *Journal of Psychological Type, 10,* 46–56.

McCaulley, M. H. (1990). The Myers-Briggs Type Indicator and leadership. In K. E. Clark & M. B. Clark (Eds.), *Measures of Leadership* (pp. 381–418). West Orange, NJ: Leadership Library of America.

Morrison, A. R., White, R. P., & Van Velsor, E. (1987). *Breaking the glass ceiling: Can women reach the top of America's largest corporations?* Reading, MA: Addison-Wesley.

Myers, I. B., & McCaulley, M. H. (1985). *Manual: A guide to the development and use of the Myers-Briggs Type Indicator.* Palo Alto: Consulting Psychologists Press.

Pearson, C. S., Shavlik, D. L., & Touchton, J. G. (1989). *Educating the majority: Women challenge the tradition in higher education.* New York: Macmillan.

Rosener, J. W. (1989). Ways women lead. *Harvard Business Review, 68*(6), 119–125.

Sandler, B. R., & Hall, R. M. (1986). *The campus climate revisited: Chilly for women faculty, administrators, and graduate students.* Washington, DC: Project on the Status and Education of Women, Association of American Colleges.

Schwartz, F. N. (1989). Management women and the new facts of life. *Harvard Business Review, 67*(1), 65–76.

Shakeshaft, C. (1987). *Women in educational administration.* Newbury Park, CA: Sage Publications.

Shavlik, D., & Touchton, J. (1983). Toward a new era of leadership: The National Identifica-

tion Program. *New Directions for Higher Education, 12*(1), 47–58.

Statham, A. (1987). The gender model revisited: Differences in the management styles of men and women. *Sex Roles, 16*(7/8), 409–429.

Stokes, J. (1987a). Exploring the relationship of type and gender Part I: Anecdotal experiences of MBTI users. *Journal of Psychological Type, 13,* 34–43.

Stokes, J. (1987b). Exploring the relationship of type and gender Part II: A review and critique of empirical research and other data. *Journal of Psychological Type, 13,* 44–57.

Touchton, J. G., & Davis, L. (1991). *Fact book on women in higher education.* New York: MacMillan.

Charlotte Jacobsen Weddle has a background in senior university administration, counseling, research, elementary and college teaching, and human resources training. She earned a PhD in Human Development from Bryn Mawr College.

Direct inquiries about this article to Charlotte Jacobsen Weddle, Human Resources Consultant, Excell Associates, 3504 Greenwood Terrace, Greensboro, NC 27410, 919/632-9535.

CHAPTER 44

The Myers-Briggs Type Indicator, Subordinate Feedback, and Perceptions of Leadership Effectiveness

Paul E. Roush

Results of this study indicate that ratings of leader effectiveness varied with the leader's and rater's psychological preferences as inferred from the Myers-Briggs Type Indicator.® Self-ratings of leaders differed significantly from ratings provided by followers. When feedback regarding follower perceptions of leader effectiveness was provided to leaders under the conditions reported in the study, the leaders altered their behavior and modified their self-perceptions of effectiveness.

Developing leaders is the most important task of the United States Naval Academy. A crucial part of that process is the plebe development program during which newly arrived civilians make the transition to full-fledged members of the Brigade of Midshipmen. The initial year at any of the service academies has assumed the role of rite-of-passage. The upper classes have approached this grand indoctrination by "doing unto the plebes what had earlier been done unto them." While the traditional view has emphasized the ultimate benefits of the plebe development process for the plebes, the greatest potential benefit probably accrues to the upperclass. It is they who are charged, as 20-year-old men and women, with the responsibility for the inculcation of a particularly demanding military culture in 18-year-old men and women for whom, initially, that culture is largely alien. Much of that inculcation occurs without direct supervision except for that of other midshipmen. The situation offers these 20-year-olds a unique opportunity to experiment with a variety of leadership styles as they attempt to accomplish their daunting task.

This combination of a considerable measure of upperclass autonomy and an emphasis on repeating time-honored

Myers-Briggs Type Indicator is a registered trademark of Consulting Psychologists Press, Inc.

rites-of-passage poses a number of risks as well as opportunities. First, it has the potential for creating a climate in which the leadership practices of the upperclass can take on forms which would not be appropriate if applied to enlisted sailors and marines in the fleet. Second, the upperclass may not realize how their leadership practices are perceived by their followers; hence, they may not make an effort to learn more productive ways of influencing the behavior of their followers.

In the fall of 1990, the Naval Academy initiated an approach to the leadership development process that was a departure from previous practice. The approach had the followers (plebes) provide feedback to the leaders (second classmen, i.e., third-year midshipmen). This feedback took the form of ratings by the followers of the effectiveness of the leadership practices to which they were exposed during the plebe development process.

In initiating this program, the academy utilized two instruments. One was the Leadership Feedback Questionnaire (LFQ); the other was the Myers-Briggs Type Indicator (MBTI™). The LFQ, the items of which are listed in Appendix A, was developed locally in order to deal with local needs. The MBTI, a self-report instrument, assesses one's psychological preferences for acquiring information and for making decisions. It categorizes those preferences into 16 MBTI types (McCaulley, 1990).

The leadership feedback project addressed two fundamental research questions: Is MBTI type a leadership factor?, and what is the effect of feedback on self-perception? Subsumed under these overarching questions are a number of lesser included issues. To what degree is MBTI type associated with followers' perceptions of leadership effectiveness? To what degree is MBTI type associated with leaders' self-assessment of leadership effectiveness? To what degree is MBTI type as-

MBTI is a trademark of Consulting Psychologists Press, Inc.

sociated with leader and follower agreement in their perceptions of leadership effectiveness? Does initial feedback from followers promote greater agreement between leaders and followers on subsequent assessment opportunities? Do followers whose MBTI type is similar to that of a given leader assess the leader more positively than do followers whose MBTI type is dissimilar to that leader?

Apart from the research aspects of the initiative, several important by-products were intended. First, the standards against which effectiveness was assessed provided a positive leadership model for emulation by the midshipmen. Second, feedback was seen as a very useful catalyst for making appropriate changes. It was hoped, in other words, that leaders would modify both their perceptions and, where appropriate, their practices on the basis of substantive, quantifiable feedback from followers. Third, since the process also required the leaders to estimate their own effectiveness, it was intended to enhance the self-assessment skills of the leaders and help them learn, while still midshipmen, how their leadership practices were perceived by their followers, rather than gaining those insights, if at all, only after reporting to the fleet as junior officers. Fourth, the process was intended to incorporate a mechanism for understanding the role and value of individual differences; hence, psychological preferences of both leaders and followers were linked to leadership variables in the project. Finally, since the feedback program was monitored in leadership classes taken by all midshipmen, it offered a powerful means of linkage between the classroom study of leadership and its concurrent application in the subordinate-development and leader-development processes outside the classroom

The leadership feedback approach was designed to incorporate the positive aspects of a number of earlier studies. For example, Bass (1985) had developed a model in which leaders attempt to have followers put aside their own self-interests in order to promote the interests of the organization. In this model, the leaders provide vision and inspiration for the organization's goals, help their people learn new ways of thinking about issues, invest deeply in the development and empowerment of their followers, and deal with them as individuals. Bass and others have labelled this approach transformational leadership. It is typically contrasted with transactional leadership, an approach in which the leader satisfies the needs of subordinates in return for performance by subordinates which satisfies the needs of the leader.

Yammarino and Bass (1990) studied Naval Academy graduates serving in the surface warfare community. They found that leaders who were rated more transformational by their followers received better performance evaluations from their seniors and were more likely to be recommended for accelerated promotion than were their peers who were assessed as less transformational. Clover (1990) reported similar results at the Air Force Academy. Officers whose squadrons performed better were rated by cadets as more transformational than the officers whose squadrons did not perform as well.

Bass and Yammarino (1989) looked at the issue of leader self-perceptions. Leaders who were rated as more transformational by their followers were more likely to see themselves as their followers saw them. Their study refers to two tasks in the effective-leader equation, namely, practicing transformational leadership behaviors and assessing accurately one's own leadership behaviors.

In a study of the leadership practices of midshipmen at the Naval Academy, Roush and Atwater (1992) built upon this earlier work by assessing the MBTI as a predictor of transformational leadership and of self-perception accuracy. The Multifactor Officer Questionnaire (MOQ), developed by Yammarino and Bass (1990), was employed to infer the presence of transformational or transactional leadership or the laissez-faire (nonleader-

ship) approach. Subjects were upperclassmen responsible for helping incoming plebes make the initial transition from civilian to military life in preparation for integration into the Brigade of Midshipmen. Transformational leadership practices and the contingent promises and rewards elements of transactional leadership were significantly associated with extra effort by the followers. The feeling and sensing MBTI preferences had high association with the transformational leadership approach, and with self-perception accuracy in the transformational subelements. A major finding of the study was that followers were less willing to produce extra effort for a leader who practiced a "hands-off" style of leadership—active or passive management-by-exception or the laissez-faire approach. Conversely, "hands-on" practices, such as those embodied in the transformational concept of individualized consideration, a style in which the leader habitually provides personal attention to the follower when needed, evoked in the followers a desire to produce extra effort.

In a study of Fortune 500 managers, feedback resulted in reduction of self/other discrepancies on at least one of three rating scales by more than 80% of the subjects of the study. More than 40% of the managers significantly revised their self-view on all three scales after receiving feedback that indicated self/other discrepancy (Van Velsor, Ruderman, & Phillips, 1991).

Method

Subjects

The subjects comprised the entire classes of 1992 (leaders) and 1994 (followers) at the United States Naval Academy, a total of over 2,200 midshipmen. When the academic year began, the class of 1994 comprised 1,232 persons, of whom 136 were women and 270 were minorities. Minorities included 106 Blacks, 55 Asians, 99 Hispanics, and 10 Native Americans. The class of 1992 numbered 995 persons. Of that number, 95 were women and 139 were minorities, including 38 Blacks, 45 Asians, 51 Hispanics, and 5 Native Americans.

Procedures

At the start of the academic year in August 1990, each member of the class of 1992 (second classmen) was provided a copy of the LFQ, a survey which was to be the basis for anonymous feedback to him or her from those plebes in the class of 1994 for whose professional training the second classman was accountable. They received an explanation about the LFQ, the goals of the leadership feedback project, and the procedures to follow in its implementation. The 26 items of the LFQ were included on a computer program written to permit data entry by midshipmen at designated times during the academic year. As part of their leadership course in the fall semester of 1990, the plebes were required to enter on their individual personal computers the responses to the LFQ items. Data entry occurred after the 8- and 16-week points of the semester. Each plebe answered all 26 questions for each second classman in his or her squad—normally four, but sometimes only three people. Thus, for each second classman there were eight entries (assuming four plebes per squad) by the end of the semester. The responses were compiled on the Naval Academy Time Sharing System (NATS) and were not accessible by any member of the chain of command.

In January 1991, the class of 1992 began the second-class, core-leadership course. In the first week of the course, they answered the same 26 items about themselves previously answered by the plebes. That is, they looked back at the first semester and assessed their own leadership practices. They were then given the opportunity to have displayed on their computer screens, adjacent to their own entries, a single score for each LFQ item representing the aggregated mean of all plebe rating entries for a given upperclassman during the first semester. This technique of data display preserved the anonymity of the followers. Additionally, the followers and leaders were no longer assigned to the same squads as in the first semester, so the likelihood of group retribution by a disgruntled upperclassman was exceedingly remote. The protections built into the process enhanced the confidence in the outcomes.

Finally, 14 weeks later (i.e., the 32-week point of the academic year) the process was repeated. Plebes rated the leadership practices of the second classmen in their respective squads during the second semester; the second classmen then rated themselves for that same time period and were subsequently given the opportunity to view aggregated scores of the plebes in their squads.

Measures

Leadership Feedback Questionnaire (LFQ). The LFQ (see Appendix A) was developed locally to address areas of interest at the Naval Academy, which ranged from providing academic assistance to using behaviors that would be appropriate if used with enlisted sailors in the fleet. Each item is a positive statement about the leadership behavior of the second classman being rated. Respondents indicated their level of agreement with the statement by assigning a number from (1) strongly agree to (5) strongly disagree. Thus, lower scores are more positive. Podsakoff and Organ (1986) pointed out a problem which arises when rating scales, particularly the self-report variety, ask raters to go beyond reporting specific facts or finite events to engage in higher-order cognitive processes involving weighting, inference, interpretation, and the like. Similarly, Wohlers and London (1989) discussed the problems in evaluating management characteristics, due to the difficulty of linking the characteristics to concrete observable behaviors. Items on the LFQ were worded to promote confidence in the responses. Rather than being asked to come to conclusions based on inferred intent or state of mind of the leader, the followers were asked, on most items, to report if they observed particular leadership behaviors by the second classman in the leader-follower relationship in which they were participants. A number of LFQ items were constructed to assess behaviors which would be indicative of transformational leadership. There was, however, no effort to assess the presence of transactional or laissez-faire approaches. The emphasis was overwhelmingly on positive leadership and on "hands-on" leadership.

Myers-Briggs Type Indicator (MBTI). All midshipmen complete Form G of the MBTI shortly after arrival at the academy and again 2 years later. Two leadership courses, one in plebe year and another in the summer preceding second-class year, include MBTI instruction as part of the formal curriculum. The instrument relies on self-report to identify how individuals become aware of their environment and how they come to conclusions on the basis of that awareness (Myers & McCaulley, 1985). The MBTI comprises four bipolar indices of one's preference for either: extraversion (E) or introversion (I), sensing (S) or intuition (N), thinking (T) or feeling (F), and judging (J) or perceiving (P).

The E/I index is based on items that differentiate between individuals whose focus is on people and things (extraversion) versus those whose focus is on concepts and ideas (introversion). The S/N index deals with the preferred manner of taking in information. Those who take in information through the five senses (sensing) are differentiated from those whose focus is on possibilities, meanings, and relationships among data and events (in-

tuition) rather than on the data or events, per se. Decision making is at issue on the T/F index. People who prefer objective analysis and logical consequences (thinking) are at one end of the continuum; those who base their decisions on the personal rather than the technical or abstract aspects of the situation (feeling) are at the other. Finally, the J/P index addresses tolerance for uncertainty. The person who seeks early closure, who wants structure, who lives by schedules and deadlines minimizes uncertainty (judging), while those who keep their options open, live less scheduled and more loosely planned lives (perceiving) are more comfortable with uncertainty (Myers & McCaulley, 1985). While each preference is important, it is necessary to bear in mind that one's MBTI type involves the simultaneous interactions of all the preferences. A key point in type theory is that all persons can use all eight preferences to some degree. The purpose of the MBTI, however, is to identify the four preferences that represent an individual's habitual choice between rival alternatives on each of the four indices (Myers & McCaulley). The four preferences identified by the instrument are combined to constitute an individual's MBTI type. Appendix B shows the distribution of MBTI types for the subjects of the study.

Results

Tables 1 and 2 address the first of the two fundamental research questions posed earlier; namely, are MBTI psychological preferences (and the MBTI types which they constitute) a factor in the leadership equation? Table 1 shows mean ratings assigned to the second classmen by the plebes. Ratings are categorized by MBTI type and by MBTI preference. The table also shows the number of ratings from which the means were derived. The reader should be aware that the number of ratings received and given represents roughly 10 times the number of leaders or followers in the study, since three or four followers each rated each leader three times.

The mean rating score for all LFQ items is 2.03. The upperclass midshipmen whose MBTI type was ISTJ received the least positive rating, with a mean score of 2.11. The MBTI type which is opposite of ISTJ is ENFP (i.e., it is the MBTI type with none of the letters I, S, T, or J). ENFPs received the second most positive rating. Type differences can be understood more fully by looking at the mean scores of the preferences which constitute these two types. Table 1 shows that the most positive ratings are received by the following preferences: feeling, perceiving, intuition, and extraversion, in that order. Introversion and thinking are less positive than these four, and sensing and judging receive the least positive ratings of the eight preferences. Obviously, it follows that mean scores of the types will reflect the mean scores of their constituent components, the preferences, assuming adequate sample size. The type rated most positively, the ISFPs, represented only 15 midshipmen (see Appendix B) and could be vulnerable to large fluctuations based on extreme ratings of just a few people.

In order to retain perspective, it is worth noting that all mean ratings are positive. On the LFQ, the most positive rating is 1 (strongly agree), 3 is neutral, and 5 (strongly disagree) is the most negative. In the current study, there is no item on the LFQ for which the mean rating drops to the level of neutral. The study, in other words, deals with varying degrees of positive feedback. Given the stress engendered by the plebe development system and the opportunity for varying levels of abuse of the system, that represents a rather remarkable achievement.

With the exception of sensors and intuitives, the followers, in giving ratings, exhibited the same pattern as did the leaders in receiving them. That is, extraverts, feelers, and perceivers gave more positive ratings than did introverts, thinkers, and

judgers. It appears that the same approaches to life that yield a more positive outlook when making judgments about other people may result in being assessed more positively by others

Table 2 goes a step farther in questioning MBTI type as a factor in the leadership equation. It does so by calculating whether the differences in mean rating scores for the 16 MBTI types tabulated in Table 1 could have occurred by chance. For each item on the LFQ, one-way ANOVA was calculated, with MBTI type of the second classmen (leaders) as the independent variable and rating scores supplied by the plebes (followers) as the dependent variable. The same process was then repeated, but the MBTI type of plebes was substituted as the independent variable while retaining the same dependent variable. Results are shown in Table 2 as F-values and probabilities associated with each LFQ item.

Table 2 offers very strong confirmation for the notion that MBTI type is a pervasive leadership factor. Follower ratings of leaders show considerable variation as a function of the MBTI type of the follower. In fact, rating differences are statistically significant for every item on the LFQ. For 19 items, $p < .001$, but in no case is $p > .05$. The results are similar when follower ratings of leaders are analyzed in terms of MBTI type of the leaders. For 21 of the 26 items on the LFQ, $p < .001$. There are only three items for which $p > .05$.

Comparison of the F-values in Table 2 offers a convenient means for assessing the magnitude and locus of the role of MBTI type in the process. The table deals with differences in ratings of leaders by followers. F-values calculated from rating differences based on MBTI types of leaders are generally larger than F-values when rating differences are derived from MBTI types of followers. It thus appears that MBTI type of the leader is a more dominant factor in leadership assessment by followers than is MBTI type of the follower.

There are also differences when one ex-

TABLE 1 Number and Mean Score of Follower Ratings Received by Leaders (by Leader MBTI Type and MBTI Preference) and Number and Mean Score of Follower Ratings Given by Followers (by Follower MBTI Type and MBTI Preference)

	Ratings Received by Leaders		Ratings Given by Followers	
MBTI Type	**n**	**Mean**	**n**	**Mean**
ISTJ	1437	2.11	1071	2.03
ISFJ	280	2.05	203	2.23
INFJ	143	1.96	221	1.95
INTJ	600	2.01	725	2.11
ISTP	679	2.05	486	1.99
ISFP	155	1.92	156	2.01
INFP	409	1.96	303	2.05
INTP	779	2.05	614	2.08
ESTP	935	2.01	565	2.08
ESFP	219	1.97	268	2.05
ENFP	575	1.94	658	1.97
ENTP	1110	2.00	1269	2.00
ESTJ	1450	2.07	1662	2.00
ESFJ	228	2.04	287	1.98
ENFJ	160	1.97	377	1.97
ENTJ	683	2.04	1099	2.08
MBTI Preferences				
Extraversion (E)	5360	2.02	6185	2.02
Introversion (I)	4482	2.05	3779	2.06
Sensing (S)	5383	2.06	4698	2.03
Intuition (N)	4459	2.00	5266	2.04
Thinking (T)	7673	2.05	7491	2.04
Feeling (F)	2169	1.97	2473	2.01
Judging (J)	4981	2.06	5645	2.04
Perceiving (P)	4861	2.00	4319	2.02

amines which items elicit the largest type-related differences. Type differences of *followers* are greatest on item 22, on which followers assessed the loyalty of their leaders to higher authority. The second greatest difference was on item 25, in which the follow-up practices of the leaders was at issue. Variation in follower ratings based on *leader* MBTI type was greatest for item 7, which dealt with respect for the leader among his or her peers. The second greatest variation occurred on item 10, dealing with the likelihood of subsequent emulation by the follower of the leadership practices of the leader. Ratings on the use of positive leadership practices (item 18) also showed significant variation by leader MBTI type.

One of the research issues subsumed under the basic question of whether or not MBTI type is a factor in the leadership equation is this: Do followers rate leaders differently based on similarity of MBTI type between follower and leader? The data portrayed graphically on Figure 1 were derived from one-way ANOVA for

TABLE 2 F-Values and Probabilities for One-Way ANOVA with MBTI
Type as Independent Variable and Follower Rating of Leaders
on LFQ Items as Dependent Variable

| Item | MBTI Type (Leaders) | | MBTI Type (Followers) | |
	F-value	p-value	F-value	p-value
#1	3.23	.001	3.57	.001
#2	2.72	.001	2.94	.001
#3	5.17	.001	3.42	.001
#4	5.22	.001	1.96	.014
#5	3.04	.001	3.71	.001
#6	4.40	.001	2.91	.001
#7	6.74	.001	2.92	.001
#8	4.94	.001	4.73	.001
#9	4.88	.001	3.80	.001
#10	5.68	.001	1.85	.023
#11	1.41	.133	3.77	.001
#12	2.78	.001	1.94	.016
#13	2.04	.010	1.97	.014
#14	2.48	.001	4.35	.001
#15	2.90	.001	3.90	.001
#16	4.50	.001	2.37	.002
#17	2.90	.001	3.37	.001
#18	5.59	.001	2.02	.011
#19	3.52	.001	4.49	.001
#20	3.56	.001	2.24	.004
#21	2.71	.001	2.85	.001
#22	2.06	.009	7.01	.001
#23	2.66	.001	4.07	.001
#24	1.32	.181	3.62	.001
#25	1.56	.078	5.04	.001
#26	4.19	.001	3.26	.001

each of the LFQ's 26 items. The calcula-
tions were repeated on 16 different data
sets, each of which contained only those
leaders who shared a single MBTI type.
Each dataset was investigated using MBTI
type of the followers as the independent
variable and the rating assigned to the
leaders by the followers as the dependent
variable. For each LFQ item on each dataset, the Games-Howell procedure (Games
& Howell, 1976) was used as a post hoc
test. The purpose was to identify any follower MBTI types whose ratings of leaders were more positive, at a statistically
significant level, than the ratings given by
at least one other MBTI type. If such follower MBTI types were identified, and if

they contained at least three letters in
common with the MBTI type of the leaders in the dataset under investigation, the
item was tabulated in Figure 1. For each
leader MBTI type, the chart shows the
number of items (from the 26 on the LFQ)
that meet the twin criteria of significance
and shared preferences. It provides a
quick visual assessment of the likelihood
that a given leader MBTI type will experience wide variation in follower ratings as
a function of shared psychological preferences.

The results were mixed. In some cases,
when follower and leader MBTI types
shared at least three preferences, leaders
were rated higher than when two or fewer

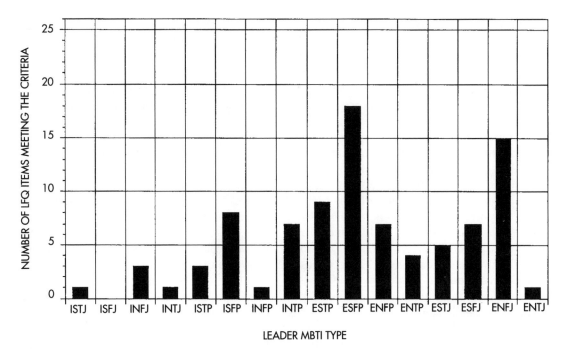

Figure 1 Frequency with which similarity of follower and leader MBTI type was associated with higher ratings from the follower.

preferences were shared. This was especially true for extraverted feeling types (ESFP, ENFP, ESFJ, and ENFJ). For other types, the similarity factor appeared to have little impact. For three of the four "TJ" types (ISTJ, INTJ, and ENTJ), probably among the most common types in the military, shared type produced a significant difference on only 1 of the 26 items on the LFQ. Another way to conceptualize the dynamic involved is to view this measure as an index of consensus. For example, there was broad agreement among followers about where ISTJs should be rated. For ESFPs, on the other hand, there was much less consensus. On 18 of the 26 LFQ items, at least one follower type shared three or four preferences with ESFP leaders and rated those leaders more positively (at a statistically significant level) than did at least one other MBTI type. There was less consensus among followers about the effectiveness of "FP" leaders, and particularly about ESFP leaders, than about "TJ" leaders. In all probability, ESFPs, true to type characteristics of the feeling preference,

invested more psychic energy in personal relationships than did the "TJs," thus making themselves more vulnerable while simultaneously opening up a host of possibilities. Those consequences may well be amplified by the greater tolerance of the perceiving preference, relative to the judgers, for living with (even inviting) ambiguity and risk. Applying type theory sheds light on the consensus phenomenon evident in the study. In general, there was more consensus (whether positive or negative) about introverted leaders than about extraverted leaders.

Table 3 deals with the second of the fundamental research questions: What is the effect of feedback on self-perception? The answer requires a comparison of leader self-assessment before and after receiving feedback. Relative to how the followers saw their leader, how did the leader see himself or herself in the fall semester (when there was no feedback)? When the leader-follower comparison was repeated in the spring, after feedback, what changes were noted? Were the leaders' self-perceptions more accurate, relative to ratings by the followers, than they were prior to receiving the feedback?

Table 3 includes three sets of difference scores and their corresponding t-values. The first two sets of mean differences were derived by comparing, on two occasions, the self-ratings of the leaders with ratings of the leaders by their followers, once at the end of the fall semester and again at the end of the spring semester. Minus signs preceding the difference score mean that the leader rated himself or herself less positively than he or she was rated by the follower. T-values were calculated for each set of differences on each LFQ item to estimate whether the noted differences could have occurred by chance. The third set of mean differences was derived by comparing leader self-ratings in the fall semester with leader self-ratings in the spring semester. Minus signs preceding the difference score mean that the leader rated himself or herself less positively in the spring than in the fall. Again, the differences were subjected to t-tests for each LFQ item.

By comparing the mean differences in the spring with those in the fall, it is clear that the discrepancies between leader and follower changed in both magnitude and direction after the leaders received feedback from the followers. For 15 of the 26 LFQ items, the difference between self-ratings and follower ratings was smaller after receiving feedback (i.e., in the spring) than it had been initially. The same propensity for change-following-feedback appeared when self-ratings were compared. On 14 items, self-ratings were less positive in the spring than in the fall. Of perhaps greater importance was the trend among the leaders toward lowered expectations on self-ratings for all items on the LFQ when taking follower ratings as a point of reference. This was true for 25 of the 26 LFQ items in the spring semester when compared with the fall. Where overestimates continued, they were smaller. Where underestimates continued, they were larger. For six items, overestimates became underestimates.

While the question at issue in Table 3 is the effect of feedback on self-perception, a major subelement is the influence of MBTI type differences on an individual's ability to assess accurately how he or she is perceived by subordinates. For each of the 16 MBTI types, the mean score for leader self-rating was determined for each LFQ item and compared with the corresponding mean rating of leaders by followers. Those differences in ratings for the LFQ items were then averaged. The mean difference across all MBTI types and for all LFQ items was 0.197. The differences were absolute. They show only magnitude, without regard to whether the self-ratings or the follower ratings were more positive. The MBTI type most accurate in self-assessment was INTP, with a mean difference score of 0.153. Least accurate were their opposite type, the ESFJs, with a mean difference score of 0.245. The fact that introverted (rather than extraverted), intuitive (rather than sensing), thinking (rather than feeling), and perceiving (rather than judging) leaders, on average, rated themselves more like their followers rated them is consistent with type theory. The inner world of contemplation, the capacity for seeing patterns, meanings, and relationships behind facts, the logical, consequential approach to making choices, and the desire to avoid premature closure all militate in favor of greater congruence.

Discussion

The results of the study confirm that follower perceptions of leader effectiveness, as inferred from the LFQ, differ significantly based on MBTI type, whether the type differences are those among the leaders or those among the followers. However, the variation was greater when leader MBTI type was the independent variable. Rating-score differences as a function of type differences were pervasive. Not only did fol-

TABLE 3 Mean Differences and T-Values by LFQ Item When Follower Ratings Are Compared with Self-Ratings in the Fall and Spring Semesters and When Self-Ratings in the Fall and Spring Semesters are Compared with Each Other

Follower Rating and Self-Ratings

| LFQ Item | Mean Differences | | T-Values | | Self-Rating in Fall and Spring | |
	Fall	Spring	Fall	Spring	Mean Differences	T-Values
#1	0.26	0.20	17.19***	9.44***	− 0.10	− 3.51***
#2	0.31	0.13	19.22***	5.81***	− 0.07	− 2.26*
#3	0.41	0.28	26.34***	13.07***	− 0.05	− 1.57
#4	0.18	0.24	11.04***	10.30***	0.28	7.92***
#5	0.14	0.12	9.54***	6.22***	0.04	1.46
#6	0.38	0.20	23.88***	9.22***	− 0.05	− 1.61
#7	0.10	0.09	6.82***	4.32***	0.04	1.19
#8	− 0.07	− 0.10	− 4.24***	− 4.72***	− 0.11	− 3.78***
#9	0.16	− 0.13	9.61***	− 5.31***	− 0.18	− 5.40***
#10	0.39	0.30	22.76***	11.78***	− 0.05	− 1.92
#11	0.02	0.00	1.88	0.06	0.02	0.67
#12	0.04	− 0.12	2.69**	− 5.21***	− 0.07	− 2.27*
#13	0.04	− 0.16	2.80**	− 7.31***	− 0.15	− 5.07***
#14	− 0.08	− 0.15	− 4.98***	− 7.26***	0.04	1.44
#15	0.00	− 0.05	0.14	− 2.07*	0.08	2.59**
#16	0.21	0.12	13.36***	5.81***	0.06	2.31*
#17	0.26	0.20	14.58***	8.14***	0.17	5.01***
#18	0.32	0.19	19.88***	8.28***	0.09	3.15**
#19	0.37	0.26	20.75***	10.86***	0.31	9.57***
#20	− 0.28	− 0.40	− 19.29***	− 18.38***	− 0.19	− 6.08***
#21	0.25	0.08	16.08***	3.49***	0.05	1.56
#22	0.00	− 0.15	− 0.11	− 6.74***	− 0.05	− 1.56
#23	0.06	− 0.05	3.70***	− 2.38*	0.00	− 0.04
#24	− 0.07	− 0.22	− 4.61***	− 10.26***	− 0.09	− 3.16**
#25	− 0.26	− 0.40	− 18.98***	− 19.72***	− 0.13	− 4.61***
#26	− 0.12	− 0.29	− 7.45***	− 12.25***	− 0.13	− 4.55

*p < .05.   **p < .01.   ***p < .001.

lower ratings vary with MBTI type; the same phenomenon occurred when leaders rated themselves. Certain MBTI type leaders found it much easier to assess accurately the effectiveness of their own leadership practices when follower ratings were taken as the point of reference.

For many midshipmen leaders, the initial rating represented the first quantifiable feedback of their leadership ability (and by those who knew how that leadership really was carried out). Leaders re-

sponded to the feedback they received in January 1990 by assessing their leadership practices much differently in April 1990. In most cases (15 of 26 items on the LFQ) they rated themselves less positively. Where they rated themselves more positively on the second self-rating opportunity, there is evidence that their performance matched the rating. In every such occurrence, their followers also rated them more positively. For 16 of the 26 items on the LFQ, when leaders changed their self-rating scores after receiving feedback, the change was statistically significant ($p < .05$).

One important issue raised by the study is that of standards. Campbell (1987) pointed out that 56% of the general officers who attended the Center for Creative Leadership's Leadership Development Program were drawn from the ranks of just two of the "TJ" types, namely ISTJ and ESTJ. These were obviously people who had performed superbly over the course of their careers. Yet in the project at the Naval Academy, ISTJs were ranked by their followers as the least effective of all the leader types, both in the aggregate and in most of the individual LFQ items. The explanation is largely in the criteria employed. Had the LFQ assessed the ability to organize, to persevere, to attend to details, to be responsible, logical, and dependable, the results may well have been quite different. Those latter qualities help define the ISTJ (Myers & McCaulley, 1985). Instead, the LFQ dealt largely with the quality of personal interactions between the leader and the follower in a setting in which the leader had almost unlimited power relative to the follower; there was minimal external supervision of the day-to-day interactions; and there was a strong presumption of the military necessity for the negotiation of a rigorous rites-of-passage. West Point has learned from recent surveys that the areas in which its new graduates performed least well included talking with troops, developing subordinates, and concern for welfare of troops (U.S. Military Academy, 1988). Annapolis graduates are probably very similar.

A survey of follower attitudes taken at the conclusion of the study in April 1991 amplifies the value of the approach for the participants. When 850 followers were polled, 82% said that responding to the LFQ items had made them more aware of the leadership qualities they were expected to achieve. Approximately 77% said it made them more aware of the practices they should employ when they become responsible for development of followers. Just over 50% said that assessing leadership practices of the leaders gave them a voice in the analysis of the plebe indoctrination program. There was agreement by 74% that feedback from followers provided a useful basis for making changes in one's approach to leading. In other words, participation in the project had an informing effect and an attitudinal effect for followers that should improve their subsequent performance in a leadership capacity.

The capacity of feedback as a change agent was a salient feature of the study. Evidence is very strong that midshipmen leaders modified their leadership behavior as a result of feedback from their subordinates. They also modified their self-assessments about the effectiveness of their leadership practices. It is probable that several factors were major contributors. One was the confidentiality factor. As the study progressed, it became clear to all participants that there was no risk in telling the truth. A second factor was consensus among the leaders that the feedback was both accurate and useful. They became convinced, in other words, that the followers knew the answers to the questions. In the main, the LFQ items allowed the followers to say that a particular, discrete behavior pattern either did or did not occur in the leader-follower relationship. When the leader was asked to respond to the same item, there was very little ambiguity—the behavior and the language were understood with clarity by both parties. Additionally, the leaders understood that the behaviors being assessed were not just an intellectual exercise but reflected skills and abilities they were using at the time of the study that would stand them in good stead in the world of the professional military officer. Given those precursors, the condition described by Van Velsor, Ruderman, and Phillips (1991) as "disconfirming data about self" had the desired effect for the leaders in the feedback project; namely, it gave them the opportunity to confront the self/other discrepancy and then use it as a motivator for change, however painful the process.

A final issue involves the scope of the Leadership Feedback Project. For purposes of this study, there was no attempt to create an instrument which represented a leadership paradigm. Items were formulated purely in response to perceived local needs. Different items may be inserted into the fundamental structure of the program in the future. While factor analysis may be undertaken to isolate a smaller number of factors that promote the goals of the current project, the project is likely to remain committed to practical responses to perceived problems rather than to the search for a more encompassing leadership paradigm. Future analysis will include greater emphasis on gender and ethnic differences in the leader-follower equation. Other potential variables include the effects of prior enlisted service and first choice for service selection (i.e., does a midshipmen whose choice is Marine Corps infantry lead differently from a midshipman whose choice is naval aviation?). Finally, there is merit in long-term follow-up in the fleet to ascertain if follower ratings at the Naval Academy contain predictive components for subsequent success that are not captured by other indicators.

The major impact of the study lies in its documentation of the positive effects of providing feedback to leaders. Provision of a simple, rational, and workable structure to accomplish that feedback function in a nonthreatening way has the potential to alter fundamentally the purposes pursued in both the leader development and follower development processes at the Naval Academy.

References

Bass, B. M. (1985). *Leadership and performance beyond expectations*. New York: Free Press.

Bass, B. M., & Yammarino, F. J. (1989). *Transformational leaders know themselves better* (Technical Report No. ONR-TR-5). Arlington, VA: Office of Naval Research.

Campbell, D. (1987, August). *The psychological test profiles of brigadier generals: Warmongers or decisive warriors?* Paper presented at the annual meeting of the American Psychological Association, New York.

Clover, W. H. (1990). Transformational leaders: Team performance, leadership ratings, and firsthand impressions. In K. E. Clark & M. B. Clark (Eds.), *Measures of leadership* (pp. 171–184). West Orange, NJ: Leadership Library of America.

Games, P. A., & Howell, J. F. (1976). Pairwise multiple comparison procedures with unequal n's and/or variances: A Monte Carlo study. *Journal of Educational Statistics, 1,* 113–125.

McCaulley, M. (1990). The Myers-Briggs Type Indicator and leadership. In K. E. Clark & M. B. Clark (Eds.), *Measures of leadership* (pp. 381–418). West Orange, NJ: Leadership Library of America.

Myers, I., & McCaulley, M. (1985). *Manual: A guide to the development and use of the Myers-Briggs Type Indicator*. Palo Alto, CA: Consulting Psychologists Press.

Podsakoff, P., & Organ, D. (1986) Self-reports in organizational research: Problems and prospects. *Journal of Management, 12,* 531–544.

Roush, P. E., & Atwater, L. (1992). Using the MBTI to understand transformational leadership and self-perception accuracy. *Military Psychology, 4(1),* 17–33.

U. S. Military Academy (1988, June). *Platoon leader performance of USMA graduates.* (Report No. 88–002). West Point, NY: Office of Institutional Research.

Van Velsor, E., Ruderman, M., & Phillips, D. (1991). *Enhancing self-objectivity and performance on the job: The developmental impact of feedback.* Unpublished manuscript.

Wohlers, A., & London, M. (1989). Ratings of managerial characteristics: Evaluation difficulty, co-worker agreement, and self-awareness. *Personnel Psychology, 42,* 235–261.

Yammarino, F. J., & Bass, B. M. (1990). Long-term forecasting of transformational leadership and its effects among naval officers: Some preliminary findings. In K. E. Clark & M. B. Clark (Eds.), *Measures of leadership* (pp. 151–170). West Orange, NJ: Leadership Library of America.

Paul E. Roush, PhD, is Associate Professor of Leadership at his alma mater, the Naval Academy, and is Coordinator of Institutional Research for the Commandant of Midshipmen. He is a retired Marine Corps Colonel with service in Viet Nam and has been a Naval Attache in Moscow and a faculty member of the National War College.

Direct inquiries about this article to Paul E. Roush, Associate Professor, Luce Hall, Room 209, U.S. Naval Academy, Annapolis, MD 21402, 410/268–1084.

Appendix A

Leadership Feedback Questionnaire

1. This 2/c knows how I am doing academically.
2. This 2/c shows me ways to do better academically.
3. It seems to me that this 2/c is concerned about my personal welfare.
4. No matter how upsetting the situation, this 2/c never loses self-control.
5. This 2/c treats me as an individual rather than a number.
6. This 2/c is willing to listen to me when I am having a problem.
7. This 2/c seems to enjoy the respect and camaraderie of his or her peers and seniors.
8. The uniform appearance of this 2/c is as good as or better than that of the 4/c.
9. The room standards of this 2/c are as good as or better than those of the 4/c.
10. When I am an upperclassman, I would like to lead in the same manner as this 2/c.
11. The compliance with regulations by this 2/c serves as a good model for me to follow.
12. This 2/c gives me feedback about both the good and bad aspects of my performance.
13. This 2/c advises me on how I can improve my performance in weak areas.
14. This 2/c requires me to back up my opinions with good reasoning.
15. This 2/c helps me by providing new ways of thinking about problems.
16. Even though the plebe indoctrination system is very demanding, this 2/c treats me with respect.
17. The leadership techniques used by this 2/c would be very appropriate if applied to enlisted sailors in the fleet.
18. Most of the time this 2/c tries to motivate me by using positive leadership techniques.
19. As a general rule, this 2/c praises in public and reprimands in private.
20. This 2/c holds me accountable for the highest personal, uniform and room standards.
21. This 2/c consistently takes advantage of opportunities to acknowledge my successes.
22. The statements of this 2/c about orders issued by higher authority reflect loyalty to that authority.
23. This 2/c treats me in a consistent rather than an erratic manner.
24. This 2/c clearly communicates what is expected of me.
25. This 2/c follows-up on assignments he or she has directed me to accomplish.
26. I feel motivated to make an extra effort in the tasks assigned to me by this 2/c.

ISTJ	ISFJ	INFJ	INTJ
n = 150 (138)	n = 29 (25)	n = 17 (29)	n = 67 (85)
% = 13.6 (11.2)	% = 2.6 (2.0)	% = 1.5 (2.4)	% = 6.1 (6.9)
ISTP	**ISFP**	**INFP**	**INTP**
n = 80 (68)	n = 18 (19)	n = 50 (44)	n = 90 (71)
% = 7.3 (5.5)	% = 1.6 (1.5)	% = 4.5 (3.6)	% = 8.2 (5.8)
ESTP	**ESFP**	**ENFP**	**ENTP**
n = 100 (72)	n = 26 (30)	n = 61 (88)	n = 125 (155)
% = 9.1 (5.8)	% = 2.4 (2.4)	% = 5.5 (7.1)	% = 11.3 (12.6)
ESTJ	**ESFJ**	**ENFJ**	**ENTJ**
n = 164 (201)	n = 27 (34)	n = 22 (43)	n = 76 (130)
% = 14.9 (16.3)	% = 2.5 (2.8)	% = 2.0 (3.5)	% = 6.9 (10.6)

Index

and managers, 362; impacts, 361–63; job
performance of graduate supervisors, 359;
methodology, 360; program evaluation, 359;
program improvement, 362; program
objectives, 361; recommendations, 361–63
Leadership-making model, 380; effective
professional work teams, 386; goals, 382;
horizontal relationships, 382; measures,
382–83; process, 380; professional project
team development, 386; professional work
teams, 382; three-component model, 381;
transactional relationships, 381; vertical
dyadic relationships, 382
Leadership Practices Inventory (LPI), 133
Leadership Style and Influence: Management
Skills Profile (MSP) subsection, 469–70
Leadership Style Indicator (LSI), 469; comparison
of scores with MSP, 473; correlation results
with MSP, 471; Latin American personal style,
488–90; procedure, 470–71; regression
conclusion, 471–72
Legitimating tactics, 419
Letter series subtest, 338
Levi Strauss, 447
Likability, 351–53
Likert: scales of managerial behavior, 121; -type
scales, 49
Linguistic analysis, 250–51
Linkages: financial health and effectiveness in
higher education, 496; leadership. See
Leadership Linkages
Locklear, J.C.: effect of stress on decision making,
100–103
Locus of control: leader-follower personality
match, 228; leadership and performance, 227
Longitudinal economic data: preferred analysis
method, 295
Looking Glass, Inc. (LGI) simulation, 433; data
collection, 434; measures, 434–35;
participants, 433; results, 435–36; role
assignments, 433; variables, 434–35
Lotus, 455
Low-performing organizations, 294
Loyalty, 238; American work force, reduction of
since World War II, 62; Japanese industry, 62;
in schools, 137
Luck, 300

Maintenance (M), 4; behaviors, 82
Management, 26: development, 199; differentiation
from leadership, 77; effectiveness defined,
49–51; interpretations of role in name change
firms, 310; risktaking, 440; roles described,
48; Senior Executive Profile. See Senior
Executive Profile; senior executives. See
Executives; subordinates perception of work of
senior, 51–55; theory, executive ideology, 284;
top management. See Executives; skills and
group effectiveness, 199–211
Management by Exception, 238; behaviors, 178
Management Skills Profile (MSP), 201, 455;

comparison of scores with LSI, 473;
correlation results with LSI, 471; correlations
with TSP, 204; definitions, 203; dimensions,
203; gender study, 508–09; intercorrelations
with TSP dimensions, 204; interrater
reliabilities, 202; item, text and factor
loadings, gender study, 510; median
correlations with TSP, 208; median and
maximum correlations with TSP scales, 209;
regression conclusion, 471–72; subordinate
ratings, 202
Managerial Grid, 17
Managers, 3; comparisons of international
locations, 355–57; health service
organizations, 400; and status quo, 178
Managers, behavior, 120; analysis, 121–22; cluster
equations, 124; commitment measurement,
121; Duncan multiple range test, 124, 127;
dynamic correlations, 124; goal pressure, 122;
matrix, 126; measures, 120–21; negative linear
relationship between performance and stress,
125; oblique cluster analysis, 123, 125;
performance, tension, and commitment,
120–28; procedures of longitudinal
observational data, 120–21; productivity
measurement, 121; static correlations, 123;
study limitations, 127–28; tension
measurement, 121; zero-order Pearson
correlations, 121–22
Managing as a Performing Art (Vaill), 429
Manipulation: experimental, 337
Manuals: how to lead, 399
March, J.G., 496
Marine Corps, 541
Marx, Groucho, 365
Masculine/aloof, 519
Maslow, Abraham, 43
Mastruzzi, Bob, 137, 138
Matrix: management, 445; structure and
alignment, 286
McDonnell Douglas, 447
Means centered research, 43
Mean utility point, 294
Measurements: use of, 8
Meglino, B.M., 120
Meier New-Truck Exercise, 7
Meindl, J.R., 294
Melbourne (Australia) Metropolitan Fire Brigade:
action-research study, 141
Mentor, 245
Methodology: jargon, 13; multiple methods, 20
Michigan Four-Factor theory, 132
Middle East: recent fighting, 400–01
Middle ground theories, 251; learning, 254
Middle managers: corporate. See Corporations
(middle managers); retail store study, 217–22
Military structures: academies, 314; discontinuous
hierarchy study, 401–412; identifying
enhancers, 414; indoctrination, 319;
leadership enhancers, 408–13; leadership
neutralizers, 408–12, 414; leadership

measurement of, 38; selective reporting, 40; special challenges, 40–42

Organizational cultures, outcomes: measurement, 217; performance, 217; shrinkage, 217; study method, 217–18

Organizational cultures, performance, 215; ambiguous conditions, 294; indices, 184; moderated on stove level, 221; and outcomes, 217

Osborn, Diana B., 12, 21–22, 487

Osborn, T. Noel, 21, 487

Ouchi, Z., 62

Outcomes: leadership change, 327–29

Overall Leadership Ratio (OLR), 488

P.O.P. syndrome, 14

Paradigms, 22–23

Participation, 156; encouraging, 347; military structures, 402; teams in higher education, 259–60

Participative leaders, 390; subordinate preferences, 396; style, 518

Participative management, 257

Passive leadership, 237–38

Path-Goal Theory, 17–18, 216

Pay-for-performance system, 461

Pearson correlations: leader self-report, 160; MBTI and LR factors, 160; product-moment, 173, 220; subordinate and leader ratings of climate, 163; subordinate report, 161; zero-order, 121–22

Penwell, Larry A., 7

Perceived stress: Japanese leadership, 91; scale, 88

Performance, 4, 238, 238; appraisal, 459–65; Chrysler, 298; classroom training and, 359–63; consolidated business unit, 228; Ford Motor Company, 298; group, 321; group under leader stress, 338–39; individual, 321; individual ratings in leadership change, 329; intergroup dynamics, 483; life-long learning and sustained, 445; managerial behavior and. See Managerial behavior; moderated by culture on store level, 221; and organizational culture, 215; personality factors and, 227; prediction, 230–31; role of industry inertia, 299; teams in higher education, 260–61; trend, 294; USAFA study, 180–81

Performance-Maintenance (PM): behaviors, 82; theory, 18

Performance-Maintenance Leadership Theory: categories derived from interviews, 86–87; critical incident interviews, 86–87; environmental factors, 88; evaluation, 85; Fundamental Interpersonal Relationship Orientation-Behavior. See Fundamental Interpersonal Relationship Orientation-Behavior (FIRO-B); individual factors, 88; Japanese utility study, 84–93; leadership models, 88–89; leadership process, 85–88; method, 84–85; Multifactor Leadership

Questionnaire, 89; procedure, 85–88; results, 8889; scoring, 85; and transformational leadership, 89; transformational leadership results, 89; work group factors, 88

Permanent white water, 429

Persistence: pattern of organizational activity, 295

Personal appeals, 419

Personal growth, 194, 322

Personal involvement. See Leadership

Personality: assessment, 346, 357; bipolar dimensions of, 519–20; extraversion-introversion, 348; judging-perceiving, 348–49; Latin American personal style, 487–92; leadership disposition, 157–61; and leadership role by gender, 519; linked to leadership styles, 227; locus of control, 227; sensing-intuition, 347; thinking-feeling, 347–48

Personality characteristics: leadership effectiveness, 469, 472–73; scales, 470; variance within work units, 231

Personality theories: crash-plan behavior, 103; dual system of interpersonal behavior, 103; emergency personality, 103

Personal style, 27

Personnel Decisions, 202

Perspectives: new, 22; structural frames, 269

Peterson, K.D., 141

Philadelphia Police Department, 107–16; Commissioner's Advisory Group, 111–12; course correction, 116–17; decision making, 117; MOVE incident, 111; training, 117; Strategic Plan, 113–16; Study Task Force, 110–11

Philadelphia and Its Police: Toward a New Partnership (1987), 111

Physical danger: and stress, 98–100

Planning, 306

Plot titles, 338

Pluralism: Catholic values in pluralistic society, 366; colleges and universities, 365

Police Executive Research Forum, 112

Police organizations, 108; big-city departments, 108; community policing emphasis, 111; external-institutional focus, 108; external advisory groups, 111–112; internal-management focus, 108; internal advisory groups, 111–112; political intrigues, 108; training, 108. See also Philadelphia Police Department

Politics, 26; dimension, 273–74; colleague ratings, 279; frames, 270; responses among educational leaders, 273

Polly Peck empire, 252

Population characteristics: leadership importance among ethnic groups, 66–67

Positive motivation, 322; curriculum, 320

Postmodern relativism, 249

Practices: and climate, 161; component of Transformational/Transactional Leadership model, 152; and disposition, 161; relationship

with school, 373; student with undergraduate program, 372; subordinate managers, 142

Saunders, David, 347

Scaled Comparison, 455

Scales: composite, 321–22

Schein, E.H., 310

Schneider, B., 150

School Culture Assessment Questionnaire (SCAQ), 135, 141

Schools: administrators, regression analyses, 276; daily routines and values, 139; leadership in, 135–41; principals, visionary leadership, 136–39; values, communication of, 138–39

Secularization: and Catholic institutions, 366

Self-analysis, 42

Self-confidence: employee, 219; subordinates, 56

Self-esteem: individual variable, 84; Japanese leadership, 90–91; measure, 88; student, 137

Self-interest, 238

Self-ratings, 5

Self-report: Transformational/Transactional Leadership model, 161–62

Self-worth: subordinates, 56

Senior Executive Profile: comparison profile of effective and ineffective executives, 56; factor analysis, 52–53; mobilizer role, 53; participants, 54; variables, 55

Senior executives. See Executives

Sensing-Intuiting (SI) 152, 347; and leadership disposition, 157; leadership requirements, 153

Sex discrimination, 518

"Ss" factors, 61, 65, 73–74; correlation matrix of, 75; possible substitutions among, 75–76

Shared values: communicating, 368–69; values, 368; feedback loop, 369; in higher education, 365–76; raising organizational, 367; targets, 369. See also Values

Shido, 81

Shipper, F., 120

Short-termism, 254

Shrinkage: moderated by culture on store level, 221; organization outcome in retail stores, 217, 219; relationships, 222

SIC Industry Codes, 307

Sisters of Mercy, 366

Sisters of Providence, 366

Situational contingency: military, 400–01

Situational engineering, 342

Situationalism: perceived leader impact, 389–91; subordinate preferences, 389–91

Situational moderator: military, 400

SKILLSCOPE, 455

Smith, Roger, 301

Sociability, 353

Social facilitation theory: performance on simple and overlearned tasks, 102

Social sciences: empirical evidence, 14

Sock Shop chain, 252

Squadron Assessment Questionnaire (SAQ): attrition, 179–80; correlations of

transformational and transactional leadership, 183–85; descriptive statistics, 182, 184; pattern matrix, 180; performance, 180–81

St. Mary of the Woods College, 370

Stalin, Josef, 26

Standards, 156

Statham, A., 519

Status quo, 178

Stogdill, Ralph M., 200, 226

Stories: telling and culture building, 140; communicating values in schools, 139

Strategic Advisory Committee, 115

Strategic business units (SBU), 282; characteristics compared with ideology, 286; managers, 282

Strategic Decision Data, 455

Strategic goal setting, 306

Strategic leadership: absence of, 108; antecedents for in Philadelphia Police Department, 109–10; constructing an emphasis, 110; course correction in Philadelphia Police Department, 116–17; creating a plan, 113–16; decision making, 117; defined, 60; internal feedback from command staff, 113; obstacles in American policing, 107–08; strategic emphasis programs, 112; training, 117; Strategic leadership. See also Police organizations; Philadelphia Police Department

Strategic Planning Group, 115

Strategies: advertising and marketing, 300

Strategies for Taking Charge, The (Bennis and Nanus), 367

Stress, 5; as activator, 120; boss stress, 97, 335; combat infantry leaders study, 97; dominant response behaviors, 336; effect on decision making, 100; as environmental factor, 84; and experience, 96–103; extensive search for information, 100; high and low correlations, 99; immediate superior, 97; information search study, 100–03; intelligence and performance scores, 98; intuition and hunch, 100; Japanese leadership, 90–91; and management, 120; measures of, 338–39; and organizational commitment, 120; and performance, 120; physical danger, 98–100; promotion, 97; reliance on intelligence, 100; social facilitation, 335–36; transfer, 97; types, 96–97; in workplace, 2, 119–20

Structural change: environment, 287–88; ideology and characteristics match, 286–88; ideology and selection, 287–89; match between characteristics, 285–87; other factors, 287; perceptions, 285; performance, 287–88; size, 287–88; technology, 287–88; from traditional bureaucracy to SBU, 282

Structural dimensions, 273–74, 282

Structural frames, 269, 306; as predictors, 279; colleague ratings, 279; responses among educational leaders, 273

Structure: and leadership, 216

Subcultures: in higher education, 366

Subjective measures, 301

Subordinates: impact of leader behavior and climate on reactions of, 194; items predicting reactions, 196; performance and leadership change, 329; ratings, 161–62; reactions contingent on leader level, 193–94; role of management towards, 56–57; training methods, 56–57; treatment of, 238

Subordinates preferences: F-ratios, 393; leader perspective, 395–96; measures, 391; model prescription, 395; normative situation analysis, 397; participative leaders, 396; preferred participation level, 395; projections of behavioral intentions, 393–94; role perspective, 395; scenario correlations, 393; scenario response, 397; scenario summary, 392; study design, 391–92; study procedure, 391; subjects, 391

Substitutes for Leadership, 17

Success: followership versus leadership, 300

Succession: in higher education, 495, 500–02; executive in name change firms, 310; external and internal, 307; planning, 199; type, 308

Summer Institute, 521; extroverts, 524; thinking dominant leaders, 524

Superleadership, 60

Supervisory ratings, 445

Supportiveness, 322; military structures, 402

Survey of Management Practices (SMP), 345; ratings, 353

Survivalism, 170

Symbols: as changes, 310; communication of values in schools, 139; dimensions, 273–74; frames, 270, 272–73, 278–79, 306; role, 51

Syntax, 447

Synthesis: teams in higher education, 260

Systematic Multiple Level Observation of Groups (SYMLOG): adjective rating scale, 479; measurements of intergroup dynamics, 479–84; measures derived from, 480–81; multiple-level field theory, 479; space, 480

Tai Ji, 253

Tannenbaum-Schmidt model, 17

Taoism, 253

Targets: shared values, 369

Task Delegation: leadership linkages project, 360

Taxonomies, 195; influence tactics, 417

Taylor and Fayol models, 257

Team-based management, 233

Teams: approach, participation and production, 396; assignments, temporary project, 445; camaraderie, 261; collaboration, 259–60; communication, 261; competence, 260–61; decisions, higher education, 263; effectiveness, correlations with leadership-making variables, 384; emotional climate, 261; enabling conditions, project team, 383, 385; enabling others, 263; evaluation, in-situ. See In-situ team evaluation; individuation, 260; internalization, correlations with leadership-making variables

and measures, 385; involvement, project team, 383, 385; leadership, 26163; members, HIHP, 262; model excellence, 263; morale, 261, 383, 385; outcomes, 385; participation, 259–60; performance, 260–61; project, 381; sustained performance, 259; synthesis, 260; teamness, 259; teamwork, 206; vision statement, 262. *See also* Groups

Team Performance (TP) checklist, 258

TEAMS Survey Software, 455

Team Success Profile (TSP): correlation matrix of subordinate ratings, 207; correlations with MSP, 204; definitions, 205; dimensions, 205; intercorrelations with MSP dimensions, 204; internal consistency, 206; interrater reliabilities, 206; items, 202–04; median correlations with MSP, 208; medial and maximum correlations with MSP scales, 210

Team Task Management: leadership linkages project, 360

Tecnología Administrativa Moderna (TEAM), 12, 21–22; personality characteristic in Latin American organizations, 487

Telecommunications: missions dependent on, 478

Teleconferencing, 477–78; intergroup dynamics, 484–85; missions dependent on, 478; prevention/intervention techniques, 484; previous studies, 479; study methods, 479; training for, 484–85

Telephone interviews: leadership linkages project, 360

Temple University, 112–113, 115

Tenacity, 57

Tension: managerial behavior and. *See* Managerial behavior

Tenure: with supervisor, 462, 462; average for American college presidents, 170; granting of ceremony, 140; organizational, 296; variable, 296–97

Term prediction: defined, 230

Terrey, J.N., 170

Theories: based on qualitative research, 17; Theory Bee, 12; theory-in-use, 254; Theory of Leader Decision Making, 18

Thinking-feeling (T-F), 152, 347–48; leadership requirements, 153; and leadership disposition, 157

Three-component model of leadership, 381

Thurston, Bill, 306

Time-series analysis, 295

Time in Service (TIS), 97

Tornow, Walter, 12

Traditional null model, 461

Traditions: communication of values in schools, 139

Training: assignments, 445; methods, 18

Traits: anxiety, 342; characteristic of theory studies, 470; theories of, 17, 469

Transactional leadership, 48, 142–43, 170; defined, 178; focus, 238; outcomes, 238; personality factors, 227; prediction outcomes, 243; rated,

Wilson's Survey of Management Practices, Form J, 120–121

Wilson, Clark L., 9, 345

Wilson, J., 281–82

Win-loss records, 200

Women administrators: comparison of leadership style distribution, 524; comparison with other groups of leaders, 522–24; dominant characteristics, 525–26; in higher education, 517–18; leadership behavior ratings, 452–53; MBTI study, 521–26; preferences, 522; self-ratings, 355; selfselection index scores, 523, 525; thinking dominant, perception of, 521; *See also* Gender

Workers: quality of, 3; effect of group on leadership, 83–84; talents, Japanese reliance on, 62

World War II, 400

Xerox, 445

Yammarino, F.J., 531

Yang, 253

Yerkes, R., 120

Yin, 253

Yukl, Gary A., 12, 19–20, 401